AA

COUNTRY ROADS OF BRITAIN

Colour Library Books

COUNTRY ROADS OF BRITAIN

Writers

Martyn Brown

Richard Cavendish

Ross Finlay

Barry Shurlock

Roland Smith

Roger Thomas

Geoffrey Wright

Cartography © The Automobile Association 1990. Reprinted with amendments 1991.
Mapping based on the AA Automaps database.

This 1992 edition produced exclusively for Colour Library Books Ltd, Godalming, Surrey by The Automobile Association.

Typesetting by Microset Graphics Ltd, Basingstoke, Hampshire.
Repro by BTB Reprographics Ltd, Whitchurch, Hampshire.
Printed and bound by Graficromo, Cordoba, Spain.

REF 3066

ISBN 0 86283 930 0

Page one: *the Trough of Bowland, Lancashire*

Pages two and three: *Scotney Castle Garden, Kent*

CONTENTS

Some of the finest traditional hay meadows in England are to be found behind the village of Muker, near the head of Swaledale in North Yorkshire

INTRODUCTION

On a fine Sunday in high summer it can seem as if the world and his wife have taken to the roads; major routes are often totally congested, traffic is either crawling along nose to tail (or speeding along at an alarming rate), and patience and good temper runs low - especially if attempted `short cuts' go disastrously wrong.

However, travelling around the countryside by car and finding new places to visit needn't be like this at all. Britain is covered with a maze of country roads that are still a pleasure to drive along and this book has been carefully designed to help you find your way around them. Moreover, it takes the worry out of planning and map reading, enabling you to sit back and enjoy the ride, confident in the knowledge that there is very little likelihood of getting lost and that a pleasant day lies ahead.

One of the aims of the book is to help the motorist explore areas of Britain that may usually be by-passed and although the authors have suggested several places to visit on each tour, part of the pleasure in venturing into unknown territory is discovering places for yourself so for the more adventurous the tours may be used as a starting point only.

As well as major tourist attractions - such as castles and stately homes - scenic walks, small museums, quiet villages and various outdoor activities are included in the book, plus a taste of the off-beat and unusual, so whatever your interests there is bound to be something to aim for on every tour that takes your fancy.

Poynings, seen here from the Devil's Dyke, is one of several villages nestling beneath the South Downs in Sussex. It is said that on a clear day Windsor Castle may just be glimpsed (with binoculars) across the Weald

THE OLD ROADS OF BRITAIN

Before the Roman came to Rye or out to Severn strode,
The rolling English drunkard made the rolling English road.
(G K Chesterton)

Above: *a typical packhorse bridge, at Conkesbury, Over Haddon, in Derbyshire. These bridges were designed with low parapets to stop them interfering with the packs slung on either side of the horses*

Below: *the Roman invasion of Britain began in* AD43 *and ended in about 410. During this period the Romans created an elaborate network of roads to link up their military and civilian towns. This is a section of a Roman road at Wansdyke in southern England*

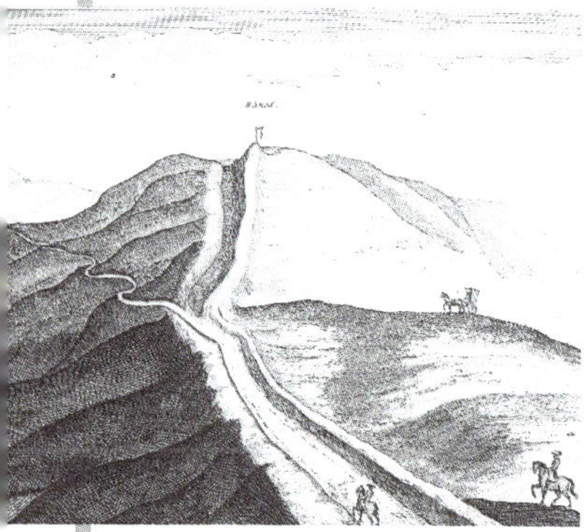

Britain's earliest roads were not constructed, but worn down over centuries untold by the feet of people and farm animals taking the easiest and safest routes across country. The paths may often have started earlier still as routes used by migrating deer and wild cattle. They were rough tracks, potholed and muddy, which might be half a mile wide or split into several branches, as travellers avoided holes and puddles, and animals spread out to browse along the way.

Ridgeways and Marsh Roads
The principal ridgeways (literally 'highways') avoided dense forests and marshy valleys by keeping to high ground. Rivers were crossed at fords, which can still be encountered by motorists on back country roads. The earliest clapper bridges, like roofed-over stepping stones, may go back this far. More substantial rivers, such as the Humber, already had ferry services in prehistoric times.

Although most prehistoric roads grew up spontaneously, people began to construct wooden trackways more than 5,000 years ago in the tangled marshes of the Somerset Levels. Posts were fixed upright every few yards so that the track could be seen from a distance. A reconstructed section of one of these early corduroy roads can be seen today near Glastonbury.

Much of today's road network may rest on prehistoric foundations, including many B roads that link quiet villages and hamlets. Country lanes that have sunk deep into the ground between high banks may have been trodden for thousands of years. Some major prehistoric cross-country routes have come back to life as long-distance footpaths: the Ridgeway Path across Wiltshire, for instance, and the South Downs Way. Other prehistoric tracks are now green lanes, such as Mastiles Lane between Kilnsey and Malham in North Yorkshire. Motorists can follow the Portway, an ancient pre-Roman route along the top of the Long Mynd in Shropshire. The A39, swooping up and down on Exmoor between Lynmouth and Porlock, follows a prehistoric road, as does the A423 from Oxford to Banbury and Coventry.

Roman Highways
The Romans introduced centralised road planning and, outside Devon and Cornwall, few places in England are more than a dozen miles from a Roman road. A byword for straightness, Roman roads were built on a bank of beaten earth, on which were laid layers of stones, lime, chalk, sand or gravel – whatever materials were locally available. A ditch on each side of the raised roadway drained off the rainwater. Milestones indicated distances and along the roads were places where travellers – officials, army officers, merchants – could rest or stay, with stabling for horses.

An exceptionally well-preserved stretch of Roman road can be seen at Blackstone Edge, off the A58 north-east of Rochdale. More often the Roman road is buried beneath its modern successor. Watling Street from London to Chester was the forerunner of much of today's A5. The scenic and solitary A68 from Hadrian's Wall north to the Scottish Border at Carter Bar follows substantial lengths of the Roman Dere Street.

Long stretches of the Fosse Way can be traced enjoyably today on a mixture of A roads and unclassified back roads. As the A37 and A367, the route crosses Somerset from near Ilchester to Radstock and Bath. Minor roads go on towards Cirencester and then the A429 picks up the Roman route across the Cotswolds to beyond Moreton in Marsh. Then it runs straight as an arrow for miles as a forgotten country road across Warwickshire past Moreton Morell and between Coventry and Rugby. From Leicester the A46 triumphantly completes the journey to Newark and Lincoln.

Road Over Water

After Roman times few major roads were built until the 18th century. Roads grew up between villages and market towns, but long-distance travellers – armies, pilgrims, traders, cattle drovers – found the existing main road network adequate. Hundreds of solid stone bridges were built in the Middle Ages, however, by landowners, monasteries and town merchant guilds whose prosperity depended on efficient communications. The bridges at Bradford on Avon, Rotherham, Wakefield and St Ives in Cambridgeshire still have their medieval chapels. A handsome medieval bridge crosses the Arun at Stopham, West Sussex, on the A283. Another is Twizel Bridge in Northumberland, with its 90ft single span across the Till, on the A698 between Coldstream and Berwick.

A tiny medieval packhorse bridge negotiates the stream at Charwelton in Northamptonshire on the A361. Packhorse bridges had low parapets to avoid bumping the panniers slung on either side of the horses as they crossed in single file. V-shaped refuges were often provided for pedestrians caught on the bridge.

Salt and Corpse Ways

Country roads and green lanes can still be found which are known as saltways, or saltergates in the North. They were once used by convoys of packhorses carrying salt from coastal areas and inland production centres such as Droitwich. The modern roads out of Droitwich are former saltways. The Roman road over Blackstone Edge was an important saltway from the Midlands into Yorkshire. The A59 coming into Harrogate from the west was another saltway along a Roman road. From the salt lagoons beside the Solent a saltway ran through the New Forest to Lymington and then turned north-west for Burley and Ringwood.

People from outlying farmsteads and remote hamlets might have to be carried miles to be buried in consecrated ground in a churchyard. Some of the routes the coffin and the mourners took are known as corpse ways. The most famous of them now is the Lyke Wake Walk over the North York Moors. The Old Corpse Road runs from Haweswater in the Lake District to Keld and the churchyard at Shap.

Along the Drove Roads

Until the railways snaffled the trade in the 19th century, herds of lowing cattle and flocks of bleating sheep used to be driven across country from Wales and Scotland to the Midlands and London, on routes now known as drove roads. More than a thousand head of cattle a week passed through Wetherby on the Great North Road in the 1770s. Covering not more than 12 miles a day, each herd would halt for the night at a 'stance', ideally a grassy area near a stream for the cattle, and hard by an inn for the drover. Some of the stances can still be identified where the roadside verge suddenly expands to twice its width.

Cattle were assembled at towns in the Scots Lowlands, shod with special shoes and driven slowly south, some of the drovers and their herds travelling down what is now the A68 south from Carter Bar. In Wales cattle from Anglesey were swum across the Menai Strait and ambled, mooing, through Snowdonia by the Nant Ffrancon Pass, where the A5 runs today. Then they went up the Conwy Valley to Llanrwst and on eastwards to Wrexham. From there a route ran south-eastwards past Birmingham to Kenilworth in Warwickshire. A country road from Kenilworth today is still marked on maps as the Welsh Road. It runs to Southam and on through the Northamptonshire landscape to Culworth, on what was once the way to St Albans and London.

In the 18th century thousands of Suffolk turkeys were driven in great noisy flocks to London every year down what is now the A11, their feet coated in a mixture of tar and sand for protection. The same route had long been a cattle drover's road. Before that it was a Roman road and earlier still a major prehistoric ridgeway, the Icknield Way. The traveller on such a road recalls past centuries with every mile.

Below: *the 'broad ford' – recorded in the Domesday Book as being the natural crossing point of the Avon at Bradford – is now spanned by a 14th-century bridge, widened in the 17th century by the addition of the lock-up*

Bottom: *crossing the River Barle on Exmoor is a low, medieval clapper bridge known as the Tarr Steps. Clapper bridges consist of flat, stone slabs laid across a series of supports*

ROADS AND THE HORSE

Good horses make short miles.
(George Herbert)

Above: *Elizabeth 1 rode in a coach for state occasions, but otherwise made her way around the country on horseback, or was carried in a sedan chair*

Below: *in spite of the introduction of the railway during the 19th century, horse-drawn vehicles, like this carriage, were still used for short journeys*

Bottom: *stage coaches, running in England by 1640, provided the first relatively swift, regular passenger transport. The service improved with turnpike roads*

For centuries the horse was the indispensable animal. Agriculture, transport and trade all depended on it. Almost until the First World War the roads were built for horses and even today the performance of a car is expressed in horsepower.

The horse-drawn stagecoaches of the 18th century transformed Britain's transport system. To go from Norwich to London had taken a week in 1700, but in 1751 the stagecoach did the journey in under two days. Changing horses every 5 to 15 miles, express coaches averaged 9 to 10mph over substantial distances, and a German visitor travelling to Scotland in 1798 complained that it was impossible to appreciate the scenery at such speed.

York, Chester or Exeter from London in only four days! People were amazed. In the 1820s 12 coaches a day ran from Leicester to London. In 1830 the regular Oxford-Southampton service via Newbury and Winchester left at 8am and arrived at 3pm that afternoon: 66 miles in 7 hours, despite the fact that the passengers had to get out and walk up several steep hills on the way.

Litter and Sledge

The coaching network reached its peak of efficiency in the 1820s and 1830s. It then fell victim to the greater speed and carrying capacity of the new railways which developed from the 1840s onwards.

The earlier history of wheeled vehicles is surprisingly obscure. In the Middle Ages people got about by walking or on the backs of horses, mules and donkeys. Gently bred ladies might be carried on a litter, a couch slung on poles between two horses, fore and aft. Less fragile ladies usually rode pillion, behind a man. Farmers had horse-drawn carts, and sledges were long used on farms. Goods in any bulk were moved by sea along the coast and inland by river wherever possible. Elsewhere strings of packhorses carried wool, tin, salt, lead, iron and other commodities across country. Four-wheeled passenger vehicles were beginning to develop and by the 14th century great ladies travelled in four-wheeler chariots.

Fit for a Queen

The coach, invented on the Continent, reached Britain somewhere about 1550. Drawn by two horses and slung on leather straps, its rear wheels were much bigger than the front ones, which made for a less uncomfortable ride. Elizabeth I, who preferred to ride side-saddle or sometimes pillion, had a state coach for great occasions. It was specially constructed to give her adoring subjects a good view of her. When she made one of her progresses across country with her retinue, anything up to 600 carts and waggons creaked and trundled along behind with the baggage.

The earliest omnibuses, four-wheeled passenger waggons which could carry 20 or 25, had made their debut by the end of the 16th century. Expensive and uncomfortable, they were slower than walking. Waggons drawn by eight or even ten horses lumbered along with wool and heavy freight. Towns of any size now had carriers, who transported people and goods.

The posting system had also evolved. Royal letters and government communications were carried by relays of riders along main roads, each covering a stage of 10 to 20 miles. A postman or postboy was originally one of these horsemen. Fresh horses were kept ready at the staging points by postmasters, who were usually substantial innkeepers. Elizabeth I allowed them to let horses to private travellers. It cost more than air travel does today, but it was the foundation of the whole staging system and many inns still call themselves posthouses.

The Turnpike Roads

Following Queen Elizabeth's example, a private coach became a status symbol, a mark of aristocracy and wealth, though except in and around London they were seldom seen until the 1660s. The introduction of steel springs took some of the jolts out of journeys, and long-distance passenger traffic was developing. The first stagecoaches in England were running by 1640, when there was a service between London and Cambridge.

The growth of a swifter system was hampered by the abominable state of the roads. Mired, rutted and pitted, they were impassable in wet weather and rarely had signposts of any kind. Holes were sometimes so deep that unfortunate travellers drowned in them or were suffocated in clinging mud.

The coaching era flowered with the improvement of roads by the turnpike trusts, the first of which was set up in 1663. They widened existing roads, improved bridges and bridged over fords. They also built new roads and in hilly country constructed easier gradients for coach traffic.

The trusts covered their costs and made a profit by charging tolls. These were collected at barriers called turnpikes, by the much-reviled pikemen, who lived in the toll houses alongside. Charges were levied on wheeled vehicles and animals, but not on farm cattle going to the fields and back. Pedestrians and people going to church or to a funeral were not charged. Travel on Sundays cost double.

The Royal Mail

In the 1780s the mails were transferred from the post riders to high-speed coaches. Drawn by four horses and carrying passengers as well as mail, they travelled toll-free and had priority over all other traffic. The guard, armed with a blunderbuss against highwaymen, would sound his horn as the coach tore towards a toll gate, which had to be hastily thrown open to let the mail career through.

Grand private coaches, adorned with the family coat of arms, were now pulled by matching teams of four or six horses. Travellers who disliked stagecoaches could hire a post-chaise, with room for two or three passengers and their luggage, the driver riding one of the horses. Sporting Regency bucks drove phaetons, high and fast and a byword for spills and recklessness.

The invention of elliptical springs in 1804 brought an advance in comfort. So did macadam road surfacing after 1815, but the railways eventually stifled the turnpike trusts. In 1890 only two were left, and the last toll gates, on the Holyhead Road in Anglesey (the A5), finally ceased operation in 1895.

The Old Order

Although the railways scooped the long-distance transport pool, carriage of passengers and freight over short distances remained horse-powered all through the 19th century, in the countryside and in towns. A great variety of vehicles met the various needs, from the light gig or pony-drawn trap to the stately landau, with a hood that folded back in fine weather. Horse-drawn cabs, trams and buses plied in cities, horse-drawn fire engines hurtled clanging through the streets. The brougham was a small private carriage for town use, driven by a coachman. Society ladies would take the air in a victoria, with a folding hood at the back, like an outsize perambulator, drawn by one or two horses. The dog cart was originally designed to carry sporting dogs, the governess cart for the children and their chatelaine.

The country carrier long outlasted the stagecoach and horse-drawn buses plodded country roads, carrying passengers and small packages. Railway parcels carts collected and delivered to stations. Shopkeepers and tradesmen made deliveries in vans. Flat, open drays bore beer barrels to pubs. Floats and lorries were lighter drays. Dust carts collected refuse.

Down into this century in country districts horse-drawn hay waggons brought the harvest home. Doctors made their rounds on horseback or in a gig and rural postmen rode ponies. Milk was still being delivered by pony and trap in the 1940s in Cornwall. The old order was a long time a-dying.

Above: *until the development of a national network of canals and railways, freight was still being moved by teams of lumbering packhorses for short-haul journeys throughout the 19th century*

Below left: *after the 1780s came the advent of the high-speed mail coaches. Drawn by four horses, they carried passengers as well as mail and had priority over all other road users*

Below: *like the carriers' covered wagons, the brewers' dray long outlived the faster stage coaches. In fact in some parts of the country horse-drawn drays are still used today*

Above: *the inn sign has its origins in the days when most people could not read and the painted picture, hung in a prominent position, could be understood by all and served to advertise the innkeeper's trade. In the 14th century publicans were required by law to exhibit a sign which resulted in fierce competition and more elaborate illustrations*

Below: *the courtyard of a typical Georgian inn, the George Hotel in Huntingdon. These large establishments provided stabling for the horses which had to be changed throughout the journey, and accommodation and food for passengers*

INNS AND TAVERNS

There is nothing which has yet been contrived by man, by which so much happiness has been produced as by a good tavern or inn.
(Dr Johnson)

There are inns in Britain which have been dispensing hospitality since before the Wars of the Roses. A typical example is the Spread Eagle at Midhurst, in West Sussex, which Hilaire Belloc hailed as the 'most revered of all the prime inns of this world'. This rambling venerable pile has entertained Elizabeth I, Edward VII and Hermann Goering in its time. Dating back to 1430, when travel was on horseback or by foot, it still does a roaring trade in the age of the car. So do other immemorial hostelries, which seem to be kept standing as much by the strength and conviviality of gallons of good ale poured out in them over the centuries as by the actual structure.

Pilgrims and Traders

In the early Middle Ages towns and villages had their alehouses, the forerunners of today's `locals', but few people travelled more than a dozen miles from home in a lifetime. Those who did stayed at monasteries, which gave passers-by a night's lodging. As prosperity grew, however, horizons widened, travel increased and the custom of going on pilgrimage to saints' shrines began to spread. Seeing an opportunity for profit, monasteries and town merchants' guilds opened the earliest English inns.

The George and Pilgrims at Glastonbury, for instance, was built by Glastonbury Abbey for the pilgrim trade in the 1470s. The Star Inn at Alfriston, East Sussex - originally the Star of Bethlehem - was run by Battle Abbey for pilgrims to the shrine of St Richard of Chichester. The primeval, half-timbered George in Norton St Philip, Somerset, was built by local Carthusian monks in 1397 to lodge the merchants who came to buy their wool.

Coaching Days

The 16th century saw a steady growth of road travel and by 1600 there were some 6,000 inns in the country altogether. Many ancient pubs called the New Inn date from this time. The stage was now set for the development of the quintessential English hostelry: the coaching inn, familiar from many a Christmas card.

Long distance coaching in Britain began in the 1600s and reached its peak in the late 1820s and `30s. Three days a week in 1706 the London coach left the Black Swan in York at 5 in the morning for the 4-day journey to the capital. All along the major routes new inns were built and existing ones enlarged to meet the demand for comfortable places where the stagecoaches could change horses and passengers could pause to eat, shave, change clothes or simply get warm by a roaring fire.

This is the period of the handsome, ample Georgian inns of so many cities and country towns, with their courtyards and stabling: the

Red Lion in Salisbury, the George at Huntingdon, the Lion in Shrewsbury. The landlord of the George and Dragon, West Wycombe, on the London-Oxford route, ran a carrier pigeon messenger service for guests stranded by bad weather. The proximity of two coaching inns at Stony Stratford, Buckinghamshire, the Cock and Bull, a few doors from each other in the High Street, is said to have inspired the phrase 'cock and bull story'.

Stand and Deliver

The 18th century was the period of highwaymen and smugglers. There are inns which look back fondly to their connections with gentlemen of the road: such as the Roebuck at Stevenage in Hertfordshire, and the Dun Cow at Dunchurch, Warwickshire, which Dick Turpin patronised.

Others have smuggling tales to tell. The best-known is probably Jamaica Inn, on the A30 in the lonely wilds of Bodmin Moor in Cornwall, made famous by Daphne du Maurier's novel. The Mermaid Inn at Rye was the headquarters of a brutal gang of smugglers in the 18th century, and later provided the novelist Henry James with his blameless pint. In North Devon, between Bideford and Clovelly on the A39 Hoops Inn was another smugglers' lair.

What's In a Name?

Inns and pubs have a rich heritage of names and signs. Pictorial signs were needed to identify them because until well down into the 19th century most people could not read. Some names are ecclesiastical: the Angel, the Mitre or the Cross Keys, which are St Peter's keys of heaven and hell.

When Henry VIII broke with Rome, hostelries called the Pope's Head prudently changed to the King's Head. The Royal Oak refers to the future Charles II hiding in the oak tree at Boscobel, and the sign usually has a picture of it. Many pubs bear the name or title and coat of arms of the local landowners: the Berkeley Arms, the Chandos Arms, the Devonshire Arms and so on. The Eagle and Child is the heraldic badge of the Stanleys, Earls of Derby. Some inns were originally built by wealthy families to house any overflow of guests' servants when entertaining: a tradition revived in 1906 by Lord Rothschild when he rebuilt the Rose and Crown at Tring in Hertfordshire.

Many names come from the animal kingdom: the Bull, the Bear, the White Hart, the Swan. The old Fighting Cocks by the River Ver in St Albans was named after a sport often carried on at inns. Other names are drawn from farming and country pursuits: the Plough, the Waggon and Horses or the Fox and Hounds.

The Bat and Ball at Hambledon commemorates that Hampshire village's cricketing fame. Other pubs are named after local heroes: the Admiral Nelson at Burnham Thorpe in Norfolk, the Edith Cavell in Norwich, the General Wolfe at Westerham, Kent. The Marquis of Cranby was a notable 18th-century soldier, forgotten now except on pub signs.

Some names are distinctly odd. The Goat and Compasses is said to be possibly a corruption of a Puritan slogan, God

Encompasses Us. The Cat and Fiddle may be descended from a medieval saint's appellation, Caterine le Fidele. Some names are wonderfully strange and romantic: Bel and the Dragon at Cookham, Berkshire; the Galley of Lorne at Ardfern in Strathclyde, Scotland; the Olde Trip to Jerusalem in Nottingham; the Green Man and Black's Head at Ashbourne, Derbyshire, with a 'gallows' sign.

The signs are sometimes of substantial artistic merit, though Charles Dickens commented unfavourably on the figure of 'an animal distantly resembling an insane carthorse' over the door of the Great White Horse at Ipswich. George Morland painted inn signs for food and bumpers of gin in the 18th century, and the sign of the Punchbowl Inn at Lanreath in Cornwall is said to have been designed by Augustus John.

Highest and Smallest

Several inns claim to be the highest in the country, among them the solitary Cat and Fiddle on the A537, west of Buxton in Derbyshire. Others claim to be the smallest, including the Nutshell in Bury St Edmunds, where there is scarcely room to swing one of the mummified cats which adorn it.

Yet other hostelries bring you close to figures of the past. The low-beamed Ship was Sir Francis Drake's favourite tavern in Exeter. Daniel Defoe met the original of Robinson Crusoe in the Llandoger Trow in Bristol. Dr Johnson and Charles Dickens both stayed at the Olde Bull's Head in Beaumaris, Anglesey. Robert Burns used to drink at the Globe in Dumfries. The Green Tree at Hatfield Woodhouse, South Yorkshire, is haunted by the ghost of a Roundhead soldier who was hanged there by a party of Cavaliers.

There are plenty of other haunted inns, half-timbered inns, waterside inns, inns with views, inns with histories. Without them, Britain would not be Britain.

Top left: *over the years pubs have sprung up in every corner of the country and many boast unusual features and vie for various claims to fame. One such establishment is the Nutshell in Bury St Edmunds, in Suffolk, which reckons to be the smallest tavern in Britain, although – naturally – there are other contenders for this title*

Top right: *as transport became more sophisticated the roads of Britain were frequented by the wealthier classes and a new breed of criminal, the highwayman, capitalised on this. The picture shows one such notorious character, Robert Smith, robbing a Hackney coachman on the way to London. Many of today's pubs claim past associations with these colourful villains who frequently bribed landlords to shelter them*

Above: *the Bat and Ball at Hambledon, Hampshire, preserves memories of this famous cricketing village. A wealthy local landowner established the Hambledon Club in the 1760s and the pub, built in the 17th century, once served as the clubhouse*

Above: *like other travelling people, circus performers moved around their native country and around the world in search of 'customers'. Originally much smaller outfits, these transient entertainers of the past were used to draw people to travelling markets*

Below: *following the improvement in transport in the 19th century, travelling animal shows – operating since the 18th century – began to team up with the performers. These shows often centred around a main tent where the public performances were held*

THE TRAVELLING PEOPLE

A fugitive and a vagabond shalt thou be in the earth.
(Genesis 4.12)

When Lord George Sanger's travelling circus made its majestic way across country every summer, it stretched along two miles of road. Seventy vehicles hauled by 150 horses conveyed the performers, the clowns and trapeze artistes, the bearded lady and the strong man, the animals, the band, the costumes and properties, and the giant marquee. The circus had its own travelling blacksmith and wheelwright, two vets and an army of grooms, carpenters and tentmen, as well as herds of Shetland ponies and liberty horses. Elephants marched ponderously in front. The populations of entire villages turned out to watch the dusty cavalcade rumble by.

`Lord' George (his title was self-conferred) was the king of the ring in the 1890s and 1900s. The son of a travelling showman, he started his career touring the country with performing mice and canaries, and married a formidable lion tamer, said to be the first woman ever to put her head in a lion's mouth. For centuries before his heyday, however, Britain's country roads had witnessed a procession of nomads, from gypsies and tinkers to itinerant actors and acrobats, hawkers and beggars. Governments passed laws against them, local authorities put them in the stocks, whipped them and tried desperately to send them back where they belonged, but in vain. They belonged on the road.

Smiths and Tinkers

Among the earliest regular travellers in Britain were Bronze Age smiths. When the craft of metalworking was introduced, before 2500BC, and stone implements were made obsolete by bronze ones, specialist smiths took to the roads, singly or in small groups. Carrying their tools and moulds and a supply of bronze, they would stay for a while at a settlement, set up a furnace and fill the local orders before packing up and moving on again. They must have brought a welcome breath of fresh air, news and gossip from the outside world, but their craft seemed uncanny to the uninitiated and they had an aura of magic about them.

Iron replaced bronze and in time most villages acquired their own resident blacksmiths, but travelling smiths were still to be found on the roads in the Middle Ages. They were the forerunners of the tinkers, or tinklers, who roamed about mending kettles and pots and pans. Travelling on foot or by horse and cart, they still had something eerie and sinister about them in the eyes of ordinary folk, or `flatties' as Scots tinkers called them.

Mass production of stainless steel utensils made the tinkers obsolete, but a few still travel the back roads of Scotland and Ireland. Fiercely independent, they keep themselves to themselves and have their own `cant' or secret language. They dislike the word tinker, with its connotations of poor workmanship, and prefer to be called travellers.

Children of Cain

`Gypsy' is a corruption of Egyptian. When these swarthy nomads first appeared in Britain, about 1500, they were believed to have come from the land of the pharaohs. They did nothing to discourage this notion or the myth that they were descended from Cain, cursed and doomed to wander the earth for ever. They actually came originally from India.

The gypsies travelled on foot or in covered carts, sleeping in tents, and made a living by a mixture of horse-dealing, casual farm labour, selling baskets and clothes pegs, poaching and begging. Gypsy women told fortunes. Palmistry was their great art, but they might also read cards or tea leaves or a crystal ball. They also traded on their knowledge of herbal medicines and folk magic, love potions and ways of inducing abortion.

The gypsies were striking figures, dark-skinned, the men with gold or silver rings in their ears, the women in gaudy finery with necklaces of gold coins. Ordinary settled folk, or `gorgios', regarded them with a combination of hostility, envy and fear. Magistrates kept moving them on.

The Gypsy Caravan

It was not until well into the 19th century, with the dramatic improvement of the roads, that the gypsies took to the brightly painted caravans that became their trademark and which are now collector's items. Normally pulled by a single horse, fitted with glazed windows, a door and movable steps, and with

a pointed stove-pipe protruding through the roof, a well equipped caravan would be furnished with an iron stove, beds or curtained-off bunks, silver and china, mirrors and ornaments. Besides the horse, the family might travel with chickens and cage-birds, and usually with one or two dogs, traditionally lurchers, which were used in taking rabbits.

The caravans were elaborately decorated with carved horses, birds, grapes, flowers and leaves, wheels and scrolls, and painted in brilliant hues. As with canal narrowboats, their style of decoration preserves the bright and cheerful popular taste of the Victorian period, also seen in fairground art.

Gypsy caravans probably reached their maximum numbers in the Edwardian era. The old Romany way of life has since fallen victim to the 20th century, to industrialisation and mass production, the welfare state and the car. An official report in 1965 put the number of gypsies in England and Wales at over 15,000 of whom more than 90% lived in car-hauled caravans or motor trailers.

Bread and Circuses

Lumped in with the gypsies for centuries by settled folk were a motley crew of travelling hawkers, card sharps, quack doctors and assorted entertainers. Pedlars, chapmen and cheapjacks went from village to hamlet to farm, selling domestic utensils, nostrums, dress materials and cheap items of all sorts. They travelled on foot or by pony with their goods in a pack, or by horse and cart.

Wandering entertainers included fiddlers, ballad singers, conjurors, tumblers and jugglers, strolling players and clowns, and showmen with performing bears. Many of them made the rounds of the country fairs.

In the 19th century, mass production and improved transport changed the character of the traditional fair, which gradually ceased to be a market of any importance for buying and selling. Entertainment, formerly only an appendage, became the main attraction. Substantial travelling shows developed, moving with a train of heavy waggons and caravans from one fairground to the next. There were rides, waxworks, magic lantern shows, boxing booths, coconut shies and shooting galleries, booths selling gingerbread and ribbons and cheap toys.

The earliest simple roundabouts were propelled by hand or by a donkey plodding round and round the inside track. From the middle of the century, however, the application of steampower to the fairground produced faster and more elaborate rides and the first switchbacks, ancestors of the modern rollercoaster.

Meanwhile, the travelling menageries which had been touring the country with wild animals since the 18th century joined forces with the travelling circuses. The pioneer of the modern circus was Philip Astley, an ex-cavalryman and trick rider who started giving regular performances in 1770. He built up a show of equestrian acts which he took all over Europe, and other showmen followed his lead. In the 19th century wild animal acts were introduced, the flying trapeze was invented and the circus became part of the entertainment round.

As the century wore on, showmen began to use steam traction engines to haul their lumbering waggons on the move. These were still a familiar sight on the roads in the 1920s, but the age of the car was at hand and cinema, radio and television were to bring travelling entertainment hard times.

Top: *gypsies first entered Britain in the 16th century and originally travelled on foot or in covered carts, and slept in tents. In the 19th century they took to the better-known painted caravans. These gypsies, c.1895, are encamped in Essex*

Above: *most gypsies changed from the traditional horse-drawn caravans to lorries and trailers when petrol rationing ceased in the 1950s. Firms began to build trailers specifically to fit gypsies' requirements, and luxury interiors reached a peak during the 1970s*

ROAD AND STREET FURNITURE

Where perhaps some beauty lies,
The cynosure of neighbouring eyes.
(Milton)

Above: *the most common relics of turnpike roads are mileposts, or stones, like this one in Barkway, Hertfordshire. Each turnpike trust equipped its roads with a set of 'posts' whose style of decoration was particular to that trust*

Below: *the tollhouse at Stanmore is a typical example of the breed – a small, compact building with on-the-job accommodation for the toll collector, and windows which gave a clear view of the road in both directions*

To drive or walk or cycle along any country road, village street or town thoroughfare is to pass a remarkable quantity and variety of road and street equipment. Much of this paraphernalia is so familiar that it is hardly noticed. It ranges from signposts and bollards to drinking fountains and horse troughs, from railings, lamp posts, clocks, pillar boxes and telephone boxes to benches and bus shelters, traffic lights and footscrapers, rubbish bins and sand or grit containers. These disregarded items are eloquent of road history and changing fashions in design.

How Many Miles to Babylon?

A few of the old tollhouses can still be found along the former turnpike roads, standing quietly forgotten by today's traffic. The homes of the pikemen who collected the tolls, they are diminutive stone buildings, sometimes hexagonal, octagonal or circular to command a view in every direction from which a carriage might approach. Most of them were designed in conventional 18th-century classical style, but some look like miniature medieval forts. There would be a ticket hole and a wooden or stone notice listing the various tolls.

It was the turnpikes which brought milestones back to British roads for the first time since Roman days. They were put in place along the Dover Road (later the A2) in 1663. In 1698 Celia Fiennes, riding through Lancashire, reported posts at the crossroads with the names of the main towns and hands pointing the way. This was unusual, however, and travellers mostly had to find their own way across country and often got lost, until in 1773 the turnpike trusts were ordered to place mile markers and direction posts on all their roads.

Most of the milestones left along country roads today date from after this provision. Many of them are simple stone slabs with elegant, deep-cut Georgian lettering. Some are shaped like obelisks and there are elaborate Victorian ones like tombs. The Victorians also installed iron milestones, often with hands pointing the way, picked out in black on a white background.

Numerous new road signs had to be introduced for motorists in this century: give way signs, no right turn signs, warning of low or hump-backed bridges and so on. Some of the older ones were studded with little round glass reflectors to show up at night. The first automatic traffic lights appeared in Britain in the 1920s, some displaying the word `Stop' on the red light and `Go' on the green. The first cat's eyes began to twinkle along British roads at night in the 1930s.

After the Second World War a change of official policy introduced visual signs - readily understandable by everyone in theory - instead of signs in words. Major Road Ahead, for example, was retired after years of honourable service and replaced by an inverted triangle.

With the coming of the car, road verges formerly productive of primroses and cow parsley began to sprout petrol stations, with their harvest of pumps and garish oil company logos. Some towns and villages have put up elaborate signs to announce themselves to the approaching motorist, generally identifying the foreign towns they are twinned with and often with a picture of the place or someone associated with it. At Biddenden in Kent, for instance, the village sign has a picture of the Biddenden Maids, a famous pair of Siamese twins who were born there.

Where Streams of Living Water Flow

Back in the horse age, milestones and direction posts sometimes doubled as mounting blocks, often placed outside churches and inns. Another relic of that time is the horse trough - the 19th-century equivalent of the filling station, as it has been called. The early ones were made of wood or iron, but the deep granite troughs have naturally lasted better. Sometimes there's a second trough, lower and shallower, for dogs.

Horse and dog troughs were an outgrowth of the great Victorian drive to provide clean water for the poor, an improvement in public sanitation which was supported by the powerful temperance movement. Local authorities in Liverpool and other northern cities began to install roadside drinking fountains in the 1850s and in London the

influential Metropolitan Free Drinking Fountain Association was founded in 1859.

Drinking fountains were soon placed in villages and towns all over the country. Most of them were solid but humble affairs in granite or marble, medieval in appearance and equipped with a metal cup on an iron chain. Some were far more grandiose, like the stupendous one erected in Dudley's market square in 1867, a triumphal arch 28ft high with water spouting from dolphin's heads into troughs for horses and from lion's heads for thirsty human passers-by. Some of the biggest and most enjoyable grotesque fountains were put up to honour Queen Victoria's golden jubilee in 1887 or the diamond jubilee of 1897, in marble of all shades, richly pinnacled and crocketed.

Many Victorian fountains have improving maxims and biblical texts inscribed on them: 'The fear of the Lord is a fountain of life', for example, or 'Whosoever drinketh of the water that I shall give them shall never die.' The Bath Temperance Society erected a 'Rebecca at the Well' fountain outside Bath Abbey in 1861, with a graceful female figure holding a pitcher, and the motto 'Water is Best'.

Some fountains doubled as memorials. A small mock-Norman one with horse and dog troughs by the road in Grasmere, Cumbria, was erected in Wordsworth's memory in 1889. The Boer War Memorial in Bellingham, Northumberland, is a fountain. You can drink Buxton spa water from the fountain in The Crescent, installed in 1940 in memory of a local councillor.

Patterns Underfoot

Some town clocks and clock towers were built to honour Queen Victoria's jubilees - the one in Brighton is an example - and it is worth keeping an eye out for the terracotta plaques which were fastened to the walls of town and village houses in patriotic salute to her. Some are still in place.

Coalhole covers, manhole covers and inspection covers provide a rich field of interest to the street furniture enthusiast. Iron coal plates have a variety of decorative patterns on them, and often the manufacturer's name and date. Some carry slogans ('Economy, Efficiency, Durability'). Covers to water, gas and electricity mains are generally less engaging, but display a variety of designs.

Nineteenth-century gas lamps can still be found here and there, now converted to electricity. The finest Victorian and Edwardian examples are magnificently decorative, with classical or Gothic lanterns, curvaceous ornamental ironwork and shapely ladder rests. Some are adorned with dolphins or galleons or cherubs. Scottish ones often had a crown on top.

Pillar to Post

Roadside postboxes are usually simpler and more severe in design. They were first introduced in the 1850s, on the recommendation of the novelist Anthony Trollope, who worked for the Post Office, and a good many 19th-century boxes are still in use. There are free-standing pillar boxes, wall boxes and lamp boxes, attached to lamp posts or telegraph poles. The pillar boxes are usually round, but some are oval or hexagonal. They almost always carry the royal cipher.

Then there are telephone boxes. The classic design was by the architect Sir Giles Gilbert Scott in the 1930s.

Much of the road and street furniture of the past has been destroyed, and too much that has taken its place seems ugly or nondescript. As the years go by, however, every decade's contribution to the scene can come to be prized. Even the humble, spindly parking meter will one day exert a nostalgic appeal.

Far left: *before the advent of piped water, domestic supplies were often collected at fountains and conduits such as this one built by Mr Hobson of Cambridge. Elaborate devices and decorations often featured in such structures*

Centre: *clocktowers developed as a natural progression from bell towers. Once the idea was born, the building of these became a much favoured way of commemorating special events. This particular example, on Marine Drive, Margate, was built in 1897 to celebrate the diamond Jubilee of Queen Victoria's reign*

Top: *with the development of gas lighting came ornate cast-iron lamps such as this one in Glasgow. The cross bar was for the lamp lighter to lean his ladder against*

Above: *pillar and letter boxes of all shapes and sizes mushroomed throughout Britain with the implementation of the penny post in 1839. Victorian examples of this type are now rare*

Above: *lovely Loch Katrine is part of the romantic area known as the Trossachs – one of the first regions to attract tourists bent on enjoying the scenery*

TOURING FOR PLEASURE

I travel not to go anywhere, but to go. I travel for travel's sake. The great affair is to move.
(Robert Louis Stevenson)

Right: *with increased mobility the visiting of stately homes as a pastime came into vogue. Contributing to this was an Act of Parliament in 1937 which enabled owners to give their houses to the National Trust and allowed them to live there provided the property was open to the public. Other owners soon followed suit by opening their homes off their own bat to raise money. Chatsworth – shown here – is one of the most visited of our historic houses*

Britain's roads were made for practical purposes. The idea of travelling for pleasure was born comparatively late and did not come of age until the roads were sufficiently comfortable to make using them anything but a purgatory. Lonely, untamed landscape was feared as late as the 1720s, when the dislike of wild scenery was still so strong that Daniel Defoe could condemn mountainous Westmorland as 'the most barren and frightful' county in all England. He made almost equally disparaging comments about the Peak District.

Enchanted Glens

Tastes were beginning to change, however, and the Georgian period saw a new appetite grow for romantic, picturesque scenery. The poet Thomas Gray visited the Lake District in 1769 and wrote of it with approval, and was followed by many other writers. Painters who included Gainsborough, Constable and Turner went there too, and found they could sell romantic Lakeland views. In the same vein Turner and other artists exploited the mountain splendours of Wales. Capability Brown, meanwhile, was busy artificially creating natural-looking vistas in the aristocracy's stately parks.

The Highlands of Scotland, whose inhabitants inspired mingled fear and contempt in the English – and in the Lowland Scots as well – as savage barbarians, acquired a new romantic aura in the immensely popular poems and novels of Sir Walter Scott. *The Lady of the Lake*, which came out in 1810, hymned the beauties of the Trossachs region of Perthshire. It inspired so many people to want to see these enchanted lochs and glens for themselves that the local landowner, the Duke of Montrose, built a new road into the area for visitors. It is still in use today as the A821.

The Road to the Isles

The new and improved turnpike roads were essential to the burgeoning tourist traffic. So were better maps and more generous provision of signposts, which made it harder to get lost.

The first metalled roads in the Scottish Highlands were built for the government by General George Wade after the Jacobite rising of 1715, to make it possible to move troops more swiftly against the rebellious natives. Today's A9, running north from Perth over the high, desolate Pass of Drumochter, follows the line of one of these military roads. So do the A822 and A826 from Crieff across Glen Almond and through the hills to Aberfeldy, where the handsome bridge over the silvery Tay was built for General Wade. Ironically, the first troops to make good use of these roads were those of the Young Pretender in 1745. After the '45 Rising the present B6318 along Hadrian's Wall in Northumberland was built by the military.

Scotland and Wales were further opened up to travellers in the next century by Thomas Telford, the great engineer wittily nicknamed 'the Colossus of Roads' for his exploits. In 18 years of unremitting effort he drove close to 1,000 miles of new roads through the Highland mountains. The romantic 'road to the isles', the A830 from Fort William to Arisaig, was built by Telford. So was the ravishingly beautiful A87 road through Glen Shiel and past the peaks of the Five Sisters of Kintail to

General Wade's elegant five-arched bridge crosses the Tay at Aberfeldy in the Scottish Highlands. Wade's metalled roads were the first to penetrate the Highlands, although it was another 100 years before visitors travelled them for pleasure

Kyle of Lochalsh. While he was at it, Telford also constructed the Caledonian Canal.

In the 1820s Telford dramatically improved the London to Holyhead road, now the A5, which carries today's motorists through the towering Snowdonian summits on gradients nowhere steeper than 1 in 22. Confronted by the Menai Strait, the great man hurled across it the first major suspension bridge in the world, soaring 100ft above the water.

Another redoubtable Scotsman, the irascible John Loudon McAdam, gave his name to the new road surfacing method he invented. Adopted after 1815, it made travel faster and more comfortable for the rest of the century. So did the railway, and Thomas Cook organised his first excursion, by rail, in 1841. Parties were now making outings by road in the first charabancs, which were large carts, drawn by two horses, with the passengers sheltered under striped awnings. Enthusiasm for the seaside spread among the middle class and down the social ladder to the working class, who had an opportunity for day trips every year after the first bank holidays were introduced in 1871.

Where My Caravan Has Rested

A new development of the 1880s was pleasure caravanning. The pioneer was a Scots naval surgeon, William Gordon Stables, who became a successful author of books for boys and was also much in demand as a sound judge of dogs, cats and rabbits. Shown round a gypsy caravan one day, he decided to have his own 'land yacht'. It was built for him in Bristol and can be seen today in the Bristol Industrial Museum. Two tons of luxury in mahogany and maple, the 'Wanderer' rolled along the country roads pulled by two horses, with stables, a coachman, a valet, a Newfoundland dog and a depressed parrot on board.

Stables wrote a book about his first expedition in 1886 and the Bristol works soon built another grand land yacht for the Duke of Newcastle, 'the Bohemian', with a built-in wine cellar. The rich Earl of Dudley owned one so heavy it took six horses to haul it: it had an aviary in the roof.

Caravans were taken up by the Salvation Army and other evangelistic Christian groups, which used them as mobile preaching and conversion centres. On the sides were slogans: 'The wages of sin is death', 'Give up sin, surrender to God', 'Where will you spend eternity?'

Caravanning slowly caught on. In 1907 eleven enthusiasts formed the Caravan Club, which by 1913 had 300 members. By this time the first motorised land yachts had appeared. A luxurious Austin model, designed for two, travelling with their chauffeur and chef, weighed 2½ tons and cost £2000 (equivalent to at least £70,000 today). The separate trailer caravan, drawn by a car, did not become popular until later on and was not seen on the roads in any numbers until the 1930s.

On Swifter Wheels

Much cheaper and more popular was the bicycle, which emerged from its prolonged chrysalis stage in the 1880s, with the introduction of the chain-driven rear wheel and the Dunlop pneumatic tyre. The fuel was free, the roads were open, and between 1890 and 1910 cycling spread with breakneck rapidity. Groups of friends went on cycling expeditions together, cycling clubs formed, flocks of cyclists wheeled and swooped through country lanes. Tradesmen and postmen made deliveries by bicycle, policemen rode their beats majestically on them, couples went courting on them, pedalling tandems or side-by-sides. Women took to cycling readily and it helped towards freeing them from the twin tyranny of the skirt and the sink. The cycling boom continued after the First World War, to reach a peak in 1935.

By this time, however, the car was outdistancing all rivals. The first crotchety, petrol-driven horseless carriages drove onto English roads in the 1890s and early 1900s – Daimlers, Wolseleys, Lanchesters. They were luxury vehicles, carrying Edwardian gentlemen in heavy overcoats and yachting caps, and ladies in furs and motoring veils against the dust. The first Rolls-Royce 'Silver Ghost' went on show in 1906, and in 1910 there were 53,000 cars in Britain.

After 1920 a new age of popular motoring dawned, which would eventually bring touring for pleasure within the reach of the vast majority of households. Ever bigger and faster roads were constructed for ever-increasing numbers of cars. With commercial and business traffic grinding along the motorways, it has become possible on the older country highways to recapture something of the pleasure of motoring for its own sake and the joy of the open road.

Top: *Telford's remodelled London to Holyhead road, now the modern A5, took tourists onto Anglesey over his Menai Suspension Bridge which was completed in 1825*

Above: *another of Thomas Telford's projects, the Caledonian Canal, seen here at Inverness, was designed to open up the Scottish Highlands*

Below: *when mass produced cars came onto the market in the 1920s and 30s motoring became accessible to the middle classes for the first time. Shown here is a 1915 Ford*

USING THE BOOK

The book is divided into six regions, as shown on the map on page 23, and a regional map at the beginning of each section locates all the tours in that area.

To help you get to the start point of each tour, a map reference to the atlas at the back of the book is given in the route directions. The National Grid is explained on page 228.

The places described in the text under the heading On The Tour are highlighted in red on each tour map. Places described under the headings Off The Tour, Off the Beaten Track and Outdoor Activities are not shown on the tour map, but the text includes location details.

A key to all the symbols and information shown on the tour maps is given on the page opposite.

This symbol, shown in the text, indicates that a place is particularly suitable for children.

The opening times of places to visit are not generally given in the text, although some entries indicate that access to a particular site is very limited. Many properties, especially those belonging to the National Trust and the National Trust for Scotland, are closed between October and Easter. It is always advisable to check the current details in advance when planning a visit to avoid disappointment.

Durham Cathedral towering above the Framwellgate Bridge over the Wear

MAP SYMBOLS

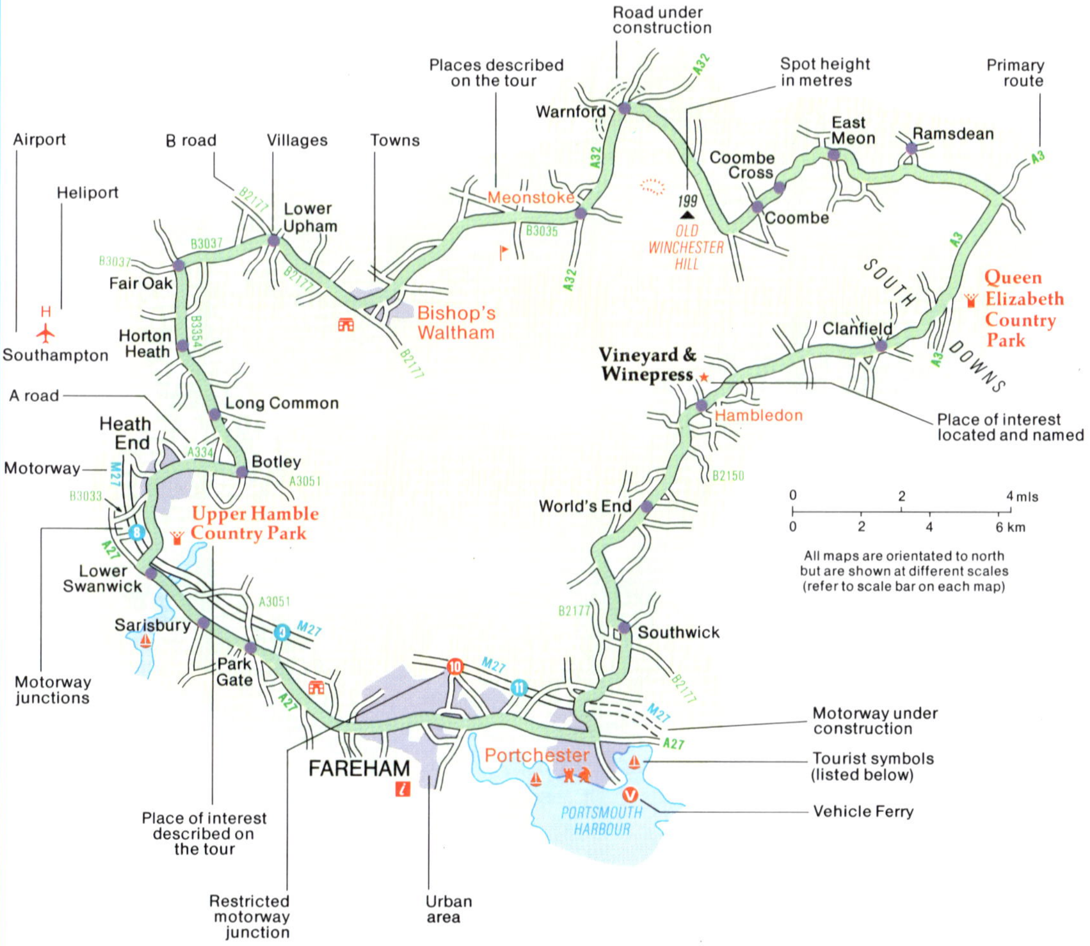

TOURIST INFORMATION

- Tourist Information Centre
- Tourist Information Centre (summer only)
- Abbey, cathedral or priory
- Ruined abbey, cathedral or priory
- Castle
- Historic house
- Museum or art gallery
- Industrial interest
- Garden
- Arboretum
- Country park
- Theme park
- Zoo
- Wildlife collection – mammals
- Wildlife collection – birds
- Aquarium
- Nature reserve
- Nature trail
- Forest drive
- National trail
- Hill fort
- Roman antiquity
- Prehistoric monument
- Battle site with year
- Preserved railway/steam centre
- Cave
- Windmill
- AA viewpoint
- Picnic site
- Golf course
- Country cricket ground
- Horse racing
- Show jumping/equestrian circuit
- Motor racing circuit
- Gliding centre
- Coastal launching site
- Ski slope – natural
- Ski slope – artificial
- Other places of interest

THE WRITERS

Britain On Country Roads has been written by professional travel writers who have an extensive knowledge of Britain's countryside and heritage, and of their own regions in particular.

Features

Richard Cavendish has written several books about Britain's past and edited *Out of Town* magazine for several years in the 1980s. He has contributed substantially to recent AA publications and is a regular contributor to *History Today* magazine and *The Literary Review*. Mr Cavendish is also an expert on magic, mythology and legends.

The West Country

Martyn Brown, born and brought up in Devon, continued his education in Dorset and from university he returned to the West Country for research projects. He trained as a museum curator and spent 10 years in Somerset creating the Somerset Rural Life Museum. He has written a number of books on West Country themes and is now Assistant Director of Leisure and Arts in Oxfordshire.

South and South East England

Barry Shurlock is a freelance writer based in Winchester, Hampshire. He has worked in publishing and journalism for more than 20 years and spent much of his time travelling the world as a medical journalist; in quieter moments he writes on topography and local history. He is a keen photographer and walker and is particularly interested in `reading' the landscape.

Central England and East Anglia

Roland Smith, Head of Information Services for the Peak National Park, lives in Bakewell. After 20 years as a journalist, he continues to write a weekly column for the *Birmingham Post* and contributes to many outdoor magazines. He has written six books on the British countryside, as well as the official Countryside Commission guide to the Peak National Park.

Wales and the Marches

Roger Thomas has written six books about Wales and contributes regularly to many periodicals. Born and raised in South Wales, he has a particular interest in the countryside and historic sites. Employed by the Wales Tourist Board for 10 years, he now works from his home near Crickhowell, in the Brecon Beacons.

Northern England

Geoffrey Wright spent the first 25 years of his life in north-east England, and after serving in the RAF taught for 26 years in Wiltshire. He took early retirement in 1976 and moved to a farmhouse in Wensleydale to concentrate on his first loves - writing and photography. Now living near Ludlow, he has contributed to over 15 books about England.

Scotland

Ross Finlay has lived in Scotland all his life work ing as a journalist and an author. Specialising in travel and motoring, he has contributed to several books about Scotland's towns and countryside, presented a BBC radio series, and currently writes a weekly motoring column for the *Glasgow Herald*. His home is in Helensburgh.

KEY TO THE REGIONS

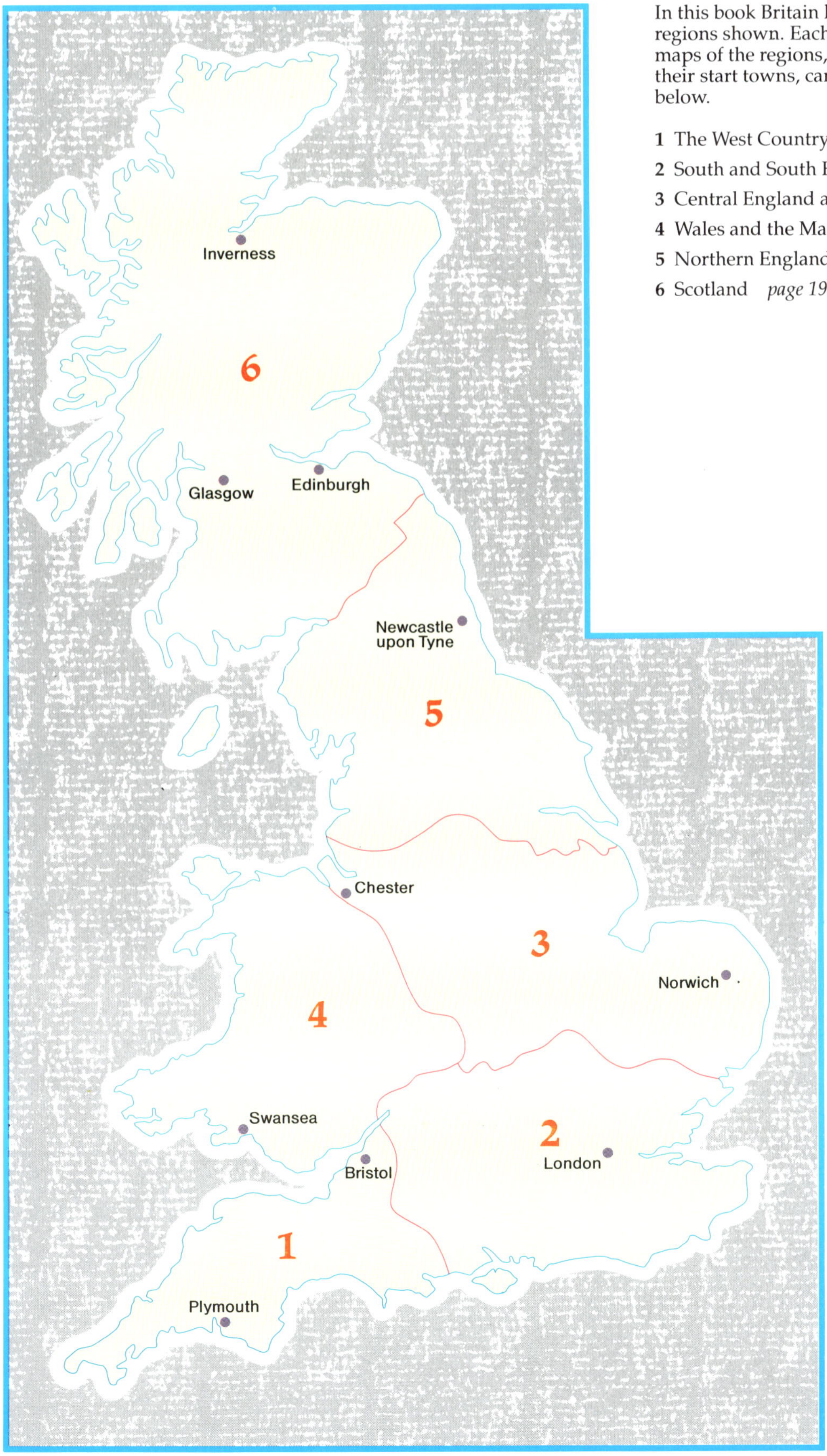

In this book Britain has been divided into the six regions shown. Each region contains 16 tours, and maps of the regions, locating the tours and naming their start towns, can be found on the pages given below.

Miller Dale from Monsal Head, Derbyshire

THE WEST COUNTRY

From the sunken lanes of Devon, where wildflowers bloom along the high banks, to the rolling sheep country of the Cotswolds and the lofty austerity of Salisbury Plain – where Stonehenge has stood in arcane majesty for 3,000 years and more – the West Country keeps a store of varied riches on its country roads. In Cornwall and North Devon, among the gorse and the bracken, you can sense the sea before you come to it, and narrow lanes lead steeply down to sandy beaches where the rollers smash and splinter under adamantine cliffs.

Cornwall is made of granite and slate, and so are its grey, diminutive churches and the gaunt cottages whose harsh lines are softened by nasturtiums and geraniums in profusion. In Devon they built their cottages of cob – clay mixed with straw and dung – and white-washed them or colour-washed them in pink and pastel shades, and pressed them down under heavy caps of thatch. Quiet roads lead deep into the tree-hung, stream-splashed valleys of the Torridge and the Taw, where Tarka the otter lived and died.

In Somerset the back roads wind their way among the apple orchards, past immemorial manor houses in the local Ham stone. Dazzlingly pinnacled church towers soar grandly above village war memorials and lines of leaning tombstones. Somerset and Dorset villages rejoice in euphonious and magical names: Ryme Intrinseca and Huish Episcopi, Bishop's Caundle and Cary Fitzpaine. Dorset always lay off the main routes between London and the west, and its green and pleasant landscape preserves something of the tranquillity of an older day.

Left: *Clovelly, Devon – a steep, cobbled street leads down to the romantic harbour*
Above: *Wells, Somerset – the lovely cathedral is famous for the statues on its west front*

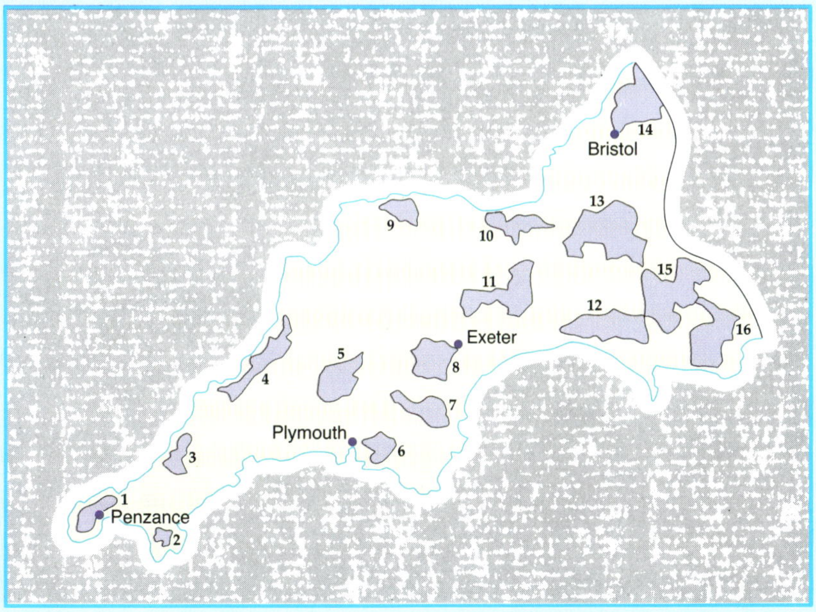

PENZANCE AND LAND'S END

46 miles

This is the western tip of England, exposed to the prevailing winds and violent storms and yet warmed by the great Atlantic Ocean.

Scattered remains of ancient settlements and abandoned mines add to the mystery of this isolated peninsula.

Penwyth means `extremity' in Cornish, and West Penwith, the Land's End peninsula, is the extremity of England - a brave toe stretching out to the Atlantic Ocean. Sea, rain and wind have battered and moulded the coastline with only the hardest rocks withstanding the force of the elements; trees and bushes have been permanently bent by the prevailing winds. Between sheer and ragged cliffs tiny coves offer havens of shelter. The scenery changes around Penzance ,where the sweeping curve of Mount's Bay frames St Michael's Mount, capped by an ancient castle and priory. The town of Penzance thrived for centuries in isolation from the rest of the country, its prosperity ensured by the rich mineral deposits mined in the area, especially tin. Ruined mine buildings dot the surrounding countryside, beside more ancient remains: stone circles, barrows and the extraordinary well-preserved Iron Age village of Chysauster.

ON THE TOUR

Penzance

The most westerly town in England, Penzance lies on the north-west corner of Mount's Bay commanding views across the sweeping expanse of water as far as Lizard Point. Away from the quay a network of lanes reveals many fine Regency buildings, especially in Chapel Street. The Nautical Museum contains evidence of the ferocity of the seas along this coast with numerous items discovered from wrecked ships. Further to the west are Morab Gardens, with a sumptuous display of sub-tropical plants; aloe, myrtle and camelias, thriving in the mild climate.

Newlyn

Numerous valleys and courtyards crowd round the pretty harbour of this busy fishing village. The beauty of the clear light attracted a group of artists at the beginning of the present century; their work is on permanent display in the Newlyn Art Gallery.

Mousehole

Regarded as the epitomy of the Cornish fishing village, Mousehole, pronounced 'Mowzel', retains its charm and feeling of history in its busy quay and granite houses hugging the hillside. From here, the view across Mount's Bay is unsurpassed.

The now-peaceful harbour at Mousehole sheltered over 400 boats when the village was a centre for pilchard fishing up to 100 years ago

Land's End

Although not the most spectacular part of Cornwall's coast, Land's End has a unique appeal; seeing the last inn, house and church in England has a satisfaction all of its own. Rocks rise from the sea like giant stepping stones leading the eye to the Longships Lighthouse almost two miles away and, on a clear day, the distant Scilly Isles. A leisure complex displays and interprets the natural history of the area.

St Just

One of the centres of copper mining in Cornwall, there are many industrial remains around St Just, especially near the coast where the shafts run up to half a mile out under the sea. In the town centre is a *plane-an-gwarry*, a circular enclosure where Cornish mystery plays were performed. The church, mostly 15th century, contains two fine wall paintings and a 5th-century inscribed stone.

Zennor

Isolated for centuries, Zennor has an ancient feel and is surrounded by tiny fields, some of which date back to the Bronze Age. A range of agricultural and mining finds in the area is exhibited in the Wayside Museum, near the car park. The square-towered church has a mermaid carved on one of the bench ends, relating to a legend about a squire's son who had such a fine voice that a mermaid spirited him away to live with her in the sea.

St Ives

Until the early years of this century St Ives was just a fishing port of grey, slate-roofed cottages packed in the lee of a hill overlooking a sheltered harbour. Then, the character of the place and surrounding countryside attracted a bevy of artists - Bernard Leach, Ben Nicholson and Barbara Hepworth amongst them. Barbara Hepworth's home is administered by the Tate Gallery; her studio is intact and the garden planted with sculptures. In summer visitors still flock to the town to enjoy the art galleries and absorb the atmosphere. The beaches south of the town are ideal for families - fine sand gently shelving to the sea.

Lelant

Lying on the Hayle Estuary, the salt flats at Lelant provide the ornithologist with a rich variety of bird life. In the grounds of Quay House is a hide constructed by the RSPB that is open to everyone. Merlin's Magic is a theme park with a wide variety of amazing attractions that appeal to children of all ages.

ROUTE DIRECTIONS

Leave **Penzance** (map 1SW43), by following the signs to Newlyn and Mousehole, beside the harbour. At **Newlyn** cross the bridge and turn left, unclassified (sp. Mousehole) to reach **Mousehole**. Here, turn left then, at the harbour, turn right and right again (sp. Paul). Ascend to Paul, continue forward to pass the church (sp. Land's End) and in ½ mile turn left on to the B3315 to Sheffield. In a further 5 miles, at the trunk road, turn left, then in ½ mile descend (hairpin bends) to the outskirts of Treen. In 1¼ miles turn right then in 2 miles further turn left on to the A30 for **Land's End**. Return along the A30 through Sennen and in 1¾ miles turn left on to the B3306 (sp. St Just). In 3 miles further, at the trunk road, turn left on to the A3071 for **St Just**. Here, go forward on to the B3306 then descend and follow signs St Ives to reach Pendeen. Continue to the edge of Morvah then at the Gurnards Head Hotel bear right then keep left to pass the outskirts of **Zennor**. Continue to **St Ives**. Here, turn right on to the A3074 (sp. Hayle) for Carbis Bay and **Lelant**. Here, turn right and in ½ mile, at the mini-roundabout, bear right (sp. Penzance). At the next roundabout take 3rd exit, A30 to Canonstown and Crowlas. In a further mile, at the roundabout, take 2nd exit, unclassified (sp. Marazion). In ⅓ mile further turn left to Marazion to view St Michael's Mount. Return, unclassified (sp. Penzance) to Longbrook. Here, at the roundabout, join the A30. Go forward at the next roundabout and turn left at the third one to re-enter Penzance.

The sheltered harbour of Penzance

OFF THE BEATEN TRACK

Cornwall has more than its fair share of ancient sites. Two of the finest are Chysauster village, an Iron Age settlement of courtyard houses along a street, and Lanyon Quoit, a burial chamber of three standing stones and a huge capstone. Sited north and north-west of Penzance respectively.

Numerous artists have been attracted to delightful Lamorna Cove, set in superb countryside. A stream rushes to the sea through a maze of giant boulders.

OUTDOOR ACTIVITIES

Reaching out into the Atlantic, Cape Cornwall promontory is a good site for picnics and coastal walks. From the summit the view south includes the Brisons, treacherous rocks that have been the scene of many wrecks and, beyond them, Land's End.

Known as Belerion – 'Seat of storms' – to the Romans, Land's End is the most westerly point of mainland England

OFF THE TOUR

Hayle

Turning on to the B3301 just after leaving Lelant, the road crosses the River Hayle and enters the town. Hayle was once an important port for the tin mining industry. Along the coast great towans or sand dunes make a fascinating walk. Paradise Park houses a large collection of exotic birds and rare-breed farm animals.

Porthcurno Bay and Minack Theatre

Signposted off the B3315 beyond Treen, Porthcurno Bay and the Minack Theatre make an interesting detour. Just to the south of the beach of fine white sand is the open-air theatre conceived by Rowena Cade. Hewed from the rock, the Roman-style auditorium is perched on the edge of a cliff, the distant horizon forming a majestic backdrop to the action. It is worth a visit even if no play is being performed.

Marazion – St Michael's Mount

Eastwards along the coast road from Penzance, Marazion is the starting point for a trip to St Michael's Mount; a stone causeway exposed at low tide leads to the 20-acre mass of rock that rises over 200ft from sea level. Crowned by an ancient castle and chapel, views stretch from Land's End to the Lizard.

CLIFFS AND COVES – THE LIZARD PENINSULA

29 miles

The Lizard Peninsula is a granite tableland 300ft above the sea, almost cut off from Cornwall by the Helford Estuary. Falling away precipitously at the coast, tiny coves and harbours are dotted along the shoreline – the former haven of smugglers and honest fishermen alike.

The tip of the Lizard peninsula is the most southerly point in Britain; the mild, moist climate attracts delicate and rare flora and in summer pink and lilac Cornish heather covers much of the ground. The west-facing coastline is wild and bashed by the full force of the Atlantic weather, while the eastern side is quite sheltered.

The sites of the peninsula offer striking contrasts; the remains of ancient tin mining ventures and the sleepy villages, unchanged for centuries, contrast sharply with the modern technology of the huge radio aerials at Goonhilly Downs Satellite Communications Station and the Royal Navy's Air Station at Culdrose, both of which have areas for visitors.

ON THE TOUR

Helston

Established as one of the five Stannary towns of Cornwall in 1305, where tin was weighed and graded, Helston was an important port until shingle blocked the entrance to the harbour. This created Loe Pool, the largest lake in Cornwall, where the thickly wooded hillsides and Loe Bar, on the coast, make a pleasant walk. Behind the Guildhall a museum houses an interesting collection of ancient agricultural implements and craft tools, as well as pictures and photographs of local scenes and events – the most famous of these events being 'Flora Day'. This festival, held on 8 May, is said to commemorate the dropping of a huge rock on the town by a dragon, the devil or St Michael, depending on the allegiance of the person you ask. The rock, miraculously, caused no damage, so celebrations are held with dances and music from dawn until late at night. Early morning sees the performance of the ancient mumming play; the main dance begins at 12 noon and processes through the town in and out of houses, bringing the place to a standstill.

Flambards Triple Theme Park

A family leisure park with three award-winning, all-weather attractions: a complete Victorian village with fully stocked shops, carriages and fashions; 'Britain in the Blitz', a wartime street; and the Cornwall Aero Park with historic aircraft, helicopters and a Concorde flight deck. There is also a 'hands-on' science playground, restaurant and gardens.

Trelowarren House

Home of the Vyvyan family since 1427, part of the house dates from early Tudor times. The chapel, part of which is pre-Reformation, and the 17th-century portion of the house are leased to an ecumenical Christian charity. Chapel and main rooms are open to the public, with guided tours. Services are held in the chapel on Sundays during the season.

Cadgwith

One of the least-spoilt coastal villages, Cadgwith is tucked neatly between rocky headlands. The picturesque cove has two small beaches divided by 'The Todden', a narrow headland with many rock pools. It is still a working fishing community and the beach is littered with small boats and their paraphernalia.

Lizard Point

The village of Lizard itself is rather plain, but just a mile further south is Lizard Point with its magnificent coastal scenery and walks. The lighthouse was first erected in 1752, and improved in 1903. It now has one of the most powerful lights in the world, at 4 million candlepower!

The village of Helford, on the south bank of the Helford River along a tidal creek. West of Helford is Frenchman's Creek, made famous by Daphne du Maurier's novel of the same name

OFF THE TOUR

Helford

Turning off the B3293 at Mawgan Cross to Mawgan, the road follows the river and then descends to a creek straddled by the village of Helford: a pretty place of neat thatched cottages in a delightful setting in the thickly wooded valley of the Helford River. Today, the sheltered waters and innumerable hidden inlets that were once the haven of smugglers attract anglers and yachtsmen. Although always attractive, the time to visit is high water when the great spread of water sets off the flowing lines of the surrounding green hills. A passenger ferry crosses the river to Helford Passage and the Ferry Boat Inn, a lively and friendly hostelry.

Coverack

Continue along the B3293 rather than turning towards Lizard Point, and then turn right on to the B3294, to reach Coverack, perhaps the archetypal Cornish fishing village; thatched whitewashed cottages overlook a tiny harbour and lifeboat station (now disused). At low tide there is a safe beach and the surrounding cliff walks provide many fine views.

Cornish Seal Sanctuary

Begun in 1958, when Ken Jones rescued a young seal, the sanctuary at Gweek has grown to include the care of dolphins and whales, the aim being to return them to the wild. There is also a donkey paddock, nature trails and exhibition hall. Also at Gweek, a maritime museum exhibits more than twenty craft from all over the world. Turn left off the B3293 after leaving Helston.

Mullion

One mile inland from Mullion Cove, the village has an interesting 15th-century church containing beautifully carved bench ends depicting the Instruments of the Passion, a jester and a monk. The cove has a sturdy granite harbour as protection from the Atlantic. On all sides ribbed and vaulted rocks pile up to form steep cliffs, and the waves send great clouds of spray into the air. At low tide there is a good, safe beach.

Poldhu Cove

Poldhu hit the headlines at the beginning of this century when Marconi sent the first transatlantic radio signal from the cliff top. All that remains of the masts and aerials is a simple commemorative stone.

There is a good sized beach at low tide and the cliffs are unusual; being made of slate and clay, they provide a contrast with the granite and serpentine which is found along the rest of the coast.

OUTDOOR ACTIVITIES

The coast, hugged by the Cornwall Coast Path, is characterised by cliffs interspersed with tiny coves – one of the most attractive being Kynance Cove. Although dominated by granite rocks there are outcrops of serpentine, a silicate of magnesium that produces strange formations with colours from red through purple to green, and these are seen at their best at Kynance. There is a good beach at Kynance but as with all the coves it is best to go at low tide to appreciate it. One of the best beaches is at Kennack Sands, where many rock pools add interest for the children. The largest beach is just south of Porthleven, a pleasant Victorian village near Loe Pool.

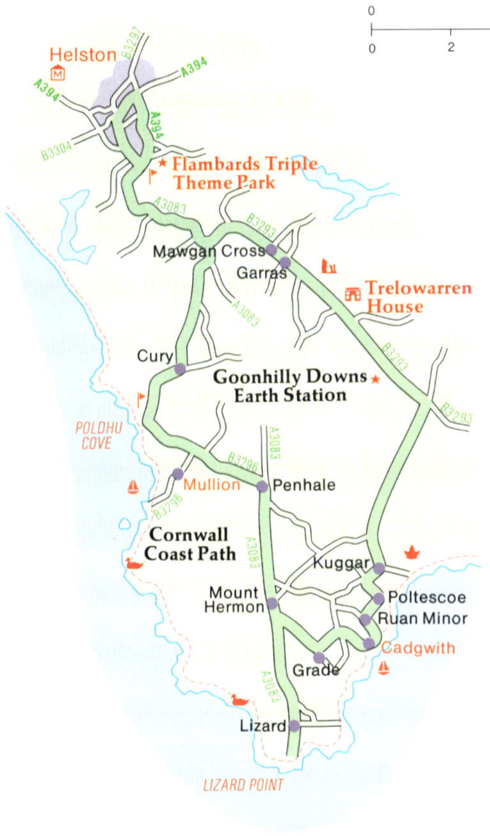

The Seal Sanctuary at Gweek, set in pleasant woodland and sloping fields on the north bank of the Helford River. Here, injured seals are cared for after being washed up on the beaches of the north coast

ROUTE DIRECTIONS

Leave **Helston** (map 1SW62) town centre by following signs Falmouth A394. In 1/2 mile, at the mini round-about, turn right (sp. Lizard). Pass the road to **Flambards Triple Theme Park** and at the ensuing roundabout go forward on to the A3083. In 1 3/4 miles, at the roundabout, take 1st exit B3293 (sp. Keverne). Pass the road to Culdrose RNAS Viewing Area on the left and in a further 1 mile, at the mini-roundabout, bear right to Garras. Pass the entrance to **Trelowarren House** on the left, pass Goonhilly Downs Earth Station and, in 3/4 mile, at the crossroads, turn right, unclassified (sp. Cadgwith). At the trunk road turn right, then in 3/4 mile, at the cross-roads, turn left for Ruan Minor. Bear right then keep left and descend (1 in 4) to **Cadgwith**. Ascend and in 1/3 mile keep left (sp. Lizard). In 1/2 mile further turn right and in 3/4 mile turn left on to the A3083 for the **Lizard Point**. Return along the A3083 Helston road then turn left on to the B3296 (sp. Mullion Cove) for **Mullion**. Here, keep left (one-way) and at the end turn right, unclassified (sp. Poldhu Cove). In 2 miles descend to **Poldhu Cove**, cross the bridge and bear right then ascend (1 in 6). Pass Cury Church on the right and in 1/2 mile turn left (sp. Helston). In 1 2/3 miles further, at the trunk road, turn left on to the A3083. In 1/2 mile at the roundabout go forward and in another 1 2/3 miles, at the roundabout, turn left on to the A394 (sp. Town Centre) to re-enter Helston.

WEST CORNWALL'S SANDY COAST

40 miles

The west-facing coast between Newquay and St Agnes is braced by rocky headlands withstanding the power of Atlantic breakers. Gently sloping sandy bays

provide perfect conditions for surfers. Truro, midway between the north and south coasts, is a fitting county town with a magnificent cathedral.

This unspoilt coast and wind-swept downland were once the heart of a thriving mining industry producing tin and copper for export. Surviving engine houses powered pumps to drain the mines and winding gear for hauling men and ore to the surface. Rough pock-marked ground, covered in gorse and brambles, often marks the site of old mine workings and should be avoided for the sake of safety.

Crantock, Perran Bay and Trevellas are 'meccas' for surfers, who, dressed in colourful Bermudas or skin-tight wet suits, sit astride their boards to wait for the best wave that will carry them in. Night clubs and discos cater for their evening entertainment. The area is also popular for family holidays – with its coastal walks, and sheltered coves ideal for young children.

One of the horse rounds to be seen at the Country Life Museum and Dairyland at Summercourt. Up to four horses worked this particular example which drove barn machinery in about 1800

ROUTE DIRECTIONS

Leave **Newquay** (map 1SW86) on the A392 (sp. Bodmin, Indian Queen's) to reach Quintrell Downs. At the roundabout take 2nd exit A3058 (sp. St Austell), then in ³/₄ mile turn right, unclassified (sp. Trevoll, St Newlyn East). Pass **Trerice Manor** on the right and in a further mile, at the crossroads, turn left. After ¹/₂ mile further, at the trunk road, turn left for **St Newlyn East**. On entering, bear right then go over the crossroads (sp. Truro) to Fiddlers Green. At the trunk road turn left, and in 1¹/₃ miles go over the crossroads (sp. Zelah) then right on to the A30 for Zelah. In ¹/₂ mile, ascend (1 in 8) then turn left, unclassified (sp. Shortlandsend). At Shortlandsend Inn turn left to join the B3284 for **Truro**. Here, at the mini-roundabout, bear left. At the next roundabout take 4th exit (sp. Redruth). Follow the A390 for 6 miles then, at the roundabout, take 2nd main exit on to the B3277 (sp. St Agnes). Pass St Agnes Leisure Park on the right to enter **St Agnes**. Go forward (one-way) then, at the church turn right on to the B3285 (sp. Perranporth) and descend to Trevellas. In 1 mile further descend to **Perranporth**, follow the signs to Newquay and ascend to **Goonhavern**. At the New Inn turn left on to the A3075 then in 2¹/₂ miles turn left, unclassified (sp. Cubert). Enter Cubert by the nearside of the village and turn right for Crantock. Here, turn right (sp. Newquay) and in ²/₃ mile turn left. In 1 mile further turn left on to the A3075, then follow the signs for Newquay Town Centre to re-enter Newquay.

OFF THE TOUR

Mawgan Porth

North of Newquay on the B3276, Mawgan Porth is a small, safe bay at the entrance to the beautiful Lanherne Valley. Remains of a 10th-century fishing settlement can be seen near the beach, including courtyard houses and a cemetery. Outside the church in the nearby village of St Mawgan is an excellent example of the granite-carved Saxon crosses that are dotted around Cornwall.

Trelissick

Leave Truro on the A39 south and turn left on to the B3289 to St Mawes. Here, Trelissick gardens provide meandering walks along the Fal Estuary; the house, rebuilt in 1825 in classical Greek style, is not open to the public. The grounds were landscaped mostly earlier this century; dense woodland and thick shrubs are relieved by expanses of lawn, with lovely views as far as Falmouth. There are camelias, rhododendrons and a collection of over 130 species of hydrangea.

Newquay's Towan beach. Now Cornwall's largest and most popular holiday resort, Newquay attracted Victorian holidaymakers with its bracing beaches. Large hotels soon sprang up in the town and on the grassy headlands

ON THE TOUR

Newquay

The major tourist centre in Cornwall, Newquay has a host of entertainments for visitors of all ages and is surrounded by fine beaches and magnificent scenery. The original Iron Age settlement was to the north-east at Porth; no remains can be seen, but it is an imposing place of towering cliffs and fascinating caves. The oldest remaining buildings of the town are around the harbour and at St Columb Minor, once a separate village but now little more than a suburb; the church, dating from the 15th century, has the second highest tower in Cornwall at 115ft.

There are two main beaches: Towan beach is a mile-long stretch of sand divided from Fistral beach by the rock-strewn promontory of Towan Head, from where there are magnificent views. Towan beach is sheltered and good for families whilst Fistral is one of the best surfing beaches in Britain with awe-inspiring breakers.

Trerice Manor

Sir John Arundel, a member of an ancient Cornish family, spent many years soldiering in the Low Countries. When he returned to Cornwall he built Trerice Manor in a style influenced by his travels. Its curved gables and E-shaped front have hardly changed since first built at the end of the 16th century. Fine plaster ceilings and original fireplaces are regarded as the finest points of the interior.

St Newlyn East

A charming village, the main interest lies in its beautiful 15th-century church dedicated to St Newlinia, a 6th-century missionary and one of Cornwall's earliest martyrs. It contains a richly carved Norman font and exquisitely carved bench ends of the 14th and 15th centuries. A two-mile round trip on the Lappa Valley Railway, the former Newquay to Chacewater line, takes in a leisure park and a former lead mine with its pumping house, East Wheal Rose. There is also a boating lake and maze.

Truro

The county town and Cornwall's only city, Truro stands where the rivers Allen and Kenwyn meet to form the Truro river. Its growth as a centre for mining and trade reached a peak in the 18th century when it became a social and cultural centre with a Philharmonic Orchestra, library and Book Society. Fine Georgian buildings survive in Lemon Street and Walsingham Place. Elsewhere back alleys with evocative names; Tippet's Backlet and Squeezeguts Alley, lead to attractive courtyards.

The cathedral was built in the 19th century in an Early English style, and incorporates some of the original Parish Church of St Mary in the south aisle. The Royal Institution of Cornwall in River Street houses the County Museum and Art Gallery. The collections are superb and include geology, archaeology and more recent antiquities as well as a surprisingly rich array of old-master drawings.

St Agnes

An attractive town, St Agnes retains much of its local character despite a hectic tourist season. Pleasant streets and by-ways surround the parish church, and a steep row of cottages called Stippy-Stappy leads down Town Hill. Just outside the village is the St Agnes Leisure Park with models of famous Cornish buildings and dinosaurs.

Perranporth

The small town has become a thriving holiday spot thanks to its magnificent beach. At the northern end, furthest from the town, wind-blown sand has created a moonscape of undulating dunes.

Goonhavern

Twelve acres of landscaped gardens here contain large models of world-famous buildings and statues. There is also a re-creation of a 'Western' street complete with horse rides and 'Saloon'.

OFF THE BEATEN TRACK

Holywell

Signposted from Cubert, the well that gives the village its name is a spring at the north end of Holywell Bay with a large and relatively quiet beach. Accessible only at low tide via steps in the cliffs, the spring falls through a series of basins in the rock like holy water stoups.

Summercourt

There is a farm park and country life museum with animals, game birds and wildfowl at Summercourt, on a minor road south-east of St Newlyn East. The animals are tame enough to be handled and a farm nature trail adds interest for the children. There is also an adventure playground and 160 cows can be seen being milked.

OUTDOOR ACTIVITIES

The 628ft headland of St Agnes Beacon is said to give a view of 23 miles of coastline and provides exhilarating walks.

BETWEEN BODMIN MOOR AND THE COAST

79 miles

In the centre of Bodmin Moor, Brown Willy rises to almost 1,400ft in as bleak a landscape as any. Towards the coast, the country softens a little but the west-facing shore is windswept and treacherous – magnificent for coastal walks.

Dramatic cliffs, created by the sea attacking the many rock types deeply folded and crushed into amazing strata, give rise to great variety in the coastline and create a haven for nesting seabirds. Cliff crevices support tiny plants like thrift and sea holly, adding a richness of colour enhanced by the deep-blue of the sea. Craggy headlands divide the coast into a jagged edge; coves and beaches are generally rocky with the exception of Widemouth Bay – a glorious stretch of silvery sand south of Bude. This is the land of King Arthur; legends abound – from his castle at Tintagel to the reputed siting of Camelot at Camelford.

Away from the coast, slate quarrying is still in evidence around Delabole. The rural coastal plateau stretches between the sea and Bodmin Moor – a counterpane of small fields bounded by low walls and hedges.

ON THE TOUR

Wadebridge

Until early this century, Wadebridge was a busy port. The 320ft-long medieval bridge that spans the River Camel is one of the finest in England. Built in about 1468, it has twice since been widened. The foundations are said to be made from bales of wool sunk into the river bed. Eddystone Road is so called because it was from here that the granite blocks for the Eddystone Lighthouse were shipped. The prosperity of the town today is largely reliant on the tourist trade; there are plenty of cafés and souvenir shops. The town also serves a large rural community for day-to-day needs. Nearby is the site of the Royal Cornwall Show, held in June.

Polzeath

With superb sands Polzeath has naturally become a favourite holiday village. Polzeath Bay offers some of the best surfing in Cornwall, whilst nearby Daymer Bay, in the shelter of the Camel Estuary, is a haven for young families.

Port Isaac

Steep lanes drop down to the tiny harbour, where fishing boats are pulled up on to the beach and the air is full of stories of the day's catch. Whitewashed cottages drip with hanging baskets.

Delabole

An inconspicuous village, Delabole is famous for its slate quarry, worked continuously for 350 years, and also Britain's deepest hole – 500ft deep with a circumference of 1½ miles.

Tintagel

Tintagel Castle is perched romantically on a rocky crag, approached by a narrow causeway and almost surrounded by steep cliffs to the crashing sea. Legend claims that King Arthur was born here and taught by the wizard, Merlin. The nearby village oozes with Arthurian souvenirs. The Old Post Office is a fine, slate-hung house dating from the 14th century; originally a small manor, and now a National Trust shop. King Arthur's Exhibition Hall is worth a visit.
Cliff walks are superb and Tintagel Head has traces of earlier Celtic settlements.

Boscastle

A picturesque S-shaped harbour at the mouth of the Valency Valley, flanked by rugged cliffs. The gruesome Witches Museum has fascinating relics of magic and witchcraft.

Crackington Haven

There is a good beach for surfers at this tiny seaside village. To the south, High Cliff drops a spectacular 700ft in a series of giant terraces to the sea.

Bude

An ever-popular seaside resort. The River Neet was once the port for the busy Bude Canal that ran to Launceston. There are plenty of amenities for visitors, and superb coastal walks in either direction. The Bude Marshes Nature Reserve reflects the flora and fauna shown in the World of Nature exhibition, and the history of Bude is depicted in the Historical and Folk Museum of Canal Wharf.

Camelford

Legend claims Camelford as Arthur's Camelot, with Slaughter Bridge (a mile to the north) as the site of Arthur's last battle. The North Cornwall Museum and Art Gallery is in a former coach and carriage works, and has well-displayed exhibits of rural crafts, with a reconstructed moorland cottage interior.

Boscastle harbour, with its narrow, fjord-like entrance is little more than a cleft in the slate cliffs. The harbour leads to a tiny 16th-century pier

OFF THE TOUR

Pencarrow House

Leave Wadebridge on the A389 to Bodmin and after about 3 miles follow signs to the left to Pencarrow to reach this historic Georgian house with its fine furniture and paintings. The long main drive passes through an Iron Age hillfort. There are woodland trails, a palm house and an ice house in the gardens, and exhibits by the Cornwall Crafts Association in the stables.

Padstow

Follow signs to the sailing village of Rock from Pityme (about 1½ miles) and from the beach take the ferry over the Camel Estuary to Padstow, an attractive village of slate houses and bustling narrow streets. It is famed for its May Day celebrations with the Hobby Horse parading the streets to the accompaniment of much merriment. Behind the town Prideaux Place, an Elizabethan mansion open in the summer, has a large deer park, and nearby are the Tropical Bird Gardens, with many exotic species.

ROUTE DIRECTIONS

Leave **Wadebridge** (map 1SW97) on the A39 (sp. Bude) and cross the river bridge. Then, at the mini roundabout, turn left, and in ½ mile further, at the traffic signals, turn left on to the B3314 (sp. Port Isaac). Pass through Trewornan Bridge and in 2 miles turn left, unclassified (sp. Rock). In 1⅓ miles keep left for Pityme, then take the next turning right (sp. Polzeath) for Trebetherick. Ascend (1 in 5) to **Polzeath** then ascend (1 in 7) and in 2 miles keep left (sp. Port Isaac). In ½ mile further, at the trunk road, turn left on to the B3314 for St Endellion. In 1 mile turn left on to the B3267 to **Port Isaac**. Here, turn right, unclassified, and descend to Portgaverne. Ascend (1 in 7) and in 2½ miles turn left on to the B3314 into **Delabole.** In 1¾ miles turn left (sp. Tintagel, B3263) and in a further ½ mile keep forward on the B3263, then keep left for Trewarmett. Continue to **Tintagel** and at the Wharncliffe Arms Hotel turn right (sp. Boscastle). In ¾ mile descend (1 in 9), ascend (1 in 6) and after 2 miles further turn left (sp. Bude). Descend to **Boscastle**, then make a long ascent (1 in 6) and after 3½ miles further turn left then immediate left again, unclassified (sp. Crackington Haven). In 2½ miles descend (1 in 5) to **Crackington Haven**, ascend (1 in 6) to Wainhouse Corner, then turn left on to the A39 (sp. Bude). Continue through Treskinnick Cross and Poundstock, then in ½ mile turn left, unclassified (sp. Widemouth). In 1 mile turn right to Widemouth Bay and continue to **Bude**. At the mini-roundabout follow the signs Bideford A39, then in ¼ mile turn right (sp. Camelford A39). In another mile turn right on to the A39, then left, unclassified to Marhamchurch. Here, turn left (sp. Week St Mary) then bear right for Week St Mary. Turn right (sp. Canworthy Water) and at the end of the village branch right. In 3½ miles at the trunk road turn left, then in 1¼ miles further turn right and cross the mill bridge into Canworthy Water. Continue with the Hallworthy road to Warbstow and Hallworthy. Here, turn right on to the A395 (no sign) and in 2¾ miles turn left on to the A39 (sp. Wadebridge) to **Camelford**. Continue past the edge of St Kew Highway for the return to Wadebridge.

The 14-arch bridge at Wadebridge, known as 'The Bridge on Wool'

OFF THE BEATEN TRACK

Take the narrow lane down to Daymer Bay from the village of Trebetherick, and walk along the sandy path to the golf course. Here, nestling in a hollow in the dunes is tiny St Enodoc Church, once totally buried by the sand. Restored in 1863, it is a delightful spot; John Betjeman was buried here in 1984. Watch out for hang gliders off Bray Hill!

Warbstow Bury

A prominent Iron Age hillfort with widely spaced defences, rising to 750ft with extensive views over north Cornwall.

Roughtor

In the valley below the car park is a stone monument to Charlotte Dymond, murdered in 1844 by a fellow servant. The path to the summit passes interesting Bronze Age huts and fields. Across the valley is Brown Willy – Cornwall's highest point. Extensive views northwards to Lundy Island and south-west to St Agnes Beacon.

OUTDOOR ACTIVITIES

Fantastic bracing walk along the promontory of Rumps Point to Cornwall's finest Iron Age cliff castle, with three ramparts and ditches. Spectacular coastal scenery either side.

Throughout this area there are many riding stables catering for experienced and novice riders who want to explore the area on horseback. Check the telephone directory and book in advance.

WESTERN REACHES OF DARTMOOR

67 miles

Wild moorland scenery with high, peaked tors rises to the east of the road linking the historic towns of Okehampton, Lydford and

Tavistock. Westwards the deeply cut valley of the River Tamar marks the boundary with Cornwall.

South of Okehampton much of the moor is inaccessible at certain times of the year, when the army uses the ground for artillery practice. Yes Tor and High Willhays rise to over 2,000ft here; a great, grey mass amid bleak and wind-swept hills. It is barren land, populated by shaggy black - faced sheep. Isolated farms and cottages of grey stone, with Cornish slate roofs, are sheltered by windbreaks. Westwards, towards the Cornish border and Launceston, the landscape mellows into a pattern of hills and deep wooded valleys, cut by a radiating fan of rivers which converge into the Tamar. The main road fringing the moor links the three historic towns: Okehampton, Lydford and Tavistock.

Below: *part of the living history of Morwellham; one of the staff is dressed as maid to the Assayer*

Bottom: *Lydford's church and wheelwright's stone*

ON THE TOUR

Okehampton

Situated on a wedge of land between the East and West Okement rivers, Okehampton is a busy market town enjoying a revival now that the long-awaited town bypass has been completed. Within a few miles to the south are High Willhays and Yes Tor, rising to over 2,000ft; Dartmoor's highest and most northerly summits. The parish church outside the town, and the tower of the chapel of St James, which dominates the High Street, date from the 15th century. An old mill is home to the Museum of Dartmoor Life. Exhibits include archaeological finds, reconstructions of local tin and copper mines and an interesting array of agricultural vehicles.

Launceston

The only once-walled town in Cornwall, it was important as the county town until 1835, when ousted by Bodmin. The Norman South Gate survives, with an art gallery in the room above the narrow arch. Castle Street's brick Georgian houses include Lawrence House (now the museum) with mementoes of the Napoleonic Wars, when captured French soldiers were billeted here. The Church of St Mary Magdalene is unique in its rich exterior of granite carvings, commissioned by grief-stricken Sir Henry Trecarrel in 1542 after the death of his wife and son.

The impressive 13th-century castle, perched on an enlarged natural mound, dominates the town, replacing an earlier timber construction of the Norman Conquest, built by William the Conqueror's brother.

Morwellham Quay

The nearest navigable point for sea-going ships to Tavistock, Morwellham became the port for huge local deposits of copper and tin. The site is now a time capsule, hidden in the wooded valley, and sensitively restored to create a sense of living history. Cottages, houses, the pub and shop have been refurbished; there are demonstrations of crafts and industrial skills and a train ride deep into a copper mine, last worked in 1868. Up the hill, the Victorian farm, complete with Shire horses, offers carriage rides along the Duke of Bedford's drive.

Tavistock

Now a pleasant market town catering for western Dartmoor, Tavistock's early prosperity relied on tin. As this declined, wool became important, until the 19th century, when copper was discovered and the town's population trebled in the first half of the century. Much of the town was owned by the Dukes of Bedford, who completely rebuilt and restyled the centre in Victorian times with their new-found wealth, creating an impression of grandeur and prosperity, with Victorian villas and elaborate Gothic façades. The only remains of the Benedictine abbey of 974 are the walls, and Still Tower, visible from riverside walks.

Lydford Gorge

Lydford Gorge, $1\frac{1}{2}$ miles long, has been scooped into a series of dramatic potholes, creating features like the thundering Devil's Cauldron. Walk the fern-dripping wooded valley to the spectacular 100ft White Lady waterfall. Paths can be slippery so wear sensible shoes. There are picnic sites above the gorge.

Lydford

Lydford is relatively small today, but originally it was established as part of a national defensive network against the Danes in the 10th century. Its natural position on a promontory above the River Lyd was used to advantage with the castle sited on a huge earth rampart. The present castle dates from 1195; the court was held on the first floor, with prisoners below. Next to the castle, St Petrock's Church is mainly 14th- and 15th-century, with a low Perpendicular tower; notice the watchmaker's gravestone beside the porch.

OFF THE TOUR

Finch Foundry Museum

Take the A382 from Okehampton, signposted to Moretonhampstead, and after $2\frac{1}{2}$ miles enter the village of Sticklepath. Seven 19th-century watermills worked in the village, with a corn mill at one end, a woollen serge factory at the other, and the Finch Foundry in the middle producing edge tools for agricultural use. The latter is now fully restored with three water wheels.

Cotehele House

Turn right off the A390 at St Ann's Chapel for Cotehele; a charming medieval manor house. Colourful gardens, with a stream, pools and fine medieval dovecote, merge with thick natural woodland in the valley. A pleasant riverside walk leads to Cotehele Quay and a restored mill, with an old inn, warehouse and limekilns.

ROUTE DIRECTIONS

Leave **Okehampton** (map 2SX59) by following the signs Launceston B3260 along the West Okement Valley. After 3½ miles skirt the village of Bridestowe, continue to Combebow and Lewdown and on to Liftondown. In ¼ mile beyond the village, turn right on to the A388 (sp. Callington) and in ¾ mile cross the River Tamar into Cornwall, and **Launceston**. At the crossroads go forward (sp. Town Centre), then shortly turn right, pass beneath the South Gate and turn left into the town square. At the far end bear right, pass the castle entrance and, at the crossroads, go forward on to the A388 (sp. Callington). In ½ mile turn left to join the bypass, A30. Half a mile further branch left (sp. Callington) and, at the T-junction, turn right on to the A388. Continue through Treburley, across the River Inny and on to Kelly-Bray, then, at the Swingle Tree take 2nd left on to the B3257 (sp. Tavistock). Skirt the summit of Kit Hill and, after 2 miles, at the crossroads, turn right, unclassified (sp. Kit Hill). In ¼ mile turn right again (no sign) to ascend to the car park and viewpoint at the summit. Descend along the approach road to the T-junction and turn right. Continue down, then turn left to join the A390 Tavistock road. In 2 miles, at St Ann's Chapel, pass the road for Cotehele House on the right and descend through Gunnislake to New Bridge on the River Tamar. Re-cross the river into Devon, ascend and at the summit turn right at the crossroads, unclassified (sp. Morwellham). In 1 mile, at the next crossroads turn right and descend to **Morwellham Quay**. Return to the crossroads and go forward (sp. Tavistock) and in 1 mile at the Harvest Home, turn right on to the A390 to **Tavistock**. Continue from the town hall crossroads, following signs Okehampton A386, to follow the Tavy Valley. Pass the Kelly College on the left and continue to Mary Tavy. Here, branch left, unclassified, on to the Brentor road. Cross the slopes of Gibbet Hill then descend to cross the bridge before climbing to North Brentor village. Pass the church and at the windmill turn right (sp. Lydford). In ½ mile bear left and in ¼ mile further, at the T-junction, turn right. After 1¾ miles make a descent, pass the car park for **Lydford Gorge** on the left, and descend a further mile to cross the River Lyd. Ascend into **Lydford** village. Pass the church and Lydford Castle on the left, then keep forward and, in 1 mile, turn left on to the A386 (sp. Okehampton). Pass beneath Great Links Tor then 1 mile beyond Sourton, turn right on to the A30. After 1 mile turn left on to the B3760 for the return to Okehampton.

The tiny Church of St Michael, Brentor, stands 1,100ft above sea level on the western edge of Dartmoor. The walls are only 10ft high, but, being made of 3ft-thick volcanic stone taken from the tor on which they stand, they are well able to withstand the elements

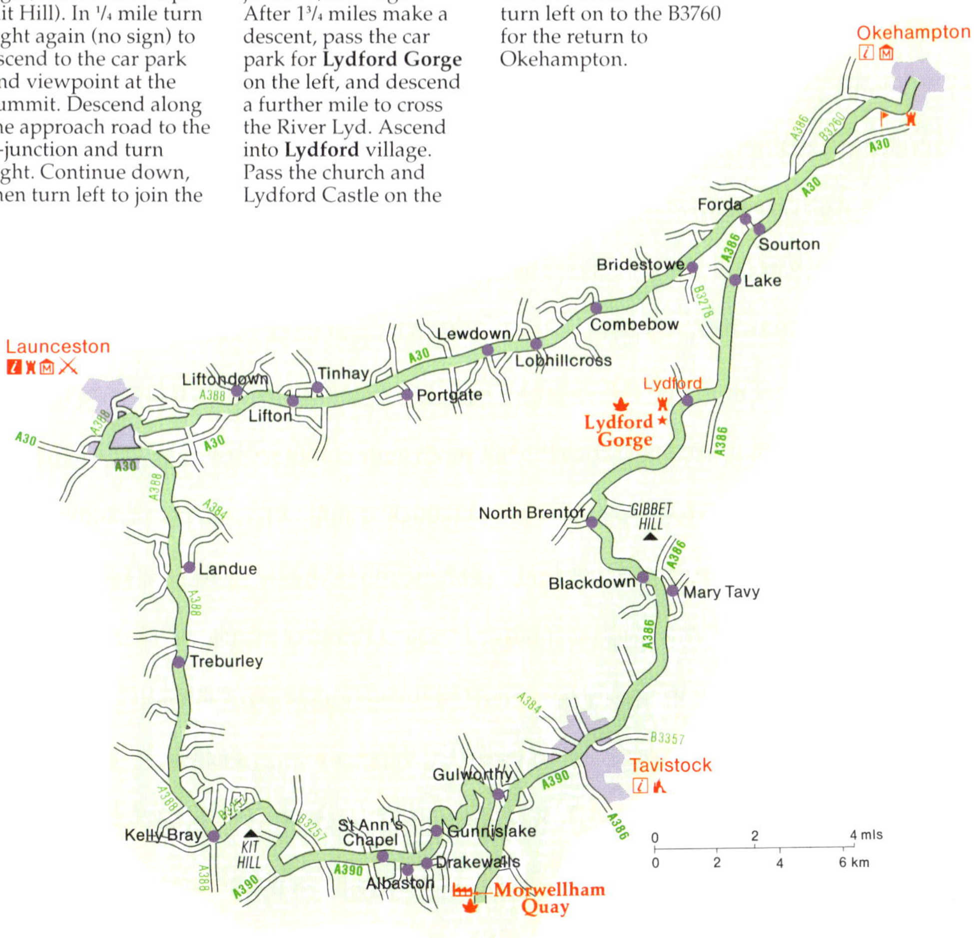

OFF THE BEATEN TRACK

Turn left at the T-junction just beyond North Brentor village for the Church of St Michael at Brentor; the car park and entrance are about 1½ miles down the road. Folklore and superstitions surround the precarious church crowning the summit, said to be the fourth smallest church in the country. The present building dates from the end of the 13th century, but there was a church here even before then.

OUTDOOR ACTIVITIES

Belstone, an attractive moorland village east of Okehampton, is an excellent starting point for moorland walks. Near Belstone Tor is a circle of standing stones known as Nine Stones (in fact 16) – a Bronze Age burial site. In the village there is a good pub and delightful cottage tea rooms for refreshment.

Just outside Okehampton is Meldon dam, a reservoir and picnic area, with disabled facilities. There are walks on to open moorland, and fantastic views back towards Okehampton and beyond.

WHERE THE RIVERS MEET THE SEA – SOUTH-WEST DEVON

39 miles

Dartmoor spawns many rivers and from Plymouth eastwards the coast is a series of convoluted estuaries between steep wooded hillsides. At Plymouth

itself two rivers, the Tamar and the Plym, have created a natural harbour: the focus of the city's prosperity and history.

The busy naval port of Plymouth dominates the south-western corner of Devon, both in size and in the rich story of its past. The fine natural harbour lies at the mouth of the River Tamar, which forms the natural boundary between Devon and Cornwall. At Plymouth the river is spanned by two bridges: the 19th-century Brunel railway bridge and a modern road bridge, both soaring high above the flotilla of pleasure craft on the secluded inlets and tributaries below. To the east of the city the rivers Yealm and Erme enter the sea in peace and quiet; too shallow to allow the development of any substantial harbour. Their appeal lies in the natural beauty of their meandering estuaries, cutting into the sheer slate cliffs. Inland, the roads skirt the mass of Dartmoor that rises impressively to the north, offering the visitor many spectacular walks.

ON THE TOUR

Plymouth

Much of the centre of historic Plymouth was destroyed by horrific bombing raids during the Second World War. Rebuilding to a grid-iron pattern has not enhanced the area. However, the quayside at Sutton Harbour, called the Barbican, survived and a taste of the city's seafaring traditions is encapsulated in the narrow streets and ancient buildings. It was from here that Drake began his circumnavigation of the world, that the Pilgrim Fathers left in the *Mayflower*, and that the first transportees set sail for Botany Bay in Australia. A 15th-century building houses the distillery for the famous 'Plymouth Gin', and two ancient custom-houses stand on Parade Quay. Leading away from the Barbican Quay is New Street, which contains many fine old buildings, including the Elizabethan House, which has been sensitively restored to its former splendour.

Two buildings that survived the air-raids are Prysten House and Merchants House, behind St Andrew's Church on Royal Parade. Both are open to the public, Merchants House offering a more conventional view of Plymouth's past.

Plymouth's sea front, the Hoe, gives wide views of the Sound which, from the top of the reconstructed Eddystone Lighthouse, are even more stunning. A high-tech visitor centre here interprets the past with exciting visual and sound effects. Radar, satellites and sophisticated cameras monitor the weather and local shipping activity.

Saltram House, a George II house (now owned by the National Trust), which was built around the remains of a late Tudor mansion

Yealmpton

Set in the wooded Yealm Valley its chief claim to fame is that it was the home of the original Old Mother Hubbard. She was housekeeper at nearby Kitley where Sarah Martin, who wrote the nursery rhyme, lived.

The church is in a lovely setting, and although modernised contains some fine marble pillars and chancel screen, brasses and, beneath the tower, the old town stocks.

National Shire Horse Centre

The National Shire Horse Centre is a farm worked solely by horse-power. Set in impressive old farm buildings, there are agricultural and craft displays and a wide variety of other farm animals.

Newton Ferrers

On a hill above a tributary of the River Yealm, this pretty village faces across the creek to Noss Mayo. The church is mostly 15th century but the tower arch and chancel are 13th century.

Ivybridge

A bridge over the River Erme was first recorded in 1280, and the town developed as a trading post on the route to Plymouth. A 19th-century paper mill survives by the fast-flowing river, and a walk north along its banks reveals the massive remains of a railway viaduct designed by Brunel. The adjacent Victorian viaduct was built in 1893 to take the doubled line of the Great Western Railway. Ivybridge is being greatly expanded and the new South Dartmoor Leisure Centre provides many sporting and recreational facilities, and includes a coffee shop and bar. The Imperial Inn, on Western Road on the way into Ivybridge, has an extensive range of bar snacks, a beer garden and children's play area.

Cornwood

Set on the fringe of the moor, all the lanes north-east from the village lead to high tors and slopes speckled with ancient hut circles, stone rows and burial mounds. Two great names in nautical history are associated with Cornwood, both Raleigh and Drake had ancestors from this parish.

Dartmoor Wildlife Park

This 25-acre park has many breeds of European wildlife: bears, deer and birds of prey, as well as lions and tigers. An observation tower gives magnificent views of the grounds and surrounding area. 'Close Encounters of the Animal Kind' is a great visual and tactile experience for the children.

OFF THE TOUR

Kitley Caves

Just off the A379 at Yealmpton are Kitley Caves, where the remains of bear, rhinoceros and woolly mammoth have been found.

Mount Edgcumbe Park

Reached via the passenger ferry from Cremyll in Plymouth. Mount Edgcumbe House, a Tudor mansion badly damaged in the Second World War, has been beautifully restored. The gardens are open all year and the house, which contains a restaurant, is open during the holiday season.

Saltram House

This fine Georgian mansion contains two rooms designed by Robert Adam and furnished in period style and a huge kitchen. In the lush grounds are two 18th-century buildings: an orangery and summer house.

ROUTE DIRECTIONS

Leave **Plymouth** (map 2SX45) on the A379 Kingsbridge road to cross the River Plym by Laira Bridge. Skim the suburb of Plymstock, keep forward at all roundabouts and then pass through Brixton. One mile further pass the road to Newton Ferrers and Kitley Caves, and enter **Yealmpton**. After ¾ mile, at the crossroads, turn right, unclassified (sp. Shire Horse Centre, Dunstone) and pass the entrance to the **National Shire Horse Centre**. At Dunstone turn right (sp. Newton Ferrers) and in ¾ mile, at the crossroads, turn left on to the B3186 Newton Ferrers road. In 2½ miles descend to the edge of **Newton Ferrers** and turn left, unclassified, for Noss Mayo, continuing the descent. In ½ mile turn sharp right to round the head of the creek, then in ½ mile further bear left and ascend through Noss Mayo on the Holbeton road. At the church bear left (no sign) and in ½ mile bear left again (sp. Holbeton). In ⅔ mile at the crossroads, turn left and in 1 mile bear right and descend to Holbeton. Bear left, ascend past the church and in ¼ mile, at the crossroads, turn right (sp. Ermington, Kingsbridge). In ½ mile bear right and in 1 mile turn right on to the A379. One mile further, at Modbury Cross, branch left on to the B3210 Totnes road to follow the Erme Valley. In ¾ mile turn left, unclassified and ascend into Ermington. Go forward on to the Ivybridge road, continue to the edge of **Ivybridge** and at the T-junction turn right to cross the A38. Then turn left on to the Cornwood road, unclassified. In 1 mile bear right and in ¼ mile turn right. One mile further bear left, then descend into the Yealm Valley to reach **Cornwood**. At the crossroads turn left on to the Sparkwell road, continue past Lutton and the entrance to **Dartmoor Wildlife Park** before reaching Sparkwell. After 2½ miles further, at the mini-roundabout, turn left (sp. City Centre), go under the railway bridge and turn right. In ½ mile, at the mini-roundabout on the edge of Plympton, turn right on to the B3416 Plymouth road. Half a mile further, pass the road to Saltram House, then the road to Plym Valley Railway. Continue forward to the Marsh Mills roundabout and take 2nd exit A374, to return to Plymouth city centre.

A modern John Piper window in St Andrew's – the parish church of Plymouth virtually destroyed by wartime bombing

OFF THE BEATEN TRACK

Signposted off the A379 just past Brixton, a lane leads to Wembury and then on to the little bay dominated by an ancient, isolated church. It was probably built here to act as a bearing for ships along the treacherous coast. On the beach the National Trust have restored an old mill where teas are served in the high season. A mile offshore stands the Mew Stone – a rocky crag inhabited by numerous seabirds, which was once the warren for the local gentry.

OUTDOOR ACTIVITIES

About 4 miles from Noss Mayo turn right at Battisborough Cross and park in the car park at Mothercombe. Continue on foot to the quiet beach at the mouth of the Erme, with lovely views across the estuary and walks up-river.

THE DART VALLEY AND SOUTH DEVON CASTLES

43 miles

The higher reaches of the River Dart tumble through stunning wooded moorland scenery, with deep pools and rounded boulders. Below Buckfast the landscape mellows into rolling farmland. The ancient market towns of Buckfastleigh and Totnes are charming and packed with history.

Fore Street, in the heart of Totnes, leading up the hill towards the broad arch over the road at the East Gate. Set in the pavement here is the Brutus Stone, where Brutus is supposed to have stood before allegedly founding Totnes and the entire British race

The Dart and Teign rivers radiate from Dartmoor like the spokes of a wheel and slice this corner of south-east Devon into a neat segment. Beneath the shadow of the moor, the hills soften; crisscrossed by high banked hedges and patchworked into tiny fields. The villages lie deep in valley bottoms linked by a maze of tortuous and narrow lanes. Predominantly pasture land with cattle and sheep, the plough-share cuts a furrow of striking red as the rich loam is exposed, and the sea is stained blood red in winter storms where new red sandstone cliffs crumble under the waves.

The principal towns, Newton Abbot and Totnes, lie at the highest navigable points of their respective rivers; both are ancient route centres. The small towns and villages between them are unspoilt and retain much rural charm. Look out for signs for cream teas.

ON THE TOUR

Newton Abbot

This is a lively and bustling town at the head of the Teign Estuary. The Wednesday market serves a wide hinterland stretching from the moors to the sea. In 1688, from the tower of St Leonard's Chapel at the centre of the town, William III, Prince of Orange, proclaimed his intention to become King of England. The tower now stands alone, the chapel was demolished in 1836. Newton expanded with the arrival of the railway in 1846, and has continued to grow both as a commercial centre and as the hub of transport routes.

Just outside the town, signposted off the A30, is Trago Mills – a huge shopping complex for cut-price goods surrounded by a bewildering array of attractions. These include a miniature steam railway, adventure playground, the largest model railway in Devon, 'sensearound' cinema, countless eating places, and picnic areas.

Ashburton

This ancient Stannary town was one of four granted a charter in 1285 for the weighing and stamping of tin mined on Dartmoor. The River Ashburn rushes through the centre of the town and once powered several wool mills – they brought prosperity in the 15th century. The magnificent Church of St Andrew reflects this affluence. Vernacular slate-hung buildings date from the 17th and 18th centuries. There are several craftshops and a free car park.

River Dart Country Park

This popular park has adventure playgrounds and nature trails, with a lake for swimming. There are picnic areas, a café and takeaway food. For an extra charge pony trekking and fly fishing are available. Special activities like caving and climbing are arranged in the summer holidays for teenagers.

Dartmeet

This popular beauty spot is situated where the road drops steeply to the convergence of the East and West Dart rivers. The valleys are thickly wooded, breaking out into bracken and heather on the higher slopes. There is a large car park but it is easy to escape the crowds by walking a short distance up or downstream. The storm-damaged remains of the old clapper bridge are next to the packhorse bridge still used today.

Holne

The attractive late-Georgian rectory was the birthplace of Charles Kingsley in 1819. The church dates from 1300 and has an hour-glass incorporated in the carved pulpit. An enjoyable walk from the west of the village along Sandy Way leads to the source of the River Avon.

Buckfast

The village is dominated by the great Abbey Church, founded in the 10th century, and rebuilt by a handful of untrained monks between 1907 and 1938. There is a magnificent mosaic inside the church. Nearby, the House of Shells demonstrates the use of shells in arts and crafts.

The Buckfast Butterfly Farm boasts tropical gardens with huge ponds under cover, where exotic butterflies fly freely. There are also birds, terrapins, fish and insects.

Buckfastleigh

Up 196 cobbled steps on the north-east side of the town, the views from the church are breathtaking. Now quiet from the noise of the wool mills that made Buckfastleigh prosperous, the town is a delight to explore; crammed with cottages around tiny courtyards behind the main street. Following the banks of the Dart between Buckfastleigh and Totnes, a steam train carries passengers through picturesque woodland. At Buckfastleigh station there is a display of rolling stock, a model railway and a café.

Cider Press Centre

At Shinners Bridge, this is a huge craft complex with demonstrations and events, and the famous Cranks restaurant. There are riverside trails and picnic areas too.

Totnes

This fascinating old town rises on a hill to the west of the river, up to the keep of the classic

Norman castle, sited on a mound at the top of the High Street and commanding far-reaching views over the roofs and beyond. The busy quay, which still takes freight and passengers travelling up and down the River Dart, has been renovated to house expensive shops and restaurants. Much of the architecture is 16th-century, notably the Elizabethan House, the town museum.

Berry Pomeroy

The ivy-clad ruins of the old castle of Berry Pomeroy stand on a rocky limestone crag beside the steep valley of the Gatcombe Brook. The outer walls date from the 14th century. Inside are the ruins of a great Tudor house, reputed to be haunted.

Compton Castle

This impressive fortified manor house was built at three periods – 1340, 1450 and 1520 – by the Gilbert family, who still live in it today. It is open Monday, Wednesday and Thursday throughout the season.

Bradley Manor

Deep in the valley of River Lemon lies Bradley Manor, now owned by the National Trust. It is a delightful 15th-century manor house with a gabled front.

OFF THE BEATEN TRACK

Crockern Tor

From Dartmeet continue along the B3357 to Two Bridges. From here a waymarked path leads up on to Dartmoor's tors. One of these, Crockern Tor, was the assembly point for the Stannary Parliament between 1494 and 1703. This was the Great Court of the Dartmoor tinners and the site was chosen as it lies approximately the same distance from the four stannary towns of Ashburton, Chagford, Tavistock and Plymouth. Representatives from each town attended the meetings.

OUTDOOR ACTIVITIES

Holne

The National Trust owns about 2½ miles of woodland along the Dart at Holne and there are numerous woodland paths which can be explored.

OFF THE TOUR

Buckland in the Moor

One of the most picturesque moorland villages, north-east of Poundsgate. The church clock face, inscribed 'My dear Mother' in place of numbers, chimes a hymn when it strikes. Tea rooms and a craft shop are located in a converted stable. The walk to Buckland Beacon can be bracing, but rewarding, with superb views, and the Ten Commandments at the top carved in stone.

Dartington

From the main A384 beyond Riverford Bridge, turn left to the Dartington estate. The 14th-century great hall is now a venue for cultural and artistic activities. The formal gardens have Henry Moore sculptures and a restored tiltyard, flanked by huge grassy terraces. There are also riverside trails and picnic areas.

ROUTE DIRECTIONS

Leave **Newton Abbot** (map 2SX87) on the A383 (sp. Ashburton) and after 4½ miles keep left to join the A38. In 1¾ miles branch left on the B3357 (sp. Ashburton) then turn right across the bridge and left to enter **Ashburton**. Keep forward and at the end turn right (sp. Dartmeet, Princetown). In ⅔ mile pass the entrance to the **River Dart Country Park**. In 1 mile turn left to cross the River Dart by Stoke Bridge. In 1¼ miles recross the Dart at New Bridge, ascend (1 in 5) and pass through Poundsgate. Ascend again (1 in 4) and in 1 mile pass Sharp Tor (1,250ft) on the left. Start the descent (1 in 5) to reach **Dartmeet**, and Dartmeet Bridge. Ascend again (1 in 6) and in ½ mile turn left, unclassified, on to the Hexworthy road. Descend and cross the river bridge before making a steep ascent (1 in 4) with hairpin bends through the hamlet of Hexworthy. At the top keep forward (sp. Holne) on to the moorland road. At the top pass Combestone Tor, then descend to cross the dam wall of the Venford reservoir. Pass a car park on the left, in 1¼ miles bear left, then in ¼ mile at the crossroads turn right (sp. Holne, Buckfastleigh) to enter **Holne**. Follow signs Buckfastleigh and in ½ mile bear right, then in another ½ mile descend (1 in 5). At the bottom keep left and in 1½ miles, at the crossroads, keep forward. In ¼ mile bear left then in ¾ mile at the next crossroads turn left (sp. Buckfast). Descend and pass the road into **Buckfast**. At the mini-roundabout turn right and in ½ mile at the T-junction, turn right again on to the B3380 (sp. Buckfastleigh) to skirt around **Buckfastleigh**. In ⅓ mile pass the road to the Dart Valley Railway. Take next turning left, unclassified (sp. Colston) and pass beneath the A38 viaduct. In ¼ mile turn left (no sign) to cross the railway and, at Austin's Bridge, cross the River Dart then turn right on to the A384 (no sign). Follow the Dart Valley and in 2¼ miles bear right to cross the Riverford Bridge. In 1½ miles pass Dartington church and the turning to Dartington Hall, and ½ mile further, at the traffic signals, keep left on to the A385, Paignton road past the **Cider Press Centre**. In 1¼ miles at the traffic signals keep forward to enter **Totnes**. In ¼ mile, at the roundabout take 3rd exit (sp. Town Centre). At the mini-roundabout turn left to cross the River Dart and in ¼ mile turn right to rejoin the A385 (sp. Paignton). Ascend and branch left, unclassified, on the road to **Berry Pomeroy**. In ½ mile, at the crossroads, turn left (sp. Marldon, Torquay). In a further 2 miles, at the edge of Marldon, turn left at the mini-roundabout on to the A3022, then immediate left again, unclassified (sp. Compton). Enter Compton village, pass **Compton Castle** and, in ½ mile, keep forward (no sign). In 1½ miles, at Park Hill Cross, turn right on to the A381 Newton Abbot road. Continue forward, passing the entrance to **Bradley Manor** before re-entering Newton Abbot.

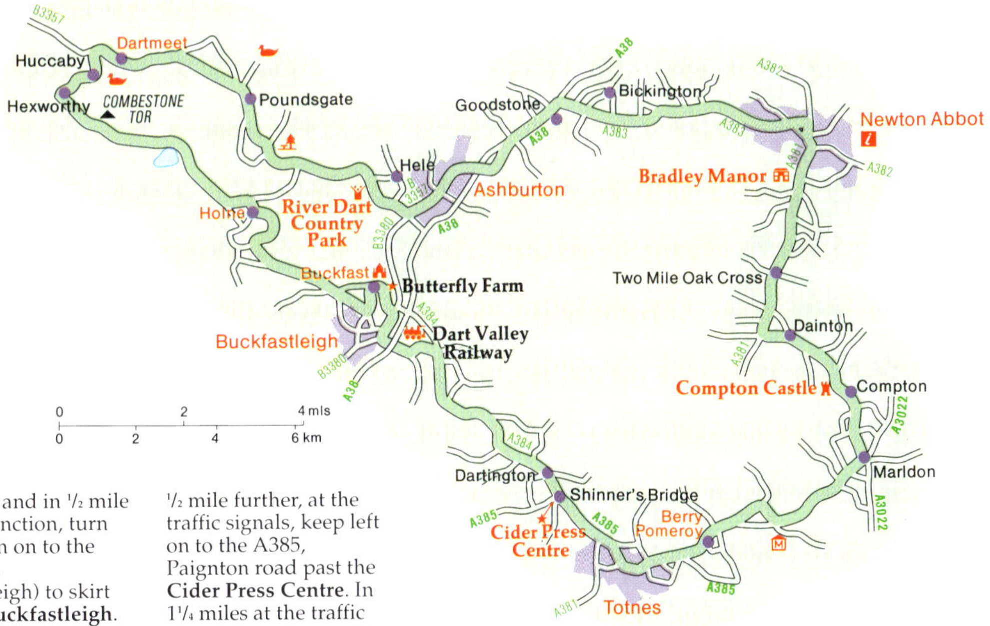

The restored Abbey at Buckfast

EXETER, EAST DARTMOOR AND THE HALDON HILLS

46 miles

West of Exeter the landscape rolls gently towards the wooded foothills of Dartmoor – rounded hills and valleys and contours marked

by low sun. The Haldon Hills are steep and bleak by comparison, planted with conifers, but with fine views over the Exe Estuary.

Established by the Romans 2,000 years ago, on a bluff overlooking the lowest fording point of the River Exe, Exeter marked the limits of civilisation. Beyond lay the realms of the brigand and outlaw; wild, wooded hills and moorland – treacherous and uninviting.

Now the landscape of eastern Dartmoor welcomes the visitor, with its network of tiny fields typical of peripheral moorland farms, giving way to wilder stretches of high, open moor, bisected by rushing streams and scattered with ancient granite homesteads, nestling in the lee of the hills. Long-established market towns survive as memorials to the industries of the past – tin, granite and copper. The land-scape is pock-marked with evidence of these activities. The original industries have died, but traditional crafts have enjoyed a revival, spurred by the increased tourist trade.

St Mary Steps Church, Exeter, with the cobbled and stepped medieval way into the city beside it

ON THE TOUR

Exeter

The site of Exeter was fortified in Roman times and the town expanded as a centre of trade with a quay on the River Exe. Most of medieval Exeter was destroyed by enemy action during the Second World War, or by post-war planners; miraculously the cathedral survived, as did several attractive old houses around the Close. The cathedral dates from 1050, when the See was transferred from Crediton to the safety of the walled city. Most of the present building dates from the 14th century. The magnificent 300ft nave has the longest span of Gothic vaulting in the world. The 13th-century Guildhall in the High Street is one of the oldest municipal buildings still in regular use. Rougemont House, dating from 1768, now exhibits a fine collection of Regency costumes and lace, and the gardens, in the moat of Norman Rougemont Castle, provide an opportunity to appreciate the strategic value of this site. In Princesshay an inauspicious entrance leads down to a maze of underground passages (open at certain times) built as medieval aqueducts to bring water to the city from beyond the walls. Down at the Old Quayside visitors to the Maritime Museum are encouraged to clamber aboard boats ranging from a Bahrain pearling dhow or Venetian gondola to a steam tug or dredger. Cross the river on the hand-hauled ferry for further exhibits.

Castle Drogo

The last 'castle' to be completed in England. Built on a rocky promontory it commands superb views over the Teign Valley. Designed by Sir Edwin Lutyens for Julius Drew, it was completed in 1930, combining modern requirements with castle tradition.

Moretonhampstead

This moorland gateway town was established as a marketing centre for the woollen trade. Main streets radiate from a central square, unchanged since the Middle Ages. From the Sanctuary Field by the church (now a recreation area) there are lovely views across the valley to Hingston Rocks. The 17th-century almshouses in Cross Street are unique in their construction; an 11-bay loggia with granite columns, above which are three tiny mullioned windows.

North Bovey

This is perhaps the epitomy of a Devon village. Thatched cottages cluster around the village green, surrounded by oak trees and complete with old pump. The Ring Of Bells Inn provides refreshments inside and out. The church, with ancient font and much notable woodwork, lies beyond, dating from the 13th and 15th centuries.

Bovey Tracey

Though small, Bovey is well supplied with a variety of shops, catering for the day-to-day needs of the locals and with an excellent range of higher quality craft and gift shops. The Devon Guild of Craftsmen has a permanent showroom and exhibition gallery here at the bottom end of the town in a converted mill, the courtyard is a pleasant open-air extension to the restaurant. On the west side of the town near the old railway station are Parke Rare Breeds Farm, and the centre for the Dartmoor National Park Authority. The farm exhibits a diverse range of poultry and animals, most so used to visitors that they can be hand fed (special food to be purchased in the shop). There is a small restaurant and craft shop, and excellent walks through the parkland down to the valley of the River Bovey, meandering with the river through deciduous woodland and meadows.

Chudleigh

The town, situated on a long ridge, ends abruptly at the Rock, a great limestone outcrop. Pixie's Cave can be safely explored – prehistoric animal bones have been found here. The old mill in Clifford Street now houses the Wheel Craft Centre, with workshops and restaurant.

ROUTE DIRECTIONS

Leave the centre of **Exeter** (map 2SX99) following the signs Okehampton, and in 1 mile, at the Exe Bridge roundabout, take the B3212 Moretonhampstead road. Pass St Thomas Station and in ½ mile, at the traffic signals, turn right, unclassified (sp. Whitestone) into Buddle Lane. In ½ mile, immediately beyond the Barley Mow, turn left (sp. Whitestone) and ascend. In 2¾ miles pass through Whitestone and continue ascent. After a long descent ascend into Tedburn St Mary and turn right (sp. Cheriton Bishop, Crockernwell). In ½ mile keep forward (sp. Crockernwell) through Cheriton Bishop. In 1½ miles, at the end of Crockernwell village, turn left, unclassified (sp. Drewsteignton, Fingle Bridge) then in 1½ miles further ascend and bear left into Drewsteignton. Cross the square and, at the T-junction, turn right (sp. Sandy Park, Chagford). In ½ mile bear left and pass the entrance to **Castle Drogo**. At Sandy Park crossroads turn left on to the A387 Moretonhampstead road, and in ¼ mile cross the River Teign. Continue to **Moretonhampstead**, turn sharp right (sp. Princetown) and right again. Then, turn left, unclassified (sp. North Bovey). In 1¾ miles enter **North Bovey**, descend through the village and bear left (sp. Manaton) to cross the River Bovey. Continue forward, then in 1 mile bear right and ascend. In ½ mile, at the top, turn left (sp. Manaton, Becky Falls). Descend through Manaton, enter woodland and cross the Becka Brook, with Becky Falls on the left. Cross Trendlebere Down and pass the Parke Rare Breeds Farm then start a long descent past the Yarner Wood National Nature Reserve. In 1½ miles turn left on to the B3387, then in ½ mile, at the roundabout, take 2nd exit B3344 to enter **Bovey Tracey**. Keep forward on to the Chudleigh road. At Chudleigh Knighton turn left and in ½ mile keep forward. Cross the River Teign, and the A38 then ascend past Chudleigh Rocks to enter **Chudleigh**. At the war memorial branch left, unclassified (no sign) into Old Exeter Street. In 1 mile, at the crossroads, go forward (sp. Exeter) to ascend. At the crossroads turn left (sp. Dunchideock, Ide) to follow the ridge. After 1 mile pass Lawrence Tower, then in ½ mile further bear right and start to descend. Pass through Dunchideock to Ide. At the T-junction at the end of the village turn right (sp. Exeter) and in ⅔ mile, at the roundabout, take the A377 for the return to Exeter city centre.

OFF THE TOUR

Chagford

To visit the ancient Stannary town of Chagford, turn right at Easton Cross, and after about 1½ miles enter this attractive town. The Three Crowns Hotel, reputedly the site of a Civil War skirmish, dates from the 16th century. There is an excellent range of traditional family run shops, and several pubs and restaurants.

Ugbrooke House

Turn right at the crossroads about ¾ mile down the road from the Wheel Craft Centre at Chudleigh, and after a further ½ mile lies Ugbrooke House, a Tudor house remodelled by Robert Adam in 1759, set in grounds designed by Capability Brown.

The converted mill at the bottom end of Bovey Tracey which houses the permanent showroom and exhibition gallery of the Devon Guild of Craftsmen

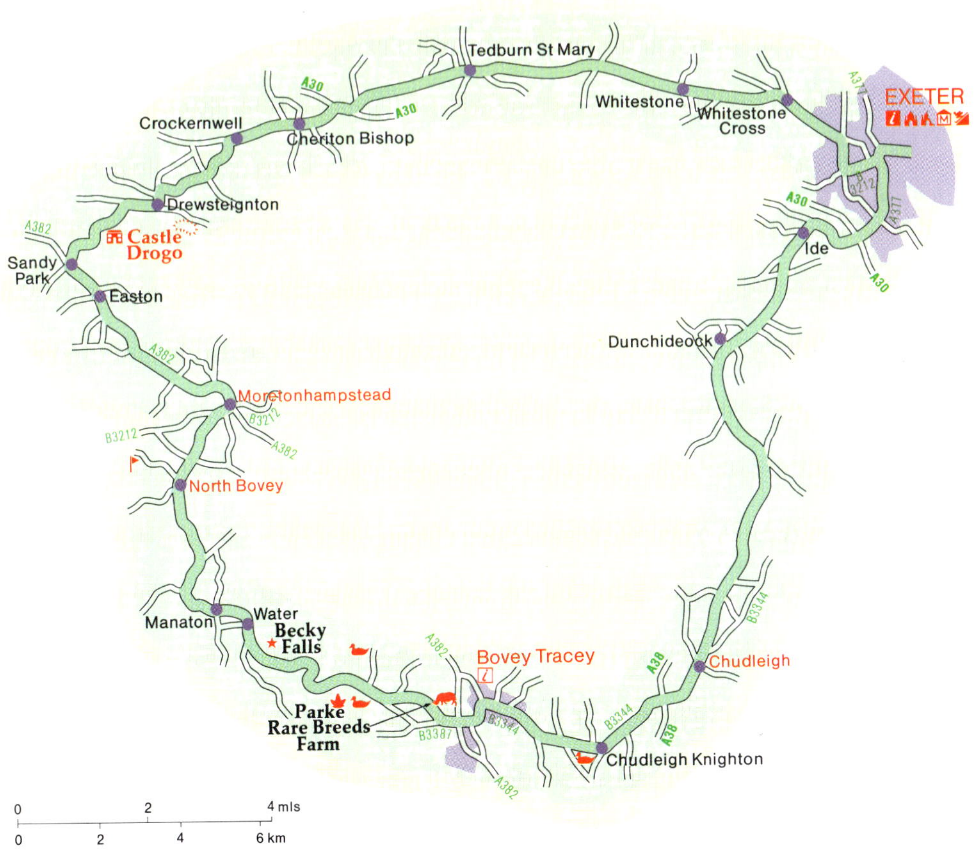

OFF THE BEATEN TRACK

Lustleigh

Just past the Yarner Wood Nature Reserve take the turning on the left at the bottom of the hill to visit the picturesque village of Lustleigh, about 2 miles away: thatched cottages tucked down leafy lanes, excellent tea rooms, a delightful church.

OUTDOOR ACTIVITIES

Fingle Bridge

Nestling deep in the wooded valley, 16th-century Fingle Bridge spans the River Teign below Drewsteignton. An excellent starting point for riverside walks, returning for well-earned refreshment at the famous Angler's Rest.

Canonteign Falls

The highest waterfall in the south of England, set in natural woodland in the heart of the Teign Valley. Refreshments.

Lawrence Tower and Forest Walks, Haldon

Lawrence Tower, built as a folly, is open throughout the summer with magnificent panoramic views of Dartmoor, Exmoor, east Devon and the Exe. Nearby access to forest walks, mostly graded and well signed according to length and difficulty.

WHERE EXMOOR MEETS THE SEA

31 miles

Astride the county boundary between Devon and Somerset, Exmoor meets the sea. Steep, wooded combes plunge from the high plateau, creating shaded bays strewn with boulders. The scenery is spectacular, both along the coast and inland.

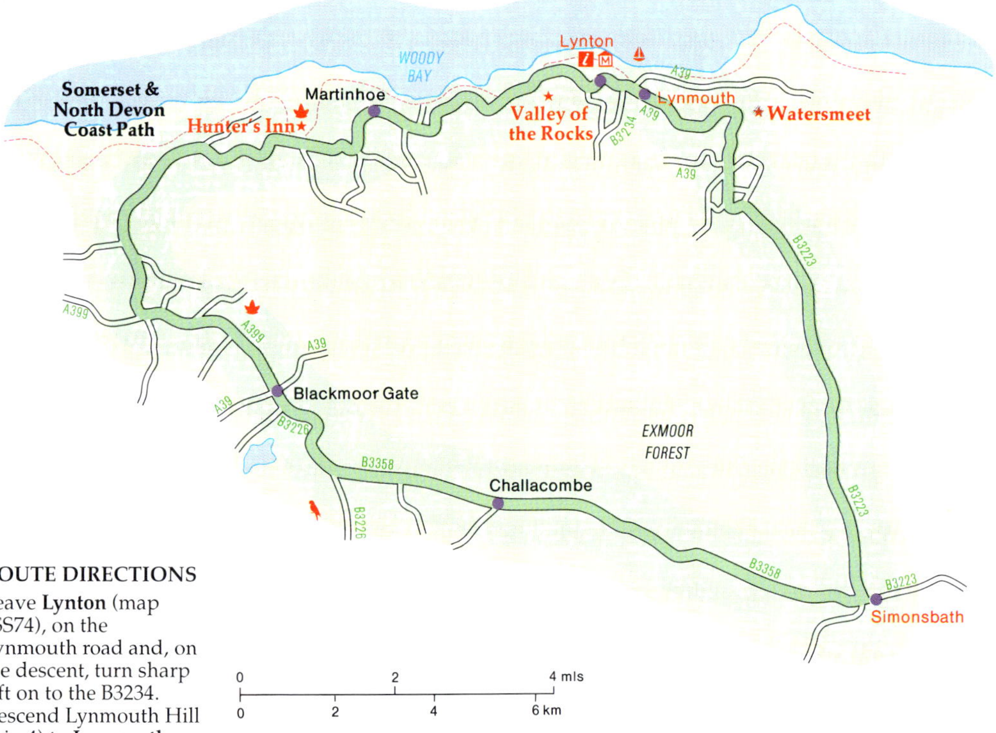

Exmoor has been dramatically affected by centuries of human activity, but still supports a diverse range of flora and fauna; purple heather, gorse and rough grassland provide a habitat for the indigenous red deer and Exmoor ponies. As early as 1200 the mineral wealth was being exploited, with extraction of iron, copper, manganese and even gold and silver. Queen Victoria is reputed to have had brooches made of Exmoor silver.

Evidence of 19th-century attempts to cultivate the moor can be seen in isolated farmsteads and field boundaries; beech hedges were planted as windbreaks, often set in low herringbone-pattern walls, particularly noticeable around Simonsbath.

The northern edge of Exmoor rises steeply from the sea to over 1,500ft, the strata of hard sedimentary rocks clearly shown in the spectacular cliffs. Tourism is the main industry now, with walking and pony trekking across the varied moorland landscape.

The farm of Lorna Doone *fame, on Exmoor. The county boundary between Devon and Somerset splits the bleak plateau of Exmoor at the point where the Doones of Exmoor legend once rampaged, at Badgworthy Water*

ROUTE DIRECTIONS

Leave **Lynton** (map 2SS74), on the Lynmouth road and, on the descent, turn sharp left on to the B3234. Descend Lynmouth Hill (1 in 4) to **Lynmouth**. Here, turn right on to the A39 (sp. Barnstable) then reach **Watersmeet**. Turn left and in ²/₃ mile turn left on to the B3223 (sp. Simonsbath) and cross the river bridge. In ³/₄ mile, at the top of the ascent, turn sharp right to **Simonsbath**. Here, turn right on to the B3358 (sp. Blackmoor Gate, Ilfracombe) for Challacombe. In 2¹/₃ miles, at the trunk road, turn right on to the B3226 to Blackmoor Gate. Turn immediate right on to the A399 (sp. Combe Martin), then in 2 miles further, turn right, unclassified (sp. Trentishoe, Hunter's Inn). After 1¹/₄ miles turn right, pass Holdstone car park on the left and in a further mile bear right (sp. Hunter's Inn). At the **Hunter's Inn** turn left and ascend (sp. Martinhoe). In ³/₄ mile, at the top, turn left (sp. Woody Bay, Martinhoe). Pass Martinhoe church and in ¹/₂ mile branch left (sp. Woody Bay) then turn left and descend. Continue with signs Lynton, via Toll Road, past the Woody Bay Hotel. Go forward with the narrow coast road and in 1¹/₄ miles, pass through the toll gate. In another mile, at the roundabout, go forward through the **Valley of the Rocks** and re-enter Lynton.

OFF THE TOUR

Malmsmead and Doone Valley

About ³/₄ mile beyond Hillsford Bridge on the B3223 Simonsbath road, turn left on a hairpin bend signposted Brendon Valley, and continue along the valley of the East Lyn River, through Brendon to Malmsmead. A handful of old stone cottages cluster here, where the road crosses Badgworthy Water by means of a narrow bridge or, for the more daring, a ford. From here either walk or hire a pony for the beautiful 2 ¹/₂ mile trek up Badgworthy Water to the famous Doone Valley.

Arlington Court

From Blackmoor Gate turn left on to the A39 signposted Barnstaple, the entrance to Arlington Court is after about 4 miles on the left. A magnificent collection of carriages is the greatest attraction, and rides are available. The house, built in 1822, contains unusual shells and model ships. There is a restaurant, and a nature trail through the park and wooded valley to the lake, complete with heronry.

Watermouth Castle

Watermouth Castle, between Combe Martin and Ilfracombe, with model railways, dairy and cider-making exhibitions, smugglers' dungeons and great granny's kitchen, has something to interest everyone.

Combe Martin Wildlife Park

The setting, west of Martinhoe, for this diverse selection of wildlife, tropical plants and rare trees is stunning. There are six breeding species of monkey in natural habitats, wallabies, seals and otters, plus a children's zoo and a huge '00' gauge model railway.

ON THE TOUR

Lynton

Set high on the cliff-top some 600ft above Lynmouth, Lynton became a fashionable resort at the time of the Napoleonic Wars. It abounds in Victorian and Edwardian architecture, epitomised by the splendid town hall, built by the publisher George Newnes, who also sponsored the unusual water-powered cliff railway. The museum in St Vincents Cottage, crammed with local interest, reflects the activities of the community. From the churchyard an orientation table identifies features on the Welsh coast. The church contains some exceptional marbles, but has been subjected to drab Victorian 'restoration'.

Lynmouth

The Victorians developed Lynmouth from a fishing village, building secluded gabled hotels and villas on the verdant hillsides, and eccentricities like the Rhenish Tower, on the quay, built to store saline bath water. Ferocious floods devastated the village in 1952; 90 houses were destroyed as the River Lyn burst its banks and swept through the sleeping village. Thirty-four people died, and a poignant exhibition records the fateful events in the Flood Memorial Hall.

The oldest area, around Mars Hill, is a medley of colour-washed cottages, and it was here that R D Blackmore stayed whilst researching *Lorna Doone*. Over the little footbridge, the pleasure gardens below the rising mass of Countisbury Hill afford a pleasant picnic area, with children's playground, bowls and a delightful grassy sward adjacent to the shingle beach.

Watersmeet

This aptly named National Trust beauty spot is located where the East Lyn river converges with Hoaroak Water, and cascades down a rocky ravine in a series of waterfalls. Watersmeet House, a fishing lodge built in 1832, offers refreshments during the summer.

Simonsbath

Note the beech hedges and herringbone walls established by John Knight in the 1820s. Access from the car park (signposted from the road) leads to a pleasantly landscaped picnic site, with local tourist information.

Hunter's Inn

At Hunter's Inn, set in mature woodland, a path continues to Heddon's Mouth, where the river rushes over smooth pebbles to the sea. For the energetic there is a climb to Heddon's Mouth Cleave, which leaves the path on the west of the river about halfway down. Relax with refreshments at Hunter's Inn afterwards – delightful gardens with ponds and greedy ducks.

Valley of the Rocks

Precarious rock formations pierce the skyline, and top the steep heather-clad hillocks standing sentinel between the sea and the moor; described by poet Robert Southey as 'rock reeling upon rock, stone piled upon stone, a huge terrifying reeling mass.'

OFF THE BEATEN TRACK

Woody Bay

Accessible only on foot. Park at the Woody Bay car park, and make the tree-lined descent. There is a sandy beach at low tide, and an old limekiln, where limestone from Wales was slaked and used to counteract the acidity of the local soil. Also, the remains of a jetty, built to attract paddle steamers that made trips along the coast.

Exmoor Brass Rubbing Centre

A wide selection of brasses is available and helpful advice on how to get the best effects. Children are welcome and encouraged to participate. The Centre is in Lynmouth.

OUTDOOR ACTIVITIES

Countisbury

Six horses were needed for the coach that made the steep ascent from Lynmouth. Park at the top of Countisbury Hill and join the spectacular coastal footpath, or walk out to Foreland Point Lighthouse (open to the public). Notice the prehistoric earthworks to the west of the Blue Ball Inn.

The picturesque village of Lynmouth, situated at the junction of the East and West Lyn

THE QUANTOCK HILLS

46 miles

Thickly wooded combes and rolling farmland lead up to a high ridge of wind-swept heather and gorse, stretching from Taunton to the coast at Kilve. There are views to the north over the Bristol Channel and on either side across the Somerset landscape.

The Quantocks are a narrow range of hills running from Bishops Lydeard to the sea near Kilve. Although only 12 miles long and rising to a maximum of 1,260ft at Will's Neck they provide a great variety of habitat; the summits are heathery moorland with gorse thickets and bracken, virtually treeless,whilst the lower slopes are heavily wooded, and foxgloves and rhododendrons pack the banks of the swift streams. Ponies and sheep graze the upper slopes, and red deer, fox and badger inhabit the combes. Villages cling to the lower slopes, some of them linked by the West Somerset Railway with restored steam engines ferrying visitors along a scenic route. Walkers enjoy the best views; from the high ridge the Somerset Levels stretch away to the south and east, and to the north lies the great expanse of the Bristol Channel, with distant Welsh hills.

ON THE TOUR

Bridgwater

Situated at the lowest crossing point of the River Parrett, where the fertile plains of Somerset meet the Severn Estuary, Bridgwater is an important industrial and commercial centre. The town has few old buildings; the most attractive street is Chapel Street built by the Duke of Chandos. Admiral Blake, who had a distinguished naval career, was born in the town and is commemorated in a museum that bears his name. The museum also contains items of local interest, particularly an exhibition on tile and brick making, which brought prosperity during the 19th century. The Arts Centre hosts touring theatre companies and travelling exhibitions.

Nether Stowey

Samuel Taylor Coleridge lived in the village for three years and it was here that he wrote *The Ancient Mariner*. He walked the Quantocks with William and Dorothy Wordsworth, who lived nearby at Alfoxton House. His cottage, tiny and thatched, was acquired by the National Trust – the parlour and reading room are open to the public.

Crowcombe

Nestling beneath the hills, the village has many finely carved bench-ends in its Perpendicular church; many symbolising fertility, to ensure productive harvests and prosperity of the villagers. Opposite is the Tudor Church House.

Watchet

A busy port as far back as the Middle Ages, when the town had its own mint; the quayside bustles with activity, and the 19th-century paper-mill is still in production. A small museum near the slipway portrays the town's history as a port and trading centre; there are also objects from the 19th-century ore mines on the Brendon Hills and the mineral railway.

Cleeve Abbey

Here, there are the remains of a 13th-century Cistercian abbey (dissolved in 1537) noted for its gatehouse, dormitory and refectory with traceried windows, timbered roof and sadly faded wall paintings. Look out, too, for the intricately decorated encaustic floor tiles.

Combe Sydenham Hall

Currently in the course of restoration by the present owners, the house was built on medieval foundations in 1580 by Sir George Sydenham. Formal gardens, 16th-century fish ponds stocked with trout and a leat through the 'Secret Valley' to a mill make an attractive setting. Walks lead through wooded combes to High Viewpoint – with panoramic views across to Wales, Exmoor and the Blackdown Hills.

Bishops Lydeard

The red sandstone church is the landmark of the village, sporting a fine tower with pierced tracery battlements and pinnacles. Inside it boasts a wonderful 16th-century fan-vaulted screen, and beautifully carved bench-ends. Outside there is a well-preserved 14th-century cross; the 12 apostles are sculptured around the base, with Christ risen and enthroned. One of the steps has been hollowed out for holy water or alms.

Gaulden Manor, south east of Monksilver, lies on the eastern edge of Exmoor. It has a magnificent plaster ceiling and fine furniture

ROUTE DIRECTIONS

Leave **Bridgwater** (map 2ST33) on the A39 (sp. Minehead) and in 3¾ miles reach Cannington. Turn left with the main road, and in a further 4¼ miles turn left, unclassified (sp. Nether Stowey) to enter **Nether Stowey**. Here, turn left, unclassified (sp. Over Stowey) and make a sharp ascent before descending to a T-junction and turning left. In ½ mile, on the ascent, bear right (sp. Crowcombe). Continue ascent and at the summit pass the Dead Woman's Ditch car park on the left. In a further mile descend (1 in 4) to **Crowcombe**. Turn right (sp. Williton, Minehead) and in ½ mile, at the end of the village, branch right then shortly turn right on to the A358. After 2¾ miles, at a crossroads, turn right, unclassified (sp. Weacombe, West Quantoxhead). In a further 1½ miles, reach West Quantoxhead, turn left in the village (sp. Williton, Minehead). In ¼ mile cross the main road (sp. Doniford, Watchet) to approach Doniford, then continue for 1¼ miles to reach the edge of **Watchet**. At the main road keep forward on to the B3191 (sp. Williton). Continue on for 3¼ miles then keep forward on to the B3190 (sp. Brampton). One mile further, at the crossroads, turn right on to the A39 to Washford. Here, turn left, unclassified (sp. Cleeve Abbey), then in ½ mile beyond **Cleeve Abbey** keep forward (sp. Monksilver). After a further ½ mile go over the crossroads on to the B3188 (sp. Monksilver, Wiveliscombe). Continue for 2 miles then pass through Monksilver. Still on the B3188 in ¾ mile pass **Combe Sydenham Hall** on the right and in 1½ miles, at the crossroads, turn left, unclassified (sp. Taunton). After 5¾ miles pass under the railway bridge, turn right on to the A358 (sp. Bishops Lydeard, Taunton) and in ¾ mile turn left, unclassified (sp. Bishops Lydeard) to enter the village. At **Bishops Lydeard** turn left (sp. Bridgwater). Continue to Enmore and, 2 miles beyond the village, skirt the Durleigh reservoir to enter Durleigh. Pass through the village and in ¼ mile, at the T-junction at the end, turn right (sp. Bridgwater) to return to Bridgwater.

OFF THE TOUR

East Quantoxhead

Turning right out of West Quantoxhead on to the A39, after about a mile there is a turning to East Quantoxhead: one of the most attractive villages in the county, with a cluster of pretty cottages, farm, church and manor house around a duck pond. The church has delightful wood carvings of berries, leaves and thistles on the bench-ends. In the circular building by the mill a horse traipsed round and round, working a cider-apple mill.

Gaulden Manor

A turning off the tour route about 5 miles from Monksilver leads to Gaulden Manor, dating from the 12th century. It is a charming manor house on a small scale, once the home of the Turbervilles (immortalised by Thomas Hardy in *Tess of the d'Urbervilles*). The peace and beauty of this secluded place is enhanced by the well cared-for gardens, including a herb and bog garden.

Hestercombe House

South of Bishops Lydeard, a turning off the A358 leads to Cheddon Fitzpaine where, at Hestercombe, Sir Edward Lutyens and Gertrude Jekyll designed the intricate copy of Elizabethan garden landscaping. Raised pathways give extensive views over the Vale of Taunton and more intimate and tranquil pleasures can be found in the sunken, formal garden.

Barford Park

Just before Enmore a turning left off the tour leads to Barford House, a Georgian house surrounded by park and gardens providing an excellent example of 18th-century landscaping. A pond, terrace, lawns and a wonderful water and woodland garden create a delightful effect of natural wilderness.

OFF THE BEATEN TRACK

Steart Point

Mud-flats extending far out into the Bristol Channel provide a haven for geese and wildfowl. An ancient means of fishing is carried out here; the 'mud-horse' fishermen push their crude sledges across the flats to retrieve the catch from nets positioned at high tide and return laden with shrimps and rock salmon.

Quantock Sheep Milking Centre

A family-run farm at Nether Stowey where visitors can see sheep being milked and go on a farm trail. There is a good children's play area.

Quantock Weavers

Craft workshops and showrooms at Over Stowey where visitors watch dyeing and spinning of wool, and fabrication to finished garments.

OUTDOOR ACTIVITIES

Fyne Court

The Somerset Trust for Nature Conservation has offices in the old coach house at Broomfield. The Trust's shop and visitor centre, with interpretation of the natural history of the area, are worth visiting before setting off on one of a number of trails to a variety of habitats – woodland, quarryland, lakeside and deadwood – all well explained by leaflets. There is a picnic site beside the lake.

This interesting red sandstone church is the landmark of the village of Bishops Lydeard

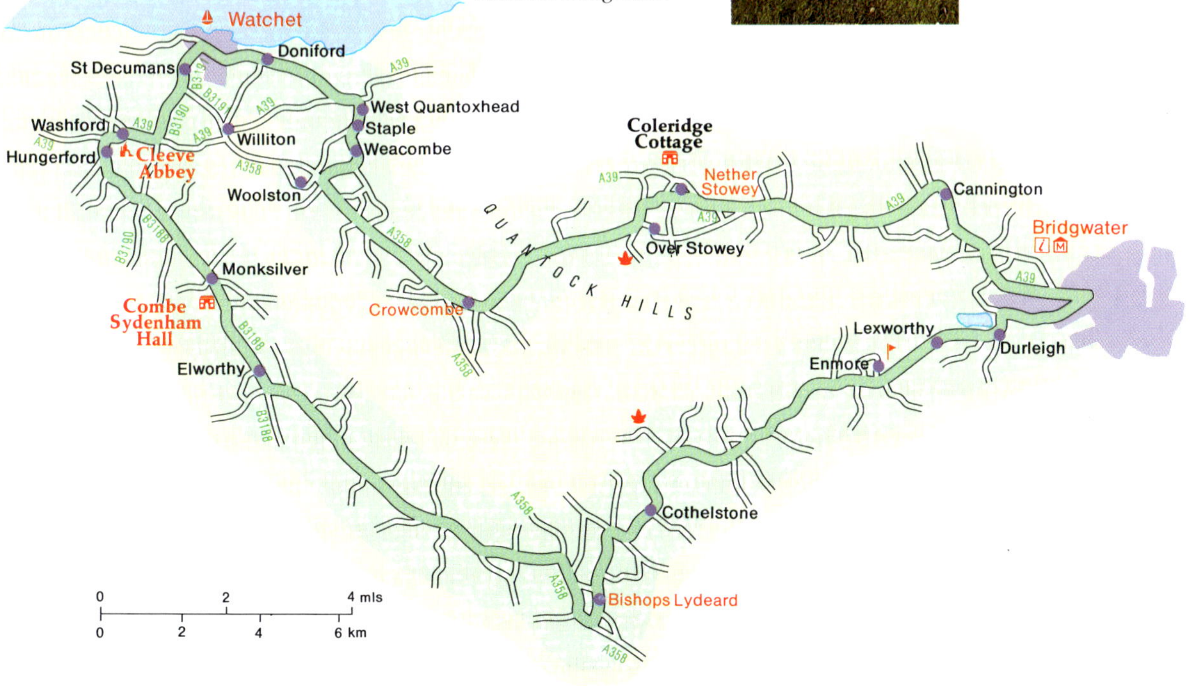

THE DEVON AND SOMERSET BORDERS

72 miles

The Blackdown Hills mark the boundary between Somerset and Devon, with the Wellington Monument at their western end.

To the north lies the Vale of Taunton Deane; south and west, rich rolling countryside is cut by the valleys of the rivers Exe and Culm.

Restoration of the Grand Western Canal began in 1971. There is now a horse-drawn service operating from Tiverton Basin

This is one of the most productive agricultural regions of the West Country; herds of dairy cattle predominate with market gardens and cider orchards. Market days in each of the principal towns bring the people to life and traffic to a halt as country traders flock in; even Taunton retains a rural character. Textile industries were once important – world famous Honiton lace and woollen cloth production bringing prosperity reflected in the quality and scale of the parish churches. The small towns and villages are generally unspoilt; most tourists, heading for the coast or further west, rush past on the motorway.

ON THE TOUR

Tiverton

The town's industrial past has bequeathed many fine buildings; St Peter's Church, Blundell's School and three sets of almshouses. From Saxon times the town was important as a fording place at the meeting of the rivers Exe and Loman. Tiverton Castle, dating from the 12th century, stands behind the parish church; it contains fine displays of Civil War armour. In St Andrew Street an award-winning museum of local history contains a comprehensive selection of agricultural and industrial artefacts.

Devonshire Centre

Housed in Bickleigh Mill, the Centre has a working water wheel and workshops for craftspeople who can be seen at work. Rare breeds of traditional farm animals, including magnificent Shire horses, are kept in the adjacent farm buildings.

Cullompton

This small, busy town, the market centre for a wide rural population, is now bypassed by the motorway. The great tower of the parish church, built in contrasting red sandstone and white Beer stone, is a dominant landmark and illustrates the medieval prosperity of the woollen manufacturing industry; inside, the wagon roof is richly gilded and painted. Behind the Showman pub in Station Road touring fairground rides and sideshows rest up for the winter.

Honiton

Situated on the main road east from Exeter, the town has several fine Georgian coaching inns; the stables behind the Dolphin and Black Lion are now a pedestrian shopping precinct. Honiton's chief claim to fame is its lace industry, which still produces fine hand-made work for royal wedding dresses. Allhallows Museum contains a history of the craft, and fine examples as well as demonstrations in the high season.

Trull

Although close to Taunton, Trull retains a village atmosphere, its church containing a mass of fine carvings from the 15th century; bench-ends depict a religious procession and the unusual wooden pulpit has five canopied niches containing carved statues.

Taunton

The county town of Somerset and its administrative centre, Taunton lies in the Vale of Taunton Deane on the meandering River Tone. It contains most modern amenities; indoor swimming pool and landscaped parks and gardens. The main historical interest is contained in the County Museum, built on the castle foundations. The most famous event to take place in the castle was the trial of supporters of the Duke of Monmouth after the Battle of Sedgemoor. In the space of two days Judge Jeffreys sentenced 146 men to death whilst presiding in the great hall. The museum contains a comprehensive exhibition of local history, the showpiece being the Low Ham mosaic – a masterpiece of Roman craftsmanship.

Wellington

A pleasant town with the main street lined by fine Georgian buildings and evidence of earlier industries in the back streets. A small museum is housed in the old Squirrel Hotel, one of a number of coaching inns that once served passing trade.

Uffculme

A large village on the River Culm, Uffculme was an important centre for the wool trade; its serges were exported to Holland. Its surviving woollen mill at Coldharbour closed down in 1981 but was then converted into a working museum.

ROUTE DIRECTIONS

Leave **Tiverton** (map 2SS91) on the A396 Exeter road, following the Exe Valley down to Bickleigh Bridge. Turn left to cross the Exe and pass the **Devonshire Centre** at Bickleigh Mill on the left, then continue along the B3185 (sp. Silverton). Enter Silverton and at the mini-roundabout, bear right then left, (sp. Broad Clyst). In 1¼ miles turn left, unclassified (sp. Brandninch) and in 1½ miles, at the crossroads turn left. Continue to Brandninch, keep forward on the Cullompton road and turn left (no sign) on to the B3181 to enter **Cullompton**. Continue along the main street and just before the King's Head turn right on to the A373 (sp. Honiton). Cross the M5 and, at the third crossroads, turn left, unclassified (sp. Sheldon). Ascend on to the Blackdown Hills, continue to the T-junction then turn right (sp. Honiton). In 1¾ miles at the crossroads, keep forward and in ¼ mile bear right (sp. Payhembury, Feniton). Descend to the crossroads, and turn left (sp. Honiton), rejoining the A373 to descend to **Honiton**. At the traffic signals turn left (sp. Town Centre) and leave by going forward down the main street (sp. Andover, Yeovil), to join the A30. Head north-east to pass through Monkton, then 1 mile further, branch left, unclassified (sp. Upottery). Pass Rawridge, cross the river and enter Upottery. Keep forward (sp. Churchinford), ascend to Churchinford village crossroads, then keep forward again (sp. Blagdon, Taunton). After 2 miles pass the radio masts of Culmhead Signal Station, then begin the descent of the Blackdown Hills. Pass through Blagdon, then Staplehay and **Trull** to reach the edge of **Taunton** town centre. Turn left (one-way) and keep forward on to the A38 (sp. Wellington, Exeter). Follow the A38 into the open country of the Tone Valley and, after 5 miles, at the roundabout, take the B3187 (sp. Wellington). In 1¼ miles enter **Wellington** and, at the traffic signals, turn left, unclassified (sp. Wellington Monument, Hemyock). In 1 mile turn right, then next left, recross the M5 and ascend. Climb (1 in 5) to reach a staggered crossroads. Turn right then left on to the Hemyock road and continue with a steep descent into the Culm Valley and Hemyock. At the centre of the village keep right (sp. Culmstock) and continue to Culmstock. At the crossroads, turn left on to the B3391 (sp. Tiverton), and continue to **Uffculme** to cross the River Culm, then bear left on the ascent to pass the church. In 2 miles turn left, then immediate right (sp. Tiverton) across the B3181 and on to an unclassified road. Pass beneath the M5 and the railway, and in 1½ miles turn left into Halberton. In ½ mile beyond the village cross the Grand Western Canal to return to Tiverton.

Bickleigh Castle, steeped in 900 years of history, lies across the River Exe from the picturesque village of Bickleigh

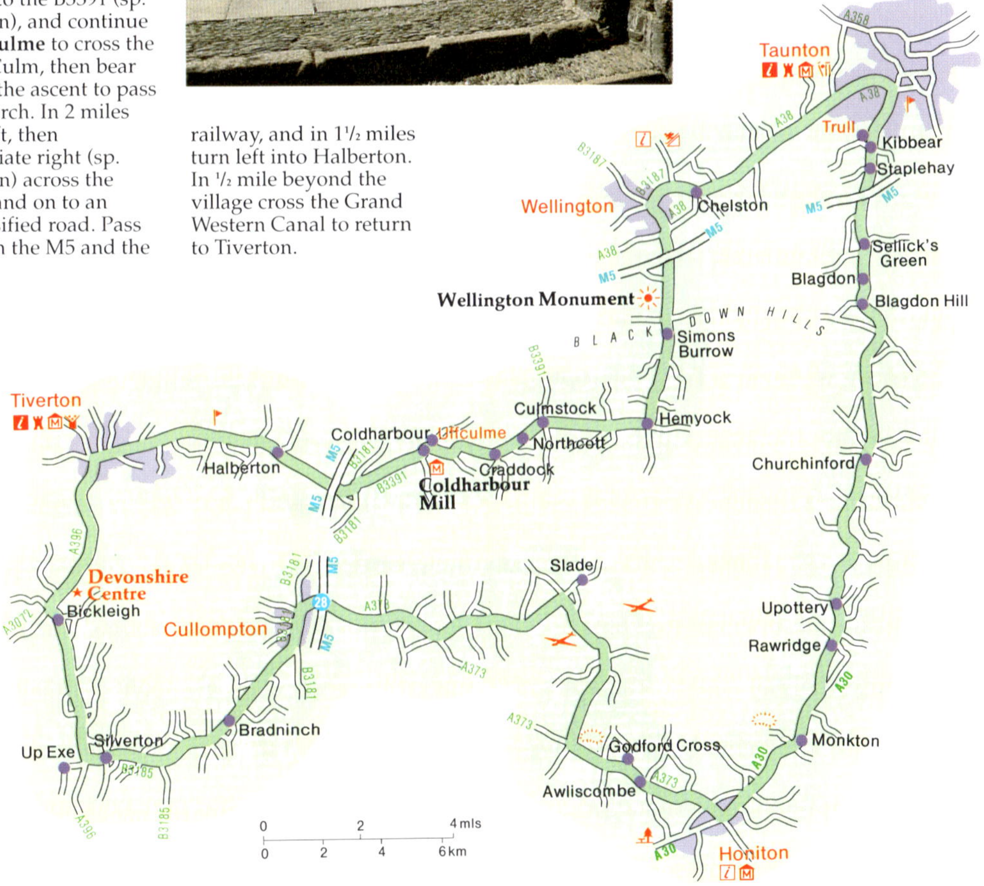

OFF THE TOUR

Bickleigh Castle

Across the river from the Devonshire Centre, Bickleigh Castle is a fortified and moated manor house with a small Norman chapel that escaped the ravages of the Reformation, and is said to be the oldest complete building in Devon. Impressive heavy oak beams and stonework.

Killerton House and Gardens

Just off the B3181, 5 miles south of Cullompton, this estate is now owned by the National Trust. The 18th-century house has an exhibition of costumes in a series of rooms, each of which depicts a style from the time the house was built to the present day. The 15 acres of gardens include formal herbaceous borders and wide lawns.

Poundisford Park

Just outside Pitminster, off the B3170 south of Taunton, this Tudor mansion has remained virtually untouched since it was built – beginning in 1546. The beautiful gardens contain an unusual 17th-century summerhouse.

Knightshayes Court

The fine 19th-century house is surrounded by some of the finest gardens and parkland in Devon, just north of Tiverton off the A396. Set out on a majestic scale, containing both native and rare plants, the open park contrasts with the formal terraces and presents a continually varied scene.

OFF THE BEATEN TRACK

Christ Cross

A rough track heading north east out of Silverton leads through rolling farmland up to Christ Cross, locally known as Criss Cross. Standing at 850ft, the superb views from here – extending into Somerset, are well worth the steep climb. Turn right, then right again to return via Greenslinch Farm.

OUTDOOR ACTIVITIES

Tiverton Canal

Ambitious plans to connect the Bristol Channel and the south coast by canal were never realised, but part of the Great Western Canal remains, and provides an easy walk through wood-lined fields. Horse-drawn boat trips make the going even easier. Pleasant tea rooms are situated at the Tiverton – end of the canal.

SOUTH-WEST DORSET – HARDY COUNTRY

65 miles

From the border with Devon at Lyme Regis, the Dorset coast is spectacular; 500ft cliffs and a footpath offering superb views. Inland,

enchanting villages of rich, golden stone and pleasant country towns are set in the lush rolling countryside loved by Thomas Hardy.

Rural Dorset retains an atmosphere of tranquillity, with a pace of life reminiscent of Hardy's 19th-century novels. It is possible to trace the footsteps of his characters through a little-changed landscape, deep into the Dorset heartland. East of Bridport the land rises dramatically to the high chalklands which run across the county to the north-east, with ancient fortifications on strategic sites like Eggardon Hill and Maiden Castle. Later settlements favoured the more hospitable valleys of the rivers Char, Brit and Frome. West of Bridport there is a landscape of contrasts; from dramatic cliffs like Golden Cap (the highest point on the south coast of England at 625ft) to the Marshwood Vale with intricate hills and valleys, rumpled fields and wooded hedgerows dotted with wild flowers.

The view towards Bridport, 12 miles away, from the top of Pilsdon Pen. This is the site of one of Dorset's many prehistoric hillforts

ROUTE DIRECTIONS

Leave **Bridport** (map 2SY49) on the Dorchester road and, at the roundabout, take 2nd exit A35. In 3 miles bear left, unclassified (sp. Maiden Newton). In 1/2 mile, at the T-junction, turn right and, beyond the Spyway Inn, ascend Eggardon Hill. At the summit turn sharp right (sp. Dorchester) on to a former Roman road. In 3 miles, at the crossroads, turn left (sp. Grimstone). In 2 miles, at the end of a long descent, at the crossroads turn right (no sign) to follow the Frome Valley through Bradford Peverell. Here, keep forward at the crossroads for Dorchester. In **Dorchester** pass the keep of the Military Museum then turn left on to the A35 and, at the roundabout, take 1st exit A37 (sp. Yeovil). Descend to the Frome Valley and in 1 mile pass a road for Wolfeton House on the right. At the roundabout take 2nd exit then branch right on to the A352 (sp. Cerne Abbas, Sherborne) to pass through Charminster. Follow the River Cerne, pass through Godmanstone and in 2 1/2 miles, at the crossroads at the edge of **Cerne Abbas**, turn left, unclassified (sp. Sydling St Nicholas). Ascend, then descend and bear left. Shortly, turn left to enter Sydling St Nicholas. Return for 1/4 mile then keep forward (sp. Yeovil) and at the next crossroads turn left (no sign). Ascend and at the top go forward (sp. Cattistock) then in 1/2 mile cross the A37 and descend into the Upper Frome Valley. Bear left to enter Cattistock, return to the edge of the village and keep forward (sp. Rampisham). Cross the railway and the River Frome, then in 1 mile bear right. One mile further, at the Tiger's Head, bear right then keep forward (sp. Beaminster). In 1 1/2 miles, at the T-junction, turn left into Benville Lane and after 2 miles cross the A356 to join the B3163. Continue to **Beaminster** then turn right on to the A3066 (sp. Crewkerne) to enter the main street. Continue through the market square and in 1/4 mile branch left on to the B3163 to Broad-

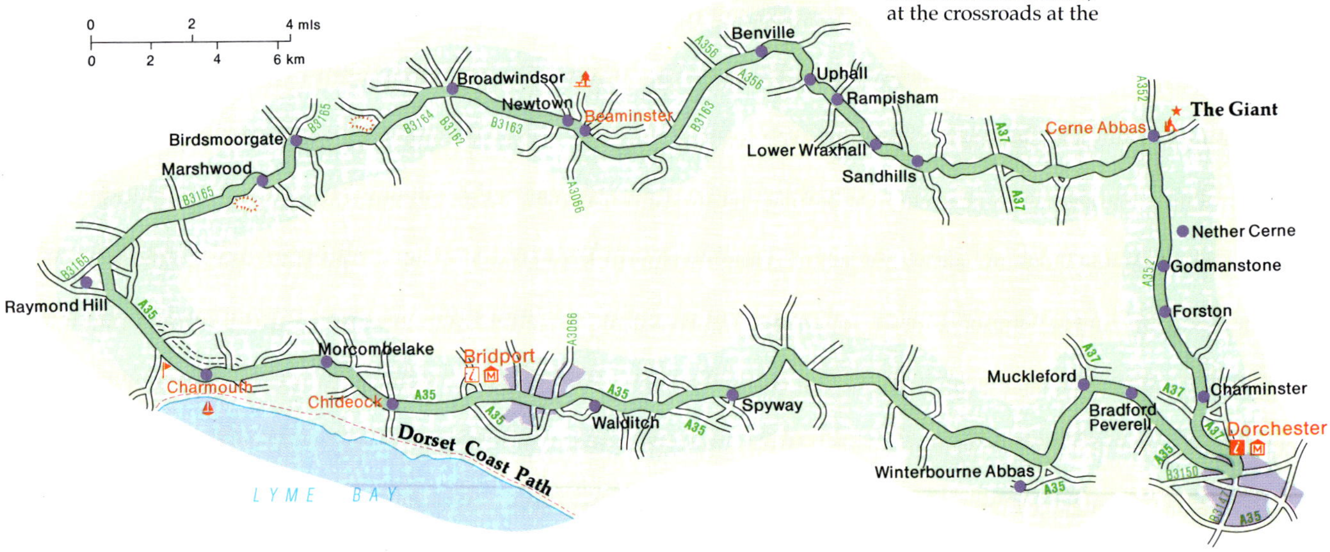

windsor. Keep forward (one-way) and at the church turn left on to the B3164 (sp. Axminster). Ascend and pass Lewesdon Hill on the left and continue forward to Birdsmoorgate. At the Rose and Crown turn left on to the B3165. Pass through Marshwood, ascend, continue and after 3 miles, at Monkton Wyld Cross, bear left (sp. Charmouth, Bridport). In ½ mile turn left on to the A35 then pass through a short tunnel. Descend to the village of **Charmouth** and continue along the A35 to reach Morcombelake. Pass the lane off to the right for Golden Cap, and, still on the A35, descend through **Chideock**. Make a final ascent and long, easy descent towards Bridport. Bear left, unclassified, to return to Bridport town centre.

OFF THE TOUR

Wolfeton House

In an isolated spot to the south of Charminster village, where the Cerne meets the Frome; a romantic 16th-century house of mellow Purbeck stone. The great hall, ceilings and fireplaces are especially notable. An added attraction is the Cider House, where visitors are offered home-produced cider traditionally made.

Hardy's Cottage

Situated about 2½ miles north-east of Dorchester, off the A35 near Higher Bockhampton. Hardy was born here in 1840. The cottage, built by his great-grandfather in 1801, is an idyllic thatched house – only open by appointment. The charming gardens to the front are open throughout the summer.

Mapperton Manor Gardens

About 2 miles before reaching Beaminster on the B3163, turn left, unclassified, to Mapperton, where the delightfully secluded gardens of Mapperton Manor can be found. The house is open to parties only. The garden comprises a valley and hillsides studded with daffodils, formal borders, specimen shrubs and trees. There are fishponds, a summerhouse and orangery.

Maiden Castle

The most famous Iron Age hillfort in southern England, 2 miles south-west of Dorchester, with massive earthworks and a complex system of entrances. Perhaps as many as 4,000 people lived here prior to the arrival of the Romans, who established nearby Dorchester for their capital.

ON THE TOUR

Bridport

Associated for the past 750 years with rope and net making, Bridport is still Europe's major centre for the production of nets. Nets were once hung across the main street (hence its unusual width) with narrow alleyways off it, used as ropewalks. An old saying is 'to be stabbed with a Bridport dagger' i.e., hanged. The museum, in an interesting 16th-century stone building, has a comprehensive display of the net industry and a huge collection of dolls in international dress. The town has much fine Georgian brick architecture, especially the town hall of 1785.

Dorchester

Founded by the Romans in AD43, Dorchester still remains prominent amongst Dorset towns. It is the county capital, bustling with activity, yet small enough to be a pleasure to explore. The course of the Roman walls can be traced, and provides an insight into its early importance. The western entrance to the town, from Bridport, is marked by the impressive stone keep of the Victorian barracks, now the Dorset Military Museum. In South Street Judge Jeffreys held his Bloody Assizes in the Antelope Hotel, following the Monmouth Rebellion in 1685. His former lodgings, in High West Street, is a superb timber-framed building, now a restaurant and tea rooms. On the opposite side of the road - above St Peter's Church and the statue of William Barnes, the local poet – is the County Museum: the best in Dorset for archaeology, natural history and geology, it includes a reconstruction of Thomas Hardy's study.

Cerne Abbas

Buried deep in the Cerne Valley, a village of quaint cottages and interesting remains from the Benedictine abbey that once flourished here. The ornate porch of the abbot's hall is still standing, with a fine oriel window. Better known is the huge Cerne Giant, cut into the chalk hillside above the village in Roman times, symbolising fertility.

St Augustine's Well, found in the churchyard, is believed to possess healing properties: the sick used to lie on the stones, hoping for a cure. See also page 55.

Beaminster

The market place forms the centre of this small, neat town, lying in a bowl of farmed and wooded hills at the source of the River Brit. Around the market are interesting 17th- and 18th-century houses of warm, honey-brown stone. A variety of shops caters for the farming communities nearby. Down a lane, St Mary's Church has a tall tower with excellent figure carvings.

Charmouth

Sadly the A35 forms the main street of Charmouth, which is otherwise a charming seaside town with grand Victorian and Regency villas creating an air of opulence reminiscent of the pre-railway era, when it was developed as a resort. It is worth visiting for the fossil shop and exhibition. There are numerous places for refreshments.

The sandy beach at the mouth of the Char is a good place for fossil hunters. Beware of the cliffs as they are prone to landslips and are very dangerous.

Chideock

Another attractive village, despite the main road which descends steeply to the cluster of thatched cottages of local golden stone. To the south a lane leads to Seatown, where there is an inn and a few houses at the mouth of the River Winniford. There are exhilarating cliff-top walks in either direction.

OFF THE BEATEN TRACK

Parnham House

A fine Tudor manor house just south of Beaminster with embellishments by John Nash in 1810, and 14 acres of gardens. Now the home of John Makepeace's exclusive hand-made furniture workshops; open Sundays, Wednesdays and Bank Holidays through the summer.

Bredy Farm Old Farming Collection

A comprehensive collection (at Burton Bradstock south-east of Bridport) of farm implements, wagons and machinery ranging from dairy to cider-making equipment.

OUTDOOR ACTIVITIES

Thorncombe Wood Nature Trail

An area of mixed woodland close to Hardy's Cottage at Higher Bockhampton. Leaflets and information boards, with a selection of walks through mature deciduous woods.

Eggardon Hill

Spectacularly sited north of Spyway at the top of this wind-swept spur, the Iron Age hillfort covers 36 acres. Worth walking to for the magnificent views across the Marshwood Vale and beyond.

Pilsdon Pen

The highest hill in Dorset at 910ft lies south east of Birdsmoorgate surmounted by an elongated hillfort at the southern end. Views to the coast, and west towards Dartmoor.

Looking towards Charmouth and Lyme Regis from Golden Cap – a National Trust coastal estate lying to the east of Lyme Regis

THE SOMERSET LEVELS

71 miles

Between the great limestone scarp of the Mendips and the gentle rise of the Polden Hills, forming a ridge between Street and Bridgwater, the Somerset

Levels form a unique area of low-lying, waterlogged peat moors, a rich agricultural region and fragile habitat for migrant birds.

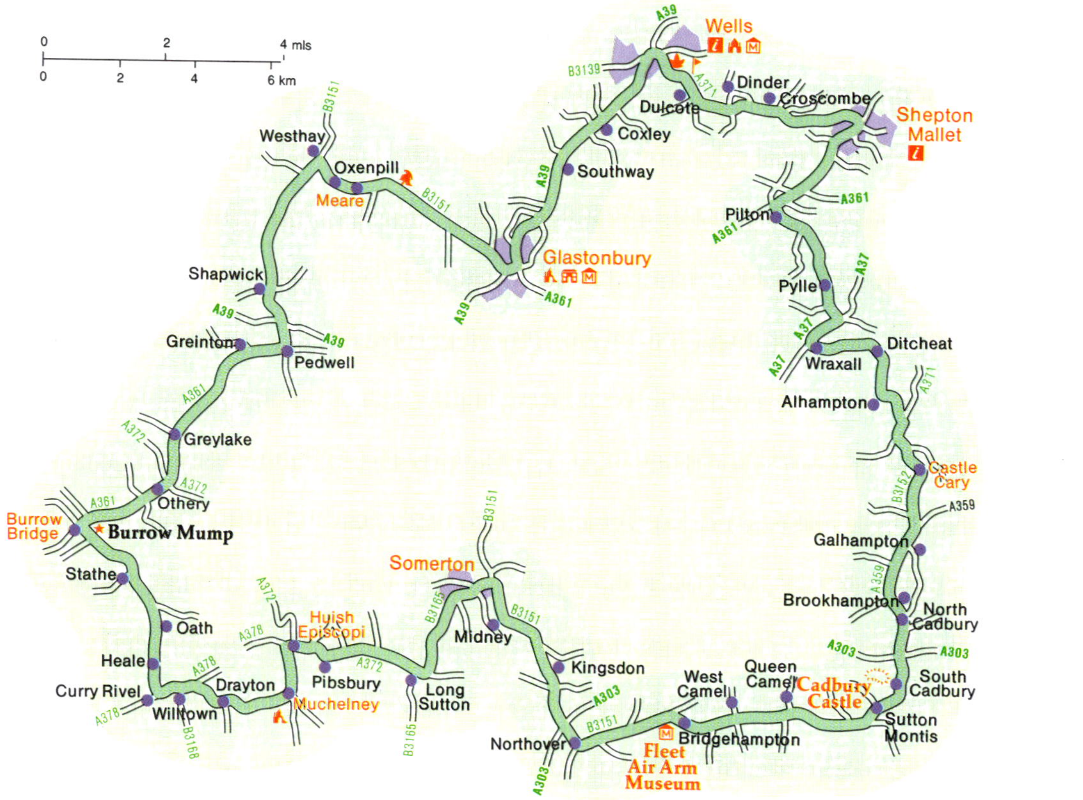

The Somerset Levels comprise the flat central core of the county that barely rises above sea level, protected from severe flooding since the Middle Ages by a complex network of drainage ditches called rhines. A magical landscape is created; flat fields stretching to a hazy horizon, often flanked by lines of pollarded willow trees bearing a distinctive spiky head-dress of new shoots. The mystical shape of Glastonbury Tor pierces the skyline (associated with King Arthur and the Holy Grail) and the bleak scarp of the Mendips rises to the north-east.

The Levels provide a vital and fragile habitat for migrant geese and other birds, which feast on the rich insect life in the damp meadows. Any settlements are confined to slight rises in the ground; until recently every family had a flat-bottomed boat by their back door in case of emergency!

ROUTE DIRECTIONS

Leave **Wells** (map 2ST54) on the A39 (sp. Glastonbury) and after 2 miles pass through the village of Coxley. Cross part of Queen's Sedge Moor and Whitelake River to enter **Glastonbury**. Turn right (sp. Bridgwater) to reach the town centre and in $^{1}/_{4}$ mile, at the market cross, turn right again (no sign) to leave on the B3151 Meare road. Continue beside the River Brue for part of the way to **Meare**. Continue on the B3151 and in 1$^{1}/_{4}$ mile, at the edge of Westhay, turn left, unclassified (sp. Shapwick). Shortly, at the T-junction, turn left again and continue to Shapwick. Here, keep forward (sp. High Ham, Langport) and beyond the village ascend to cross the Polden Hills. In $^{3}/_{4}$ mile at the T-junction turn left on to the A39, then at the Albion Inn, turn right, unclassified (sp. Redwell, High Ham, Langport). Descend, and in $^{1}/_{2}$ mile at the bottom, turn right on to the A361 (sp. Taunton). After 1 mile pass through Greinton, and cross King's Sedge Moor to reach Othery. In $^{3}/_{4}$ mile round Burrow Mump reach **Burrow Bridge**. Cross the River Parrett then turn left, unclassified (no sign). In just under $^{1}/_{4}$ mile keep forward (sp. Stathe, Langport) to Stathe. Continue with the Curry Rivel signs then in $^{3}/_{4}$ mile turn right and cross the railway bridge. In 1 mile make a sharp ascent. At the top turn right and in $^{3}/_{4}$ mile turn left on to the A378 to enter Curry Rivel. In $^{1}/_{4}$ mile from the centre of the village turn right, unclassified (sp. Drayton, Muchelney). After $^{3}/_{4}$ mile pass through Drayton and on to **Muchelney**. Here, bear left at the Abbey with the Langford road. In 1 mile, at the T-junction, turn right and pass **Huish Episcopi** church, then turn right on to the A372 (sp. Wincanton, Yeovil). In 1$^{3}/_{4}$ miles pass the edge of Long Sutton, then in $^{1}/_{2}$ mile turn left on the B3165 (sp. Somerton). In 2$^{1}/_{4}$ miles turn right (sp. Ilchester) and enter **Somerton**. Beyond the main square turn right into New Street, unclassified (sp. Ilchester). In $^{1}/_{4}$ mile turn right on to the B3151. After 2$^{3}/_{4}$ miles turn right then left, crossing the A372. Continue on the B3151 and in 1$^{1}/_{2}$ miles, at the mini-roundabout, take 1st exit (sp. Yeovilton). Pass the **Fleet Air Arm Museum** and in $^{1}/_{4}$ mile turn right, unclassified (sp. Queen Camel) then in 2$^{1}/_{2}$ miles reach the edge of Queen Camel. Keep left to join the A359 then turn right, unclassified (sp. Sutton Montis). In 2 miles pass through Sutton Montis and at the end of the village turn right (sp. South Cadbury). Continue round the mound of **Cadbury Castle**, through South Cadbury and in $^{1}/_{2}$ mile cross the main road (sp. North Cadbury, Castle Cary). After $^{3}/_{4}$ mile pass through North Cadbury and continue with the Castle Cary road. In $^{3}/_{4}$ mile turn right on to the A359 and $^{1}/_{4}$ mile beyond Galhampton branch left on to the B3152 (sp. Castle Cary). In 1$^{1}/_{4}$ miles enter **Castle Cary** and turn left (one-way) then left again (sp. Bath, Bristol A371). In $^{3}/_{4}$ mile turn left on to the A371 (sp. Shepton Mallet) then bear right across a railway bridge. In $^{1}/_{2}$ mile at the Brook House Inn turn left, unclassified (sp. Alhampton). In $^{3}/_{4}$ mile enter Alhampton and turn right (sp. Ditcheat) then in 1 mile enter Ditcheat and turn left (no sign) at the T-junction. At the Manor House Inn turn right (sp. Glastonbury). Keep left (sp. East Pennard, Glastonbury) and continue to Wraxall. At the crossroads turn right on to the A37 (sp. Shepton Mallet) then immediately ascend Wraxall Hill (1 in 7). In 1 mile, at the crossroads, turn left, unclassified (sp. East Pennard). After $^{1}/_{2}$ mile turn right (sp. Pilton) and descend. In 2$^{1}/_{2}$ miles enter Pilton, turn left and, beyond the church, turn left again (sp. Shepton Mallet). Shortly, reach a T-junction and turn right on to the A361 (sp. Shepton Mallet). In 1 mile turn left on to the B3136 to reach **Shepton Mallet**. Leave by the A371 (sp. Wells) and continue to Croscombe. Pass the Old Manor on the right, then the church, and continue, to re-enter Wells.

ON THE TOUR

Wells
In a superb, open setting the cathedral and its environs have scarcely changed since their foundation and development in the medieval period. Magnificent sculptures adorn the west front, more reminiscent of a French cathedral. Beside the cathedral is the Bishop's Palace, which, despite its moat and drawbridge, was never a defensive site. Swans on the moat have been trained to ring a bell for their food. Through a gateway called the Bishop's Eye is the market place; an irregular L-shape, dominated by the Market House. On the north side a fine row of 15th-century houses is disguised by elegant 18th-century façades. There is a good range of small shops, numerous cafés and large hotels in the town.

Glastonbury
Dominated by Glastonbury Tor and the tower of St Michael's Church on its summit, the town has grown up at its foot; above the area liable to flooding and around the ancient site of the abbey. Joseph of Arimathea reputedly brought Christianity to England when he planted his Holy Thorn here. King Arthur's tomb is marked in the ruins of the chancel of the great church. Although little remains intact of the abbey, save the Abbot's Kitchen, its prosperity and influence throughout the county are visible in the many important properties associated with it. Notable ones in the town include a 14th-century barn, now housing the excellent Rural Life Museum, and the Tribunal, now the local history museum with fine exhibits from the Iron Age lake villages at Meare and Glastonbury. The town has become a centre for alternative and mystical activities, with a wealth of fascinating shops to browse around.

Meare
Fishermen for the Glastonbury monks lived here in the Abbot's Fish House in the 14th century, and the contemporary manor house was a summer residence for the abbots.

Burrow Bridge
There are extensive views from the summit of the 'Mump'. The old pumping station opposite has a collection of Victorian engines.

Muchelney
The 10th-century Benedictine abbey was founded on the site of a Saxon chapel. The Priest's House is a rare survival of a 14th-century house, scarcely altered after 600 years.

Huish Episcopi
The 15th-century church tower is considered to be the finest in the county; it has a superb Burne Jones window and Norman doorway.

Somerton
An attractive small market town built of local blue lias stone, whose centrepiece is the market place with battlemented market cross. The town hall, *c*1700, is surrounded by elegant town houses and old inns; Broad Street is reminiscent of a tree-lined city boulevard. The church has a magnificent 15th-century tie-beam roof.

Fleet Air Arm Museum
Fleet Air Arm Museum portrays the history of naval aviation since 1903, with over 50 historic aircraft, including *Concorde*.

Cadbury Castle
A strategic site overlooking principal routes to the West Country, occupied intermittently from neolithic to Saxon times. A great chieftain, reputedly Arthur, had his palace here; and Ethelred the Unready established a mint.

Castle Cary
Several fine old houses and an attractive duck pond form the heart of Castle Cary. Behind the old market hall, which houses the tiny museum, is the old lock-up – a circular structure, only 7ft in diameter, for petty criminals.

Shepton Mallet
Beautifully sited at the foothills of the Mendip plateau, the town was once important for its woollen industry supplied from flocks grazing the wind-swept hills. The fine market cross and several good 17th- and 18th-century buildings reflect this prosperity. The superb 15th-century church has an intricately carved nave roof, and a pulpit hewn from a single piece of stone.

OFF THE BEATEN TRACK

Peat Moors Visitor Centre
Between Westhay and Shapwick, this excellent and comprehensive display relates to all aspects of the Peat Moors, with sections devoted to different subjects: archaeology; history; dealing with commercial extraction of peat; and finally natural history with photos and samples of the unique flora and fauna of the wetlands.

Above: *the moat and wall around the Bishop's Palace and gardens at Wells Cathedral*

Below: *the famous Somerset landmark, Glastonbury Tor. Once surmounted by St Michael's Church, all that now remains of the building is the tower*

OFF THE TOUR

Westonzoyland Pumping Station
Turn right off the A361 on to the A372 for Bridgwater to reach Westonzoyland, about 2½ miles away. The site of the first pumping station in the county to drain the Levels, a restored pump of 1861 is still working. A blacksmith's forge and narrow gauge railway are also here.

Pilton Manor Vineyard
This historic vineyard outside Pilton was one originally planted by the abbots of Glastonbury in 1189. Guided tours of the winemaking process are available, with the produce on sale in the restaurant.

Wookey Hole Caves
A bizarre tourist complex north-west of Wells, bought by Madame Tussaud in 1973. The gigantic system of caves was hollowed out of the limestone by the River Axe. Cave dwellers lived here between 250BC and AD400; a tour through the caves is enlightened by a small exhibition of finds.

Sparkford Motor Museum
Dedicated to restoring and preserving its huge collection of veteran and vintage vehicles in working order: the museum ensures each one is driven at least twice a year.

THE SOUTHWOLDS AND VALE OF BERKELEY

63 miles

North-east of Bristol the land rises steadily towards the Cotswold Hills, a limestone landscape cut by winding rivers and dotted with stone-built villages.

Networks of fields on the steep slopes are marked by low dry-stone walls - sheep country that brought wealth to medieval merchants.

Bristol is a cosmopolitan city of international stature; rich in culture and history and thriving as an established engineering and high technology centre, and yet only a few miles to the north is the peace and beauty of ancient 'golden' villages and spectacular rural scenery. Avonmouth, Bristol's port, lies on the Severn Estuary; the surrounding area is a flat vale of agricultural land, when the urban spread of the city has been left behind. Here, the villages have an industrial as well as an agricultural history; coal mining, brass and copper working were all important up to the 19th century. Now, the villages act as dormitory areas for Bristol.

In the east the steep escarpment of the Southwolds (the southern Cotswolds) rises, surmounted by a plateau of gently rolling limestone. This provides the golden-yellow stone out of which everything is built; the field boundaries, houses, churches and even the roofs are made from limestone tiles.

Dyrham, a splendid William and Mary house set in a 265-acre park

ON THE TOUR

Bristol

From the 16th century Bristol was an important international port, opening trade routes to the East and America. Today, the city docks are only used by pleasure craft; huge modern ships cannot enter the narrow, twisting and silted Avon Gorge. The area around the old docks has been transformed into an attractive arts and leisure complex, and has seen the return of one of its most famous creations: the SS *Great Britain*, built by Brunel and the largest iron ship of its time, now renovated and open to visitors with an exhibition recording its creator and the city of its birth.

Much of the centre of Bristol was devastated by bombing during the Second World War, so isolated surviving buildings feel lost in a sea of post-war development and ring roads. The church of St Mary Redcliffe was built during the 13th and 15th centuries, boasting a massive tower and 285ft spire. Two houses have been furnished and decorated in the style of their respective periods: the 16th-century Red Lodge and the 18th-century Georgian House. A more modern attraction is the Exploratory, at Brunel's Temple Meads Station – a hands-on science 'museum', with 150 experiments to perform.

Bristol manages to retain a 'country town' feeling, largely due to over 4,000 acres of open space notably 'The Downs' at Clifton, where Brunel's famous suspension bridge spans the Avon Gorge and leads to Leigh Woods and the Ashton Court Estate.

Badminton

Established by Edward Somerset, the first Duke of Beaufort, in the 17th century, the imposing house and parkland is open on Wednesdays during the summer. The interior is richly decorated and contains many fine paintings and furniture. The huge 15,000-acre park has superb wooded areas and is the home of the famous three-day event horse trials. The villages of Little and Great Badminton are typical of the Cotswolds; weathered, golden-stoned cottages in an unspoilt setting.

Wotton-under-Edge

This is an attractive town in a beautiful setting, under the 'edge' of the steep Cotswold escarpment and overlooking the Severn Valley. Well-signposted walks from the town are worth following. In the town the main streets are in a rectangle and show both traditional and unusual architectural features; on the corner of Market Street is the Queen Victoria Jubilee clock, an elaborate landmark. Of special note are the Perry and Dawes Almshouses, graceful 17th-century buildings containing a courtyard and contemporary chapel, a tranquil place.

Berkeley

The town lies close to the Severn where the river has exposed beds of clay used for brick making; hence the predominant brick architecture of the wide main street, contrasting with the mellow Cotswold stone found on the higher ground. Behind the church is Berkeley Castle, a massive stone keep with great hall, chapel and dungeon, where the ill-fated Edward II was murdered. Nearby is the Jenner Museum, where the first smallpox vaccination was performed, housing a collection of Jenner memorabilia. See page 61 for Slimbridge.

ROUTE DIRECTIONS

Leave **Bristol** (map 2ST57) by following signs M32, and in $1\frac{1}{4}$ miles join the M32. Leave the motorway at junction 2 and follow signs Fishponds, B4469. In $\frac{1}{4}$ mile, at the mini-roundabout, turn left on to the A432 and in $1\frac{1}{4}$ miles reach Fishponds. In $\frac{1}{4}$ mile, at the traffic signals, branch right to pass the Cross Hands, then in $1\frac{3}{4}$ miles reach Mangotsfield. At the mini-roundabout turn left, then, at the church, turn right (sp. Pucklechurch) and continue forward to Pucklechurch. Bear right, unclassified (sp. Hinton) and in 200 yards turn left. Continue through Hinton and on reaching the main road, turn left on to the A46 (sp. Stroud). In $\frac{3}{4}$ mile, at the roundabout, take 2nd exit to cross the M4, then in 2 miles, at the traffic signals, turn right on to the B4040 (sp. Malmesbury). In $1\frac{1}{2}$ miles turn left, unclassified (sp. Badminton) then, in another $1\frac{1}{2}$ miles turn left again to enter **Badminton**. Turn left (sp. Stroud) and in $2\frac{1}{2}$ miles cross the main road for Hawkesbury Upton. In $\frac{3}{4}$ mile pass the Hawkesbury Monument then bear right for Hillesley. Continue through Alderley and in $1\frac{1}{2}$ miles bear left into **Wotton-under-Edge**. Follow signs Dursley B4060 to reach North Nibley and at the Black Horse Inn turn left, unclassified, into 'The Street'. In $\frac{1}{4}$ mile, at the church, bear right (sp. Berkeley), descend and, after $2\frac{3}{4}$ miles, at the main road, turn left on to the A38. In nearly $\frac{1}{2}$ mile turn right, unclassified, and at the following T-junction turn left to join the B4060. After $1\frac{3}{4}$ miles go forward, unclassified, for **Berkeley**. At the crossroads turn left (no sign) and in $2\frac{1}{4}$ miles turn right, unclassified (sp. Thornbury). Continue through Rockhampton and in $1\frac{1}{2}$ miles turn right on to the B4061. About 1 mile further turn right, unclassified, into Church Road, to reach Thornbury Castle Hotel. Turn left past the church and keep left for Thornbury town centre.

Turn right on to the B4061 (no sign) and in 1¼ miles turn right on to the B4461 (sp. Aust). In ½ mile turn right again then in 3¾ miles, at the junction roundabout with the M4, take 1st exit A403. Continue for 3 miles then turn left on to the B4055 into Pilning and go forward (sp. Bristol) through Easter Compton. Ascend to reach a roundabout and take 3rd exit A4018, then in a further 1½ miles, at the next roundabout, take 3rd exit (sp. Blaise Castle) along the B4057 (no sign) to Henbury. At the crossroads turn right then keep forward (one-way) to pass the road to Blaise Castle House on the left. Continue on the B4057 for 2 miles then, at the traffic signals, turn right on to the A4162 into Sylvan Way (sp. Avonmouth). At the next traffic signals turn left on to the A4 (sp. City Centre). Enter Avon Gorge and pass beneath Clifton Suspension Bridge to return to Bristol.

OFF THE TOUR

Chepstow

Cross the Severn Bridge and leave the M4 at junction 22. This ancient fishing and trading port contains a Norman church with an especially fine west door, but the most important building is the ruined Norman castle on a rocky promontory high above the River Wye. Huge circular towers remain, offering splendid views in all directions.

Dyrham House and Park

Off the A46 just south of the M4 junction 18, the house, church, stables and orangery make a pleasant group of varied architectural styles all set in the huge deer park on the southern edge of the Cotswold escarpment. Of special interest is one of the earliest surviving greenhouses. A well-signposted walk from the wood leads to Hinton Hill, the site of a turning point in British history. In AD577 the Saxons defeated the Celts here and forced them to withdraw to Wales and Cornwall, leaving England to the English.

Horton Court

The village of Horton lies west of the A46, five miles north of the M4. The Court has Norman origins, but the main construction is 16th century. It was built for Dr Knight, who negotiated with the Pope on behalf of Henry VIII in his attempt to divorce Catherine of Aragon. The Roman influence can be seen in the loggia in the garden. Owned by the National Trust, it has limited opening times.

Dodington Park

The history of the horse and carriage is celebrated here; over thirty coaches, a blacksmith and carriage museum as well as cowboy gear are displayed. A narrow gauge railway, pets' corner and adventure area provide energetic entertainment, whilst the peace and beauty of the parkland, laid out by Capability Brown, supply tranquil relaxation. North of Hinton, off the A46.

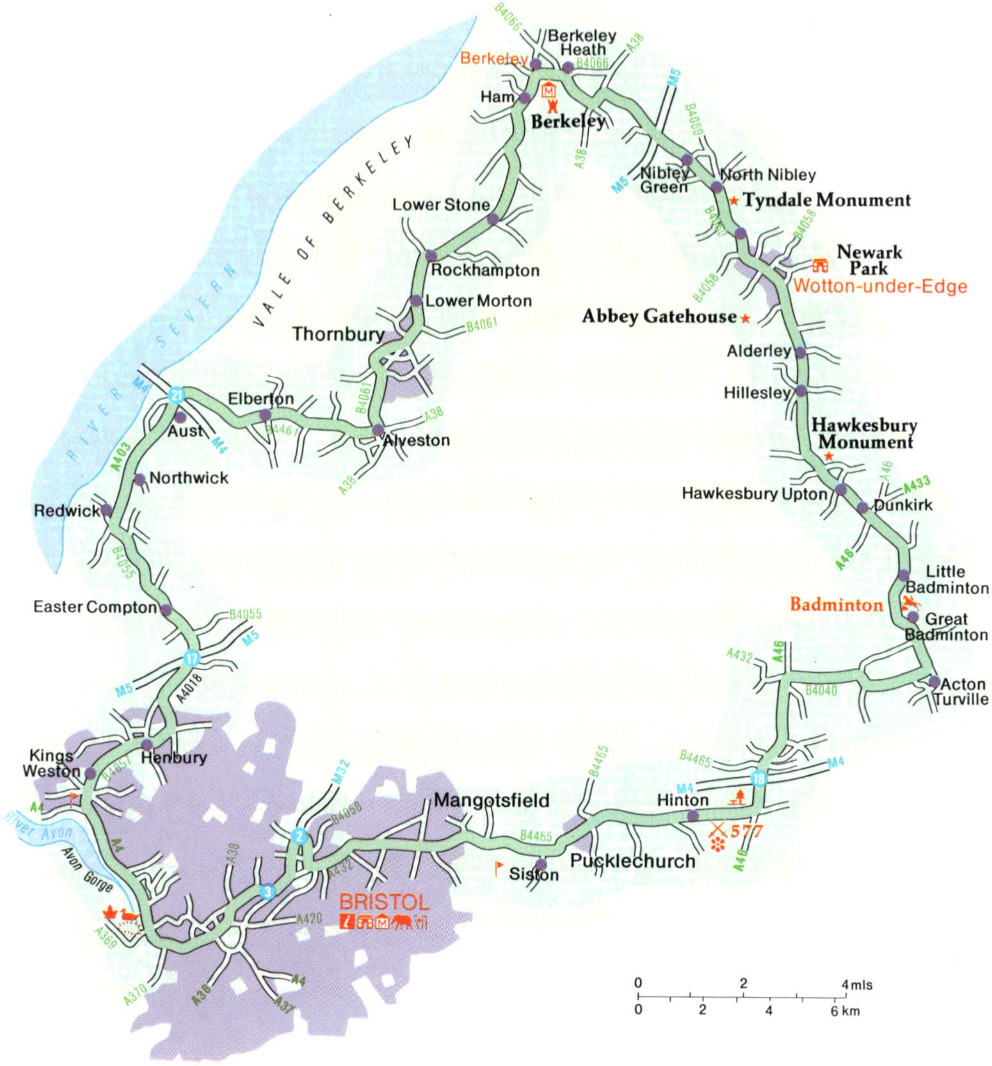

Brunel's famous Clifton Suspension Bridge, soaring 245ft above the River Avon with a span of 702ft

OFF THE BEATEN TRACK

Blaise Castle House

Blaise Castle House, at Henbury on the north-west outskirts of Bristol, was built in 1796 by William Paty, its plain style appropriate for J S Harford, a Quaker banker; today it houses Bristol's Museum of Social History. The grounds were laid out by Humphrey Repton and include a restored watermill, thatched dairy and woodland walks. Blaise Hamlet nearby is a picturesque group of thatched cottages around a green built for estate workers and old retainers from the Castle estate.

HILLS AND VALES OF THE DORSET HEARTLAND

83 miles

Blackmoor Vale, between Sherborne and Shaftesbury, is a landscape of undulating pasture; rich dairying country, dotted with

pretty villages. Cranborne Chase, south of Shaftesbury, is wilder and wooded - it once provided private hunting for royalty.

The enduring nature of rural Dorset life has left abundant evidence of ancient settlements, and bears witness to centuries of fluctuating prosperity. Shaftesbury, perched on a high spur of greensand, overlooks the fertile clay soils of the Blackmoor Vale, characterised by small fields with tree-lined hedges, scattered with rural hamlets.

The Vale is bounded on the south by a dramatic escarpment of high chalk hills; a mixture of pasture, arable and woodland, disected by long, deep valleys cut by the south-flowing streams of the Cerne and Piddle. Important strategic sites can be seen in numerous earthworks such as Bulbarrow, Hambledon and Hod Hills, and the more obvious Cerne Giant.

Beyond Blandford, the landscape softens into the grasslands and beech woods of Cranborne Chase, between Shaftesbury and Salisbury, with more superb vistas towards Poole Harbour and the Isle of Wight.

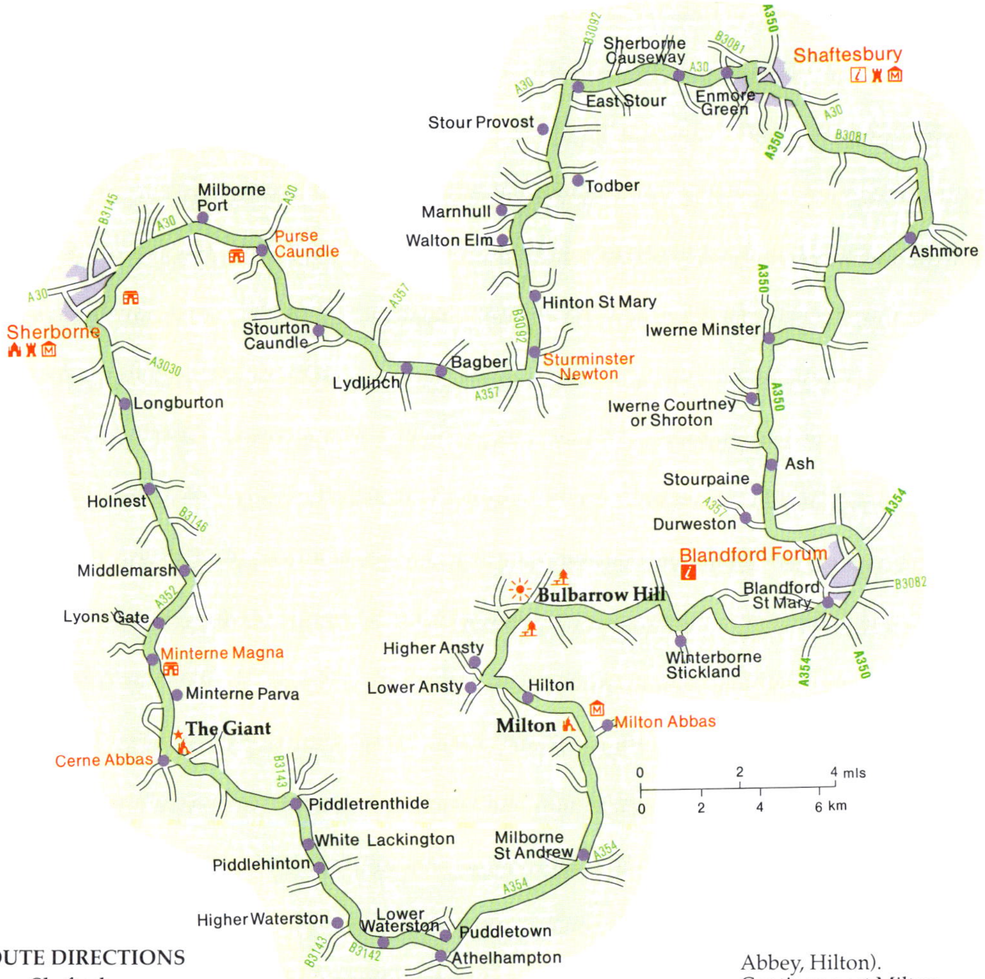

The 18th-century cottages of Gold Hill, Shaftesbury – one of the few cobbled streets left in England

ROUTE DIRECTIONS

Leave **Shaftesbury** (map 3ST82) on the A30 Yeovil road. At East Stour crossroads turn left on to the B3092 (sp. Sturminster Newton) and pass through Stour Provost and Todber to reach Marnhull. Here, bear left at the church and pass Hinton St Mary to reach **Sturminster Newton**. Keep forward then, at the end of the town, cross the River Stour and turn right on to the A355 (sp. Sturbridge). In $^{3}/_{4}$ mile branch left, unclassified, on to the Stourton Caundle road, keep forward to reach **Purse Caundle**. Here, go forward on to the A30 (sp. Sherborne). Pass Ven House and enter Milborne Port before reaching **Sherborne**. In $^{3}/_{4}$ mile, at the crossroads, turn left (sp. Dorchester) and 1 mile further turn left on to the A352. Ascend to reach Middlemarsh, climbing to the downs and passing High Stoy Hill on the right before reaching **Minterne Magna**. Pass Minterne House on the left and continue down the valley to the edge of **Cerne Abbas**. Here, turn left, unclassified (sp. Village Centre) and at the T-junction turn left then in $^{1}/_{4}$ mile turn right (sp. Piddletrenthide). Ascend steeply and, at the crossroads on top of the ridge, turn right then immediate left (no sign). Descend in to the Trent Valley and at Piddletrenthide, turn right on to the B3143 (sp. Dorchester). Continue through Piddlehinton then in $1^{1}/_{2}$ miles further, after crossing the river, turn left on to the B3142 Puddletown road. At the edge of Puddletown turn left on to the A354 (sp. Blandford) and continue to Milborne St Andrew. Pass the Royal Oak then turn left, unclassified (sp. Milton Abbas) and follow the valley for $2^{1}/_{2}$ miles to reach **Milton Abbas**. At the foot of the village turn left (sp. Milton Abbey, Hilton). Continue past Milton Abbey to Hilton. In a further $^{3}/_{4}$ mile turn right (sp. Hazelbury Bryan) then in $^{1}/_{4}$ mile further turn right (sp. Bulbarrow). In $1^{1}/_{4}$ miles bear right then in $^{1}/_{2}$ mile further at the crossroads, reach the car park and viewpoint at Bulbarrow Hill. Turn right (sp. Blandford Forum) and in $^{1}/_{2}$ mile bear left (sp. Winterbourne Strickland). Descend to a T-junction and turn right then, 1 mile further on, at the edge of Winterbourne Strickland, turn left (sp. Blandford Forum). In 1 mile bear right and descend, then at Blandford St Mary turn left and cross the Stour into **Blandford Forum**.

ON THE TOUR

Shaftesbury

Steep, cobbled Gold Hill flanked by old cottages, and the buttressed precinct wall of the abbey set against the rolling Dorset scenery, has won Shaftesbury a role in many films. At the top is the museum, with well-displayed collections of local archeaological finds including a Roman child's coffin. The town still supports a thriving market on Thursdays, and a friendly local atmosphere pervades. There are excellent views across the Blackmoor Vale from the wide Park Walk, and on the north side from Castle Hill to the Mendips, Glastonbury and the Quantocks. Little remains of the abbey founded by Alfred the Great – after the Dissolution it became a welcome source of building stone.

Sturminster Newton

Attractively situated on a spur, within a meander of the River Stour, the town is sleepy every day of the week except Monday when there is a huge cattle market and the streets are packed with lorries and farmers. Across the river the working water mill is open to the public.

Purse Caundle

A small village, a backwater with an attractive church and a superb manor house. The manor is noted for its graceful oriel window and magnificent Perpendicular great hall; it is open to the public on certain afternoons.

Sherborne

Glimpses down winding streets of mellow golden Ham stone houses offer a wealth of history at every turn. The magnificent abbey dominates the town, dating in part from Norman times and completed in the 15th century. Many of the original abbey buildings have been incorporated by Sherborne School, founded in 1550. The main thoroughfare, Cheap Street, offers an excellent selection of small local shops, and innumerable cafés, well used to an influx of children. The museum, housed within the abbey gatehouse, has exhibits covering the abbey and the role played by Sherborne castles in the Civil War.

Minterne Magna

Minterne Gardens, around Minterne House, have miles of woodland walks, with a great variety of trees – rhododendrons, acers, azaleas and many more. Below the house is a beautiful lake. There is a semi-wild shrub garden, with bamboo-lined walks.

Cerne Abbas

The Cerne Giant is best seen from the Sherborne road; an imposing figure cut into the chalk hillside, 180ft high, dating possibly from pre-Roman times, and believed to be associated with fertility rites. A Benedictine abbey was founded here in 987. Remains include the 15th-century Guest House, and the tithe barn. A picturesque village with welcoming tea rooms. See also page 49.

Milton Abbas

This planned 'model' village of regular, thatched, whitewashed cottages was built between 1771 and 1790 by George Damer, who moved the village from its original site around Milton Abbey as it spoilt the outlook from his mansion! The 1674 almshouses were moved stone by stone. The abbey, rebuilt into a magnificent house, is now a public school. Park Farm Museum has a comprehensive collection of Dorset farm implements. The picnic site has views to Poole Harbour.

Blandford Forum

A pleasant town with much elaborate Georgian brickwork, the result of extensive rebuilding after a severe fire in 1731. Note the magnificent pump, a memorial erected by John Bastard in 1760. The museum contains displays of buttons and chimney pots as well as the ubiquitous agricultural bygones.

OUTDOOR ACTIVITIES

Bulbarrow Hill

Bulbarrow Hill, the second highest point in Dorset, is one of the county's best viewpoints, with a stone giving directions of towns and features far beyond the Blackmoor Vale. There is a good picnic site at Ibberton Hill, a little lower and to the north-east.

Hambledon and Hod Hills

Rising steeply to 622ft and surmounted by superb earthworks, created at various times between the Stone Age and Roman times, Hambledon Hill was an important strategic site. There are tremendous views from the top. General Wolfe trained troops here before embarking for Quebec. Next to Hambledon is Hod Hill, also with ancient earthworks. Hod Hill was a defensive site before the Roman invasion; then later, in AD63, the Romans established a camp here.

The working watermill, beside the weir on the River Stour, at Sturminster Newton

Here, bear left on to the B3052 and in 1¼ miles turn left on to the A350. Follow the Stour Valley, passing Hod Hill and Hambledon Hill before reaching Iwerne Minster. At the war memorial turn right, unclassified (sp. Tarrant Gunville) and skirt the village. Pass the church then, in 1¼ miles at the crossroads, turn left (sp. Shaftesbury). Continue through Cranborne Chase and after 1¾ miles, at the crossroads, turn right (sp. Ashmore). Descend then ascend to enter Ashmore. At the pond, bear left (no sign) and in 1 mile turn left on to the B3081 (sp. Shaftesbury). Continue across the Charlton Downs before descending the Zig-Zag Hill then, at the T-junction, turn right and in 1¼ miles turn left on to the A30 to re-enter Shaftesbury.

OFF THE TOUR

Sherborne castles

Follow signposts from the town centre for the Old Castle ½ mile to the east of the town. Dating from the 12th and 13th centuries it was reduced to a romantic and evocative heap of ruins in the Civil War, when the defending force of 500 was overcome by some 7,000 Parliamentarians.

The New Castle, across the artificial lake to the south of the Old Castle, was built in 1594 for Sir Walter Raleigh. It has been owned by the Digby family since 1617, when Sir John Digby added four wings and towers.

Athelhampton House

Turn right instead of left on to the A354 for Puddletown, and Athelhampton House is about a mile down the A35 towards Tolpuddle. This is the legendary site of King Athelstan's palace, and one of England's finest medieval houses, set in 10 acres of formal landscape and water gardens.

Royal Signals Museum, Blandford

Follow the A354 off the Blandford ring road to the east (sp. Salisbury) and a couple of miles beyond the town turn right to Blandford Camp, where the Royal Signals Museum is found. A comprehensive history of all types of communications equipment.

Worldwide Butterfly Farm

Within the historic setting of Compton House are live butterflies, in exotic settings with tropical plants. Walk in the butterfly house with its free-flying butterflies, or enjoy the gardens, especially planted to attract native species. Here also is the Lullingstone Silk Farm, unique in Britain, where silk worms are reared and their silk reeled.

DORSET COAST AND HILLS

56 miles

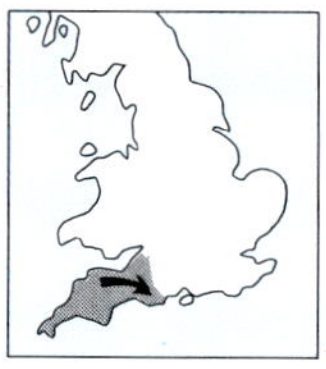

From the gently undulating, fine-turfed chalk uplands, to rolling heathland and curiously twisted rock formations on the coast, this is a tour of great variety including some of Hardy's Wessex and the Purbeck Hills.

Thomas Hardy's descriptions of rural Dorset are revitalised in the landscape and villages of this unspoilt stretch of country. The underlying geology has created an area of contrasts: chalk downlands scored by deep valleys in the north, heath and forest land west of Wareham. Once a wild and mysterious spot, the latter is now dominated by the roar of tanks in training on military exercises. The rivers Piddle and Frome meander through the broad valley to Poole Harbour, and to the south lies the great spine of the Purbeck Hills. On the coast, limestone adds to the variety, twisted into strange shapes beside sheer cliffs.

A wide range of local building materials enhances the towns and villages; Purbeck stone, tough and resistant, makes an ideal building stone, and when polished resembles marble; elsewhere bricks are mixed with sparkling flint to create pattern and texture.

ON THE TOUR

Blandford Forum

In 1731 the town was gutted by a fire and almost wholly rebuilt between 1732 and 1760, creating one of the most attractive and complete small Georgian towns in England. The Corn Exchange, on the north side of the large rectangular market place, is particularly fine. The bridge over the River Stour leads to the Hall and Woodhouse Brewery, the home of Badger beer.

Bere Regis

This was the village of `Kingsbere' in Thomas Hardy's *Tess of the d'Urbervilles*, where Tess discovered the tombs of her ancestors. The church contains a crypt belonging to the Turberville family, from which Hardy adapted the name. The church has Norman origins; richly carved pillars with grotesque figures and a 15th-century timber roof.

Tank Museum

The museum of the Royal Armoured Corps and Royal Tank Regiment houses the largest collection of armoured fighting vehicles in the world, dating from 1915 to the present day. There is a self-service restaurant and bookshop.

Wool

By the ancient bridge over the River Frome is Woolbridge Manor, which Hardy called 'Wellbridge' and where Tess and Angel Clare spent their tragic wedding night. The village itself lies on a slight hill above the river. Just to the east is the ruined Bindon Abbey, founded in the 12th century.

Kingston Lacy

Belonging to the National Trust, this is one of Dorset's finest houses. There is a room packed with treasures from Spain, and a fine collection of paintings.

Lulworth Cove

An almost circular bay of chalk and limestone cliffs set in spectacular surroundings makes this a very popular site for visitors. Nearby Stair Hole shows how the cove was formed: the sea has broken through the limestone and is gradually eroding the softer clay and sand beneath. Paths east and west provide magnificent coastal walks. To the west is Durdle Door, a natural limestone arch rising from the sea.

Wareham

Formerly an important port, until eclipsed by Poole in the 13th century, Wareham lies in a strategic position between the rivers Piddle and Frome. It was fortified in Saxon times and the massive earthworks still surround the town between the rivers. Much of Wareham was rebuilt after a great fire in 1762, so the place has a distinctly Georgian feel despite its ancient origins. Behind the town hall, in East Street, is the local museum, which contains a fascinating exhibition of photographs and documents connected with Lawrence of Arabia, who died in 1935 following a motor-bike accident near Bovington Camp.

Wimborne Minster

The old town lies between the rivers Allen and Stour and has some attractive Georgian and Victorian architecture, but the main interest is the twin-towered minster, believed to have been built on the site of a Saxon nunnery. The combination of greensand, red heathstone and pale limestone creates a colourful exterior, complemented by the 'quarter-jack', a brightly painted grenadier guard who strikes the quarter hours high up on the north side.

A view of Wareham and the Church of Lady St Mary. The original building, which was Saxon, was replaced in Victorian times

OFF THE TOUR

Poole

Poole is a busy, prosperous town with all the amenities you would expect to find in a tourist resort: indoor swimming pool, zoo and the natural attractions of a good beach and sheltered harbour. The most interesting area is around the quay, the older part of the town, where there are two museums of local life: the guildhall covering the 18th and 19th century and Scalpen's Court dealing with earlier history. There is also a maritime museum and one tracing the development of the RNLI.

Corfe Castle

On the A351 south of Wareham the village was the centre of the Purbeck marble industry in the Middle Ages and most of the houses, even the roofs, are made from Purbeck stone. Rising behind the village is an almost symmetrical hill surmounted by the imposing remains of the castle that gives the village its name. Occupying a prominent position in a gap in the Purbeck Hills, it was probably first fortified by Alfred against the Danes. The present ruins, dating from the 12th to 15th centuries, were the scene of the murder of King Edward the Martyr, on the orders of his stepmother, in 978, and were subsequently blown up by Cromwell after a lengthy siege.

ROUTE DIRECTIONS

Leave **Blandford Forum** (map 3ST80) by following the signs for Poole. After crossing the River Stour turn left, and at the roundabout, go forward on to the A350 to pass through Blandford St Mary. Continue to Spetisbury and, at the end of the village, turn right on to the B3075 (sp. Dorchester). In $1\frac{3}{4}$ miles turn right on to the A31, pass through Winterbourne Zelston, continue past the Red Post crossroads and on to **Bere Regis**. At the bypass roundabout take 2nd exit to reach the village centre. At the traffic signals turn left, then immediate right, unclassified (sp. Wool), then in $\frac{3}{4}$ mile turn right (sp. Turners Puddle). In $\frac{1}{2}$ mile further at the crossroads go forward (sp. Briantspuddle), cross the River Trent and in 1 mile, at the crossroads, turn left (sp. Bovington Camp). In 1 mile, at the T-junction, turn left (sp. Cloud's Hill, Bovington) and in $\frac{1}{4}$ mile turn right. Continue through Bovington Camp, passing the **Tank Museum** on the left. Then, in $1\frac{1}{2}$ miles, at the T-junction, turn right. In $\frac{1}{2}$ mile further turn right again on to the A352 (sp. Dorchester). Shortly, cross the River Frome and continue to **Wool**; pass Wool Bridge and Woolbridge House. At Wool station go over the level-crossing, turn left on to the B3071 (sp. West Lulworth) and pass through the village. Ascend, then descend past Lulworth Camp into West Lulworth, keeping forward for **Lulworth Cove**. Return to Lulworth Camp. From here there may be closure of the army firing range. If the route is not possible because of closures, return to Wool and take the A352 to Wareham. If the route is open turn right on to the B3070 (sp. East Lulworth, Wareham) and in $1\frac{1}{2}$ miles at the edge of East Lulworth, turn right, unclassified (sp. Whiteway Hill). In $\frac{1}{4}$ mile branch right (no sign) to pass through an Army barrier. Ascend Whiteway Hill, keep forward at the summit, then at the junction bear left (sp. Wareham), passing the Steeple picnic area on the right. Descend through Great Wood, past Tudor Creech Grange (no sign) and on to Stoborough. Here, turn left on to the A351, then immediate right, unclassified. At the junction with the B3075 turn left to re-cross the River Frome and enter **Wareham**. At the traffic signals, keep forward (sp. Poole) and in $\frac{1}{2}$ mile cross the River Trent and at the roundabout take 3rd exit. At the next roundabout take 2nd exit and in $\frac{3}{4}$ mile, at the third roundabout, take 2nd exit and keep forward. In $2\frac{3}{4}$ miles, at the A35 junction roundabout, take 2nd exit on to the B3067 on to Lytchett Minster. Continue forward, and in $\frac{1}{2}$ mile turn left, unclassified (sp. Corfe Mullen). At the next crossroads, go forward (sp. Wimborne Minster) and in $\frac{3}{4}$ mile, at the T-junction, turn left then right, unclassified (sp. Corfe Mullen). In 1 mile further branch left (sp. Corfe Mullen church), descend and at the T-junction at Corfe Mullen Church turn right, then immediate left then right (sp. Wimborne) on to the A31. Continue down the valley then, at the bypass roundabout take 1st exit. Recross the River Stour, to enter **Wimborne Minster**. Leave on the B3082 Blandford road and continue past **Kingston Lacy** before re-entering Blandford Forum.

OUTDOOR ACTIVITIES

Steeple Picnic Site

Situated on the narrow spine of the Purbeck Hills, the site has magnificent views both inland and along the coast.

Kimmeridge

The Smedmore Estate, reached by a minor road to the south of Grange Gate, includes the nearby village of Kimmeridge and the land around has retained the charm of an ancient holding. A folly, Clavell's Tower, overlooks the bay, and the Ledges are well known for fossils.

Arne Peninsula

The tiny village of Arne lies alone in wild and colourful heathland on a promontory jutting into Poole Harbour. It is lovely walking country with views around the whole of the bay.

Badbury Rings

A large Iron Age hillfort of over 17 acres north west of Wimborne with three rings of earthworks. The fort stands at the meeting point of the ancient roads from Bath, Dorchester and Poole.

The ruins of Corfe Castle dominate its village

SOUTH AND SOUTH EAST ENGLAND

Seabirds cry and wheel over Beachy Head and the white cliffs of Dover, while palm trees bring a feathery touch of tropical luxuriance to the Isle of Wight coast towns. Wildfowl in multitudes haunt the muddy creeks and inlets of the Essex shore, as sailing barges tack and fill their brown sails across the estuary of the Blackwater.

Inland along the country roads lies some of the sweetest scenery in Britain. In Hampshire the trout streams where Izaak Walton cast his fly glide and chuckle below the beech hangers on the downs. Drives in the New Forest lead to glades where deer and wild ponies browse. Cattle chew the contented cud on the flat pastures of Romney Marsh, where the inns are alive to the sound of smugglers' tales. Up on the Lambourn Downs in Berkshire racehorses of impeccable pedigree stretch their slender, extravagantly expensive legs on the gallops.

This is a prosperous region of cricket squares on village greens, of Kentish orchards and oasthouses in the 'garden of England', of charming country towns: Midhurst, Lewes, Tenterden, Faversham, Amersham, Hungerford. In Saffron Walden you can admire some of the best traditional pargetting, or ornamental plasterwork, in Essex. In Abingdon they eccentrically throw buns from the top of the County Hall to the waiting populace on great occasions.

Hammer ponds can still be found in the Weald, where once the forest glowed to the ironmasters' furnaces. A clutch of Rothschild stately homes imports grace and luxury to rural Buckinghamshire. Sir Winston Churchill sleeps among his ancestors in the peace of Bladon churchyard.

Left: *Alum Bay, Isle of Wight – the cliffs here are famous for their coloured sands*
Above: *Leeds Castle, Kent – a former royal residence built on two islands in a lake*

Where the tours start **page**

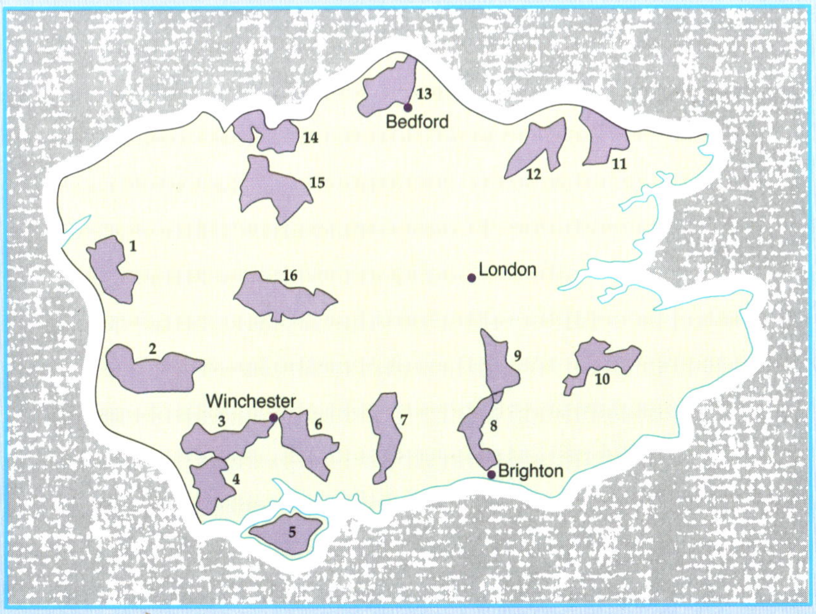

ALONG THE COTSWOLD ESCARPMENT

65 miles

With the exception of the south-east corner, this tour remains on the Cotswold Hills. It is a mellow land of drystone walls and dramatically steep valleys, the land of Cider with Rosie, *well-dressing and elver-eating.*

This is one of those parts of Britain blessed with natural stone; most of the area is underlain by Oolitic limestone and its golden colour gives this region its charm. Author Laurie Lee lives in the village of Slad, near Stroud.

A large part of the tour runs along the Cotswold escarpment, where the hills fall steeply to the Vale of Berkeley and the River Severn. The escarpment exposes the various layers of the Jurassic rocks of the region, including Inferior Oolite and the sands and iron-bearing marlstones of the Liassic series. Views of the lands below are truly breathtaking, with the silver waters of the River Severn and the Welsh hills beyond.

In recent years the Cotswolds have been favoured by the royal family. Princess Anne and Prince Charles have both taken up residence in the region.

Malmesbury's splendid, partly ruined abbey shows Norman and Decorated workmanship. The richly carved south porch is particularly outstanding

ON THE TOUR

Stroud

Lying in a deep bowl and fed by four fast-flowing streams, Stroud is a natural mill town. The great mill buildings still stand beside the Nailsworth Stream, the Stroudwater Canal of 1779 and the Thames and Severn Canal. The latter was opened in 1789 but was never a success. Most of the cloth trade has gone and the valleys have become an industrial heritage area.

The towpaths alongside the old canals are gradually being restored. They provide a chance to explore the locks and wharves used by the clothiers, who bought Cotswold wool, organised local weavers and grew rich on the 'Golden Fleece'.

Stroud has some fine civic buildings, including the Subscription Rooms and the nearby Congregational Chapel. There is a small industrial display in a former chapel in Landsdown Street.

Stratford Park has a lake, picnic areas, miniature railway and swimming pool.

Nympsfield and Uley

These villages have lent their names to prehistoric remains, perched nearby on the edge of the Cotswold escarpment. A stop at Nympsfield long barrow is ideal for taking in the views or a picnic. Uley Bury is a spectacular Iron Age hillfort, with a long barrow nearby called Hetty Pegler's Tump!

Tyndale Monument

Overlooking North Nibley, the Tyndale Monument is a local landmark 111ft high. It commemorates William Tyndale, the martyr who was the first to translate the Bible into common English. For his pains he was strangled and burned for heresy in 1536 at Vilvorde, near Brussels.

The Cotswold Way crosses the tour here. It runs for 100 miles along the scarp, between Chipping Campden and Bath.

Wotton-under-Edge

'Wotton-undridge', as it is called locally, is an old mill town. It once had 13 mills, making woollen cloth and silk.

Great Badminton

Badminton House is the seat of the Dukes of Beaufort; descendants of John of Gaunt and renowned for their hunting. The grounds of the house are famous for their annual horse trials.

Malmesbury

A very pleasant small town, with a famous abbey and several other interesting buildings. The Saxon king Athelstan is buried in the abbey, which has an extremely ornate porch. The town has a fine market cross.

There is a waymarked river walk along the two branches of the River Avon.

Westonbirt Arboretum

Founded in 1829, and run, since 1956, by the Forestry Commission, this is one of the largest collections of temperate trees in the world. There are more than 15,000 specimens set in 600 acres. Good facilities for visitors.

Tetbury

All the streets in this pleasant market town lead to the market place laid out in the 13th century. The celebrated Woolsack Races are held at Gumston Hill every Spring Bank Holiday Monday. They involve two local teams carrying sacks of wool, and form part of the Tetbury Festival.

Chavenage House

An unspoilt Elizabethan house, dated 1576, with Cromwellian connections, Chavenage contains some 17th-century, and earlier, stained glass, furniture and tapestries.

Avening

An old mill town, Avening is famous for its pig-roasting ceremony held each year on 'Pig Face Sunday' in mid September.

Minchinhampton

A stone-built village-cum-small town, with narrow streets, a fine market house and a church with half-steeple, half-tower – the result of an over-ambitious builder. Half of the steeple had to be taken down in 1563.

The church contains memorials to past owners of nearby Gatcombe Park, now the home of Princess Anne.

ROUTE DIRECTIONS

Leave **Stroud** (map 7SO80) by the A46 Bath road and in 3/4 mile, at the crossroads, turn right, unclassified, into Dudbridge Hill (sp. Dursley). At the end turn right then immediate left on to the B4066. Make an ascent to the viewpoint at Frocester Hill then descend to **Nympsfield** and **Uley**. Continue on the B4066, turn right on to the A4135 to enter Dursley, then in 1 mile turn left on to the B4060 (sp. Wotton-under-Edge). In 1/2 mile, at the Yew Tree Inn, bear left and skirt Stinchcombe Hill to reach North Nibley. Continue, past the **Tyndale Monument**, to **Wotton-under-Edge** and branch left (sp. Bath). At the war memorial go forward then immediate right, unclassified, on to the Alderley road. Pass through Alderley and Hillesley and continue past the Hawkesbury Monument to Hawkesbury Upton. In another mile cross the main road to enter **Great Badminton**. In the village turn right for Acton Turville to join the B4039 Chippenham road to Yatton Keynell, then in 1 mile turn left, unclassified (sp. Malmesbury). In 2 1/4 miles go over crossroads on to a narrow road and at the end turn left on to the A429. In 1 1/2 miles, at the roundabout, take 2nd exit. Continue through Corston then in 1 3/4 miles, at the roundabout, turn left on to the B4014 to enter **Malmesbury**. Follow the B4040, Bristol road to Sherston, pass the church and turn right, unclassified. At the end bear right on to the Knockdown road. In 1 3/4 miles turn right on to the A433 Cirencester road and in 1 1/2 miles further pass the entrance to **Westonbirt Arboretum** before entering **Tetbury**. Here, turn left and, at the end of the main street, go forward on to the B4104 Avening road. Shortly branch left, unclassified (sp. Chavenage) and after 1 1/2 miles pass **Chavenage House** on the left. Take the next right turn (no sign) on to a narrow by-road, then in 3/4 mile turn left to re-join the B4104. Descend to **Avening**, turn right at the Cross Inn , unclassified (sp. Minchinhampton) and make a long ascent to **Minchinhampton**. Continue on the Stroud road to Minchinhampton Common and turn right then immediate left. After another mile pass the Bear Inn, branch left (sp. Rodborough) and cross Rodborough Common. Descend through Rodborough and, at the foot, turn right on to the A46 to return to Stroud.

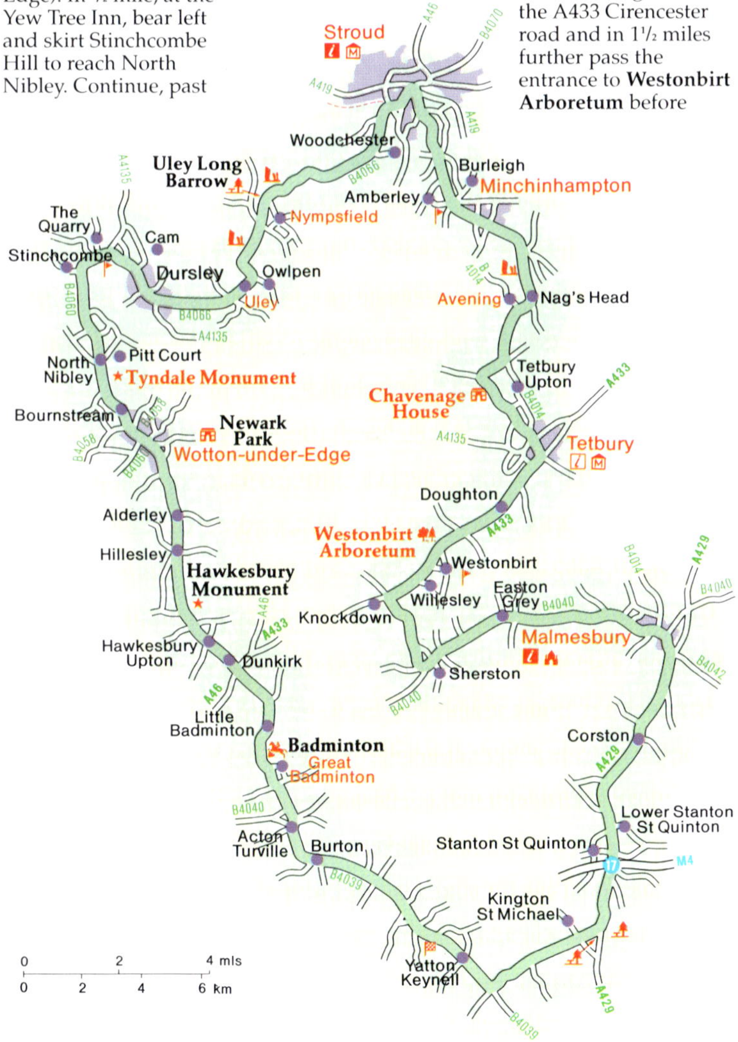

OFF THE TOUR

Slimbridge

The Wildfowl and Wetlands Centre is set in 800 acres. Here, visitors can watch birds in their natural habitat from specially constructed hides and observatories. Follow the A4135 through Dursley until it meets the A38. Slimbridge is northwest of the T-junction.

Berkeley

Berkeley lies to the west of the A38 on the B4066, and contains a classic example of the Englishman's castle, home of the Berkeley family since 1117. Edward II was horribly murdered at Berkeley Castle in 1327.
The Jenner museum at Berkeley tells the story of Edward Jenner (1749-1823), who introduced vaccination for smallpox.

Castle Combe

A beauty spot a short distance off the B4039. Ideal for sophisticated eating. Nearby is the well known Castle Combe motor racing circuit.

OFF THE BEATEN TRACK

Selsey

At the end of a lane that runs beside the Bell Inn, with dramatic views of Stroud, is Selsey Herb and Goat Farm - a must for herb lovers.

OUTDOOR ACTIVITIES

There is plenty of good walking to be had in this area, including the towpath that stretches along the Frome Valley at Stroud, and sections of the Cotswold Way.

The Malmesbury Civic Trust have waymarked a two-mile walk beside two branches of the River Avon.

Just outside the village of Minchinhampton are the Great Park and commons. They offer good walking and fine views and are scattered with prehistoric remains.

Castle Combe's delightful honey-coloured cottages are seen to best advantage overlooking Bybrook

WEST WILTSHIRE AND SALISBURY PLAIN

74 miles

This tour is based on Bradford-on-Avon, one of the finest small towns in the country. Salisbury Plain is scattered

with prehistoric remains, including the most famous one of all – Stonehenge.

The home of fine sausages, earthworks, Sarsen stones, 'Moonrakers' and dewponds. The land of Wiltshire (with a touch of Somerset) and the valleys of the Wylye and the Hampshire Avon, two of the five rivers that meet at Salisbury.

The tour starts at the delightful town of Bradford-on-Avon, a mill town with a strong industrial tradition. The rows of hill-perched, stone-built cottages - many of them once lived in by weavers - make it one of the prettiest places in the country.

Salisbury Plain is an uplifted chalk plateau, the westernmost part of the chalk downs that end in the east at the cliffs of Dover. Much of its interior is in the hands of the military, but the distant `crump-crump' of shellfire rarely interferes with the peace of its water meadows, open downlands and herb-rich grasslands. The northern part of the tour runs along the rim of the Vale of Pewsey.

ROUTE DIRECTIONS

Leave **Bradford-on-Avon** (map 3ST86) on the A363 (sp. Trowbridge). Cross the River Avon and branch right on to the B3109 (sp. Frome). In $\frac{2}{3}$ mile turn right, unclassified (sp. Westwood), and in a further $\frac{1}{2}$ mile, at the trunk road, turn right for **Westwood**. At the New Inn turn left, pass Westwood Manor and continue along a narrow road for 1 mile before turning right on to the A366. Ascend and pass Farleigh Castle on the right and **Farleigh Hungerford** on the left, then in 1 mile turn left on to the A36 (sp. Warminster) to reach Woolverton. In $1\frac{1}{3}$ miles, at the roundabout, take 2nd exit then in $\frac{2}{3}$ mile, at the roundabout, take 1st exit. In $4\frac{3}{4}$ miles further, at the next roundabout, take 2nd exit B3414 for **Warminster**. Here, follow the signs for Salisbury (A36) to leave by the B3414 and in $3\frac{1}{4}$ miles at the roundabout, take 1st exit A36. In $\frac{2}{3}$ mile turn left on to the B390 (sp. Shrewton) to reach Chitterne, then follow signs Amesbury and in $4\frac{3}{4}$ miles turn right on to the A360 (sp. Salisbury) into Shrewton. In a further 2 miles go forward on to the A344 (sp. Amesbury). Pass the **Stonehenge** car park and in $\frac{1}{2}$ mile turn left on to the A303. In $1\frac{3}{4}$ miles further, at the roundabout, take 1st exit A345 (sp. Marlborough). Pass **Woodhenge** on the left and in $\frac{1}{2}$ mile, at the roundabout, take 2nd exit. In 3 miles, at the Dog and Gun, turn right, unclassified (sp Everleigh) and keep left into Netheravon. Continue through Haxton to Everleigh and at the trunk road, turn left on to the A342 (sp. Devizes) for Upavon. Go forward (sp. Devizes) and in $\frac{1}{3}$ mile at the trunk road turn right. Skirt the edge of Rushall, turn left, then in $4\frac{1}{3}$ miles turn left on to the B3098 (sp. Westbury). Continue to Urchfont and on through Easterton and Market Lavington to West Lavington. Here, go over the crossroads (sp. Westbury) and continue to **Edington**, then on to **Bratton**. At the end of Bratton turn right, unclassified (sp. Steeple Ashton) and in 1 mile, at the crossroads, go forward. In $\frac{1}{2}$ mile, at the trunk road, turn left for **Steeple Ashton**. In 1 mile further turn left (sp. Hilperton) and in $\frac{1}{2}$ mile go over the crossroads to Hilperton. Then, turn left on to the A361, then right on to the B3105 (sp. Bradford). In a further $1\frac{1}{4}$ miles at the mini-roundabout, bear right to Staverton. In $\frac{1}{2}$ mile turn left on to the B3107 to return to Bradford-on-Avon.

Recorded in the Domesday Book, Bradford-on-Avon's mellow stone cottages lead to the Saxon Church of St Lawrence

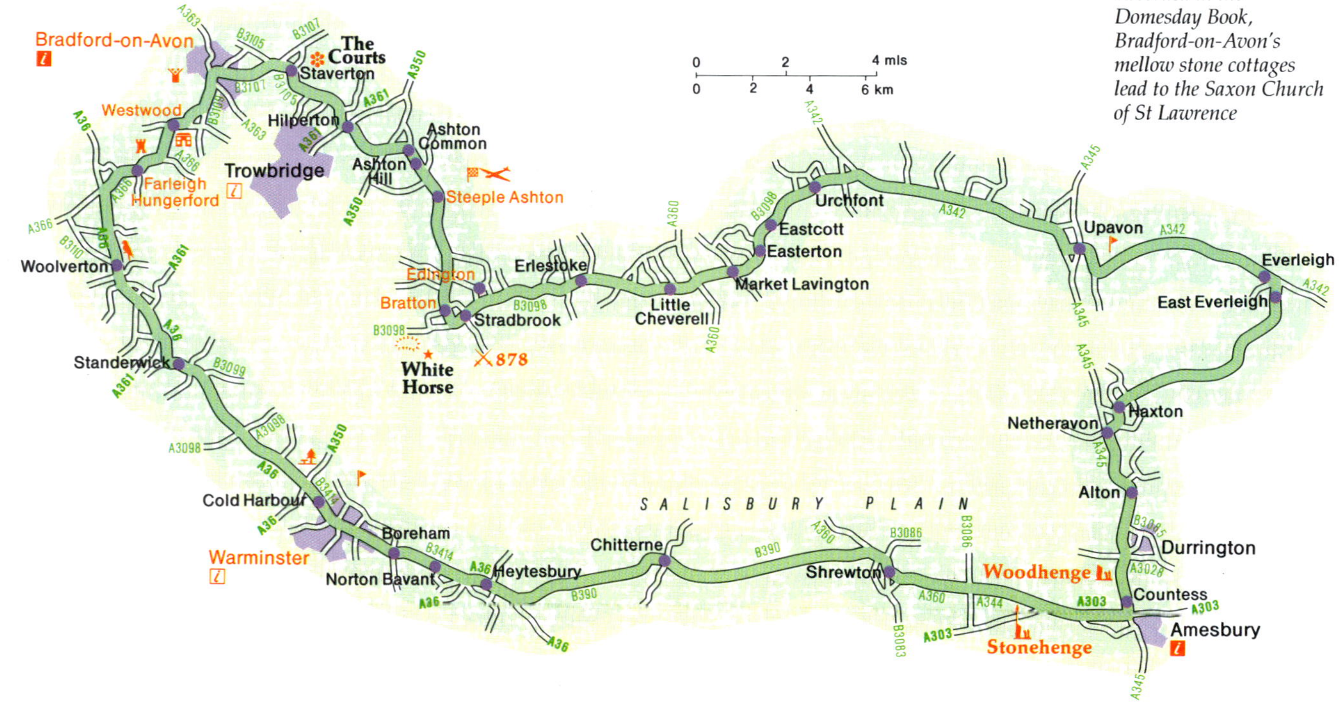

ON THE TOUR

Bradford-on-Avon
This is a mini-Bath; a delightful town on the edge of the Cotswolds, the home of the Moulton bike and a centre of considerable interest to architecture buffs and industrial historians. It made its money from weaving woollen cloth and you can still see the old mill buildings beside the Avon. Housed in one of them is the largest company in the town, Avon Industrial Polymers (formerly the Avon Rubber Company).
The Saxon church of Bradford is an extremely rare relic and the finest of its kind in the country. It stands close to the parish church in the centre of the town and yet was 'lost' until 1857.
A huge medieval tithe barn still stands to the south of the river, a short distance from the Frome road.

Westwood
Beside the church is a fine 15th-century stone-built manor house, now owned by the National Trust (limited opening hours).

Farleigh Hungerford
On a commanding site beside the A366 are the ruins of a 14th-century castle, once the home of the Hungerfords. The chapel is particularly well preserved. A skein of murder and adultery eventually led to the downfall of the family.

Warminster
A shopping centre and former market town, now the home of the School of Infantry and the workshops of the Royal Electrical and Mechanical Engineers.
Dr Arnold, the famous headmaster of Rugby, attended Warminster School, which still exists.

Stonehenge
This famous monument is visited each year by more than 700,000 people. It is thought to have been built as a huge astronomical calculator, to set the annual calendar. The major axis of the rings are in line with the rising of the sun at mid-winter and mid-summer.
Some of the great stones came from Marlborough, 20 miles away, but the 'bluestones' came from the Preseli Mountains in south-west Wales.

Woodhenge
The site of a look-alike wooden Stonehenge. The positions of the post holes are shown by concrete markers. There is a picnic area and an interesting mini-display about Salisbury Plain.

Edington
The famous priory church of this village was founded by a bishop of Winchester, William of Edington. Amongst the monuments is one that shows the bright colours that were once the norm in churches. A rebus, or visual pun, of a bay leaf growing out of a barrel (a tun) suggests that it commemorates a Baynton. The nearby hamlet of Baynton was the home of the wife of the poet George Herbert, who was married in the church.

Bratton
A minor road leads up to Bratton Camp, the finest viewpoint in Wiltshire. Its double banks and ditches are the remains of an Iron Age hillfort that lasted from 300BC to AD43.
The north slopes of the hill contain the famous Westbury White Horse, an 18th-century re-cutting of an ancient monument.

Steeple Ashton
A lock-up and a market cross with four sundials stand opposite the Longs Arms pub in this pretty stone-built village.

OFF THE BEATEN TRACK

Imber
In the priory church at Edington can be seen effigies brought from the church at Imber, which stands at the centre of Salisbury Plain. The village has been in the hands of the military for almost 50 years. It was commandeered for training battle troops during the last war and never returned to its inhabitants. Much of the village, including the virtually undamaged church, still stands.
Imber is generally open to view only on public holidays.

OUTDOOR ACTIVITIES
Barton Country Park on the southern outskirts of Bradford-on-Avon has a pleasant four-mile walk alongside the River Avon.

The area around Stonehenge is also fine walking country. The National Trust have waymarked walks that take in such curiosities as the processional way, or cursus, that marches for a mile and a half across the downs.

A new marina has opened at Hilperton on the Kennet and Avon Canal. Narrowboats can be hired.

St John's Court and Church at Devizes. This area of the town was built by the prosperous wool merchants in the 18th century. Many buildings from that period, and earlier, can still be seen

OFF THE TOUR

Rode
A short distance east off the A36 are 17 acres of gardens with more than a thousand rare tropical birds of more than 200 different species. Flamingos, penguins and macaws run 'wild' in a chain of small lakes. There is a children's play area, a cafeteria and a 'woodland steam railway'.

Longleat
The home of the Marquess of Bath, the first of the great stately homes of England to open its doors regularly to visitors, found west of the A36 at Warminster. There are the sumptuous rooms of the Elizabethan mansion itself, and also the famous lions and other wild animals in the safari park. Longleat also has a butterfly house, an adventure park and much else.

Devizes
Due east of Bradford-on-Avon, at the junction of A361 with A342, the streets of this historic town still reveal the circular pattern of the defences that once surrounded the medieval castle. It is an ideal place for a stroll; along Monday Market Street and the oddly named Brittox, and into the fine Market Place. There are two museums, on opposite sides of the town. In Long Street is the prize-winning Devizes Museum, exhibiting finds from classic archaeological digs. The Wharf Centre, alongside the Kennet and Avon Canal, tells the story of the canal in a waterside setting, complete with craft shops, places to eat and, at peak times, boat trips and small boats to hire. West of the town is the 16-lock flight down Caen Hill.

WINCHESTER TO SALISBURY VIA THE NEW FOREST

69 miles

Two historic cathedral cities, a world-famous arboretum, beautiful abbeys, a Roman villa and the stamping ground of the

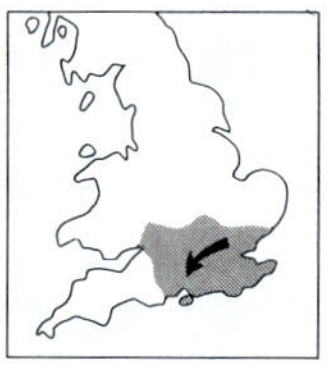

racehorse Desert Orchid all come into view in this part of Wiltshire and Hampshire.

This is a part of the country that is often missed by people hurrying to Dorset and the West Country. Much of it was originally settled by the church. The influences of the cathedrals at Winchester and Salisbury, and of the smaller houses at Romsey and Breamore, are still apparent 400 years after the Reformation.

The tour touches the northern edge of the New Forest which here consists of wide open, rolling heathland. The Martin Peninsula, a little-known corner of Hampshire to the north of Fordingbridge, is full of interest. It contains a Saxon church and a mansion-house at Breamore, a Roman villa at Rockbourne and the village of Whitsbury, where the racehorse Desert Orchid is trained. Above all, this tour passes through some beautiful small villages, including Hale, Mottisfont, Kings Somborne and many others.

Early examples of tractors in the Breamore Countryside and Carriage Museum, which traces agricultural history

ROUTE DIRECTIONS

Leave **Winchester** (map 3SU42) on the A3090, Romsey road (sp. Romsey A31) and pass through Hursley. In $\frac{1}{3}$ mile keep forward on to the A31 through Ampfield to **Romsey**. Here, at the roundabout, take 1st exit, then at the next roundabout take 2nd exit (sp. Ringwood). Continue past Broadlands on the left and, at the roundabout, go forward. In 3 miles, at the roundabout, take 3rd exit A36 (sp. Salisbury), then in $1\frac{1}{2}$ miles turn left, unclassified (sp. Bramshaw). Go over the cattle grid to **Bramshaw**. Continue over the crossroads (sp. Bramble Hill, Fordingbridge) and in $1\frac{1}{4}$ miles, at the crossroads, turn right on to the B3078 (sp. Fordingbridge). Pass the Bramble Hill Picnic Area and in a further $1\frac{2}{3}$ miles turn right on to the B3080 (sp. Downton). Pass the Pound View Car Park and in 1 mile turn left, unclassified (sp. Hale, Woodgreen) into Tetherington Row. After a further $\frac{1}{2}$ mile, at the crossroads, go forward, then at the next crossroads turn left for Hale, then Woodgreen. Continue forward (sp. Breamore) and in $\frac{1}{2}$ mile cross the River Avon. At the T-junction turn right on to the A338 (sp. Salisbury) into **Breamore**. Here, turn left, unclassified (sp. Whitsbury, Breamore House) then in $\frac{1}{3}$ mile turn right on to a narrow road (sp. Breamore House). After $\frac{1}{2}$ mile turn left and pass Breamore House on the right. Continue, unclassified (sp. Whitsbury) and in $\frac{1}{2}$ mile, at the crossroads, turn right (sp. Whitsbury). In 1 mile go over the crossroads (sp. Rockbourne) then in a further mile, at the T-junction, turn right (sp. Rockbourne, Salisbury). Pass the entrance to Rockbourne Roman Villa on the left and enter **Rockbourne**. In a further $4\frac{1}{2}$ miles turn right on to the A354 (sp. Salisbury) and continue to Combe Bissett and **Salisbury**. Leave on the A36 (sp. Southampton) and in $2\frac{1}{4}$ miles, at the start of the dual carriageway, turn right, unclassified (sp. Alderbury) for Alderbury. In $\frac{3}{4}$ mile, at the end of the village, turn left (sp. West Grinstead) and cross the bridge. At West Grinstead go forward (sp. West Dean) and in 3 miles, at the T-junction, turn right for West Dean. Here, turn right for Lockerley and in $\frac{1}{2}$ mile, at the T-junction, turn right (sp. Dunbridge). In $\frac{1}{2}$ mile turn left for Dunbridge, then at the T-junction turn left on to the B3084 (sp. Mottisfont). Go over the level crossing and in $\frac{1}{2}$ mile turn right, unclassified, for **Mottisfont**. At the Abbey gates turn right (sp. Kings Somborne) and in $\frac{2}{3}$ mile at the T-junction, turn left on to the A3057 for **Kings Somborne**. Here, turn right, unclassified (sp. Farley Mount, Winchester), shortly turn left, and in $\frac{2}{3}$ mile turn right (sp. Farley Mount). Pass the **Farley Mount Country Park** and in $\frac{2}{3}$ mile bear left (sp. Winchester). Go over all the crossroads for 3 miles, then turn left and return to Winchester.

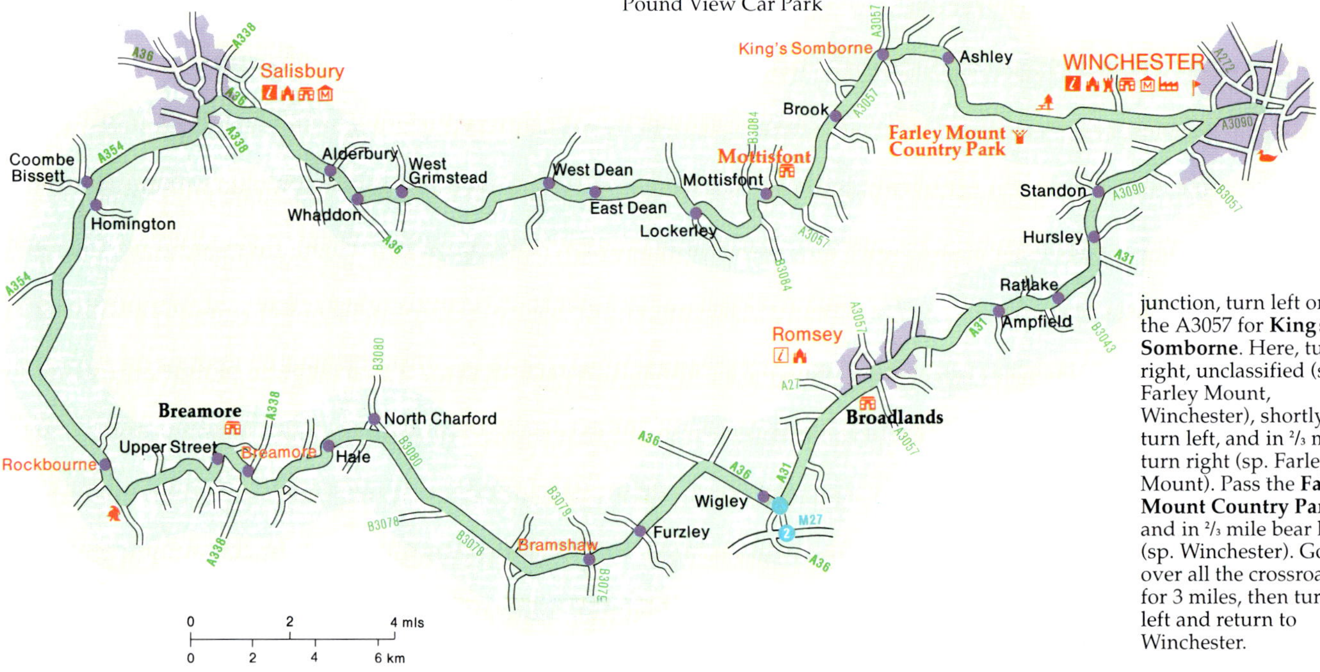

OFF THE TOUR

The Hillier Arboretum

The country's largest collection of temperate trees and shrubs, started in 1953 by the late Sir Harold Hillier, with the broadcaster Roy Lancaster doing a stint as curator. It covers 160 acres and contains many thousands of species of woody plants. There is something to be seen at all seasons, but the spring and early summer are probably best. The arboretum is in Jermyns Lane, Ampfield, off the A31, just beyond the village.

Paulton's Park and Bird Gardens

A treat for all the family. The attractive gardens that once surrounded a mansion are now a peaceful scene of ponds and aviaries, with many different kinds of birds. The park is on a minor road off the roundabout at Ower, just north of the M27 (Junc 2).

Wilton House

The home of the Earls of Pembroke for more than 400 years, this is one of the finest houses in the country. There are eight superb 17th-century state rooms by Inigo Jones, including the famous double-cube room. The splendid grounds are watered by the River Nadder and contain giant cedars and an adventure playground. Wilton House is 3 miles west of Salisbury on the A3094.

Old Sarum

The site of Salisbury until the 13th century, 3 miles north of the city on A345, with remains of a Norman fortress, a cathedral and fine views.

The Walton Canonry, in Salisbury's Cathedral Close. The painter Constable was once a guest here

ON THE TOUR

Winchester

The county town of Hampshire and the former Saxon capital of England. Don't miss the Crusades Experience; a great show for the children, about bounty-hunting and religious war. Further details of this historic city will be found in the tour on page 71.

Romsey

A charming country town on the River Test, with a famous abbey. Once the church of a nunnery, founded in the Saxon period, it is now the parish church. Its Norman and Early English architecture is a must. Below the altar steps is the pew used by Lord Romsey, the owner of Broadlands, whose visitors have often included royalty. In the south transept is the grave of Broadlands' most famous owner, Lord Mountbatten, who was killed by Irish extremists in 1979. The market place contains a statue of Palmerston, another illustrious owner of Broadlands. The house stands beside the A31 and is open to the public.

Bramshaw

Bramshaw is the site of a telegraph used in the Napoleonic Wars. It involved a system of shutters and was part of a signalling system which stretched from Whitehall to Plymouth. There are fine views of the New Forest here.

Breamore

An unspoilt corner of Hampshire with Breamore House and Countryside Museum, and a Saxon church of great interest. The house is Elizabethan and built in the form of an `E'. It is still the home of the Hulse family, who have lived here since the late 17th century. The museum contains a superb collection of carefully displayed bygones, with special exhibits on village crafts and farm machinery. There is a 1,200ft brick maze that won a *Sunday Times* competition.

Rockbourne

The home of General Sir Eyre Coote (1726-83), whose lofty monument overlooks the site of the Rockbourne Roman Villa, said to be the largest in the country. There is an excellent small museum on the site.

Salisbury

This famous cathedral city moved down to its valley site in the 13th century. Its grid of streets still reflect the medieval layout, with isolation of the cathedral close (locked each night) from the commercial area around the market place. Salisbury cathedral is rare for being almost entirely built in one short period, between 1220 and 1258. The most significant addition was the spire, which weighs 6,400 tons and soars 404ft. The beautiful chapter house contains one of the copies of the Magna Carta. Also in the Close is the Salisbury and South Wiltshire Museum, which has a reconstruction of Old Sarum, the Museum of the Duke of Edinburgh's Royal Regiment, and Mompesson House, a fine Queen Anne house owned by the National Trust.

Mottisfont

Tea on the lawn at Mottisfont is one of the joys of visiting the Test Valley. Mottisfont Abbey is a National Trust property known for its Rex Whistler 'optical illusion' decorations. The house, which shows obvious signs of its monastic origins, has a national collection of roses, including many old and rare varieties. The splendid grounds are set around a spring which feeds the river. Open-air theatrical productions take place here in the summer.

Kings Somborne

Once owned by John of Gaunt, who had a deer park here. The war memorial is by Sir Edwin Lutyens. The school was a model Victorian establishment visited by Mathew Arnold, Florence Nightingale and the prime minister Lord John Russell.

Farley Mount Country Park

More than 1,000 acres of glorious open downland, ancient woodland and Forestry Commission plantations. The focal point is a pyramidal memorial to a horse named Beware Chalk Pit!

OFF THE BEATEN TRACK

East Wellow was the home of 'lady of the lamp' Florence Nightingale. She lies buried in the churchyard, to the south of the porch. Her tall spire-like memorial is simply engraved 'FN 1820-1910'. Inside the church is another poignant memorial to the famous nurse; a cross made from bullets from the Crimean War, in which she eased the passage of the dying, and nursed so many back to health.
This is an isolated village reached by turning west off the A31 south of Romsey. There is a vineyard at nearby West Wellow.

OUTDOOR ACTIVITIES

The Test Way cuts the route at Mottisfont and at Romsey. These points provide access to lovely walks along the banks of the River Test. Similarly, the Clarendon Way is waymarked out of Salisbury and in the village of Kings Somborne. This walk follows a ridge between Salisbury and Winchester and takes its name from Clarendon Palace, the little-known royal residence that once stood three miles east of Salisbury.

THE NEW FOREST AND THE HAMPSHIRE AVON

56 miles

Open moorland, wild ponies and ornamental woodlands are the hallmarks of the New Forest. The valley of the Hampshire Avon is famous for its water meadows, its fishing and its pretty villages.

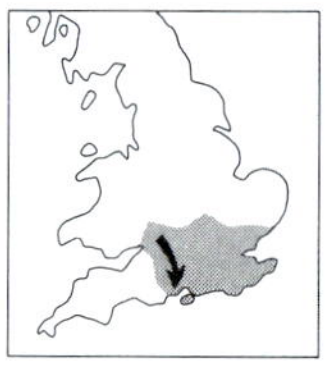

Despite appearances to the contrary, the wide open spaces of the New Forest are intensively managed, and have been for nearly a thousand years. The traditional tool of management has been the commoner and his ponies, though fewer people now want to keep livestock. The word 'forest' means an area for hunting, where special forest laws operate, rather than an area of woodlands. However, timber production has long been an important aspect of the forest. When wooden warships were essential for defence, the oak of the forest started to be protected from its deer in special inclosures, some of which still remain. The forest hides a vast number of other archaeological relics, from Bronze Age barrows to the scars of the last war, when the Luftwaffe dropped fire bombs.

The Hampshire Avon, famous with coarse and game fishermen, reaches the sea at Christchurch.

ON THE TOUR

Christchurch

The historic town of Christchurch, which has been in Dorset since 1974, lies between the estuaries of the Hampshire Avon and the Dorset Stour. Its great harbour is almost closed off by the spit called Hengistbury Head, which was used as a trading wharf in the Iron Age. Later the port moved to Christchurch Quay, which is near the famous Norman priory church. The quay is a delightful spot for a picnic. Christchurch Priory is of major architectural importance. It was built in the 11th century, on the site of a Saxon church, by Flambard – William the Conqueror's chancellor. Amongst its memorials are one, under the tower, to the poet Shelley and another, at the north-east corner of the choir, to the Countess of Salisbury. To the north of the church are remnants of the Norman castle (on a marked motte) and the substantial remains of a medieval hall, the Constable's House.

The Christchurch Tricycle Museum is the only one of its kind in the world. It is housed in former monastic buildings to the south-west of the church. A short distance away to the north, in Quay Road, is the Red House Museum and Art Gallery, a fine local museum with an excellent section devoted to fashion and costume.

Brockenhurst

This pleasant village has several eating places and pubs, including the Snake Catcher. This is named after the legendary local snakecatcher 'Brusher' Mills, whose ornate gravestone is in the local churchyard, to the north of the church. He earned a living by catching adders to feed to animals at zoos.

Beyond Brockenhurst on the route of the tour are two delightful waymarked forest trails, namely, the Ober Water Walk and the Tall Trees Walk. The latter runs alongside Rhinefield Ornamental Drive, planted in the middle of the last century. There are huge specimens of Redwood, Douglas Fir and Wellingtonia.

Further on the route passes the Knightwood Oak, said to be 400 years old, and follows the Bolderwood Ornamental Drive.

The Rufus Stone

This marks the spot where, traditionally, William II (son of William the Conqueror) was killed by an arrow in 1100. Ever since, people have been debating whether he was killed accidentally, or murdered.

Fordingbridge

Two miles before the town is Godshill, where domestic earthenware pottery is made. Fordingbridge is a comfortable little town with a seven-arch medieval bridge that crosses the River Avon. The artist Augustus John lived near here and a statue of him by Sir Ivor Roberts stands in the recreation field, on the east side of the river. Branksome China Works are in Shaftesbury Street, Fordingbridge. Here you can watch the making of fine English porcelain chinaware and animal models. There are regular factory tours.

Ringwood

One of the main towns of the forest. An extensive street market is held here every Wednesday. There are several restaurants and pubs and good local shops. In 1685, after the Battle of Sedgemoor, the ill-fated Duke of Monmouth – Charles II's eldest son – hid in the house in West Street (off the attractive Market Place) that bears his name.

The New Forest has, to many people, the appearance of a truly wild, natural landscape, although it has, in fact, been carefully 'managed' for centuries

OFF THE TOUR

Lyndhurst

The capital of the New Forest (north of Brockenhurst), with a superb new Museum and Visitor Centre. The Forestry Commission has its headquarters here, in the Queen's House, which includes the ancient Verderers Courtroom. The Holidays Hill Reptiliary, near Lyndhurst, contains local reptiles.

Fritham

At the end of a lane, past a pub and the village green, is Eyeworth Lodge Pond; alive with ducks, and with a convenient car park. It was once used for the gunpowder factory which stood nearby, and locally made charcoal was used in the manufacture. Fritham can be reached by turning north off the tour route, 3 miles after it first crosses the A31.

Dorset Heavy Horse Centre

Here the rare breeds of horse that once pulled the plough are kept, including Shire, Clydesdale, Ardennes, Percheron and Suffolk Punch. It also has the only Canadian-Belgian heavy horses in Europe. Turn right instead of left, at the B3081, to Verwood, where a minor road, left, leads to the Centre.

Fishing on the river in Christchurch is a popular pastime. The ruins of the 11th-century Priory make a picturesque backdrop

OFF THE BEATEN TRACK

Peterson's Tower is a striking, early concrete construction 218ft tall. It stands half a mile south of the road between New Milton and Sway. It is definitely a folly, and some say that its builder wanted to be buried beneath it, but his wishes were not granted.

OUTDOOR ACTIVITIES

The New Forest is a walker's paradise, criss-crossed with paths. There are waymarked trails, with explanatory leaflets, starting from the following car parks: Bolderwood, Brock Hill, Blackwater, Puttles Bridge (the Ober Water Walk), Whitefield Moor, Knightwood Oak and Wilverley, which is a short walk suitable for the disabled. The valley bottoms of the forest are boggy and it is unwise to stray off the marked paths.

ROUTE DIRECTIONS

Leave **Christchurch** (map 3SZ19) on the A35 (sp. Lyndhurst, Southampton) and in 2 miles, at the roundabout, take 1st exit for Hinton. In 3 miles turn right on to the B3058 (sp. Wooton, New Milton) and pass Brown Hills Car Park and Picnic Site. Enter Wooton and turn left, then left again, unclassified (sp. Brockenhurst). Pass Broadley Picnic Site and Wooton Bridge Car Park and Picnic Site then, in ¼ mile at the T-junction, turn right (sp. Brockenhurst). Pass Hincheslea Viewpoint and at the edge of **Brockenhurst** continue forward (sp. Rhinefield). Continue to enter Rhinefield Ornamental Drive and in 1¼ miles further cross the main road and enter Bolderwood Ornamental Drive. Pass Knightwood then Bolderwood Car Parks and Picnic Sites and in ¼ mile, at the T-junction, turn left (sp. Linwood, Stoney Cross). In 2 miles turn right (sp. Stoney Cross, Fritham) and in 2½ miles, at the T-junction, turn right (sp. Stoney Cross, Cadnam). Pass Stoney Cross Plain Car Park and, in 1 mile, turn left on to the A31 (sp. Southampton). In 1 mile turn left, unclassified (sp. Rufus Stone) to pass the **Rufus Stone**. Continue to Brook then take a sharp left on to the B3078, Fordingbridge road, to **Fordingbridge.** Turn left into High Street, B3078 (sp. Damerham) then bear right to Sandleheath. Turn left, unclassified (sp. Alderholt) to Alderholt Mill and the edge of Alderholt. At the T-junction turn right then immediate left (sp. Ringwood, Ibsley). In 5¼ miles join the B3081 (sp. Ringwood) and in ¾ mile further turn left and join the A31. In ½ mile branch left (sp. Ringwood) then, at the roundabout, take 3rd exit B3347 to enter **Ringwood**. At the roundabout take 2nd exit (sp. Sopley) then at the next roundabout turn left to leave by Christchurch Road (one-way). In 2½ miles, at the roundabout, take 3rd exit A35 and return to Christchurch.

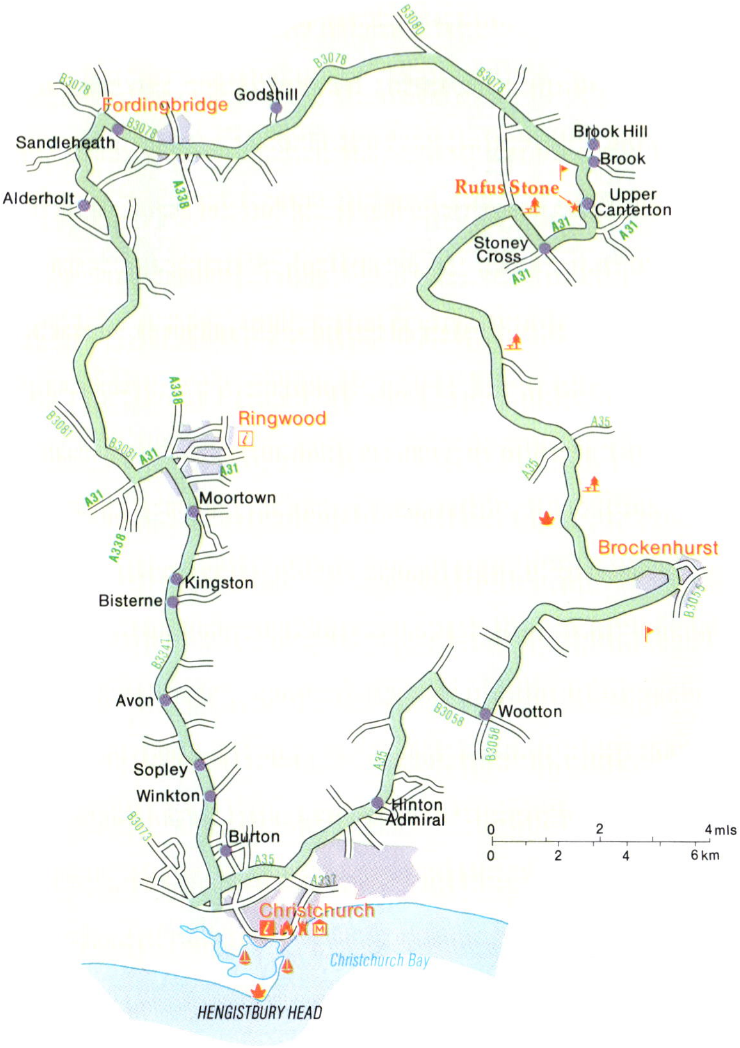

A TICKET TO THE ISLE OF WIGHT

72 miles

The place that claims to have more sunshine than anywhere else in England! An island which in parts is quite unspoilt, a place

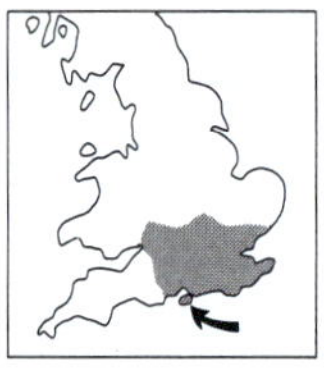

of lofty downs with pretty thatched villages, set between the Solent and the English Channel.

The Isle of Wight can be reached from Portsmouth, Southampton or Lymington. To the north it is a place of busy harbours, yachts and gently sloping beaches. The south is generally quieter, with tall cliffs and steep chines. The capital of the island is Newport, defended by nearby Carisbrooke Castle, the seat of the Governor of the Isle of Wight. His main job used to be to defend the island, which has always been vulnerable to capture by the French. This is why so many forts were built around the coast. The island now depends on tourism, with all that that entails. Yet, it is still a place of peace, with medieval churches and fine manor houses.

Whether you want quiet empty beaches, seaside fun, vineyards, soaring cliffs or pretty walks – the island can supply it. At the height of the season its roads can be very busy.

Cowes Week traditionally starts with a bang from the Royal Yacht Squadron cannons at West Cowes

ON THE TOUR

Newport

This is the capital of the Isle of Wight and its busiest town. A memorial to Princess Elizabeth, the second daughter of Charles I, can be found in the church. She died whilst in captivity in Carisbrooke Castle. The monument was commissioned by Queen Victoria. The town hall is by John Nash, who had a country retreat at nearby East Cowes Castle. A fine 3rd-century Roman villa in the town has brightly painted, reconstructed rooms.

Cowes

Famous for Cowes Week, held in August, when thousands of yachtsmen – and landlubbers – flock to the town. The focal point is the Royal Yacht Squadron in West Cowes Castle, an exclusive gentlemen's club founded in 1815.

Alum Bay and the Needles

The multicoloured sands of Alum Bay helped put the island on the tourist map. The beach is reached via a continuous chairlift. From the cliffs are dramatic views of the Needles, the famous chalk stacks.

Freshwater

Beloved by Tennyson, who lived at Farringford (now a hotel). On the north side of Freshwater is Golden Hill Fort, a Victorian fortress with a pleasant sheltered courtyard and a variety of entertainments. The nearby Needles Pleasure Park is a must for children.

The Undercliff and Ventnor

This part of the island was developed after 1829, when the physician Sir James Clarke recommended the area for those suffering from lung disease. The Undercliff is part of a complicated series of landslips in the Gault clay between St Catherine's Point and Ventnor. The lighthouse at the point is open at limited hours, subject to the fog signal not sounding. The Old Park at nearby St Lawrence houses a fascinating tropical bird garden and glass-making display, and there is a smuggling museum in the Ventnor Botanic Gardens.

Shanklin and Sandown

There is almost a continuous strip of seaside development here, with a cliff lift at Shanklin. The old village sits at the head of the chine. Keats came here for his health and stayed at what is now 76 High Street. Sandown is a mecca of seaside fun, with a zoo and a dinosaur 'museum'. It also has a Geology Museum, run by the county council and well worth visiting to learn about the interesting fossils and rocks of the Island.

Ryde

A large town that was once a small fishing village, Ryde is famous for its entertainments, its sandy beaches and its half-mile-long pier built in 1824, which made it possible to land from large vessels.

Whippingham and East Cowes

Here is a riot of genuine Victoriana, including Osborne House, the mansion built by Queen Victoria and Prince Albert in 1845-51. In the garden is a Swiss cottage used by the children as a playhouse and also the Queen's bathing machine. Nearby is Whippingham church, where the royal party worshipped, crammed with royal relics. Barton Manor Gardens were laid out by Queen Victoria and Prince Albert. They are a delight to visit and now contain a vineyard.

OFF THE TOUR

Carisbrooke Castle

This story-book castle west of Newport is approached across a moat with a great gatehouse and a keep. It was to Carisbrooke that Charles I withdrew at the end of the Civil War. The Governor of the Isle of Wight at first treated him with respect, but later became his gaoler. Despite help from Parliamentary traitors, Charles I failed to escape and on 30 November 1649 left the island for London and execution. The gatehouse contains a fascinating exhibition telling his story.

Godshill

The jewel of the island, this pretty village has an interesting church packed with memorials to the Worsleys, a prominent Isle of Wight family that lived at Appuldurcombe House (see Off The Beaten Track) It can be extremely busy. The model village at Godshill contains a miniature model village, and within that there is an even smaller miniature village! It is reached from Ventnor by turning north on the B3327 and turning left on the A3020.

ROUTE DIRECTIONS

Leave **Newport** (map 3SZ58) by the A3020 (sp. Cowes) and in 3/4 mile, at the roundabout, go forward. In a further 2 miles, at Northwood, branch left on to the B3325 then in 1/2 mile bear right to skirt **Cowes**. After another 3/4 mile, at the mini-roundabout, turn left, unclassified (no sign) and in 1/4 mile go over the crossroads and descend Church Road. Shortly, turn right into Lower Church Road and, at the next T-junction, turn left (sp.

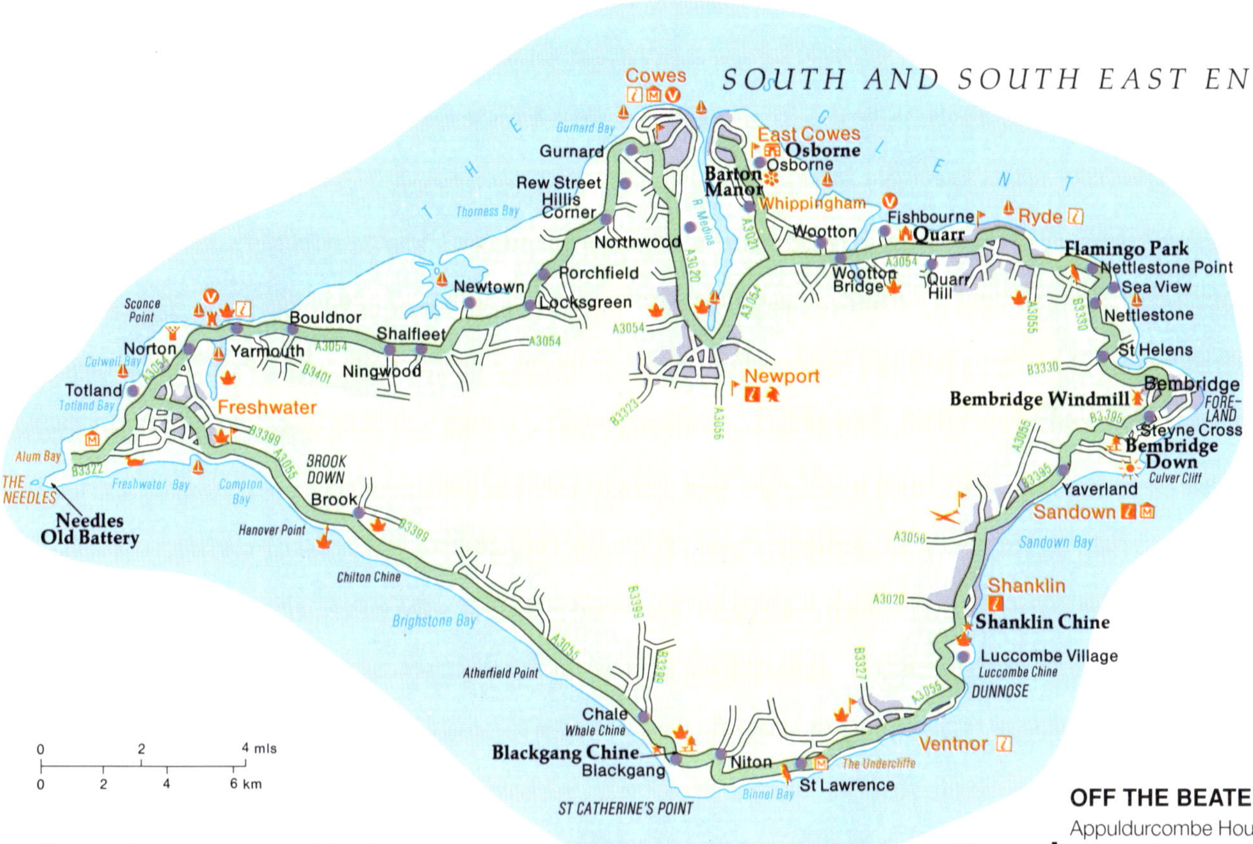

Yarmouth) to pass Gurnard Bay. In 1¼ miles turn right at the T-junction, bear right and in a further 1½ miles bear right again and continue to Porchfield. Continue and, in ½ mile, bear right, then in a further ½ mile turn right (sp. Newtown). Continue past the inlet of the Newton River and, at the T-junction turn right (sp. Yarmouth). In ¾ mile, at the next T-junction, turn right again on to the A3054 and enter Shalfleet. Follow signs to Freshwater and cross the Yar Bridge. Stay on the A3054 and continue through Colwell Bay. Shortly go forward on the B3322, Alum Bay road and enter Totland. At the roundabout keep forward and enter **Alum Bay**. Return along the same road and in ½ mile pass the Museum of Clocks, then branch right, unclassified (sp. Freshwater Bay). In a further ½ mile, at the High Down Inn, bear right then turn left and continue to **Freshwater** and Freshwater Bay. Here, bear right to join the A3055 (no sign) and skirt Compton Bay. Continue along the coast road (sp. Ventnor) to reach Chale. Half a mile beyond the village, at the roundabout, take 2nd exit for Blackgang. Return to the roundabout and turn right with the A3055 (sp. Ventnor). Then, pass beneath St Catherine's Hill and continue to Niton. Here, keep left (one-way) then turn right. Continue through St Lawrence, pass the **Undercliffe** and Ventnor Botanic Gardens and proceed to **Ventnor** town centre. Leave on the A3055 (sp. Shanklin) and descend to **Shanklin**. Follow the main road through the town to Lake. Here, pass the Stag Inn and in ¼ mile at the war memorial, bear right. Pass beneath the railway and in just over ½ mile turn right (sp. Town Centre) to enter **Sandown**. Leave by the sea-front B3395 (sp. Bembridge) and in 1¼ miles, at the T-junction, turn right. Continue along the B3395 and in 1¼ miles pass Bembridge Airport. Bear left and after a further mile, at the mini-roundabout, turn left, unclassified, and continue to Bembridge. Follow the Ryde signs B3395 to skirt Bembridge Harbour, and at St Helens, at the T-junction, turn right on to the B3330 (sp. Nettlestone). In just over ¼ mile turn left (sp. Ryde) and continue to Nettlestone. Here, branch right on to the B3340 (sp. Seaview) and in almost ¼ mile further, branch right again, unclassified (sp. Sea Front). Continue to Seaview, descend the High Street, follow the Esplanade then keep forward into Bluett Avenue. At the T-junction turn right then keep left along the shoreline. Continue on the coast road, veer inland and in ½ mile further turn right on to the B3330. Shortly, turn right again, with the A3055 then join the Esplanade to enter **Ryde**. Leave on the A3054 (sp. Newport) and after 1½ miles pass through Binstead. Continue to Wootten Bridge and in 1½ miles, at the roundabout, turn right on to the A3021 (sp. East Cowes). In a further mile turn left unclassified (sp. Whippingham Church) then in ½ mile pass the church at **Whippingham**. Continue to the T-junction and turn left into Victoria Grove. Join Adelaide Grove and at the end turn right, on to the A3021 into **East Cowes**. Leave by the A3021 (sp. Newport, A3054). Continue on the A3021 and in ½ mile pass the road to Barton Manor Vineyard and Gardens on the left. In 1½ miles, at the roundabout, take 2nd exit A3054 and return to Newport.

Artists are often inspired by the spectacular scenery of Freshwater Bay, with Stag Rock and Tennyson Bay beyond

OFF THE BEATEN TRACK

Appuldurcombe House, once the home of the prominent Isle of Wight family of Worsley, is now a majestic ruin. It stands at Wroxall, north of Ventnor, in fields to the west of the B3327 road. The Palladian-style house is reached via a short footpath and is managed by English Heritage. It has a link with Quarr Abbey, which is seen from the car ferry at Fishbourne. Exiled from their native France in 1901, the monks of Solesmes came first to live at Appuldurcombe House.

OUTDOOR ACTIVITIES

There is a network of footpaths on the island, including several long-distance walks, such as the Tennyson trail between Freshwater and Newport. The coast between Shanklin and Ventnor and the Needles cliffs are fine areas for walking.

THE SOLENT HINTERLAND

65 miles

The valleys and downland of Hampshire make a peaceful refuge from the bustle of its seaboard. Strings of pretty villages, with

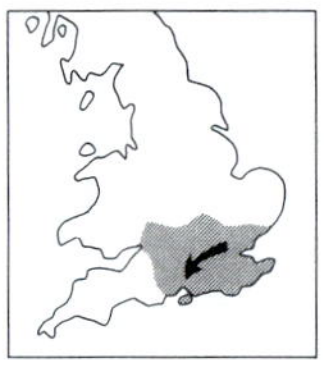

staddlestone granaries and thatched brick-and-flint cottages, stand on the banks of sparkling chalk streams.

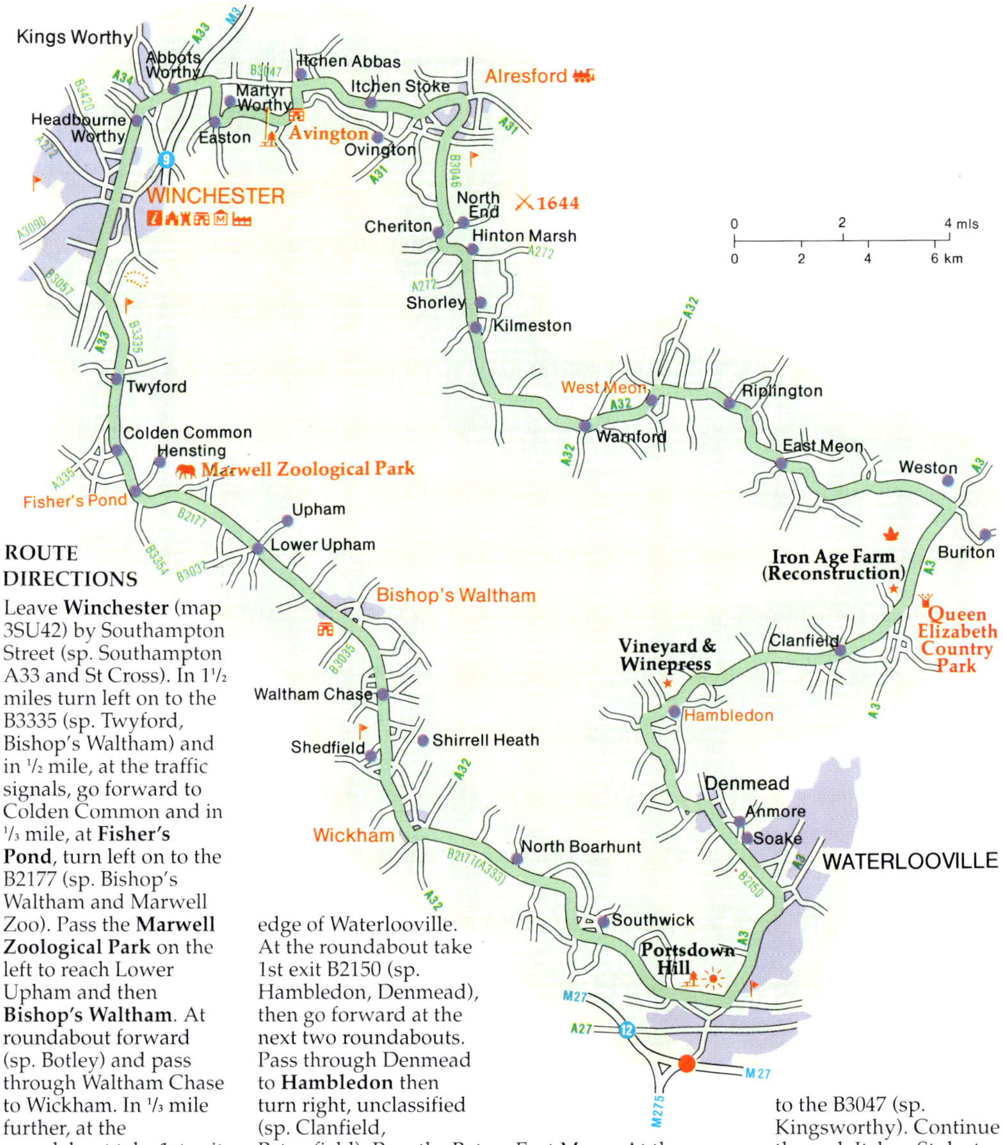

Hampshire's heartlands are its Downs, which once held the vast flocks of sheep that fed the coffers of Winchester cathedral. Although the Hampshire coast has been extensively developed (some call it 'Solent City'), its interior is quite unspoilt.

Starting at Winchester, the old Saxon capital of England, the tour strikes across the southern edge of Hampshire chalklands, through remnants of the Forest of Bere to the isolated ridge of Portsdown Hill. From here there is a dramatic bird's-eye view of the naval city of Portsmouth.

East Hampshire is an area of folded chalk downs, with ancient hollow-ways and patches of ancient yew, locally called 'the Hampshire weed'.

The tour picks up the River Meon near its source at East Meon and follows it to Warnford. Here it branches off towards Kilmeston and the source of the River Itchen, a world-famous trout stream, which it follows back to Winchester.

King Alfred's statue is a prominent landmark at the bottom of the busy High Street in Winchester, and a useful meeting place for tourists

ROUTE DIRECTIONS

Leave **Winchester** (map 3SU42) by Southampton Street (sp. Southampton A33 and St Cross). In 1½ miles turn left on to the B3335 (sp. Twyford, Bishop's Waltham) and in ½ mile, at the traffic signals, go forward to Colden Common and in ⅓ mile, at **Fisher's Pond**, turn left on to the B2177 (sp. Bishop's Waltham and Marwell Zoo). Pass the **Marwell Zoological Park** on the left to reach Lower Upham and then **Bishop's Waltham**. At roundabout forward (sp. Botley) and pass through Waltham Chase to Wickham. In ⅓ mile further, at the roundabout take 1st exit A32 (sp. Southwick), through **Wickham,** then in ⅓ mile turn right on to the B2177 (A333) (sp. Southwick). Pass the road to Southwick, and in ⅓ mile, at the roundabout take 2nd exit (sp. Portsmouth). In 1¾ miles at the roundabout take 1st exit (sp. London, Petersfield) and in ½ mile pass Fort Widley and Portsdown Hill viewpoint. In ⅓ mile turn left (sp. London) then left again to join the A3. In 1 mile further, at the roundabout, go forward (sp. Waterlooville) to the edge of Waterlooville. At the roundabout take 1st exit B2150 (sp. Hambledon, Denmead), then go forward at the next two roundabouts. Pass through Denmead to **Hambledon** then turn right, unclassified (sp. Clanfield, Petersfield). Pass the Bat and Ball Inn and in 1⅓ miles, at the T-junction, turn left into Clanfield. Follow the signs Petersfield and in ½ mile turn left into Petersfield Road (sp. Butser Hill). Pass the road to Butser Hill and Picnic Area and in ¼ mile turn left (sp. Petersfield and London). In ½ mile join the A3 and pass the **Queen Elizabeth Country Park**. In 1⅔ miles turn left, unclassified (sp. East Meon) and in 3⅓ miles, at the T-junction, turn right and continue to East Meon. At the George Inn bear right, then at the T-junction turn left (sp. West Meon) for **West Meon**. Turn left on to the A32 (sp. Fareham) to Warnford. Turn right, unclassified (sp. Winchester) and in 1¾ miles at the crossroads turn right (sp. Kilmeston, Alresford) to Kilmeston. In 1 mile further cross the main road to join the B3046 to Cheriton, then **Alresford**. Here, at the T-junction, turn left on to the A31 (sp. Winchester) and in 1 mile turn right on to the B3047 (sp. Kingsworthy). Continue through Itchen Stoke to Itchen Abbas and turn left, unclassified (sp. Avington). Pass the entrance to Avington House and enter **Avington**. At the end of the village turn right (sp. Easton, Winchester) and enter Avington Park. At Easton at the T-junction, turn right (no sign) and in ½ mile turn left on to the B3047 and continue to Kingsworthy. Here, turn left on to the A33, then immediately right on to the A3090 (sp. Winchester). Follow the signs Town Centre to re-enter Winchester.

ON THE TOUR

Winchester

The streets of this ancient city were laid out more than a thousand years ago by Alfred the Great, King of Wessex, who made it his capital. William the Conqueror respected its status and chose to be crowned here, as well as at Westminster. Here too, the Domesday Book was compiled in 1086. During the Middle Ages the bishops of Winchester were amongst the richest men in England. One of them, William of Wickham, gave some of his wealth to founding New College, Oxford, and the famous boys' public school, Winchester College.

The jewel of Winchester is its cathedral, a Norman church with a 15th-century 'facelift' which would have made it unrecognisable to its original builders. A new triforium gallery and the library display some of the medieval treasures of the cathedral, including the famous Winchester Bible; a masterpiece of monastic illumination. The novelist Jane Austen is buried here.

There is much more to see in Winchester, including St Cross Hospital, the city museum, several military museums and The Crusades Experience – an account of the holy wars.

Fisher's Pond

This is an attractive place to stop for a drink and a meal. The pond is the former fish pond of the Bishops of Winchester.

Marwell Zoological Park

A zoo with a difference; devoted to rare and endangered species, such as the Scimitar horned oryx and the Przewalski horse. It also has an impressive collection of other wild animals, including 'big cats' (Asian lion, Siberian tiger, snow leopard, etc.) and birds.

There is a 'farmyard' area for children and good family facilities.

Bishop's Waltham

The impressive ruins of one of the several palaces of the bishops of Winchester are here, together with an interesting interpretative exhibition.

On the opposite side of the B2177 is the town of Bishop's Waltham with places to eat and a small local museum (limited opening).

Wickham

Birthplace of William of Wickham, the famous prelate, who spent his last days at Bishop's Waltham Palace, Wickham is an extremely pleasant large village set around a square.

Hambledon

The cradle of cricket and the home of the famous village side that once beat an All-England team! The Bat and Ball pub alongside Broadhalfpenny Down, where matches were played, is a mile beyond the village. White wine from Hambledon has a national reputation. The vineyard was planted by Sir Guy Salisbury Jones in 1951; the very first of the new wave of English vineyards.

Queen Elizabeth Country Park

A pay-to-leave country park in a delightful downland setting with the novel sport of grass skiing, regular country displays and miles of footpaths. On the same site is a unique experiment in Iron Age farming, with recreated buildings used by Britons before the Roman occupation.

West Meon

The quiet churchyard hides two surprises. Below the church is the tabletop tomb of Thomas Lord, who retired to West Meon after founding the famous London cricket ground. Also, on the north side of the church, opposite the tower, stands a great cross that marks the Burgess family grave, where the ashes of the spy Guy Burgess are scattered. He was born in the village.

Alresford

The home of the Mid-Hants Railway, resurrected by enthusiasts and operating real steam loco's as far as Alton.

'New' Alresford was a borough 'planted' in the early 13th century by the bishop of Winchester. It prides itself on politeness and civic tidiness. The old town is a mile to the north. Here Mary Sumner, the wife of the rector, founded the Mothers' Union, as commemorated in the brick-built church.

Avington

An estate village with an interesting Georgian church with box pews, Avington stands beside the mansion where Charles II entertained Nell Gwynne when he was living in the cathedral close at Winchester, from which the dean had barred her. The house dates mainly from the 18th century. It has fine iron-framed orangeries and is open to the public at limited times.

Through the village is a charming small country park with a picnic site overlooking Avington lake.

'All aboard' the Mid Hants Railway

OFF THE BEATEN TRACK

Warnford Park

Warnford Park, with its church and ruined medieval hall, 'King John's House', is a place where the ambitions of past owners have come to naught. Traditionally founded by St Wilfrid, Archbishop of York in exile, in the late 7th century, and refounded in the 12th by a feudal lord, Adam de Port, it now stands isolated from its village. A public footpath leads to the ruined house and the church from the east side of the A32, just beyond the turning in the opposite direction to Winchester. It should be approached on foot, from the village. The church has fine 17th-century family memorials.

OUTDOOR ACTIVITIES

The Wayfarer's Walk, a long-distance footpath from Inkpen Beacon to Emsworth on the coast, crosses the tour's route two miles south of Kilmeston.

A particularly interesting walk to the deserted medieval village of Lomer, and beyond to Beacon Hill, starts on the Wayfarer's Walk (SU591239) and continues via a farm track, eventually leading to Exton, three miles away.

OFF THE TOUR

Titchfield Abbey

A turning to the south just before Wickham leads to the splendid remains of a Tudor mansion, where Shakespeare's patron, the third Earl of Southampton lived. Recent research has shown that the house had a 'Play House Room'; perhaps the Bard came here and had his plays performed.

Portchester Castle

A 3rd-century Roman fort of the 'Saxon shore', the finest in Northern Europe, with a medieval castle built within it by Henry II. It is reached by turning south off the B2177 near Southwick. The English crown mustered troops for Crécy and Agincourt at Portchester.

Portsmouth Naval Heritage Area

There is a great deal to see in this famous naval city, reached via the A3 and M275. A flying visit could take in one of the sights, such as Nelson's flagship HMS *Victory*, the Tudor *Mary Rose*, or the ironclad HMS *Warrior*.

Portchester Castle is a really splendid 3rd-century Roman fort, with fine sea views from the top

CHICHESTER AND WEST SUSSEX

58 miles

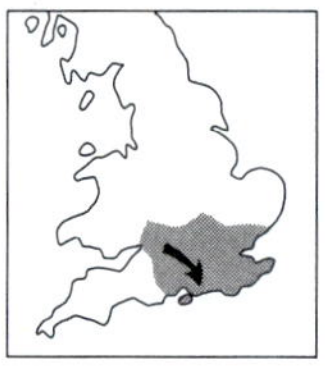

Luxurious English country life is a living advertisement for conservation here. Pretty malmstone villages blend into the dramatic landscape of the South Downs and, on the edge of Surrey, there is the grandeur of the Devil's Punchbowl.

From Chichester this tour climbs up over the South Downs and then crosses the valley of the river Rother to Petworth. It circles through the western tip of the Weald and returns to the downs via Midhurst.

The tour slices through a very wealthy part of Southern England; an area of stud farms, clay shoots, Range Rovers and gentlemen farmers. It extends from Chichester, one of the artiest cathedral towns in the country, to the sandy woodlands of Surrey. Malmstone is a fairly common building material in the south, while the Surrey part is almost all built in brick, often of a very fancy and attractive design.

This is the cradle of the 'civilized pub', where eating and drinking have generally become irresistibly pleasant experiences.

The landscape around Hindhead is so beautiful that it is not surprising to find that its preservation was one of the early successes of the conservation movement.

Chichester's 19th-century spire replaced one designed by Sir Christopher Wren

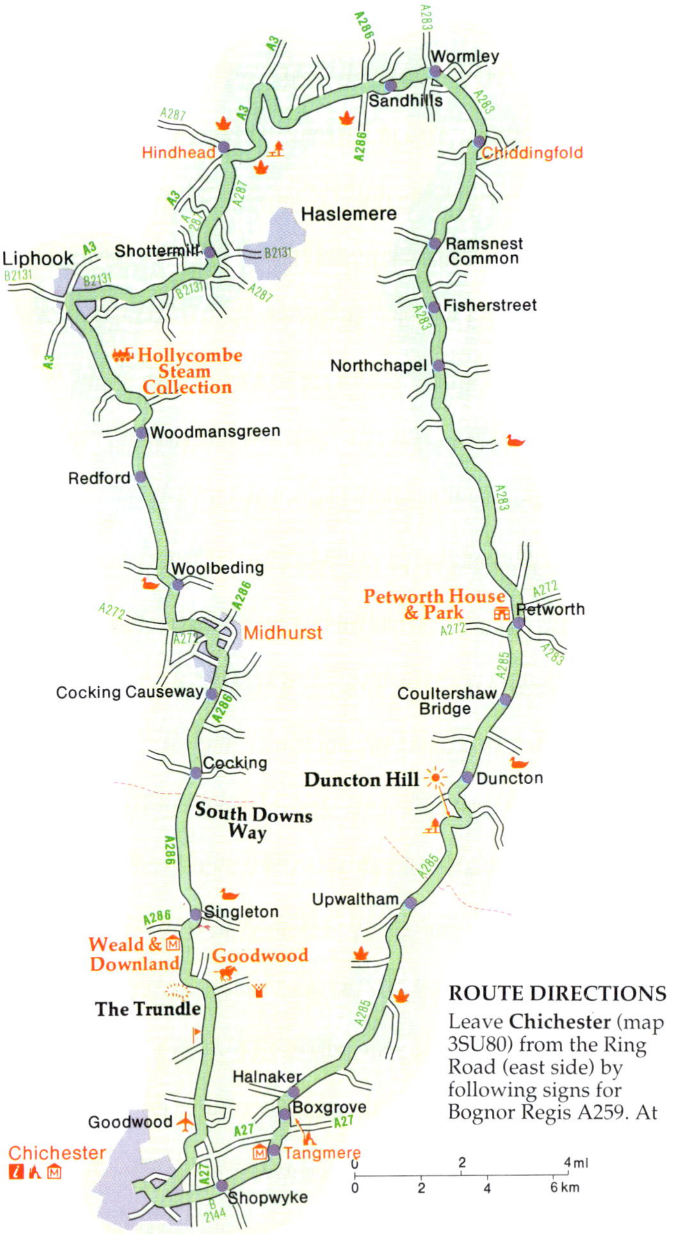

ROUTE DIRECTIONS

Leave **Chichester** (map 3SU80) from the Ring Road (east side) by following signs for Bognor Regis A259. At the Four Chestnuts keep forward (no sign) into Oving Road (B2144). In a further ½ mile, at the traffic signals, go forward (sp. Oving) over the Chichester By-Pass, then in ½ mile go forward, unclassified (sp. Tangmere). In 1¼ miles bear left to pass the airfield at **Tangmere** and the entrance to the Military Aviation Museum. At the end of the village turn right on to the A27 then take the first turning left, unclassified (sp. Boxgrove, Halnaker). Continue through Boxgrove to Halnaker and turn right on to the A285 Petworth, Guildford road. Ascend to reach the top of Duncton Hill and descend through Duncton. Cross the River Rother to enter **Petworth**, and leave by following the A283 Guildford road to enter Surrey. Continue to **Chiddingfold** and in a further 2¼ miles cross a railway bridge then turn immediate left, unclassified (sp. Sandhills, Brook). In ½ mile bear left and 1 mile further, at the edge of Brook, cross the main road (no sign). After 2½ miles turn sharp left on to the A3 (sp. Petersfield, Portsmouth). Ascend and pass Gibbet Hill on the left and Devil's Punchbowl on the right before entering **Hindhead**. At the traffic signals turn left on to the A287 (sp. Midhurst) and descend. After 2 miles, at Shottermill, turn right (sp. Midhurst) then at the traffic signals turn right again on to the B2131 Liphook road. In ¼ mile at the roundabout turn right, then 2 miles further on bear right to enter Hampshire and Liphook. At the town centre turn left, unclassified (sp. Hollycombe, Midhurst). In 1¼ miles re-enter West Sussex and pass the entrance to

OFF THE TOUR

Fishbourne

Two miles to the west of Chichester, at the head of its harbour, stands the Roman palace of Fishbourne. This is a site of major archaeological importance and a truly interesting relic of life almost 2,000 years ago. There are extraordinarily well-preserved Roman mosaics and a 'Roman' garden.

Lurgashall

This attractive village stands about 5 miles north of Petworth, to the west of the A283. Nearby, at Windfallwood Common is Lurgashall Winery, where country wines can be tasted. A speciality is 'Love Potion', the product of a secret recipe. The winery is reached by leaving the village with the Noah's Ark pub on the right and turning right at a T-junction after a mile. It is half a mile further on, on the left.

ON THE TOUR

Chichester

There are many who, with good reason, think that Chichester is the finest cathedral city in the country. Once the largest town in Sussex, it is proud of its past but at the same time looks forward. Its modern Festival Theatre, which stands on the northern outskirts, presents all-star performances of plays and musicals.
The cathedral is worth visiting for its historic architecture, but also to see the stained glass of Marc Chagall, the modern font by John Skelton, the painting by Graham Sutherland and the tapestry designed by John Piper. Its greatest treasures are the two 12th-century carvings in the south choir aisle.
Near the cathedral are a brass-rubbing centre, a splendid tea-room and the peace of St Richard's Walk and the Bishop's Palace Gardens. The streets to the south of East Street are also extremely pleasant and contain Pallant House, a superb Queen Anne town house and art gallery. On the outskirts of the city is the well-known Mechanical Music and Doll Collection in Church Road.

Tangmere

Beside a famous disused airfield is Tangmere Military Aviation Museum. Amongst its exhibits are an operative flight simulator and a diorama of working models, as well as photos, uniforms and other relics.

Petworth House and Park

The road winds round the ragstone walls of the Petworth Estate, owned by the National Trust. Petworth House was built in the 17th century by the Duke of Somerset. It houses paintings by Turner, Van Dyck, Gainsborough and Reynolds and is noted for the Great Room, with its fine carving.
The deer park was designed by Capability Brown and is entered separately from the house; from the A283, to the north of Petworth.

Chiddingfold

This extremely pretty village set around a green is a good place to watch cricket. The Crown Inn has been in business since at least 1285.
Glass-making was once an important local industry. The church has a lancet window made from fragments of ancient medieval glass made locally.

Hollycombe Steam Collection on the left. Continue with the Midhurst signs and in 1½ miles turn left (sp. Woolbeding, Midhurst). Descend to Woolbeding and bear right to pass the church. In ½ mile re-cross the River Rother and turn left on to the A272 for **Midhurst**. At the mini-roundabout turn right on to the A286 (sp. Chichester). Pass through Cocking and, on the far side of Singleton, turn left, unclassified, on to the Goodwood road.

Pass the entrance to the **Weald and Downland Open Air Museum** on the right. Ascend on to the Downs and pass beneath a hill called The Trundle (675ft). Keep forward and descend, passing the grounds of **Goodwood House** on the left then, 1 mile beyond the entrance to the house, turn right (sp. Chichester). In ½ mile, at the by-pass junction roundabout, take 3rd exit A285 to re-enter Chichester.

John Piper's modern altar screen tapestry brings colour to Chichester Cathedral's otherwise sober interior

Hindhead

Hindhead Common and the Devil's Punchbowl are part of the 1,000 acres of common owned since 1906 by the National Trust and dominated by the viewpoint of Gibbet Hill (895ft).

Hollycombe Steam Collection

A collection of steam-driven equipment, including a 2ft-gauge railway in a woodland setting. Also, Hollycombe tramway, bioscope show, fairground organ and steam roundabout. There are demonstrations of threshing and steam rolling, traction engine rides and much more. A festival of steam is held here on Spring Bank Holiday. There are pleasant woodland walks and gardens.

Midhurst

The yellow-painted houses hereabouts belong to the Cowdray Estate, today known for its polo matches. The ruins of the fortified Tudor mansion, Cowdray Castle, and its museum stand half a mile from the town.

Weald and Downland Open Air Museum

World famous for its collection of rescued buildings from the south-east of England, this is the place to learn how to 'read' old buildings and discover what went on inside. It is also a country park, with picnic sites and walks, and occasional displays of country crafts, such as smithing, horse-ploughing and charcoal burning.

Goodwood

The name 'Goodwood' dominates the downs to the north of Chichester. There is the famous racecourse, the ducal mansion and a private aerodrome and race circuit. Goodwood House has limited opening hours but its parkland is generally open.

OFF THE BEATEN TRACK

The Trundle

Just off the tour, a mile out of Singleton, a minor road leads up to St Roche's Hill and The Trundle, a prehistoric hillfort. A fine picnic spot, with views of Chichester and the coast.

Witley

Half a mile to the south of Witley Station is the factory of Cooper and Sons Ltd, makers of fine walking sticks – visitors welcome to buy. Copses of ash and sweet chestnut are specially grown hereabouts for an industry with (so to speak) deep roots in this corner of Surrey.

OUTDOOR ACTIVITIES

There is a fine 6-mile (or less) walk along the towpath of the Chichester Canal – from the basin in the north (just south of the city railway station) to Birdham in the south. The South Downs Way provides opportunities for way-marked walks of any required length. It crosses the route of the tour 5 miles south of Petworth at Duncton Down, a fine viewpoint.
The Sussex Border Path is a newly created, long-distance footpath that follows the county boundary and crosses the route 3 miles south of Chiddingfold. The commons of Hindhead make fine walking country too.

BRIGHTON AND THE SUSSEX 'LAKE DISTRICT'

67 miles

Sussex is a feast for serious gardeners and lovers of fine landscape, with the unexpected sight of extensive freshwater lakes and the delights of 'London-by-the-sea', as Brighton is sometimes called, thrown in for good measure.

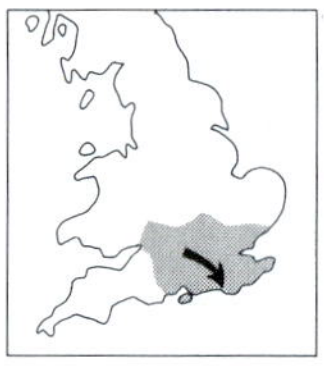

This tour stretches from the Channel coast to the Wealden forests, where ironmakers once worked. They needed water to power their forges, which is why freshwater ponds are still abundant in this part of Sussex. Ironstone, too, is often seen, particularly in the great Perpendicular towers of the churches and in the older houses. The man-made reservoirs at Ardingly and near Forest Row are a pleasant addition to a fine landscape and have abundant wildlife and opportunities for watersports.

There are lofty viewpoints on the South Downs at Devil's Dyke and Ditchling Beacon, where the road falls dramatically – almost down a cliff – to the village below. The downs are also especially steep to the north and east of Brighton. The seaside resort itself is an anomaly in Sussex, albeit one that has spawned the largest population in either East or West Sussex. However, it and its suburbs have surprisingly little impact on their surroundings.

Brighton's now-derelict West Pier was once deservedly popular with those seeking the more down-to-earth amusements found at the seaside

ON THE TOUR

Brighton

Until 1939 the local water company supplied some houses in Brighton with both fresh and salt water. Belief in the restorative properties of sea water was the basis of the hype that created the resort. The chief barker was a physician, Dr Richard Russell, who had settled in the fishing village of 'Brighthelmstone' in 1754. The future of Brighton was sealed a generation later when the Prince of Wales, later George IV, built the Royal Pavilion, an exotic folly with onion-shaped domes and minarets typical of India and a Chinese-style interior. The Regency architecture for which the town is famous can be found in such places as Brunswick Terrace and Brunswick Square (to the west of the derelict West Pier) and in Royal Crescent and Lewes Crescent to the east. This part of Brighton is called Kemp Town. Today the town's waterfront is rather faded, but on sunny days the prom, the Palace Pier and the beach are crowded. Brighton is also famous for The Lanes, a grid of tiny streets with numerous speciality shops and restaurants to the south of the Royal Pavilion. On the north side of the Pavilion is the museum and art gallery.

Ditchling

The beacon above Ditchling is a famous view-point that looks north towards the borders of Sussex. It is on the South Downs Way and has a small flint-strewn car park. The road down to the village of Ditchling, once travelled by stagecoaches, is truly hair-raising! The village used to be favoured by famous artists and craftsmen, a period marked by the founding of the Ditchling Press in 1916. It has its own small museum.

Legh Manor

There are some great architectural features in 16th-century Legh Manor, although access to the house is limited. The lovely gardens were laid out by Gertrude Jekyll.

Cuckfield

A lovely village with a fine church and views of the Jack and Jill windmills to the south, near Clayton. The roof of the nave was painted by the well-known Victorian stained glass artist C E Kempe. Cuckfield Museum is on the way out of the village, in the fine Queen's Hall.

Borde Hill Garden

Gardens and parkland well known for their rhododendrons and camellias, with a lake, rare trees and shrubs and woodland walks. Many of the species were collected in the 1920s when plant hunting came back into favour.

Wakehurst Place

A superb National Trust collection of exotic trees, extensive water gardens and the Loder Valley Nature Reserve managed by the Royal Botanic Gardens, Kew; a must for gardeners.

Standen House

A large Victorian house designed by Philip Webb, with William Morris furnishings. Owned by the National Trust, with a fine hillside garden and breathtaking views of the Medway Valley. See also page 76.

East Grinstead

See the tour on page 76.

Leonardslee Gardens

The Leonardslee Gardens are superb in the spring and famous for their camellias. There are also animals – Sika deer and wallabies – to be seen here.

ROUTE DIRECTIONS

Leave **Brighton** (map 4TQ30) by following signs Lewes A27. In $3\frac{1}{4}$ miles, at Moulsecoomb traffic signals, turn left, unclassified (sp. London, Crawley) and ascend past Coldean. After $1\frac{1}{4}$ miles turn right (sp. Ditchling), pass a picnic site on the right, and ascend to Ditchling Beacon on the left. Descend and, at the bottom, keep forward. In 1 mile turn right on to the B2112 (sp. Haywards Heath) into **Ditchling**. At the first crossroads turn left (no sign) into West Street (B2116) and pass Anne of Cleves House on the left. In $\frac{1}{2}$ mile enter West Sussex and pass through Keymer, Hassocks and Hurstpierpoint. There, at the mini-roundabout by the church, turn right, unclassified (sp. Ansty, Cuckfield). After $2\frac{1}{4}$ miles, at the Sportsman, keep ahead at the crossroads then in $1\frac{1}{2}$ miles pass the entrance to **Legh Manor** on the left. In a further $\frac{1}{2}$ mile turn left on to the B2036 (sp.

Cuckfield) and, at the mini-roundabout at Ansty, go forward (sp. Haywards Heath). Continue to **Cuckfield** and, at the mini-roundabout, go forward on to the B2036 (sp. Hawley) and ascend. In 1/2 mile at another mini-roundabout, turn right, unclassified, into Ardingly Road (sp. Cuckfield Hospital). Bear right past the hospital and in 1 mile, at the T-junction, turn left (sp. Balcombe). In 1/2 mile pass the entrance to **Borde Hill** on the left, then take the next right turning (sp. Ardingly). In 1 mile, at the T-junction, turn left and pass Ardingly College before entering Ardingly. Here, turn left on to the B2028 (sp. Lingfield). Pass the entrance to **Wakehurst Place** on the left, then in 1 3/4 miles turn sharp right, unclassified, on to the West Hoathly, Sharpthorne road. Pass through West Hoathly to Sharpthorne and after a further 1/2 mile turn left (sp. East Grinstead, Standen) and descend into the Medway Valley. Cross into West Sussex, ascend and then pass the entrance to **Standen House** on the right. Enter the outskirts of **East Grinstead** and, at the mini-roundabout, bear left. At the town centre turn left into West Street B2110 (sp. Turners Hill). Descend and continue to Turners Hill. Here, keep forward (sp. Handcross). Continue to the T-junction and turn left on to the B2036, then turn right on to the B2110 (sp. Handcross). After 4 miles turn left into Handcross then at the end turn right on to the A279 (sp. Horsham, Cowfold). Three miles further on at Lower Beeding, turn left (sp. Cowfold). In 3/4 mile turn left again on to the A281 and pass the entrance to **Leonardslee Gardens** on the left. At the mini-roundabout in Cowfold keep left (sp. Brighton and Haywards Heath, A272). In 2 miles at the crossroads turn right, unclassified (sp. Wineham). Pass through Wineham (not signed) and, at the end of the village cross the infant River Adur. In 1 mile at the T-junction turn left on to the B2116 Hurstpierpoint, Lewes road and in a further mile turn right, unclassified, on to the Poynings road. Pass through Shaves Wood and at the T-junction turn left on to the A281 Brighton road (no signs) and bear right. In 1 mile, at the roundabout, take 2nd exit, unclassified, on to the Devil's Dyke road, and ascend to the South Downs. After 1 mile turn right (sp. Devil's Dyke), climb past the Devil's Dyke on the right, pass the golf course and, at the T-junction, turn left (sp. Hove, Brighton). Continue over the downs and turn right before re-entering Brighton suburbs. Keep forward across the A2038 on the Dyke Road. Later, pass the Booth Museum of Natural History on the left and keep forward across the A27. At the next roundabout take 2nd exit (sp. The Station) to reach the town centre of Brighton by the Queens Road.

OUTDOOR ACTIVITIES

A swim from Brighton beach or a day at its races might satisfy some appetites for exercise! But real leg-stretching needs one of the superb downland walks in the area – perhaps a section of the South Downs Way, which crosses the route at the Devil's Dyke and Ditchling Beacon. The West Sussex Border Path also crosses the tour at the Devil's Dyke, which is a local beauty spot with fine views. Another fine path runs from East Grinstead to the famous Saxon church at Worth.

The view from Ditchling Beacon – at 813ft one of the highest points of the South Downs. A road climbs almost to the summit

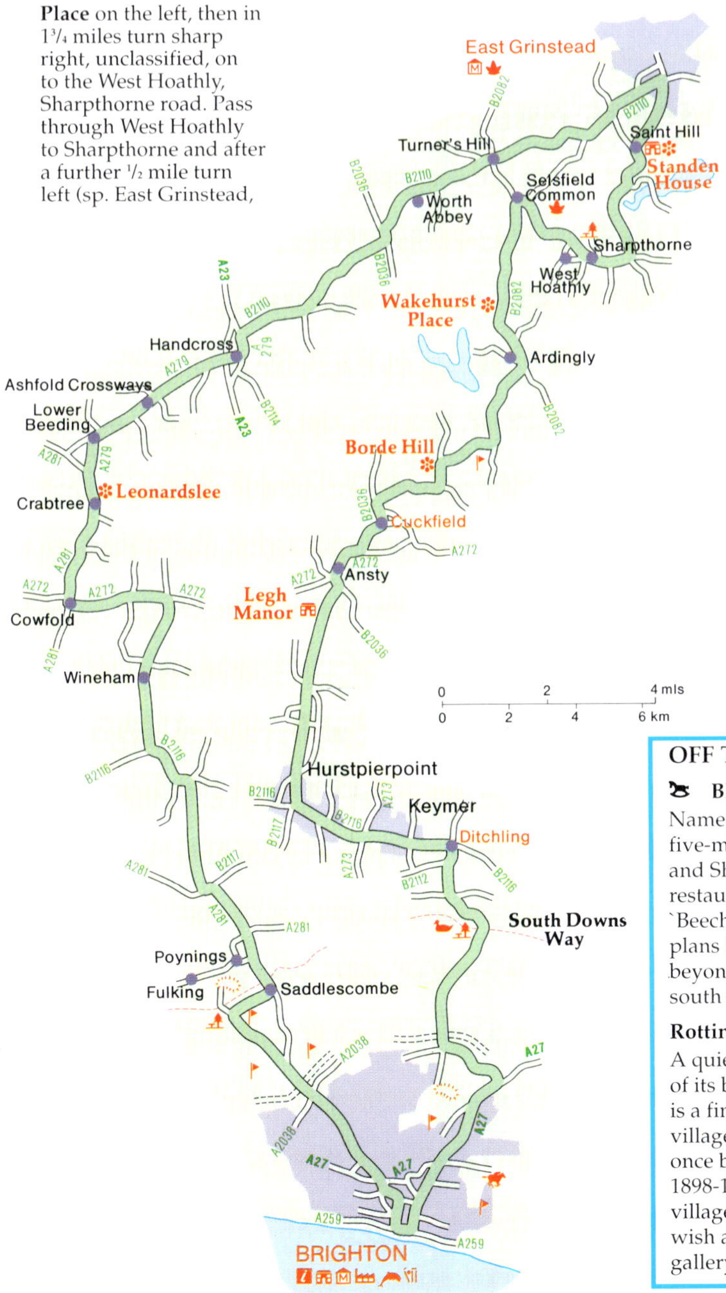

OFF THE TOUR

Bluebell Railway

Named after the flowers which grow alongside the track in the spring, this five-mile stretch of Puffing Billy nostalgia runs between Horsted Keynes and Sheffield Park (north of Lewes on the A275), where the main offices, restaurant and buffet can be found. The line was reopened in 1960 after the 'Beeching axe' had been blunted by a local resident, who discovered that plans to shut it down were illegal. A short stretch of line has been relaid beyond Horsted Keynes, which is reached by turning east off the B2028, just south of Ardingly.

Rottingdean

A quieter taste of the Sussex coast than Brighton, Rottingdean is 4 miles east of its big neighbour and is reached by keeping to the A259 coast road. There is a fine walk along the promenade beneath the undercliff. It still has its village green and pond. The Kipling Gardens, which are open to the public, once belonged to the famous writer and poet, who lived at 'The Elms' from 1898-1902. All wishes (except money) are granted at the Wishing Well in the village, where locals stroke their nose with their right forefinger, make a wish and then turn round thrice. Rottingdean has a small museum and art gallery and miniature golf and putting courses.

ACROSS THE SURREY-KENT BORDERS

61 miles

Sussex, Surrey and Kent, probably the three richest Home Counties, include a rural landscape that has not been overpowered by the nearness of London; this is an area peppered with fine houses, like Winston Churchill's Chartwell, and prosperous villages.

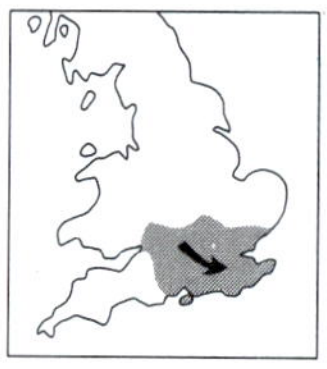

From the north-east corner of West Sussex, this tour passes through the borders of Kent into Surrey, crosses the M25 and gets within 'shouting distance' of London, before returning to the peace and tranquillity of rural Surrey and Sussex. It is a journey that encompasses the chalk of the North Downs and the underlying eroded strata of Greensand and Wealden clays. The River Eden-cum-Medway drains it to the east.

This has long been an area of comfortable living, not only because of the proximity of London but also because of the nearness of Northern Europe, an effect that is likely to increase when the Channel Tunnel is completed. Even the yeomen's houses hereabouts were particularly fine long before City stockbrokers sought them out. However, large estates in the hands of one person have been few, particularly in Kent, where flourished the custom of gavelkind (equal division of wealth between sons).

ON THE TOUR

Purley and Coulsdon

These two suburbs merge at the edge of the 'concrete jungle', only 11 miles from London. Farthing, or Fairdean, Down to the south was the site of an ancient ridgeway settlement on the slopes of the North Downs.

Bletchingley

The parish church, which lies just north of the A25, contains a hermit's cell and a hugely extravagant early 18th-century monument by Richard Crutcher, an artist otherwise unknown. It stands in the south chancel chapel and depicts the over-lifesize figure of Sir Robert Clayton, once lord mayor of London. He is shown wearing his robes and chain of office, whilst his wife wears a splendid gown and gold jewellery.

Outwood

This hamlet sits on a tiny cap of limestone. Its famous post-mill, which is surprisingly small, dates from 1665.

West Hoathly

This 'ironmakers village' is well-known for its Priest's House, administered by the Sussex Archaeological Society. It lies just off the through route.

Beautiful, moated Hever Castle was the girlhood home of the ill-fated Anne Boleyn. It was painstakingly restored earlier this century by the wealthy Astors

Standen House

Two miles south-west of East Grinstead stands this National Trust property and its 10-acre garden; fine examples of country comfort from the end of the last century. The furnishings of Morris and Co and the original details of the architect Philip Webb have been lovingly maintained. The rooms are beautifully light and airy. Especially memorable is the blue-green panelled dining room.

East Grinstead

A busy town on a small sandstone hill in the heart of the Weald. The key building of many in its historic centre is Sackville College, which is at the east end of the High Street and is open during summer afternoons. It was founded in 1609 as a charity for elderly people under the terms of the will of Robert Sackville, second Earl of Dorset. It is still used for sheltered housing. One of its wardens was John Mason Neale (1818-66), the hymn-writer, whose High Church ideas once drew the mob outside Sackville College.

Cowden

A major centre of Wealden ironmaking in the 17th century. Many local memorials were cast in iron, the same moulds often being used for firebacks. There is a memorial slab of 1622 in the church and two later ones in the churchyard, to the north of the chancel.

Edenbridge

An important crossing point on the Roman road between London and Lewes, built in the 1st century AD to get iron and corn out of Sussex. Honours Mill in Edenbridge and Haxted Mill to the west are notable survivals, both now attractive restaurants.

Watermill Museum

A late 16th-century mill on 14th-century foundations; weather-boarded, with a mansard roof and adjoining the mill house on Eden Water. The museum contains mill machinery, two working waterwheels and a picture gallery.

Limpsfield

This Surrey village contains the grand house called Detillens, ostensibly of the 18th century, but at its core a 15th-century hall-house with a massive king-post roof. The English composer Frederick Delius (1862-1934) is buried in Limpsfield churchyard.

OFF THE TOUR

Hever Castle

The splendours of Hever Castle and its gardens are largely due to the American millionaire William Waldorf Astor, who bought the estate in 1903. He created the 40-acre lake, the loggia and the sculpture-crammed Italian garden. Hever Castle is off the B2026 west of Edenbridge.

Chiddingstone Castle

Two miles east of Hever Castle stands Chiddingstone Castle; a Gothic house on the outskirts of a pretty hamlet of that name, noted for its fine 16th- and 17th-century Kentish cottages. A short footpath south-east of the church leads to an ancient 'chiding stone', from which the place takes its name.

Chartwell

The property bought by Churchill in 1922 and lived in by him for more than 40 years. Owned since 1945 by the National Trust, the house still contains the great statesman's studio, the drawing room where he played bézique and his library. Above all there is his study, where he pondered his political fate and wrote or dictated his books. From Limpsfield take the A25 east and turn right on the B2026 at Westerham.

ROUTE DIRECTIONS

Leave **Purley** (map 4TQ36) on the A23 (sp. Redhill) to reach **Coulsdon**. In a further 1/4 mile branch left (sp. Caterham B2030) and pass under two railway bridges. Shortly branch right, unclassi-fied into Downs Road. Ascend and in 2 2/3 miles cross the main road into Hill Top Lane. In 1/2 mile descend and in a further mile, at the T-junction, turn left (sp. Bletchingly). In 1 3/4 miles, at the T-junction, turn left on to the A25 (not shown) and con-tinue to **Bletchingley**. Here, at the Prince Albert turn right, unclassified, to **Outwood**. Continue forward to Smallfield and in a further 1 1/3 miles, at the traffic signals, turn left on to the B2037 (sp. East Grinstead). In a further mile turn right on to the B2028 (sp. Haywards Heath). In 1/2 mile, at the roundabout, take 2nd exit to Crawley Down. Continue to Turners Hill, go forward, and in 1 mile branch left, unclassified (sp. West Hoathly). In 1 1/2 miles turn right (sp. Priest's House) and continue to **West Hoathly**. At the church turn left and in 1/3 mile, at the T-junction turn right to enter Sharpthorne. In a further 2/3 mile, turn left (sp. East Grinstead) and continue past **Standen House**, on the right. In a further mile, at the mini-roundabout, branch left into Ship Street then after 1/3 mile, at the T-junction, turn right to **East Grinstead**. Here, at the mini-roundabout, turn right and in 1/3 mile, at the roundabout, take 2nd exit A22 (sp. Eastbourne). In 1 1/4 miles branch left, unclassified, for Ashurstwood. Here, turn left into Woodhall Lane and in 1/2 mile, at the Maypole, turn left. In a further 1 3/4 miles at the T-junction turn right, on to the A264 (sp. Cowden). Pass the road to Hammerwood Park on the right, pass Hammerwood church and in 1 mile branch left, unclassified (sp. Cowden) to **Cowden**. Continue for a further 1/2 mile and cross the main road (sp. Penshurst). One mile further on turn left to Markbeech. Here, go over the crossroads (sp. Hever Castle), pass the road to Hever Castle on the right and continue forward (sp. Edenbridge). In 2 miles, at the T-junction, turn right on to the B2026 (not shown, sp. Wester-ham). Continue to **Edenbridge**, then in 1/4 mile, turn left, un-classified (sp. Haxted), then in a further 1/4 mile, at the T-junction turn left. In 1/4 mile turn right then immediate right again for the **Watermill Museum**. In 1 1/2 miles turn right into Bowerland Lane (sp. Crowhurst) and, after a further 2/3 mile, at the T-junction turn right. In 1/2 mile turn right into Pikes Lane (sp. Oxted, Limpsfield). Pass the Royal Oak and in 2 3/4 miles at the traffic signals, go forward on to the B269 to **Limpsfield**. In 1/10 mile bear right (sp. Titsey), pass Titsey church, and ascend. At the top turn left, unclassified (sp. Woldingham) and in 1 3/4 miles bear right. In a further mile, bear left past Woldingham church and Woldingham Station, then bear right (sp. Caterham). In 1/2 mile bear left then in a further 2/3 mile, at the roundabout, take 4th exit A22 (sp. London). Pass the Wyteleafe Tavern and Kenley, before re-entering Purley.

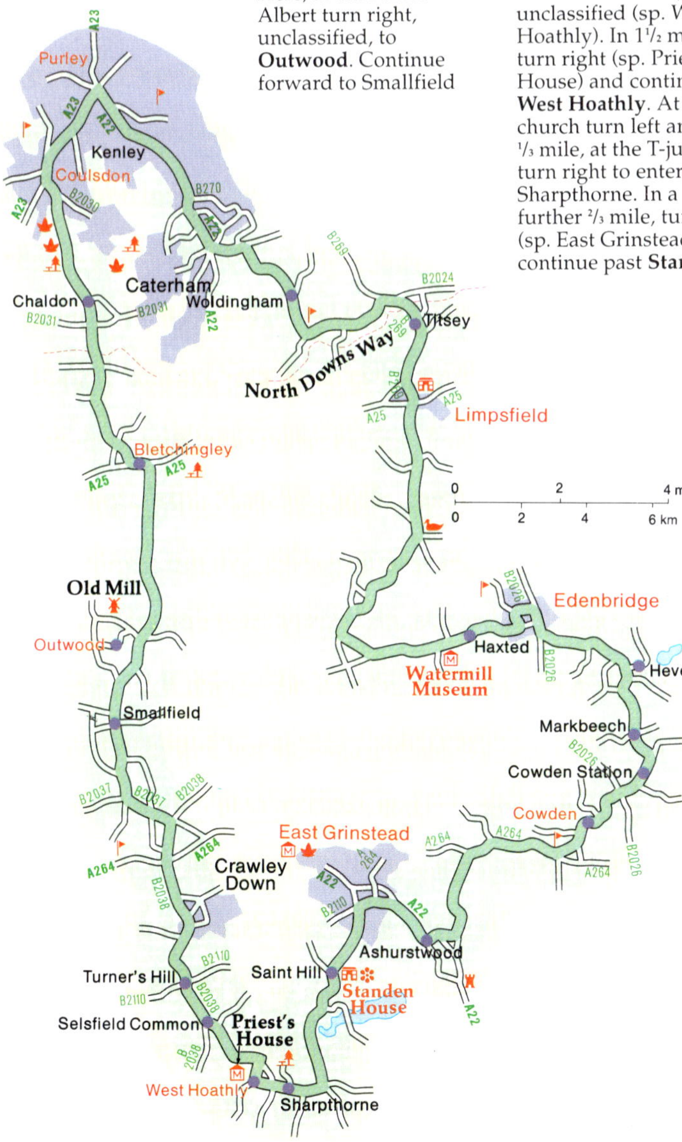

The weatherboarded watermill at Haxted is a museum and gallery

OFF THE BEATEN TRACK

Fen Place Mill is a rare relic of rural Sussex, three miles south-west of East Grinstead (not open to the public). It can be viewed most easily from footpaths reached from the B2110. The timber-framed miller's house and the weather-boarded mill make a composition that is worthy of a Constable. Nearby is the mill pond, which spreads out in three segments along the spine of the small brook which feeds it.

OUTDOOR ACTIVITIES

This is an area rich in footpaths, several of which are waymarked over a long distance. The Sussex Border Path passes through East Grinstead, from the north-east to the south-west, where it passes 1/2 mile north of Fen Place Mill (see above). Worth Way runs from the west side of East Grinstead, along a former railway track, to Worth Abbey. The North Downs Way runs east-west, partly overlapping the so-called Pilgrims' Way. It crosses the Vanguard Way (East Croydon to Seaford) just north of the M25 near Limpsfield. The tour crosses both of these long-distance paths in the vicinity of Titsey.

Weir Wood Reservoir

This large artificial lake was created in 1950-55 by damming the River Medway near Forest Row. The narrow west end has a small car park which can be reached from the tour (TQ383342). There is a footpath along the north shore, accessible from the road (TQ385352) and from Standen. At the east end of the lake is a sailing club and a small car park, reached by turning right off the A22 at East Grinstead church.

MAIDSTONE AND THE WEALD OF KENT

68 miles

A tour through the Garden of England, with its unique mix of hop fields, orchards and vineyards. The area is studded with oast-houses, charming villages and fine houses; white weather-boarded cottages, great timbered Wealden hall-houses and pleasure gardens aplenty.

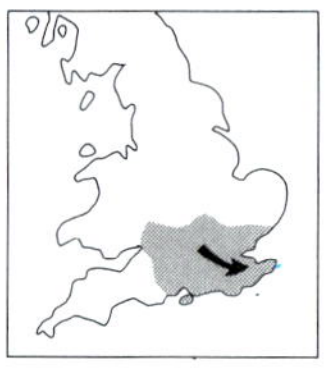

This tour starts at the county town of Kent, travels up the valley of the Medway, then takes a route to the High Weald at Goudhurst. It returns via a string of pretty villages and the `fairy-tale' castle at Leeds. This is a part of Kent where orchards, hop fields and market gardens are constant companions. It is, by general agreement, a very civilised part of England; the land of H E Bates, and one that has always been under the twin spells of London and the Continent. Also, a place of Wealden hall-houses and tile-hung or weatherboarded cottages (thatch is rare), built in local ragstone or sandstone. Hops and cricket are two of its passions.

The people of Kent have always been strongly independent. It was from here that Wat Tyler (egged on by `mad' John Ball from his prison in Maidstone) led the Peasants' Revolt of 1381, whilst Jack Cade did the same nearly 70 years later.

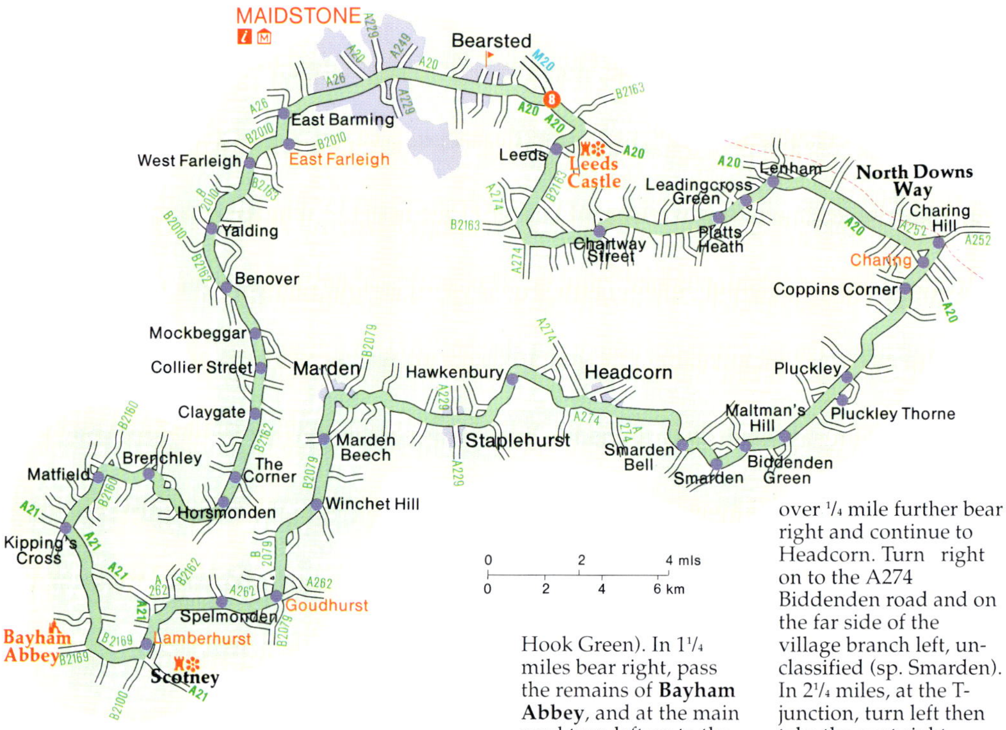

Henry VIII's first wife, Catherine of Aragon, lived at beautiful Leeds Castle. It was a royal palace for 300 years

ROUTE DIRECTIONS

Leave **Maidstone** (map 5TQ75) on the A26 Tonbridge road, and in $1\frac{3}{4}$ miles, at the Fountain, turn left, unclassified (sp. East Farleigh Station) into Farleigh Lane. Go over the railway and cross the River Medway to enter **East Farleigh**. At the church turn right into Lower Road (B2010) then continue on to Yalding. Cross the River Beult and turn left on to the B2162 Horsmonden road. Continue through Collier Street to reach Horsmonden. Here, at the crossroads, turn right, unclassified, to Brenchley. Continue for $1\frac{1}{4}$ miles then, at the Standing Cross, turn left on to the B2160 to pass through Matfield. Climb to reach the junction with the A21. Here, at the roundabout, turn left on to the Hastings road and in 1 mile turn right, unclassified (sp. Hook Green). In $1\frac{1}{4}$ miles bear right, pass the remains of **Bayham Abbey**, and at the main road turn left on to the B2169 (sp. Lamberhurst). In $1\frac{1}{4}$ miles turn left again on to the B2100 and descend into **Lamberhurst**. Leave by the A21 Sevenoaks road and at the end of the village turn right on to the B2162 (sp. Goudhurst A262). In a further $\frac{1}{2}$ mile turn right on to the A262 and after $1\frac{3}{4}$ miles pass Finchcocks. Continue to **Goudhurst** and at the Vine Hotel turn left on to the B2079 Marden road (no sign). In $1\frac{1}{4}$ miles bear right and pass the orchards to reach Marden. At the Unicorn continue forward, unclassified, on the Staplehurst road, and in 1 mile, at the T-junction, turn right then take the next turning left. Nearly 2 miles further, go over the crossroads on to the Headcorn road. In 1 mile cross the River Beult and in another mile turn right. Just over $\frac{1}{4}$ mile further bear right and continue to Headcorn. Turn right on to the A274 Biddenden road and on the far side of the village branch left, unclassified (sp. Smarden). In $2\frac{1}{4}$ miles, at the T-junction, turn left then take the next right turning for Smarden. Leave on the Charing road and climb to Pluckley. In 3 miles cross the A20 and enter **Charing**. Continue through the village then turn left on to the A252 (sp. Maidstone). At the roundabout turn right on to the A20 then, 3 miles further, turn left, unclassified, to enter Lenham. At the village crossroads turn left on to the Platts' Heath road. After $2\frac{1}{4}$ miles, at Platts' Heath, turn right by the Swan (sp. East Sutton). Continue (sp. Sutton Valance and Langley) for $4\frac{1}{2}$ miles to reach the junction with the A274. Turn right on to the Maidstone road and, half a mile further, turn right again on to the B2163 (sp. Leeds). Continue to Leeds village, pass **Leeds Castle**, and at the junction with the A20, turn left, then in $\frac{1}{2}$ mile branch left for the return to Maidstone.

OFF THE TOUR

Bedgebury National Pinetum
This is the Forestry Commission's collection of specimen conifers, set in 150 acres 3 miles south of Goudhurst off the B2079. A small lake, forest streams and a visitor centre are all here, and it is a fine place for a picnic.

Sissinghurst Castle Garden
These are the gardens created by the writer Victoria Sackville-West and her husband Sir Harold Nicholson. She once described it as 'a series of "outdoor rooms" connected by "corridors" open to the sky'. Each garden is different: the white garden, the herb garden, the lime walk - and all grow in surprising profusion around the relics of a ruined Elizabethan house built within an earlier medieval moated house. There is a splendid rose garden surrounded by a circular yew hedge and a spiral staircase in an Elizabethan tower. Dreamland for gardeners and romantics. The property, which is owned by the National Trust, lies 5 miles south of Staplehurst. It can be reached from Staplehurst by taking the A229 south, turning left on to the A262, and turning left again after 1 mile.

Owl House Gardens
A mile to the east of Bayham Abbey, west of the A21, is Owl House, a tilehung smugglers' cottage (not open) surrounded by gardens and lawns.

Chatham Dockyard
The historic dockyard at Chatham, 6 miles north of Maidstone, where HMS *Victory* was built, is well worth visiting. There is a working ropery, an ordnance collection, a mast house and mould loft, together with extensive displays of the Royal Navy in the days of sail.

ON THE TOUR

Maidstone
Sitting at the foot of the North Downs, Maidstone is the gateway to the hop fields and orchards of the Medway Valley and the Weald of Kent. The best part of the town is by the river, where there is a pleasant walk beside the Archbishop's Palace and the Dungeons. There are river cruises from the quay at Maidstone, which once handled hops and fruit, ragstone, Wealden iron, fuller's earth, paper and much else. Maidstone's law courts speak of its other role, as the county town of Kent. Early shire courts were held on Penenden Heath, which is now in the northern suburbs of the town.
Worth seeking are the marvellous Tyrwhitt-Drake Museum of Carriages, which is close to the old palace, and the Maidstone Museum and Art Gallery, which is housed in a fine Elizabethan manor house to the north, next to Brenchley Gardens. Kent plays county cricket in Mote Park to the east of the town, an extensive area of 450 acres of parkland with fishing and sailing on a lake formed by damming the River Len.

East Farleigh
The Medway above Maidstone is one of the finest parts of the Kentish Weald. This is where Eastenders once came in droves to pick hops in the summer. A cross in East Farleigh churchyard commemorates 43 of them, who died of cholera in 1849. Cricket balls are made at Teston (pronounced Teeson), which faces West Farleigh. The medieval bridge over the River Beult at Yalding is one of several hereabouts and is 100yds long.

Bayham Abbey
Ruins dating back to the 13th century, including parts of the church, cloistered buildings and gatehouse. The abbey is sited in the wooded River Teise valley on the Kent border, and was occupied by an order of monks from Prémontré in France. This is a good place for a picnic.

Lamberhurst
Here the railings for St Paul's churchyard were made; one of several local ironmaking villages. It also has the largest vineyard in Kent, which produces a fine, white German-style wine. To the east is the National Trust property of Scotney Castle, where the romantic ruins of a 14th-century moated castle, and a later house, provide the setting for a wonderful garden.

Goudhurst
The local family of Culpeper bred so prolifically that few local churches are without memorials to them; Goudhurst's is overflowing, with one family group numbering 19! Two miles south-west of the village is the redbrick mansion of Finchcocks, built in 1725. It contains a marvellous collection of early keyboard instruments, which are played whenever the house is open (limited times).

Charing
Formerly a manor of the archbishop of Canterbury, with the remains of the palace or 'church barn' (now used as farm buildings) where Cranmer lived and Henry VIII stayed in 1520 – on his way to 'Field of the Cloth of Gold', a dignified 'knees-up' in France.

Leeds Castle
One of the wonders of Kent; a beautiful castle, sitting on two islands in the middle of a lake formed by damming the River Len, with grounds laid out by Capability Brown. The site has Saxon origins, but the existing buildings date from the Norman period. The castle is crammed full of fine furnishings and paintings and there is a bizarre Dog Collar Museum in the gatehouse. The parklands include a maze, a grotto and a vineyard.

Top: *the house at Scotney Castle was added to the 14th-century tower three centuries later*
Above: *Bayham Abbey, the best of Sussex's monastic remains*

OUTDOOR ACTIVITIES

Rowing boats can be hired at Tovil Boatyard, upstream from Maidstone, where there is also a fine towpath walk along River Medway. Villages such as Smarden, Headcorn and Charing are a delight to stroll about, and there is a forest trail in Chingley Wood.

Bewl Water, the largest reservoir in south-east England, was created in the mid 1970s by damming the River Bewl. It is now an area of outstanding unnatural beauty, with a visitor centre, boat cruises and waterside walks, including part of the Sussex Border Path. The lake is used for fishing and sailing. Access off the A21, a mile south of Lamberhurst.

NORTH ESSEX AND THE SUFFOLK BORDERS

51 miles

This part of England was 'built to last'; a legacy of the great wealth that came from the woollen cloth trade. The clothiers

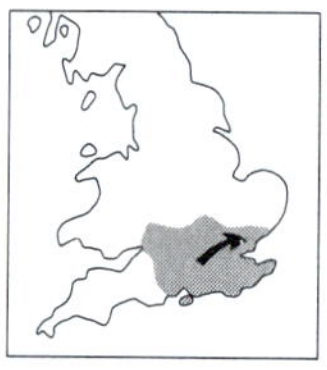

and weavers left behind fine houses, ornate churches and unbelievably pretty villages.

The Colne Valley Railway runs restored steam and diesel trains on most Sundays

Although the countryside is generally flat, and almost all under the plough, the counties of Essex and Suffolk have an extremely rich heritage. Not only do they have a fair share of stately homes, but they have remarkably rich and well-preserved villages and small towns. Almost every one of them is worth exploring. The Suffolk borders are particularly fine; the long villages of Clare and Cavendish are only out-stripped by the aptly named Long Melford. The churches are truly splendid, many of them with fine brasses of local grandees; a brass-rubber's paradise!

The main town of Braintree is very busy – and the growth of East Anglia will probably make it busier. However, there are quiet parts, at Bocking and Coggeshall, which make it easy to forget that London is so close.

ON THE TOUR

Braintree and **Bocking**

The home of Francis Crittall and his metal windows, the Courtauld textile family and the famous naturalist John Ray (1627-1705), who was born at nearby Black Notley. There is a statue of him in Bank Street, unveiled by the botanist David Bellamy in 1985. Bocking is two miles west of Braintree and is known for its fine post mill. The Braintree town story is told in a heritage centre in the town hall. Traditionally a wool town, in the last century it became famous for its silk, made by the Courtauld company and others. There are plans to restore a working silk mill.

Castle Hedingham

The keep of the Norman castle that gives the village its name is one of the best preserved in Europe. It was built in 1140 by Aubrey de Vere, who was killed in a riot a year later. In the Matilda and Stephen wars of the 12th century, de Vere's son supported the empress, who created him Earl of Oxford and died at the castle. Henry VII and Elizabeth I were also entertained here.

Colne Valley Railway

A mile of the Colne Valley and Halstead line has been restored and now runs steam trains, operated by enthusiasts. The original railway buildings have been rebuilt on the site (between Castle Hedingham and Great Yealdham).

Clare

The heart of the village is Market Hill, the church and the castle – which is now the centrepiece of an attractive country park. There is a small museum near the church in a house which dates from 1473. The castle was the home of the lords of Clare, who gave their name to the Royal Duchy of Clarence, Country Clare and Clare College, Cambridge. Near the castle stand the peaceful precincts of the Catholic priory church; founded in 1248, suppressed in 1538 and rededicated in 1954.

Cavendish

A charming Suffolk village put on the map by Sue Ryder, foundress of the charity, and the vintner Basil Ambrose. There is a small museum and tea-room at the Sue Ryder HQ, which is in the main street. Cavendish Manor Vineyards are centred on Nether Hall, behind the church.

Long Melford

The famous village that just goes on and on along the A134, for more than a mile. The superb 'wool' church reflects the wealth created by the Flemish weavers who settled here. The National Trust owns Melford Hall, a Tudor mansion in the village. It has a Beatrix Potter display and fine gardens.

Sudbury

A busy town, whose famous son is Thomas Gainsborough (see also page 116). The Church of St Gregory in the town was built by an Archbishop of Canterbury who was beheaded in the Wat Tyler poll tax riots of 1381; his skull is kept in the vestry.

Chappel

Here, on a 4-acre site beside Chappel rail station, is the East Anglian Railway Museum. This is the place to lay hands on signalling equipment and get a whiff of steam trains. Nearby is the dramatic 32-arch viaduct across the Colne Valley.

Coggeshall

A very pleasant town with some extra-ordinary timbered buildings. The National Trust owns Paycockes, a merchant's house of about 1500, and also the recently restored Grange Barn, dating from around 1140.

ROUTE DIRECTIONS

Leave **Braintree** (map 5TL72) by following the signs Sudbury (A131) to **Bocking**. In 1 mile further, at the roundabout, go forward on to the A131, then in a further mile bear left on to the A1017 (sp. Cambridge). Pass through Gosfield and in 2 miles join the A604. In a further mile turn right on to the B1058 to **Castle Hedingham**. Here, turn left, unclassified, and shortly pass the road to the castle on the right. In $^2/_3$ mile turn right and re-join the A604 (no sign). Pass the **Colne Valley Railway** on the right and continue to Great Yeldham. Turn right, unclassified (sp. Little Yeldham), then immediate left (sp. Clare). In 1 mile turn left for Ovington. Continue for a further $^1/_3$ mile, bear left, at the trunk road, turn right. In $^1/_2$ mile turn right again on to the A1092 for **Clare**. Follow the signs to Sudbury and pass the road to Clare Castle Country Park on the right, before reaching **Cavendish**. In a further $1^1/_2$ miles turn left on to the B1065 for Glemsford. Bear right through the village (sp. Bury St Edmunds) and at the end turn left past the church. In $^1/_2$ mile, at the trunk road, turn right on to the B1066 (sp. Long Melford). Bypass Stansted and in $1^2/_3$ miles, at the trunk road, turn left on to the A1092 (sp. Long Melford). In $^2/_3$ mile further turn right and pass Melford Hall on the left. Cross the river bridge to enter **Long Melford**. In $1^2/_3$ miles, at the roundabout, take 2nd exit A134 (sp. Sudbury). In 1 mile further, at the roundabout, the A131 to **Sudbury**. Follow the signs to Bures on the B1058 then, at Bures, follow the signs to Colchester and bear left. In $^2/_3$ mile turn right, unclassified (sp. Wakes Colne) to Mount Bures. Go over the level crossing and bear left to Wakes Colne. At the main road turn right on to the A604 (sp. Halstead). Across the road is **Chappel.** At the edge of Earls Colne bear left on to the B1024 (sp. Coggeshall). Reach the junction with the A120 and turn right, then immediate left to **Coggeshall**. Turn right, unclassified (no sign), and in 1 mile turn left on to the A120 (sp. Braintree). In a further $3^3/_4$ miles, at the roundabout, go forward to re-enter Braintree.

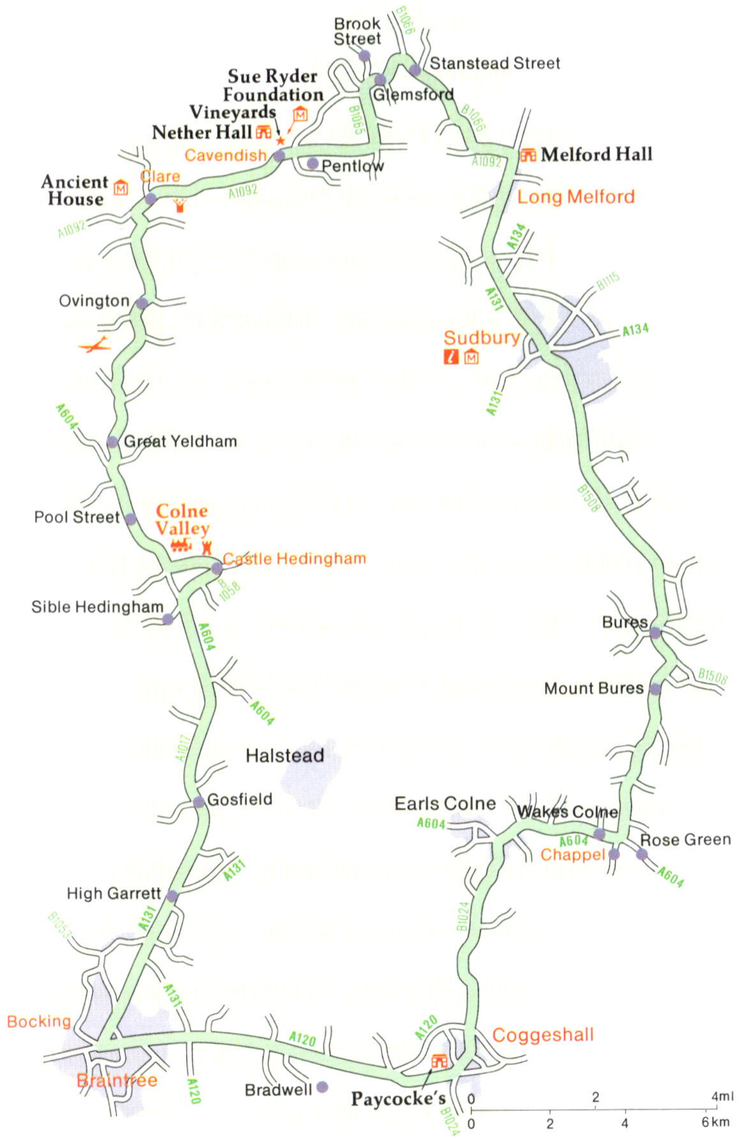

OFF THE TOUR

Colchester Zoo

The highlight of this zoo is Tiger Valley, where Siberian tigers have an extended territory. The zoo covers 40 acres and houses more than 150 species. It is south-west of Colchester, just south of the B1022.

Kentwell Hall

Turn left on to the A134 before Long Melford to reach the great Tudor house, which has a rare breeds farm, gardens and a brick-paved maze.

OFF THE BEATEN TRACK

There is a great rarety in Little Maplestead, which can be reached by tiny lanes from Castle Hedingham. This Essex village contains one of the few round churches in the country. It was built more than 600 years ago by the military order of the Knights Hospitallers. Their 'preceptory' at Little Maplestead was suppressed more than 400 years ago by Henry VIII.

OUTDOOR ACTIVITIES

Novices can try their hand at water skiing on Gosfield Lake, where there is a pay-as-you-enter water sports centre. Fishing and pitch and putt are among the other activities. The lake is overlooked by Gosfield Hall, a Tudor house where textile magnate Samuel Courtauld lived from 1854-81. It is reached by turning left in the village of Gosfield.

There are pleasant walks at Clare Country Park, alongside the River Stour and the 'new cut' made nearby for the priory mill. There is also a walk along the route of a former railway track, between Long Melford and Sudbury. Sudbury has facilities for outdoor, and indoor, bowling.

The Augustinian priory buildings, founded in 1248, seen from the top of Clare's Norman castle

BISHOP'S STORTFORD AND TURPIN'S COUNTRY

59 miles

Although the M11 and Stansted airport are nearby, this north-western corner of Essex has some of the most beautiful villages in

England. Saffron Walden is a fascinating small town and nearby Audley End numbers among the country's greatest houses.

This is one of two tours in the beautiful countryside of Essex. It actually starts just in Hertfordshire, at Bishop's Stortford, where the county boundary makes a wide detour around the town. The route passes through an area of winding lanes, gently rolling hills and great arable fields, seemingly stretching to the sky. With the exception of the busy towns of Bishop's Stortford and Great Dunmow – and the delightful town of Saffron Walden – this tour passes through countryside where villages scarcely seem to have changed for centuries. The finest are Thaxted and Finchingfield, but almost anywhere is worth exploring. There are plenty of pubs and restaurants, including Turpins at Hempstead, where the notorious highwayman was born.

Although the tour is cut by the M11 and the occasional aircraft is seen coming in to land at Stansted, the area is almost entirely unspoilt.

ON THE TOUR

Bishop's Stortford

Cecil Rhodes is the most famous son of Bishop's Stortford. His father was the local vicar and he was born in Netteswell House, which now houses the Rhodes Memorial Museum (half a mile south of the town centre, beside the A184). He was the founder of Zimbabwe, as Rhodesia is now called. At the age of 17 he went to southern Africa and got bitten by the diamond-hunting bug.
The mound of Waytemore Castle still stands in pleasant gardens beside the River Stort, to the east of the town.

Stansted Mountfitchet

Pilots circling Stansted Airport may blink in wonderment at the Norman village, complete with domestic animals, that stands on a hillock two miles from the runways. Adjacent is the only reconstructed motte-and-bailey castle in the world. The original was built after 1066 by the Duke of Boulogne, a cousin of the Conqueror.

Thaxted

One of the great villages of Essex, with a medieval guildhall and a famous windmill, built in 1804. It has a huge, airy church, with a fine bronze of a former vicar; Conrad Noel (1910-42), a leading Christian Socialist. The composer Gustav Holst lived at Thaxted between 1914-25 and often played the church organ.

Great Dunmow

Famous for the 'Flitch of Bacon' ceremony, which now takes place every leap year. It was once given as a right to any couple in the neighbouring village of Little Dunmow who could swear, after a year and a day of marriage, that they had not had a cross word or engaged in a 'household brawl'!

Great Bardfield

A pretty village with a cottage museum containing an interesting collection of bygones and corn dollies.

Finchingfield

A fine example of a show village, with a guildhall and local museum, a post mill, a river, and a 'causeway' giving views of the whole village. The gardens of the Elizabethan mansion, Spain's Hall, are open on Sunday afternoons in the summer.

Hempstead

Dick Turpin was born here in 1705 in the former Bell Inn. A 'better' claim to fame is that William Harvey, who discovered the circulation of the blood, was also born here, in 1578. The church contains his bust, beside the family vault.

Saffron Walden

Named after the Saffron crocus which was grown here to make dyestuffs in the middle ages. Much of the medieval plan of the old town survives and there are hundreds of fine buildings, many timbered with overhanging upper floors and decorative plasterwork (pargeting). There is a lavishly decorated 15th- and 16th-century church, and to the east a fine museum with many interesting items, including a Viking necklace. Bridge End Gardens, to the north, include a maze.

Audley End

Once a royal palace, the house was originally built in 1605 by the Earl of Suffolk on a site given by Henry VIII to Chancellor Audley. The grounds, landscaped by Capability Brown, include a 19th-century French garden. This is one of English Heritage's finest properties.
Audley End narrow-gauge railway offers pleasant rides through woodland.

With its post mill, its duck pond and its charming village green, Finchingfield is generally thought to be one of the most unspoilt villages in England. It appears in many 'beauties of Britain' calendars

OFF THE TOUR

Little Dunmow

Sister of Great Dunmow, one of the many 'Little' villages in Essex, reached by staying on the B184 through Great Dunmow. The church is of particular interest as it holds the original chair used in the ancient Flitch of Bacon 'marital bliss' ceremony (see page 82). Buried here is Robert Fitzwalter, who died in 1225 and played a prominent role in the Magna Carta. He was one of the 25 barons appointed to make sure that King John obeyed its provisions.

Linton Zoo

This is a wildlife conservation centre, founded in 1972. It has a string of breeding successes to its credit, including a variety of big cats, Bengal eagle owls, snapping turtles and bird-eating spiders. Set in 10 acres of countryside with full family facilities, it can be reached from Saffron Walden by taking the B1052 north.

Duxford Airfield

An arm of the Imperial War Museum and a centre of aviation history and aircraft restoration of international importance. Anyone with the faintest interest in aircraft must come here. Visitors can climb aboard a Concorde, or watch restoration experts at work. Regular special events are held during summer weekends. Duxford was an RAF station in the Second World War. Fighter ace Douglas Bader flew from here in the Battle of Britain. The 'Ops Room' of 1940 has been painstakingly restored. Go north-west from Saffron Walden to reach Duxford, off the M11.

Widdington

Here is Mole Hall, a 20-acre wildlife park surrounding a 13th-century moated manor house (not open). There is a splendid butterfly and insect pavilion too. Left off the B1383 from Newport.

ROUTE DIRECTIONS

Leave **Bishop's Stortford** (map 5TL42) on the B1383 Newmarket road and in 1½ miles, pass a Tower-mill before entering **Stansted Mountfitchet**. Turn right on to the B1051 (sp. Thaxted) and at the Kings Arms, turn left then bear right. Continue to Elsenham and on to **Thaxted**, then turn right on to the B184 Chelmsford road to reach **Great Dunmow**. Follow signs Colchester to join the A120 and in 2 miles turn left, unclassified (sp. Stebbing). In 1¼ miles, at Stebbing church, turn left to enter Stebbing. In 1 mile turn right on to the B1057 for **Great Bardfield**. Continue on the B1057 to **Finchingfield**, cross the bridge then turn left (sp. Haverhill) and in ½ mile turn left again. Continue to Steeple Bumpstead. Leave by the B1054 Saffron Walden road to reach **Hempstead**. In 1½ miles go forward on to the B1053 for Radwinter and then **Saffron Walden**. Follow signs London B1052 then bear right, unclassified, for **Audley End**. Continue to the B1383 then turn left for Newport. Turn right on to the B1038 Buntingford road and pass through Wicken Bonhunt to reach Clavering. Turn left, unclassified, to Manuden. Continue with the Bishop's Stortford signs, and in 2¾ miles, at the Red, White and Blue Inn, join the B1004 for the return to Bishop's Stortford.

OFF THE BEATEN TRACK

Hadstock

North of Saffron Walden on the B1052 is Hadstock, where the village church has a north door reputed to have been covered with a piece of human skin which can now be seen in Saffron Walden's museum. The skin is believed to have belonged to a Viking who had been flayed alive. The door itself dates from before the Norman Conquest. There are also 11th-century carvings in the church.

OUTDOOR ACTIVITIES

This is not an area with ready-made, long-distance footpaths, though there are plenty of local paths. Thaxted is a good place to start from. There are paths from the centre of the village past the windmill; from the Bull Ring in Watling Lane; and from Copthall Lane, which is beyond the Tanyard.

Finchingfield is a fine village for walks. There are paths from the Bardfield Road across the river; from the guildhall, past the south side of the church; and from Duck End, past the post mill.

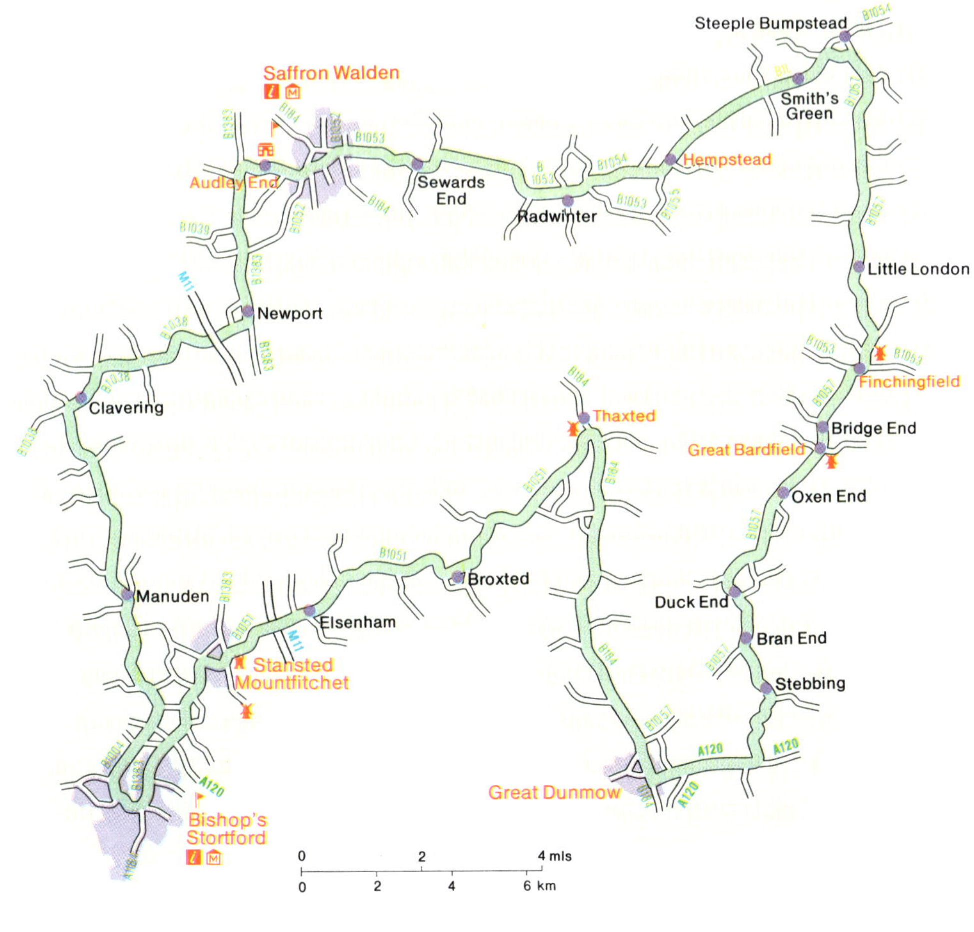

This attractive windmill, found at Stansted Mountfitchet along with other relics of bygone days, is typical of those dotted throughout this part of England

'FIVE COUNTIES' IN A DAY

62 miles

Here there is wide, open countryside that has a hint of Cambridgeshire and the Fens, with a belt of stone houses

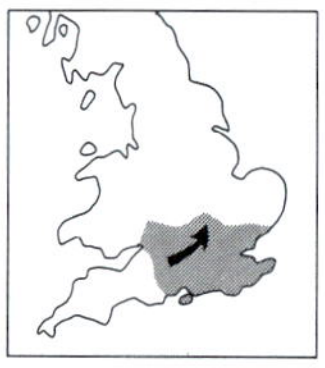

to the west and, at the start of the tour, the county town of Bedford and the Great Ouse.

The reservoir created by the water authority near the small village of Grafham has become a mecca for sailors and fishermen, as well as swimmers and windsurfers

This is a tour through the heartlands of England; the landscape of John Bunyan, with fine manor houses and pretty villages and, more recently, memories of GIs and wartime air-bases. The wealth of its traditional estates are seen at Castle Ashby, the home of the Marquesses of Northampton, and Woburn Abbey, the home of the Dukes of Bedford. Many of the cottages in the area have gabled thatched roofs; in the east they are mainly of brick and in the west of stone.

The eastern landscape is open, with large arable fields, generally without hedges, but invariably with drainage ditches. It was by draining the land that East Anglian farmers made it work. The water finishes up in the Great Ouse, a river that is already large at Bedford, but still has a long way to go before it reaches the sea at King's Lynn.

At Kimbolton the route enters Cambridgeshire, which in 1974 swallowed up Huntingdonshire – hence the title of this tour.

ROUTE DIRECTIONS

Leave **Bedford** (map 8TL04) on the B660 (sp. Cambridge, Kimbolton) and pass through Keysoe and Pertenhall. Skirt Kimbolton Park and turn left on to the A45 Northampton road to enter **Kimbolton**. Continue on the A45 to Tilbrook, then in 1 mile turn left, unclassified

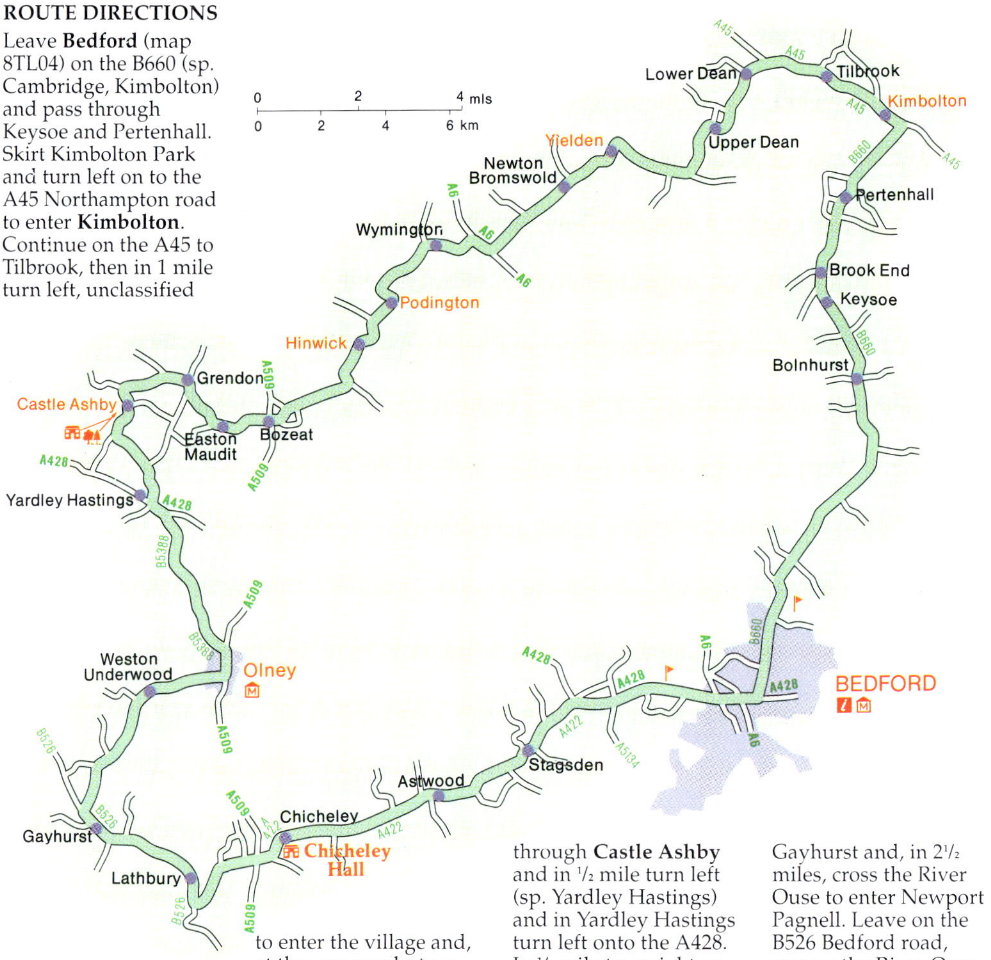

(sp. Lower and Upper Dean). Pass through Lower Dean to reach Upper Dean and continue on the Melchbourne road for 1¼ miles. At the T-junction turn right (sp. Yielden and Rushden) and continue to **Yielden**. Continue on the Rushden road and in 1¼ miles, at the T-junction, turn right then immediate left. In a further mile turn left into Avenue Road (sp. Wymington) then in a further mile turn right on to the A6. Take the next left turn, unclassified, for Wymington. At the New Inn join the Podington road to reach **Podington**. Continue, unclassified, and in ¾ mile, at the edge of **Hinwick** bear right. In 1¼ miles turn right and continue to Bozeat. At the T-junction turn left to enter the village and, at the crossroads, turn right into High Street. At the next road turn right again, then immediate left (sp. Grendon). Beyond Easton Maudit bear right for Grendon. Here, branch left on to the Earls Barton road, then in ½ mile turn left (sp. Castle Ashby) and cross the park. Continue through **Castle Ashby** and in ½ mile turn left (sp. Yardley Hastings) and in Yardley Hastings turn left onto the A428. In ½ mile turn right on to the B5388 Olney road. Pass through Yardley Chase and then turn right on to the A509 to enter **Olney**. Here, turn right into Weston Road, unclassified (sp. Weston Underwood). Enter Weston Underwood, and follow the Newport Pagnell road to join the B526. Pass through Gayhurst and, in 2½ miles, cross the River Ouse to enter Newport Pagnell. Leave on the B526 Bedford road, recross the River Ouse, and turn right. In 1½ miles go forward at the roundabout to join the A422 for **Chicheley Hall** and Chicheley. Continue to Stagsden, then at the edge of Bromham, at the roundabout, turn right on to the A428. Cross the River Ouse and re-enter Bedford.

OFF THE TOUR

Stagsden Bird Gardens

A collection of rare species of birds kept in a delightful rural location. Reached from the A422 by turning north beside the church at Stagsden.

Elstow

John Bunyan was born in this village, beside the Bedford-Luton road (now the A6). His family had lived at Elstow for 400 years when the author of *The Pilgrim's Progress* was born – in 1628 in a cottage that no longer exists, though a stone marks the spot. He rang the bells in the nearby church, which once belonged to a nunnery. The nuns organized an important fair for merchants on Elstow Green, which Bunyan used as a model for his *Vanity Fair*. The fair's Moot Hall is now a small museum of Bunyan bygones (limited opening).

Bedford Suspension Bridge forms a graceful arc over the river

ON THE TOUR

Bedford

The county town of Bedfordshire is generally associated with the Dukes of Bedford, the Whitbread family, and its famous son, the preacher and writer John Bunyan. Another famous local man is John Howard, the prison reformer who gave his name to the Howard League. His statue stands to the east of St Paul's Church. Opposite, on the Embankment, is the Swan Hotel, a fine building designed by Henry Holland for the Duke of Bedford. Nearby is Town Bridge, which dates from 1813 and is by another of the duke's architects, John Wing. Embankment Gardens is linked at its eastern end to Mill Meadows by Bedford's other famous bridge, an elegant suspension bridge of 1888. The most interesting part of Bedford for 'culture vultures' is around the east end of Mill Street, which runs east off High Street. Here is the Bunyan Meeting House (and museum), where Bunyan preached from 1671 to 1688; the Cecil Higgins Art Gallery, with its fine collections of ceramics and prints; and the Bedford Museum. Bunyan's statue is further north, near the Saxon Church of St Peter.

Kimbolton

The grand building here is Kimbolton Castle, used since 1950 by the local grammar school. It is open to the public, and Robert Adams' gatehouse of *c*1766 is prominent. Kimbolton's fine medieval church is full of relics of the castle's owners, the Dukes of Manchester. There is also a memorial to the US Army Air Force, which flew from a local airfield.

Yielden

The prominent earthworks at the entrance to this pretty village are all that remain of a Norman castle, ruined at least 600 years ago.

Podington and Hinwick

In 1985 Podington church had its organ restored as a memorial to `Fames Favored Few', the nickname of the 92nd Bombardment Group of the US 8th Air Force, which flew from a local airfield (now the Santa Pod Raceway at Hinwick). The superb Georgian mansion Hinwick House has been the home of the Orlebar family since 1714. Nearby is Hinwick Hall, a beautiful water-girt Tudor house, which has a garden centre in the grounds.

Castle Ashby

A classic estate village, home of the Compton family, Marquesses of Northampton. The house is not open to the public, though the façade, with its rather kitsch lettered balustrades, is easily viewed and the gardens and hot houses are open. A charming setting, where a real welcome is extended. Many Comptons are commemorated in the church nearby, which also has huge family memorials in the churchyard. Inside, against the north wall of the nave, is a moving sculpture by Marochetti of Lady Margaret Leveson Gower, a daughter of the second Marquess.

Olney

A town strung out along the main road, with The Cowper Memorial Museum in the market place. The poet lived here in the solid Georgian house for 18 years and his manuscripts and other relics are on display. One of the friends he entertained here was John Newton, the author of *Amazing Grace*.

Chicheley Hall

A grand house dating from 1719, with mementos of Lord Beatty, the First World War admiral. Look out for the hidden library, believed to be unique.

OFF THE BEATEN TRACK

To the north-east of Bedford, near the village of Colmworth, is Bushmead Priory, one of the most charming small properties managed by English Heritage. It was founded in 1195 and is still lived in by the descendants of the Gery family who built a mansion here after the priory had been suppressed. Of special interest is the refectory, which has a rare crown-post roof of 1250. There are also 14th-century wall paintings and an old brewhouse. Colmworth is itself a pretty village, a mile east off the B660.

OUTDOOR ACTIVITIES

This is not countryside for demanding walks, but there are plenty of footpaths to be found. There is a gentle 15-minute stroll around Grendon Quarter Pond, which is three miles beyond Bozeat and belongs to the Compton Estates. Emberton Park and Lake, to the south of Olney, provides pleasant walks.

Grafham Water

A few miles from Kimbolton is the great lake at Grafham, which is 10 miles in circumference; the largest artificial lake in England. It was created between 1962 and 1968 by damming a small brook and is in parts 70ft deep. Although principally a reservoir, it is a splendid place for a picnic. Part of the area is a nature reserve and there is sailing and fishing. From Kimbolton the lake is reached by taking the A45 south and turning left after three miles.

'BANBURYSHIRE' AND THE OXFORD CANAL

58 miles

Pastoral tranquillity and unspoilt, rolling countryside cut by the River Cherwell and the Oxford Canal. Fine country houses,

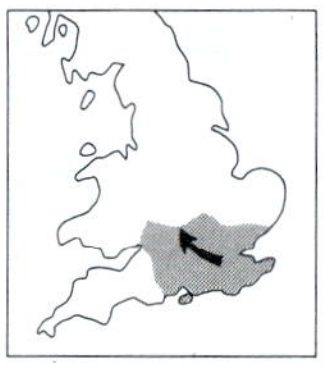

homely churches, and stone-built villages; scarcely an obvious trace of the 20th century outside the main town of Banbury.

This tour passes through corners of the counties of Oxfordshire, Northamptonshire and Warwickshire. It is unpretentious, solidly agricultural countryside, with ample traces of ancient ridge-and-furrow tillage. Its villages are almost all built in ironstone, with roofs of thatch or blue Welsh slate. There are fine stone-built churches, mostly of the 14th and 15th centuries, rich with carvings and with ornate tombstones in their graveyards. Great three-lock parish chests are common. At Wroxton there is a thatched church, at Swalcliffe a huge 14th-century tithe barn.

The area is cut by the River Cherwell, with its sister waterway the Oxford Canal; built in the late 18th century to link Oxford with the north. Its own special way of life was captured by L T C Rolt in his classic book Narrow Boat.

The Civil War was fought bitterly hereabouts, notably at Edgehill. Nine of the dead from this battle are buried at Warmington, in the churchyard on the hill.

Banbury Cross was immortalised in the rhyme 'Ride a cock-horse'

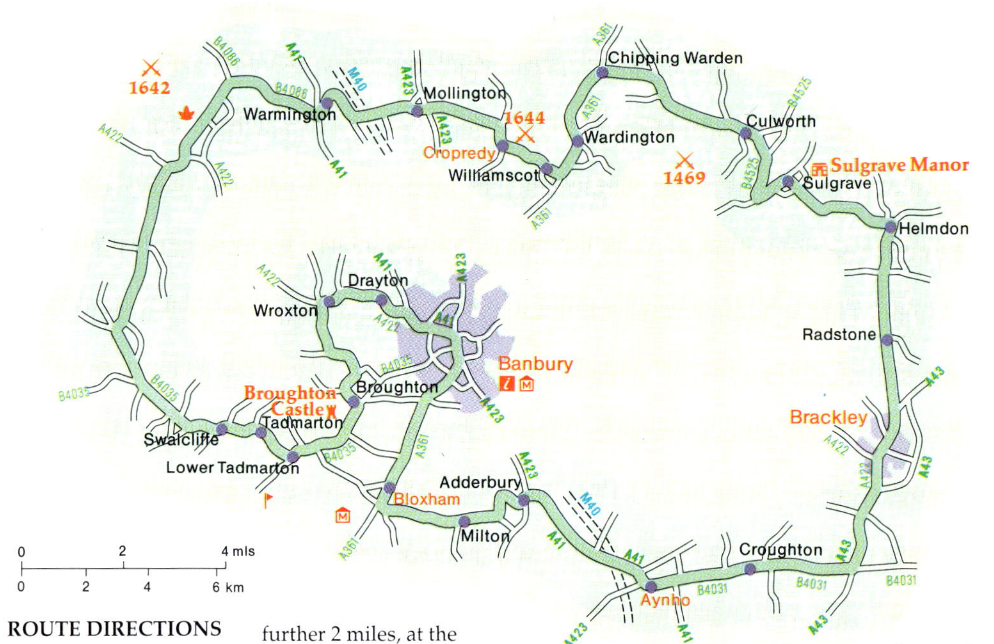

ROUTE DIRECTIONS

Leave **Banbury** (map 4SP44) on the A361 Swindon road to reach **Bloxham**. Here, at the end of the village, turn left, unclassified on to the Adderbury road, then left again into Milton Road. Pass the edge of Milton then in 1 mile turn left for Adderbury. Turn left on to the A423 then, at the traffic signals, turn right on to the A41 (sp. Aylesbury). Enter Northamptonshire and reach **Aynho**. In ¾ mile branch left on to the B4031 (sp. Buckingham) to reach Croughton. In a further 2 miles, at the roundabout, turn left on to the A43 for **Brackley**. At the roundabout take 1st exit, then turn right into the town. Keep forward and ¾ mile beyond the town turn left, unclassified (sp. Helmdon and Sulgrave) to reach Helmdon. Here, cross the bridge and turn left to pass **Sulgrave Manor** and reach Sulgrave. Continue on the Culworth road through the village and, in 1 mile, turn right on to the B4525. In a further ½ mile, at the T-junction, turn left into Culworth. In 1¾ miles turn right and cross a bridge, then in ½ mile turn left for Chipping Warden. Join the A361 Banbury road for Wardington then, in 1 mile, turn right, unclassified (sp. Cropredy). Skirt Williamscott to enter **Cropredy** and, at the Brasenoes Arms turn right. In ¼ mile turn left (sp. Mollington) and then at the main road, go over a staggered crossroads into Mollington. Continue to Warmington and on entering, bear left, cross the green and ascend through the village. At the top turn left on to the A41, pass the church and then turn sharp right on to the B4086 (sp. Kineton). Continue for 2 miles then, at the T-junction, turn left, unclassified (sp. Edge Hill). Continue for 1¾ miles to reach the A422. Turn right (sp. Stratford) then take the next left, unclassified (sp. Compton Wynates). Continue forward for 3½ miles and, at the crossroads, turn left (sp. Banbury). In another mile turn left on to the B4035 and continue through Swalcliffe and Tadmarton to Broughton. Here, turn left, unclassified (sp. North Newington) and bear right to pass the entrance to **Broughton Castle**. Shortly, bear right again then in ½ mile turn left for North Newington. At the end of the village turn right (sp. Wroxton) then in 1¼ miles turn right on to the A422 and skirt Wroxton. Continue through Drayton, then join the A41 for the return to Banbury.

OFF THE TOUR

Edgehill Battle Museum

Alongside the 18th-century mansion of Farnborough Hall is a museum which tells the story of the first battle of the Civil War. This involved a total of 30,000 men and was fought nearby on 23 October, 1642, on the dramatic slopes of Edgehill. There are maps, graphic dioramas of the battlefield and a display of costumes and armour.

Burton Dassett Hills Country Park

A spur of rugged ironstone hills topped by a late medieval beacon, with extensive views - 52 miles to the Clee Hills, 40 to the Malverns, with sights of Warwick Castle and Coventry on a clear day. There is an AA viewing point on Magpie Hill (630ft). Reached from the A41 at Warmington, turning east towards Northend after 3 miles.

The imposing façade of stately Upton House is softened by the beautiful plants and shrubs

ON THE TOUR

Banbury

Situated near the meeting point of three counties, Banbury is the centre of the unofficial county of `Banburyshire'. Known for its cakes and `riding cock-horses', Banbury itself has been criticised for destroying its own heritage, including its famous cakeshop. However, the centre of the town is still extremely pleasant. The famous Banbury Cross was first made popular by a local publisher of books of children's verse. The present cross is Victorian. Banbury Museum has an attractive display of local history and a coffee shop. The town is overlooked by the verdigris tower of its grand Georgian church. Jonathan Swift took the name of his hero, Gulliver, from the tombstones of a local family buried in the churchyard.

Bloxham

A fine village with many 16th- and 17th-century buildings in local ironstone. Seal Cottage was built for an Elizabethan yeoman farmer. The former Court House is still held by local feoffees, and is now an attractive museum of bygones. The church at Bloxham is rich in stone sculpture and has a spire 200ft high.

Aynho

The 'Cartwright corner' of Northamptonshire, where the family's splendid house, Aynhoe Park, stands beside the Georgian church that was grafted on to a medieval tower. The house, which is open at limited times, was sold in 1960 and partly converted to flats. *Lili at Aynho* is Elizabeth Cartwright-Hignett's charming account of life as it was once lived here.

Brackley

A fine unspoilt market town, as pleasant a pitstop as you will find. Plenty of places to eat, shop and draw money. The Duke of Bridgewater lost his `pocket borough' of Brackley in 1832. A forebear had built the fine town hall in 1706. Stone buildings line the Market Place, including Winchester House School (1875-8) and the medieval chapel used by Magdalen College, Oxford, whose scholars sought refuge here during epidemics.

Sulgrave Manor

This is the birthplace of the father of Colonel John Washington, a forebear of the first president of the US. In 1656 he left his native Oxfordshire to farm at Mount Vernon, Virginia. The 'Stars and Stripes', which hangs outside the house, is said to have been based on the Washington family's coat-of-arms.

Cropredy

A well-known stop-off on the Oxford Canal. The Battle of Cropredy Bridge took place near here in 1644. One of the brass feet of the lectern in the huge local church was lost at the time. It still `looks different' because the replacement was cast in bronze. The remains of a preaching cross near the church are called the `cup and saucer', for obvious reasons.

Broughton Castle

This moated manor house dates from 1306. Incredibly, the effigy of its builder, Thomas Broughton, is in the church, which he also built. It later became the home of the Fiennes family, forebears of the present day explorer, Sir Ranulph. Broughton Castle has a fine medieval hall and intricate Elizabethan plasterwork. Opening times are limited, but the park is generally open to the public.

OFF THE BEATEN TRACK

Edgcote House

Edgcote House was built in the 18th century and has belonged to the Courage family since 1926. The house is not generally open to the public, but a nearby church can be visited. It contains two superb Elizabethan tombs of the Chauncey family, so finely carved that the ruffs and the petticoats of the ladies look freshly starched. There are box-pews and a large square squire's pew.
Edgcote is at the end of a narrow lane and is reached by turning left at Wardingtòn, then taking a fork left after about a mile.

OUTDOOR ACTIVITIES

Wigginton Heath

There is a wildfowl sanctuary here which is reached by turning south off the B4035 at Tadmarton.

Oxford Canal

TThe towpath of the Oxford Canal doubles as a footpath along much of its length, and there is a convenient section at Cropredy. To the north the locks are extremely close together.

OXFORD AND THE EAST COTSWOLDS

69 miles

The sheer homeliness of Oxfordshire is its greatest asset. Gentle and unspectacular, the countryside is made up of farming land, low hills

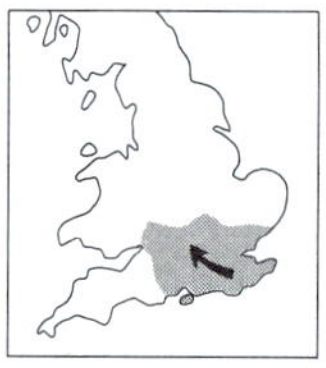

and sluggish rivers. North of Oxford's dreaming spires the tour follows a belt of limestone stretching across from the Cotswold Hills.

The first part of this tour edges into Buckinghamshire, where the red brick of Brill contrasts with the mellow stone of the rest of the trip. Small Cotswold towns and villages such as Deddington, Charlbury and Great Tew have a sense of classic timelessness that reflects their long history.

Bicester and Witney on the other hand, although sizeable towns with strong historical associations, are definitely not period pieces. Witney is the seat of the West Oxfordshire District Council, whose latest claim to fame is that in 1990, 18 of its councillors resigned in protest against the community charge.

The whole area is, however, dominated by Oxford, a city of international repute that has too much to 'bite off' in one visit. Much of its greatness can be seen to have come from the countryside, and from the headstreams of the Thames which have fed it.

ON THE TOUR

Oxford

Probably the best way to savour Oxford in a short visit is to start at the Carfax, walk along High Street and Broad Street and wander in and out of one or two of the colleges (there are 30 *in toto*). Then, perhaps, pick one item of particular interest.

The Carfax has a tower from which there is a superb view of the city. Nearby is the City Museum of Oxford and the High Street, which contains the Frank Cooper Shop and Museum of Marmalade.

In Broad Street is the Museum of the History of Science and also the Oxford Story, a popular audio visual/olfactory (smells!) production that tells the history of the university. The Ashmolean Museum in Beaumont Street is world famous and contains one of the country's greatest collections of art and antiquities.

More specialised interests are served by the University Museum, the Pitt Rivers Museum in Parks Road, and the Botanic Gardens at the foot of High Street.

Peace and quiet are to be found in the famous meadows of Oxford, whilst there are steamer trips from Folly Bridge and (for the adventurous) punts for hire at Magdalen Bridge.

Stanton St John

According to the inscription above the door of a stone-mullioned house opposite the church, Oxford don John White, the 'chief founder' of the New England colony of Massachusetts, was born here.

Brill

Once the centre of the royal forest of Bernwood and a Royalist stronghold. In the Battle of Brill, fought in 1643, 5,000 Parliamentarians were kept at bay.

A fine post mill stands on the common, which betrays the clay diggings of the town's once extensive brickworks. The mill dates from the end of the 17th century.

Bicester

A garrison town, with modern facilities and eating places. The oldest parts of the town are around the Market Square (actually a triangle) and St Edburg's Church. 'Edburgers' is the local name used for the parishioners of Bicester.

Deddington

The heart of this village-cum-town is off the main road. The town hall, with open arches beneath, is virtually the only brick building in the place. In the centre of the 'bull-ring' is a former blanket factory. Nothing of the castle still stands; its outer bailey holds a football pitch. Very pleasant pubs and antique shops.

Minster Lovell and oilseed rape

OFF THE TOUR

Rousham House

Just beyond Lower Heyford the route crosses the Cherwell via a four-arch medieval bridge. Rousham is reached by turning left at the far side of the bridge. The house dates from 1635 but was refashioned by William Kent in the 18th century. Its famous ornamental gardens, which cover 20 acres, are in the early Romantic style, largely as Kent left them. The house has limited opening times.

Minster Lovell Hall

The ruins of this fine English Heritage medieval hall stand to the north of the B4047, west of Witney. They are part of a classic landscape of manor house and church which still survives in a beautiful setting beside the River Windrush.

In 1431 William, the 7th Baron Lovell, came back from soldiering in France in bad health and had both the house and the church built. A fine alabaster tomb in the church, surmounted by the effigy of a knight, is almost certainly that of Lord William.

Near Minster Lovell, along the Brize Norton road and elsewhere, are the Charterville cottages and allotments; relics of the benevolent but ill-fated land settlement schemes of the Cork MP and Chartist, Feargus O'Connor.

Blenheim and Woodstock

Turning left at the A34 after Bladon leads to the famous Blenheim Palace, completed in 1722 for John Churchill, Duke of Marlborough. It should not be missed, if time allows.

Woodstock is the charming village that grew up 'about' the palace. It contains the Oxfordshire County Museum.

Great Tew

Too good to be Tew! The classic English village, with masses of thatched stone-mullioned cottages. The one pub, the Falkland Arms, commemorates Lucius Cary, Lord Falkland, Secretary of State to Charles I, who died at the Battle of Newbury. His memorial, erected more than 250 years after his death, can be seen in the church, which is on the southern outskirts of the village. It also has a particularly fine sculpture of a lady, by Sir Francis Chantrey .

Charlbury

At the heart of this small, stone-built town is a charming green called The Playing Close. The Duke of Marlborough once lived at Lee Place on the southern outskirts, and the emancipated Quaker preacher, Anne Downer, was born at Charlbury vicarage in 1624. She married the famous Quaker leader George Whitehead.

Witney

Witney is famous for making blankets, though the only working mill is Early's, founded in 1669, in the north of the town. A short distance away in High Street is Blanket Hall, where the blankets were weighed and measured.

At the southern end of the town is Church Green, a pleasant spot, where the remains of the late Saxon palace of the bishops of Winchester have been excavated (and back-filled) in recent years.

Bladon

Sir Winston Churchill (1874-1965) is buried in the churchyard at Bladon, beside other members of the families Soames and Churchill. The church is touchingly plain.

ROUTE DIRECTIONS

Leave **Oxford** (map 3SP50) city centre, following signs The East, then at the end of the High Street cross Magdalen Bridge and, at the roundabout, branch left then leave by the A420 Headington road. Pass through Headington then at the roundabout take 2nd exit, unclassified (sp. Stanton St John) into Bayswater Road. In ¾ mile turn right then in 1 mile further, at the T-junction, turn right then immediate left into **Stanton St John**. At the church turn left and follow the signs to Oakley. At the main road turn right on to the B4011 then take the next left turn, unclassified, for **Brill**. At the war memorial keep left and at the Sun Hotel turn left into Windmill Street. Pass the old windmill and after 1¾ miles join the B4011 to Blackthorn. In 1 mile turn left on to the A41 to reach **Bicester**. Follow the signs Oxford A421, then turn right on to the A4095 (sp. Witney) and in 1 mile go forward on to the B4030 Enstone road to Middleton Stoney. Cross the main road and continue to the edge of Lower Heyford. Turn left and in 1 mile cross the River Cherwell. At Hopcrofts Holt Hotel turn right on to the A423 (sp. Banbury) and continue to **Deddington**. Turn left on to the B4031 Chipping Norton road, pass through Hempton and in 3 miles turn left on to the A361. In ½ mile turn left on to the B4022 (sp. Enstone) and in 1 mile further turn left, unclassified, for **Great Tew**. Here, bear right then in ½ mile turn right, and at the next crossroads turn left to re-join the B4022 (sp. Enstone). After 3 miles go over a staggered crossroads and skirt Enstone, then cross the A34 (sp. Charlbury). In another 3 miles keep forward to enter **Charlbury**. Go over the staggered crossroads (sp. Witney) and at the end of the town turn right, then immediate right again. Continue on B4022 to **Witney**. Turn left to avoid the Town Centre and leave by the A4095 Bicester road. Continue though Long Hanborough to **Bladon** and, 1 mile beyond the village, at the junction with the A34, turn right (sp. Oxford). In 4 miles, at the roundabout, take 2nd main exit to join the A43. At the next round-about follow signs City Centre for the return to Oxford.

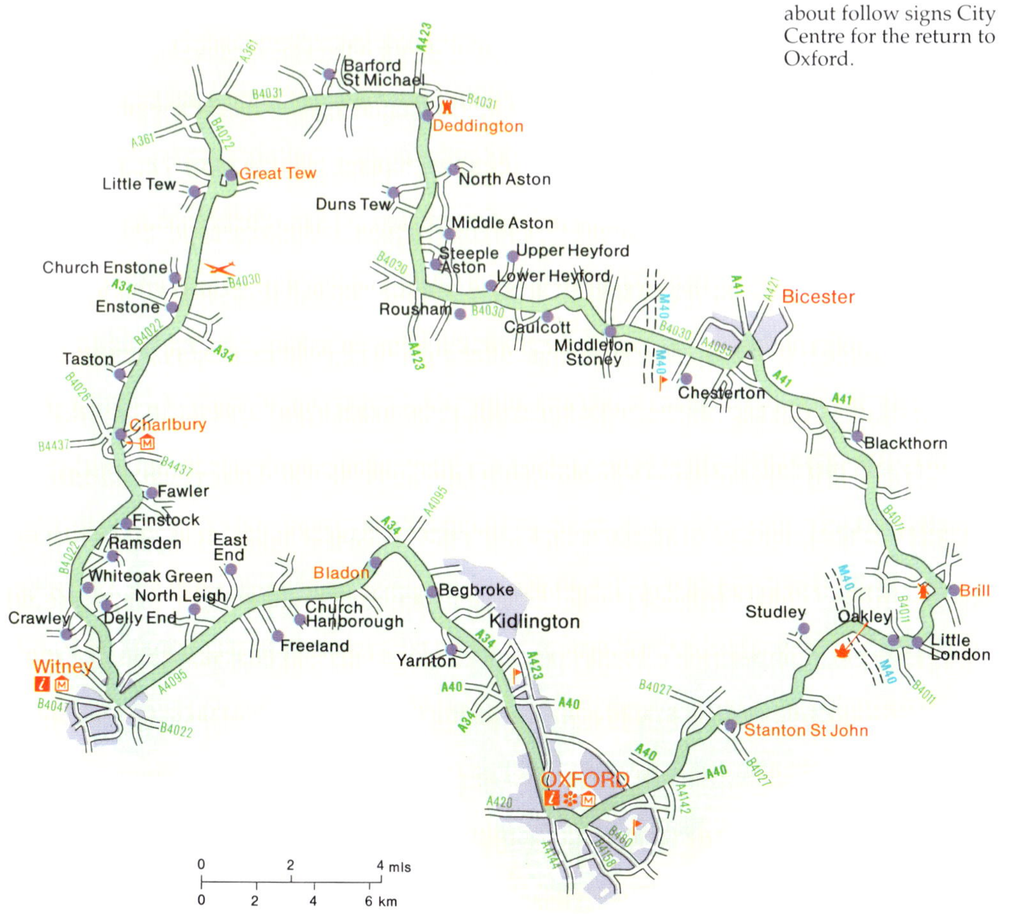

This ornate drinking fountain is Charlbury's memorial to Queen Victoria, and well worth closer inspection

OFF THE BEATEN TRACK

Ot Moor

Turn left off the B4011 just past the village of Blackthorn to reach Ot Moor – a strangely isolated area covering about six square miles of marshy farmland. Bowl shaped, with many streams, the Moor is rich in wildlife – especially water plants and butterflies. Despite the presence of the army now, a visit here gives some idea of how much of England would have looked two or more centuries ago. Two bridleways cross the Moor, one following the course of a Roman road.

OUTDOOR ACTIVITIES

There is punting at Oxford and canoeing at Charlbury. There is also the much drier alternative of walking a sector of the Oxfordshire Way, which passes through Charlbury, *en route* between Bourton-on-the-Water in Gloucestershire and Henley-on-Thames.

Bernwood Forest Nature Reserve

At Oakley, just past the newly built M40, is Bernwood Forest Nature Reserve, one of the most important British habitats for butterflies. This is an ideal picnic site with waymarked trails designed to last 45 or 90 minutes. There are more than 40 species of butterfly to be spotted in the reserve, which is an SSSI in the hands of the Forestry Commission and a relic of the once-extensive Forest of Bernwode.

THE BEST OF BERKSHIRE

71 miles

Whether you prefer cosy river valleys with pretty cottages and fine manor houses, or wide open downs, Berkshire has it all. Water

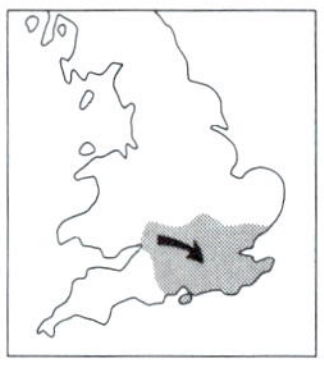

is rarely far away... the lush water meadows of the Lambourn Valley, the stately banks of the Thames, and village ponds galore.

Think of Berkshire and you generally think of busy towns like Reading and Newbury. Yet most of the county has a relaxed and comfortable air about it – even slightly scruffy.

The early part of this tour runs between the valleys of the Bourne and the Pang (hence Pangbourne) through a large open area of commons. It then winds itself past Newbury in a part of the country where the smoke of the Civil War scarcely seems to have cleared.

The valley of the Lambourn is dotted with small villages of thatched cottages and old mills. A few sheep still graze the meadows that once supplied the raw material for the vital clothmaking industry of Jack of Newbury, and other wealthy clothiers. The high-profile business today is training racehorses.

After Lambourn the route is virtually all across downland until, with dramatic suddenness, the road falls down to Streatley and the Thames Valley.

Bluebell time at Basildon Park

ON THE TOUR

Reading

A place for river rats and shoppers, Reading is justly proud of the little bit of its ruined abbey that remains. This was an important royal foundation and the place where Henry I was buried. Here too, the earliest known song – *'Summer is a-coming in'* – was written down. In the nearby gaol (not the one used today) Oscar Wilde languished and wrote his famous *Ballad*.
The Museum of English Rural Life on the southern outskirts of the town is nationally known and a joy for country lovers.
Reading's Museum and Art Gallery in the town hall is undergoing a major facelift. It is noted for the Roman remains of the deserted town of Silchester or Calleva.
For canal buffs, the Blake's Lock Museum, also being rejigged, is a must.
There are beautiful walks along the southern banks of the Thames and its tributary the Kennet.

Donnington

Famous for its castle, which was involved in a celebrated Civil War siege. Cromwell never took it, but after the king's surrender in April 1646 much of it was destroyed. The great gatehouse remains; it and the beautiful hill on which it stands are in the hands of English Heritage and open to the public. However, they are closed during the lunch hour.
Nearby Donnington Priory was once the family home of Thomas Hughes, author of *Tom Brown's Schooldays*.

Lambourn

A small town devoted to racehorses, with 25 training stables in the area. The West Berkshire Downs have become a major national centre for training horses and several hundred races are won each year by Lambourn mounts.
There are several excellent pubs in the town, but don't believe all the tips offered at the bar! Drivers are asked to slow down when approaching horses.

Childrey

A classic village and a pleasant place for a stop. The church has a fine collection of brasses, which can be rubbed for a small fee – permission given at the village garage. Some of them are of the Fettiplaces, a famous Berkshire family, whose arms are above the west door and who lived in the lovely Elizabethan manor house nearby.

Wantage

Birthplace of Alfred the Great and a place of some importance in Saxon and medieval times, it later became noted as a haunt of criminals. A Victorian statue of Alfred stands in the town's fine market place.
A pleasant place for a stroll, with plenty of eating places. One of these is the coffee shop at the Vale and Downland Museum, which has a well-displayed collection of local material. Apparently, Wantage was the first place in the country to have a steam tram – which ran to the nearest railway station.
The 'Wantage Sisters' is a religious community, founded in 1847, and now active throughout the world.

Aldworth

The village church is perched on a hill and contains the celebrated `Aldworth Giants', an astonishing collection of nine recumbent stone effigies of the De la Beche family, dating from 1300-1350. It's like stumbling into catacombs or a reserve sculpture collection of the V & A! Elizabeth I once rode over from Ewelme to see the Giants.

Basildon Park

A fine Georgian mansion in 406 acres of parkland. Still lived in by its former owners, Lord and Lady Iliffe, but now owned by the National Trust. The fine Shell Room contains a collection of rare shells, land and sea. There is a tea room and a shop.

Child Beale Wildlife Park

This peaceful spot beside the Thames is more than a bird park. As well as housing flamingos, owls, parrots and pheasants, it is also home to rare breeds of sheep, Highland cattle, llamas and Shetland ponies. There is an adventure playground and paddling pools, and fishing tickets can be purchased.

ROUTE DIRECTIONS

Leave **Reading** (map 3SU77) on the A4 (sp. Newbury) to reach the junction with the M4. At the roundabout take 2nd exit (sp. Theale) then in $1\frac{1}{3}$ miles, at the roundabout, take 2nd main exit A340 (sp. Pangbourne). In $\frac{1}{4}$ mile, turn left, unclassified (sp. Bradfield). Continue towards Bradfield then turn left (sp. Southend, Bucklebury). In 1 mile, at the trunk road, turn right to Southend, Bradfield and continue to Upper Bucklebury. At the end turn right (sp. Cold Ash) and continue to Cold Ash. Here, at the crossroads, turn right (sp. Hermitage) and in $1\frac{1}{2}$ miles, at the trunk road, turn left on to the B4009 (sp. Newbury). After $2\frac{2}{3}$ miles, turn right, unclassified into Love Lane (sp. Donnington) and reach **Donnington**. Here, at the crossroads, turn right on to the B4494 (no sign) and in $\frac{1}{4}$ mile at the mini-roundabout branch left (sp. Wantage) to pass Snelsmore Common Country Park. Take the next turning on the left, unclassified (sp. Winterbourne, Boxford) and descend. In $\frac{2}{3}$ mile at the trunk road turn right (no sign) to reach the edge of Winterbourne. Turn left (sp. Boxford, Shefford) and enter Boxford. Here, turn left, cross the road bridge, and keep left. At the next crossroads turn right (sp. Welford, Great Shefford), to reach Great Shefford. Go forward on to the A338, then forward again, unclassified (sp. Lambourn) to reach **Lambourn**. Here, at the crossroads, turn right on to the B4001 (sp. Wantage) and in 6 miles, at the crossroads at **Childrey**, turn right on to the B4507 (sp. Wantage). Enter **Wantage** and follow the signs Newbury, B4494. In $2\frac{1}{4}$ miles ascend. Then, in a further $2\frac{1}{3}$ miles turn left, unclassified (sp. Farnborough) to reach Farnborough. Continue forward (sp. East and West Ilsley through West, and then East Ilsley. Keep left, (sp. Compton) to reach Compton, and continue forward (sp. Pangbourne). In $2\frac{1}{3}$ miles, at the trunk road, turn left on to the B4009 (sp. Streatley). Pass the outskirts of **Aldworth** and descend to Streatley. At the traffic signals, turn right on to the A329 (sp. Reading). Pass **Basildon Park** on the right, and **Child Beale Wildlife Park** on the left before entering Pangbourne. Here, at the mini-roundabout, turn left, then left again on to the B471 (sp. Whitchurch). Cross the River Thames via the Toll Bridge, into Whitchurch, and ascend Whitchurch Hill. Turn right, unclassified (sp. Goring Heath) and in $1\frac{1}{3}$ further, at the trunk road, turn right (sp. Reading). At the trunk road turn right on to the A4074 for Caversham. Here at the traffic signals turn right (sp. Town Centre) and cross the River Thames to re-enter Reading.

OFF THE TOUR

Uffington

A fork to the left off the B4001 road between Lambourn and Wantage leads past Seven Barrows (there are actually 39) to White Horse Hill, famous for its carved outline of a horse. This is said to commemorate Alfred's victory over the Danes in AD871, at Ashdown, on the Ridgeway. However, the style of the carving suggests that it predates the battle by more than a thousand years. There is a car park and a path to the top of White Horse Hill and on to Uffington Castle, one-time prehistoric camp.

Mapledurham House

A fine Elizabethan mansion which can either be reached by road (right off the A329 north-west of Reading) or by taking a riverboat from Caversham Bridge, Reading. Opening is restricted to weekend afternoons and public holidays. The grand house was built in 1588 by Sir Michael Blount, whose descendants still occupy it. One of its regular visitors was the poet Alexander Pope. There is a working water mill in the grounds, which also has a picnic area. Home-made cream teas are served.

OUTDOOR ACTIVITIES

The ancient Ridgeway Path crosses the tour three miles beyond Lambourn where a section to the west leads to the White Horse Hill.

Other places for leg-stretching include the towpath of the Kennet and Avon Canal, which is soon to be open along its entire length; the Bucklebury Estate, between Theale and Thatcham; and Snelsmore Common Country Park – 146 acres of heathland between Donnington and Winterbourne that has remained as uncultivated commonland. There is a pleasant, wooded, picnic area and a network of footpaths and bridelways.

Wantage has an attractive market place and a church with old woodwork and a 15th-century roof

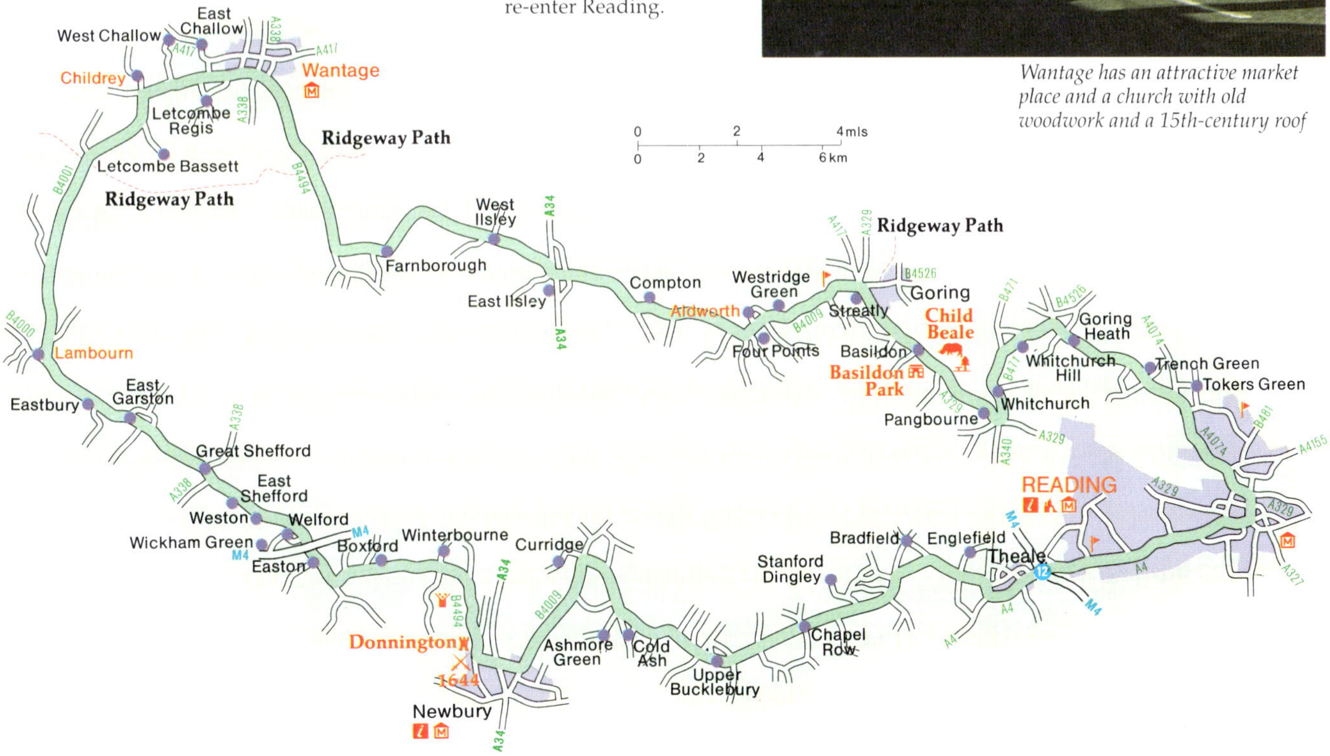

TOLLESBURY

CENTRAL ENGLAND AND EAST ANGLIA

Staffordshire's byways run to the cemetries tucked away on Cannock Chase, where the ranks of Second World War dead lie peacefully in winnowed rows under the sheltering trees, hostility long spent. Further north, the Churnet, the Dane and the Dove glide sweetly through the Staffordshire moorlands in a landscape as quintessentially English as a pack horse bridge across a sparkling stream. The Manifold meanders in its gorge and minor roads tumble down hills into the valley of the hamps. To the north again loom the Peak District moors, with their drystone walls and high, lonely inns. You can stop for traditional gingerbread in Ashbourne or a pudding made to a secret recipe in Bakewell.

The rolling Leicestershire countryside still echoes to the huntsman's horn of the Quorn and the Pytchley. North-east are the Lincolnshire Wolds that the young Tennyson knew, and the North Sea shore running down to the bird-haunted desolation of Gibraltar Point. The once impenetrable fen country lies open now, with its church towers and windmills, its sinuous rivers and straight, shining drainage cuts. Southwards are the Norfolk Broads. Otters disport themselves merrily at Earsham, while avocets amble and bitterns boom at Minsmere, on the way down the shingly Suffolk shore to Flatford Mill and the Constable country on the Essex border.

Left: *Pin Mill, Suffolk – old Thames barges and modern sailing boats on the Orwell Estuary*
Above: *Lincoln, Lincolnshire – medieval buildings by the Witham, in the city centre*

Where the tours start **page**

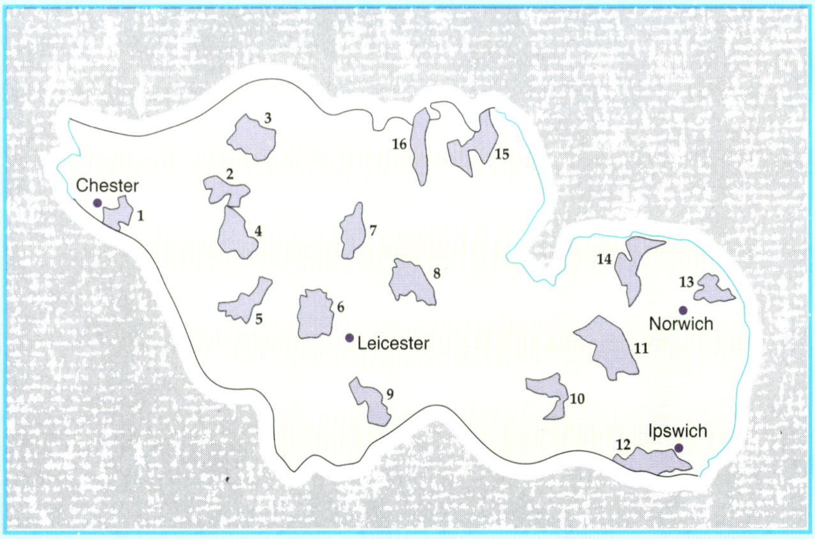

CHESHIRE'S DEESIDE

54 miles

From historic Chester, the River Dee flows south, passing through quiet Cheshire countryside where charming villages invite

exploration. The well-wooded Peckforton Hills are dotted with historic sites, and run north to the ancient Forest of Delamere.

The River Dee was once as important a seaway as the Mersey, and the foundation of Chester's fortune. Now largely a silted-up bywater used by pleasure boats and bird-watchers, it runs south between the Clwydian Range of Wales and the low, red Triassic sandstone ridge of the Peckforton Hills; the most prominent natural feature of central Cheshire.

Ancient fortifications, from Iron Age hillforts to the 13th-century Beeston Castle, stud the wooded heights, while below charming black-and-white 'magpie' villages built of the native rock and half-timbered, nestle close for shelter.

Further north, the ancient Forest of Delamere, once hunted by the Earls of Chester, is separated from the Peckforton ridge by the tiny River Gowy, whose course is followed by the Shropshire Union Canal. 'Meres', or lakes left by salt-mining subsidence, dot the rich pastoral landscape.

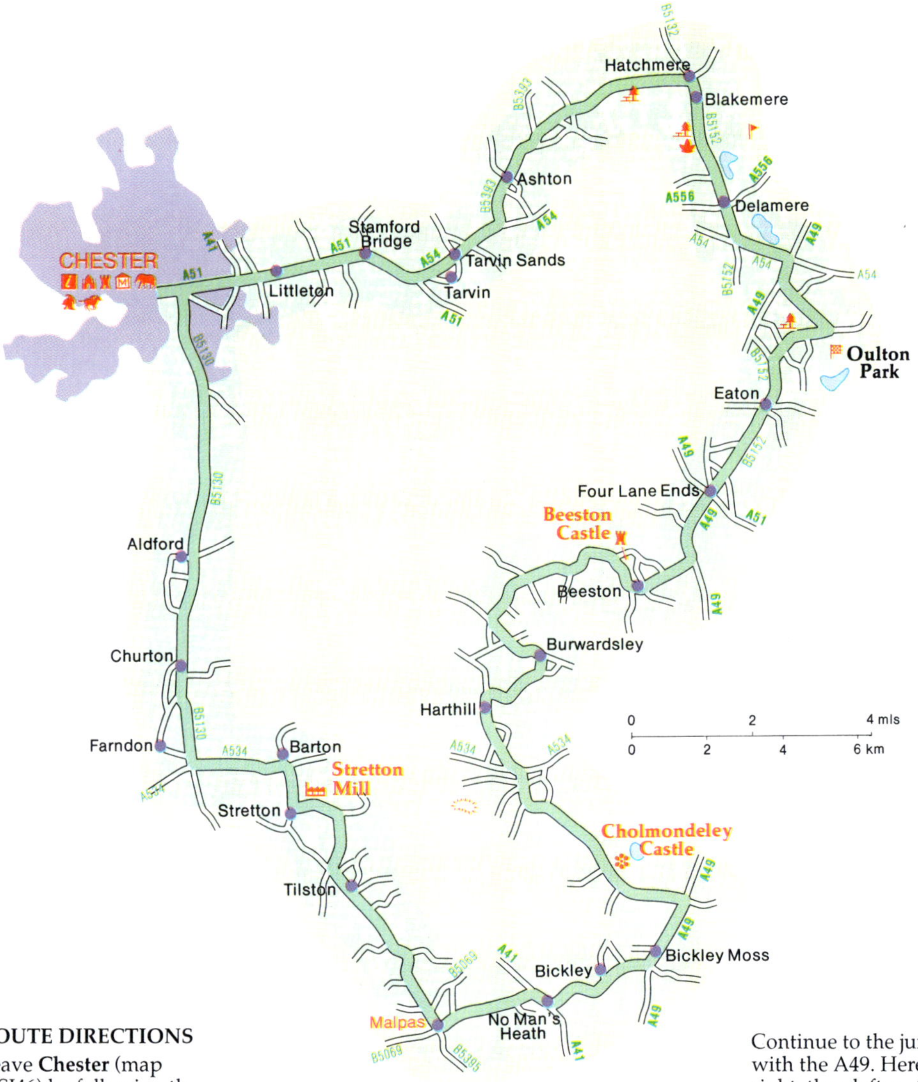

Malpas is a small town of half-timbered, box-framed 'magpie' houses and hilly streets set in rich farming country

ROUTE DIRECTIONS

Leave **Chester** (map 11SJ46) by following the Whitchurch road from the Ring Road. At the gyratory system follow the signs to Farndon to leave on the B5130. At Farndon, turn left on to the A534 (sp. Broxton). In $2\frac{1}{4}$ miles, at the edge of Barton, turn right, unclassified (sp. Tilston). After a further $\frac{3}{4}$ mile turn left on to a narrow by-road (sp. Stretton Water Mill). Pass **Stretton Mill**, keep forward and in $\frac{1}{2}$ mile turn right (sp. Tilston). At Tilston turn left (no sign) and continue to **Malpas**. From the market cross, turn left to No Man's Heath. Cross the A41 (sp. Bickley) and after 2 miles turn left on to the Warrington road, A49. In $1\frac{1}{4}$ miles turn left again, unclassified (sp. Bickerton). Pass the grounds of **Cholmondeley Castle** and continue, unclassified, for 2 miles. At the T-junction turn right, then at Bickerton church keep left (sp. Broxton). After $\frac{1}{4}$ mile cross the A534 to join the Harthill road. Pass the church and in $\frac{1}{4}$ mile turn right for Burwardsley. Continue for a further mile then turn right (sp. Beeston). In $2\frac{1}{2}$ miles, at the foot of the castle hill, bear right (sp. Peckforton), for the village of Beeston, passing **Beeston Castle**. At the end of the village keep left (sp. Tiverton) and in 1 mile further turn left on to the Warmington road, A49. Pass the edge of Tiverton and in $\frac{3}{4}$ mile go forward on to the B5152 (sp. Eaton). Continue through Eaton and in $\frac{3}{4}$ mile turn right, unclassified (sp. Oulton Park and Winsford). Pass the picnic site beside a small mere, and the entrance to Oulton Park Motor Racing Circuit, then turn sharp left (no sign). Continue to the junction with the A49. Here, turn right, then left on to the A54 (sp. Chester). One mile further, at the Fishpool Inn, turn right on to the Delamere Forest road, B5152. In $\frac{1}{2}$ mile cross the A556 (sp. Frodsham) then cross the railway bridge at Delamere Station to enter Delamere Forest. In 1 mile, at the crossroads, turn left, unclassified (no sign) and after $2\frac{1}{4}$ miles, go over the crossroads (sp. Tarvin). In $\frac{3}{4}$ mile turn left on to the B5393 (no sign) and pass through the village of Ashton. After $\frac{3}{4}$ mile turn right on to the A54 (sp. Chester). After skirting Tarvin, join the A51 for the return to Chester.

ON THE TOUR

Chester

Of all British cities, Chester has the finest complete set of walls, and the 2-mile walk around the ramparts of this ancient city on the Dee is not to be missed. King Charles I is said to have watched the defeat of his forces at the Battle of Rowton Moor in 1645 from the tower (now a museum) which takes his name.

First settled by the Romans, who knew it as Deva, Chester has a fascinating, continuous history, the story of which is comprehensively told in the Grosvenor Museum in Grosvenor Street, and the associated Castle Street Georgian House. The Chester Heritage Centre, in the former St Michael's Church, is another good interpretation centre. The red sandstone cathedral dates mainly from the 14th century, and was a Benedictine Abbey until its dissolution in 1540. The following year it became the cathedral for the newly created diocese of Chester. Don't miss Chester's unique galleried streets, known as The Rows, or the street market behind the Town Hall.

North of the city is one of the country's most famous, and best, zoos, noted for the spacious enclosures for its animals and its enlightened policies on endangered species. Extremely popular with children, there is literally something for everyone here, from delightful gardens to waterbus trips and a fascinating aquarium.

Stretton Mill

The name of this village gives a clue to its ancient history; it was on the Roman road north from Whitchurch to Chester. Today it is famous for its 17th-century water-powered corn mill, restored to working order by Cheshire County Council.

Malpas

A small town on the edge of the Peckforton Hills, Malpas has black and white half-timbered cottages, a row of almshouses and an interesting 14th-century parish church dedicated to St Oswald.

Cholmondeley Castle

A Gothic-style 18th-century `castle' (not open to the public) with romantically landscaped gardens (which are open) full of rhododendrons, a lakeside picnic area, and a collection of rare breeds of farm animals.

Beeston Castle

A landmark for miles around on its wooded crag, Beeston Castle was started by Ranulf de Blundeville in 1220, and further fortified against the Welsh by Edward I. Now in ruins, the castle has a small museum telling its history, but it is worth the visit for the view alone, which extends across eight counties to the Pennines in the east and westwards to the Welsh hills.

OUTDOOR ACTIVITIES

Delamere Forest

Originally the medieval hunting grounds of Mara and Mondrum, the 4,000 acres of modern Delamere Forest is managed by the Forestry Commission for the production of softwood timber. It is dotted with attractive meres, such as Hatchmere and Oak Mere, and there are miles of way-marked walks, with picnic areas at Linmere, Hatchmere and Barnesbridge Gates.

Chester's galleried streets, known as The Rows, date from the Middle Ages. Shops open on to balustraded walkways which are reached by steps from the road

Below: *handsome red-brick Erddig House, built in the 1680s*

OFF THE TOUR

Ellesmere Port Boat Museum

Take the M53 motorway from Chester city centre to junction 9, to reach this, the world's largest floating collection of canal craft – over 50 in number. This is a working museum at the junction of the Shropshire Union and Manchester Ship Canals, where you can re-live the days when the `The Cut' was king.

Dorfold Hall

Dorfold Hall, one mile west of Nantwich on the A534, is a privately-owned Jacobean country house, with beautiful plaster ceilings, a cobbled courtyard and attractive gardens.

Erdigg House

Turn westwards from Wrexham along the A534 to reach this handsome country house. The garden has been restored to its 18th-century design, and there are several domestic outbuildings in working order.

BUXTON AND THE WESTERN PEAK

47 miles

Bleak, high moors shelter secret, hidden valleys in the western fringe of the Peak District, where the counties of Derbyshire, Cheshire and Staffordshire meet. To the east of the spa town of Buxton, spectacular limestone dales cut through the White Peak plateau.

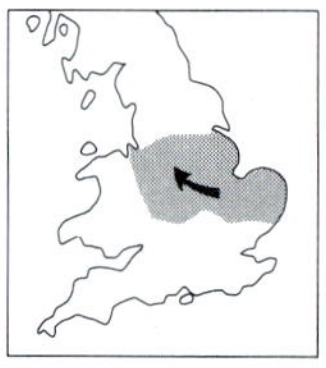

Buxton, perched in a fold of the Pennines at over 1,000ft, is one of the highest market towns in England. It is almost completely surrounded by the glorious scenery of the Peak National Park, although the town itself is excluded.

To the west, forbidding gritstone moors, purple with heather and golden with bracken, frown down, and are split by deeply-incised valleys, like the popular Goyt Valley, with its twin reservoirs and glorious displays of rhododendrons in early summer.

To the east of the A53 Leek road, the scenery changes dramatically from gritstone to limestone - Dark Peak to White Peak. The valley of the Upper Dove is less well-known than its lower reaches, but just as beautiful, while the Derbyshire Wye, which rises a few yards from the source of the Dove, boasts some of the finest limestone river scenery in Britain.

ON THE TOUR

Buxton

The Romans knew Buxton and its warm mineral springs as Aquae Arnemetiae, and the town enjoyed a period of high fashion in the 18th century, when the fifth Duke of Devonshire made it a spa which briefly rivalled Bath. He constructed the magnificent Crescent and the stables – now the Royal Devonshire Hospital – which has one of the largest unsupported domes in the world. Today, Buxton is the cultural capital of the Peak, with a superbly-restored Opera House which hosts an annual Arts Festival as well as numerous theatrical entertainments.

There are two Buxtons – Upper and Lower – and many attractions for the thousands who use the town as their holiday base to explore the Peak District. The museum has a fine collection of archaeological finds, and a fascinating display which takes you back in time to explore the Wonders of the Peak.

In St Anne's Well, opposite the Crescent, a warm spring still gushes from the ground at 28°C and the building now houses the Micrarium, an interesting insight into the world of microscopics.

Bollington

On the edge of ancient Macclesfield Forest and the hunting ground of the Earls of Chester, Bollington was originally a scattered group of medieval farmsteads which developed quickly in the early 19th century. St John's church was consecrated in 1834.

Rainow

The attractive, gritstone hillside village of Rainow, east of the bulky shape of Kerridge, is renowned for its 18th-century custom of having a `Mayor for the Day'. The unfortunate dignitary had to ride through the village sitting backwards on a donkey!

Wildboarclough

Formerly known as Crag, this charming hamlet nestling under the sharp peak of Shutlingsloe used to boast one of the most imposing sub Post Offices in Britain. It was housed in the Georgian offices of Crag Mill, which wove silk for the Great Exhibition of 1851. Wildboarclough suffered badly from a severe flood in 1989.

Flash

At 1,518ft, Flash claims to be the highest village in England, and the term `flash money' is thought to have come from the fact that the village was once famous for its production of counterfeit coins.

Longnor

The imposing Market Hall, complete with list of tolls, is now the home of a ceramic artist whose company delights in the name of Woodstringthistlefoss! Longnor, high on a ridge between the Dove and Manifold, is an ancient market centre, with a cobbled square and many delightful nooks and crannies.

Chelmorton

A one-street village which rises to the church of St John the Baptist on the slopes of Chelmorton Low, Chelmorton is famous for its regular pattern of limestone walls, which 'fossilise' medieval strip cultivations. The stream which runs through the centre of this attractive village is charmingly known as Illy Willy Water.

Lyme Park, home of the Legh family since Tudor times, is a large and imposing stone mansion set in a huge park. Stag hunting was the traditional occupation at Lyme and herds of deer still roam the parkland

OFF THE TOUR

Errwood Hall

Now in ruins, this was the ornate mansion of the Grimshawe family. It was demolished in the interests of water purity when the Errwood Reservoir was constructed in the valley below. The Grimshawes were great collectors of plants; the surrounding grounds are a blaze of colour when the rhododendrons and azaleas are in flower. A car park just off the route beside the Errwood Reservoir gives easy access.

Lyme Park

Palladian mansion of the Legh family, Lyme Park lies within a 1,300-acre deer park just off the A6 between Whaley Bridge and Stockport. The house contains Grinling Gibbons woodcarvings, Mortlake tapestries and a wonderful collection of clocks. Lyme is now in the hands of the National Trust and popular `living history' re-creations of Edwardian life, upstairs and downstairs, are regularly featured.

Miller's Dale and Chee Dale

Turn right off the A6, less than a mile from Taddington, towards Blackwell and the road descends sharply into the valley of the River Wye. The large car park at Miller's Dale is on the site of the old Midland line railway station, and the track is now converted to a pleasant walking route known as the Monsal Trail. It is a short step to the dramatic limestone buttresses of Chee Dale.

Part of the 23 acres of lovely public gardens at the Buxton Pavilion that was built in 1871. As well as admiring the plants, visitors can enjoy a swim in spa-water charged with nitrogen and carbon gas

ROUTE DIRECTIONS

Leave **Buxton** (map 11SK07) by following the signs to Leek, A53, then bear right on to the A5002 (sp. Whaley Bridge). *In 2 miles branch left, unclassified (sp. Goyt Valley). Descend to Errwood Reservoir Dam, continue to the T-junction and turn right (sp. Kettleshulme). Make a long ascent and at the summit turn right (sp. Whaley Bridge) for Kettleshulme. At the T-junction turn left on to the B5470 (sp. Macclesfield) and in 1¼ miles, at the top of the ascent (1 in 10), turn right, unclassified to Port Shrigley. At the church turn left (sp. Bollington) and in ¼ mile bear right into **Bollington**. Here, branch left into Church Street then, at the Crown bear right and ascend. At the top, bear right into Chancery Lane, and at the next T-junction turn left. In ¼ mile turn left into Redway. Ascend, bear right and in 1 mile branch left into Lidgetts Lane. Descend to the T-junction and turn left on to the B5470 (not signed) and pass **Rainow**. Take the next turning right, unclassified (sp. Buxton) and in ½ mile, at the T-junction, turn left on to the A537 (not signed). Pass the Setter Dog and the road to Teggs Nose Country Park then, in 1½ miles at the crossroads, turn right, unclassified (sp. Wildboarclough), to **Wildboarclough**. After ¾ mile turn right then, in 1 mile, bear left (sp. Wincle). Half a mile further, at the crossroads, turn left on to the A54 (sp. Buxton). Pass the Rose and Crown and turn right, unclassified (sp. Quornford). In 2 miles go forward (sp. Flash). At **Flash** go forward and in ⅓ mile, at the T-junction, turn left on to the A53 (sp. Buxton). In ¼ mile turn right, unclassified (sp. Longnor). At the edge of **Longnor** turn left on to the B5033 (sp. Buxton) and in ⅓ mile descend (1 in 7). After a further 2½ miles, at the T-junction, turn right on to the A515, then left on to the A5270 (sp. Bakewell). In 1 mile branch right, unclassified (sp. Chelmorton) to pass **Chelmorton**. Keep forward for 3¼ miles then, at the crossroads, turn left for Taddington. Here, turn left (sp. Buxton) and in ⅓ mile, at the T-junction, turn left again on to the A6 (not signed). Enter the Wye Dale and return to Buxton.

**NB*. When the Goyt Valley is closed, continue with the A5002 for 5 miles to Horwich End, then turn left on to the B5470 to reach Kettleshulme.

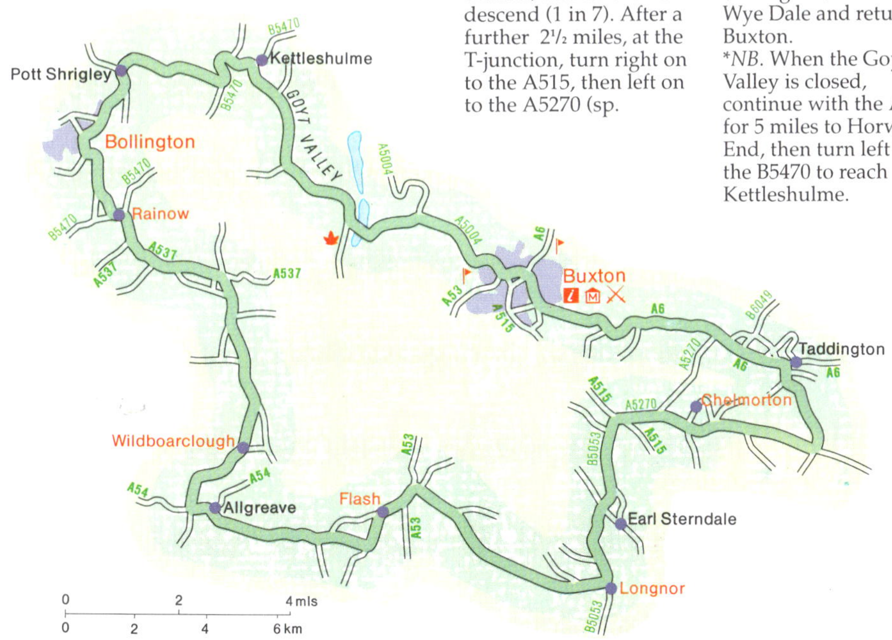

OFF THE BEATEN TRACK

Macclesfield Forest Chapel

This tiny remote building high in the hills west of the A537 - Wildboarclough road, is the scene of an annual rush-bearing ceremony, when rushes are strewn in the aisles in lieu of carpets.

OUTDOOR ACTIVITIES

Upper Dove Valley

A paradise for walkers, geologists and lovers of spectacular scenery, with sharply-pointed reef limestone summits like Chrome and Parkhouse Hills. The best starting point is Longnor, where good paths lead into the hills, or Earl Sterndale, just off the tour.

NORTHERN MOORS OF THE PEAK

49 miles

Few roads cross the highest and wildest moors of the Peak where, despite the fact that you are less than 20 miles from the centres of Manchester or Sheffield, you enter the nearest thing to a wilderness in England. Industrial mill towns fringe the moors, and peaceful reservoirs flood many valleys.

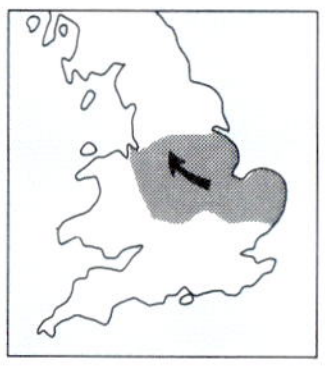

Kinder Scout and Bleaklow only just top the 2,000ft mark as the highest points of the Peak District; but make no mistake, these peat-covered plateaux are real mountains, and a severe first-day challenge to those hardy souls setting out on the 250-mile Pennine Way long-distance path from Edale.

The Snake Pass, well-known to anyone who listens to road reports in winter, threads between these two hills, reaching over 1,600ft in the process. At the foot of the Snake the cul-de-sac valley of the Upper Derwent winds towards Bleaklow, flooded by the triple reservoirs of Howden, Derwent and Ladybower.

To the west, the industrial town of Glossop stands at the foot of Longendale, while to the north you enter Last of the Summer Wine *country around Holmfirth. The Strines road marks the eastern limit of these high moors, where a cluster of tiny villages reach up from the Don Valley and Sheffield.*

ON THE TOUR

Glossop

Glossop is largely a planned town of the early 19th century; created to the blueprint of the Lord of the Manor, the 11th Duke of Norfolk. Originally known as Howard Town (after the family name), Glossop expanded rapidly from its ancient heart – now known as Old Glossop – which still has many 17th-century cottages and a quiet, village-like air.

By the early 1880s, Howard Town had outgrown its aristocratic masterplan, and more than 30 mills were producing cotton goods for the colonies. It was said that each mill owner built a mill, a church and a school in Glossop; certainly by the end of Victoria's reign, there were 21 chapels in the town!

Today, Glossop surprisingly retains an air of dignity, with good municipal buildings and spacious squares – and the Duke of Norfolk's lion still stands proudly over the entrance to the station.

Torside

A Peak National Park information centre overlooks Torside Reservoir and its colourful yachts, on the Devil's Elbow road from Glossop. Interpretive displays tell the story of the Longdendale Valley; flooded by a string of five reservoirs which, at the time of their building (1848 to 1875), were the greatest man-made expanse of water in the world.

Holme Moss and Holme

The 725ft needle mast of the Holme Moss television transmission station – one of the largest in the country – is a familiar sight on these bleak and inhospitable moors and a landmark for many miles around. The tiny hillside village of Holme clusters on the side of the valley of the Rake Dike, and the solid, gritstone cottages are well equipped to face the ravages of the Pennine winters.

Holmfirth

If the reservoir-dotted landscapes around here seem familiar, it's because they have become known to millions of television viewers through the long-running series *Last of the Summer Wine*. Wandering round the charming mill town of Holmfirth, you can visit Sid's Cafe, see Nora Batty's house, and you almost expect you might bump into Foggy, Clegg or Compo. Holmfirth rivalled Hollywood as a centre for moving pictures in the years before the First World War, and it is still the home of the world-famous picture postcard firm of Bamforths.

Langsett

Situated in an important junction of ancient packhorse routes, Langsett is a popular week-end resort of Sheffielders. The crenellated design of the valve tower on the nearby reservoir was based on that of Lancaster Castle. The village has a youth hostel and Peak National Park information centre.

Ladybower Reservoir

This is the biggest of the three reservoirs which flood the Upper Derwent Valley and was officially opened by King George VI in 1945. As the A57 crosses the southern arm of the huge reservoir, it passes over the site of the village of Ashopton, which was depopulated as the waters rose.

Snake Pass

This is the highest and wildest road in the Peak, rising to over 1,600ft at Snake Summit, where the Pennine Way crosses between Kinder Scout and Bleaklow. The road is a 19th-century turnpike constructed by Thomas Telford, and it takes its name from the Snake Inn, which in turn is named after the figure in the coat of arms of the Duke of Devonshire.

Derwent dam, Derbyshire. When the winding valley of the Upper Derwent was flooded by the three reservoirs of Howden, Derwent and Ladybower, two villages were engulfed and the surrounding countryside was transformed into an attractive panorama of lakeland and coniferous forest

OFF THE TOUR

Melandra Castle Roman Fort

Turn left off the A57 Glossop-Hyde road and onto the A626 Marple road to reach the huge Gamesley housing estate where, somewhat incongruously, you will find one of the most important Roman Forts in the Peak. Built to command the Longdendale Valley, Melandra covered 19 acres and was occupied until AD140.

Dinting Railway Centre

One mile west of Glossop off the A57 is the Dinting Railway Centre, where the heady whiff of nostalgia is carried in the steam of the working locomotives. Nearby, the impressive five-arched Dinting viaduct carries the line over Dinting Vale.

Bradfield

This superbly sited gritstone village is just east of the Strines road and stands in a commanding position above the Loxley Valley. The Church of St Nicholas is one of the grandest in all Peakland, with splendid views towards the Agden and Damflask Reservoirs.

Derwent Dams

Turn north off the A57 Snake Road to enter the valley of the Upper Derwent, which has been dammed three times to create an unnatural but not unlovely landscape of reservoirs and coniferous forest. The villages of Derwent and Ashopton disappeared under the rising waters, and the valley was later used by the Dambusters practising for their wartime raids.

ROUTE DIRECTIONS

Leave **Glossop** (map 11SK09) following the signs to Barnsley via Woodhead on the B6105; passing **Torside**, a Peak National Park Information Centre. In 5½ miles, at the T-junction, turn right on to the A628 (sp. Barnsley), then after a further ½ mile turn left on to the A6024 (sp. Holmfirth). Ascend (1 in 8) to **Holme Moss Summit** then descend to **Holme** and Holmbridge. After 1½ miles beyond Holmbridge church, at the traffic signals, turn right on to the A635 to enter **Holmfirth**. Leave by crossing the river bridge, and immediately branching right on to the B6106 (not signed). In 1 mile bear right (sp. Penistone). In 4⅓ miles, at the crossroads, turn right on to the A616 (not signed). At the Flouch Inn go over the crossroads (sp. Sheffield) to **Langsett**. Then in 1¾ miles, at the crossroads, turn right, unclassified (sp. Bradfield) for Midhopestones. Continue forward and follow the signs for Strines and Derwent Valley to Strines Inn. After a further 2 miles, at the T-junction, turn right on to the A57 (sp. Glossop, Manchester via Snake Pass) and pass **Ladybower Reservoir**.

Continue on the A57 **Snake Pass**, beyond the Snake Pass Inn, to the summit, and on for the return to Glossop.

The view towards Derwent Dale from Over Owler Tor near Hathersage (south of the tour). This sturdy Peak District village was the inspiration for 'Morton' in Charlotte Brontë's Jane Eyre. *Robin Hood's friend Little John is said to be buried in a 14ft grave in the churchyard*

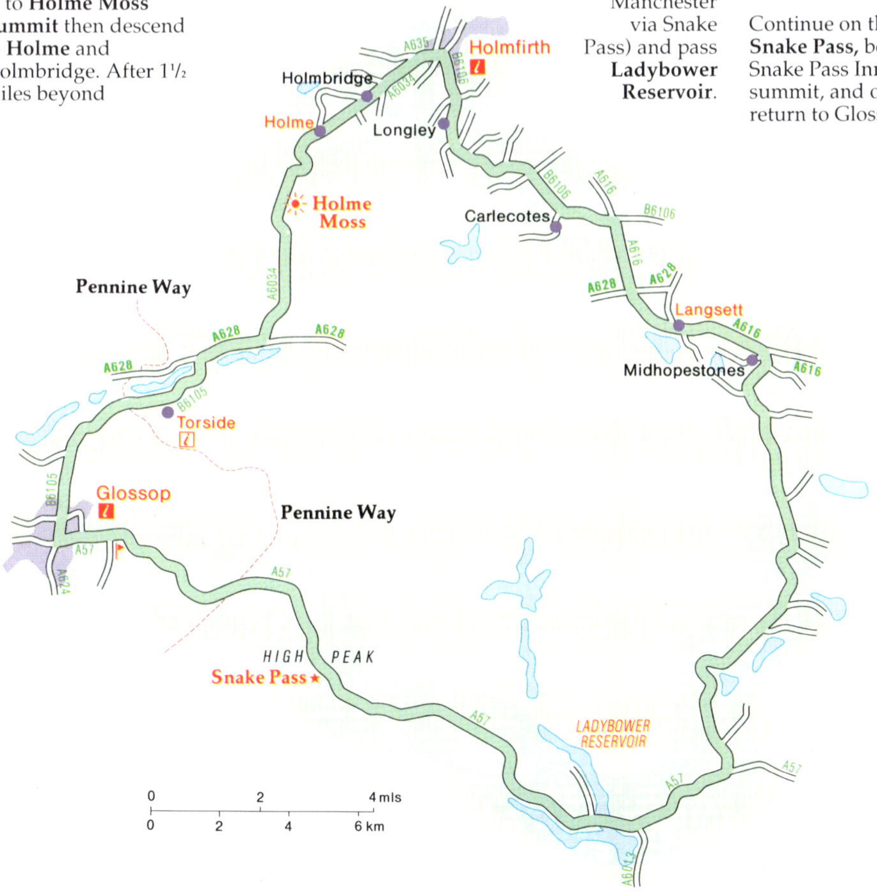

OUTDOOR ACTIVITIES

Pennine Way

This gruelling, 250-mile route runs up the spine of the Pennines from Edale to Kirk Yetholm just across the Scottish Border. It was the brainchild of the late Tom Stephenson, and is recognised as the hardest long-distance walk in Britain. It should only be attempted by experienced and fit walkers.

Doctor's Gate

Linking Glossop to the Derwent Valley, this ancient track was named after Dr John Talbot of Glossop, who may have paid for the original Roman route to be paved.

STAFFORDSHIRE PEAK AND PLAINS

55 miles

North and west of Ashbourne lies the Staffordshire part of the Peak District, less well-known than its Derbyshire counterpart but equally beautiful. One bank

of far-famed Dovedale lies within this under-rated county, and the towns and villages on the edge of the hills are full of interest.

Ashbourne is known as the Gateway to Dovedale and is a favourite centre for exploring this beautiful valley, first made famous by Izaac Walton and Charles Cotton in The Compleat Angler. *Ashbourne is also convenient for the equally lovely Manifold Valley, and the rest of the limestone White Peak country. Quiet country lanes lead west to the rich, dairying country of north Staffordshire, and the lovely wooded Churnet Valley.*

Further north lies the ancient silk-weaving and dyeing town of Leek, one of the most southerly of the northern industrial towns. North of Leek is some of the most dramatic gritstone scenery in the Peak National Park; with challenging outcrops like the Roaches, Hen Cloud and Ramshaw Rocks enticing the rock-climbing tigers, and bleak, sepia moorlands stretching to the horizon.

ON THE TOUR

Ashbourne

Ashbourne has been described as the most perfect Georgian town in Derbyshire, and its long main street leading up to the sloping market place has many fine examples of town houses. Walking in the other direction, you enter Church Street, with the beautiful Tudor mullions of Queen Elizabeth's Grammar School on your right.

The Parish Church of St Oswald's is an elegant building with a shapely, 212ft spire, but perhaps it is most famous for its touching memorials to the Cokayne and Boothby families, particularly that created by Thomas Banks to Penelope Boothby, who died in 1791 aged five.

Ashbourne is also famous for its Shrove Tuesday Football Game, which takes over the entire town as the opposing teams attempt to score goals which are 3 miles apart!

Nineteenth-century Ilam Hall, now the property of the National Trust, was partly demolished 60 years ago but today serves as a popular youth hostel. The village of Ilam is a favourite starting point for walkers

Mayfield

Just over Hanging Bridge – so called because some of Bonnie Prince Charlie's Scottish rebels were hanged there in 1745 – as you leave Ashbourne, is the village of Mayfield. This was the home of the Irish poet, Thomas Moore, who wrote the oriental romance *Lalla Rookh* while living there.

Alton Towers

Former estate of the Earls of Shrewsbury and set in 500 acres of beautifully wooded grounds, Alton Towers is now much better known as the biggest pleasure park in Europe. Attractions among the 125 rides include the Corkscrew, Log Flume and fearsome Black Hole, which are guaranteed to turn anyone's stomach. But there are many other, more gentle attractions, including a children's farmyard, a 3D cinema, boat rides and an aerial monorail.

Cheddleton Flint Mill Museum

Two restored red brick watermills straddle the River Churnet at Cheddleton. They once ground flint for the pottery industry of Stoke-on-Trent, and are now open to the public during summer weekends. Nearby is the Cheddleton Railway Centre, complete with Victorian station and steam loco's.

Leek

Often described as `The Queen of the Moorlands', Leek is an important centre for the surrounding countryside, with weekly cattle and street markets on Wednesdays. Its modern importance was founded on silk products and dyes, now largely superceded by synthetic fabrics. Modern industry still uses the old mill buildings and the old water-powered corn mill in Mill Street, which was built by the famous canal builder James Brindley in 1752, has recently been restored to working order. A museum illustrates mill-wrighting, and tells the story of this brilliant, though illiterate, engineer.

Wetton

An ancient settlement high above the Manifold Valley, Wetton is a convenient place to explore the numerous caves and crags which punctuate its length. The church has an unusual exterior staircase to the belfry.

Ilam

A strangely spick and span estate village which bears little resemblance to Peak District vernacular architecture, modern Ilam is the creation of Jesse Watts Russell who lived at the Hall. The elegant `Eleanor' Cross was built in 1840 in memory of Mrs Watts Russell. The Victorian Gothic Hall, now in the hands of the National Trust, was partly pulled down in the 1930s, but still serves as a youth hostel.

ROUTE DIRECTIONS

Leave **Ashbourne** (map 11SK14) on the A52 (sp. Stoke) and after $1\frac{1}{2}$ miles at the Queen's Arms, **Mayfield**, turn left onto the B5032 (sp. Uttoxeter) to Ellastone. Here, bear left then in 1 mile branch right (sp. Denstone, Alton). At Denstone, bear right and in $1\frac{3}{4}$ miles turn right, unclassified (sp. Alton, Farley) at Alton. Here bear left and descend (1 in 10) to cross the Churnet Valley. At the entrance to **Alton Towers** bear left and continue to Farley. In 1 mile, at the crossroads, turn right (sp. Ashbourne A52). Ascend and in 1 mile, at the crossroads, turn left, unclassified (sp. Winkhill, Leek). In 1 mile at the crossroads, turn left on to the A52 (sp. Stoke) and pass the Green Man. Continue through Whiston and on to Froghall, and Kingsley. At Kingsley bear right and in $1\frac{1}{2}$ miles, at the T-junction, turn right. In $1\frac{1}{4}$ miles further branch right on to the A522 (sp. Wetley Rocks). At Wetley Rocks turn right on to the A520 (sp. Leek). Continue through Cheddleton and past the **Cheddleton Flint Mill Museum**. After a further 3 miles, at the traffic signals, turn right on to the A53 (sp. Buxton) and enter **Leek**. At the roundabout take 2nd exit into Ball Haye Street then , at the traffic signals, turn right (sp. Buxton). After 3 miles turn left, unclassified (sp. Upperhulme), then shortly branch left and keep left. After $2\frac{1}{2}$ miles keep forward at two gates and in 2 miles keep left, then at the T-junction keep right for another $\frac{1}{2}$ mile to cross the main road. In 1 mile bear right (sp. Leek, Bottomhouses) and after another mile branch left (no signs). In $\frac{1}{2}$ mile, at the T-junction turn left (sp. Warslow) and after $1\frac{1}{2}$ miles bear right into Warslow. In $\frac{1}{4}$ mile, at the T-junction, turn left on to the B5053 (sp. Longnor, Buxton). Take the next right, unclassified (sp. Manifold Valley) and in $\frac{1}{4}$ mile turn right again, descend to the T-junction and turn right. In $\frac{1}{2}$ mile, cross the river bridge and turn right (sp. Wetton) then turn immediate left through the tunnel. In $1\frac{1}{2}$ miles keep ahead, then in $\frac{1}{3}$ mile bear left and ascend (1 in 7). At the top keep forward (sp. Alstonefield) into **Wetton**. Bear right, and at the end of the village, branch right (no sign). In $\frac{1}{2}$ mile, at the crossroads, turn left and descend. In $\frac{1}{4}$ mile further go forward, then turn right (sp. Dovedale, Ilam). At **Ilam**, turn left (no sign), pass Dovedale Car Park on the left and continue forward for the return to Ashbourne.

OFF THE TOUR

Foxfield Light Railway

Turn left off the A52 at Blakeley Lane towards Dilhorne, where a lovingly-preserved collection of steam locomotives and rolling stock give leisurely, 5-mile rides into the Staffordshire countryside on summer Sundays and Bank Holiday weekends.

The Roaches and Hen Cloud

The tour encircles this impressive gritstone outcrop, north of Leek, off the A53. There are a number of convenient lay-bys and parking places where paths lead up and you can stop and stretch your legs to enjoy some of the finest viewpoints in the Peak. It's an easy stroll to reach the crest of the Roaches, and the view west extends across the Cheshire Plain to the distant Mersey.

Thor's Cave

This enormous, gaping hole in an imposing limestone cliff 300ft above the River Manifold is an easy stroll by well-marked footpaths from Wetton. It really is the archetypal caveman's dwelling (prehistoric remains have been found there), and the stiff climb up from the Manifold track is well worth the effort.

OUTDOOR ACTIVITIES

Churnet Valley

The industrial village of Froghall is a good centre from which to explore the beautiful and peaceful waters of the Caldon Canal, which threads its way through the lovely Churnet Valley.

Dovedale

Perhaps the most famous dale of all, Dovedale is best avoided on summer weekends, when the path up from the famous Stepping Stones can be unpleasantly crowded. Much work has been done on the main path in recent years, and it is now possible to walk the length of the dale to Milldale and keep your feet dry.

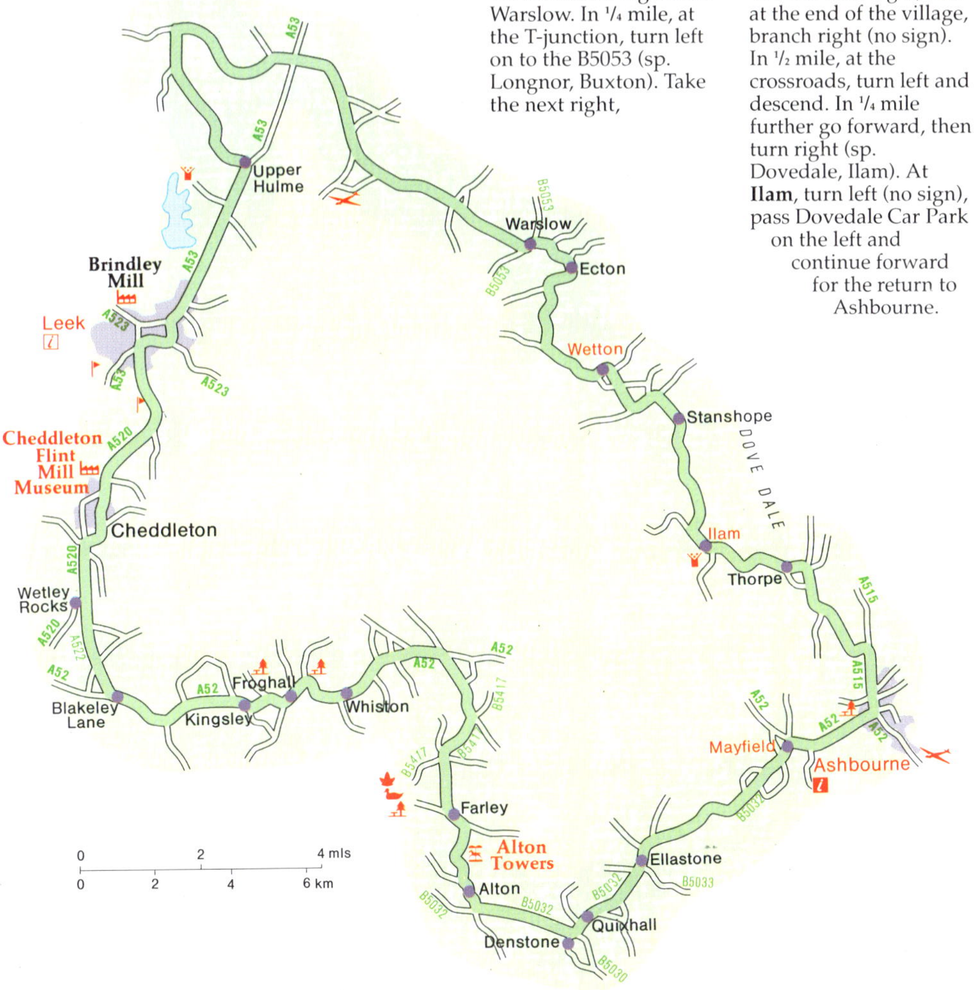

Below: *the River Dee as seen from the Dove Holes, one of the caves in Dovedale's rocks. Dovedale itself is a lovely twisting limestone gorge in the gentler, southern part of the Peak National Park*

Bottom: *away from the fun of Alton Towers pleasure park there is the quieter delight of 600 acres of trees and flowering shrubs, interspersed with lakes and fountains that surround the 19th-century mansion*

STAFFORDSHIRE FOREST AND CHASE

59 1/2 miles

North of the cathedral city of Lichfield, the ancient hunting grounds of Needwood Forest and Cannock Chase provided sport for medieval kings and nobles. Today, those

wildernesses are tamed under rich farming country or extensive forestry plantations, but they still provide a vital `lung' for the industrial parts of the county.

Lovely, unspoilt villages, stately country mansions, and unrivalled recreational opportunities in the Cannock Chase Area of Outstanding Natural Beauty - all these are not usually associated with industrial Staffordshire.

However, there is much more to Staffordshire than the Black Country and the Potteries. Our tour takes us deep into unexplored country, through villages where ancient customs still survive. To a castle where a queen was imprisoned, through the ancient Forest of Needwood, and past the heathlands and forest rides of Cannock Chase; rich in wildlife, and inviting the active visitor to further exploration.

We start from the proud cathedral city of Lichfield, whose three spires so dominate the landscape that they are known locally as `the Ladies of the Vale.'

ON THE TOUR

Lichfield

The three lovely red sandstone spires of the cathedral, best seen from across the still waters of the 17-acre Stowe Pool, mark a spot first consecrated by St Chad. The present cathedral, standing in a quiet close, is an outstanding example of Early English and Decorated architecture with a magnificent, restored west front.
Lichfield was the birthplace of Dr Samuel Johnson, and his home in Breadmarket Street is now a museum devoted to his life and works. His statue stands in the busy cobbled Market Place, beside that of his biographer, James Boswell.

Tutbury

A pleasant little town on the banks of the River Dove, with a wealth of Tudor and Georgian houses and a magnificent half-timbered inn, the Dog and Partridge. The priory church, which was built in 1100, has splendid Norman arcades, clerestory and triforium, and is without doubt one of the finest Norman churches in the Midlands. Towering above the town is John of Gaunt's castle ruined by Parliamentary forces in the Civil War, but retaining a dignified presence. Mary Queen of Scots was an enforced visitor on several occasions, and held captive in the High Tower.

Magnificent 17th-century Sudbury Hall is remarkable for its fine state of preservation, but the apartments look out over beautiful gardens that have changed a great deal over the centuries

Sudbury Hall

The pretty red brick village of Sudbury is perhaps best-known for its magnificent Charles II Hall, now in the hands of the National Trust. This former home of the Vernon family is sumptuously decorated, and now contains a fascinating Museum of Childhood, with old toys and reconstructed classrooms.

Abbots Bromley

A black and white, half-timbered village clustered around an ancient Butter Cross. The village is famous for its annual Horn Dance performed every September, which is perhaps an echo of a pagan hunting dance. Nearby is Blithfield Hall, ancient home of the Bagot family and their black and white wild goats, and the extensive Blithfield Reservoir.

Shugborough Hall

Eighteenth-century seat of the Earl of Lichfield, Shugborough (National Trust) now also houses the Staffordshire County Museum, in the servants' quarters, with a fascinating insight into life `downstairs.' A working Rare Breeds Farm and restored corn mill are included in the extensive parklands, which are dotted with neo-classical monuments. Walks and trails are organised through the estate throughout the summer, so there is plenty to do for all the family.

Cannock Chase

Cannock Chase was originally the Royal Forest of Cannock, hunted by Norman kings, before it passed to the Bishop of Lichfield in 1290 and became Cannock Chase. Today it is an Area of Outstanding Natural Beauty and, with about 6,000 acres planted with conifers by the Forestry Commission, has reverted to the generally-accepted definition of a forest. Herds of fallow deer frequent the dense forest, and Staffordshire County Council have provided car parks, trails and an information centre at Milford, where the history and wildlife of the Chase is explained. The Forestry Commission has provided a Wildlife and Forest Centre south west of Rugeley on the Penkridge Road.

OFF THE TOUR

Hanch Hall

Originally the seat of the Aston family, the present mansion exhibits architecture from Tudor times through to the Georgian period. Hanch Hall is 4 miles north of Lichfield on the B5014.

Bass Museum of Brewing

Burton is the home of brewing, and this fascinating museum celebrates 7,000 years of ales and beers with a reconstruction of an Edwardian bar and a display of pumping engines. Burton is also the home of the prize-winning Bass Shire horse teams. Turn right on the B5017 beyond Rangemore to Burton. The museum is next to the Bass Brewery.

Wall Roman Site

Go south from Lichfield on the A5127, and turn right just before reaching the A5 for these remains of a Roman posting station (Letocetum) on the line of Watling Street. There is a small museum of finds.

The calm waters of Stowe Pool reflect Lichfield Cathedral's graceful sandstone spires, known as 'the ladies of the vale'. The largest was destroyed by Cromwell's men during the Civil War, and later rebuilt

ROUTE DIRECTIONS

Leave **Lichfield** (map 7SK10) on the A51 (sp. Stone). In $1\frac{3}{4}$ miles, at the roundabout, take the A515 (sp. Ashbourne) and continue to King's Bromley and Yoxall. Here, turn right on to the B5016 (sp. Barton-under-Needwood). In 2 miles, at the Top Bell, turn left, unclassified (sp. Tutbury). After $3\frac{1}{4}$ miles further go over the crossroads to **Tutbury**. Here, go forward into High Street (sp. Uttoxeter) and at the roundabout join the A50 continuing forward. At the end of the town cross the River Dove and in 2 miles, at the trunk road, turn left. After $3\frac{1}{3}$ miles at Sudbury turn left on to the A515 (sp. Lichfield) to pass **Sudbury Hall**. Continue through Draycott in the Clay, ascend, and in $\frac{1}{2}$ mile at the crossroads, turn right, unclassified (sp. Newborough). At Newborough go over the staggered crossroads (sp. Yoxall, Hoar Cross) to Hoar Cross. Here, at the crossroads, turn right (sp. Abbots Bromley). In $2\frac{1}{4}$ miles join the B5234 (not signed). After a further mile turn right on to the B5014 into **Abbots Bromley**. Continue with Uttoxeter signs and in $\frac{3}{4}$ mile turn left on to the B5013 (sp. Rugeley). In $2\frac{1}{2}$ miles turn right, unclassified, into Bellamoar Lane (sp. Leisure Drive). Continue for $1\frac{1}{2}$ miles, then, at the crossroads turn left (sp. Stafford). At the trunk road turn left on to the A51, cross the River Trent and, at the roundabout, turn right on to the A513 (sp. Stafford). Continue, past **Shugborough Hall** on the right, to Milford. Here turn left, unclassified (sp. Brocton) to pass through Brocton. Continue forward (sp. Stafford). In $\frac{1}{2}$ mile turn left on to the A34 (sp. Cannock) then, in $\frac{1}{3}$ mile turn left, unclassified (sp. Hednesford). Ascend through Cannock Chase German Military Cemetary and, at the crossroads, turn left (sp. Rugeley). In 1 mile pass **Cannock Chase** Visitor Centre. Continue past the forest centre and museum then turn right into Post Office Lane (no sign). At the end turn right and pass The Horns and continue to the trunk road. Here, turn left on to the A460 (no sign). In $\frac{3}{4}$ mile turn right, unclassified (sp. Upper Longdon). Ascend and in $1\frac{1}{3}$ miles go over the crossroads into Startley Lane. Continue to ascend to Upper Longdon and in $\frac{1}{2}$ mile turn right on to the A51 (no sign) and return to Lichfield.

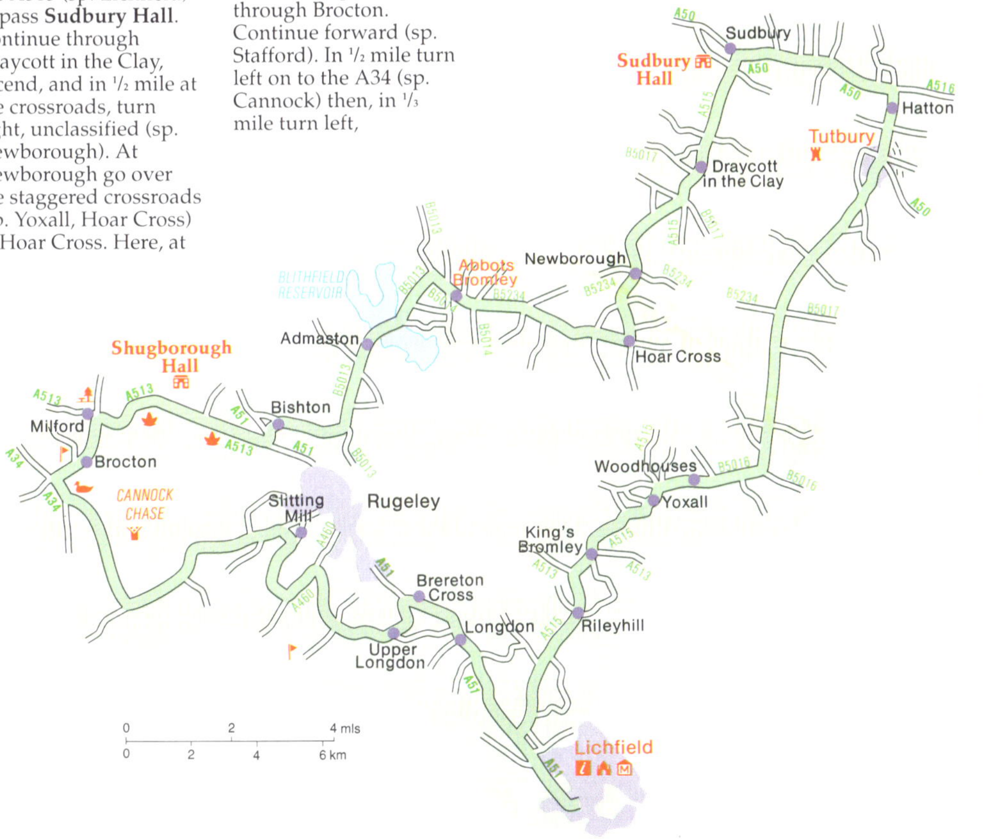

OUTDOOR ACTIVITIES

Blithfield Reservoir

Bring your binoculars, for Blithfield Reservoir is one of the best bird-watching sites in the West Midlands, with impressive species lists of visiting migrants each year. The Reservoir can be found just south west of Abbots Bromley.

Cannock Chase

Active visitors will want to explore the many trails which lead into the forest for glimpses of the wildlife which include fallow deer, red squirrels and woodland birds such as crossbills and nightjars.

LEICESTERSHIRE'S UPLANDS

56 1/4 miles

Threaded by the M1 Motorway, this unheralded part of north Leicestershire is often ignored by the visitor. Yet, off the beaten track, there are lovely views, craggy outcrops, and fascinating villages where the long history of the area is never far below the surface.

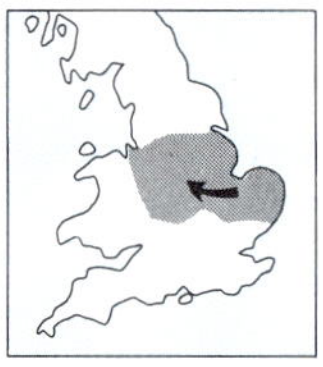

Some of the oldest rocks in Britain outcrop in the splintered crags of Charnwood Forest, north-west of Leicester. Geologists know these multi-coloured slates as pre-Cambrian, and they date from the very dawn of life on the planet; a staggering 500 million years ago!

Country parks such as those at Bradgate and Beacon Hill make these airy uplands accessible to the visitor and command breathtaking views across the rich Quorn fox-hunting country of this part of the county. Many of the woodlands, spinneys and coverts which add so much to the quality of this countryside have been created and maintained purely to encourage the quarry of the Quorn.

Further west lie the ancient market town of Ashby-de-la-Zouch, and the well-interpreted Battlefield of Bosworth, where the Plantagenet dynasty gave way to the Tudors, and the course of English history was changed.

ON THE TOUR

Ashby-de-la-Zouch

The town's unusual name was adopted to honour a local land-owning family and to differentiate this Ashby from the many others in the district. Mentioned by Sir Walter Scott in *Invanhoe*, Ashby Castle is on the site of a Norman stronghold, but the present ruins are mainly 15th century, 'slighted' by Parliamentary forces during the Civil War. St Helen's Parish Church has an unusual 300-year-old finger pillory, designed to punish miscreants in church services, including anyone who interrupted the sermon!

Calke Park and Abbey

Untouched by the Harpur-Crewe family for 100 years, Baroque Calke Abbey became a time-capsule, with everything left just as it was before the National Trust took over its administration. The cluttered, magpie-style collections of natural history exhibits, caricatures and Victoriana are amazing. Admission is by timed ticket, so be prepared to wait. The Park is open to visitors during the hours of daylight.

Ruined Ashby-de-la-Zouch Castle stands behind the main street. This Royalist stronghold was besieged for 15 months during the Civil War

Melbourne Hall

Former home of Victoria's prime minister, Lord Melbourne, Melbourne Hall boasts one of the most famous formal gardens in Britain. The house itself contains important works of art, and the Melbourne Crafts Centre is also well worth a visit.

Beacon Hill Country Park

Spectacular views over the immeasurably-old landscape of Charnwood Forest can be had from the 800ft summit of Beacon Hill, once an Iron Age stronghold.

Bradgate Country Park

Over 850 acres of natural parkland, and woodland – where herds of red and fallow deer roam – can be enjoyed here. The ruins of Bradgate House, birthplace of Lady Jane Grey, are open during the summer.

Market Bosworth

A pleasant, stone-built market town with a mainly 14th-century church featuring many memorials to the Dixie family. The town's light railway operates to Shackerstone, 5 miles to the north-west, where there is a railway museum and rolling stock.

OFF THE TOUR

Breedon-on-the-Hill

A landmark for miles around, Breedon Hill is the site of an Iron Age hillfort, gradually being eaten away by a quarry in its side. The village which nestles below the hill has a circular lock-up, and an interesting hilltop church with a fine collection of Saxon sculptures, which probably came from an earlier monastery. Breedon is on the A453 Ashby road.

Donington Motor Museum

The world's largest collection of Grand Prix racing cars traces the history of the sport from pre-war times to the present day, in this comprehensive museum, adjacent to the Donington Park Racing Circuit. Take the minor road from Isley Walton.
This area also houses the East Midlands Airport Aeropark. As well as close-up views of aircraft taking off and landing, the Aeropark offers the opportunity to walk around full-scale aircraft and exhibits, with explanations of how the airport works. A fascinating place for children.

Cadeby Light Railway

One of the smallest working narrow gauge railways in Britain, this offers steam train rides amongst its attractions. Check opening times on (0455) 290462. South of B585 on A447.

Bosworth Battlefield Centre

The final, conclusive battle of the War of the Roses was fought here in 1485, when the future Henry VII defeated Richard III and founded the Tudor dynasty. The visitor centre, based in a red brick farmhouse, provides the most comprehensive interpretation of any battle site in England, with battlefield trails and special events in the season. One mile south of Market Bosworth on a minor road.

Twycross Zoo

Home of the 'PG' chimps, Twycross Zoo has one of the finest collections of gorillas, orang-utans, gibbons and chimpanzees in Britain. There are many other animals and attractions too. Continue on the A444 at Twycross to reach the Zoo.

ROUTE DIRECTIONS

Leave **Ashby-de-la-Zouch** (map 8SK31) by following the signs to Burton, then Ticknall, on the B5006. In 4¾ miles turn right on to the A514 into Ticknall. At the end of the village, the nearside of the bridge, turn right, unclassified (no sign) and enter **Calke Park**. Continue for 1 mile, then bear left on the B587 towards Stanton by Bridge. After ¾ mile turn right, unclassified, to Melbourne. Turn right (sp. Wilson) and pass **Melbourne Hall** on the right. At Wilson turn left (sp. Castle Donington). After ¾ mile further turn left on to the A453, pass the turn to Castle Donington and in 1 mile turn right on to the B5401 (sp. Hathern) for Diseworth. Continue to Long Whatton, then turn right, unclassified (sp. Shepshed). In 1 mile turn right on to the B5324 and after ¾ mile turn left, unclassified (no sign) to Shepshed. On entering Shepshed turn right into Britannia Street, shortly keep left then, at the mini-roundabout, keep forward (sp. M1 Motorway). In 1 mile turn left on to the A512 (sp. Loughborough). At the M1 junction round-about take 2nd exit and, in ½ mile, turn right, unclassified (sp. Nanpantan). At Nanpantan cross the main road (sp. Woodhouse Eves), at the trunk road turn right on to the B591 and ascend **Beacon Hill**. In ⅓ mile turn left on to the B5330 (sp. Cropston) and ¾ mile further on go over the crossroads, unclassified (sp. Newtown Linford) passing **Bradgate Country Park**. After 1 mile turn right and pass Hunts Hill Car Park. In 1 mile, join the B5327 and enter Newtown Linford. Here, turn right, unclassified (sp. Groby) and continue to Groby, under the A50. At Groby turn right, then left (sp. Ratby). At the end of Ratby turn right (sp. Desford) and in ¾ mile turn right on to the B5380 to Desford. Here, turn right on to the B582 (sp. Barlestone) to the edge of Newbold Verdon. In ½ mile turn left on to the B585 (sp. Market Bosworth). After 1½ miles turn right and immediately left across the A447 and on to **Market Bosworth**. Turn right into the Town Centre then left (sp. Sheepy). Pass Market Bosworth Light Rail-way Station and in 2½ miles turn right on to the A444 (sp. Burton). Continue to Twycross then turn right on to the B4116 (sp. Snarestone). Pass the edge of Snarestone and in ¾ mile bear right (sp. Ashby). One mile further on go over the crossroads then, in another mile, turn right on to the B4006 to return to your starting point at Ashby-de-la-Zouch.

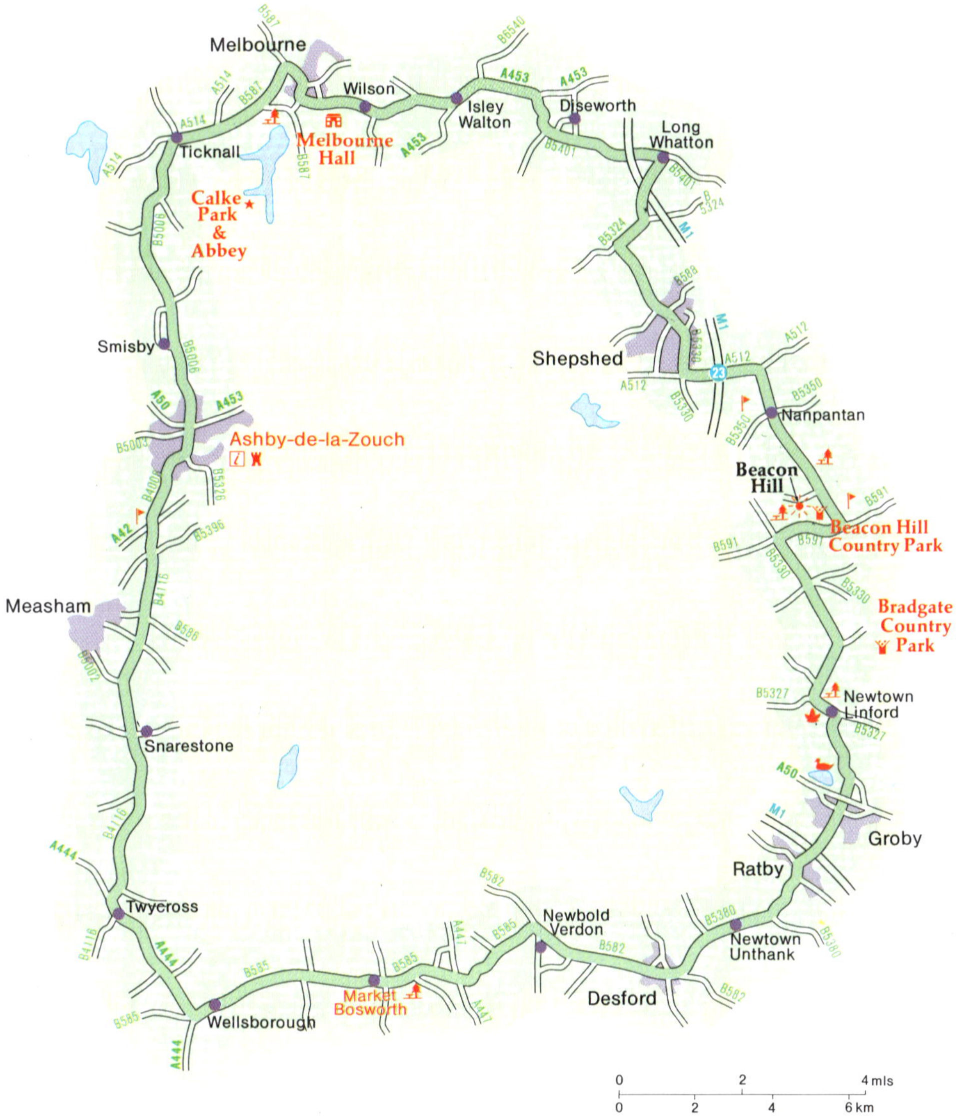

OFF THE BEATEN TRACK

Whatton Garden

A minor road north from Long Whatton leads to these beautiful, 25-acre gardens containing both formal and wild areas and magnificent trees. The Manor House, dating from 1804, is not open to the public.

Mount St Bernard's Abbey

The only monastic settlement left in Charnwood Forest, which once boasted several former priories and abbeys, such as those at Grace Dieu and Ulverscroft. Mount St Bernard's, near Coalville, was founded in 1835.

Just a sample of some of the superb exhibits at the Donington Motor Museum, which has the largest collection of Grand Prix cars in the world: essential viewing for motorsport enthusiasts

SHERWOOD AND THE DUKERIES

55 miles

Minor roads thread north from the county of Nottingham through the ancient Forest of Sherwood, now consisting mainly of farmland with Forestry Commission plantations, but

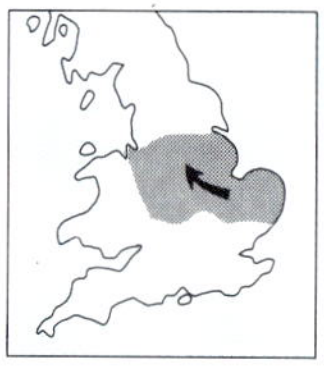

forever associated with the legendary tales of Robin Hood and his Merrie Men. Won from that medieval forest were great estates and houses of the so-called `Dukeries.'

Hollywood has given us a totally false impression of the real *Robin Hood, if there ever was one such 'rob the rich to give to the poor' hero. On the evidence of placenames alone, Robin Hood must have roamed far and wide from his traditional home in Sherwood, and the truth is he was probably more of a universal hero than a local one.*

In the remaining oak and birch woods of Sherwood, and the imaginative visitor centre near Edwinstowe, you can still feel the magic of the Greenwood, although extensive Forestry Commission plantations have destroyed much of the atmosphere. Further north, a district of large country estates and houses such as Thoresby, Clumber and Welbeck have long been known as the Dukeries, because of their aristocratic connections. At nearby Laxton are the last examples of the medieval open field and rotation systems of farming.

ON THE TOUR

Nottingham

Nottingham's life has centred around the castle, high on its sandstone crag overlooking the city, ever since William the Conqueror's first building on the site in 1086. The present 17th-century building doubles as the Castle Museum, and houses collections of fine and decorative art.

Beneath the castle walls in Castle Road, the Nottingham Lace Centre documents one of the city's best-known products, and there are examples of all types of Nottingham lace on display. Close by is the Trip to Jerusalem, reputedly one of the oldest public houses in the country, which is built into the Castle Rock. Five 17th- and 18th-century cottages form the nearby Brewhouse Yard Museum, where authentic room settings chart the everyday life of Nottingham citizens through the ages.

Burntstump Country Park

The park's curious name is taken from one of the oldest trees in the Forest. Open all year round, this is a pleasant area for walking and there are good views from the top of Burntstump Hill.

The present 17th -century Nottingham Castle (of Player's cigarette packet fame) was a ruin until 1875, when the corporation restored it. It is now the city's museum and art gallery

Longdale Rural Craft Centre

A bygone way of life is recalled here with reconstructions of timbered buildings and narrow streets. Workshops are always kept busy producing a wide range of traditional craft items.

Rufford Abbey

Site of a Cistercian Abbey founded in 1146, Rufford was dissolved by Henry VIII and eventually purchased by Nottinghamshire County Council and made a country park in 1969. The Craft Centre often has craft demonstrations, and there are lakeside and woodland walks throughout the estate. The formal gardens include a fine collection of sculpture, and there are many picnicking opportunities.

Sherwood Forest Visitor Centre

Traditionally the scene of Robin Hood's marriage to Maid Marion, Edwinstowe may have got its name from being a resting place of the Saxon King Edwin.

Today, Edwinstowe is at the heart of the Robin Hood `industry', and the nearby visitor centre features the story of the world's most famous outlaw through exciting interpretive displays. The centre is situated in 450 acres of ancient oak woodland, with many waymarked walks leading to the famous Major Oak, now fenced off to protect its roots from trampling feet.

Thoresby Hall

One of the famous Dukerie estates, Thoresby has a history of rebuilding, but the present magnificent Victorian house was designed by Anthony Salvin for the third Earl of Manvers, a successor of the original Dukes of Kingston. The Library fireplace features the Major Oak with Robin Hood and Little John. Set in lovely landscaped grounds.

Southwell

Southwell's twin-towered Norman Minster is probably the least-known and least-visited of all England's cathedrals, but it is a gem of 12th-century architecture. Some of the finest stone foliage carving in Britain adorns the Minster, and the chapter house is one of the most beautiful in England.

The village – for Southwell (pronounced `Suth'l') is the only village in England which boasts a cathedral – grew up around the Minster, but never achieved urban status.

Almost opposite the Minster is the Tudor, timber-framed Saracen's Head Hotel, where Charles I surrendered to the Scots in 1646 to end the Civil War. Bramley Cottage, in Church Street, has *the* original Bramley apple tree.

ROUTE DIRECTIONS

Leave **Nottingham** (map 8SK53) on the A60 (sp. Mansfield) and pass the Old Spot. In 1³/₄ miles, at the roundabout, take 1st exit, and in 2¹/₄ miles turn right, unclassified (sp. Calverton). Pass **Burntstump Country Park** on the right then turn left to Papplewick Pumping Station. In ¹/₄ mile, at the crossroads, turn left (no sign) and pass the **Longdale Rural Craft Centre** before reaching Ravenshead. Turn right on to the A60 (sp. Mansfield) and in ¹/₂ mile, at the traffic signals turn right on to the B6020 (sp. Blidworth). Pass through Blidworth and in ¹/₂ mile bear right to Rainworth. At the trunk road turn left, then immediate right at the traffic signals on to the A617 (sp. Newark). In 2¹/₂ miles, at the roundabout, take the A614 (sp. Doncaster). Continue past **Rufford Abbey and Country Park** and in ¹/₄ mile turn left on to the B6034 (sp. Edwinstowe). In ¹/₂ mile, at the traffic signals, keep forward. In Edwinstowe keep left and after ¹/₄ mile, at the trunk road, turn right on to the A6075 (sp. Ollerton) then at the traffic signals turn left on to the B6034 (sp. Worksop). Pass the **Sherwood Forest Visitor Centre**, then in 1 mile turn left on to the A616 (sp. Sheffield and Worksop). Pass through Budby, then in ¹/₄ mile turn right, unclassified (sp. Thoresby Park) to pass **Thoresby Hall** on the right. In 1 mile turn right on to the A614 (sp. Nottingham) and in 3 miles, at the roundabout, take the A616 (sp. Newark). Enter Ollerton and at the roundabout take 2nd exit (sp. Newark). Continue to Wellow. At the Durham Ox turn right, unclassified and continue to Eakring. Here, turn left (sp. Kirklington) and in ¹/₄ mile turn right. In 2³/₄ miles further, at the trunk road, turn left on to the A617 to Kirklington. Turn right, unclassified (sp. Southwell), pass the Picnic Site on the right, and in 2 miles turn right (sp. Southwell). In ³/₄ mile, at the trunk road, turn left into **Southwell**. Here, turn right into the Market Place and join the A612 (sp. Nottingham). In ¹/₄ mile turn left and continue through Thurgarton. In Lowdham, at the roundabout, take 2nd exit for Burton Joyce and continue on the A612 back to Nottingham.

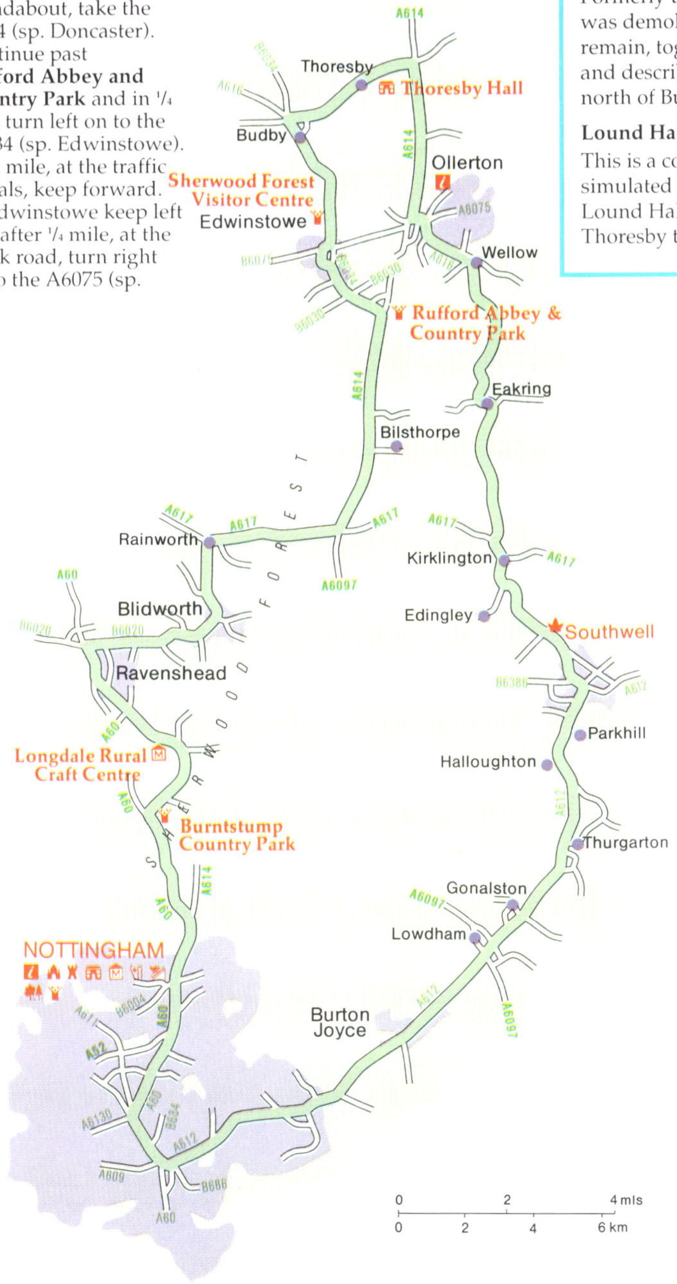

OFF THE BEATEN TRACK

Laxton

Three miles east of Ollerton, Laxton is the last surviving example in England of the medieval system of strip farming, now explained by a visitor centre and interpretive trail. The land was farmed on a three-year rotation basis, with one of the three strips lying fallow each year.

OFF THE TOUR

Newstead Abbey

Home of the poet Lord Byron in the early 19th century, and now a treasurehouse of his possessions, Newstead was originally an Augustinian priory converted to a family house in the 16th century. Open afternoons daily, Easter to September, Newstead is set in glorious gardens and parkland, open daily, about 4 miles from Papplewick off the A60 Nottingham to Mansfield road.

Creswell Crags

This is one of the classic archaeological sites of Britain. Here, in caves in a narrow limestone gorge on the borders of Nottinghamshire and Derbyshire, remains of the first men to inhabit the area have been found, dating back 100,000 years. There is an excellent visitor centre. Creswell is on the A616 north of Budby.

Clumber Park

Formerly the family seat of the Dukes of Newcastle, the house of Clumber was demolished in 1938, but 3,700 acres of parkland, lakes and woodland remain, together with a fine late-Gothic Revival chapel, built a century ago and described as 'a cathedral in miniature.' Clumber (National Trust) is north of Budby off the B6034, 4 miles south of Worksop.

Lound Hall

This is a coal-mining country and the National Mining Museum, with simulated mine shaft, coal face and other interesting exhibits, is housed at Lound Hall. It can be reached by continuing on the minor road east from Thoresby to Haughton.

Southwell Minster is a superb Norman cathedral with these magnificent twin towers on the west face. It is famous for its beautiful stone carvings depicting different types of foliage

VALES AND WOLDS OF THE DANELAW

53 miles

Lovely stone villages with superb churches and sweeping views characterise the southern Lincolnshire Wolds, which overlook the broad and

fertile Vale of the Belvoir, in the ancient county of Rutland (now in Leicestershire), and its dominating sham-medieval castle.

It is a common misconception among those who do not know the county that Lincolnshire is flat. In fact the oolitic limestones of the Lincolnshire Wolds, in the south and west of the county, give the northbound traveller – on the A1 Great North Road – his first taste of stone-built towns and villages, and a gently rolling countryside which offers commanding views. Placenames ending in 'by' or 'thorpe' abound on the borders between Lincolnshire and Leicestershire; at the foot of the Wolds and in the Vale of Belvoir. They give us a clue to the origins of the first settlers of this fertile countryside, for they are both pure Scandinavian; Old Danish words for villages or small settlements in this heartland of the former Danelaw. Also common here is the Gothic lettering on the map which indicates former villages; deserted during the Middle Ages through pestilence, or for the greater profit obtainable from sheep.

ON THE TOUR

Grantham

Fine old coaching inns and an attractive market square echo the days when Grantham was a major stopover on the Great North Road – which now thankfully by-passes the town. St Wulfram's Parish Church, dating from the 12th century, is one of the finest in England, and its 282ft spire dominates the town.

Grantham House, east of the church, dates from 1380, but now presents a pleasing mixture of architectural styles. The gardens are a pleasant open space in the heart of the town. The Grantham Museum on St Peter's Hill has a special exhibition on the life of Sir Isaac Newton – who was a pupil at Grantham Grammar School – as well as displays illustrating the history and natural history of the town and its district.

Belvoir Castle

Red-brick, mock-medieval castle home of the Duke of Rutland, Belvoir lords it over the broad Vale of Belvoir from its commanding wooded bluff. It was rebuilt in 1816 after a terrible fire had destroyed what was left of Robert de Todeni's Norman castle. Most of what you see today is the 19th-century work of James Wyatt, but inside the house is a treasure trove of works of art. Regular medieval-style 'events' such as jousting and mock-battles are held in the grounds on most Sundays during the summer season.

Waltham on the Wolds

At the centre of Leicestershire's little-known Wold country, Waltham's hilltop site has revealed evidence of settlement going back to Roman and Saxon days. A typically elegant Wolds church spire and a smock windmill are landmarks for miles around as is the less-elegant modern addition of a television transmitting mast.

Woolsthorpe Manor

This charming, small 17th-century farmhouse was the birthplace and family home of Sir Isaac Newton. Certainly, he did much of his pioneering work here, but whether it was under an apple tree in the garden that he discovered the theory of the force of gravity is best left to the imagination.

Castle Bytham

One of the candidates for the title of Lincolnshire's loveliest village, Castle Bytham gets its prefix from the massive earthworks of the Norman castle east of the village across the stream which flows into the River Glen. It is well worth the steep climb to the top of the motte to get an overall view of the village street, full of hidden byways, which runs under a limestone edge and up to a tiny village green.

The cruciform Church of St James is one of the best in the county too, and treasures an 18th-century sundial inscribed with the pun 'Bee in Thyme', and the village maypole.

Oakham Castle's great hall contains a unique collection of horseshoes dating, it is thought, from the 11th century

OFF THE TOUR

Belton House

Three miles north-east of Grantham on the A607, Belton House is described by its custodians, the National Trust, as the crowning achievement of Restoration country house architecture. It was built between 1685 and 1688 for Sir John Brownlow, with later alterations by James Wyatt in 1770. It has an interesting exhibition which focusses on the abdication of Edward VIII.

Allington Manor

Unoccupied for 80 years from the 1860s, this Dutch-gabled ironstone house dates from about 1660 and has been lovingly restored by its present owner. It can be reached by turning right off the tour at Sedgebrook.

Oakham

Former 'capital' of the tiny county of Rutland, Oakham retains an air of its past importance. It makes a pleasant diversion to visit this charming ironstone town, with its well-preserved market square, interesting County Museum and Norman Banqueting Hall in the Castle, which is hung with hundreds of horseshoes left by visiting nobility. Take the minor road due south from Wymondham.

ROUTE DIRECTIONS

Leave **Grantham** (map 8SK93) on the A52 (sp. Nottingham). In 1½ miles cross the A1, and in 2½ miles further turn left, unclassified (sp. Stenwith and Woolsthorpe). In 1½ miles cross the Grantham Canal and turn left (sp. Belvoir). At the edge of Woolsthorpe, at the crossroads, turn right and then pass the entrance to **Belvoir Castle**. Continue on the Knipton road and, after 1 mile, at the T-junction, turn left. At the edge of Knipton turn right (sp. Branston). At Branston turn left into Main Street (sp. Melton) and at the far end turn left to leave by the Waltham Road. Turn right on to the A607 and continue to **Waltham on the Wolds**. Here, turn left, unclassified (sp. Stonesby and Sproxton) and at the end of the village turn right then keep forward with the Garthorpe road (sp. gated road) to the outskirts of Garthorpe and join the B676. Then take the next turning left, unclassified, for Wymondham. Here, turn left on to the South Witham road and in nearly ½ mile turn left again (sp. Sewstern). Pass through Sewstern then, at the far end of the village, go over the crossroads and continue to Gunby. Keep forward on the North Witham road and, in ¾ mile at the crossroads, turn left (sp. Colsterworth). After a further mile, cross the B676 to reach Woolsthorpe. Pass **Woolsthorpe Manor** on the left and at the T-junction, turn right (no sign), then at the next T-junction go right again on to the B6403 to enter Colsterworth. Go through the village, over the crossroads (sp. Stamford) and then turn right on to the A1. After 2 miles pass the Fox Inn and take the next left, unclassified (sp. Castle Bytham). At the next T-junction turn right and pass the picnic area at East Marlany Wood on the right, to reach **Castle Bytham**. Go forward with the Stamford road and in ½ mile, at the crossroads, turn left for Little Bytham. Here, go forward on to the B1176 (no sign), and continue to the outskirts of Creeton. Here, bear right to reach Swinstead, turn left (sp. Grantham) and continue to Corby Glen. Turn left on to the A151 and in ½ mile turn right to re-join the B1176. Pass through Bitchfield and Boothby Pagnell. Beyond Old Somerby, at the roundabout, take the A52 for the return to Grantham.

The beautiful 14th-century spire of St Wulfram's Church is a landmark for miles around the ancient farming and hunting town of Grantham. The church was left a chained library in 1598

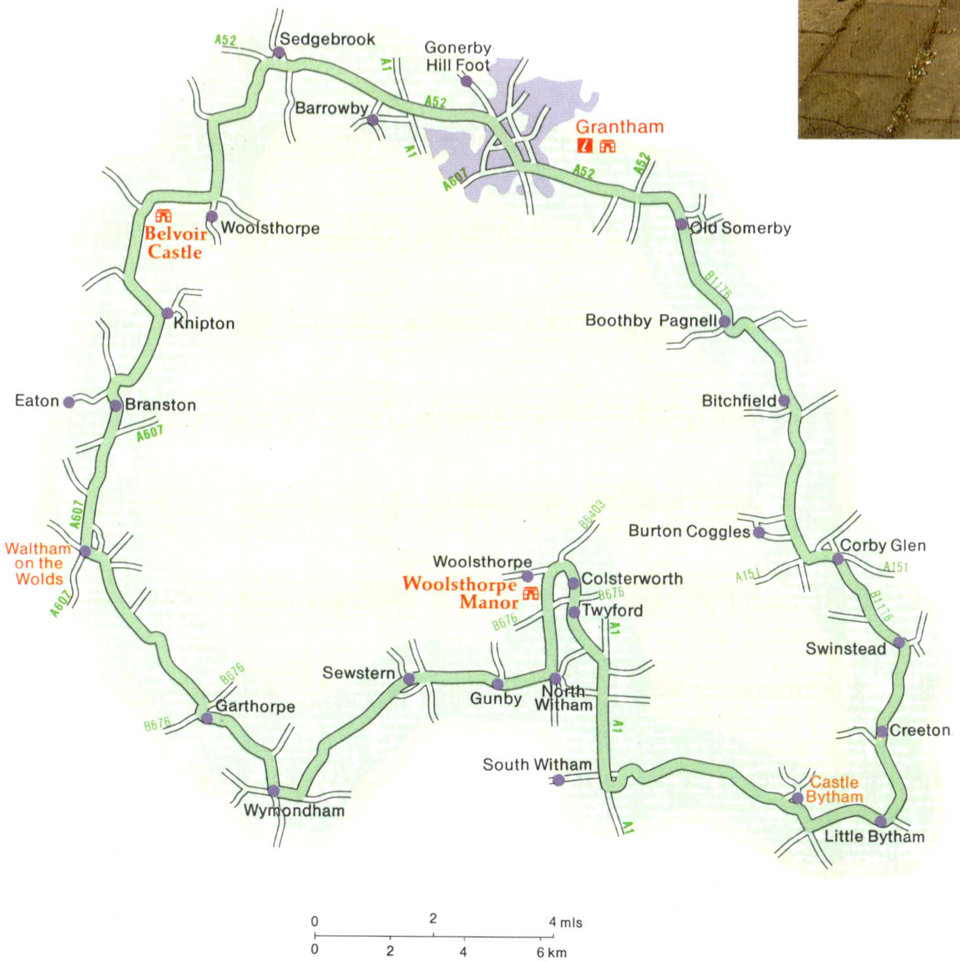

OFF THE BEATEN TRACK

Croxton Kerrial

A small, stone-built village on the A607 south-west of Grantham, curiously named Croxton Kerrial is the site of the former Croxton Abbey, founded in 1150. It can be reached by a pleasant 3-mile walk through the fields from Waltham on the Wolds.

OUTDOOR ACTIVITIES

Rutland Water

Claiming to be the largest man-made lake in Western Europe, Rutland Water near Oakham covers 3,100 acres and has 27 miles of shoreline. The Regency-style former church of Normanton, on an isolated peninsula left by the rising waters, now houses a splendid museum depicting the history of the flooding of the valley. There are picnic sites, adventure playgrounds and opportunities for angling, sailing, canoeing and windsurfing, as well as cycle hire at the Whitwell and Normanton car parks.

NORTHAMPTONSHIRE UPLANDS

50 miles

The quiet villages and roads east of the M1 are seldom visited by the motorist in his headlong dash north or south. They remain an unspoilt rural backwater, with lovely, golden-stone villages set in rich, prosperous farmland.

The Northamptonshire Uplands lie in the middle of the belt of oolitic limestone which starts with the Cotswolds and ends in the Lincolnshire Wolds. This warm-coloured building stone has been used to create beautiful villages which seem to grow almost naturally from the underlying rocks.

Northamptonshire is often known as the county of 'spires and squires' – a reference to the fine country churches, often with elegant spires, and large country houses and estates which make up the landscape. It was also a cockpit of history; as witnessed by the momentous part it played in the Civil War, when the county town was a Parliamentary stronghold, and the decisive battle was fought, in 1645, on rolling countryside near the village of Naseby.

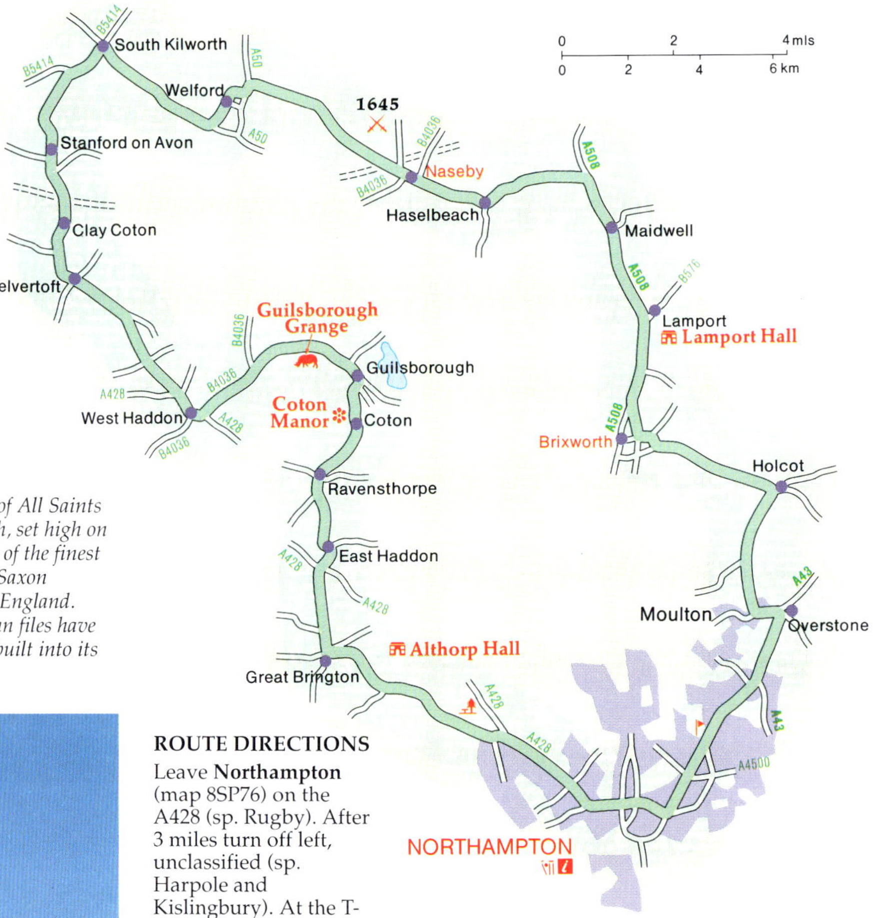

The church of All Saints at Brixworth, set high on a hill, is one of the finest and largest Saxon churches in England. Many Roman files have been found built into its arches

ROUTE DIRECTIONS

Leave **Northampton** (map 8SP76) on the A428 (sp. Rugby). After 3 miles turn off left, unclassified (sp. Harpole and Kislingbury). At the T-junction turn right on to the Brington road. After 2 miles turn right again (sp. Great Brington and Althorp Hall) to pass the entrance to **Althorp Hall**. In ¾ mile turn left, then at Great Brington church turn sharp right on to the East Haddon road. After 1 ¾ miles cross the A428 and enter East Haddon. At the church, turn left, then next right (sp. Ravensthorpe). At Ravensthorpe keep forward (sp. Coton and Guilsborough), pass Ravensthorpe Reservoir and the entrance to **Coton Manor Gardens**, and bear right. In ¾ mile, at the T-junction, turn left in to Guilsborough. Continue on the West Haddon, pass **Guilsborough Grange** and, 1½ miles on, join the B4036 and enter West Haddon. Keep forward on the A428, and bear right, then, at the end of the village, turn right, unclassified (sp. Yelvertoft). Cross the Grand Union Canal three times before reaching Yelvertoft. Continue to Clay Coton and bear right across the bridge with the Stanford road to Stanford-on-Avon. Here, turn on to the South Kilworth road, continue past Stanford Reservoir, and turn right on to the B5414 to reach South Kilworth. Here turn right, unclassified (sp. Welford). In 1¼ miles turn left to enter Welford. Keep forward and at the end of the main street turn left on to the A50, then next right on to the unclassified Naseby road. At **Naseby** join the Market Harborough road, B4036 and, at the end of the village, turn right, unclassified (sp. Haselbach and Maidwell). At Haselbach keep left and after 2 miles turn right on to the A508 (sp. Northampton). Continue through Maidwell and Lamport, passing **Lamport Hall**, then in 2¼ miles, at the **Brixworth** roundabout, take 1st exit, unclassified (sp. Holcot and Sywell). In ¼ mile, at the T-junction, turn right then after ¾ mile, at the T-junction, turn left. Cross the Pitsford Reservoir for Holcot. Here, at the crossroads, turn right (sp. Moulton) and at Moulton turn left (sp. Northampton). In ½ mile turn right on to the A43 for the return to Northampton.

ON THE TOUR

Northampton
Considering its important place in English history, the county town of Northampton is disappointing to some visitors. Unfortunately it was the victim of a disastrous fire in 1675, which destroyed much of the old town.
In a town famous for its boot and shoe industry, Northampton Museum and Art Gallery has, appropriately, the largest collection of boots and shoes in the world. There is also a Museum of Leathercraft in the Old Bluecoat School in Bridge Street. The 12th-century St Sepulchre's Church in Sheep Street is one of only four round churches in England, built by returning Crusaders as a replica of the Church of the Holy Sepulchre in Jerusalem.

Althorp Hall
Famous as the family home of the Princess of Wales, Althorp has been the seat of the Spencer family since 1508, when the first house was built on this site. Family security means that the house, which contains some priceless works of art, can be closed without notice, but it is usually open all year.

Coton Manor Gardens
Rather incongruously, wildfowl, flamingos and tropical birds fly free in this traditional English country house garden. The 17th-century house is not open to the public.

Guilsborough Grange
More than 400 domestic and exotic animals and 70 species of birds are kept in the beautiful grounds of this 19th-century country house. There are special birds of prey demonstrations, and a children's corner.

Naseby
The Battlefield of Naseby Battle and Farm Museum at Purlieu Farm are now unfortunately threatened by a motorway. It was here, in 1645, that General Fairfax's Parliamentary forces defeated the Royalists of Charles I and Prince Rupert in one of the most decisive battles of the Civil War. A monument, erected in 1936, marks the site of the battle.

Lamport Hall
Well-known for its programme of drama, music and other artistic events staged throughout the summer, Lamport Hall was the home of the Isham family from 1560 to 1976. The classical house is mainly 17th and 18th century, and the gardens include one of the oldest-established Alpine gardens in Britain, featuring the first British garden gnomes!

Billing Aquadrome provides boating and watersport fun for all the family as well as amusements on dry land

Below right: *Holdenby House was claimed to be the largest private house in England during Elizabeth I's reign*

Brixworth
Another classic Saxon church, in this county of rare and beautiful places of worship, Brixworth church dates from the late 7th century and is the largest mainly Saxon church to survive in the country. It has a typically lofty nave, a presbytery, a polygonal apse and a two-storeyed porch. The spire and rare stair turret were added six centuries later. Nearby is the 750-acre Pitsford Reservoir, with its picnic site, information centre and nature reserve.

OFF THE BEATEN TRACK

Rushton Triangular Lodge
There are three walls with three windows and three gables in each, in this three-storeyed building topped by a three-sided chimney. Sir Thomas Tresham's obsession with the symbolism of the Holy Trinity prompted him to create this extraordinary building in 1593. You can find it by taking the B576 north from Lamport.

OUTDOOR ACTIVITIES

Billing Aquadrome
On the A45, 4 miles east of Northampton, this is the place for active members of the family, with boating, fishing and watersports, together with a pleasure park and other amusements.

OFF THE TOUR

Holdenby House Gardens and Falconry Centre
In Elizabeth I's day, this was said to be the largest house in England. It later became the prison of Charles I during the Civil War. The original gardens remain and are complemented by a falconry centre, where birds of prey are put through their paces. Turn right at East Haddon on an unclassified road for Holdenby.

Stanford Hall
This William and Mary house of 1690 can be found at Lutterworth after a short detour, across the River Avon, from Stanford-on-Avon. It houses, among other things, a replica of an 1898 flying machine. There is also a walled rose garden, a motorcycle museum and a nature trail and opportunities for anyone keen on fishing.

Earl's Barton
The village, left off the A45 east of Northampton, is famous for its wonderful Saxon church tower – probably the best in Britain – to which battlements were added during the 15th century.

THE FENS AROUND ELY

55 miles

The towering octagonal lantern of Ely Cathedral stands out like a lighthouse over the fertile, flat fenlands of Cambridgeshire. No longer an island, the Isle of Ely is surrounded

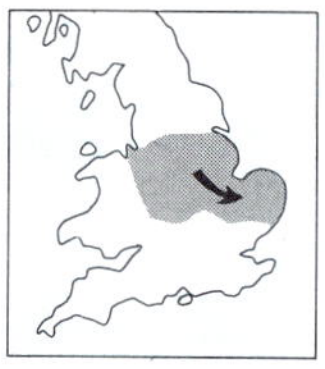

by vast, hedgeless fields, hard-won after centuries of drainage. To the south, the flat, open heaths around Newmarket in Suffolk are the home of British horse-racing.

The abundance of placenames containing the word `fen' gives a clue to the watery origins of this part of north Cambridgeshire. For although today this is one of the driest parts of Britain, until the 17th and 18th centuries when Dutch engineers were brought in, most of the land north of Newmarket was peat bog and marsh. Only in isolated, protected places such as Wicken Fen can you still see the natural fenland environment.

Many of the villages the tour passes through are slightly raised above the general level of the land, because they, like Ely, were once islands standing above the marshes.

We enter the chalk downland of the East Anglian heights near Newmarket, then cross the border into Suffolk, where the 7th-century Devil's Dyke is thought to mark a border of the central kingdom of Mercia.

Fourteenth-century Cranden's Chapel at Ely. The ancient building has a lot of fine carving, particularly in the chapels and choir stalls, but during the Reformation many statues were badly damaged

ON THE TOUR

Ely

Cathedral city capital of the Fens, Ely's Saxon name means `Eel island' - a reference to an important part of the diet of its original settlers. Alan de Walsingham's magnificent lantern tower of the cathedral was one of the great engineering feats of the Middle Ages, replacing a tower which collapsed in 1322. The rest of the cathedral, a landmark for miles around across the flat, fenland landscape, stands on the site of a 7th-century Benedictine abbey; it is a masterpiece of Norman architecture. Don't miss the interesting Museum of Stained Glass in the north triforium, or Ely Museum in the High Street, which vividly recalls the history of the Isle of Ely.

Haddenham

Haddenham Farmland Museum, showing farming equipment, rural crafts and bygones, is in the High Street. Limited opening during the summer only.

Wicken Fen

Wicken Fen is a unique survival of the great Fens of East Anglia, and one of the most important wetland reserves in Western Europe. It is kept in its primeval state by a windmill which now pumps water into, rather than out of, the 600-acre raised site. Owned by the National Trust, the fen is well-interpreted at the William Thorpe centre, and nearly a mile of well-built boardwalk makes access to the heart of the fen quite easy.
Look out for the magnificent swallowtail butterfly in summer, one of the staggering 5,000 species of insects found here.

Burwell

Burwell's beautiful Parish Church of St Mary was described by Nicolas Pevsner as 'the most perfect example in the county of the Perpendicular ideal of the glasshouse.' Light and airy, it has a commanding tower – perhaps inspired by Ely. The earthworks of the Norman castle of Burwell are to the west of the church.

Anglesey Abbey

Formerly an Augustinian abbey founded in the reign of Henry I near Lode, Anglesey was converted to a Tudor manor house standing in 100 acres of beautifully-kept gardens, and is now in the hands of the National Trust. Lode Mill is nearby and still grinds corn, using water power, on the first Sunday of each month.

Newmarket

The 'headquarters' of British horse-racing, Newmarket was made famous as `the sport of Kings' by James I, who first organised races on the open heaths surrounding the town in the 17th century. The town has a few good Georgian buildings, notably the Rutland Arms. The National Horse-racing Museum, housed in the Regency Subscription Rooms in the High Street, tells the story of racing through the ages and equine tours are arranged from here. Also in the High Street is the 18th-century home of the Jockey Club; the controlling body of British racing, while the National Stud is next to the famous racecourse south-west of the town. Also outside the town, the impressive earthwork known as the Devil's Dyke stretches for seven miles across the heath where the racehorses gallop.

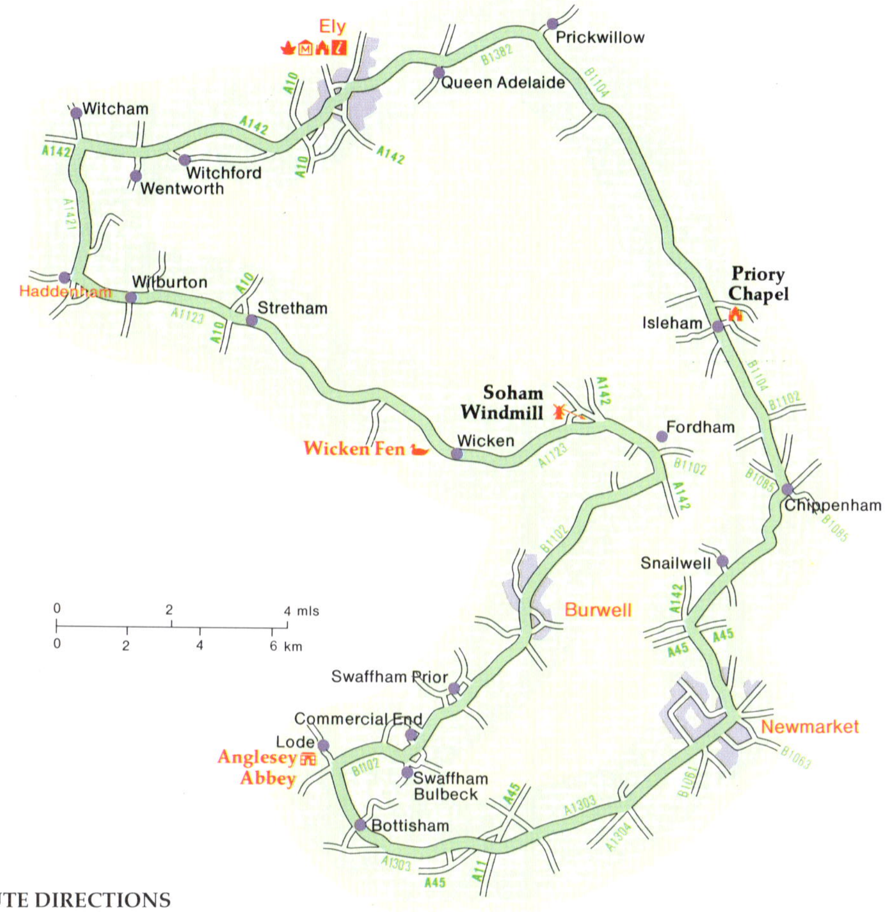

OFF THE BEATEN TRACK

Reach

Between Burwell and Swaffham Prior, the tiny village of Reach was once the principal medieval port for the city of Cambridge, although the 'lode' or canal which linked it with the Cam was of Roman origin. The grass covered Hythe was where the quays were, but nothing now remains apart from the names to remind us of Reach's past importance.

Below: Zorba *the pleasure cruiser on Wicken Fen. The fen, owned by the National Trust, survives largely unchanged from centuries ago, although its mere, or open water, was created in 1955 to attract wildfowl to the area*

Bottom: *Newmarket's elegant Regency Assembly Rooms are the home of the National Horse-racing Museum. Exhibits include famous racing silks, paintings and equine equipment and memorabilia of all sorts to appeal to racing buffs*

ROUTE DIRECTIONS

Leave **Ely** (map 9TL58) on the Cambridge road, and in 3/4 mile turn right, unclassified (sp. Chatteris, March). In 1/2 mile, at the roundabout, take the A142. In 4 1/4 miles turn left on to the A1421 (sp. Cambridge) to reach **Haddenham**. Here turn left on to the A1123 (sp. Cambridge) and continue through Wilburton. In 1 3/4 miles, at the roundabout, take 2nd exit and enter Stretham. Stay on the A1123, to cross the Rivers Ouse and Cam. In 1 1/4 miles pass Spinney Abbey, and later **Wicken Fen**, before passing through Wicken. Beyond Wicken pass within view of Soham Windmill and then turn right on to the A412 for Fordham. Here turn right again on to the B1102 (sp. Cambridge) and pass through **Burwell**. Continue to the edge of Swaffham Prior, stay on the B1102 and, at the outskirts of Swaffham Bulbeck, bear right. After 1 1/4 miles, at the crossroads with the entrance to **Anglesey Abbey** on the right, turn left, unclassified, for Bottisham. Pass the church and, at the main road, turn left on to the A1303 (sp. Newmarket). After 2 miles cross the Newmarket Bypass. Later, at a roundabout, take the A1304 and re-cross the Devil's Ditch, before entering **Newmarket**. From the clocktower leave by the A142 (sp. Ely). In 1 3/4 miles recross the Newmarket Bypass and take 2nd turning on the right, unclassified (sp. Snailwell). Continue on the Chippenham road to reach Chippenham. Here, turn left then take the next right turn on to the B1104 (sp. Prickwillow). Continue through Isleham to the edge of Prickwillow. Here, turn left on to the B1382 (sp. Ely) and at Queen Adelaide cross the River Great Ouse and three level crossings before re-entering Ely.

OFF THE TOUR

Denny Abbey

Originally a Benedictine priory, the abbey passed to the Knights Templar and eventually to the Francescan order. Most of the buildings were demolished in the 16th century but there are remains of the 12th-century church, with 14th-century additions. Denny, near Waterbeach, is reached by taking the A10 south from Ely.

Cambridge

One of the great university cities of the world, founded as early as the 13th century, Cambridge is a treasurehouse of wonderful medieval architecture. There are some fine museums, notably the Fitzwilliam in Trumpington Street, and the Cambridge and County Folk Museum in Castle Street. Don't miss The Backs, where the college lawns come down to the River Granta. Cambridge is two miles west down the A1303 from Bottisham.

Wimpole Hall and Home Farm

The refined 18th-century mansion of Wimpole Hall, 8 miles south west of Cambridge on the A603, is one of the most sumptuous country houses in the county. Next to it is the Home Farm, which is an approved Rare Breeds Survival Centre, with a special area set aside for children to visit, and a woodland adventure playground.

Mildenhall

One of the largest church porches in Suffolk is just one of many outstanding features of the parish church here. There is a fine Lady Chapel and roof elaborately carved with Biblical scenes. Mildenhall, a market town serving the Fens on the River Lark, is on the A11 north-east from Newmarket, or the B1102 through Freckenham.

HEATHLANDS AND FLINT VILLAGES

68 miles

The great dry, sandy heaths of Breckland form one of Eastern England's last true wildernesses, although more recent forestry plantations have taken away much of its natural grandeur. It was not always so, and for early man, this was one of the major flint-knapping `industrial' centres of Britain.

From the ancient priory town of Thetford pleasant country lanes head east and north to encircle the great 300 square miles of Breckland - which gets its name from its `brecks' or `brakes' of sandy heathland which once covered even more of this part of East Anglia.

A string of flint-faced villages edge the heaths, and many of the inhabitants now find work in the extensive Forestry Commission plantations which blanket the area in a monotonous monoculture. However, there is wildlife interest even in these apparently sterile ranks of conifers, and if you are lucky, you may spot roe deer, the increasingly rare red squirrel, and colourful crossbills. In the still of the summer twilight, you may hear the low, liquid churring of the nightjar along the ruler-straight forestry rides.

ON THE TOUR

Thetford

See of the Bishops of East Anglia until 1091, Thetford's past goes back even further, for it lies on an important crossroads of the Icknield Way; one of the country's oldest trade routes. The Priory is now in ruins, but the Ancient House Museum, housed in an early Tudor, half-timbered building in White Hart Street, contains fascinating collections which illustrate the history and natural history of both Thetford and its surrounding Brecklands.

Euston

A lovely street of half-timbered, red-brick and thatched cottages leads up to the church within the park gates of Euston Hall, home of the Dukes of Grafton for many centuries.

Swaffham

This pleasant little market town lies on the edge of Breckland, with some fine, 18th-century red-brick houses and a huge market place dominated by a rotunda-style 'market cross' erected by the Earl of Orford in 1783. The church is particularly interesting, with its angel-studded roof and rare Book of Hours in the Priest's Chamber.

Cockley Cley Iceni Village

This is an imaginative reconstruction of an Iceni village as it might have looked in the days of Boudicca, the warrior queen of the native tribe whose 1st-century revolt shook the foundations of the Roman Empire. This native village as it may have looked around 60 AD is a `must' for anyone who is interested in ancient history.

Inside the stockade and drawbridge are the chief's round house; and the long house which may have been occupied by the warrior elite, beside the simple huts which were the home of the common folk. Nearby is the Forge Museum of local history.

Oxburgh Hall

The splendid red-brick gatehouse leads to a fine, 15th-century castellated and moated manor house, now in the hands of the National Trust. Oxburgh, one of Norfolk's finest medieval buildings, has been the home of the Bedingfeld family for generations. It contains needlework reputedly done by Mary, Queen of Scots and, outside, there are fine woodland walks to enjoy and a traditional herbaceous garden.

Grime's Graves

A 34-acre clearing in the forestry plantations, just north of Brandon, marks the site of one of Britain's earliest industrial sites. Here, some 4,000 years ago in the late Neolithic period, men worked in pits dug through the chalk, to extract the shiny black flints which were the basis of Stone Age technology. Two of the 700 pits are open to the public; going down them is an eerie experience.

This gilded statue of Thomas Paine was installed in front of the King's House, Thetford, in 1964

OFF THE TOUR

Bressingham Steam Museum and Gardens

Hundreds of steam-related exhibits can be seen here, including three different narrow-guage railways and standard guage locomotives from all over Europe. Footplate rides are available. The Norfolk Fire Museum is also here, with Adrian Bloom's famous nurseries and gardens. The village is easily reached by turning right on to the A1066 at Garboldisham.

Castle Acre Priory and Castle

About three miles north of Swaffham on the A1065. For a fuller description see page 120.

Denver Mill

Turn right on the A134 at Stoke Ferry, then left on minor roads through Wereham to reach this splendid example of a smock windmill, a mile south of Downham Market. You are on the edge of the fertile soils of the fens here, where most of the land has been reclaimed by drainage schemes which started in Roman times.

ROUTE DIRECTIONS

Leave **Thetford** (map 9TL88) on the A134 (sp. Bury St Edmunds) and in 2½ miles, at the crossroads turn left, unclassified (sp. Euston). Continue through Barnham, then in a further 1¾ miles, turn left on to the A1088. Pass Euston Hall on the right and bear left into **Euston.** In 2 miles, at the T-junction, turn right (sp. Knettishall) and then branch left to Hopton. At the crossroads turn left (sp. Garboldisham) on to the B1111. Pass through Garboldisham and continue forward to cross the main road (sp. Watton) and bear left through East Hurling. In 2 miles, at the main road, turn right then left and in 5 miles join the A1075 for Watton. Turn left (sp. Swaffham) and keep forward on to the B1077 (sp. Ashill). In 3 miles, at the edge of Ashill, bear left to reach South Pickenham. Bear right with the Swaffham road and in 3¾ miles turn right, A1065, to enter **Swaffham.** Leave on an unclassified road (sp. Cockley Cley, Oxborough), pass through **Cockley Cley** and Oxborough, passing **Oxburgh Hall**, and continue on the Stoke Ferry road. In 1¾ miles, at the T-junction, turn left for Stoke Ferry. Here, turn left on to the A134. At the roundabout take 1st exit (sp. Thetford). In 7½ miles, at Mundford Roundabout, take 2nd exit and, 1 mile further, pass the Lynford Picnic Area. At the next crossroads turn right, unclassified, and, having passed the entrance to **Grimes Graves**, turn left on to the A1065 (no sign). Cross the level-crossing to enter Brandon. In the town centre, at the crossroads, turn left on to the B1107 (sp. Thetford). Continue forward and after 4 miles pass the track, on the right, to Thetford Warren Lodge. At the roundabout take 2nd exit for the return to Thetford.

Adrian Bloom's colourful heather and conifer gardens at Bressingham Hall, where alpine plants and perennials are also lavishly displayed during the summer. A number of old engines draw passenger trucks on a tour of the extensive gardens and nurseries at a leisurely pace

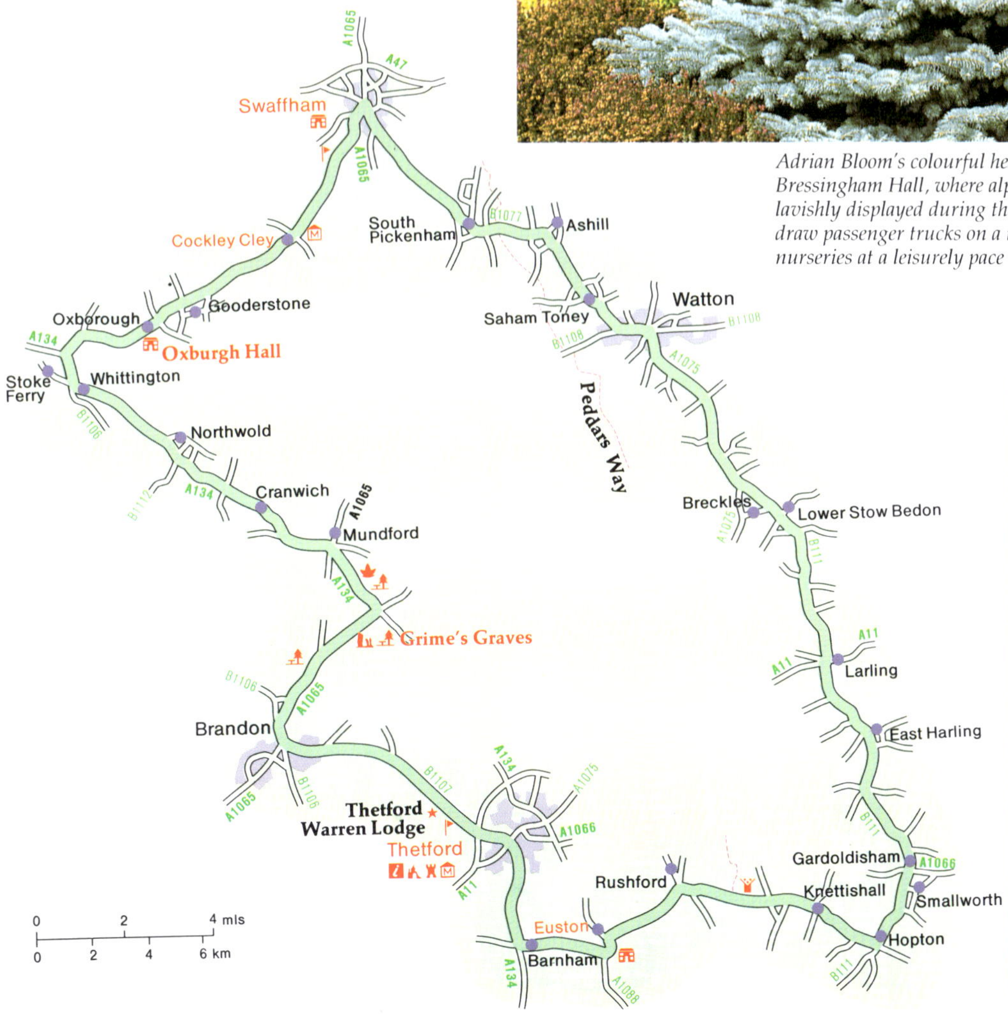

OUTDOOR ACTIVITIES

Breckland

Exploring Breckland is best done on foot, and forest rides and tracks take you into the heart of things. There are nature reserves run by the Norfolk Naturalists' Trust at Weeting and West Wretham, which has two beautiful meres (lakes). Waymarked walks run from the Forestry Commission's visitor centre at Santon Downham, and there are many picnic sites. Some of the central areas are closed to the public and used by the Ministry of Defence for military training – look out for signs.

The Peddar's Way, a waymarked long-distance footpath between Thetford and the North Norfolk Coast, can be picked up just before South Pickenham where it crosses the B1077.

ARTISTS' SUFFOLK

70 miles

East of the ancient county town of Ipswich, a string of unspoilt, colour-washed villages dots the Suffolk landscape. Lovely half- timbered inns promise a warm East Anglian welcome,

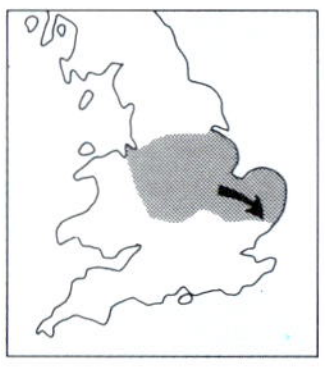

and huge, cathedral-scale churches tell of a past importance founded on the wealth gained from wool in the Middle Ages.

Flatford Mill at East Bergholt. Nearby, and meticulously preserved, is Willy Lott's little white cottage, one of Constable's most celebrated subjects

The unique clarity of light in the vast East Anglian skies has attracted artists for centuries. But it was artists John Constable and Thomas Gainsborough, both born and bred in Suffolk, who first attracted world-wide attention to these wonderful skyscapes. Constable country, as the Vale of Dedham has become known, is a Mecca for students of English landscape painting, and some scenes are still recognisable from his famous works. Thomas Gainsborough, better known as a portrait painter, is honoured in his birthplace of Sudbury on the Suffolk Stour.

Although the farmed landscape of Suffolk has been changed almost out of recognition by the prairie fields of the `barley barons', you'll still find picture-postcard villages such as Kersey, Boxford and Hadleigh on those `Beautiful Britain' calendars. Others just off the route, such as Lavenham and Long Melford, are equally famous as examples of largely unspoilt medieval villages.

ON THE TOUR

Ipswich

It is significant that the pub adjacent to Ipswich's football ground is called the Sporting Farmer. It reflects the continuing importance of agriculture to this thriving county town on the River Orwell. Ipswich was the birthplace of Cardinal Wolsey, and the Great White Horse Inn was featured in Dickens' Pickwick Papers. Nearby in the Butter Market is the Ancient House, built in 1567 (also known as Sparrowe's House after a one-time occupant). This has an exuberant display of pargeting; a form of decorated plasterwork peculiar to East Anglia.
Christchurch Mansion and Museum, in its spacious park on the outskirts of the town, includes the Wolsey Art Gallery, which features work by Constable, Gainsborough and other Suffolk artists. The Ipswich Museum in the High Street gives visitors a fascinating insight into the history and prehistory of Suffolk.

Hadleigh

A busy little market town on a tributary of the River Stour, Hadleigh's High Street offers an example of just about every type of local domestic architecture. There is half-timbered woodwork, pink-washed pargeting and Georgian red brick. The three-storeyed, 15th-century Guildhall in Church Square has overhanging eaves, and the neighbouring church – mainly Early English in style – houses some fine brasses.

Kersey

One of the most photographed villages in England, Kersey, with its outstanding range of half-timbered houses running down to the duck-filled watersplash, gave its name to a type of woollen cloth that was popular in the Middle Ages.

Boxford

Another beautiful Suffolk village, nestling in a hollow where the eponymous ford crossed the tiny stream. Colour-washed cottages cluster around the mainly 15th-century Church of St Mary, which has a fine timber porch and a flint-faced tower.

Sudbury

Locally known as `the Borough', Sudbury was once an important inland port on the wide River Stour. It was the birthplace of Thomas Gainsborough, who is honoured by a bronze statue on Market Hill, and his Georgian house in Gainsborough Street is now an arts centre and museum containing examples of his work. The porticoed Corn Exchange now houses the Quay Theatre and Arts Centre and stands opposite the mainly 15th-century parish church of St Peter's on Market Hill. The town was immortalised, as the rotten borough of Eatonswill, in Dickens' *Pickwick Papers.*

East Bergholt

Birthplace of John Constable, in 1776, East Bergholt has many fine Tudor cottages clustering around the 14th-century parish church, which has a rare, timber-framed belfry in the churchyard. The tower of nearby Dedham church features in many Constable paintings, and Flatford Mill, scene of one of his most famous paintings, *Willy Lott's Cottage*, is now a field studies centre. Here students learn about the fascinating wildlife of the river in idyllic surroundings.

OFF THE TOUR

Lavenham

Often described as England's most perfect medieval village, Lavenham looks as if it has slipped into a time-warp. The narrow streets are lined with leaning half-timbered houses, and the parish church of St Peter and St Paul reflects the wealth of its founding wool-merchants. The Guildhall (1530) in the Market Place is in the hands of the National Trust, and includes an exhibition of 700 years of the woollen trade. Lavenham is easily reached by turning right on the A1141 from Hadleigh.

Dedham

South of Holton St Mary and reached by turning left off the A12. The silhouette of the tall tower of St Mary's Church in Dedham appears in many of the paintings of John Constable. The artist was educated at the old grammar school in the village, founded about 1570; the fine building survives. The ancestors of General Sherman, the American Civil War hero, are buried in St Mary's, and the elegant Georgian town house directly opposite is Shermans Hall – one of the many period buildings in this popular village. In the Marlborough Arms are some beautiful carved beams, and the Master Weaver's house is half-timbered, built in the 15th century with a courtyard. Another noted artist, Alfred Munnings, went to live in nearby Castle House in 1920 and his widow, Lady Munnings, offered the house as a gallery to the public in 1961. The collection of paintings it contains spans the artist's turbulent life. Dedham Vale – a small but beautiful tract of low-lying, leafy watermeadow country – is an Area of Outstanding Natural Beauty.

Lavenham's magnificent Guildhall, built in 1530, is now a museum recalling the cloth trade

ROUTE DIRECTIONS

Leave **Ipswich** (map 9TM14) by following signs to Colchester, A12. In 2 miles, at the traffic signals, turn right on to the A1071 (sp. Hadleigh). In ½ mile, at the roundabout, take 2nd exit and go forward through Hintlesham. In 3¾ miles turn left on to the B1070 and enter **Hadleigh**. At the trunk road turn right (sp. Lavenham). Keep left to cross the river bridge then bear right. In ½ mile, at the trunk road, turn left, then immediate right on to the A1141. After 1 mile, at the crossroads, turn left, unclassified (sp. Kersey) and continue to **Kersey**. Just beyond the church turn right (sp. Boxford). In 3⅓ miles, at the trunk road, turn right and continue to **Boxford**. Leave by turning left (sp. Sudbury) and in ¼ mile turn right on to the A1071. In 2⅓ miles, turn right on to the A134 into Newton. After a further 2½ miles, at the roundabout, take the A131 to enter **Sudbury**. Leave by following the signs Bures B1508. In Bures, at the church, turn left, unclassified (sp. Nayland). Pass Wissington church on the right and, in 1 mile, turn right then left on to the B1087 to cross the main road and enter Nayland. Continue on the B1087 to Stoke-by-Nayland, then turn right on to the B1068 (sp. Ipswich). Continue through Thorington Street and Higham, then in 2 miles turn left on to the A12. After ½ mile branch left on to the B1070 (sp. East Bergholt). At the ensuing trunk road turn 2nd left and pass under the A12. In 1 mile, at the Carriers Arms turn right, unclassified. At **East Bergholt**, with the road to Flatford Mill on the right, bear left (sp. Manningtree). In 1 mile continue forward on to the B1070 and, in 1⅓ miles further turn left on to the A137 (sp. Ipswich). Continue past Brantham then bear left, still on the A137. At the crossroads turn right, unclassified (sp. Tattingstone). Continue through Tattingstone and, in 1⅓ miles, at the trunk road, turn left into Stutton. At the trunk road turn left on to the B1080 (sp. Ipswich), pass the Royal Hospital School and, after ½ mile, at the mill, turn right, unclassified (sp. Ewarton). In ⅓ mile at the trunk road, turn right and continue forward through Harkstead and Ewarton. In 1¼ miles past Ewarton, turn right on to the B1456 and continue through Shotley Street to Shotley Gate. Return through Shotley Street and continue on the B1456 to Chelmondiston and Woolverstone. In 3 miles, at the roundabout, take the A137 (sp. Ipswich) and, by the Wherstead Road, re-enter Ipswich.

OFF THE BEATEN TRACK

Polstead

Reached from Boxford or Stoke-by-Nayland, Polstead gained notoriety as the scene of the Murder in the Red Barn, a 19th-century crime of passion which became the subject of a popular Victorian melodrama. Nothing now remains of the barn.

Belchamp Hall

This gem of a Queen Anne period home lies just across the Essex border, 5 miles west of Sudbury, at Belchamp Water. It is open by appointment only - phone Sudbury (0787) 72744.

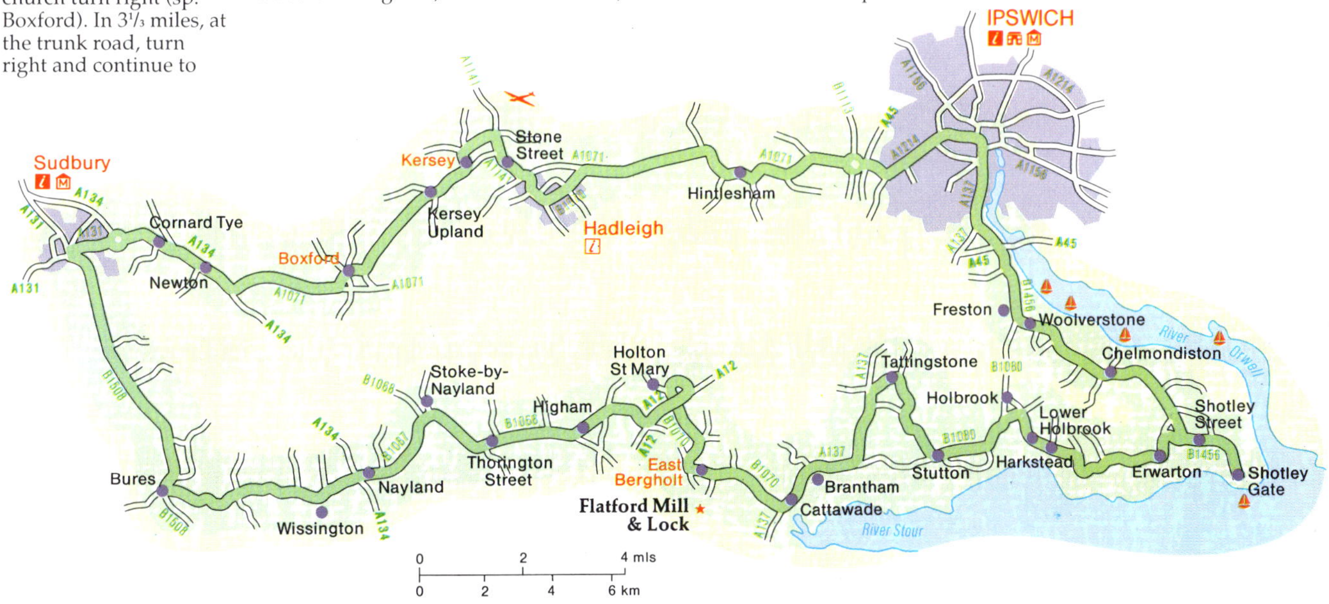

AROUND THE BROADS

46 miles

The Norfolk Broads have been called the last enchanted land of lowland Britain. The subtle mixture of winding, reed-fringed waterways punctuated by the stark silhouettes of water-pump windmills makes this a landscape par excellence *for those who enjoy nothing better than messing about in and around boats.*

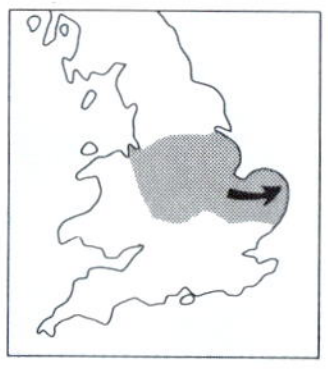

Forty years ago, if anyone had suggested that these 80 square miles of watery wilderness which are the Norfolk and Suffolk Broads, were anything other than a beautiful, natural landscape, they would have been laughed out of court. However, research by a team of historians and geographers in the 1950s proved conclusively that the Broads are almost entirely man-made, created by the large-scale flooding, from the 13th century onwards, of huge medieval peat diggings.

Today, the Broads enjoy the same protected status as a National Park and are enjoyed by millions of visitors every year. Just as popular are the charming reed-thatched villages which fringe the waterways; they provide a welcome rural antidote to the popular and commercialised holiday resorts of Great Yarmouth and Caistor-on-Sea, on the North Sea coast.

ON THE TOUR

Wroxham

A popular centre for hiring boats to explore the Broads, with easy access to Hoveton, Ranworth and South Walsham Broads, Wroxham can be a busy place in high summer. Situated on the River Bure, this bustling little town also has the Barton House Miniature Railway giving steam rides.

Ranworth

This is a convenient centre for exploring Ranworth and Cockshoot Broads, both of which have nature trails. Ranworth's Broadland Conservation Centre is a floating, reed-thatched building reached by a wooden walkway leading from the village. It provides a fascinating introduction to the wildlife of the Broads and the upstairs gallery provides excellent views.

Another magnificent view is that from the tower of St Helen's Church. It is also worth noting that this church has one of the finest and best preserved painted rood screens in the country; medieval craftsmanship in all its original colour and richness, with painted figures of saints and the twelve apostles.

South Walsham

Unusual in that the Church of St Mary's shares it beautifully kept churchyard with the ruined church of St Lawrence, South Walsham is also home to the beautiful gardens of the Fairhaven Garden Trust.

Potter Heigham

Best-known for its single-lane, humped-back bridge (now by-passed) across the River Thurne, Potter Heigham (pronounced High-am) provides boating access to Martham, Hickling and Horsey Broads. This is a busy place, with its shops mainly catering for the boating trade.

Hickling Broad

This is the largest expanse of water in Norfolk, and a National Nature Reserve. The Norfolk Naturalists' Trust has provided a nature trail and birdwatching hides on the north bank near Hickling Heath. From May to July, this is the best place to see Britain's biggest and rarest butterfly, the beautiful swallowtail. In the village of Hickling, the Pleasure Boat Inn still has its own 'staithe', or landing stage.

Beeston Hall

This 18th-century, mock-Gothic country house stands just north of Hoveton and can be reached on foot from Barton Broad. Refreshments are served in the Orangery, and there are woodland walks.

The curious combination of abbey ruins and a windmill; St Benet's near Ludham.
Opposite: *Hickling Broad, the widest stretch of water in Norfolk, is one of the five major Broads that prove a haven for sailing and motor-boat enthusiasts. The Norfolk Naturalists' Trust has observation hides here*

OFF THE TOUR

Berney Arms Windpump

On the north bank of the River Yare, 3 1/2 miles north east of Reedham, this seven-storey working tower mill – the tallest in the country – can either be reached by boat or by a half-mile walk from the railway halt. Reedham is six miles south of Acle on the B1140.

Caistor-on-Sea

Originally the capital of the Iceni and later the Roman town of Venta Icenorum, Caistor has been a place of importance for nearly 2,000 years.
The Caistor Castle Motor Museum, in the grounds of the 15th-century castle, has one of the finest collections of automobilia in the country, reached by continuing forward on the A1064 at Filby.

Great Yarmouth

One of the great holiday resorts in England, with many attractions and entertainments throughout the year. The 16th-century Elizabethan House Museum in South Quay is well worth a visit, as is the Maritime Museum of East Anglia in Marine Parade, which includes a shipwrecked sailor's home. All the fun of the seaside fair is here for the children, plus a fine, sandy beach. Wrap up warm if the wind is from the east.

ROUTE DIRECTIONS

Leave **Wroxham** (map 9TG31) on the Norwich road, A1151. In 1 mile turn left, unclassified (sp. Salhouse, Plumstead) for Salhouse. Here keep left for Woodbastwick. Continue into **Ranworth** and on to **South Walsham**. Here turn left on to the B1140 and continue towards Acle. After 1 mile, at the roundabout, take the A1064 to cross Acle Bridge. Go forward through Burgh St Margaret and on to Filby. Continue for a further mile then, at the crossroads, turn left, unclassified, for Ormesby St Margaret. Here, turn left on to the A149 and continue to Rollesby. At the Horse and Groom turn right, unclassified, to Martham. Here, turn left on to the B1152 (no sign) and, in 1½ miles turn right on to the A149. Pass through Bastwick then branch left, unclassified, to cross the Potter Heigham Bridge. Continue forward to **Potter Heigham** and join the A1062 for Ludham. At the King's Arms turn right, unclassified (sp. Catfield). Keep forward in to Catfield then turn right (sp. Hickling, Sea Palling). In ¼ mile at the main road, turn right then left. After a further ½ mile, at the T-junction, turn left past **Hickling Broad**. Continue, unclassified, to Hickling Green, then turn right (sp. Sea Palling). In ¼ mile turn left (sp. Stalham, Sutton) and continue forward for 1½ miles. At the crossroads, turn right and next left for Stalham. Here go left (sp. North Walsham) and shortly turn right on to the A149 to cross the River Ant. In ½ mile keep forward (sp. Norwich) on the A1151. Pass Beeston St Lawrence Church and **Beeston Hall** and, in ¼ mile, at the crossroads, turn left on to a narrow by-road (sp. Neatishead). After ¼ mile further, at the T-junction, turn left, then in ½ mile turn right for Horning. In 2 miles turn right on to the A1062 for Hoveton, then left on to the A1151 to return to Wroxham.

OFF THE BEATEN TRACK

How Hill

The How Hill estate, near Ludham, has been described as 'Broadland in microcosm', for every habitat of the Broads is seen in this one small area. Based on one of the finest Edwardian houses in Norfolk, How Hill is run by a charitable trust and managed by the Broads Authority. The children will love Toad Hole, a tiny, thatched marshman's cottage restored to exactly how it was at the turn of the century, and reached by one of the many footpaths which thread the estate.

St Benet's Abbey

Reached by a footpath from Ludham, this monastery was founded 1,000 years ago by King Canute. Inside the evocative ruins the remains of a century-old windmill can be seen.

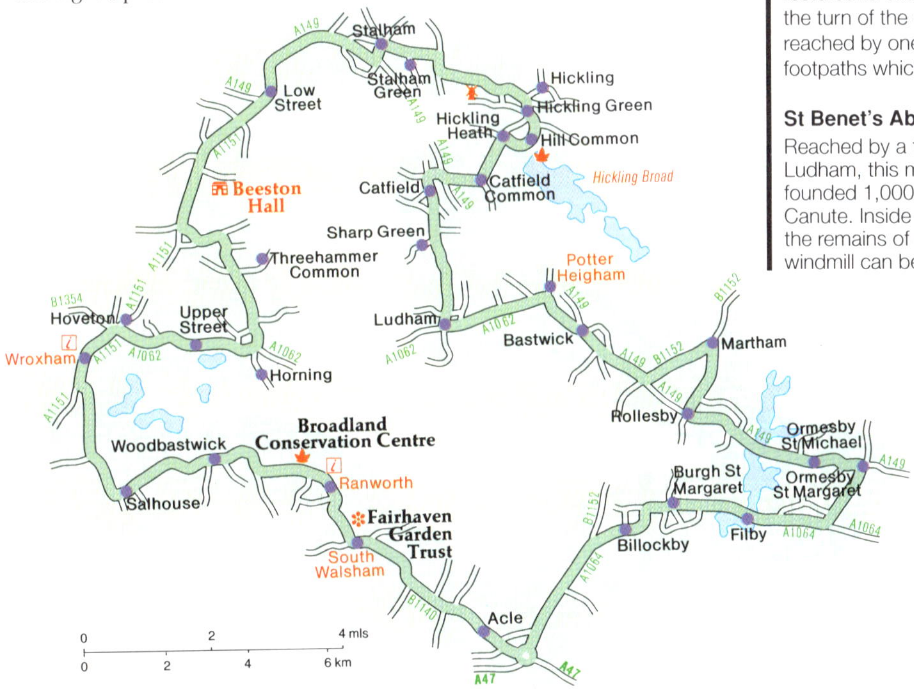

NORFOLK COAST AND COUNTRY

71 miles

Bracing, deserted beaches and delightful, unspoilt villages nestling in prosperous farming country are the attractions of north

Norfolk; an area often omitted from the tourist trails, and waiting to be discovered by the discerning visitor.

The Norfolk Coast long-distance path threads through the Norfolk Coast Area of Outstanding Natural Beauty; two clues, through their official designations, to the scenic qualities of this vastly under-rated area. The wide salt-marshes of the coast are the home of more than 250 species of birds, including many national rarities.

Inland, the ancient market towns of Fakenham and Dereham serve a huge agricultural hinterland - Britain's bread basket - with vast fields of wheat and barley stretching to the horizon and the enormous, breathtaking East Anglian skies.

This is pilgrim's country too, for Walsingham with its shrine to Our Lady has become the most important Roman Catholic place of pilgrimage in England, attracting thousands of visitors every year.

The fine old windmill at Cley-next-the-Sea – a pretty village which, in fact, is a mile from the sea because of land reclamation in the 17th century. Much of the marsh here is a bird sanctuary

ON THE TOUR

Sheringham

Sheringham owes its present importance to the coming of the railway when the old fishing village of Lower Sheringham developed into a holiday resort. The ebb tide reveals extensive sands beyond a pebbly beach. Nearby is the Regency mansion of Sheringham Hall, designed by Humphry Repton. The grounds, now in the hands of the National Trust, are famous for their rhododendrons and azaleas, in flower from late May to June.

Cley-next-the-Sea

Land reclamation in the 17th century made Cley's (pronounced Cly) suffix inaccurate, like that of neighbouring Wells, but it is still a pretty village of flint-faced houses leading down to the quay and harbour. The nearby nature reserves draw bird watchers from far and wide.

Blakeney

Separated from Cley by extensive salt-marshes – the haunt of numerous flocks of wildfowl – Blakeney and the long, low sheltering shingle peninsula of Blakeney Point is a bird-watcher's paradise (see Off the Beaten Track). The brick and flint village of Blakeney has a waterfront usually crowded with yachts and cruisers which ply the twisting inlet of the River Glaven.

Little Walsingham

It was in 1061 that Lady Richeld, lady of the manor, saw a vision of the Virgin Mary at Walsingham. The shrine she built was added to by Augustinian and Franciscan friars, but later destroyed by Henry VII. The present shrine dates from the 1930s, when there was a revival of interest which has continued.
The 18th-century Shirehall contains a museum, the principal exhibit in which is the Georgian courtroom and prisoners' lock-up. The history of the pilgrimage is also told.

Fakenham

An important market town for the local farming community, with a 15th-century church and some fine Georgian buildings. There is a racecourse on the southern edge of the town.

Norfolk Rural Life Museum

Two centuries of the rural life of the county, particularly concentrating on life on the farm, is graphically illustrated in this fascinating museum at Beech House, Gressenhall Green.

East Dereham

The commercial capital of central Norfolk, East Dereham has some fine old buildings; notably the colourfully plastered Bishop Bonner's Cottages, which may originally have been a Tudor guildhall. The large, partly Norman Church of St Nicholas stands on the site of a nunnery founded in the 7th century.

Holt

Sir Thomas Gresham, founder of London's Royal Exchange, set up Gresham's School in his birthplace in 1555. Its Tudor-style buildings of 1858 still grace the square of this largely 18th-century market town.

OFF THE TOUR

Wells-next-the-Sea

Not quite `next-the-sea' anymore, Wells nevertheless has a quayside where shrimp and whelk fishermen take their harvest from the sea. A pleasant, Georgian town reached by following the A149 from Stiffkey, this is convenient for visiting nearby Holkham Hall; the Palladian mansion which was the home of the agricultural reformer Thomas Coke. The Holkham Bygones collection gives a flavour of life `below stairs'.

Castle Acre Priory and Castle

This tiny village, reached by following the A1065 south from Fakenham, is dominated by the massive earthworks which protected the Norman keep built by William de Warrene, son-in-law of William the Conqueror. At the other end of the steep village street are the ruins of the 11th-century Clunaic priory, probably founded by William's son, and dissolved by Henry VIII.

Norfolk Wildlife Park

Turn right on the A1067 at Bawdeswell for this 40-acre wildlife park, founded by naturalist Phillip Wayre to breed rare species and re-introduce them into the wild. This is also the home of the Pheasant Trust.

Mannington Hall Gardens

Reached by turning right off the B1110 on to the B1354, just past Swanton Novers, this is a 15th-century moated manor house with the ruins of a Saxon church set in its beautiful rose gardens.

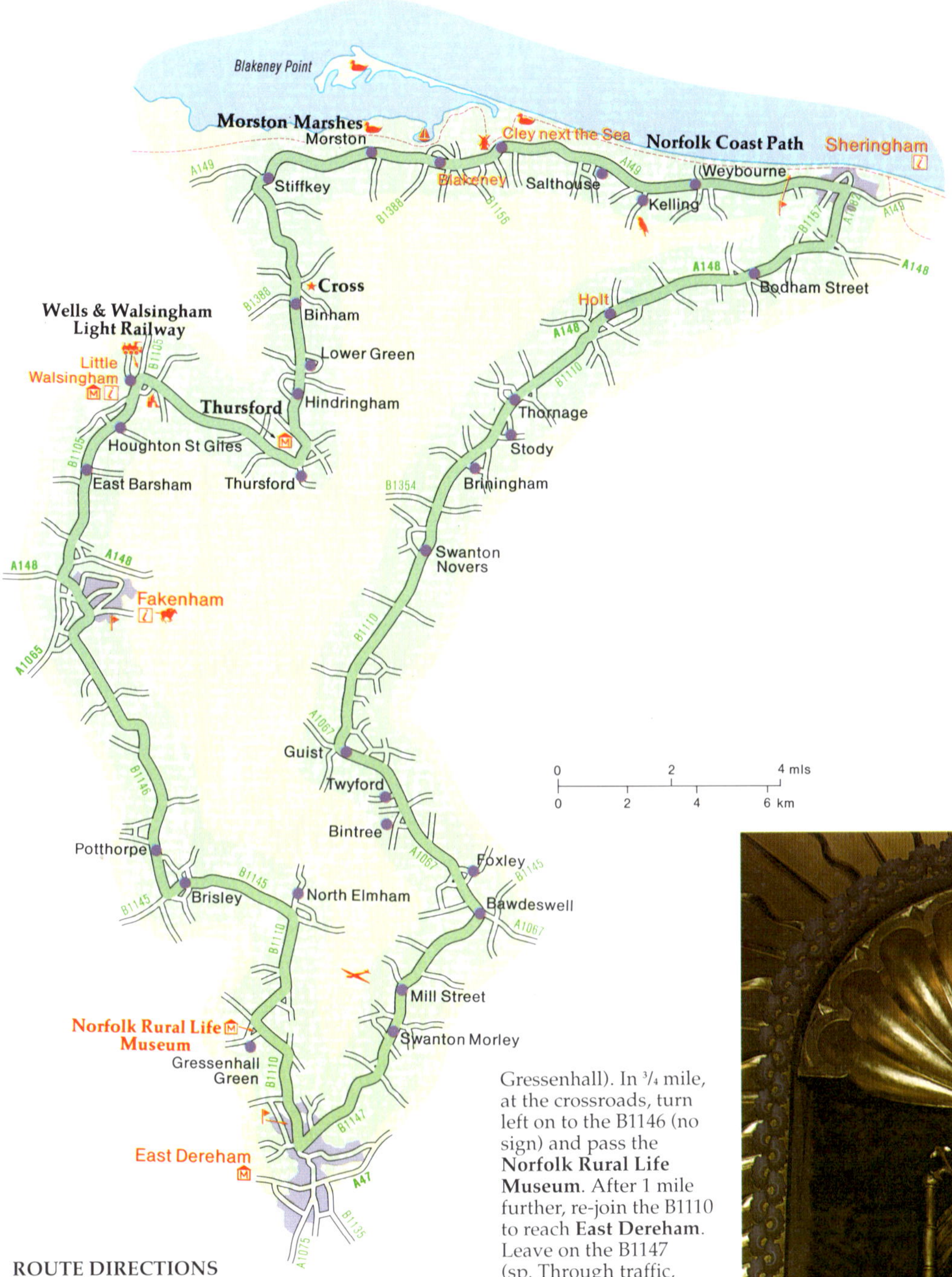

ROUTE DIRECTIONS

Leave **Sheringham** (map 9TG14) on the A149 Wells road, and in 2¾ miles pass a restored windmill before entering Weybourne. Continue through Salthouse to **Cley-next-the-Sea** and, still on the A149 (sp. King's Lynn), pass through **Blakeney** and Morston to Stiffkey. Here, turn left, unclassified (sp. Binham) and in ¾ mile turn right continuing past the Cross at Binham. Keep forward with the B1388 and continue on the unclassified road through Hindringham towards Thursford. In 1 mile, at the crossroads, turn right. At the next crossroads turn right again to enter Thursford. Continue on the Walsingham road and in 3 miles turn right to enter **Little Walsingham**. Leave on the Fakenham road B1105, and pass through Houghton St Giles and East Barsham. Go forward 2 miles, turn right on to the A148 and, at the roundabout, take 2nd exit to enter **Fakenham**. Leave on the B1146, and in ½ mile turn left. Continue for 6 miles, then at the T-junction turn left on to the B1145 (sp. Bawdeswell). In ½ mile bear right through Brisely to North Elmham. Turn right on to the B1110 (sp. Dereham) and in 1½ miles turn right, unclassified (sp. Gressenhall). In ¾ mile, at the crossroads, turn left on to the B1146 (no sign) and pass the **Norfolk Rural Life Museum**. After 1 mile further, re-join the B1110 to reach **East Dereham**. Leave on the B1147 (sp. Through traffic, Bawdeswell) for Swanton Morley. After 1 mile further turn right across the River Wensum to Bawdeswell Bypass. Turn left on to the A1067 (sp. Fakenham) and continue to Guist. At the clock tower turn right on to the B1110, and in 5¼ miles cross the main road. Continue to Thornage, then, at the roundabout take the A148 (sp. King's Lynn). In under ¼ mile turn right, unclassified (sp. Town Centre) to enter **Holt**. Follow signs to Sheringham and Cromer and at the end of the town turn left on to the A148, and pass through Bodham. After 1¾ miles turn left on to the A1082 and descend to Sheringham.

OUTDOOR ACTIVITIES

Blakeney Point

Bring your binoculars and walking boots for some fine views of common and sandwich terns, oystercatchers and ringed plovers on this National Trust property. The 3½-mile sand and shingle spit can be reached by a 3½-mile walk from Cley beach, or by ferry from Morston Quay or Blakeney. There is also a common seal colony.

West Runton

Between Cromer and Sheringham, south of the A149, the National Trust owns 110 acres of heath and woodland. Numerous public footpaths thread the area.

The Norfolk Coast Path, which provides plenty of opportunities for walking and bird watching, can be joined at several points along the coastal stretch of the tour, including Weybourne, Cley and Sheringham.

The Shrine of Our Lady of Walsingham has been a pilgrims' centre since the 11th century, when Lady Richeld built a shrine. The present Italianate workmanship dates from 1931

AROUND THE WOLDS

75½ miles

The Lincolnshire Wolds give the lie to the idea that the county seems flat The easternmost chalk carp of the Wolds runs south for 40 miles; from the mouth of the

Humber almost to the shores of The Wash. These breezy uplands rise to over 550ft, in gently rolling, sheep-cropped hills sheltering deep valleys with hanging beechwoods.

A prehistoric trackway follows the scarp of the Wolds and a Roman road crosses it near Belchford, indicating the ancient importance of these uplands. Placenames again tell of Danish settlement, with many 'thorps' and 'bys' among village names. Today, this is rich, peaceful farming country, and the busy market towns of Market Rasen, Horncastle and Louth serve a mainly agricultural community.

The land is lightly populated, and the roads are usually quiet, except when they approach the popular seaside town of Cleethorpes; with its wide beach, and views of distant Spurn Head across the busy waters of the Humber.

Alfred, Lord Tennyson, who was born at Somersby at the southern end of the Wolds, described the lonely horizons of his homeland in his In Memoriam:

'Calm and deep peace on this high wold,
And on these dews that drench the furze.'

ROUTE DIRECTIONS

Leave **Cleethorpes** (map 13TA30) pier and follow the sea-front along Alexandra Road. In ½ mile at the Lifeboat Hotel turn right into Queens Parade and on to the A1098 (sp. Louth). In 1½ miles, at the roundabout, take 2nd exit and after 1½ miles further, bear right into New Waltham. In ½ mile, at the roundabout, take 1st exit. A16 (sp. Boston). After 3¼ miles, at the crossroads, turn right, unclassified (sp. Grainsby). Continue forward, in ¾ mile go through the gateway into Grainsby Park and after a further mile go over the crossroads and continue to **Wold Newton**. At the trunk road turn left (sp. Louth) and in 3 miles at the crossroads, turn right, (sp. Market Rasen). In ½ mile keep left and then in a further ½ mile, at the trunk road, turn right (sp. Binbrook). Shortly, at the crossroads, go forward (sp. Ludford). In 2½ miles, at the trunk road, turn right on to the A631 (sp. Ludford, Market Rasen) and into Ludford. In 1 mile, at the crossroads, turn right on to the B1225 (sp. Caistor) and after 2¼ miles, at the crossroads, turn left on to the B1203 passing through **Tealby** on route to **Market Rasen**. Here, go over the crossroads on to the B1202 (no sign), through Linwood, Lissington and Holton cum Beckering to Wragby. Here, turn left on to the A158 (sp. Skegness) and continue to Baumber. In ¼ mile turn left, unclassified (sp Hemingby) then in ¼ mile further, at the trunk road, turn left again (sp. Caistor). Continue forward, passing Belmont TV mast on the right, then in 1½ miles turn right on to the A157 (sp. Louth) and go forward to Burgh on Bain. In 2½ miles turn right, unclassified (sp. Cadwell Park), then, after 4¾ miles turn left on to the A153 (sp. Louth). In 5½ miles, at the traffic signals, turn left on to the A16 (sp. Grimsby) then shortly, turn right, unclassified, into the Town Centre of **Louth**. Continue forward to leave by Eastgate, and in 1¾ miles turn left (sp. Alvingham). In ½ mile, at the trunk road, turn right to the edge of **Alvingham**. Turn left (sp. Fulstow, Tetney) and continue through Yarburgh to Covenham St Mary. Turn right (sp. Fulstow, Grimsby) to Covenham St Bartholomew and Fulstow. At the end of the village keep left and in 1⅓ miles, at the trunk road, turn right on to the B1201 (sp. Tetney). In ¾ mile, at the trunk road, turn left on to the A1031 (sp. Grimsby) to Tetney and Humberstone. In ½ mile, at the roundabout, turn right, unclassified, into North Sea Lane (sp. Humberstone Fitties). In 1 mile, at the roundabout, take 1st exit to return to Cleethorpes.

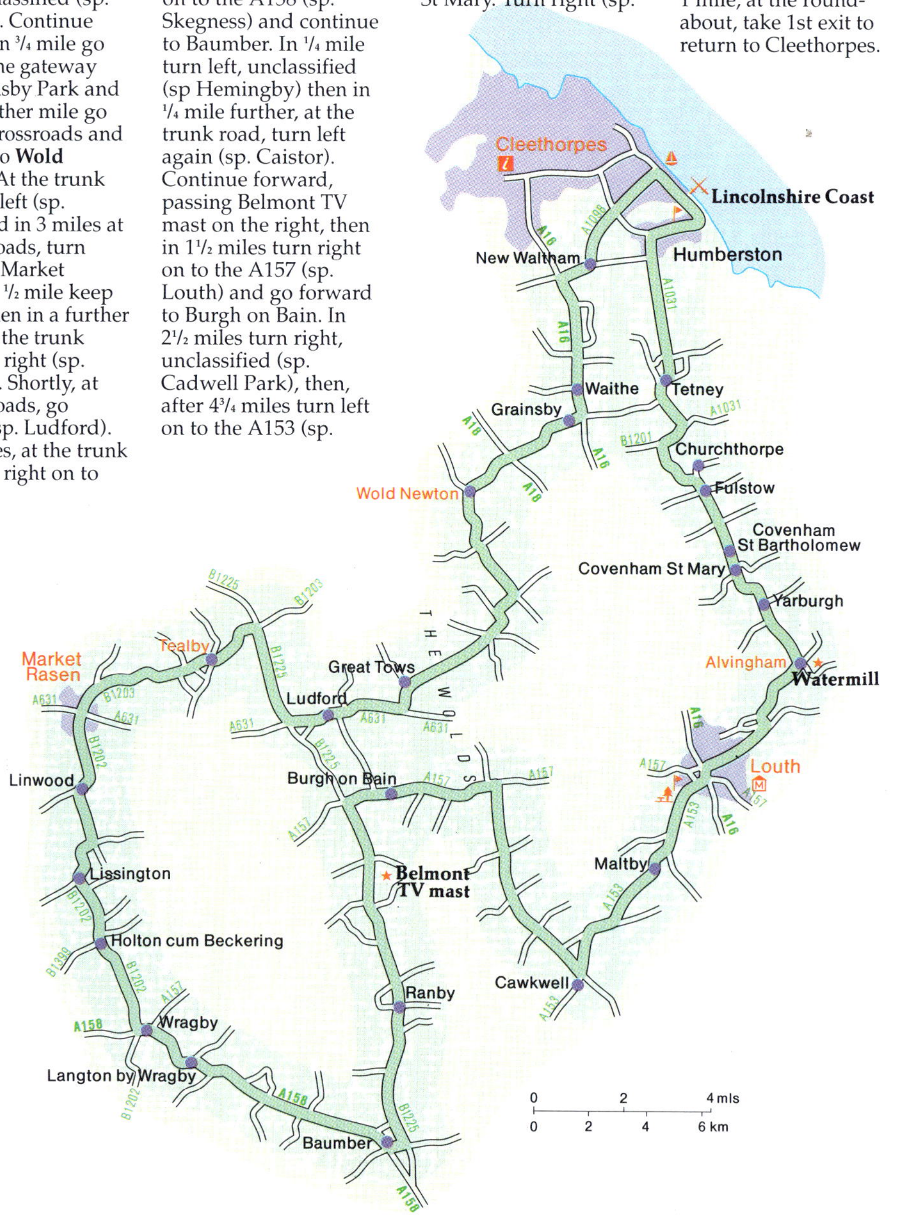

Somersby church, which contains memorials to Lord Tennyson who was born in the village in 1809

Tattershall Castle, a 15th-century fortified house, is one of the most splendid examples of medieval brick building. There are magnificent views from the square and massive keep

OFF THE TOUR

Horncastle
A pleasant, leafy market town on the River Bain, on the site of the Roman town of Banovallum, of which some walls are partly preserved. Among a number of old inns is The Fighting Cocks, which still has the cockpit where this now illegal sport was practised. St Mary's Church, near the market-place, has some Civil War relics, such as pikes and scythes. Keep south on the A158 from Baumber for Horncastle.

Tattershall
Take the A153 south from Horncastle for Tattershall Castle, the best example of a fortified brick keep in Britain. It was built c1440 for Ralph Cromwell, Lord Treasurer of England, more for show than defence. There are displays in the turret rooms and a museum in the guardhouse.
Easily combined with a visit to Tattershall Castle, this is a `must' for young aero-buffs. If you are lucky, you could see some classic aircraft in flight, or as they take off and land.

Coningsby
Just north of Tattershall, this former Second World War airfield is now the home of the famous RAF Battle of Britain Memorial Flight. Hangars contain the only flying Lancaster bomber in Europe (The City of Lincoln), five Spitfires, two Hurricanes and other memorabilia.
The Church of St Michael and All Angels in the village is notable for its early 17th-century, one-handed, red-faced clock. At 16$^1/_2$ft in diameter, it is the largest one-handed clock in the world.

Old Bolingbroke
One of the finest of the Wold villages, set in a hollow and overlooked by the impressive ruins of Bolingbroke Castle, the birthplace of Henry IV in 1367. It was `slighted' by Cromwell's men in 1643. Bolingbroke is off the A155 south-east of Horncastle.

ON THE TOUR

Cleethorpes
The many fine houses in Cleethorpes' suburbs reflect the wealth produced by neighbouring Grimsby's once-great fishing industry. Today, the town is a holiday resort - especially popular with people from the industrial East Midlands - with a wide promenade, good beaches and fine views across the Humber to Spurn Head. The resort is very friendly and the beach popular with children.

Wold Newton
Almost hidden from view, in a well-wooded valley in a shoulder of the Wolds, Wold Newton enjoys splendid views north and east towards the Humber. There is a church with a Norman tower.

Tealby
Many times a winner of the county's best-kept village competition, Tealby has a great deal of charm. Cottages of red-brown ironstone lead down to a watersplash – known as the Beck – where the River Rase gurgles by. The Church of All Saints, dating from the 12th century, overlooks this charming village.

Market Rasen
Best-known nationally for its racecourse, Market Rasen is a busy Wolds market town serving a large area of rural Lincolnshire. Originally called East Rasen and one of three Rasens (Market, West and Middle), the town's unusual name comes from the Old English 'raesn', which meant `plank', and was probably a reference to a former plank bridge.

Louth
One of the most perfectly preserved and complete Georgian market towns in England. The Grammar School, founded by Edward VI, had existed as an endowed school three centuries before. Its scholars included Arctic explorer Sir John Franklin, Captain John Smith the first President of Virginia, and Alfred, Lord Tennyson.
The elegant, 300ft crocketed spire of St James's Church stands out like a beacon across the flat marshlands of the Humber Estuary. It was built from local Ancaster stone in 1506. The museum of the Louth Naturalists, Antiquarian and Literary Society in Broadbank is full of local bygones, and has a specially impressive collection of butterflies and moths.

Alvingham
Alvingham, with its ancient 18th-century three-storey watermill in Church Lane (open at certain times) and links with Louth via the Louth Navigation Canal, has one other exceptional claim to fame. The yew-shaded churchyard contains two churches; 14th-century St Adelwold's, the only church in Britain dedicated to this Saxon saint, and St Mary's, an originally 12th-century priory chapel which actually belongs to the neighbouring village of North Cockerington.

OFF THE BEATEN TRACK

Dogdyke Pumping Station
A land drainage pumping station south west of Tattershall, worked by an 1855 Bradley and Craven steam-driven beam engine – the only one of its kind in the country. Limited opening, usually the first Sunday of each month – watch out for signs.

Burgh le Marsh Windmill
A fine, five-sailed tower windmill, built in 1833 and still in full working order, thanks to the good offices of Lincolnshire County Council and a dedicated band of volunteers. Corn is still milled (wind permitting) on the second and last Sundays of the month from April to October.

OUTDOOR ACTIVITIES

Gibraltar Point National Nature Reserve
Reached by a minor road from Skegness (take the A158 from Baumber through Horncastle), these 1,500 acres of sand dunes, saltmarsh and shoreline on the edge of The Wash are famous for their breeding colony of little terns and little plovers on the Spit. A birdwatchers' paradise, Gibraltar Point also has a fine interpretative centre for visitors.

Somersby
Reached by country lanes off the A158 east of Horncastle, the Old Rectory was the birthplace of Lord Tennyson, Poet Laureate in 1850.

EITHER SIDE OF ERMINE STREET

90 miles

Ermine Street, one of the great highways of Roman Britain, leads, ruler-straight, north from the ancient cathedral city of Lincoln to the banks of the Humber, now spanned by the elegant Humber Suspension Bridge. Either side are villages which have been off the beaten track for 2,000 years.

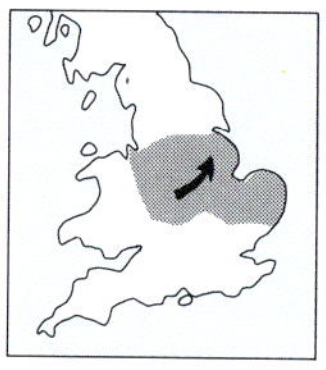

Steep Hill in Lincoln is one of the most fascinating old streets in a city whose historic centre is remarkably well preserved. Two of the oldest domestic buildings are Norman

Lincoln's magnificent triple towered, medieval cathedral stands high where the ridge known as Lincoln Edge is breached by the River Witham. The Roman city of Lindum Colonia was founded here, at the junction of two famous Roman highways, the Fosse Way and Ermine Street, and the modern city is steeped in its ancient past.

The fertile countryside to the north runs up to the great estuary of the Humber. The villages – small, isolated communities often with Danish names – stand back to a respectful distance below, and on either side of, the Imperial line of Ermine Street, which follows the ridge of Lincoln Edge. This is a countryside where farming is pre-eminent, and from where much of the nation's vegetables are obtained. If you are driving through the area at night in summer, you will see harvesting of wheat and peas going on round the clock under the glare of floodlights.

ON THE TOUR

Lincoln

Lincoln, a busy city with an abundance of Roman and Norman remains, is dominated by the three towers of the magnificent cathedral, which stand 365ft high on a 200ft ridge above the rest of the city.

The cathedral was founded by Bishop Remigius and is recognised as a masterpiece of the Early English style. A copy of the Magna Carta is preserved in the chantry. Look out for the celebrated Lincoln Imp carved high in the beautifully decorated Angel Choir. Among many other remarkable sights, Lincoln has two superb Norman domestic buildings, the Jew's House and Aaron the Jew's House, which date from around 1170 when the Normans were encouraging the Jews to finance trade. The castle was founded by William the Conqueror on this strategic site. The Newport Arch has been in use since Roman times, and the High Bridge has houses built over it, in the medieval manner.

There is a good local museum covering city and county in Broadgate, while the Usher Gallery in Lindum Road includes the Usher collection of watches, and a Peter de Wint gallery.

Thornton Abbey

The great crenellated gatehouse shows that this was one of the more important abbeys of the Augustinian order. It was founded in 1139 by William de Gros, Earl of Albemarle, who is buried within the walls.

Barton-upon-Humber

Once important as a river port, Barton has been overshadowed and overtaken by the Humber Bridge. Baysgarth Hall, on the Caistor Road, is an 18th-century town house which is now a museum with displays of porcelain, local history and geology.

Humber Bridge

Dubbed 'the bridge to nowhere' when it was bypassed by the motorway network, the Humber Bridge remains an impressive sight and the longest single-span suspension bridge in the world. The main span is 4,626ft long, suspended on 144,355ft of wire, and the reinforced concrete piers rise 510ft above the river. The bridge was opened in 1981 after nine years' construction.

Elsham Hall Country Park

Set in the magnificent grounds of Elsham Hall, with its three lakes and 400-acres of woodland, this is a great stopping-off place for all the family. There are woodland nature trails, a wild butterfly walkway, a walled garden containing rare breeds of livestock, a carp lake where the giant carp will come and feed from your hand, and an adventure play-ground for the children. Excellent, award-winning tearooms.

Glentworth

Neat stone cottages nestling against the foot of Lincoln Edge. The Parish Church of St Michael has a magnificent tomb to Sir Christopher Wray, Chief Justice to Elizabeth I, who died in 1592. The church has a notable Saxon tower.

Scampton

The permanent showground of the Lincolnshire Show, held in June, and a famous wartime airbase of Bomber Command are both on the outskirts of this village of stone-walled cottages under Lincoln Edge. Among the squadrons to be based at RAF Scampton was No. 617 - the famous 'Dambusters'.

ROUTE DIRECTIONS

Leave **Lincoln** (map 8SK97) on the A46 (sp. Grimsby) passing Nettleham before bearing left, unclassified (sp. Welton). In Welton bear right (sp. Dunholme) then in 1/3 mile turn left (sp. Spridlington). In 3 miles, at the trunk road, turn right into Spridlington. Here, turn left (sp Normanby) and in 2 1/3 miles turn right into Normanby Road. In Normanby turn left for Glentham. Here, turn right on to the A631 (sp. Grimsby) and at The Crown Inn turn left, unclassified for Bishops Norton. Continue forward (sp. Waddingham) to Atterby then turn right (sp. Snitterby, Brigg) to Snitterby and on to Waddingham. Here, turn right on to the B1205 (sp. Caistor) to South Kelsey. At the crossroads, turn left, unclassified (sp. North Kelsey, Brigg) for North Kelsey. Go forward (sp. Brigg) and in 1 mile go forward on to the B1434. In 1 mile turn right, unclassified (sp. Searby). At Searby, at the trunk road, turn left (sp. Caistor), ascend, and at the trunk road turn left on to the A1084 (sp. Brigg). Descend 1 mile and in 1/3 mile further turn right, unclassified to Bigby. In 2 1/3 miles, at the trunk road, turn right on to the A18 (no sign), then in another mile turn left, unclassified (sp. Barton A1077). After 2 1/2 miles turn left (sp. Barton-upon-Humber) to Wootton. Here, keep left on the A1077 (sp. Barrow) and in 1 mile turn right, unclassified (sp. Thornton Abbey). Pass **Thornton Abbey** and, in 1 1/4 miles, at the trunk road, turn left (sp. Barrow), then continue for 2 1/2 miles and go forward over the crossroads on to the B1402 (sp. Barton) to the edge of Barrow upon Humber. In 1/2 mile, turn right on to the A1077 for **Barton-upon-Humber**. At the mini-roundabout go forward (sp. Humber Br. Viewing Area) then bear right, shortly left, and at the end turn left. In 1/3 mile at The Sloop Inn turn left into Far Ings Road. In 1/3 mile pass under the **Humber Bridge** and in 1/2 mile turn left (sp. Scunthorpe). In 1 mile, at the roundabout, turn right on to the A1077. Descend, then branch left on to the B1204 into South Ferriby, Horkstow and Saxby All Saints. At the end of this last village, turn left, unclassified (no sign) and ascend. At the top, at the trunk road, turn right and in 3 miles, at the crossroads, turn right on to the B1206 (not shown – sp. Brigg). Descend past **Elsham Hall Country Park** and in 1 mile go over the level crossing, then in ¾ mile turn left, unclassified, into Wrawby. At the trunk road turn right on to the A18 (no sign) to Brigg. Here, at the roundabout, take 2nd exit (sp. Lincoln) and in 1 mile go forward on to the A15. In 1 mile further turn right, unclassified for Scawby. At the trunk road turn left on to the B1207 (not shown – sp. Hibaldstow) and in ½ mile, at the crossroads, turn right, unclassified (sp. Kirton). In 2 miles, at the trunk road, turn left on to the B1398. Pass Mount Pleasant Mill on the right, and continue to Kirton in Lindsey. Go forward (sp. Lincoln) and in 6 miles go over the crossroads (sp. Burton). Pass **Glentworth** and in 5 miles, bear right (sp. Lincoln) and continue through Cammeringham, Brattleby and **Scampton**. Pass the viewpoint on the right then, at the trunk road, turn right, then left to return to Lincoln.

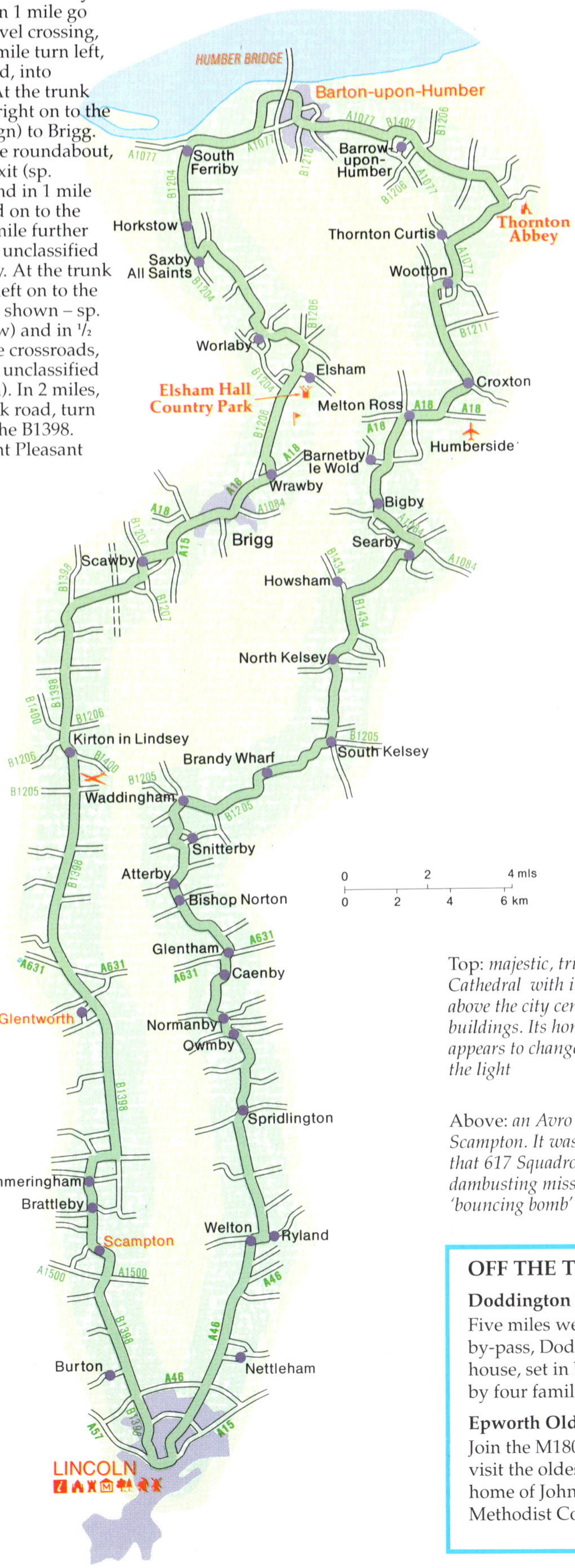

Top: *majestic, triple towered Lincoln Cathedral with its fine west front towers high above the city centre, surrounded by medieval buildings. Its honey-coloured limestone appears to change colour, according to the light*

Above: *an Avro Lancaster on display at RAF Scampton. It was from this base in May 1943 that 617 Squadron flew its successful dambusting mission with the famous 'bouncing bomb'*

OFF THE BEATEN TRACK

Stow Saxon Church

St Mary's at Stow is one of the most complete Saxon churches in the country, founded around 975 as the Cathedral Minster for Lindsey, by Earl Leofric of Mercia. The crossing arches are the largest Saxon arches in the country. Turn right off the B1398 at Cammeringham.

OFF THE TOUR

Doddington Hall

Five miles west of Lincoln on the B1190 and signposted off the A46 Lincoln by-pass, Doddington Hall is a superb and complete Elizabethan mansion house, set in beautiful gardens. Its contents reflect a continuous occupation by four families over four centuries.

Epworth Old Rectory

Join the M180 at Scawby (Junction 4) and take the A161, at Junction 2, to visit the oldest Methodist shrine in the country. Built in 1709, this was the home of John and Charles Wesley; lovingly restored by the World Methodist Council in 1957.

WALES AND THE MARCHES

Wales has a wealth of back country roads that snake their way between steepling mountainsides or politely accompany rushing torrents through wooded glens. Take the routes which penetrate the deep green valleys of the Clwydian Hills in the north-east, for example. At the opposite corner of the Principality, in Dyfed, are the Preseli Hills, where the roads cross the stony moorland grazed by mountain sheep and ponies, and sprinkled with prehistoric remains. East from here, by contrast, the massed regiments of conifers in the Brechfa Forest conceal swift trout streams.

Well worth investigating by lesser roads are the former coal-mining valleys of South Wales, which have been reclaimed and 'greened'. In Snowdonia, on the other hand, industry has left an unreconstructed legacy of roads running dramatically along hillsides black, jagged and gleaming with slate. From Rhayader in Powys, meanwhile, minor roads explore the chain of man-made reservoirs in the Elan Valley, among bare mountains and clustering woods.

Across the border in the Marches, Herefordshire country lanes will conduct you, if you let them, to England's weirdest collection of gargoyles, monstrous heads and strange stone carvings. Adorning the little church of Kilpeck, they include a sheelagh-na-gig and a rabbit of doubtful sanity. Another maze of back roads, further north, will take you to A.E. Housman's 'quietest places under the sun' – Clunton and Clunbury, Clungunford and Clun. The minor byways of Shropshire penetrate some of Britain's least spoiled scenic landscape.

Left: *Senni Valley, Powys – the river winds between The Black Mountain and the Beacons*
Above: *Tenby, Dyfed – a resort with two beaches divided by a headland: this is North Beach*

SNOWDON AND THE MENAI STRAIT

80 miles

Snowdon, the highest mountain in England and Wales, rises abruptly from the coast. The mountain and its equally formidable neighbouring peaks form a massif of

boulder-strewn screes and fearsome rock faces. Yet within 10 miles, the mountains decline to a coastal plain along the Menai Strait.

Mount Snowdon stands at 3,559ft, the high point of a rocky mountain range of razor-sharp ridges and pinnacles. The Glyders and Tryfan a few miles to the north-east are equally well known to climbers and outdoor enthusiasts, as are the smooth rock faces along the Llanberis Pass where some of Britain's greatest mountaineers developed their skills.

Snowdon gives its name to the large Snowdonia National Park, an 845-square-mile parkland that extends southwards, way beyond the mountain, all the way to Machynlleth in Mid Wales. However, it is Snowdon that invariably captures the limelight. Walkers make for its summit in their thousands each summer, joined by those who take the easy option and enjoy a ride to the top on the Snowdon Mountain Railway from Llanberis.

The mountain range fills the skyline above the Menai Strait: the narrow passage separating the Isle of Anglesey from mainland Wales guarded by two famous castles.

ROUTE DIRECTIONS

Leave **Caernarfon** (map IOSH46) on the A487 (sp. Bangor) and continue to the slate port of Port Dinorwic. In 1½ miles further, at the roundabout, turn left (sp. Holyhead) and in ¾ mile at the next roundabout take 1st exit on to the A5. Cross Britannia Bridge into Angelsey. On the far side branch left, turn right on to the A4080 and continue to the outskirts of Menai Bridge Town. Follow signs to Bangor to cross the **Menai Bridge** then, at the roundabout, join the A5122 for **Bangor**. Leave on the A5122 (sp. Betws-y-coed) and in 2½ miles pass the entrance to **Penrhyn Castle**. In ¾ mile, at the roundabout, take 2nd exit on to the A5. Turn right almost immediately on to the B4366 (sp. Caernarfon). In 3½ miles, at a roundabout, turn left on to the B4547 (sp. Llanberis) and 3½ miles further on, at the T-junction, turn left on to the A4086. Skirt the shore of Llyn Padarn and the village of **Llanberis** and continue past Dolbadarn Castle. At Nant Peris ascend the Pass of Llanberis to the Pen-y-Pass car park at its 1,169ft summit. Descend and, after 1 mile, at the T-junction by the Pen-y-Gwryd Hotel, turn right on to the A498 (sp. Beddgelert). Continue the descent, passing the viewpoint of Snowdon Peaks before Llyn Gwynant. Beyond the hamlet of Nant Gwynant follow the valley which skirts Llyn Dinas to pass the **Sygun Copper Mine** and approach **Beddgelert**. Keep forward on the A4085 Caernarfon road to skirt Beddgelert forest to Rhyd-Ddu. Pass by the shore of Llyn Cwellyn and ascend through Betws Garmon and Waunfawr. Two miles further, at the roundabout, go forward to return to Caernarfon.

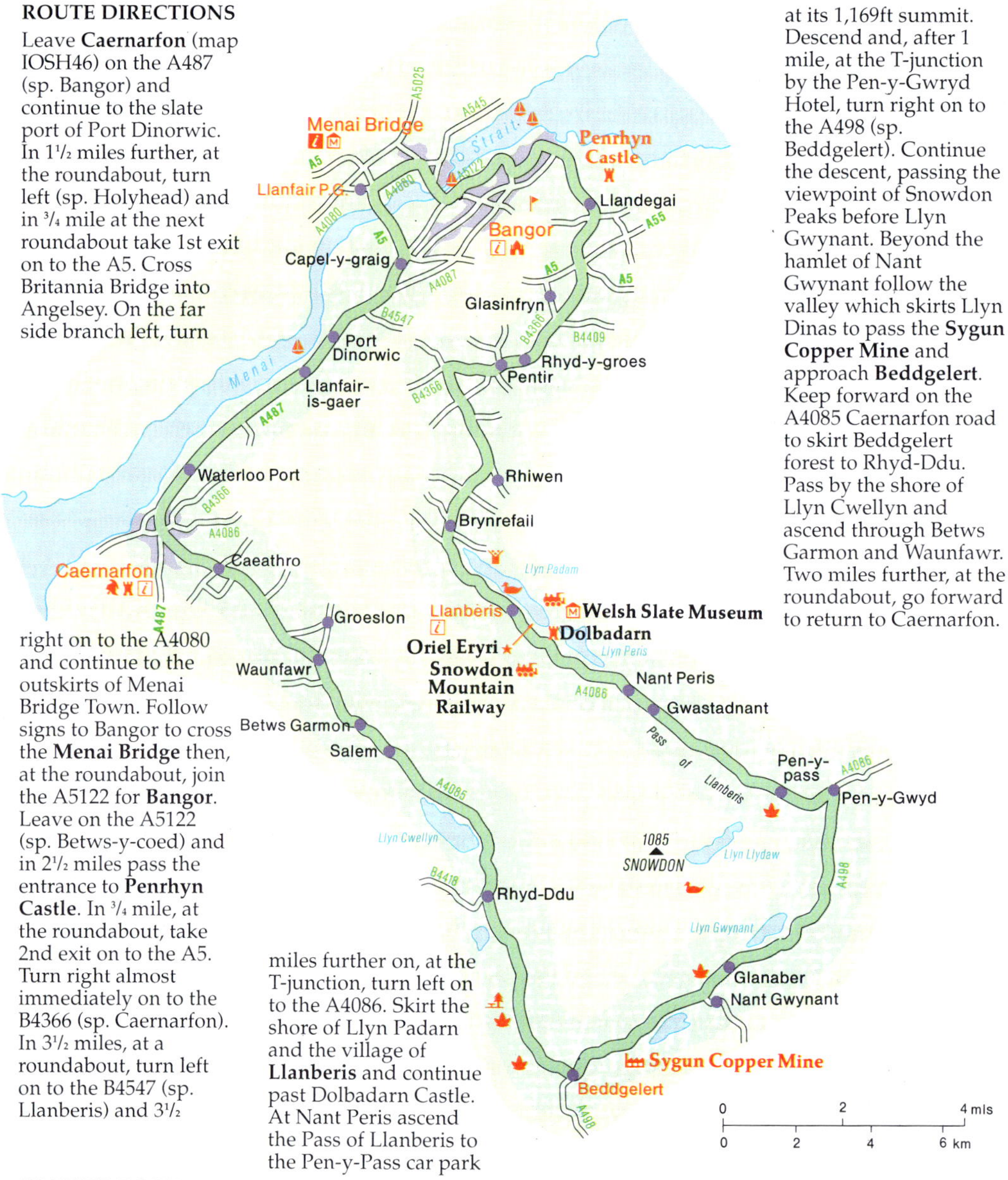

Telford's graceful engineering masterpiece, the 1,000ft-long Menai Bridge, was opened in January 1826 to carry the London to Holyhead turnpike across the Menai Strait

ON THE TOUR

Caernarfon

Caernarfon is undoubtedly the most famous castle in Wales. Its mighty towers were designed to intimidate and impress, for Caernarfon was built by Edward I as a statement of his power over the Welsh. The castle, begun in 1283, served as both royal palace and military fortress. Decorative bands of coloured stonework are amongst the features that set Caernarfon apart from Edward's other North Wales castles.

Stylish, majestic Caernarfon Castle bristles with angular towers, the most exceptional of which is the Eagle Tower with its three tall, slender turrets. An audio-visual presentation in this tower explains the castle's history, while the Queen's Tower houses the Regimental Museum of the Royal Welch Fusiliers. There are historical exhibitions in the North-east and Chamberlain Towers. Caernarfon achieved worldwide publicity as the setting, in 1969, for the investiture of Prince Charles as Prince of Wales.

The castle was not the first stronghold at Caernarfon. The Roman fort of Segontium, dating from around AD78, stands on a hill above the town.

Menai Bridge and Llanfair P.G.

The tour crosses over to Anglesey by the 'new' Britannia Road Bridge, returning to the mainland by Thomas Telford's famous Menai Suspension Bridge. The world's first iron suspension bridge, it was built in the 1820s to complete the road link from London to Holyhead.

The longest place name in the world can be seen nearby. Llanfairpwllgwyngyllgogerychwyrndrobwllllantysiliogogogoch has been shortened by the locals to a more manageable Llanfair P.G. The name, in its full glory, adorns the James Pringle Woollen Mill: a large visitor centre selling a wide range of quality crafts, woollens and gifts.

Bangor

The university town of Bangor is at its most attractive down by the old pier, which has been refurbished to its original Victorian splendour. Bangor Cathedral, a restored medieval church, stands on an ancient religious site founded in the 6th century.

Penrhyn Castle

This castle, in attractive grounds on the outskirts of Bangor, is an elaborate `sham'. Built between 1820 and 1837 by a local slate- and sugar-trading magnate, it symbolises the exuberant self-confidence of 19th-century Britain. A huge, four-storeyed neo-Norman keep dominates the outside, while slate is much in evidence in the lavish interior - there is even a bed, weighing over a ton, made from it! The castle, which also contains a doll collection and railway museum, is in the care of the National Trust.

Llanberis

Visitors can catch two trains here. The Swiss locomotives of the Snowdon Mountain Railway climb four and a half miles by rack-and-pinion line to the summit of Snowdon. The Llanberis Lake Railway follows an altogether gentler route of two miles along the shores of Llyn Padarn. The terminus for this latter line is near the Dinorwic Quarry, one of the biggest slate quarries in Wales prior to its closure in 1969. Its former workshops, with their giant waterwheel and original machinery for sawing, splitting and trimming slate, have now become the Welsh Slate Museum.

The hillsides above Llanberis are riddled with the giant tunnels of the Dinorwic Hydro-electric Power Scheme. All is explained at Llanberis's Power of Wales Exhibition, which also looks at the development of Wales from early times. Llanberis stands at the junction of two lakes, Llyn Padarn and Llyn Peris. Dolbadarn Castle, on a headland above this meeting place, is a single-towered fortress built by the Welsh leader Llywelyn the Great in the early 13th century.

Sygun Copper Mine

The mine, last worked in 1903, is in the hillside on the approach to Beddgelert. Visitors can take guided tours through the old workings, which bring to life the underground world of the Victorian miner. Stalactites, stalagmites and copper ore veins containing traces of gold and silver can be seen within Sygun's large chambers.

Beddgelert

See page 131.

OUTDOOR ACTIVITIES

Walks and trails can be taken in Llyn Padarn Country Park.

Snowdon Mountain Railway

The only public rack-and-pinion railway in Britain. It climbs $4^{1}/_{2}$ miles to the summit of Snowdon to give magnificent views of North Wales, the Isle of Man and the Wicklow Mountains of Ireland on a clear day.

Below: *mighty 13th-century Caernarfon Castle combined palatial living quarters with sophisticated defensive designs*
Bottom: *many of the trains at the Llanberis Lake Railway are hauled by vintage steam engines which used to shunt slate wagons along the narrow quarry galleries*

OFF THE TOUR

Plas Newydd

This sumptuous National Trust property is located off the A4080 a mile or so north-west of the Britannia Road Bridge over the Menai Strait. Plas Newydd stands in a magnificent spot overlooking the Strait and Snowdonia. The elegant 18th-century house contains many treasures. Pride of place goes to the wall painting by Rex Whistler, a frequent visitor to the house. The artist's celebrated painting - a highly romanticised Italianate scene - fills a 58ft-long stretch of wall. Plas Newydd's cavalry museum contains a real oddity: the wooden limb (one of the first articulated limbs to be invented) used by the First Marquess of Anglesey after he had lost a leg at the Battle of Waterloo.

Anglesey Sea Zoo

The zoo, near Brynsiencyn just off the A4080, presents the sea life of Anglesey in an imaginative way. Visitors can wander through a shipwreck, watch the ebb and flow of the waves in a `tide tank', see a rock pool in action, view large and small seascape environments, and even get to grips with lobsters and crabs in the zoo's `touch pools'. This enterprising attraction is popular with all the family. In addition to the sea creatures, the children can enjoy water games, model boats, a playground and playboat.

Beaumaris

Before returning to the mainland, drive along the A545 to Beaumaris, a handsome little resort and sailing centre on the north-eastern approach to the Menai Strait. The town owes its existence to its medieval castle, the final - and some say, the finest - of the North Wales fortresses built by the English King Edward I.

IN THE FOOTHILLS OF SNOWDON

40 miles

The southern and western flanks of the Snowdon mountain range are full of wooded valleys, rushing rivers, open moorlands and rocky crests. Two of the rivers - the Dwyryd and the Glaslyn - meet at a beautiful sandy estuary over looked by Portmeirion, one of the strangest villages in the world.

The highest peak in these parts is Moel Hebog, the 2,666ft summit of a lumpy mountain mass which dominates the landscape north of Porthmadog. The roads steer well clear of this high ground, taking advantage of the valleys carved by fast-flowing rivers - most notably just south of Beddgelert where the A498 squeezes through the narrow Aberglaslyn Pass.

The best way to travel along the Vale of Ffestiniog, the lovely valley of the River Dwyryd, is by riding on the narrow-gauge railway which follows its northern slopes. For all its scenic grandeur, this corner of North Wales has in the past relied as much on industry as on farming for its livelihood. The narrow-gauge Ffestiniog Railway was originally constructed to carry slate from Blaenau Ffestiniog's huge quarries and mines to the coast at Porthmadog. Around Nantlle and the beauty spot of Beddgelert there are more reminders of industrial activity.

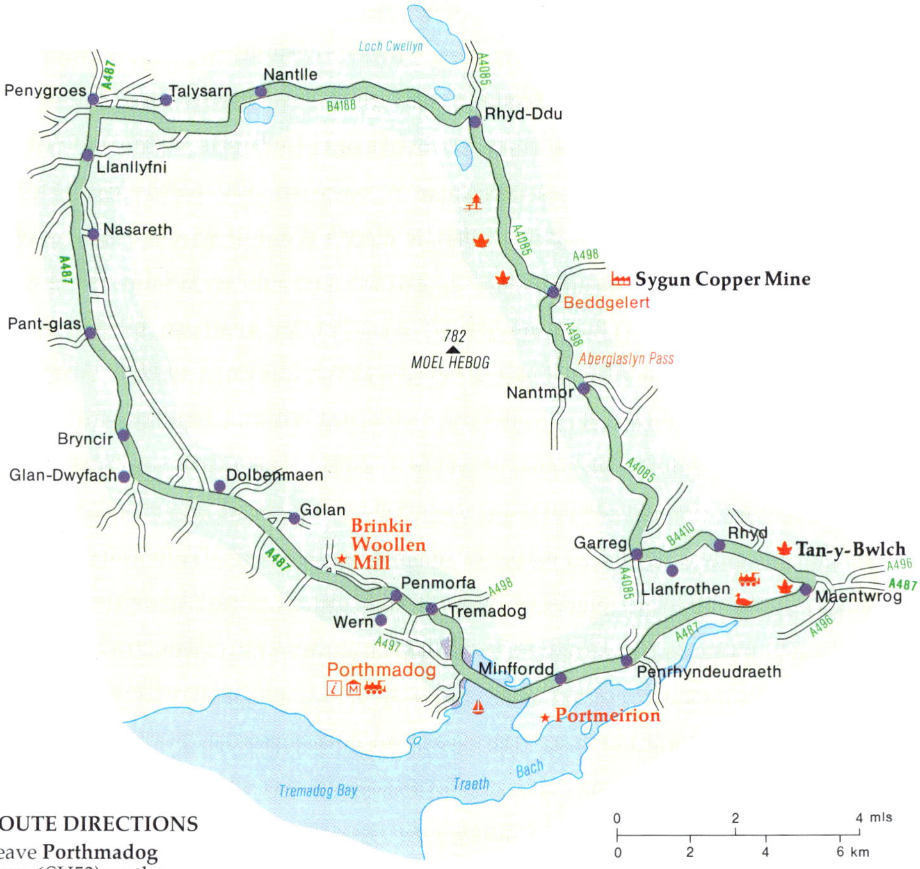

The slate memorial in Blaenau Ffestiniog, the 'slate capital of North Wales', where crags overhang many of the houses

ROUTE DIRECTIONS

Leave **Porthmadog** (map 6SH53) on the A487 (sp. Caernarfon) and in ¼ mile go over the level crossing to Tremadog. At the T-junction turn left and in ⅓ mile bear right to Penmorfa. Pass the **Brinkir Woollen Mill** on the right and continue to Dolbenmaen. Pass the road to the Pennant Valley and go forward to Bryncir, then on to Llanllyfni and Penygroes. Here, at the crossroads, turn right on to the B4418 (sp. Rhyd-Ddu) and in ¹⁄₁₀ mile turn right (no sign) to the edge of Talysarn. In ½ mile, at the T-junction, turn right for Nantlle. Skirt Llyn Nantlle and make an ascent and descent to Rhyd-Ddu. At the T-junction turn right on to the A4085 (sp. Beddgelert). Pass Snowdon on the left and continue into **Beddgelert**. Here, bear right on to the A498 (A487) (sp. Porthmadog) and cross the river bridge. Bear right again and in ⅓ mile go forward to the **Aberglaslyn Pass**. Pass the AA telephone and in ½ mile turn left on to the A4085 (sp. Penrhyndeudraeth) and cross Aberglaslyn river bridge. In 1 mile ascend (1 in 10) and in 2 miles cross the hump-back bridge and bear right to Garreg. Here, at the crossroads, turn left on to the B4410 (sp. Rhyd and Ffestiniog Railway). In 2 miles descend to Rhyd. Reach the road to Tan-y-Bwlch Station (Ffestiniog Railway), pass Llyn Mair then descend (1 in 6) to the T-junction and turn right on to the A487 (sp. Porthmadog). Pass through Penrhyndeudraeth and Minffordd Station and the road to **Portmeirion** village on the left. In ¾ mile pass through the tollgate and cross The Cob causeway to re-enter Porthmadog.

ON THE TOUR

Porthmadog

Tall-masted ships used to sail from the harbourside at Porthmadog laden with slate quarried at Blaenau Ffestiniog. The slate was brought down the valley by the Ffestiniog Railway, a narrow-gauge line built in 1836. Nowadays, this steam-powered railway - one of the most scenic of the `Great Little Trains of Wales' - carries tourists along its 14-mile route from its main station on the harbour at Porthmadog. Railway enthusiasts have a double helping at Porthmadog: the Welsh Highland Railway operates a limited service on a short route from the outskirts of the town.

Another reminder of Porthmadog's slate-exporting past lies berthed along the harbour wall. This is the S.S. *Garlandstone*, a sailing ketch which is part of the Gwynedd Maritime

Museum, whose main building is located on the quayside. The *Garlandstone*'s neighbours are modern holiday craft, for Porthmadog's harbour now has a new lease of life as a popular sailing centre.
Porthmadog Pottery in the town is a craft shop where visitors are encouraged to `have a go' and throw their own pot.

Brinkir Woollen Mill

Just after Penmorfa, a minor road off the A487 loops through Golan. Along the way is the Brinkir Woollen Mill. The entire process of making cloth in the traditional Welsh way is on display at this mill. Visitors can follow the manufacturing process from raw wool to final weaving in a mill that has been operating continuously for over 150 years. Even the waterwheel is still working, though today it provides the mill's machinery with electric power rather than direct-drive.

Beddgelert

It says a lot for the power of myth and legend that many people are familiar with the story of the faithful hound Gelert, who is supposedly buried here. The fact that the `grave' was invented by an 18th-century inn-keeper intent on boosting trade should not dissuade visitors from calling in on this beautifully situated village. Surrounded by steep slopes and towering rock slabs, it stands at the meeting place of three valleys and two rivers. Nearby is the Sygun Copper Mine, open to the public (see Tour 64 for description).

Aberglaslyn Pass

The Glaslyn tumbles through this rocky, narrow defile south of Beddgelert. The trackway and tunnels on the bank beside the road were the route of the Welsh Highland Railway: an overly ambitious enterprise which ended in failure (a short section of the line has been revived by enthusiasts at Porthmadog). The famous old stone bridge at the foot of the pass was once a significant river navigation landmark. Before the embankment at Porthmadog was built, the River Glaslyn was tidal up to this point, and boats were built here.

Portmeirion

This village has been described in many ways. Some find it bizarre, strange or other-worldly; to others it appears enchanting, delightful or downright puzzling. Sir Clough Williams-Ellis, the iconoclastic architect who created Portmeirion, would undoubtedly approve of the reactions invariably provoked by his unique village.
Sir Clough, who died in 1978 aged 94, was said to have adopted a 'gay, light-opera sort of approach' to his work, an attitude reflected in the whimsical, humorous way in which building styles from Renaissance Italy rub shoulders with oriental and traditional English influences.
The architect chose well the setting for his dream-world village. Portmeirion stands in a stunning spot on its own wooded peninsula next to the tidal sands of Traeth Bach. On the slopes above the beach Sir Clough created a maze of colour-washed buildings, statues, pathways, fountains, arcades, gardens, towers and columns. The village, which has its own self-catering and hotel accommodation, is also open to day visitors. It is an intriguing place that is well worth a visit.
Portmeirion is famous the world over through its use in films, television and advertisements. Indeed, many would argue that Portmeirion was the true star of that cult 1960s television series *The Prisoner*, in which the unfortunate Patrick McGoohan was trapped in a surreal prison-domain.

OFF THE BEATEN TRACK

About 6 miles north-west of Porthmadog, the minor road close to the junction between the A487 and B4411 leads westwards to the village of Llangybi. The village's historical interest is reflected in its name. Llangybi is associated with Cybi, a 6th-century saint who travelled widely in Wales. The peaceful fields behind the village church were a place of pilgrimage for centuries, for here is located Ffynnon Gybi, St Cybi's Well. This ancient well, whose waters are believed to have healing powers, became a small spa in the 18th century. The ruins of the well chambers-cum-spa can still be seen by following a footpath from the church which drops down into a delightful little valley.

OUTDOOR ACTIVITIES

Waymarked forest trails through the Beddgelert forest take in mountain streams, high woodland forest and open hillside. The starting point is the Forest Park Campsite off the A4085, north-west of the village.

Beddgelert is a beautiful wooded village deep in the heart of the Snowdonia National Park. The approach to it is breathtaking, with rushing rivers, sparkling lakes and towering peaks

OFF THE TOUR

Criccieth

Criccieth, along the A497 from Porthmadog, is a smallish seaside resort which has altered little from its days as a Victorian watering place. Looking down from its headland perch above the resort's two beaches is Criccieth Castle, an interesting fortress that has, in its time, been in both Welsh and English hands. Its origins are obscure, though the main part of the castle was probably built in about 1230 by the Welsh leader Llywelyn the Great. The stronghold's most outstanding feature is its twin-towered gatehouse, a formidable defensive structure which emphasises the castle's strategic siting.

Blaenau Ffestiniog

At Maentwrog, take the A496 for Blaenau Ffestiniog, the `slate capital of North Wales'. The town, almost surrounded by huge mounds of slate debris, is not to everyone's taste. Yet visitors flock here in their thousands, for Blaenau Ffestiniog offers an exciting and thought-provoking glimpse into an industry which once dominated the lives of so many North Walians. Conditions for the slate miners of old must have been damp and dangerous, as can be seen from a visit to one or both of the two mines open to the public. The Llechwedd Slate Caverns offer tramway rides through the old chambers and a `Deep Mine' trip into the lower workings. The neighbouring Gloddfa Ganol Mountain Centre, based at `the largest slate mine in the world', has an underground passageway accessible on foot, working slate mill, miners' cottages and exhibitions.
The Stwlan Dam is accessible by a road which climbs to a height of 1,000ft above the town. The dam and Ffestiniog Power Station below generate electricity as part of a pumped hydro-electric storage scheme, the first of its kind in Britain (the water is pumped back up the mountain during the off-peak hours for re-use). There is a visitor information centre for the scheme at Tanygrisiau on the approach to the station and dam.

AROUND THE RHINOGS

44 miles

The Rhinog mountains inland from Harlech are one of Britain's last true wilderness areas. Land meets water in a spectacular fashion along the lovely Mawddach Estuary, where gold was once mined. The Snowdonia National Park extends southwards encompassing this area's forests, sandy coastline and barren uplands.

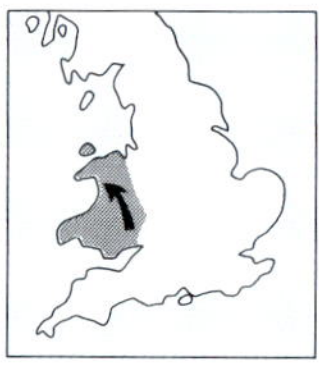

The 845-square-mile Snowdonia National Park, although named after Mount Snowdon in the far north, extends into much of Mid Wales. The Rhinog mountains and the expansive, open coastline along Cardigan and Tremadog bays are within the park. The Rhinogs are an upland mass of rocky moorlands dotted with remote lakes. Rising to a consistent height of well over 2,000ft and traversed by no roads, they pose a strenuous challenge to those who venture into their rough, rugged heights on foot.

The landscape is much more inviting along the Mawddach Estuary: a luxuriant blend of thick woodland, riverbank and sand. The coastal strip north of the estuary has a long history of human settlement. Prehistoric sites are joined by a famous medieval castle and slate quarry along this sandy, mountain-backed shoreline. East of the Rhinogs, the A470 charts a straight-as-a-dye course southwards through the Coed-y-Brenin forest; a woodland of waterfalls and long-abandoned gold mines.

ON THE TOUR

Barmouth

Barmouth is a well-established holiday resort with a pretty harbour and long, sandy beach. Its most attractive feature is its location. The resort stands on the mouth of the Mawddach estuary below the Dinas Oleu headland. Dinas Oleu is highly significant in the history of conservation in Britain: it was the first acquisition, in 1895, ever to be made by the National Trust.

For the best view of the area, take the path alongside the railway bridge which crosses the mouth of the Mawddach Estuary.

Dyffryn Ardudwy Burial Chamber

This stone tomb dates from about 3500BC. A large capstone rests on uprights to form the chamber, which would originally have been covered with a cairn. The chamber is one of many ancient sites in this area, indicating intensive settlement by prehistoric tribes.

Maes Artro Tourist Village

An ex-RAF camp at Llanbedr is the home of this entertaining family complex. Maes Artro has an excellent selection of craft shops, a large aquarium, a re-created 19th-century Welsh village street, a model village and a host of children's attractions.

Llanfair

The mounds of slate on the hillside above Llanfair mark the entrance to the caverns. Roofing slates were produced by the million from this mine in the 19th century. The mining techniques used become evident to visitors as they walk through the maze of tunnels.

The steady hand of the silversmith at work at the Maes Artro craft village

Harlech Castle

At one time, the sea lapped around the base of this spectacularly sited fortress. Seaborne access was an important strategic consideration to its builder, Edward I. The castle, which dates from the 1280s, still has its steep 'Way from the Sea', a fortified stairway cut into the cliff.

Over the centuries, the sea receded leaving the castle stranded on its rocky outcrop above the dunes. It is, perhaps, the most impressive of all the castles built by Edward in North Wales. An authentic medieval atmosphere greets visitors as soon as they enter through Harlech's massive gatehouse. The views from the castle's lofty battlements are breathtaking, extending seawards across Tremadog Bay to the Lleyn peninsula and landwards to the angular peaks of Snowdonia.

For all its strength, the castle was taken by Owain Glyndwr during the early 15th-century rising against English rule.

Trawsfynydd

The giant complex north of the village is the Trawsfynydd Nuclear Power Station. Opened in 1965, it was the first nuclear station in Britain to be located inland. It was built on the shores of Llyn Trawsfynydd, a large man-made reservoir whose waters cool the plant.

Maesgwm Forest Visitor Centre

Pleasantly located just off the A470 in the Forestry Commission's Coed-y-Brenin woodland, this centre takes a wide look at its surroundings. In addition to explaining the role of the Forestry Commission, the centre covers local wildlife and tells the story of those who live and work in the forest. The most interesting feature of all is the display which deals with this area's 19th-century gold rush. The gold-bearing rocks around the Mawddach attracted prospectors from far and wide. One of the mines – the Clogau at Bontddu - has provided the gold used in royal wedding rings. The abandoned Gwynfynydd mine is hidden away east of Maesgwm near two waterfalls in the heart of the forest.

Cymer Abbey

The abbey, standing in green fields on the banks of the Mawddach at Llanelltyd, was founded by Cistercian monks in 1198. Its ruins are the remains of a modest religious settlement which never really achieved its planned stature. Its suffering during troubles in the 13th century probably caused the abandonment of the original plans to build a larger church. Interesting features include the arched windows in the east wall.

OFF THE TOUR

Cwm Bychan and the Roman Steps

From Llanbedr, take the minor road north-eastwards which follows the banks of the River Artro to an isolated little lake at Cwm Bychan. This is as far as any vehicle can go into the Rhinogs. The mountains' heather-covered slopes and rock slabs rise up in an unkempt, jagged mass above the lake. A trackway known as the Roman Steps leads upwards into the wilderness from the end of the road. Despite its name, this well-made stone staircase is probably medieval in origin and part of a pack-horse trackway.

Portmeirion

A mile or so north of Talsarnau, take the toll bridge across the River Dwyryd for Penrhyndeudraeth and the village of Portmeirion (see page 131 for description).

Porthmadog

From Portmeirion, continue along the A487 on another stretch of toll road to Porthmadog (see page 130 for description).

Blaenau Ffestiniog

From Maentwrog, take the A496 for Blaenau Ffestiniog, whose slate caverns are open to the public (see page 131 for description).

Dolgellau

Turn off the A470 just south of Llanelltyd for Dolgellau. This old market town has a distinctive personality, thanks to the use of huge slabs of the local dark stone in its buildings. The town, which displays many interesting architectural features, has led an eventful life. In its time, it has hosted a Welsh medieval parliament, and been a wool, tanning and gold rush town.

Penmaenpool

Cross the Mawddach by a rickety toll bridge for Penmaenpool. Its signal box, a leftover from a disused railway, now serves as a wildlife centre and observation point for the bird life of the estuary.

One of the most magnificently sited of Welsh castles, Harlech commands fine views of Cardigan Bay and, inland, the mountains of Snowdonia. Completed in 1290, it was said to be impregnable, but Owain Glyndwr thought otherwise

ROUTE DIRECTIONS

Leave **Barmouth** (map 6SH61) on the A496 (sp. Harlech) and continue forward through Taly-bont, **Dyffryn Ardudwy** and past **Maes Artro Tourist Village** to Llanbedr and **Llanfair**. One mile further branch right on to the B4573 (sp. Harlech) to pass **Harlech Castle**, and in 3½ miles go forward on to the A496 (sp. Maentwrog). Go forward through Maentwrog and in ¼ mile turn right on to the A487 (sp. Dolgellau) and in 2 miles further go forward on to the A470 to pass Llyn Trawsfynydd and **Trawsfynydd**. Continue to Bronaber and, in 2 miles, enter Coed-y-Brenin Forest. Pass the track to **Maesgwm Forest Visitor Centre** on the right and continue past Ganllwyd to Llanelltyd, passing the ruins of **Cymer Abbey**. Here, turn right on to the A496 (sp. Barmouth) and pass through Bontddu before returning to Barmouth.

OFF THE BEATEN TRACK

Shell Island

Take the road across the flat coastal plain west of Llanbedr for Shell Island. An island in name only – and otherwise known as Mochras – Shell Island is a peaceful little cone-shaped peninsula. Over 200 varieties of shells can be found amongst its dunes and beaches.

Ganllwyd

Park the car here, just off the A470 north of Llanelltyd, and walk along the narrow road for a short distance up into the hills, following the course of the River Gamlan to the waterfall of Rhaeadr Du.

OUTDOOR ACTIVITIES

Over 50 miles of waymarked walks can be enjoyed in the Coed-y-Brenin forest.

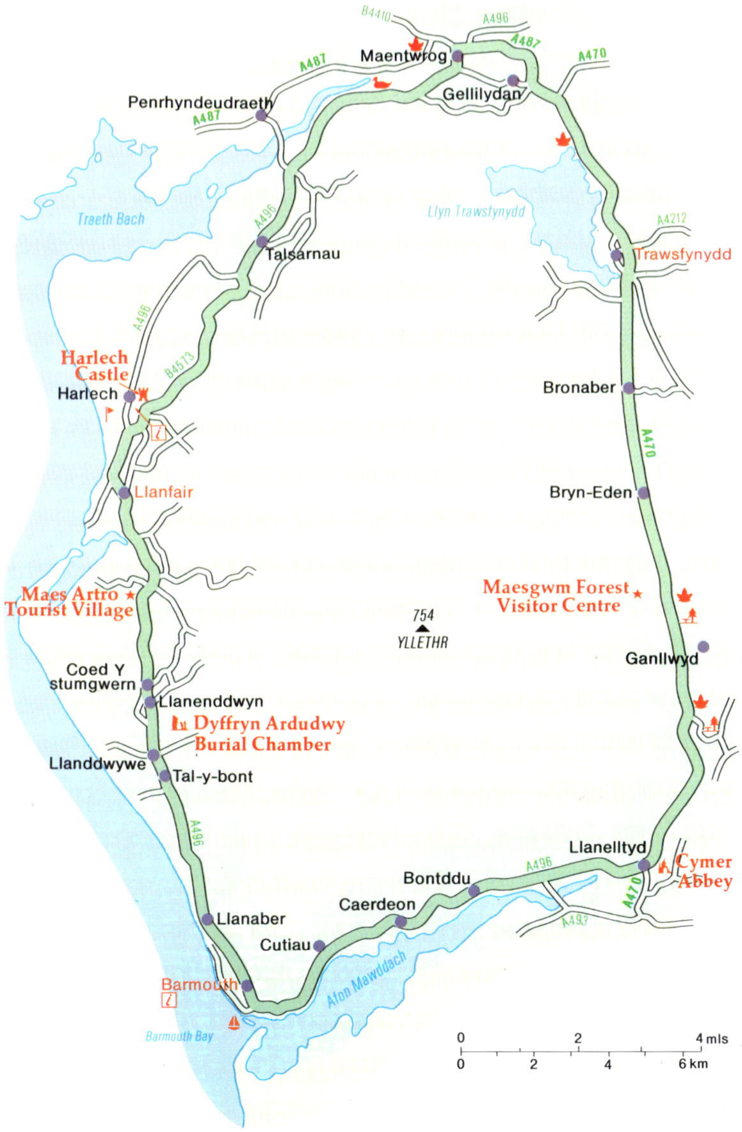

HEART OF WALES – COAST AND COUNTRY

42 miles

Aberystwyth occupies the middle ground along Cardigan Bay, that great arc in the Welsh coast stretching from north to south. Inland, green farming country rises to the

high plateaux and peaks of Plynlimon, a mountain range in the centre of Wales clothed in empty moorland and coniferous forest.

Aberystwyth, the unofficial 'capital' of Mid Wales, is on the doorstep of an exhilarating coast and country. The Cardigan Bay shoreline hereabouts consists of grassy headlands, beaches large and small, and an extensive duneland nature reserve at the mouth of the River Dovey.

A patchwork of farmers' fields begins almost next to the sea, spreading upwards to the foot-hills of the Plynlimon mountain range. As the altitude increases, the quality of land declines. Cultivated countryside is replaced by exposed moorlands, treeless apart from the blocks of conifer planted by the commercial forester. Like other parts of Mid Wales, pine trees share the high ground with man-made lakelands - in this case, the waters of the Nant-y-Moch reservoir.

Historically, this far-flung part of Wales has seen a surprising amount of activity. Early Christians founded a settlement here, the Normans marched in and built an important coastal castle, and early industrial innovators operated a smelting furnace in the farmlands.

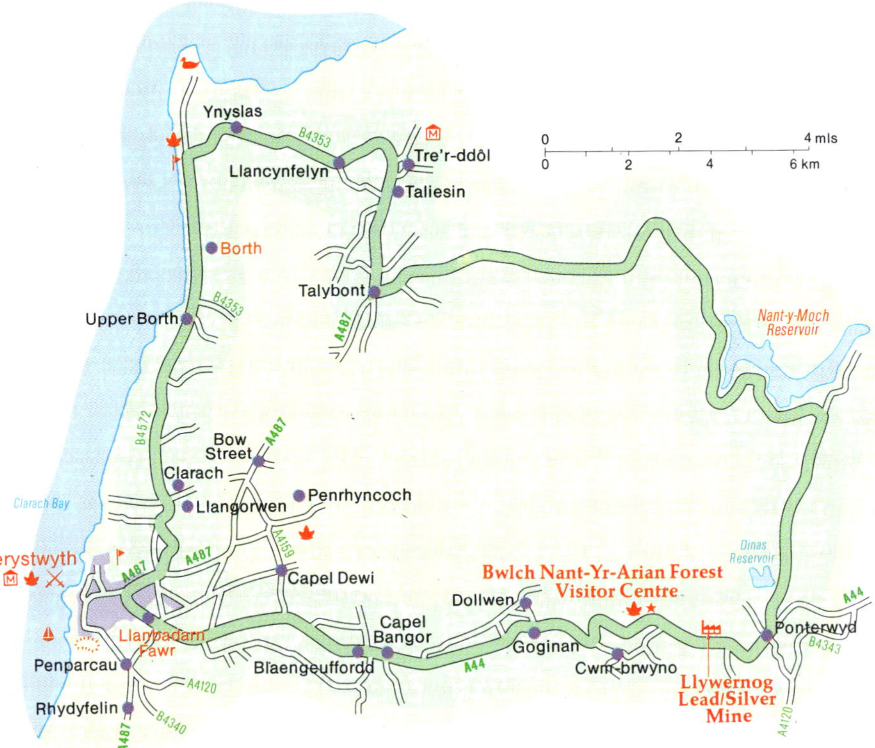

The well preserved ruins of Aberystwyth Castle, built in 1277 by Edward I and destroyed by Cromwell's forces in 1649

ROUTE DIRECTIONS

Leave **Aberystwyth** (map 6SN58) on the Pen-Glais road (sp. Machynlleth, A487) and in 1 mile turn left on to the B4572 Llangorwen road. In 1 mile turn sharp right before passing through Llangorwen. Continue to the junction with the B4353 and turn left into the resort of **Borth**. Continue on the B4353 and bear right at the edge of Ynyslas. In 3/4 mile cross the Afon Leri, then the railway and the reclaimed marshland to Tre'r-ddôl. Turn right on to the A487 (sp. Aberystwyth) and pass through Tre-Taliesin to reach Talybont. At the White Lion turn left, unclassified, then left again and follow the signs to Nant-y-Moch. Soon after bear right, then in 200 yards bear left and make a gradual ascent up the side of Cwm Ceulan. At the summit bear right, pass through a forested area, then beside **Nant-y-Moch Reservoir**. Cross the top of the dam, climb to 1,300ft then pass the Dinas Reservoir before reaching Ponterwyd.

Here, turn right on to the A44 Aberystwyth road. Pass **Llywernog Silver–Lead Mine** and after a further mile on the A44 pass the **Bwlch Nant-yr-Arian Forest Visitor Centre**.

Continue with the A44 and make a long winding descent down the Melindwr Valley. Pass through Goginan, Capel Bangor and **Llanbadarn Fawr** before re-entering Aberystwyth.

OFF THE TOUR

Dyfi Furnace

At Tre'r-ddôl, turn left along the A487 for the hamlet of Furnace, named after its roadside metal-smelting plant. Do not expect to see an ugly industrial complex. At first sight, the furnace looks more like a watermill. The stone chimney on the slate roof gives the game away, for its purpose was to remove the fumes from a charcoal-fired furnace.

The Dyfi Furnace's waterwheel powered the bellows which maintained the fierce heat necessary for metal smelting. In the 17th century, silver was refined here, though the present building was an ironmaking furnace dating from the mid-18th century. The site is open to the public.

Devil's Bridge

From Ponterwyd, continue southwards on the A4120 to Devil's Bridge (see page 137 for description).

Cwm Rheidol

Turn left at Capel Bangor and follow the minor road along the floor of the Rheidol Valley to Cwm Rheidol. The road shadows the course of the River Rheidol to the rushing Rheidol Falls. The stone building on the roadside just before the falls is the control centre for the Rheidol Hydro-electric Power Scheme (guided tours are available in summer).

ON THE TOUR

Aberystwyth

This dignified seaside resort is also a university town, and a shopping centre for the villages scattered between the mountains and the sea. Once known as the fashionable 'Biarritz of Wales', Aberystwyth preserves its Victorian character most convincingly. The view along the promenade, a curving seafront lined with pastel-shaded, bay-windowed hotels and guest houses, has changed little over the years.

The seafront ends at Constitution Hill, which can be climbed on foot or - more appropriately - by the Cliff Railway: 'a conveyance of gentlefolk since 1896' and the only one of its kind in Wales. The hill's 430ft summit has another attraction redolent of the Victorian Age - a Camera Obscura, whose all-seeing lens scans Cardigan Bay and over 25 mountain peaks.

Aberystwyth's 'museum within a music hall' is another convincing period piece. The Ceredigion Museum, which is housed in an ornate, immaculately preserved Edwardian theatre, recalls the coastal and rural history of the region. The headland at the southern end of the promenade close to the harbour is occupied by the ruins of Aberystwyth Castle. The fortress, begun in 1277, was one of Edward I's first castles in Wales. In 1404, it was captured by the Welsh leader Owain Glyndwr, though it suffered its greatest damage during the Civil War.

A large university campus is spread out across the hillside above the town. It is the home of the National Library of Wales, whose collection of over two million books includes some of the oldest manuscripts in the Welsh language.

Aberystwyth Station is the starting point of the narrow-gauge Vale of Rheidol Railway, which runs for 12 miles to a mountain terminus at Devil's Bridge (see Tour 58 for more details).

Borth

Borth is a straggling seaside centre on a flat coastal plain with a huge three-mile sandy beach. It consists mainly of caravan parks located close to a long main street.

Nant-y-Moch Reservoir

The mountain road from the square at Talybont climbs up into the wastes of Plynlimon. Here, below the mountain range's 2,468ft summit, a huge man-made lake of over 7,000 million gallons has been created. Unlike the other lakelands in Mid Wales, Nant-y-Moch's inky black waters are not used for consumption, but as a source of power. The lake plays a central role in the Rheidol Hydro-electric Power Scheme. The road runs across the top of a 172ft-high dam before following the River Rheidol southwards to the smaller Dinas reservoir, also part of the hydro-electric scheme.

Llywernog Silver–Lead Mine

The A44 westwards past Ponterwyd runs through peaceful countryside in which it is difficult to imagine that any form of industrial activity once took place. Yet in the 17th to 19th centuries, the minerals of Mid Wales were mined extensively. The overgrown spoil heaps at Llywernog are evidence of mining activity dating from the 1740s. Llywernog's mine closed in the 1880s, lying derelict until its restoration and reopening as an open-air museum in the 1970s. The seven-acre site contains old buildings, waterwheels, a 'Miner's Trail', prospecting tunnel, exhibition and audio-visual display.

Bwlch Nant-yr-Arian Forest Visitor Centre

The centre is located a little further along the A44 from Llywernog. Perched on the edge of a steep slope, it enjoys breathtaking views down the valley towards Aberystwyth. A well laid-out exhibition area introduces visitors to local history and the landscape, while the surrounding forests contain waymarked walks and picnic sites.

Llanbadarn Fawr

This village, now a suburb of Aberystwyth, reveals its historic and religious significance through the size of its church. The unexpected grandeur of the church reflects the influential role which Llanbadarn Fawr once played in Welsh affairs. A religious community founded here in the 6th century became a celebrated centre of scholarship. The present church, which is one of the largest in Wales, dates from around 1200.

OUTDOOR ACTIVITIES

Ynyslas and the Dyfi National Nature Reserve

Go straight on through Ynyslas for the sand dunes at the mouth of the River Dovey. The large beach and dune system, extending northwards as a spit which funnels the Dovey through a narrow estuary mouth, is known as the Dyfi National Nature Reserve. An information centre tells visitors about the wildlife which can be seen amongst its saltmarshes, dunes and sands. Butterflies are common in summer, while winter visitors include wildfowl and waders.

Waymarked forest walks can be taken from the Bwlch Nant-yr-Arian Forest Visitor Centre.

Below: *Aberystwyth – Cardigan Bay's largest seaside resort*

Bottom: *the Llywernog silver-lead mine museum near Devil's Bridge*

MID WALES LAKES AND MOUNTAINS

51 miles

The Elan Valley's man-made lakes blend in well amongst the thinly populated folds of the Cambrian Mountains. Traditional towns and villages serve the surrounding

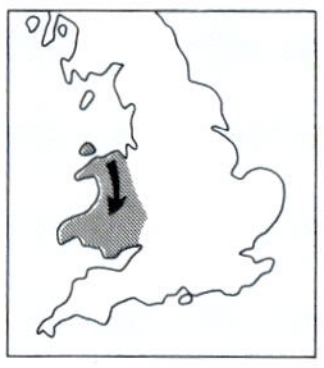

sheep farming country. The area is not immune to change: commercial forestry has joined the reservoirs in altering the landscape.

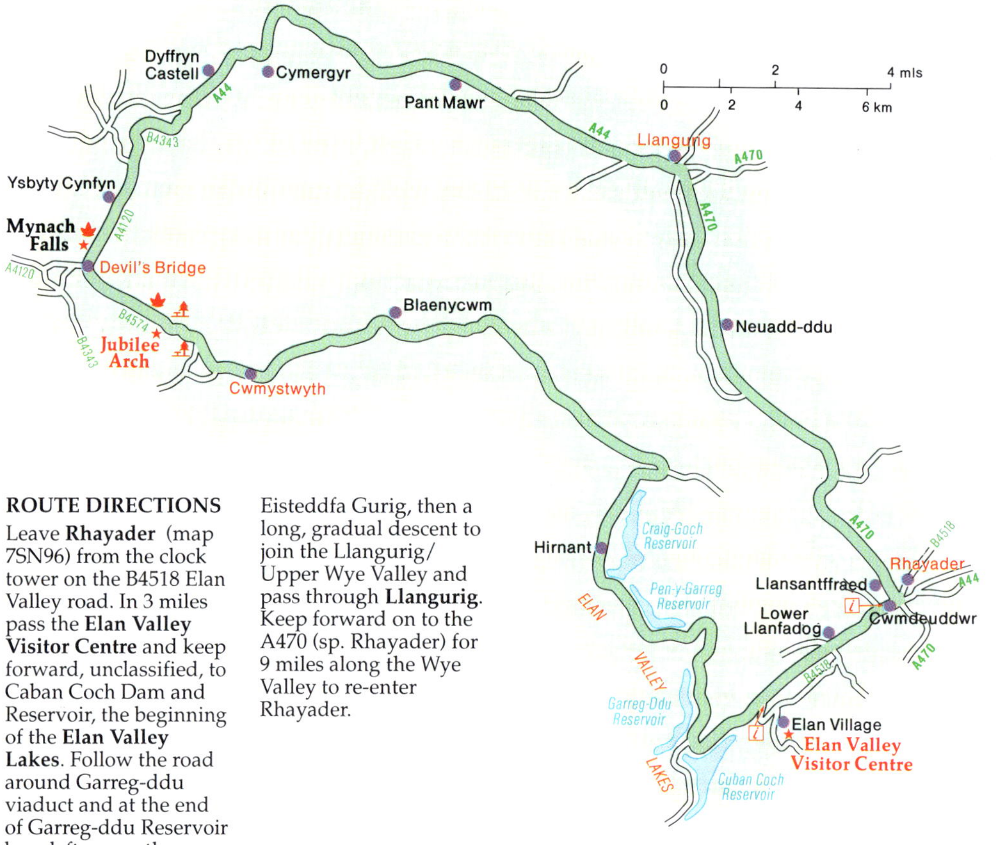

When the engineers built the Elan Valley dams in the early 1900s, they did not only secure a water supply for the city of Birmingham. The Elan Valley lakes, the first of Wales's major reservoir systems, opened up a previously inaccessible area to visitors. Soon, tourists were flocking by bus to see these lakelands in the hills just west of Rhayader.

Tourists have been beating a path to the foothills of these wild, remote mountains for many years. On the other side of the Cambrian Mountains, passengers have travelled by steam-powered narrow-gauge railway from Aberystwyth to Devil's Bridge since the line opened in 1902.

Such influences, together with the effects of forestry and a surprisingly vibrant metal-mining past, have not changed the essential character of this area. It remains, for the most part, a wilderness of poor moorland where hill-sheep farmers live a tough existence.

Just beyond Devil's Bridge the River Mynach plunges dramatically through a deep gorge. The first stone bridge over the Mynach was built in the 12th century

ROUTE DIRECTIONS

Leave **Rhayader** (map 7SN96) from the clock tower on the B4518 Elan Valley road. In 3 miles pass the **Elan Valley Visitor Centre** and keep forward, unclassified, to Caban Coch Dam and Reservoir, the beginning of the **Elan Valley Lakes**. Follow the road around Garreg-ddu viaduct and at the end of Garreg-ddu Reservoir bear left across the bridge and up to the Pen-y-garreg Dam and Reservoir. Continue to the Craig Goch Reservoir and on across moorland before ascending to a T-junction and then turning left. Continue to a summit of 1,320ft and then make a descent into the Ystwyth Valley and to **Cwmystwyth**. Ascend to leave the village and bear right, joining the B4574 Devil's Bridge road. Climb to reach the stone **Jubilee Arch** over the road then descend to **Devil's Bridge**. Turn sharp right on to the A4120 Ponterwyd road, crossing the Devil's Bridge. In 2¼ miles branch right on to the B4343 and in a further 1¾ miles join the A44 (sp. Llangurig). Make a gradual ascent up the Castell Valley to Eisteddfa Gurig, then a long, gradual descent to join the Llangurig/Upper Wye Valley and pass through **Llangurig**. Keep forward on to the A470 (sp. Rhayader) for 9 miles along the Wye Valley to re-enter Rhayader.

OFF THE TOUR

Claerwen reservoir

Although thought of as one of the Elan Valley lakes, Claerwen is an outsider on two scores. It was built 50 years after the Elan valley reservoirs; and it is not on the Elan valley 'circuit'. The 4-mile-long reservoir is located in its own valley a few miles west of the other lakes. It is accessible by a cul-de-sac road from the bridge at the meeting point of the Caban Coch and Garreg-ddu reservoirs. The construction of the Claerwen reservoir doubled the storage capacity of the lakes in this area from 11,000 to 22,000 million gallons of water.

Llywernog Silver–Lead Mine

Take the A44 westwards past Ponterwyd for the Llywernog Silver–Lead Mine (see page 135 for description).

Bwlch Nant-yr-Arian Forest Visitor Centre

This centre stands one mile west of Llywernog (see page 135 for description) off the A44.

Llanidloes

The influences of the gentle, rolling Welsh border country are finally shrugged off at Llanidloes, a town on the approach to Mid Wales's inhospitable uplands. Llanidloes's most striking building – a black-and-white half-timbered market hall – is typical of the 'magpie' architecture of the borderlands; a style of building replaced by sturdy, stone-built farmhouses in the hills further west. The town is west of Llangurig on the A470.

ON THE TOUR

Rhayader

The market town of Rhayader, on the banks of the River Wye and at the gateway to the Elan valley lakelands, is a popular fishing and pony trekking centre. The town-centre cross-roads is a meeting place of two major routes through Wales. It is marked by a neat and decorative clock tower, a well-known land-mark for those travelling from north to south or east to west.

Elan Valley Visitor Centre

This visitor centre is located at Elan Village, a 'model' settlement built below the Caban Coch dam from 1906 to 1909 to house waterworks maintenance staff. The centre serves as an informative starting point on a visit to the five lakes and their surrounding 45,000-acre estate; an area renowned not only for it beauty but also as the best inland site in Wales for birds. The centre contains an exhibition and audio-visual theatre.

Elan Valley Lakes

The four Elan Valley lakes - Caban Coch, Gareg-ddu, Pen-y-garreg and Craig Goch - form a watery chain about nine miles long. During their construction, 18 farmhouses, a school and Baptist church were submerged by their waters. Unlike the functionally built dams of today, those in the Elan Valley demonstrate attractive turn-of-the-century touches in their design and decorative stonework. The Elan valley's waters flow through a 73-mile aqueduct to Birmingham at the rate of 25 million gallons a day.

Cwmystwyth

The narrow road from the Elan valley to Devil's Bridge travels across isolated moor and mountain. On the approach to the hamlet of Cwmystwyth a strange sight comes into view – a ramshackle ghost town of mine-workings. The Cwmystwyth mine was one of the largest lead mines in Mid Wales. At its height during the 17th and 18th centuries it was one of Europe's most advanced mines, producing both lead and silver. Its skeletal, rusting workshops and mine buildings, standing in a lunar-like landscape of spoil heaps, were closed in 1916. Because of its dangerous condition, close inspection of the site is not advisable – it is best viewed from the road.

Jubilee Arch

The 1,223ft crest of the road between Cwmystwyth and Devil's Bridge is marked by a slender, rough-stoned archway, erected to commemorate George III's jubilee in 1810.

Devil's Bridge

The River Mynach takes a 300ft plunge through a deep chasm at this famous beauty spot. Devil's Bridge has a surfeit of bridges – three in all – though the only one immediately visible is the road bridge across the top of the narrow gorge. Beneath this is a second bridge, put up in the 18th century, while further down still is a stone archway – the original crossing point – which dates from medieval times. The gorge, called a 'dread chasm' by William Wordsworth, is accessible by a steep footpath – only recommended to those who do not mind climbing long staircases!

Pen-y-garreg Dam is one of a series of dams begun in 1892 and completed in 1952. They hold back the four Elan Valley lakes that supply water to the Midlands

Below the falls, the Mynach joins the River Rheidol, which has carved a steep valley for itself on its way to Aberystwyth and the sea. The narrow-gauge Vale of Rheidol Railway, one of the `Great Little Trains of Wales', runs along the side of this lovely valley for 12 miles between Aberystwyth and Devil's Bridge.

Llangurig

Tiny Llangurig is only a scattering of dwellings, though its location at an important road junction allows it to boast a large Welsh crafts shop. The village stands on the upper reaches of the River Wye, whose source lies in the hills to the north-west (within two miles, incidentally, of the source of the River Severn). The road follows the infant Wye - later to become Wales's grandest river - as it flows through a beautiful valley down to Rhayader.

OUTDOOR ACTIVITIES

Rhayader

Rhayader Pony Trekking Association, Nantserth House, Rhayader, Powys. Tel: (0597) 810298. Rhayader is also a good mountain biking centre.

Guided walks are available in season from the Elan Valley Visitor Centre. Tel: (0597) 810898/ 810880 for full information.

WILD WALES

59 miles

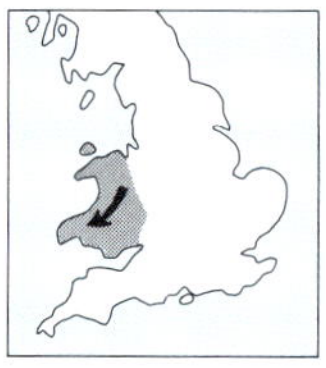

The 19th-century traveller and writer George Borrow called one of his books Wild Wales. *The title also applies to this tour. The remote hills between Llandovery and Tregaron are still a true wilderness area, infiltrated by few roads and populated by many more sheep than people.*

Although quiet here, Llandovery is a busy market town and an excellent fishing centre. It is also a good point for exploring part of the Brecon Beacons National Park

The southern block of the Cambrian Mountains dominates the landscape here. This high plateau has been dubbed the `roof of Wales' and `great Welsh desert', the latter description a reflection of its solitude. In between Llandovery and Tregaron there are only a handful of villages and a thin scattering of farms, but man is beginning to leave his mark on these mountains. Conifer plantations now occupy some of the poor, marginal lands where hill-sheep farmers previously eked out a living, and a massive reservoir was opened here in the 1970s.

Despite these developments, the area remains essentially a wilderness. It is the haunt of the rare red kite, and the only way to explore much of its moor and mountain vastness is on foot or horseback.

Historical forces have touched the landscape only lightly. Romans, the only invaders to show any real interest in these hills, were attracted by the lure of gold.

ON THE TOUR

Llandovery

In his book, *Wild Wales*, George Borrow called Llandovery `the pleasantest little town in which I have halted in the course of my wanderings'. The centre of town, with its cobbled square, covered marketplace and clock tower, has changed little since Borrow's time. Llandovery still relies on the local farmers for its livelihood. Weekly livestock sales are held in the open area below the shell of an ancient castle, precariously perched on a steep earthen tump. On the outskirts of town, occupying the site of a Roman camp, stands a hilltop church with a 13th-century tower.

Rhandirmwyn

This village is beautifully located in the upper Towy Valley. It is difficult to believe that sleepy Rhandirmwyn was the home of one of Europe's largest lead mines a few hundred years ago. Until the early 1970s, this scattered village – then on the road to nowhere – was largely ignored by the outside world. However, with the construction of the Llyn Brianne reservoir, came the building of a new road across remote, previously inaccessible uplands linking Rhandirmwyn to the Abergwesyn Pass.

The surrounding countryside is fascinating. A thickly wooded conical hill stands a few miles to the north above a spectacular stretch of the Towy where the river rushes down a narrow, rocky gorge. This is Dinas Hill, the hiding place of Twm Shon Cati, the 16th-century 'Welsh Robin Hood'. Twm, alias Thomas Jones, hid in a cave amongst the hill's upper slopes from the Sheriff of Carmarthen.

The little roadside church at Ystrad-ffin is dedicated to St Paulinus. Built in 1117 and restored in the 1820s, it originally served as a resting place for Cistercian monks following a trail to Strata Florida Abbey 15 miles to the north. Their ancient pathway is now partly submerged by the waters of Llyn Brianne.

Llyn Brianne

The view from the car park overlooking the dam captures the enormity of this reservoir. The huge rock-filled dam, reputedly the highest of its type in Britain, holds back 13,500 million gallons of water. Opened in 1973, it supplies Swansea with its water. A scenic road winds around the eastern shores of the lake.

Abergwesyn Pass

You drive along the western stretch of this memorable mountain road on your way to Tregaron. The pass, a thin ribbon of tarmac laid out across the desolately beautiful 'roof of Wales', follows a famous drovers' route along which Welsh farmers once led their sheep and cattle to markets in the English Midlands.

Tregaron

The drovers would congregate at Tregaron's town square before setting off on their arduous journey. Tregaron is a staunchly Welsh place, still much involved with the buying and selling of sheep. A statue of Henry Richard, local MP and Victorian 'apostle of peace', looks out across the square, beside which there is an excellent Welsh crafts shop.

Lampeter

After the emptiness of Abergwesyn, Lampeter seems a large place. This town, a pleasant mixture of old coaching inns and Georgian and Victorian architecture, has grown up at a busy crossroads. The scant remnants of a castle are all that survive of a medieval stronghold, put up to defend a strategic crossing point on the Teifi. Lampeter is now a busy university town. The University College of St David's, founded in 1822, is the third oldest university in Britain after Oxford and Cambridge.

Pumsaint

The lure of Welsh gold brought the Romans to these remote hills. Their Dolaucothi Gold Mine, now in the care of the National Trust, was fully operational for about 100 years from AD75. A sophisticated arrangement of adits and aqueducts was used to extract the gold, which was then transported to the Imperial Mint at Lyon. The mines were also worked in the 19th and 20th centuries.

Visitors can explore the site by following a waymarked walk or taking a guided tour (in summer) which includes some of the underground workings.

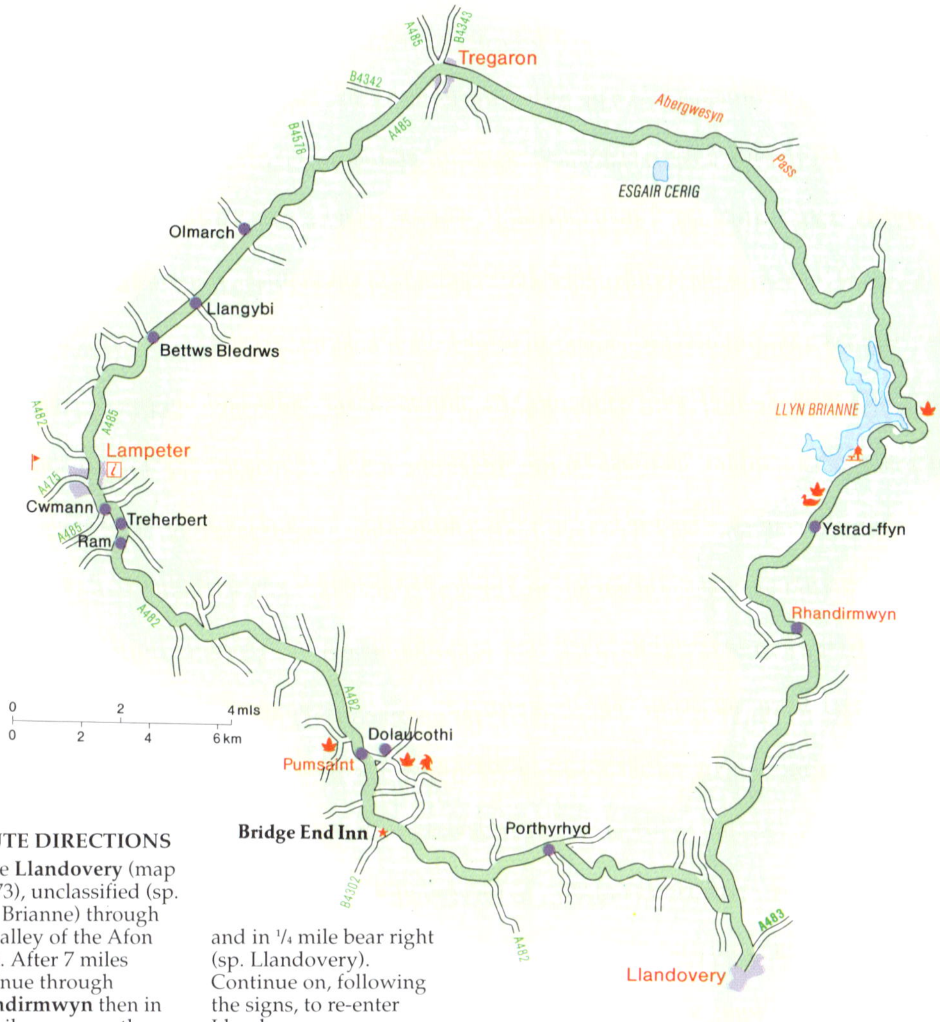

ROUTE DIRECTIONS

Leave **Llandovery** (map 6SN73), unclassified (sp. Llyn Brianne) through the valley of the Afon Tywi. After 7 miles continue through **Rhandirmwyn** then in $4\frac{1}{2}$ miles pass, on the left, the turning to Llyn Brianne dam. Bear right along the east side of **Llyn Brianne** and, after 7 miles, turn left (sp. Tregaron) and cross the river bridge. At the T-junction, turn right (sp. Tregaron). After 3 miles further the road narrows to a single track. Continue for a further mile and, near the telephone kiosk, keep left to join the **Abergwesyn Pass** drove road. Later, make a gradual descent to **Tregaron**. Keep forward, then turn left on to the A485 (sp. Lampeter). Continue through Llangybi and Bettws Bledrws then, in $2\frac{3}{4}$ miles turn left to enter **Lampeter**. At the T-junction turn left and at the far end of the town take the A482 (sp. Llanwrda), and ascend through Tre-Herbert. Later, descend to **Pumsaint**, remain on the A482 and, in $1\frac{1}{2}$ miles, pass the Bridge End Inn. After $2\frac{1}{2}$ miles further turn left, unclassified (sp. Porthyrhyd). Pass through Porthyrhyd and in $\frac{1}{4}$ mile bear right (sp. Llandovery). Continue on, following the signs, to re-enter Llandovery.

OFF THE TOUR

Tregaron Bog

This strange area just north of Tregaron is one of Britain's few raised, dome-shaped peat bogs. This reedy expanse of wetland is a nature reserve supporting a wide variety of plants, and over 40 species of breeding birds. A railway once ran along the eastern edge of the bog parallel to the B4343. Visitors can follow a nature trail along the abandoned line to a bird observation post.

Llanddewi Brefi

Turn left off the A485 about 3 miles south-west of Tregaron for Llanddewi Brefi. Students of the Welsh language will know that this little village has associations with David, patron saint of Wales, for Llanddewi means 'the church of Dewi (David)'.

The church stands on high ground above the houses and village square. According to legend, David denounced heresy at this spot in AD519, the ground rising so that he could be better seen and heard by his audience. Llanddewi Brefi's ancient church has a 12th-century tower and contains a statue of the patron saint.

Caeo

Welsh country villages do not come any more typical than this one. Tucked away on a minor road off the A482 and surrounded by green hills, Caeo is little more than a collection of cottages served by a post office, chapel, church and pub. The church, dedicated to St Cynwl, is the village's most substantial building: a powerful structure of Norman origin with a tall, castellated west tower.

For such a small place, Caeo has had more than its fair share of excitement. It was the scene of an infamous 19th-century murder, after which the murderer committed suicide. This was followed by an even more macabre episode during which the murderer's body was removed for some time from the graveyard.

OFF THE BEATEN TRACK

Myddfai

The maze of lanes south-east of Llandovery between the A40 and A4069 is centred around Myddfai, a village famous in Welsh history as the home of the Physicians of Myddfai. These medieval doctors and their descendants were responsible for many cures and remedies, some well in advance of their time. Myddfai's tradition of healing was a long one; the last physician was doctor to Queen Victoria.

OUTDOOR ACTIVITIES

Dinas Hill

Dinas Hill is now an RSPB Nature Reserve. A delightful footpath, running around the hill from an information centre at Ystrad-ffin, has a detour – it is a short, sharp climb – which leads to Twm Shon Cati's obscure hiding place, its walls covered with graffiti dating back to the 18th century.

Tregaron

Pony trekking is available from Maesglas Mountain Riders, Penpontbren, Tregaron.
Tel: (09744) 584.

There is a nature trail along the edge of Tregaron Bog.

Lampeter

Pony trekking from Oxenhall Riding Centre, Llanfair Clydogau, Lampeter. Tel: (057045) 519.

Below: *close to the hamlet of Abergwesy lies what was once the loneliest country in South Wales, known as the Green Desert*
Bottom: *Caeo may look now like a typical Welsh village, but it has an infamous past . . .*

BETWEEN THE TEIFI AND THE TOWY

56 miles

The River Teifi flows through a lovely, thickly wooded vale, while the Towy charts a more languorous, looping course on its approach to Carmarthen

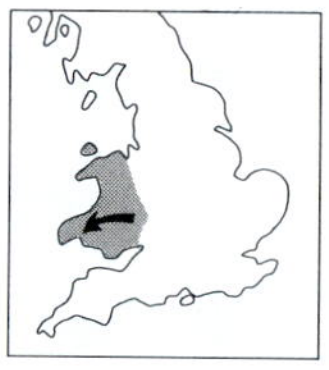

and the sea. The high countryside in between, peaceful and undisturbed, is clothed with moorland and the conifers of the Brechfa Forest.

Scenic valleys, green fields, windy moorlands and thick forests are the ingredients which make up this peaceful part of south-west Wales. Carmarthen, the largest town, continues to play its role as a busy market-place for the surrounding farming community while also serving as the administrative centre for the large 'super-county' of Dyfed.

The hills and vales are dotted with small villages and the stone-built, whitewashed farmsteads typical of rural Wales. This countryside is sandwiched between the rivers Teifi (to the north) and Towy (to the south). These are two of Wales's finest fishing rivers, famous for their salmon and sewin (sea trout).

The centre of this area is dominated by an exposed, empty plateau rising to over 1,000ft. Much of this upland is covered by the Brechfa Forest, one of the largest man-made conifer plantations in Wales. Traditional Wales lives on undisturbed in the valleys, especially along the Teifi, which preserves its links with the weaving industry.

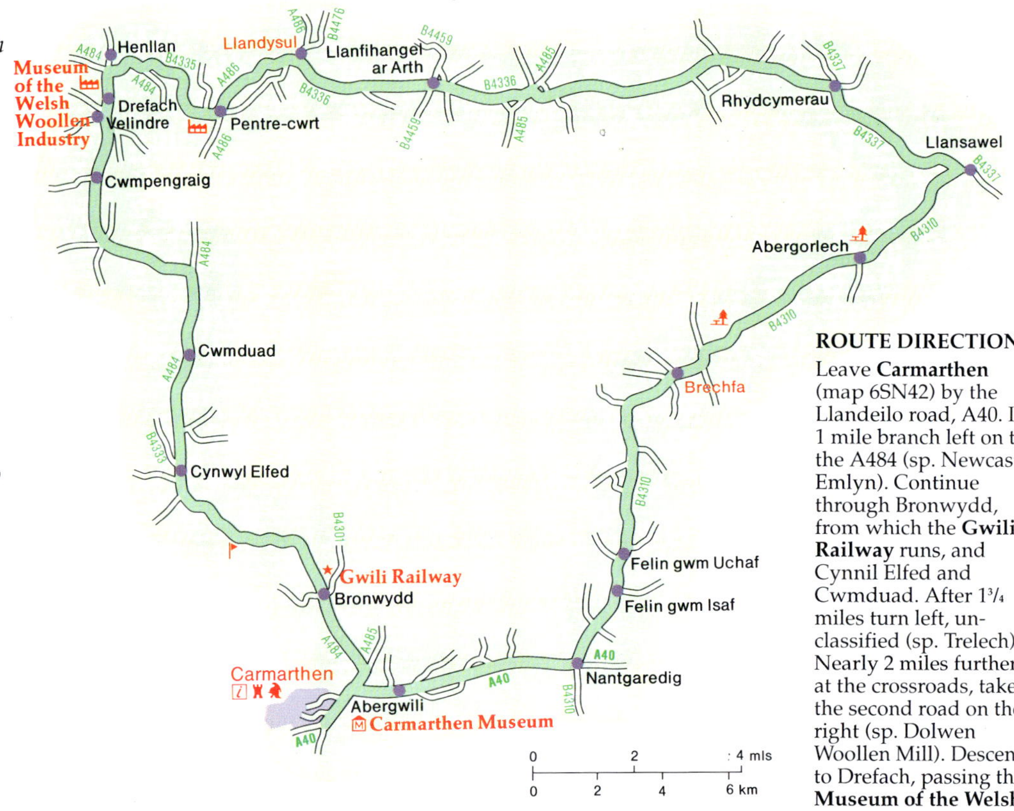

Only two arches and part of the tower remain of Talley Abbey

OFF THE TOUR

Newcastle Emlyn

Visitors to this old riverside market town, along the A484 from Henllan, should not expect to see a pristine castle. Newcastle Emlyn's fortress is a tumbledown ruin. Despite its non-warlike design, it saw its fair share of action during the Civil War when it was blown up with gunpowder.
A mile downstream, the Teifi is joined by a tributary, the Ceri. The Felin Geri Mill is to be found 2 miles north-west of Newcastle Emlyn along the secluded little valley carved by this small river. Its waters power the wheel of a 17th-century flourmill, saved from dereliction in the 1970s.

Llanybydder

At the junction of the B4336 and A485, stay on the 'A' road for Llanybydder. This place might justify the description 'one-horse town' were it not for its celebrated horse sales held on the last Thursday of each month. Buyers from all over Britain and the Continent gather here for the sales.

Talley Abbey

The village of Talley lies a few miles south of Llansawel. This serene collection of houses enjoys a beautiful setting beside twin lakes in the folds of the hills. The village church and ruined abbey are worth visiting.

Dryslwyn Castle

Follow the B4310 to Nantgaredig and travel east along the A40, turning on to the B4297 for Dryslwyn Castle. This ruined fortress, standing on a steep mound in the middle of the fertile Vale of Towy, can be seen for miles around. It was built by Welsh noblemen to control one of the few major crossings of the river, and in 1287 was the scene of a famous siege when its Welsh lord rose in revolt against the English crown. Irregular humps and bumps in the ground to the north of the castle betray traces of a medieval township that grew up beside its walls.

ROUTE DIRECTIONS

Leave **Carmarthen** (map 6SN42) by the Llandeilo road, A40. In 1 mile branch left on to the A484 (sp. Newcastle Emlyn). Continue through Bronwydd, from which the **Gwili Railway** runs, and Cynnil Elfed and Cwmduad. After 1¾ miles turn left, unclassified (sp. Trelech). Nearly 2 miles further, at the crossroads, take the second road on the right (sp. Dolwen Woollen Mill). Descend to Drefach, passing the **Museum of the Welsh Woollen Industry** on the left. Cross the river bridge and turn right. At the main road, A484 (no sign), turn sharp right. In ½ mile turn left on to the B4335 (no sign). Two miles farther, at Pentre-cwrt, turn left on to the A486 (sp. Llandysul). At the edge of **Llandysul** turn right on to the B4336 (sp. Llanybyodder). In 2 miles turn left on to the A485, then immediately right, unclassified (no sign). Go over the crossroads (sp. Rhydcymerau) and in ¾ mile, at the fork, bear right. At Rhydcymerau turn right (sp. Llansawel) on to the B4337. At Llansawel chapel turn sharp right (sp. Abergorlech) on to the B4310. Continue through **Brechfa** to Nantgaredig. At the main crossroads turn right on to the A40, and continue past the **Carmarthen Museum** at Abergwili for the return to Carmarthen.

ON THE TOUR

Carmarthen

The early history of this town was written by the Romans. Carmarthen - or Moridunum - was the most westerly Roman fort in Wales. All that remains from these times is a steep-sided amphitheatre, one of only seven known in Britain, which occupies a grassy hollow on the eastern approaches to the town next to the busy A40.

The centre of town is based around a hill overlooking the River Towy. The remains of Carmarthen Castle do little justice to its medieval role as an important seat of power in south-west Wales. Its most impressive feature is a twin-towered gatehouse, almost lost amongst the shops and houses. The castle shares its hilltop location with imposing offices from whence the affairs of the county of Dyfed are administered.

Despite modern development, Carmarthen is unmistakably Welsh - especially on a market day when farmers' trucks and Land Rovers invade the large livestock mart behind the shopping centre. Nearby is the town's covered market hall, full of interesting stalls selling everything from choice Welsh lamb to antiques and curios.

Carmarthen is the `Merlin's City' of Arthurian legend. During redevelopment an ancient tree known as Merlin's Oak was removed, despite the prophecy `When Merlin's Oak shall tumble down, then shall fall Carmarthen town'. Perhaps Carmarthen has survived by displaying a piece of the tree in the Civic Hall!

Gwili Railway

The Gwili Railway is a standard-gauge steam train operating (mainly in summer) on a renovated section of a Great Western Railway branch line. Run entirely by volunteers, it chuffs along the valley of the River Gwili for just over 1½ miles, from Bronwydd Arms to a riverside halt which has a picnic site, waymarked nature trail and facilities to keep children amused.

Museum of the Welsh Woollen Industry

The Teifi Valley's historic role as Wales's main textile-producing area is remembered at this museum, located in the village of Drefach Felindre. The museum, in a mill which was established here at about the turn of the century, incorporates working machinery which gives visitors an insight into present-day production methods.

The museum links present to past by tracing the development of the woollen industry - Wales's most important rural enterprise - from its humble domestic origins to the noisy factories of the 19th century. There are displays of hand tools, machinery and old photographs, and demonstrations are given of the various processes employed, including spinning and weaving.

Llandysul

The Teifi rushes through a rock-strewn chasm at Llandysul, attracting canoeists intent on taking up the challenge of a white-water slalom course. Llandysul's woollen mills, which once took advantage of the river's waters to wash the fleece and drive the waterwheels, have disappeared. However, a working mill, which is open to the public, survives at Maesllyn, 5 miles to the north-west off the A486.

St Tysul's, at the foot of the town, is a sturdy 13th-century church with a tall, battlemented Norman tower. This religious site may have very ancient origins, for it is dedicated to a saint believed to have been a cousin of David, patron saint of Wales.

Brechfa

This little village gives its name to the huge Brechfa Forest, a Forestry Commission plantation which covers much of the upland to the north. Brechfa stands on the Marlais, a tributary of the Cothi, and both rivers boast good fishing for sea trout and salmon. Walkers can explore parts of the forest by following waymarked trails from the nearby village of Abergorlech.

Carmarthen Museum

The Carmarthen Museum, at Abergwili on the outskirts of Carmarthen, is housed in a grand building previously used by the bishops of St David's as a country seat. Its wide-ranging exhibits, covering local history, culture and the countryside, include delicately carved butter patterns, old Welsh dressers, a wooden weaving frame, ceramics, costumes, early Christian memorial stones, Roman artefacts and a preserved upstairs chapel once used by the bishops.

OFF THE BEATEN TRACK

Paxton's Tower

This folly sits on the crest of the hill above Llanarthney, a mile or so from Dryslwyn Castle, and can be reached by a minor road off the B4300. It was put up by Sir William Paxton during the early 19th century in commemoration of Lord Nelson. From a distance this tall, castellated tower looks substantial and solid. A close-up view reveals the truth: its strangely slender walls enclose nothing but thin air. Paxton chose his location well. His tower commands magnificent views across the verdant Vale of Towy to the hills and mountains of central Wales.

OUTDOOR ACTIVITIES

A number of waymarked walks through Brecha Forest begin at Abergorlech.

Pencader

Pony trekking and riding from Blue Well Riding Centre, Ffynnonlas, Llanllwni, Pencader Tel: (026789) 274.

Spinning a yarn at the Museum of the Woollen Industry at Drefach Felindre

NORTH PEMBROKESHIRE COAST AND COUNTRY

45 miles

Pembrokeshire's rugged northern coastline from Fishguard to Cardigan lies in the shadow of the Preseli Hills. The only substantial upland range

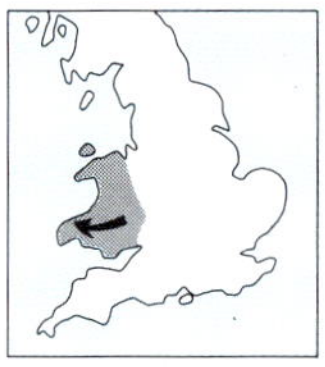

in south-west Wales, these hills rise to almost 1,800ft. Their open, largely treeless slopes, are scattered with a wealth of prehistoric sites.

North Pembrokeshire maintains a much stronger Welsh identity than its neighbouring `Little England beyond Wales' in the south. The coastline here is serrated and full of solitude, the country villages are traditional in character, and the bare slopes of the Preselis still support hardy hill farmers.

The coastal towns of Fishguard and Cardigan are this area's largest settlements. Elsewhere - especially in the Preseli Hills - the villages are small and sleepy, unchanged by the passage of time. The roads that climb across the Preselis command panoramic views over open, sparsely populated moorlands.

However, the countryside here was not always so empty. The exceptionally high concentration of stone tombs, circles and forts to be found in the Preselis is a testament to the area's popularity with prehistoric settlers. The most famous ancient monument in these hills is the Pentre Ifan Cromlech, which was made of the same Preseli `bluestones' used at Stonehenge.

ON THE TOUR

Fishguard

The prettiest part of the town is to be found at the bottom of a steep hill, where Lower Fishguard's old harbour, lined with a row of gabled cottages, nestles beneath a gorse-covered hill. The centre of town is on high ground above the sea. There is an excellent little covered market in the town hall; a building which also contains reminders of Fishguard's seafaring past, amongst which is a record of ships rescued by the local lifeboat. Opposite stands the Royal Oak Inn, a pub which contains memorabilia of the last invasion of British soil in 1797; when French troops embarked on an ill-conceived, tragi-comic military venture after landing at nearby Carregwastad Head.
Fishguard's modern port and terminus for the London to south-west Wales rail-link are to be found at neighbouring Goodwick, the embarkation point for the ferries which sail across the Irish Sea.

Newport

Despite its name, Newport is no longer a port. The quay, once busy with trading schooners, was at Parrog, a little way from the town centre on Newport Bay. Newport today is an attractive little holiday centre. Newport Sands are wide and extensive, with a golf course amongst the dunes.
The town still reveals something of its medieval ancestry. A gateway and flanking tower are the most substantial remains of Newport's refurbished Norman castle (in private ownership). The town also preserves some arcane old customs. Its mayor presides over a Court Leet, and a Beating of the Bounds ceremony takes place in August when the borough's ancient boundaries are retraced by a group of walkers and riders.

St Dogmaels

The B4546 on the southern outskirts of Cardigan travels along the bank of the River Teifi to St Dogmaels. This village grew up around a Benedictine abbey founded in 1115, the remains of which are still visible. The Pembrokeshire Coast National Park boundary begins on the sandy Teifi Estuary just north of St Dogmaels.

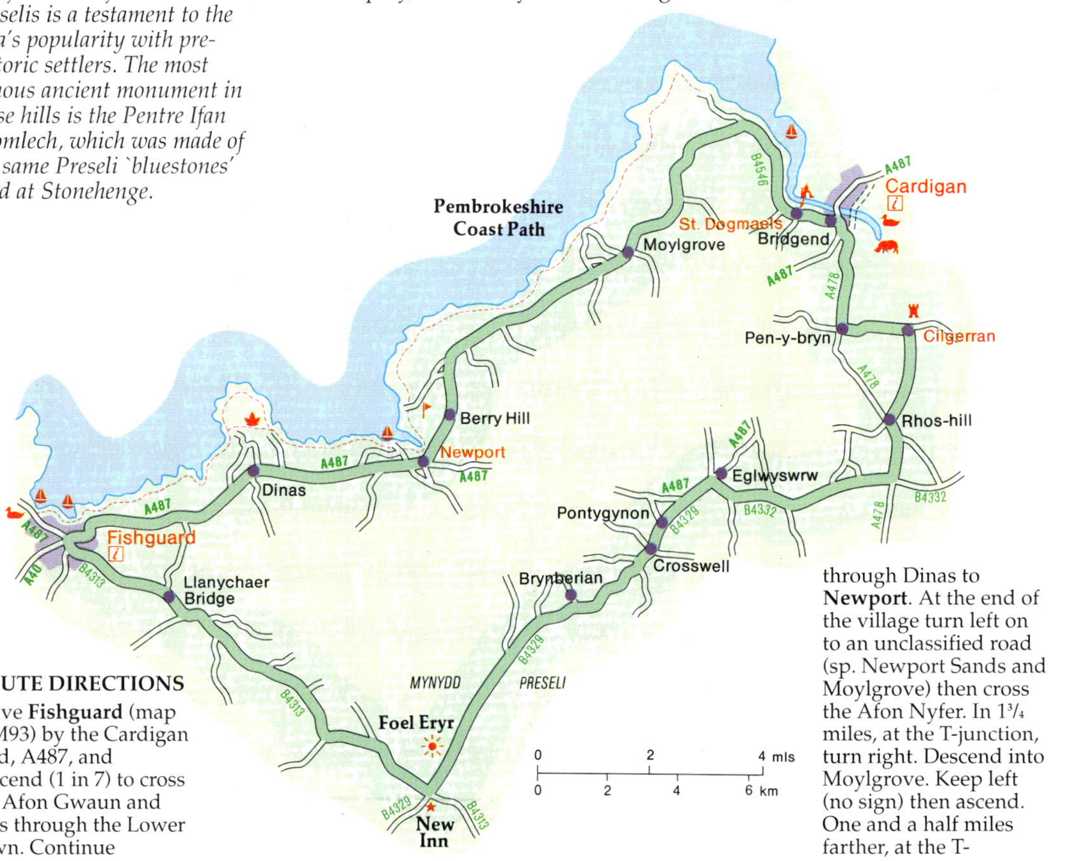

ROUTE DIRECTIONS

Leave **Fishguard** (map 6SM93) by the Cardigan road, A487, and descend (1 in 7) to cross the Afon Gwaun and pass through the Lower Town. Continue through Dinas to **Newport**. At the end of the village turn left on to an unclassified road (sp. Newport Sands and Moylgrove) then cross the Afon Nyfer. In 1³/₄ miles, at the T-junction, turn right. Descend into Moylgrove. Keep left (no sign) then ascend. One and a half miles farther, at the T-junction, turn left (sp. Poppit). Turn right on to the B4546 (no sign). At **St Dogmaels** turn left with the B4546 to reach the edge of **Cardigan**. (For the town centre turn left and cross the river bridge.) Turn right with the Fishguard road, A487, then branch left on to the A478 (sp. Tenby). In 1³/₄ miles, at Pen-y-bryn, turn left on to an unclassified road for **Cilgerran.** Bear right with the main street then take the next turning right (no sign). Continue to Rhos-hill and turn left to rejoin the A478. One mile farther turn right on to the Fishguard road, B4332. At Eglwyswrw turn left on to the A487. In ³/₄ mile turn left again on to the Haverfordwest road, B4329, for Crosswell. After undulating the road climbs and passes the National Park viewpoint of Foel Eryr in the Preseli Hills. Descend to the crossroads at the New Inn and turn right on to the Fishguard road, B4313, for the return to Fishguard.

Cardigan

The River Teifi flows into the sea at Cardigan. A castle was built here by the Normans to give them control of the river mouth. Its ruins (not open to the public) look down over the riverside and Cardigan's most picturesque feature, an elegant stone bridge of 17th-century origin.

In later times, Cardigan flourished as a trading port. Tall wharfside buildings, now mostly converted, are reminders of that period before the coming of railways, when Cardigan was one of the busiest ports in Wales. The town still survives on trade, aided by tourism. Cardigan is now a market town serving the needs of the local farming community.

A covered market is ingeniously incorporated into the mid-19th-century Guildhall. The largely rebuilt St Mary's Church, with its 14th-century chancel, stands in a pleasant riverside location next to the site of an old Benedictine priory.

Cardigan is famous in Welsh history as the place which played host to the first eisteddfod (a festival of literature, music and the arts). The tradition can be traced back to 1176 when the Lord Rhys ap Gruffydd held a Christmas-tide gathering here.

Cilgerran

The castle, in this little village, is one of few that truly deserves the description 'romantic'. Its superb location was a great favourite with Victorian tourists and a source of inspiration to the artists of the 18th and 19th centuries. The ruined battlements stand on a sheer crag above the River Teifi as it flows in a graceful loop through a wooded, narrow gorge.

Coracles, the traditional one-man fishing craft used in Wales for at least 2,000 years, can still be seen occasionally on the waters of the Teifi, here. A Coracle Regatta is held at Cilgerran each August.

OFF THE BEATEN TRACK

Take the minor road off the B4313 for Pontfaen and the Gwaun Valley. Although this secluded valley has a timeless air about it, the locals are devout clock-watchers. They come together on the 13th - not the 1st - of January to celebrate the New Year; perpetuating the traditions of the pre-1752 calendar.

Below left: *low water at Fishguard, a picturesque port with a fine bay surrounded by steep cliffs*

Below right: *the valley of the Teifi is renowned for its salmon and trout. Here, near Cenarth, in the spawning season, salmon leap their way upstream past the rushing, tumbling falls*

OFF THE TOUR

Dinas Head

The minor road northwards after Dinas leads to Cwm-yr-Eglwys (the valley of the church), a pretty village tucked away on the south-eastern approach to Dinas Head. Cwm-yr-Eglwys's ruined church stands on a grassy bank overlooking the sea. Its position was its downfall, for this 12th-century religious site was wrecked by a huge storm in October 1859. The village is also a convenient starting point for a circular 3¼-mile walk. Although the walk is not difficult, special care needs to be taken of young children on certain clifftop sections of the route.

Pentre Ifan Cromlech

This striking burial chamber stands in a field in the foothills of the Preseli Hills, accessible by country lane south of Newport (follow the signposts off the A487 east of Newport). Possibly the finest prehistoric burial chamber in Wales, Pentre Ifan is a collection of angular stones which support a massive 16ft capstone across the roof of the chamber.

The tomb was constructed by Neolithic tribesmen around 3000–4000BC for the burial of their dead. The monument's original covering of a long earthen mound has weathered away to reveal the stone framework. No one has yet explained conclusively how the local Preseli 'bluestones', from which Pentre Ifan was made, were transported all the way to Stonehenge.

Cenarth

Coracles are also used to catch salmon and sewin (sea trout) at Cenarth, a few miles east of Cilgerran on the A484. In the spawning season, salmon struggle upstream past the rocks and rushing waters of Cilgerran's falls.

Castell Henllys Iron Age Village

From Eglwyswrw, take the A487 westwards then follow the minor road north for Castell Henllys, a reconstructed Iron Age village which recreates living conditions as they would have been 2,000 years ago. A tall, conically roofed roundhouse, made from oak and reeds, provides the main accommodation, around which are scattered smaller structures such as a forge and goat house. The site is an authentic one: the reconstructed village occupies a genuine Iron Age settlement that is currently being excavated.

Below: *the remains of 12th-century Cilgerran Castle stand on a steep bluff overlooking the dark river*

PEMBROKESHIRE'S COUNTRY LANES

55 miles

The old county of Pembrokeshire - now part of the large new `super-county' of Dyfed - still preserves a strong individual identity. Although renowned for its

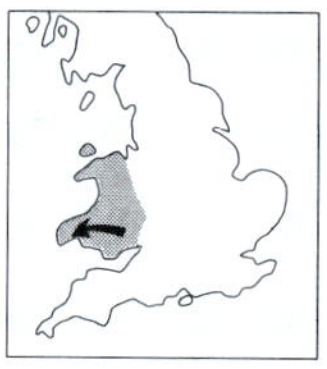

coastline, Pembrokeshire also has its inland charms and away from the sea there lies a green, hilly countryside dotted with historic places.

The tall, tangled hedgerows and open, grassy hillsides in the far south-west of Wales are green for much of the year as the climate here, under the influence of the sea, is mild and mellow. With winter arriving late and spring coming early, early potatoes are a valuable crop for many a farmer in this part of the country.

Pembrokeshire is a region of two distinct characters. In the south there is the so-called `Little England beyond Wales', where English place-names and customs have been retained. In the 11th and 12th centuries the Normans colonised this area, building a frontier of castles across the middle of Pembrokeshire behind which the Welsh retreated. In the Normans' wake came Anglo-Saxon and Flemish immigrants, creating an `Englishry' in the south in contrast to the `Welshry' in the north. The dividing line between the two is known as the Landsker or `land-scar'; this ghostly border does not actually appear on any map, though it corresponds very approximately to the route of the A40.

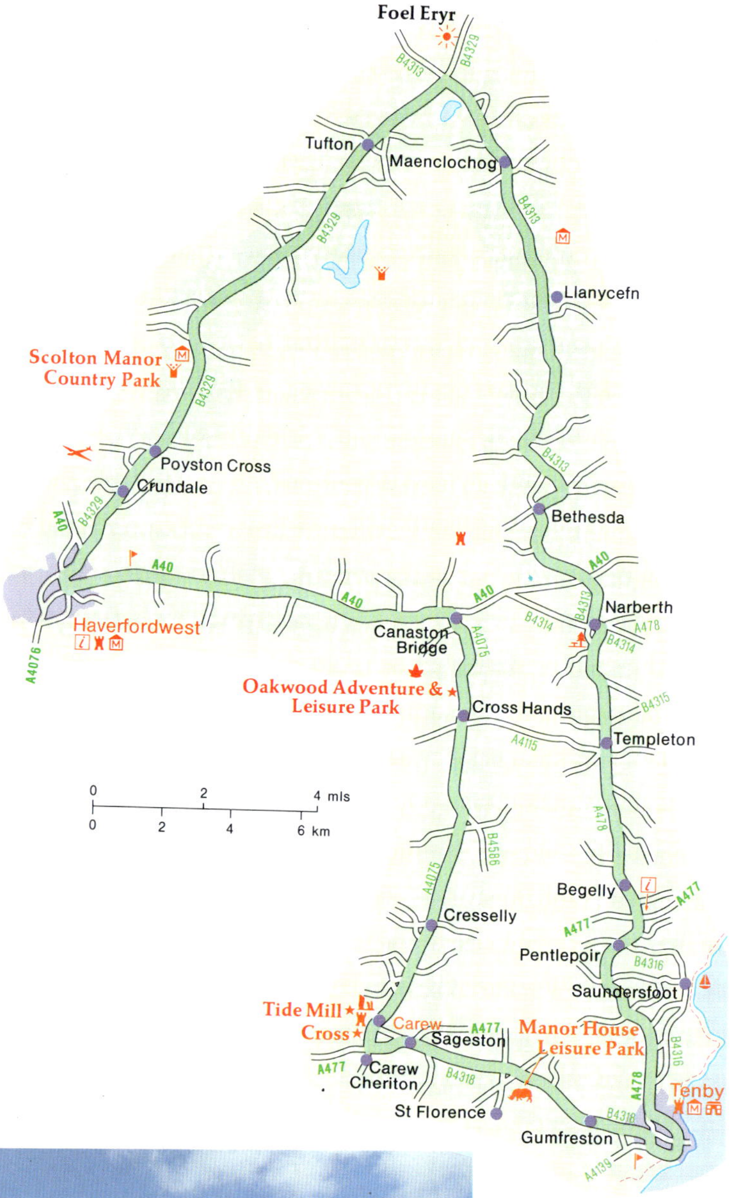

ROUTE DIRECTIONS

From **Tenby** (map 6SN10) follow the Carmarthen road, A478, then turn left (sp. Pembroke) to leave by the B4318. Half a mile later, at the T-junction, turn right passing **Manor House Leisure Park** on the left. In $2\frac{1}{4}$ miles turn left on to the A477. Nearly 1 mile further turn right on to the A4075 (sp. Haverfordwest) for **Carew**. Continue through Cresselly, passing the **Oakwood Adventure and Leisure Park**. At the A40 junction turn left. Continue to **Haverfordwest**. Leave Haverfordwest by the Cardigan road, B4329. Continue through Crundale and on past the **Scolton Manor Country Park** to Tufton. In $1\frac{3}{4}$ miles, at the crossroads by the New Inn, turn right on to the B4313. Descend to Maenclochog and after 5 miles pass under the railway bridge and turn left. In 1 mile, at the crossroads, turn right. Two and a half miles further turn left then right across the A40 into Narberth. Here, turn left (one way system), then right on to the A478 (sp. Tenby). Pass through Templeton and later, at the Begelly roundabout, take 2nd exit for the return to Tenby.

Picton Castle. The first fortress was built here in 1302 and although often altered and modernised, it has been inhabited continuously ever since – a British record!

ON THE TOUR

Tenby

There are not many British seaside resorts which manage to preserve their appearance as well as Tenby. Pastel-shaded Georgian houses rise elegantly above the old stone quayside, the cliffs are lined with bay-windowed hotels, and the town is a charming maze of narrow medieval streets enclosed by ancient walls.

The Victorian view of Tenby – a resort 'whose every view is picturesque in the extreme' - still holds good today. Tenby's ancestry is on display everywhere. The town's well-preserved medieval walls, with their imposing 'Five Arches' gateway, are the most complete

circuit in South Wales. The Tudor Merchant's House (a National Trust property) gives visitors an insight into the lifestyle of a prosperous trader during Tenby's busy seafaring days of old. A museum on local history and the environment stands on the headland next to the remains of a castle.
The beaches, at the foot of a spectacular, cliff-backed coast, are extensive. From the harbour, boats set off on the short crossing to Caldey Island – famous for its monastery where perfume is made.

Manor House Leisure Park

Set in wooded grounds outside the village of St Florence, this 12-acre park is a great favourite with families. Attractions include animal collections, a pets' corner, exhibitions and adventure play areas.

Carew

It is worth stopping off at this small village, on the upper reaches of the tidal Carew River, for at least three reasons. The first is the Carew Cross, a roadside Celtic cross decorated with intricate interlacing patterns. This exceptional cross has been adopted as the official symbol for Cadw-Welsh Historic Monuments, the organisation responsible for many of Wales's historic sites.
Across the field from the cross stands Carew Castle, a riverside fortress built in the late 13th century that gradually evolved into a splendid Tudor home.
Carew's third place of interest utilised the effects of the tide. The early 19th-century Carew Tidal Mill, the only one of its kind remaining in Wales, was driven by high-tide waters trapped in a mill pond.

Oakwood Adventure and Leisure Park

This is Wales's answer to the well-managed theme parks of the USA. Although not in the Disney mould, Oakwood has enough to keep the most demanding of children happy. The extensive 80-acre grounds contain – amongst many other things – a miniature railway, bobsleigh run, boating lake, assault course, go-kart circuit, cyclo-cross and nature pavilion.

Haverfordwest

The 'capital' of old Pembrokeshire, Haverfordwest is a town of great character where steep-sided streets, lined with handsome old houses, rise from the riverside. This was once a busy port and trading ships sailed down the Cleddau to the Milford Haven waterway and the open seas. Tall warehouses and the Bristol Trader Inn are reminders of the times when the quayside handled cargoes of wool and wine.
Haverfordwest's skyline is dominated by its ruined Norman castle, perched on a windy hilltop above the town. It shares the summit with a grim gaol, built in 1820, which now serves as the home of the County Museum whose wide-ranging exhibits include noteworthy military displays. It is well worth wandering around this fascinating town of nooks and crannies, narrow streets and riverside walks. St Mary's, the most impressive of its three churches, has an early 13th-century arcade of arches dividing the nave.

Scolton Manor Country Park

This park is based around a late-Georgian mansion built in about 1840. Parts of the house, together with rural craft workshops, exhibition hall and countryside centre are open to the public. The house looks out across a 40-acre parkland of landscaped grounds, spruce and fir plantations, deciduous trees, a 19th-century arboretum, butterfly garden and pond. Pembrokeshire's past, from prehistoric times onwards, is the theme in the exhibition hall. The grounds contain railway memorabilia from the 19th century.

OFF THE BEATEN TRACK

Penrhos Cottage

You will need to be a good navigator to find this little cottage in the narrow lanes east of the B4313 between Maenclochog and Llanycefn (it is best approached from the former village). This traditional Welsh thatched cottage, which contains original furniture, is thought to be a *Ty'n nos* (moonlight house). This is a reference to an old custom that allowed a house to be built overnight on common land as long as there was a fire burning in the hearth by the morning.

OUTDOOR ACTIVITIES

Llys-y-Fran Country Park

Take the minor road off the B4329 through Walton East for the attractive Llys-y-Fran Country Park. This park is based around the wooded shores of the scenic Llys-y-Fran reservoir, completed in 1971. Recreational activities include sailing, windsurfing, canoeing and fishing, while walkers can follow an attractive lakeside footpath along a complete circuit of the reservoir of some 7½ miles.

Tenby

A stretch of the long-distance, 180-mile Pembrokeshire Coast Footpath can be followed from Tenby, and the National Park runs many guided walks in summer.

OFF THE TOUR

Manorbier

'The pleasantest spot in Wales' is to be found a few miles south of St Florence. This is the description of Manorbier, penned by Wales's first travel writer, the medieval monk Giraldus Cambrensis. Giraldus was born at Manorbier Castle, a fortress-by-the-sea which, although around 900 years old, is in an excellent state of preservation. A little village-cum-resort has grown up around the castle, close to excellent beaches and coast walks.

Llawhaden Castle

A country lane off the A40, close to its junction with the A4075, leads to Llawhaden Castle. This interesting site, imposingly situated on a grassy knoll overlooking rolling countryside, is not a fortress in the conventional sense. Llawhaden was originally built as a castle to guard the Landsker and in later years it became a fortified mansion, serving as a secure country palace for the bishops of St David's. Its 14th-century gatehouse, which still stands to its full height, is particularly impressive.

Sutherland Art Gallery and Picton Castle Gardens

The artist Graham Sutherland had a special affinity with Pembrokeshire. This area inspired many of his finest paintings, so it is only fitting that the largest permanent display of his works is to be found here. The Sutherland Gallery is adjacent to Picton Castle, just off the A40 on the approach to Haverfordwest. The castle gardens are also open to the public.

Saundersfoot

This busy little resort is just a short detour off the main road on the way back to Tenby. It has grown up around its harbour, which is the main attraction along the South Wales coast for holiday yachtsmen. Few of those who relax on Saundersfoot's sheltered, sandy beach are aware that this pretty resort was once a coal-exporting port.

Haverfordwest: the castle, old bridge and Fishguard Arms hotel

TWO VALES AND THE WESTERN BEACONS

49 1/2 miles

The industrial past of the vales of Neath and Dulais provides a contrast with the untouched countryside in the western flank of the Brecon Beacons National Park. The park, though predominantly an upland area, has a corner of limestone scenery characterised by deep valleys, waterfalls and caves.

Industry arrived early in the Vale of Neath. Despite this fact, the valley never suffered the devastating effects of concentrated industrial activity which so badly blighted other parts of South Wales.

The coal measures of the South Wales valleys meet the limestone and sandstone of the Brecon Beacons National Park near Glyn-Neath. The band of outcropping limestone along the southern rim of the park defines a distinctive area of labyrinthine cave systems, steep-sided, wooded valleys and a string of spectacular waterfalls. Further north old redstones - the 'backbone' of the Brecon Beacons - take over, creating a landscape of high, open moorland.

This is an area of contrasts: old mining villages and scattered farmsteads, airy mountainsides and gloomy chasms, industrial remnants and popular tourist attractions.

ON THE TOUR

Neath

To the Romans, Neath was known as Nidum. Unfortunately, little remains of their fort. Neath's ruined medieval castle has suffered less from the ravages of time, though the town's most significant historic monument is its Cistercian abbey founded in 1130. Once known as `the fairest abbey in all Wales', this religious site did not escape the effects of the Industrial Revolution. When Neath became a copper smelting area in the 18th century, furnaces, a casting workshop and lodgings for the workers were set up amongst the abbey buildings.

Pont-Nedd Fechan

This little village, near the confluence of the Neath, Mellte and Sychryd rivers, offers an exceptional choice of walks taking in everything from waterfalls to abandoned gunpowder works. One delightful path, suitable for all the family, starts just beyond the Angel Inn. A well-established footpath follows the banks of the River Neath for a mile or so to its confluence with the River Pyrddin and Sgwd Gwladus, a tumbling waterfall of almost primeval beauty in a mossy, cliff-backed setting.

Ystradfellte

This hamlet – a church, pub and a handful of houses – is better known than its size may suggest. Its celebrity derives from its position in the heart of South Wales's 'Waterfall Country'.

Dan-yr-Ogof Caves

The action of water on limestone rock over millions of years has created the underground spectacle on display here. The showcaves complex, which claims to be the largest in western Europe, has three separate caves open to the public.

The main showcaves are full of weird and wonderful formations including a wealth of stalactites and stalagmites. Discovered in 1912, they represent but a fraction of the vast system of passageways which riddle this mountainside. The second chamber open to the public is the Cathedral Cave, a 42ft-high subterranean `Dome of St Paul's'. The history of settlement in this region – both by wild animals and man – is reflected in the contents of the Bone Cave. Dan-yr-Ogof is a versatile attraction suitable for all ages. Other features on site include a Dinosaur Park populated by life-sized prehistoric beasts, and a dry ski slope.

Craig-y-nos Country Park

The park was created as the ornamental grounds of Craig-y-nos Castle, a rambling 19th-century sham (not open to the public) which was the home of the famous opera singer Madame Adelina Patti. Her 'pleasure grounds' beside the River Tawe – a 40-acre swathe of wood, lake and meadow – are now open for all to enjoy.

Henrhyd Falls

These are the most easily accessible of all the waterfalls in this area. It is only a short walk

A restored steam winding engine at the Cefn Coed Coal and Steam Centre. Mining tools and equipment are also featured

OFF THE TOUR

Porth-yr-Ogof

Less than a mile south of Ystradfellte is Porth-yr-Ogof, a gaping cave entrance - probably the largest in Wales - which swallows up the River Mellte. The river, which reappears 1/4 mile downstream, flows through an increasingly narrow valley to tumble down a magnificent series of falls - Sgwd Clun-gwyn, Sgwd Isaf Clyn-gwyn and Sgwd y Pannwr. A riverside footpath leads from Porth-yr-Ogof to the falls.

A fourth waterfall is on the River Hepste, which joins the Mellte a short distance downstream from Sgwd y Pannwr. This is Sgwd yr Eira, possibly the most famous fall of them all, which allows walkers the novelty of following a path that leads between the overhang and behind the curtain of water without getting wet.

Penscynor Wildlife Park

This park, at Cilfrew just off the A465, is a very popular family attraction. The park is home to hundreds of animals and birds from all over the world. Penscynor's many attractions include tropical and chimpanzee houses, sea-lion and penguin pools, an alpine slide and an exciting bob-sleigh ride down the hillside above the animal enclosures.

ROUTE DIRECTIONS

Leave **Neath** (map 6SS79) on the B4434 (sp. Tonna) and in 3/4 mile turn left (sp. Resolven). Pass through Tonna and continue on to Resolven. Here, bear left (sp. Merthyr A465) and in 1/2 mile at the trunk road, turn right on to the A465. In 3 3/4 miles, turn left on to the B4242 (sp. Glyn-Neath) and enter Glyn-Neath. After 1/3 mile, at the traffic signals go forward (sp. Pont Nedd Fechan) and in 1/4 mile further branch left (sp. Ystradfellte). Continue through **Pont-Nedd Fechan** and keep forward, unclassified. In 1/10 mile keep left and ascend, passing the road to Porth-yr-Ogof Caves on the right. Continue to **Ystradfellte** and turn left (sp. Sennybridge) a gated road. Reach the summit (1,470ft) and in 1/4 mile descend (1 in 4) around hairpin bends. In 1 1/4 miles turn right (sp. Heol Senni), then after 2 miles, at the trunk road, turn left (sp. Crai) for Heol Senni. Here, cross the river bridge, go forward and ascend. In 2 1/2 miles turn left on to the A4067 (sp. Swansea) and pass through Glyntawe. Continue past the **Dan-yr-Ogof Caves** and **Craig-y-nos Country Park** to Pen-y-Cae. Here, turn left, unclassified (sp. Henrhyd Waterfall, Coelbren) and in 1/10 mile cross the bridge, bear right and ascend. After 2/3 mile keep left and in 1/10 mile, at the trunk road, turn left. Pass the car park for **Henrhyd Falls** on the right, cross the river bridge and in 1/4 mile turn right (sp. Abercraf). Pass Colbren post office, in 1/4 mile turn left (sp. Onllwyn) and in a further 1/4 mile cross the main road to Onllwyn. At the trunk road turn right on to the A4109 (sp. Neath) to **Seven Sisters**. Here bear right to cross the railway bridge, then right again to Crynant. Continue on past the **Cefn Coed Coal and Steam Museum** and in 2 1/2 miles turn right on to the A465. Pass **Aberdulais Falls** on the right and in 1/4 mile, at the roundabout, take 1st exit. In 2 miles branch left on to the A474 and, at the roundabout, take 1st exit to re-enter Neath.

OFF THE BEATEN TRACK

Sarn Helen and Maen Madoc

The wilderness between Coelbren and Ystradfellte is crossed by a Roman road known as Sarn Helen (Helen's Causeway), part of the link between Roman forts at Neath, Coelbren and Brecon. Although there is a vehicular right of way across the road, its route - interrupted by a deep, rocky ford - is for the most part very poorly surfaced.

Sarn Helen is much better suited for walking. It joins the mountain road to Heol Senni about 2 miles north of Ystradfellte. Along Sarn Helen a mile to the south-east is Maen Madoc, a 9ft-high standing stone which reflects the fusion of invading and native cultures. Originally, Maen Madoc was probably a plain Celtic standing stone. After Roman occupation, an inscription (in Latin) was added: '[The stone] of Dervacus, son of Justus. He lies here.'

OUTDOOR ACTIVITIES

Footpaths and nature trails from Aberdulais Basin, Pont Nedd Fechan, the Ystradfellte area, and Craig-y-nos Country Park.

In the glorious open countryside not far from Ystradfellte is the standing stone known as Maen Madoc. This slender 9ft pillar of stone is a rare example of the way in which Roman and native Celtic cultures must inevitably have intermingled during the hundreds of years of occupation

from the car park to the viewing point for this waterfall (despite the name, there is only the one). The Nant Lech takes an unbroken 90ft plunge into a wooded chasm which stands on the dividing line between industrial and rural South Wales. The abrupt change between the two is nowhere better visualised than from the car park: to the north are the inviolate solitudes of the Black Mountains, while the southern horizon is filled with a lunar-like landscape of open-cast mineworkings.

Seven Sisters

The museum here, in the Dulais Valley, traces the evolution of woodworking methods and machinery, brought right up-to-date with a look at a modern sawmill. Other attractions at this multi-faceted site include one of the country's largest collections of mining lamps, a 'Gunsmoke Cowboy Town', children's adventure playground and street of three-quarter-sized houses.

Cefn Coed Coal and Steam Museum

Visitors can walk through a simulated mining gallery at this museum, based at Blaenant Colliery near Crynant. The museum also has a preserved steam winding engine and displays of mining tools and equipment housed in authentic colliery buildings.

Aberdulais Falls

The National Trust's Aberdulais Falls epitomise the Vale of Neath's unusual blend of industrial heritage and natural beauty. The waters of the Dulais tumble down a rocky, romantically beautiful gorge which has attracted artists, including JMW Turner, from far and wide. However, this spot is also a site of early industry; the Dulais drove a waterwheel which in turn powered the bellows of a pioneering smelting works, the remains of which can still be seen. Aberdulais is important as one of the earliest industrial sites in South Wales. It started life in 1584 as a copper works, later moving on to iron and tin. Across the road is the Aberdulais Basin. This attractively restored basin, at the meeting place of the Neath (1795) and Tennant (1824) canals, is adjacent to the 340ft, ten-arched Tennant Canal Aqueduct. It is also a starting point for pleasant towpath walks.

THE CENTRAL BEACONS

64½ miles

The 520-square-mile Brecon Beacons National Park is made up of four mountain ranges. The Park takes its name from its central uplands, a mountain block sandwiched between the two very different towns of Brecon and Merthyr Tydfil. This central range contains the highest summit in South Wales.

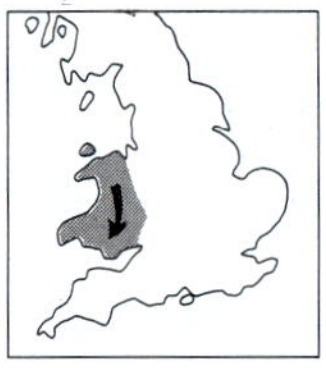

For the most part, the Brecon Beacons are made up of old red-sandstone rocks. This softish rock has formed a landscape of wide, open spaces, rounded uplands, gradual gradients and windy, treeless horizons. The Beacons are deceptive. Their grassy slopes and consistent height - much of it over 2,000ft - disguise the fact that these are 'mountains' in every sense of the word. Although relatively gentle, the gradients on the footpath from the A470 at Storey Arms take walkers to the exposed summit of Pen-y-Fan; at 2,906ft the highest peak in South Wales.

Pen-y-Fan's distinctive, flat-topped summit looks northwards to Brecon, a charming old country town. The rich Usk Valley, its sheltered river-meadows a lush contrast to the bare, unproductive flanks of the Beacons, winds its way south-eastwards. Man's influence in the park is at its greatest along the Beacons' southern slopes, where reservoirs and coniferous forests have been created.

Brecon, a charming old market town with a medieval castle, is a convenient centre for exploring the National Park. Pen-y-Fan, the highest peak in Wales, can be seen in the distance

ON THE TOUR

Brecon

Narrow streets, Georgian houses, riverside walks, a ruined castle, covered marketplace and hilltop cathedral are some of the ingredients of this charming market town. Brecon's Welsh name, Aberhonddu (the mouth of the Honddu), describes its position at the junction of the rivers Honddu and Usk. The Normans built a castle here in the late 11th century, around which grew up a walled medieval town.

Echoes of old Brecon still remain in its maze of cramped streets, though the castle has been unceremoniously cut in two by a road. The museum, housed in the classically designed former Shire Hall (1842), preserves the old assize court intact. It also contains a collection of love-spoons (symbols of betrothal in the rural Wales of bygone times) and a lake dweller's canoe of *c.* AD800, carved from a single oak trunk, found at nearby Llangorse.

A second museum in the town is dedicated to the South Wales Borderers.

Brecon Beacons Mountain Centre

At Libanus, follow the signs for the Mountain Centre. This beautifully located national park visitor centre, on Mynydd Illtud Common, provides an informative introduction to the Beacons. Displays and exhibition material focus on the countryside, wildlife, conservation and the role of the national park. On a clear day views from the terrace, looking across the valley to Pen-y-Fan and its neighbouring peaks, are superb. The centre is also the starting point for a number of pleasant walks across the common.

Talybont Reservoir

This large, attractive reservoir has become such an important refuge for birdlife – especially winter wildfowl – that it has been designated a local nature reserve. Bird watchers enjoy good vantage points from the road running along its western shores.

Talybont-on-Usk

This village should really be called Talybont-on-canal. Many of its houses are closer to the Monmouthshire and Brecon Canal than to the River Usk. The canal, completed in 1812, connected Brecon with Newport and the Severn estuary. By the 1930s it had fallen into disuse. Following restoration, a 32-mile stretch was reopened in 1970 between Brecon and Pontymoile (near Pontypool). This is now popular with canal cruising boats, many of which pull up alongside the pubs on the towpath at Talybont.

Crickhowell

The stagecoaches on the way from London to West Wales used to stop in the cobbled courtyard of Crickhowell's Bear Hotel (the bar still contains mementoes from the days of stagecoach travel). The pretty little town takes its name from Crug Hywel (Howell's fort), an Iron Age stronghold on a 1,481ft, flat-topped spur above the rooftops.

Streets lined with Georgian houses lead down to a picturesque 13-arched stone bridge over the Usk. The town's St Edmund's Church, with its needle-sharp spire, dates from the 14th century. Even older – and looking its age – is Crickhowell's ruined castle.

Tretower Court and Castle

Tretower is an unusual two-in-one historic site. A starkly simple round tower, plainly military in purpose, stands next to a substantial manor house which must have been a comfortable residence in its time. The castle - or keep - was put up in the troubled 12th century when life in Wales was full of threat. The court, in contrast, was built in the more settled 14th and 15th centuries when greater consideration could be given to home comforts; its woodwork and timber fittings in the hall and gallery are exceptional. Tretower was the home of Henry Vaughan, the 17th-century metaphysical poet who is buried at nearby Llansantffraed Church.

Llangorse

One-mile-long Llangorse Lake is the largest natural lake in South Wales. Fringed by fields and reed banks and almost surrounded by mountains, it is a popular beauty spot and sailing centre. The village of Llangorse, a short distance from the lake, is clustered around the ancient Church of St Paulinus, a religious site dating from the 6th century.

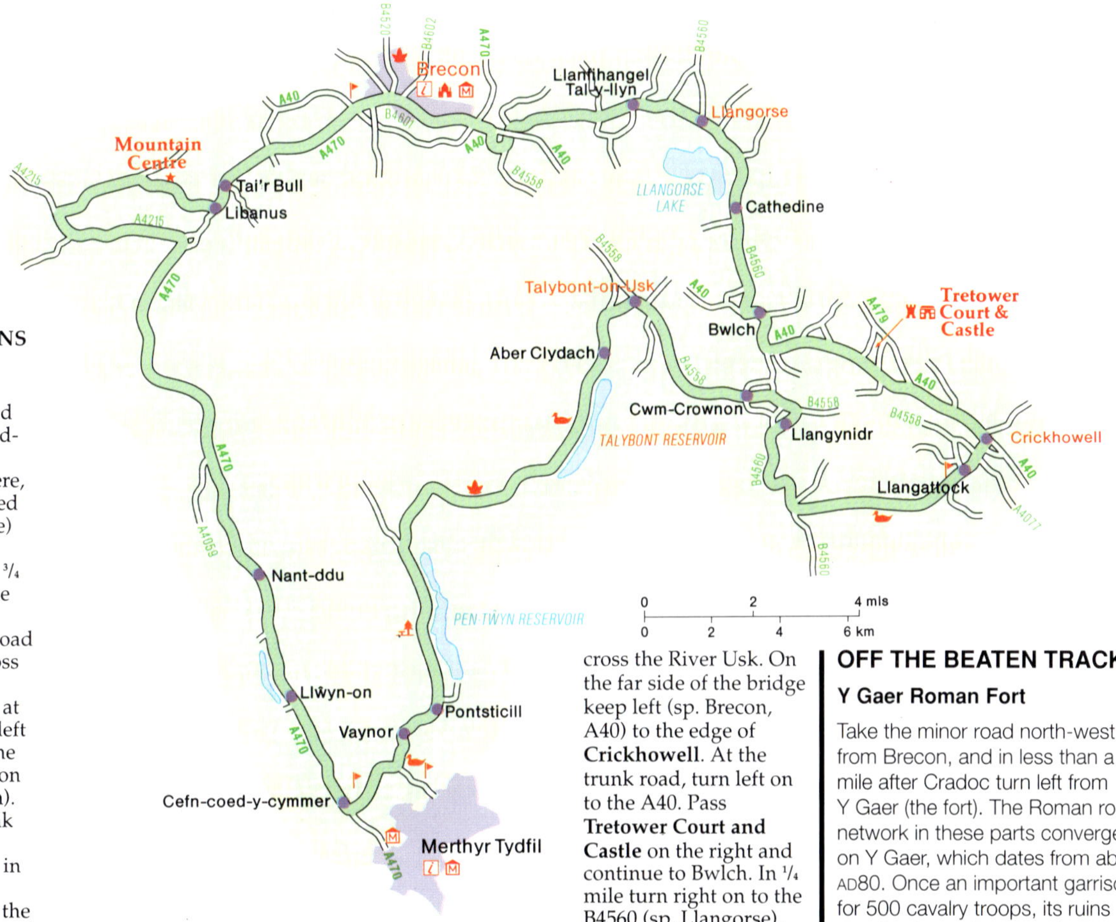

ROUTE DIRECTIONS

Leave **Brecon** (map 7SO02) on the B4601 (sp. Cardiff A470) and in 1 mile, at the roundabout, take 2nd exit A470, to Libanus. Here, turn right, unclassified (sp. Mountain Centre) and in 1/3 mile bear right. After a further 3/4 mile turn right for the **Mountain Centre**. Return to the trunk road then turn right to cross Mynydd Illtud Common. In 1/2 mile, at the trunk road, turn left and in 1 3/4 miles, at the trunk road, turn left on to the A4215 (no sign). In 1/2 mile, at the trunk road turn left (sp. Merthyr Tydfil) then in 2 1/3 miles, bear right, then turn right on to the A470. Continue forward through Nantddu, and on to Cefn-coed-y-cymmer. Turn left, unclassified (sp. Talybont) and in 2 1/3 miles bear left. After 2/3 mile further descend (1 in 9) to Pontsticill. Pass the road to the Brecon Mountain Railway Centre on the right and bear left. Pass the Pontsticill Reservoir car park and in 1 mile turn left. One mile further on turn right and descend to cross the river bridge, then make an ascent, and another descent (1 in 5) to **Taly-bont Reservoir** dam. In 1 1/3 miles bear right, then in 1/2 mile cross the canal. At the trunk road, turn right on to the B4558 (no sign) in to **Talybont-on-Usk**. In 1/4 mile go forward (sp. Crickhowell) and in 3 miles bear right into Llangynidr. In 1 mile turn right on to the B4560 (sp. Beaufort). In 3 miles pass the quarry then turn left, unclassified (sp. Crickhowell). In 3 1/3 miles cross the bridge and, at the trunk road, turn left to Llangattock. In 1/3 mile turn left on to the A4077 (no sign), then at the traffic signals, turn right and cross the River Usk. On the far side of the bridge keep left (sp. Brecon, A40) to the edge of **Crickhowell**. At the trunk road, turn left on to the A40. Pass **Tretower Court and Castle** on the right and continue to Bwlch. In 1/4 mile turn right on to the B4560 (sp. Llangorse), pass Cathedine church on the left and enter **Llangorse**. In 1/10 mile, bear right and in another 1/10 mile turn left, unclassified (sp. Brecon). In 1 mile keep left and after a further 1/2 mile bear left into Llanfihangel Tal-y-llyn. In 1/10 mile keep right, then in 2 1/3 miles, at the trunk road, turn left. In 1/4 mile pass under the bridge and turn right to join the A40. In 3/4 mile further on, at the roundabout, take 2nd exit B4601 to re-enter Brecon.

OFF THE TOUR

Taf Fechan Reservoir and Brecon Mountain Railway

The Taf Fechan Reservoir at Pontsticill is a beautiful stretch of water fringed with woodland. The buildings on the eastern side of the reservoir, overlooking the dam, are those of the Brecon Mountain Railway. This narrow-gauge line – the only one of Wales's 'Great Little Trains' to be found in South Wales – runs on part of the trackbed of the old British Rail Merthyr Tydfil to Brecon route. It operates from a main station at Pant on the northern fringes of Merthyr, running for a mile or so along the side of the valley to its lakeside terminus at Pontsticill.

Garwnant Forest Visitor Centre

The work of the Forestry Commission is featured at this centre, set amongst the trees above the Llwyn-on reservoir and reached by turning right off the A470 on to an unclassified road. Visitors are also attracted by Garwnant's scenic forest walks, picnic sites and children's adventure playground.

Merthyr Tydfil

From Cefn-coed-y-cymmer, stay on the A470 for Merthyr Tydfil. In the 19th century Merthyr was the undisputed 'iron and steel capital of the world'. Most of the evidence of its industrial heyday has vanished, though the grand house built by one of its wealthiest ironmasters, William Crawshay, still stands. Crawshay's Cyfarthfa Castle dates from 1824. Today, part of his mock-military mansion houses an excellent local museum.

OFF THE BEATEN TRACK

Y Gaer Roman Fort

Take the minor road north-west from Brecon, and in less than a mile after Cradoc turn left from Y Gaer (the fort). The Roman road network in these parts converged on Y Gaer, which dates from about AD80. Once an important garrison for 500 cavalry troops, its ruins now lie almost forgotten in a farmer's field above a loop in the River Usk.

OUTDOOR ACTIVITIES

There are many walks over the common from the Brecon Beacons Mountain Centre, and also a footpath to Pen-y-Fan - from Storey Arms on the A470.

Waymarked trails leave from the Garwnant Forest Visitor Centre, and the Talybont Forest (at Blaen-y-Glyn above the Talybont reservoir), where there is a most attractive waterfall walk.

Llandasty church by Llangorse Lake; there is a rich variety of plant, animal and bird life around the shoreline

WYEDEAN

73 miles

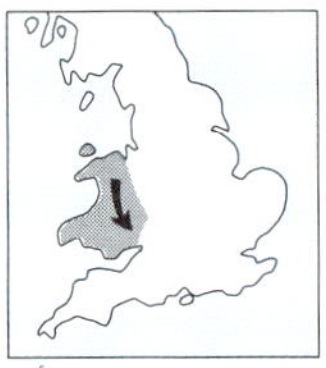

The Forest of Dean occupies the high ground between two great rivers, the Wye and the Severn. The Wye is at its most scenic along the thickly wooded valley between Monmouth and Chepstow, a stretch that has been declared an Area of Outstanding Natural Beauty.

This tour, starting and finishing in England, touches Welsh border country along the lovely Wye Valley. The Forest of Dean is a strange, fascinating place; a no-man's land locked away between the Wye and Severn. It retains a strong sense of its own identity, neither English nor Welsh, which has roots going back a thousand years to the time when it was declared a royal hunting ground by King Canute.

Despite the commercial conifers, the Forest of Dean is still a beautiful woodland where mature deciduous trees and thinly planted glades hark back to the days of Britain's medieval forests. The forest has been called 'one of the most beautiful coalfields in the world'. Coal has been mined here for centuries by its Freeminers.

The Wye, which more or less follows the England/Wales border between Ross-on-Wye and Chepstow, loops through rolling countryside past spectacular outcrops, wooded riverbanks and historic sites.

Tintern Abbey, on the banks of the Wye, is one of the finest relics of Britain's monastic age

ON THE TOUR

Ross-on-Wye

The soaring spire of St Mary's Church pierces the skyline above this charming town, built on a hill beside the curving Wye. The town's centrepiece is the Market House, constructed of local red sandstone in the 17th century, with an open ground floor and upper storey supported by columns and arches. Ross's historic role as a busy coaching town is reflected in the black-and-white inns and buildings along its main streets. The scant remnants of 13th-century Wilton Castle can be seen from the Banky Meadow gardens.

Symonds Yat

There are two Symonds Yats, east and west, separated by the Wye as it enters a spectacular gorge. Yat Rock stands above Symonds Yat East, a panoramic perch looking down into the gorge and beyond to a glorious loop in the river. The Wye Valley Farm Park, located below the rock, is the home of rare and old-fashioned breeds of farm animals.

To visit Symonds Yat West, drive via the A40 or take the passenger ferry across the river. The Wye Valley Visitor Centre at the northern edge of the village, near Whitchurch, incorporates the entertaining Jubilee Maze and the World of Butterflies.

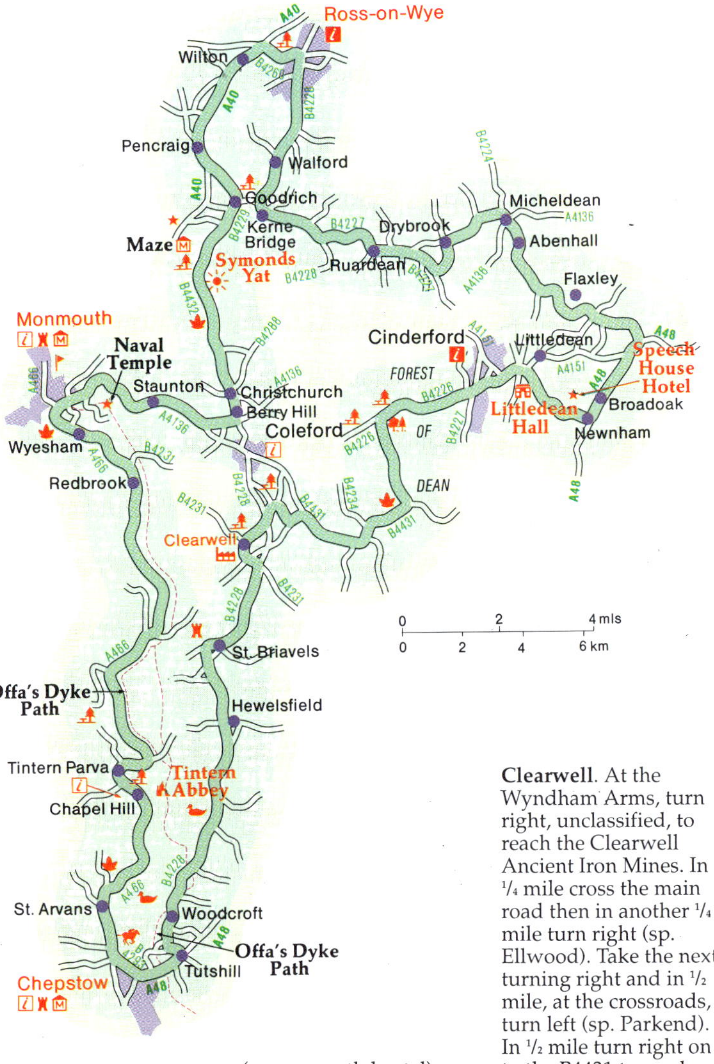

ROUTE DIRECTIONS

Leave **Ross-on-Wye** (map 7SO52) on the B4260 (sp. Monmouth). In $^3/_4$ mile cross the River Wye, then at the Wilton roundabout take 1st exit to reach Pencraig. In $^1/_2$ mile turn left, un-classified, for Goodrich. Bear right then turn right on to the B4229 (sp. Symonds Yat) to enter the **Symonds Yat** area, then in $^3/_4$ mile turn left, unclassified (sp. Symonds Yat East) to cross the Huntsham Bridge. In 1 mile keep forward and ascend (1 in 5) to reach Symonds Yat Rock. Join the B4432 (sp. Coleford) to reach Christchurch. Turn right on to the B4228 and in $^1/_2$ mile, at the crossroads, turn right again on to the A4136 (sp. Monmouth) for Staunton. After a long descent turn left on to the A466 (sp. Chepstow) to skirt **Monmouth** and enter the Lower Wye Valley, passing through Redbrook. In another $3^1/_2$ miles, cross the River Wye by the Bigsweir Bridge to reach Llandogo. Continue to Tintern, passing **Tintern Abbey** and after 3 miles pass the road to the Wyndcliff Viewpoint. Beyond St Arvans pass Chepstow racecourse then, at the roundabout, take 1st exit for **Chepstow**, B4293. Turn left and descend through the town, joining the A48 to cross the River Wye into England. Ascend and in 1 mile turn left on to the B4228 (sp. St Briavels). At St Briavels branch left, unclassified, and pass the restored castle (now a youth hostel). Continue to the cross-roads then turn left to rejoin the B4228 (sp. Coleford). In 2 miles turn left on to the B4231 and continue to **Clearwell**. At the Wyndham Arms, turn right, unclassified, to reach the Clearwell Ancient Iron Mines. In $^1/_4$ mile cross the main road then in another $^1/_4$ mile turn right (sp. Ellwood). Take the next turning right and in $^1/_2$ mile, at the crossroads, turn left (sp. Parkend). In $^1/_2$ mile turn right on to the B4431 to reach Parkend, continue and in $1^1/_2$ miles, turn left, unclassified (sp. Speech House). Turn right on to the B4226, pass **Speech House Hotel** and the

Monmouth

The town is steeped in history. Monmouth Castle, now a ruin, was the birthplace of Henry V. A statue of the king occupies a niche in the handsome Shire Hall overlooking Agincourt Square. The statue to another celebrated son, Charles Rolls of Rolls-Royce fame, also looks down on to the busy square. The Monnow Bridge, guarding the western approach to Monmouth, is an important medieval monument. This 13th-century fortified bridge gateway (a very effective bottleneck to traffic) is reputedly the only one of its kind in Britain. Monmouth's museum contains a section dedicated to the life of Admiral Lord Nelson.

Tintern Abbey

Many artists and poets have been inspired by the beauty of this serene ruin on the banks of the Wye. Tintern Abbey, founded by Cistercian monks in the 12th century, was praised in a famous sonnet by Wordsworth and painted by Turner. Its tall arches and windows point skywards in perfect harmony with its setting below the steep-sided, wooded slopes of the valley.

The Old Station at Tintern (previously a Victorian railway station) is now a countryside visitor centre and starting point for a number of lovely walks.

Chepstow

The town has grown up around a major landmark in the evolution of medieval military architecture. Chepstow Castle, begun shortly after the Norman Conquest of 1066, was the first stone-built castle in Britain. Its significance does not end there. The castle's stonework is a history lesson in the refinement of building techniques, for Chepstow was improved and modified over the next 500 years. A local history museum stands near the castle, as does a Stuart Crystal Centre where glassware is decorated.

Clearwell

More insights into the Forest of Dean's fascinating history are revealed at Clearwell. Clearwell Caves are ancient iron mines where ore was dug for nearly 3,000 years before their closure in 1945. Eight large caverns, part of Clearwell's vast complex of underground workings, are open to the public. Mining equipment and engines are also on display.

There are more ancient iron workings – this time above ground – at nearby Puzzle Wood. This jumbled, irregular area, overgrown with woodland and landscaped in the 1800s, is infiltrated by a maze of pathways arranged as a puzzle.

Speech House Hotel

This hotel, standing alone in the heart of the forest, was originally built in 1680 as a keeper's lodge and court house to administer the forest's affairs, including those of the Freeminers, whose unique mining rights date back to medieval times. The old court room is still used to transact local business.

Littledean Hall

Littledean's 17th-century front stands over a site of great antiquity. The Lords of Dene lived here from the 11th century, in a dwelling that contains the only known remains of a Saxon hall in England. A Roman temple, discovered here in 1984, displays a large, fully restored ground plan.

Evening sunlight brings a glow to the 14th-century church at Ross-on-Wye. From The Prospect, a public garden nearby, there are superb views of the river and distant hills

ROUTE DIRECTIONS continued

picnic area, and in 2¼ miles ascend before turning right on to the A4151 (sp. Gloucester) and descend to Littledean. At the T-junction turn right, unclassified (sp. Newnham) and pass the entrance to **Littledean Hall**. Make a long descent to reach Newnham then turn left on to the A48 and in 2 miles turn left again, unclassified (sp. Mitcheldean). Take the by-road to Flaxley then, in 1 mile turn right. In 1¾ miles cross the main road (sp. Hereford) to enter Mitcheldean. At the church turn left and ascend to reach Drybrook. At the crossroads turn left (sp. Coleford) then, in ¾ mile, at the T-junction, turn right on to the B4227 for Ruardean. At the end of the village bear right and descend. In 1½ miles turn right on to the B4228 (sp. Ross). Follow the River Wye before reaching Kerne Bridge. From here, return via Walford and the B4228 to Ross-on-Wye.

OFF THE TOUR

Goodrich Castle

Goodrich's crumbling, red sandstone towers were put up in the 12th century to guard an ancient crossing point on the Wye. The castle paid dearly for its role as a Royalist stronghold during the Civil War; after its surrender in 1646 Cromwell's forces inflicted severe damage. Sited south of Ross-on-Wye off the A40.

Caldicot Castle

Take the A48 from Chepstow to Caldicot. The castle, which dates from the 12th century, has a fine 14th-century great gatehouse. It was restored as a comfortable home in Victorian times and is now the venue for medieval banquets. The castle contains a local museum and pretty garden.

Dean Forest Railway

From Parkend, take the B4234 south towards Lydney for the Dean Forest Railway at the Norchard Steam Centre. The station is an original building of the Severn and Wye Company, which ran trains laden with coal in the boom period of the 19th century. Full-size locomotives, coaches and wagons are on display, together with a small museum collection of railway memorabilia, photographs and drawings. Regular 'steamdays' are held each summer.

Lydney Park Gardens

These gardens, off the A48 just south-west of Lydney, are renowned for their rhododendrons and azaleas. Set in a lakeland valley, they also contain a Roman temple site and museum.

Dean Heritage Centre

The centre is on the B4227, 2 miles south of Cinderford. It is based at Camp Mill, a most interesting site which has, in its time, been an iron foundry, corn mill, leatherboard mill, timber yard, piggery and scrapyard! The centre's displays explain the exploitation of the Forest of Dean's wood, iron ore and coal and looks at the forest's natural history.

Westbury Court Garden

This National Trust garden at Westbury-on-Severn along the A48 is a formal Dutch-style water garden, the earliest of its kind remaining in England.

OUTDOOR ACTIVITIES

Symonds Yat

The forest trail from Yat Rock has spectacular viewpoints looking down into the gorge.

Tintern

There are several short walks through the woods and the Old Station visitor centre has information on the long-distance Wye Valley Walk.

Forest of Dean

Many beautiful woodland walks can be enjoyed here. The most intriguing is the 4-mile 'Art in the Forest Sculpture Trail', which features 18 sculptures, starting from the Beechenhurst picnic site near Speech House.

EAST WORCESTERSHIRE

59 miles

Gently undulating countryside, watered by small rivers and streams between the Severn and Avon, reaches a hillier climax in the north at the Clent and

Waseley Hills. Woodlands, historic houses and attractive villages with half-timbered or mellow brick cottages add distinctive charms.

The ancient city of Worcester, compact enough to wander round comfortably, is rich in old buildings. This is Greyfriars in Friar Street, a timbered Franciscan house of 1480. The guildhall displays Civil War armour used at the Battle of Worcester in 1651

OFF THE TOUR

Coughton Court
Keep on the B4092 at Holberrow Green and join the B4090, which heads towards Coughton Court, a moated and mainly Elizabethan house.

Hanbury Hall
Turn left immediately past Hanbury's Jinney Ring Craft Centre. First right again leads up-hill to Hanbury church. Descend to the original lane for Hanbury Hall, an attractive Wren-style house in red brick.

Hagley Hall
Reached by a minor road from Lower Clent, Hagley Hall, completed in 1760, has superb plasterwork, paintings and furniture.

Severn Valley Railway
Kidderminster, north of Stourport along the A451, is the southern terminus of Britain's premier steam railway. The station (adjoining BR station) is off the A456, Birmingham road.

Eastwards from the valley of the River Severn and northwards from the Vale of Evesham a landscape of subtle contours, hedged fields and scattered woodlands rises gradually to a northern crest where, from their 1,000ft-high windy summits the popular Clent Hills overlook the great conurbation of the West Midlands. It was the various iron industries of the Midlands that, in earlier centuries, gradually depleted the former great royal forest of Feckenham to its present scattered fragments. Most of the area covered in this tour is now good agricultural land.

Nucleated villages occur every few miles. Fine 18th-century mansions stand at the centre of their landscaped parks. The M5, almost bisecting the area, impinges remarkably little, while its late 18th-century equivalent - the nearby Worcester-Birmingham Canal - parallels its route and, at the canal town of Stourport-on-Severn, completes the waterway link between Birmingham and the Severn.

ON THE TOUR

Worcester
Watered by the Severn, Worcester is a busy county capital and cathedral city set among rich farmland of meadows, orchards and hopfields. The cathedral, Norman in origin but today showing mainly 14th-century architecture, still dominates the skyline. The city centre has many fine medieval buildings, including the Commandery, used by Charles II in 1651 as his headquarters during the Battle of Worcester, when the Royalists were defeated. Friar Street is a remarkable 15th and 16th century survival. Among its many timber-framed houses are Greyfriars (NT), built in 1480 as a hostelry for travellers, and Tudor House, now a folk museum. New Street, which continues the half-timbered theme, has its own treasures including Nash House and King Charles House, where the king hid temporarily after his defeat.
Worcester's 18th-century prosperity saw handsome brick buildings added to its streets, with the Guildhall in High Street outstanding. Edgar Street, College Precincts and The Tything also have fine buildings of this period. The local porcelain industry was started about 1750, and the Royal Worcester Porcelain Company's showrooms in Severn Street are open to the public, as is the Lea & Perrins Sauce factory.

Spetchley Park Gardens
These 30 acres of gardens are a plantsman's delight, especially beautiful in spring. In addition to many fine trees, shrubs and plants there are red and fallow deer.

Feckenham
High Street is lined with black and white timber-framed cottages and neat, red brick Georgian houses. There is also a small, attractive green. Feckenham's ancient Court Leet, a medieval form of local government, met until as recently as 1935. South of the village, reached by a field-path, Wylde Moor is a small Nature Reserve with undrained peat marsh and an artificial lake to attract the wetland birds, which can be conveniently viewed from a hide.

Hanbury
This village of widely-scattered houses, cottages and farms has gained unusual fame for being, apparently, the location for 'Ambridge' the fictitious village setting for the BBC serial *The Archers*. The Jinney Ring Craft Centre (open all year Wed-Sun), housed in beautifully-restored farm buildings, has craftsmen working in woodcarving, pottery, jewellery, stained glass, leather, fashion design, crystal and glass. There is a wildlife artist. Exhibitions, a gift shop, and a licensed restaurant complete an unusual enterprise.

Avoncroft Museum
Off the A38 Bromsgrove bypass the Avoncroft Museum of Buildings on an open-air site displays rescued buildings and relics from the past, including a merchant's house, granary, windmill, cockfighting theatre, chain shop and nail shop. There is also a picnic area.

Hartlebury Castle
This historic home of the bishops of Worcester, rebuilt after the Civil War and 'Gothicised' in the 18th century, has a medieval great hall and elegant state rooms, showing fine plasterwork and portraits.

Stourport-on-Severn
Stourport is England's only town created directly as the consequence of a canal; in this case, Brindley's building of the Staffordshire and Worcestershire Canal 1766–71. Pleasure-boats and traditional narrow boats add colour and life to the great canal basins, dominated by the old canal warehouse. Locks drop the canal past the Tontine Inn to the Severn.

ROUTE DIRECTIONS

Leave **Worcester** (map 75085) on the A44 (sp. Evesham). In 1½ miles at the roundabout keep left on to the A422 (sp. Stratford-upon-Avon). Pass **Spetchley Park Gardens** and continue through Broughton Hackett to Inkberrow. In 1 mile take the second turning on the left on to the B4092 (sp. Redditch), then in a further mile turn left, unclassified (sp. Feckenham). In ½ mile turn left again on to the B4090 (no sign) to **Feckenham**. Continue on the Droitwich road to **Hanbury**. There, turn right on to the B4091 (sp. Bromsgrove) to pass the road to Hanbury Hall. Go forward through Stoke Prior, passing **Avoncroft Museum**, to Stoke Heath and, at the traffic signals, turn right on to the A38 (sp. Birmingham). Continue forward and at the ensuing roundabout and traffic signals (sp. Birmingham), to the junction with the M42. Here, at the roundabout, take 1st exit to the junction with the M5. At the roundabout take 2nd exit A491 (sp. Stourbridge) and in ½ mile turn right on to the B4551 (sp. Romsley). Pass the road towards Waseley Hills Country Park and in 1 mile, at the start of the descent turn left, unclassified (sp. Clent). In ½ mile further at the trunk road, turn left and in another mile turn left again (sp. Clent) into Chapel Lane, Clent. At the crossroads turn right (sp. Lower Clent) and at the Fountain Inn, with Clent Hill Country Park off to the right, turn left (sp. Broome). In ¼ mile at the roundabout, take 1st exit (sp. Bromsgrove) and in ½ mile further, at the crossroads turn right into Belbroughton Road, for Belbroughton. Go forward on to the B1488 (sp. Chaddesley Corbett) and at the end branch left, unclassified for Chaddesley Corbett. At the far end turn right on to the A448 (sp. Kidderminster). At the Mustow Green roundabout take 1st exit, A450 (sp. Worcester) and in 1¾ miles at the roundabout, go forward. In ⅓ mile go under the railway bridge and turn left on to the A449. In another ⅓ mile turn right on to the B4193 (sp. Stourport) to Hartlebury. Bear right and pass the turning to **Hartlebury Castle** on the right, then in 1½ miles, at the roundabout go forward on to the A4025. Shortly, turn left (one way) and follow the Town Centre signs into **Stourport-on-Severn**. Leave on the A451 (sp. Great Witley) and cross the River Severn. In ½ mile turn left on to the B4196 (sp. Worcester). Continue on to Shrawley, and Holt Heath. Go over the crossroads on to the A443 (sp. Worcester) to Hallow. In 2¼ miles join the A44 and cross the River Severn into Worcester.

South-east of Stourbridge lie the hills of Clent and Lickey, which provide fine walking country that rises to 1,000ft. The views are magnificent

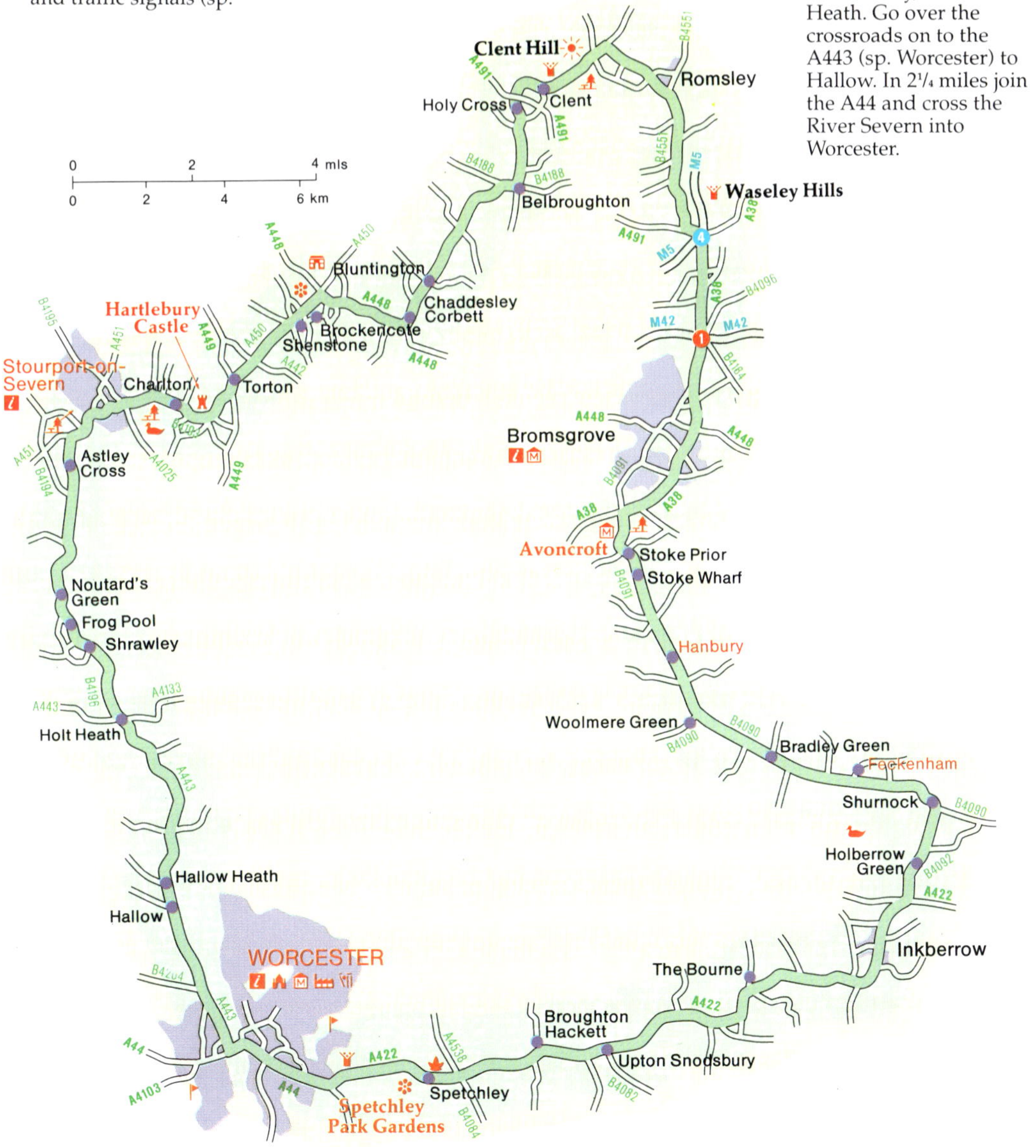

OFF THE BEATEN TRACK

North Worcestershire Path

This 15-mile route across part of the old county of Worcester consists of public and permissive paths, and links four Country Parks - Lickey Hills, Waseley Hills, Clent Hills and Kingsford - which offer good access points.

Hartlebury Common

Minor roads from Hartlebury village lead to Hartlebury Common, where 200 acres of sandy heath with coppiced woodland, together with Hillditch Pool, contain a wealth of interesting plants, birds and insects. This important Nature Reserve has a car park with picnic areas, while many public footpaths cross the common.

OUTDOOR ACTIVITIES

Worcester Woods Country Park

Adjoining the A422 on the eastern edge of the city, two ancient oakwoods, together with open fields, are ideal for enjoying open-air exercise. The Countryside Centre has displays and exhibitions, a café, and picnic and play areas for children.

Waseley Hills Country Park

Reached by a minor road off the B4551 south of Romsley, 150 acres of grass-covered hills with small woods and ponds offer good walking, with spectacular views. There is a Museum of Buildings, and the north car park has a Visitor Centre, with information, refreshments and toilets.

Clent Hill Country Park

Over 500 acres of wooded, brackeny hills, interspersed with farmland, are owned by the National Trust but managed by the county council. Among the footpaths there are two trails with easy access for everyone, including those in wheelchairs. Three main car parks have picnic areas and toilets.

LEOMINSTER, LUDLOW AND THE BORDERS

61 miles

The history-laden border country west of Leominster and Ludlow is dotted with castles, medieval halls and stately homes. Its villages, set amongst undisturbed hills and green meadows, display strong links with the past through their perfectly preserved timber-framed, black-and-white architecture.

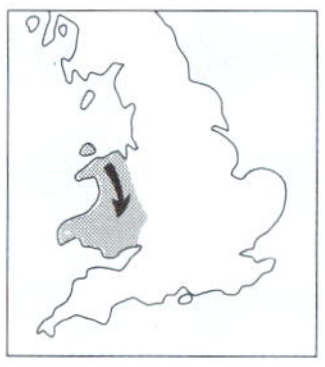

Three colours - green, black and white - dominate the English lowlands as they approach the Welsh hills across the border in Powys. Timber-framed buildings many hundreds of years old stand out strikingly against the verdant tones of this gently undulating landscape. The poet A E Houseman, author of A Shropshire Lad, *evoked the unchanging, unhurried nature of this area when he wrote:*
`Clunton and Clunbury,
Clungunford and Clun,
Are the quietest places under the sun.'

This countryside was not always so peaceful. England meets Wales along a line of hills which were first fortified by the building of a massive earthen dyke in the 8th century. The high concentration of castles along this vulnerable border testifies to a troubled past. Today, however, any thoughts of trouble and strife seem misplaced in this quietly prosperous farming area.

ON THE TOUR

Leominster

Leominster, on an important crossroads and surrounded by rich farming country, has been a busy wool and cattle town for centuries. The old town hall - built, inevitably, in the half-timbered style typical of these parts - was moved from the town centre in the 19th century to its present location on the lawns of The Grange. Leominster's Church of St Peter and St Paul, much restored in the 19th century, stands on a pre-medieval religious site. A magnificent building with a huge west window and buttresses, it contains an ancient ducking stool that was last used in 1809. Leominster's Folk Museum displays many items of agricultural interest.

Eardisland

The River Arrow flows gently through this lovely village - another small settlement of exceptionally picturesque black-and-white houses. Staick House, built in about 1300 as a yeoman's hall, is particularly fine. Medieval St Mary's Church stands next to the remnants of a castle. Burton Court, just south of the village, is mainly Georgian with a 14th-century great hall. It houses an exhibition of costumes and many old curios.

Pembridge

Time seems to have passed tiny Pembridge by. Its 16th-century market hall has an early 14th-century inn as a neighbour. These are amongst the village's many marvellously well-preserved, timber-framed buildings. Pembridge's medieval church has an unusual timber belfry tower detached from the main building. Villagers would shelter here during border raids by the Welsh.

Kington

Sheep sales are held in this small border town, whose narrow passageways reflect Kington's medieval ancestry. Hergest Croft Gardens, half a mile to the west, are beautiful from spring to autumn; their rhododendrons and azaleas are particularly fine.

Knighton

Knighton's Welsh name, Tref-y-Clawdd (the town on the dyke), reflects its location on the great earthen border built between England and Wales by King Offa of Mercia in the 8th century. The hills to the north-west contain some of the best-preserved stretches of Offa's Dyke, whose north-south route is now the basis of a 170-mile footpath. Information on the dyke and path is available at Knighton's Offa's Dyke Centre.
The town itself, ranged around a 19th-century clock tower, is a jumbled mixture of black-and-white and Victorian architectural influences. Knighton is unusual because it stands right on the border: although the main body of the town is in Wales, its railway station is in England.

Splendid views unfold along Offa's Dyke long-distance footpath

OFF THE TOUR

Dilwyn

From Eardisland, drive south for a few miles to Dilwyn, found off the A4112 one of the many pretty villages on this tour. Dilwyn's village green, immaculate half-timbered houses, gables and medieval St Mary's Church create the perfect picture of an old Herefordshire settlement.

Weobley

From Dilwyn continue down the A4112 for Weobley, another ancient black-and-white village - considered by many to be England's finest - with a Norman church and remains of a motte-and-bailey castle.

Clun

Take the A488 north from Knighton for Clun, one of the quartet of sleepy border villages whose timeless character was captured by A E Houseman in *A Shropshire Lad*, published in 1896.

Stokesay Castle

Stokesay is just off the A49, about 6 miles north-west of Ludlow. The detour is well worth it, for this historic site is one of the finest evocations of medieval England. The castle is a fortified manor house.

Croft Castle

From the B4361 south of Ludlow, take the B4362 west for Croft Castle. The castle, now an ornate country house in the care of the National Trust, began life as a border fortress.

Ludlow

The River Teme loops around a rocky outcrop at Ludlow, creating a naturally defensive site that was exploited to the full by Roger de Lacy, the Norman lord who founded Ludlow Castle in 1086. Much of de Lacy's original keep and bailey survives, though the castle, which subsequently played an influential role in borderland affairs, was altered over the centuries. Its Elizabethan buildings, for example, served the Council of the Marches: a body that was set up to govern Wales and the border country.

Ludlow has been a prosperous wool and cloth town, market place, and administrative and social centre. This favoured and fashionable past is reflected in its wealth of fine Tudor, Stuart and Georgian houses. The Feathers Hotel in the Bull Ring, one of England's most famous timber-framed buildings, has an amazing façade, quite overpowering in the detail of its ornamental carvings.

The centre of Ludlow is dominated by the 135ft tower of St Laurence's Church, one of England's largest parish churches. The thoroughfare that best captures Ludlow's assured sense of style is Broad Street, a handsome street running down from the Butter Cross (location of the town's museum) to Broad Gate, the only surviving medieval gate into the town. There are fascinating alley ways too, with little antiques and book shops to delight browsers and buyers.

Berrington Hall

The classical simplicity of Berrington Hall's exterior belies it elegant interior. The hall, a National Trust house, was built in the late 18th century for Thomas Harley, a banker and ex-Lord Mayor of London. Marble floors, painted ceilings, delicate plasterwork, fine furniture and works of art decorate its main rooms. The porticoed entrance looks out over extensive parklands, landscaped by Capability Brown, to the distant hills of Wales.

OFF THE BEATEN TRACK

The Clee Hills east of Ludlow are quarry-scarred hills accessible off the A4117. They rise to Titterstone Clee, a 1750ft hillfort site which commands superb views of the border country.

OUTDOOR ACTIVITIES

Exhilarating hill-walking is available in the uplands above Knucklas a few miles northwest of Knighton, where the Offa's Dyke Path follows a well-preserved section of the ancient earthen bank.

Berrington Hall near Leominster was built in 1783 for an ex-Lord Mayor of London, Thomas Harley. Its rather austere appearance is deceptive, for inside it is elegantly decorated and has fine works of art

ROUTE DIRECTIONS

Leave **Leominster** (map 7SO45) on the A44 (sp. Rhayader) and in 5 miles reach **Eardisland**. Continue with the A44 through **Pembridge** and in 6 miles, at the roundabout, take 2nd exit, unclassified, to enter **Kington**. At the Midland Bank turn right into Duke Street and in 1/2 mile, at the roundabout, take 2nd exit, B4355 (sp. Presteigne). Continue through Titley, enter Wales and at the T-junction turn left (sp. Industrial Estate, or Knighton). At ensuing T-junction turn right (sp. Knighton). Pass the turning to Presteigne and in 1/2 mile turn right (sp. Knighton) and cross the River Lugg. Beyond Norton climb around Hawthorn Hill (1,328ft) to reach the summit of over 1,200ft. Descend to the edge of **Knighton**. Turn right (sp. Ludlow) along the A4113 (no sign). Follow the Teme Valley, passing Stow Hill, and re-enter England before Brampton Bryan. In 1 1/2 miles turn right (sp. Hereford A410) and in a further 3/4 mile turn right on to the A4110. Pass through Adforton and enter Wigmore. At the Old Oak Inn turn left, unclassified (sp. Ludlow). Pass Leinthall Starkes. Descend through Whitcliffe Wood and, after the woodland, take the first turning left (no sign). Continue the descent. Soon after, turn sharp right to cross the River Teme below **Ludlow**. Turn right into Broad Street, pass through Broad Gate (archway) and at the traffic signals go forward (sp. Richard's Castle, B4361) to cross the ancient Ludford Bridge. In 1 mile branch right to reach Richard's Castle, then branch left and keep forward with the B4361 to Luston. Turn left, unclassified (sp. Eye, Morton) and in 1 3/4 miles pass the entrance to **Berrington Hall**. Continue forward to the main road and turn right on to the A49 to return, beside Berrington Park, to Leominster.

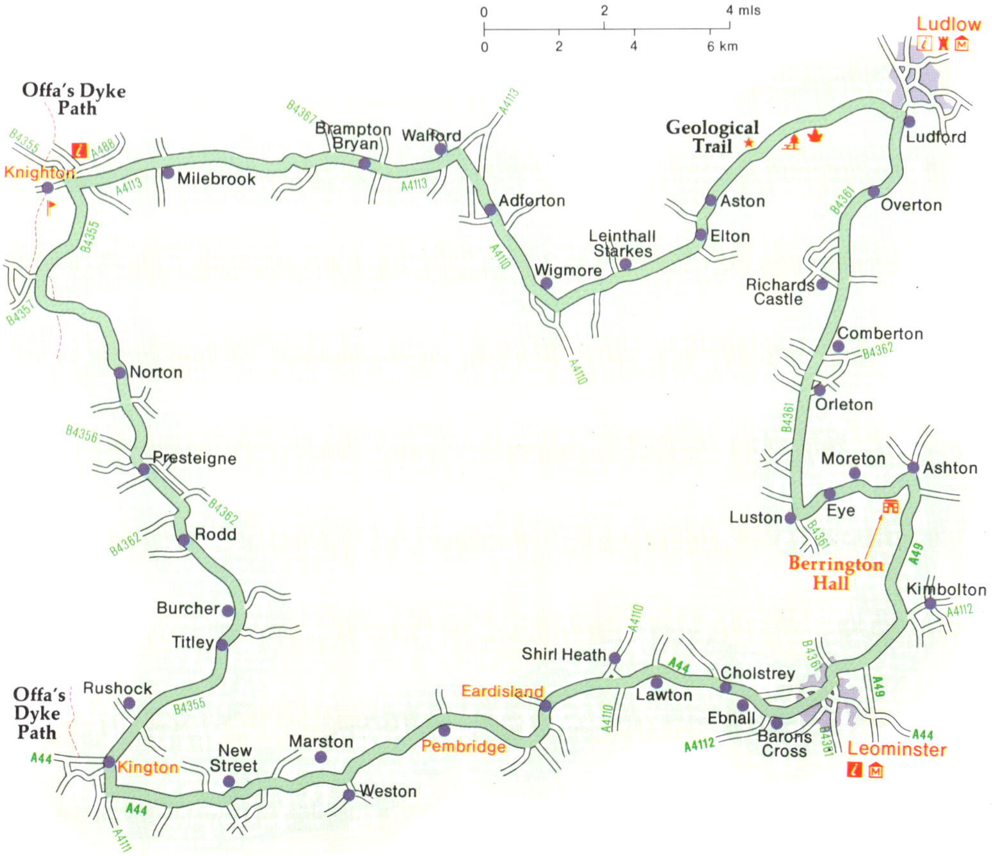

BETWEEN THE LONG MYND AND THE WELSH BORDER

57 miles

The spine of The Long Mynd runs south-westwards from Shrewsbury, an upland barrier facing the Welsh hills beyond Welshpool. The countryside sandwiched between this high country is green and gentle, bordered by the broad valley of the River Severn.

The lowlands along the England/Wales border are broken by patches of hill country. The 10-mile ridge of The Long Mynd and the crags of the neighbouring Stiperstones rise to around 1,700ft, dominating the horizon to the east. To the west, Montgomery and Welshpool stand at the gateway to the wild Welsh uplands, a border first defined by the 8th-century earthwork of Offa's Dyke.

The River Severn loops around in a broad arc from Welshpool to Shrewsbury, Shropshire's long-established county town. Shrewsbury's well-sited castle and wealth of black-and-white, timber-framed buildings are typical of these parts. Ancient strongholds, some ruined, others turned into opulent country houses, occupy almost every strategic spot along this historically troubled border country. Change is slow amongst this area's traditional towns and villages, which continue to go about their business as farming and market centres.

Old Hall is one of three Tudor houses to be seen in the ancient border town of Bishop's Castle

ROUTE DIRECTIONS

Leave **Shrewsbury** (map 7SJ41) by following signs to Welshpool, then Bishop's Castle, A488. At **Pontesbury** go forward (one way) and at the Railway Inn turn left to **Minsterley**. At the roundabout take 1st exit. Ascend through Hope Valley to 1,020ft then descend into Wales. In ½ mile beyond Lydham continue forward to the crossroads. Here, turn right on to the B4385 (sp. Bishop's Castle). Shortly after, at the church, turn right to enter **Bishop's Castle**. Keep forward into Church Street and ascend. Pass the clock tower to reach the T-junction then turn left with the B4385 (sp. Montgomery). Later cross the A489 and in another 3 miles arrive in Montgomery. Continue on the B4385, past **Montgomery Castle**, for ¼ mile then, at the Cottage Inn turn right on to the B4388 (sp. Welshpool). Beyond Forden go forward on to the A490 and in ¼ mile turn right on to the B4388 (sp. Leighton). In just over ¼ mile, at the corner, turn right, unclassified (no sign) and ascend on to the flat-topped Long Mountain. At the crossroads keep forward and in 1 mile pass Beacon Ring hill-fort. Continue forward then make a descent to Westbury on the Shropshire Plain. Here at the T-junction, turn right, then right again on to the B4387 (sp. Shrewsbury). At the main road turn left on to the B4386 for the return, through Yockleton to Shrewsbury.

ON THE TOUR

Shrewsbury

The town's two main bridges, the English Bridge and the Welsh Bridge, neatly sum up Shrewsbury's borderland location. The bridges cross the River Severn, whose course forms a protective loop around much of the town. This strategic position was seized upon by Norman warlords. Their castle, mainly built during the 12th century, formed the nucleus of a town which has aged very well, preserving a wealth of period architecture amongst narrow streets still lined with black-and-white buildings. Rowley's House, originally the home of a Tudor merchant, is now a museum of local history and archaeology. The Clive House Museum is within a beautifully proportioned Georgian house on College Hill where Clive of India once lived. There are statues in the town of Robert Clive and another of Shrewsbury's famous sons, 19th-century naturalist Charles Darwin.

Other architectural gems to be seen in Shrewsbury include the Council House, Bear Steps Hall and the delightful Victorian

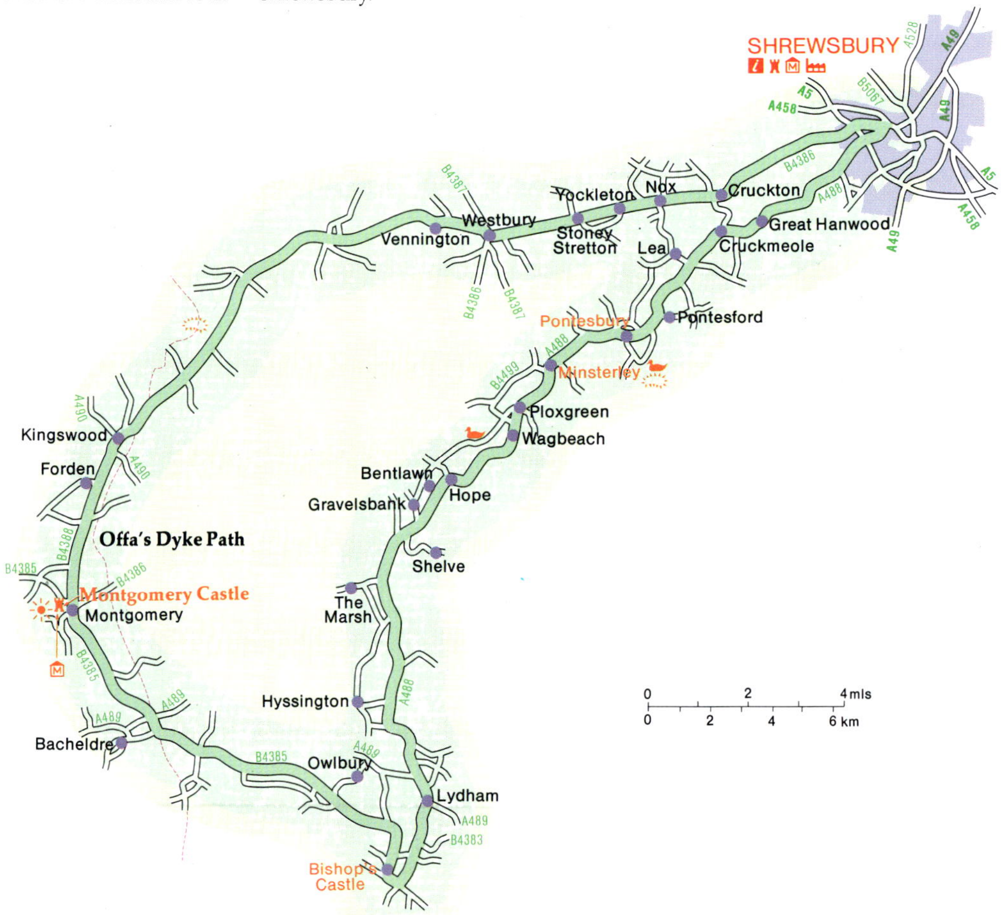

Arcade. The castle, restored by Thomas Telford in 1790, contains a military museum. Coleham Pumping Station across the river has a display of carefully restored Victorian beam pumping engines. See also page 158.

Pontesbury

Shropshire authoress Mary Webb (1881–1927) lived at Rose Cottage, Pontesbury, from 1914–1916, later moving for a short time to a nearby dwelling called The Nills. Her experiences here served as background to what is possibly her most famous novel, *Precious Bane*, published in 1924.
Above the village stands the thickly wooded Iron Age stronghold of Earl's Hill, now a nature reserve.

Minsterley

Stone skulls and crossbones adorn the `death's head doorway' of the Holy Trinity Church, Minsterley, a large red brick building put up in the late 17th century.

Bishop's Castle

Visitors have to look hard to find anything of the castle which was built here, in the late 11th and early 12th centuries, by the Bishop of Hereford as a defence against the Welsh. The Three Tuns Inn, which serves beer from its own small brewery next door, is well known to connoisseurs of real ale. The medieval `House on Crutches' is one of a number of the town's well-preserved half-timbered buildings.

Montgomery Castle

The weatherbeaten ruins of Montgomery Castle look down on to an attractive Georgian town square of red brick houses. The castle was a key border stronghold built by Henry III in the early 13th century to guard the Severn Valley as it enters Wales. Although demolished after a siege in the 1640s, the castle has kept its twin-towered gatehouse (one of the earliest in Britain), massive rock-cut ditch and 220ft-deep well.

OFF THE BEATEN TRACK

Mitchell's Fold Stone Circle

The minor road off the A488 about 6 miles north of Bishop's Castle leads to this Bronze Age circle of 37 stones, 14 of which remain standing, on the gorse and grass of Stapley Hill.

Stiperstones

The A488 south-west of Minsterley travels along the foothills of a 1,762ft ridge known as the Stiperstones. From Black Marsh, take the minor road which climbs into these hills where, according to legend, the witches of Shropshire used to meet. There is certainly something eerie about the pyramids of rock – one of which is known as the Devil's Chair – scattered across a heather-covered summit. These jagged, dramatic formations, created during the last Ice Age, were made a National Nature Reserve in 1983.

Dolforwyn Castle

The ruined medieval castle of Llywelyn the Last lies 1 mile west of Abermule, south-east of Montgomery.

OFF THE TOUR

Attingham Park

This National Trust house is located a few miles from Shrewsbury off the A5. Its grand façade, designed in the 1780s, is dominated by an impressive portico with columns 40ft tall. Inside, the mansion lives up to its external appearance. Attingham Park's treasures include magnificent state rooms, delicate plasterwork and a splendid collection of Regency silver. The picture gallery created by John Nash and the painted boudoir are particularly impressive. The mansion's splendid grounds, landscaped in the 1790s, contain a deer park.

Wroxeter Roman City

Just beyond Attingham Park lies Viroconium, Britain's fourth largest Roman city, which was mostly built around AD150. Excavations have revealed a great deal, including an outdoor swimming pool, sauna-style indoor baths of different heat gradations and an amazingly upstanding section of wall, 26ft high from the exercise hall. These remains, once the social centre of the city, are part of the area where people came to relax, exercise, eat and talk. Many fascinating artefacts unearthed during excavation are displayed at a museum on site.

Haughmond Abbey

The remains of this abbey can be seen off the B5042 on the eastern approaches to Shrewsbury. The church, founded in about 1135 for Augustinian canons, was dismantled in 1539 during the Dissolution of the Monasteries by Henry VIII. Other parts of the abbey were spared. The 14th-century abbot's house (which became a private residence) is quite well preserved, as are the Norman arches at the entrance to the chapter house and a 15th-century oriel window.

Powis Castle

The A490 from Kingswood leads to the A483. The National Trust's Powis Castle, on the southern approach to Welshpool, is a red-stone mansion which evolved over many hundreds of years from a military stronghold, to Elizabethan manor, to 19th-century country home. Beyond its medieval great gatehouse and keep lies a sumptuous interior, the high point of which is a 1688 gilded state bedchamber. The castle is also noted for its Clive of India Museum. Spread out below Powis's mock-military battlements are magnificent terraced gardens of Italianate design. Created between 1688 and 1722, they are the only formal gardens of this date in Britain which survive in their original form.

Welshpool

The partially restored Montgomery Canal runs into Welshpool. A canalside warehouse on the town wharf now houses the Powysland Museum of local history. Welshpool, a pleasant mix of half-timbered, Georgian and red brick houses, has been a busy marketplace since it was granted a charter in 1263. The early 18th-century hexagonal brick building off the main street is the only pit for cockfighting remaining in its original position in Wales. The narrow-gauge Welshpool and Llanfair Light Railway operates from the outskirts of town on a scenic eight-mile track to Llanfair Caereinion.

The Welshpool and Llanfair Light Railway, one of the 'Great Little Trains of Wales', gamely puffs its way through 8 miles of lovely pastoral countryside

NORTH SHROPSHIRE

71 miles

North of the Severn the Shropshire plain extends to the winding course of the River Dee and the Welsh border. Several low sandstone ridges break up the level landscape of winding lanes and scattered farms. There are but few villages or towns.

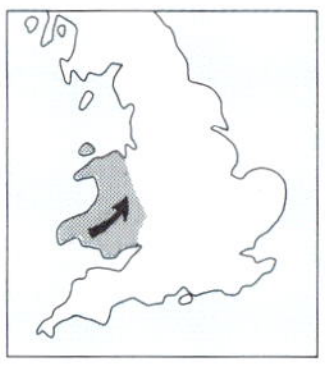

Hodnet Hall, a 19th-century mansion of Tudor style, is surrounded by lawns, flower displays and a chain of pools and ornamental lakes

Only at two places, Grinshill and near Hodnet, does the land in this tour reach 600ft. To the west of the area, however, the so-called 'Shropshire Lakes' provide particular distinction. These meres, centred on Ellesmere, are thought to have originated at the end of the Ice Age, about 12,000 years ago. Many are Sites of Special Scientific Interest, and are accessible Nature Reserves with a wealth of bird, plant and insect life. Much of this north Shropshire landscape has changed over the last three centuries, as a result of drainage and land reclamation. Scattered red brick farms and cottages are linked by a maze of roads threading through acres of pasture and arable land. Some black-and-white half-timbering can be seen in most villages.

The Llangollen arm of the Shropshire Union Canal, constructed by Telford and Jessop between 1793 and 1806, winds across the area, passing through remote but pleasant countryside. It is one of the most popular leisure waterways.

ON THE TOUR

Shrewsbury

Beautifully situated within a horseshoe loop of the River Severn, Shrewsbury, Shropshire's county town, is an ancient and historic centre, with a 12th-century castle restored in 1790 by Thomas Telford, and again in 1926. Although some modern buildings and shop-fronts intrude, Shrewsbury's flavour, provided by its many handsome half-timbered buildings and narrow streets, is essentially 16th-century, with Queen Anne, Georgian and Victorian overtones added. Rowley's House Museum has a collection of prehistoric Roman, and medieval material, and a good natural history display. Book and antique shops are good for browsing in, friendly pubs and restaurants abound, and extensive, colourful gardens reach to the river. Here, a delightful path runs round the length of the river's loop, which is crossed by four bridges. Among Shrewsbury's churches, Holy Cross in Abbey Foregate survives from a great Benedictine abbey. It has gained recent fame through the fictional exploits of the medieval monk-detective, Brother Cadfael, whose fans can now buy a leaflet and follow 'In the Steps of Brother Cadfael' to discover some of the places he knew – allowing for the differences that 850 years can make. See also page 156.

Haughmond Abbey

Below a low wooded hill the extensive remains of a 12th-century Augustinian abbey include the abbot's lodging, infirmary and kitchens. The façade of the chapter house is magnificent, but one wonders what the mansion, into which the abbey was converted after the dissolution, was like.

Moreton Corbet Castle

Only part of the keep of the medieval castle survives. The ruins of the south range of a great, brick-built Elizabethan house (1579) dominate a flat landscape. It was never completed as the Corbet house; Parliamentary forces during the Civil War ensured it would not be by removing the roof.

Hodnet Hall Gardens

From 1922 Brigadier A G W Heber-Percy spent about 30 years transforming a shrubby, marshy valley into the beautiful landscaped garden seen today. The 60 acres of forest trees, lawns and ornamental lakes are an idyllic setting for the wonderful flower displays which mark the passing of the seasons. Water-birds and other wildlife add to the pleasures.

Bangor-is-y-Coed

The name means 'monastery-under-the-wood', a reference to an early Dark Age religious settlement destroyed about AD600 by Saxon invaders. The river is more attractive than the town, and regular meetings are held at the nearby Bangor racecourse.

Ellesmere

This is a pleasant, small market town with mellow Georgian houses, some half-timbering, and a wharf at the end of an arm of the Llangollen Canal. The mere, at 116 acres, is the largest of a group of seven such lakes and offers the widest range of facilities, including fishing and boat hire. The mere and its surrounds are rich in bird life, both resident and winter visitors. Over 30 species can be seen in adjoining Cremone Gardens, which also has various recreational facilities.

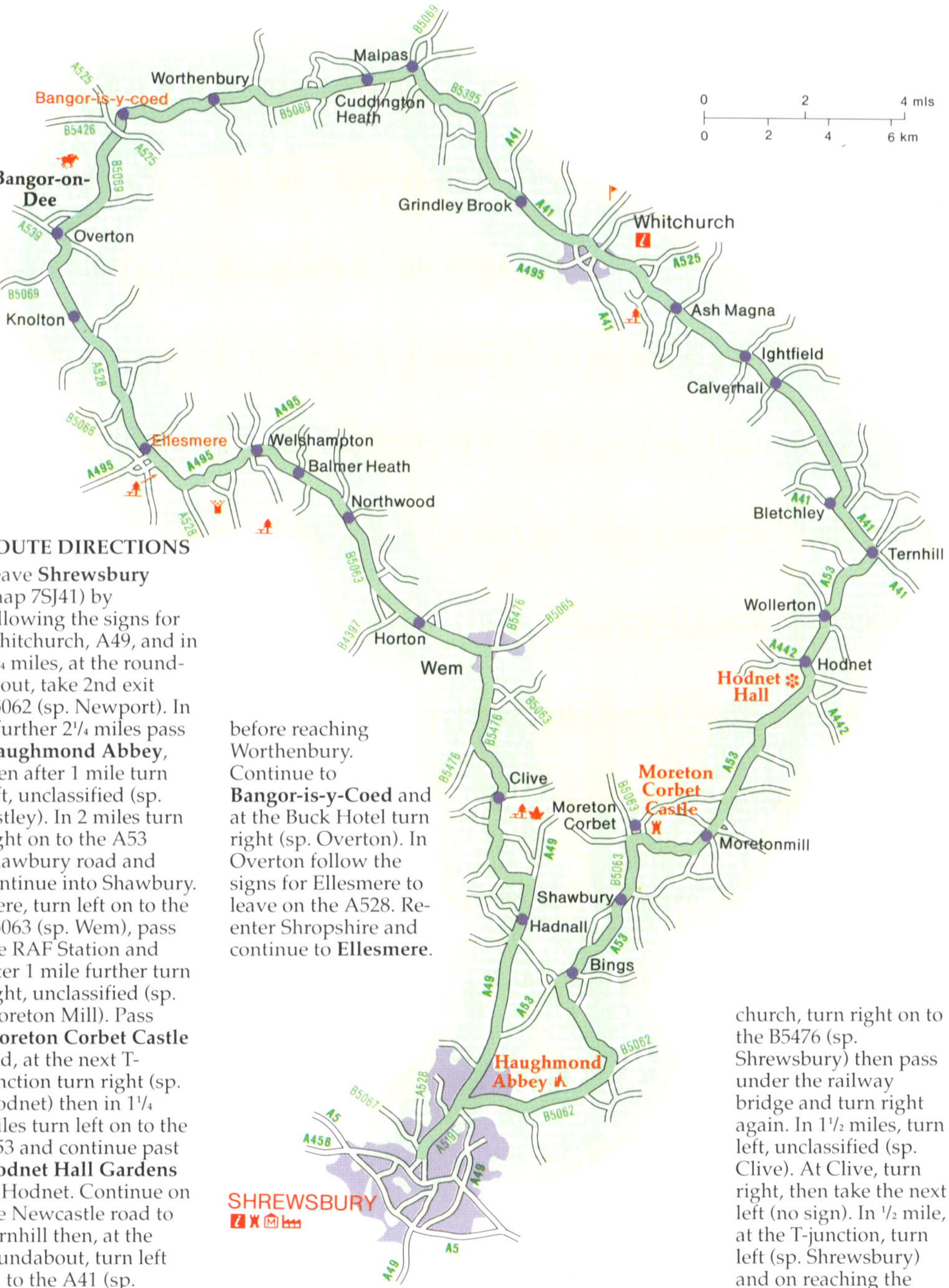

ROUTE DIRECTIONS

Leave **Shrewsbury** (map 7SJ41) by following the signs for Whitchurch, A49, and in 1¼ miles, at the roundabout, take 2nd exit B5062 (sp. Newport). In a further 2¼ miles pass **Haughmond Abbey**, then after 1 mile turn left, unclassified (sp. Astley). In 2 miles turn right on to the A53 Shawbury road and continue into Shawbury. Here, turn left on to the B5063 (sp. Wem), pass the RAF Station and after 1 mile further turn right, unclassified (sp. Moreton Mill). Pass **Moreton Corbet Castle** and, at the next T-junction turn right (sp. Hodnet) then in 1¼ miles turn left on to the A53 and continue past **Hodnet Hall Gardens** to Hodnet. Continue on the Newcastle road to Ternhill then, at the roundabout, turn left on to the A41 (sp. Whitchurch). At the beginning of the dual carriageway turn right, unclassified (sp. Calverhall) and enter the hamlet of Bletchley. Skirt the grounds of Cloverley Hall (not open) and pass through Calverhall to reach Ightfield. Here, turn left (sp. Whitchurch) and continue to Ash Magna. In 1½ miles turn left on to the A525 and enter Whitchurch. At the traffic signals turn right on to the A41 (sp. Chester) and in ½ mile, at the roundabout, take 2nd exit. In a further 1½ miles turn left on to the B5395 (sp. Malpas) to enter Malpas. Leave on the B5069 Wrexham road and enter the Welsh county of Clwyd before reaching Worthenbury. Continue to **Bangor-is-y-Coed** and at the Buck Hotel turn right (sp. Overton). In Overton follow the signs for Ellesmere to leave on the A528. Re-enter Shropshire and continue to **Ellesmere**. Join the Shrewsbury road and pass the mere. In ½ mile turn left on to the A495 (sp. Whitchurch). At Welshampton turn right on to the B5063 and continue to Wem. At the church, turn right on to the B5476 (sp. Shrewsbury) then pass under the railway bridge and turn right again. In 1½ miles, turn left, unclassified (sp. Clive). At Clive, turn right, then take the next left (no sign). In ½ mile, at the T-junction, turn left (sp. Shrewsbury) and on reaching the main road, turn right on to the A49. Pass through Hadnall before re-entering Shrewsbury.

OFF THE TOUR

Market Drayton

By staying on the A53 at Ternhill roundabout, this attractive market town is soon reached. Livestock and street markets are held regularly. A number of half-timbered houses survive, and on top of the Butter Cross hang the old fire bells, a reminder of the disastrous 1651 fire which destroyed so much.

Errdig

Continue on the A525 beyond Bangor-is-y-Coed, and Errdig is signposted on the left in 4 miles. This late 17th-century house retains most of the furniture and textiles supplied for it in the 1720s. It has a remarkable range of outbuildings and workshops, and its walled garden has been restored.

Sleap Airfield

A minor road leads off the B5476 from Wem to the home of the Shropshire Aero Club, which was formed in 1955. In addition to a number of resident aircraft operated by the club, gliding takes place regularly, and model aircraft enthusiasts also use the available facilities.

OFF THE BEATEN TRACK

Grinshill

Although car parking at Clive is limited, it is worth stopping here to enjoy the best viewpoint on the whole tour. Walk up the steep, stony lane by the north of the church and continue ahead on reaching the top. Corbet Wood covers 23 acres of hillside above disused quarry workings. Wide views open out east and south from the short summit ridge, which is covered with heather. There is a fine wood of Scots pine, and Grinshill village lies below.

OUTDOOR ACTIVITIES

Holly Coppice

At the top of the hill above Haughmond Abbey, on the right of the B5062, this Forestry Commission plantation has a car park, and there are two short waymarked walks.

Brown Moss Nature Reserve

Turn left immediately after Ash; in 1 mile turn right and shortly after right again. The minor road soon reaches Brown Moss Nature Reserve, comprising 80 acres of flat heathland, scrub woodland - mainly birch - surrounding a series of pools with locally uncommon wetland plants, and 30 species of breeding birds.

Grindley Brook

Two miles beyond Whitchurch the A41 crosses the Llangollen Canal, which here negotiates two flights of three locks each: a good place from which to watch the crews of canal leisure boats operate lock gates and paddles, to navigate the flights successfully.

Colemere

Reached by a minor road from the A528, this is a 68-acre mere among 57 acres of woodland and fields, with pleasant walks, picnic areas and facilities for fishing and day sailing.

White Mere at Ellesmere – popular for boating and fishing

NORTHERN ENGLAND

England's grandest mountain scenery is packed into an area an hour or so's drive across, in the Lake District. Bald fells tower above long, gleaming lakes, tumbling waterfalls and massive Ice Age boulders, in a landscape held in a magical clarity of light. South-east of Carlisle country roads curl their way down the delectable valley of the River Eden. Further south, in Lancashire, a minor route crosses the empty, solitary moors of the Forest of Bowland.

To the east rise the Pennines, England's knobbly backbone, where the distant bleating of sheep or the mournful call of the curlew comes with the wind sighing in the heather. Rivers hurl themselves boiling down rocky cascades or disappear suddenly underground. Walls of fissured limestone run above miles of subterranean caverns. Squat farmhouses butt their whitewashed walls against the wind under heavy stone-tiled roofs.

In the Yorkshire Dales – Swaledale, Wharfedale, Wensleydale – old limestone villages shelter below the high moors where veteran shepherds still use an archaic lingo of their own for counting sheep. A succession of Yorkshire mill towns huddles along the narrow valley of the Calder, as road, canal and railway line squeeze their way through. Up to the north are the bleak moors that inspired *Wuthering Heights* and 'On Ilkley Moor Baht 'At'. Black cottages in the local millstone grit add grimness to the scene. To the east are the solid brick farmhouses of the Vale of York.

A country road keeps Hadrian's Wall company as it swoops daringly across the Northumbrian crags. Roads peter out among the far Cheviots, and pele towers and frowning castles guard the buffer zone between England and Scotland.

Left: *Tarn Hows, Cumbria – one of the Lakes' most famous, but least spoilt, beauty spots*
Above: *Castle Howard, North Yorkshire – surely England's most palatial stately home*

BERWICK-UPON-TWEED AND BORDER COUNTRY

56 miles

Seventh-century missionary saints brought the Christian message to Northumbria. Ruined castles and fortified houses are reminders of centuries of Anglo-Scottish strife and battles, but today the rich farmlands between the Cheviots and the Tweed are gentle landscapes of wide views and quiet villages, with an unspoilt coast along the eastern margin.

Between the North Sea and the Cheviot Hills, whose rounded summits reach well over 2,000ft, Northumberland's coastal plain shows a man-made landscape, created largely over the past two centuries. Arable crops ripen in large, hedged fields; planted woodlands and shelter-belts add their darker shades. There is conifer afforestation on the Kyloe Hills near the coast, and the heathery slopes above Doddington are a marvellous viewpoint across the Vale of Till to the Cheviots.

Prehistoric man has left some mark, the Romans scarcely any. For the centuries before the Union of Crowns all this area was any man's kingdom, squabbled and fought over until the English and Scots finally agreed a boundary, partly along the Cheviots, partly along the Tweed. Farm-towns are the characteristic form of settlement but there are few large villages and fewer towns. In an area rich in history Berwick-upon-Tweed claims pride of place and is one of England's most fascinating small towns.

ON THE TOUR

Berwick-upon-Tweed

England's northernmost town is also one of the most exciting. Its strategic position at the mouth of the Tweed gave it key importance, especially during the Border wars 1287-1603, during which it changed hands thirteen times, finally surrendering to the English crown in 1482. Red-roofed, grey stone houses are grouped and aligned on different levels, as are the heights of its various bridges. The town hall spire constantly focuses attention, but historically Berwick's greatest treasure is its remarkably intact Elizabethan fortifications - ramparts, bastions and citadels - encountered in a two-mile circuit. The Barracks are one of the earliest such purpose-built structures in Britain, and the parish church is a rarity, having been built during the Commonwealth, and thus having neither tower nor spire, these being forbidden by Cromwell. With its modern shops, a lively market, a salmon-fishing industry, good hotels and inns and riverside setting, Berwick is a rewarding town to explore.

Union Suspension Bridge

Spanning the Tweed at Horncliffe, Sir Samuel Brown's graceful structure, over 360ft long, was Britain's first major suspension bridge. Built in 1820, its level roadway has six chains on each side, anchored in stone pylons - those on the English side are built into a rocky cliff. Brown invented the special wrought iron chain link used on the bridge.

Norham

Stone houses and cottages surround two triangular greens; on one stands a 19th-century cross on a stepped medieval base. The salmon surmounting its weathervane is a reminder of the days of village dependence on Tweed fisheries for its trade. A lane leads to the parish church which shows powerful Norman architecture of the early 12th century - the creation of Bishop Flambard - who also built the first castle here. Norham was the northern stronghold of the Prince Bishops of Durham, and Bishop Pudsey started the present castle in about 1160, as a palace and a fortress against the Scots. By the late 16th century it had fallen into decay.

The Church of the Holy Trinity at Berwick-upon-Tweed was built during the Commonwealth

OFF THE TOUR

Coldstream and The Hirsel

Keep right on A698, onto A697 crossing the Tweed into Coldstream, and passing the former Marriage House at the Scottish end of the bridge. The Guards' House in the Market Square houses the Coldstream Museum. Beyond the town The Hirsel Grounds, open all the year, have displays of flowers, shrubs and trees for all seasons. There are picnic areas, a museum, workshops and a craft centre.

Flodden Field

Turn left on to an unclassified road at East Learmouth (sp. Branxton) to reach Flodden Field in 2 miles. A Celtic cross in a cornfield, reached by a short path, is simply inscribed 'Flodden 1513. To the brave of both nations'. Here, 15,000 men, more Scots than English, were killed on a September day in the bloodiest battle ever fought on English soil. A commemoration service is held annually in early August.

Lady Waterford's Hall

Before Lowick turn left on to the B6353. Ford is largely a mid-19th-century estate village. The former school (1860) contains a series of highly-detailed watercolours on Biblical themes, painted by the widowed Louisa, Marchioness of Waterford, a follower of the pre-Raphaelites. Figures were drawn from village people of the time.

Holy Island

From A1, turn right, unclassified, for Holy Island. This twice-a-day island is reached by a causeway passable for a few hours between the tides. Missionaries from Iona, led by St Aidan, founded a monastery here in 634. St Cuthbert became prior, and for a few years before his death in 687, Bishop of Lindisfarne. The worn, pink sandstone ruins make a memorable scene. Beyond is Lindisfarne's tiny 16th-century castle now restored as a comfortable house, shows the architectural genius of Lutyens and contains antique furniture. Lindisfarne mead is made on the island.

Kirknewton

Standing in the shadow of Yeavering Bell, the village church has two intriguing survivals; its chancel and south transept are both tunnel-vaulted almost from the ground, suggesting these may have supported a fortified tower in the 14th century. Behind the lectern is a primitive carving depicting the *Adoration of the Magi*, with the three kings tastefully attired in kilts. Josephine Butler (d.1906), the Victorian social reformer is commemorated in the churchyard. In a roadside enclave a short distance towards Wooler a neat inscription records 'At this place was Gefrin, royal township of seventh-century Anglo-Saxon Kings of Northumbria. Here the missionary Paulinus in AD627 instructed the people in Christianity for thirty-six days and baptised them in the River Glen close by'.

Wooler

Close-clustered stone houses and inns, grey-pink and rather dour in appearance, are grouped round a small triangular market place at the southern end of High Street. Hill and arable farming meet here, by the Wooler Water, where the Cheviots descend to Milfield Plain, so that a market inevitably developed. The livestock mart is of special importance, and the town serves the wide area of Glendale. There are plenty of friendly inns and small hotels. Shops are workaday rather than outstanding, but it is the hill scenery which provides the greatest attraction.

ROUTE DIRECTIONS

Leave **Berwick-upon-Tweed** (map 15NT95) by following the signs Edinburgh A1167 and in 1/3 mile cross the railway bridge and bear left on to the A6105 (sp. Duns). In 1/2 mile bear right and, at the trunk road, turn left on the A1 (sp. Alnwick). In 1 mile further turn right on to the B6461 (sp. Kelso) then in 1 2/3 miles cross the Border and in 1/2 mile keep left. After a further 1 1/2 miles turn left, unclassified (sp. Horncliffe) and in 1 mile cross the **Union Suspension Bridge** (Border). In 1/2 mile further at the trunk road, turn right, pass the road to Horncliffe on the right. In 1 mile turn right (sp. Norham) to pass Norham Castle on the right. Enter **Norham** and turn left on to the B6470 (sp. Cornhill) then in 1/2 mile turn right, unclassified, and in a further 3/4 mile, at the trunk road, turn right on to the A698. Two miles further on cross Twizel Bridge and continue to Cornhill-on-Tweed. Here, at the roundabout, take 2nd exit (sp. Coldstream) then, shortly, turn left, unclassified (sp. Learmouth). In 1 1/3 miles go over the crossroads then take 2nd left turning (sp. Yetholm). After 2 1/2 miles, at the crossroads, turn left on to the B6352 (sp. Kilham) then in 2 1/3 miles bear right (sp. Wooler). At the trunk road turn right on to the B6351 and in 1/3 mile, at the trunk road, turn left and continue to **Kirknewton**. At the end of the village bear right, pass Plaque on the left and in 2 miles, at the trunk road, turn right on to the A697 (sp. Morpeth). At the edge of **Wooler** turn left on to the B6525 (sp. Berwick-on-Tweed). Continue to Doddington then in a further 4 3/4 miles, turn right on to the B6353 (sp. Lowick). Pass through Lowick and Fenwick then, shortly, turn left on to the A1 (sp. Berwick). Continue to West Mains and pass the road to Holy Island on the right. Continue past the car park and toilets on the right and in a further 4 1/2 miles, at the roundabout, take 2nd exit on the A1167 to return to Berwick-upon-Tweed.

OFF THE BEATEN TRACK

St Cuthbert's Cave

Turn right off B6525, 3 miles north of Doddington and head for Holburn, a farm group. A 1 1/2 mile walk leads to St Cuthbert's Cave in some open woodland. The body of the saint is said to have been rested beneath these sandstone crags during its long wanderings from Lindisfarne to Durham. There are wide views west to the Cheviots.

OUTDOOR ACTIVITIES

Northumberland National Park

The B6351 running along the foot of the Cheviot Hills by the Bowmont Water and River Glen forms for much of the way the northern limit of the Northumberland National Park. The Cheviot's northern flanks are broken by long, lovely valleys, those of the College Burn beyond Hethpool, near Kirknewton, and the Harthope Burn near Wooler, the best-known. Narrow roads provide limited access; these valleys are for walkers, who will appreciate many miles of glorious walks, with waymarked tracks leading to the hills.

Lindisfarne National Nature Reserve

Over 8,000 acres of sand-dunes, salt-marshes and mud-flats make this, particularly in winter, a site of international importance. Large flocks of whooper swans, many kinds of geese, mallard, eider, shelduck, wigeon, together with thousands of shore-loving waders create spectacular sights and sounds which delight bird-lovers.

The curtain wall at Norham Castle; one of the strongest border fortresses with a still-impressive Norman keep

JEDBURGH AND THE BORDER FORESTS

76 miles

Two lovely rivers, the North Tyne and its tributary the Rede, flow south-eastwards from the high Cheviot Hills through spacious landscapes which saw centuries

of Border strife. Vast forests now cover huge areas of uplands and Britain's largest man-made lake reflects peaceful skies.

For mile after windy mile the Anglo-Scottish border runs along the wave-like crests of the Cheviots, rarely dipping below 1,300ft and reaching over 2,000ft towards its north-eastern climax from Windy Gyle to the Cheviot. To the north the land drops steeply to calm, well-farmed landscapes with the historic town of Jedburgh their focal point. On the English side of the border Forestry Commission plantations, initiated in 1926 in the North Tyne Valley above Falstone, now extend across both sides of the border. The four blocks in Tynedale and Redesdale form the continuous sweep of Kielder Forest, embracing over 100,000 acres of former upland country of poor-quality grazing. Much of Redesdale, where unplanted, retains a timeless quality. History's roots here are deep, with many Roman survivals, but centuries of strife which did not end until 1603 have left their marks. Villages are few and, on this tour, Jedburgh is the only town. Fortified farms and pele towers were local defences against raids and forays on both sides of the border, but new man-made landscapes help to erode melancholy memories.

ON THE TOUR

Jedburgh

Beautifully situated in the valley of the Jed Water this ancient Royal Burgh was for centuries a pivot in the wars between the Scots and the English, changing hands many times. To prevent the English from keeping it as a valuable base the Scots destroyed it in 1409. The County Prison of 1823 occupies the former castle site. Jedburgh Abbey was founded by David I in 1138. It, too, was sacked seven times between 1300 and 1523, but the present exquisite ruins survived from *c.*1150-1200, a background to delightful gardens.
Mary Queen of Scots stayed in a 16th-century tower-house in 1566. This is now a museum containing relics associated with the unhappy queen. At its heart Jedburgh is a small, mainly 18th-century town with many handsome buildings, inns and good shops, some specializing in the local knitwear and clothing. The Border Games, held annually in July, attract international athletes and the town is an excellent centre for angling and walking.

Rochester ('Roe-chester')

By the side of the A68 the former village school has a porch built almost wholly of Roman masonry, with ballister projectiles as decoration. All this came from the fort of Bremenium, a short way up the adjacent minor road, where squared stones, wall footings and grassy mounds reveal the outline of what was, after the last withdrawal from Scotland in AD213, the most northerly fort in the Roman Empire. It was abandoned in 343.

Bellingham ('Bellin-jum')

This village-sized market town is the capital of north Tynedale, at the heart of raiding and reivers country, still surrounded by wild, remote landscapes. Buildings have no pretentions to architectural style. St Cuthbert's Church was frequently burned, but its 13th-century chancel survives. Rebuilding in 1609 gave it a remarkable roof of heavy stone slabs supported by massive transverse arches of stone, producing a very primitive appearance. Among churchyard stones commemorating Northumbrian Charltons, Dodds, Milburns, Robsons, and Scottish Armstrongs and Elliots is one of a pedlar who featured in an unusual robbery 200 years ago.
Old inns dispense traditional hospitality to increasing numbers of visitors attracted to Kielder Water, and Bellingham's former great annual wool fair has been replaced by a lively agricultural show at the end of August.

Kielder Water

Created by the Northumbrian Water Authority and opened in 1982, Kielder Water covers 2,684 acres (nearly $6^{1}/_{2}$ square miles) and has a 27-mile shoreline. Controversial in concept, it is increasingly recognised as an asset, visually lightening the darkness of blanketing plantations and providing a unique recreational facility for all types of water activities. The southern shore is for the general visitor and Tower Knowe Visitor Centre is an excellent starting point, with car parks and a wide range of information and other facilities.

Kielder

From the Kielder village car park a short walk along the old North Tyne Railway leads to the famous 'skew' viaduct and Bakethin Reservoir, a Nature Reserve at the head of Kielder Water. Nearby, an 18th-century hunting-lodge houses displays and exhibitions about forestry and woodland crafts. Waymarked walks and nature trails provide opportunities for local exploration.

OFF THE TOUR

Elsdon

Follow the A696 south at Elishaw, taking the B6341 after Otterburn. Elsdon encapsulates the past, with a large green which could be used as a cattle stockade, a pound, a former drovers' inn, a marvellous vicar's pele tower built about 1400, and a notable church. Vast earthworks of a Norman motte-and-bailey castle guard the northern approach.

Gatehouse and Black Middens Bastle

Baronial landowners built castles, lesser gentry and some rectors built peles, and farmers built bastle-houses - which resembled two-storeyed fortified barns giving temporary protection during a border raid. Turn right off B6320 Bellingham road for Greenhaugh, then right again for Gatehouse (sp. Black Middens Bastle House). A splendid bastle-house is seen by the roadside at Gatehouse. Farther on, that at Black Middens is restored.

Hermitage Castle

Turn left at Saughtree on to the B6357, then right on to the B6399 for Hermitage. The formidable, unusual, Border fortress is where in 1566, Queen Mary hurried to from Jedburgh to visit her wounded lover the Earl of Bothwell.

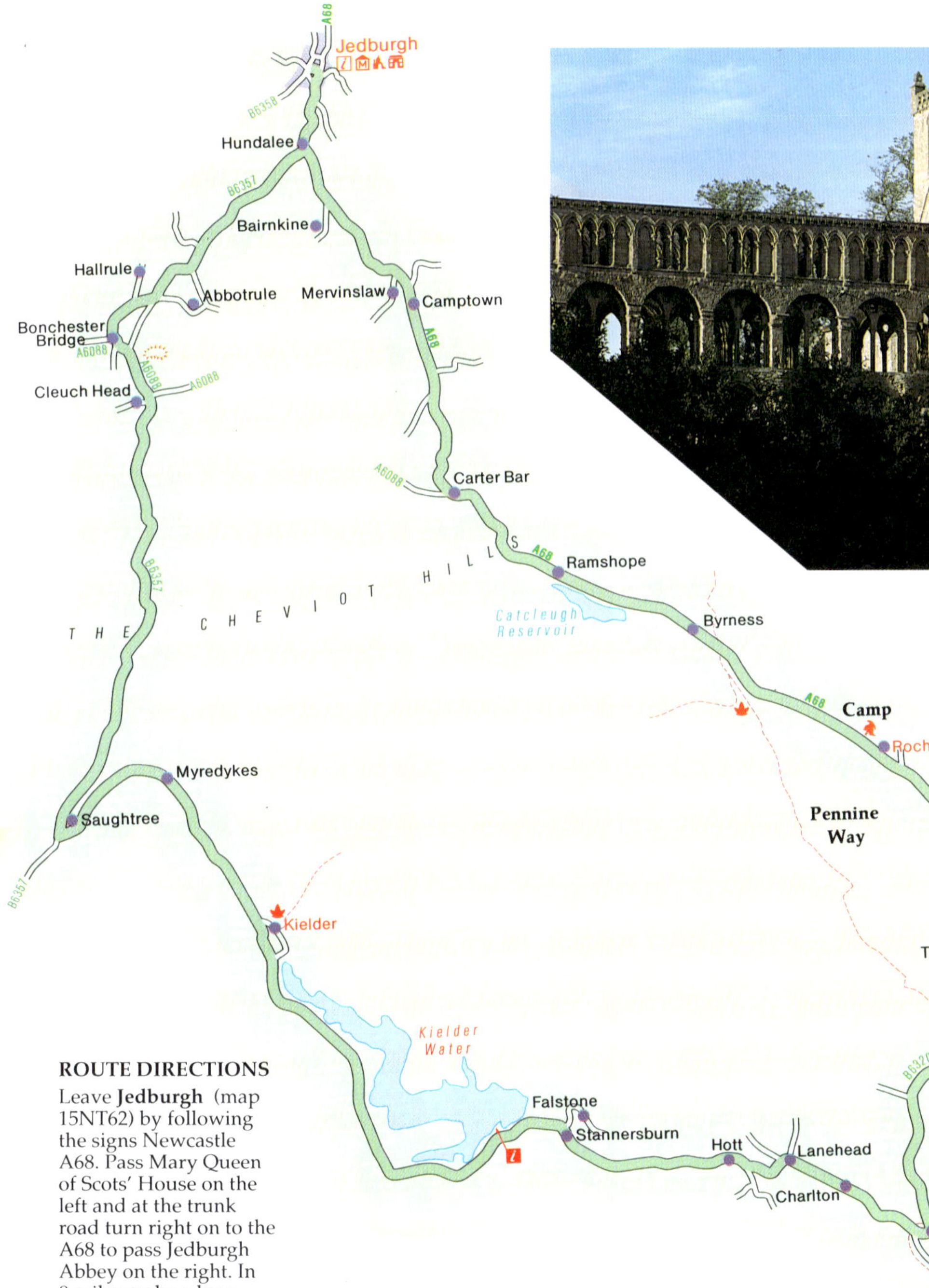

Red sandstone Jedburgh Abbey is believed to occupy the site of a 9th-century church

ROUTE DIRECTIONS

Leave **Jedburgh** (map 15NT62) by following the signs Newcastle A68. Pass Mary Queen of Scots' House on the left and at the trunk road turn right on to the A68 to pass Jedburgh Abbey on the right. In 8 miles make a long ascent to Carter Bar. Continue to Catcleugh Reservoir and on to the edge of Byrness. Pass the Forest Drive, toll road, on the right and enter **Rochester**. In a further 2½ miles turn right on to the A68 (sp. Corbridge) then cross the River Rede. In 2 ½ miles turn right on to the B6320 (sp. Bellingham) then in ½ mile ascend (1 in 10) and pass the Picnic Site, at **Bellingham**, on the right. In ½ mile turn right, unclassified (sp. Kielder Water) and continue to Lanehead. Here, turn left and in ¾ mile cross the river bridge and bear right past Ridley Stokoe Picnic Site to Kielder Dam. Continue beside **Kielder Water**, pass the Tower Knowe Visitor Centre, and on for just over 8 miles to reach **Kielder** itself. Then, in 1 mile bear right to cross the river bridge to the border. In 3½ miles at the trunk road, turn right, on to the B6357 (sp. Jedburgh) then in 4 miles further descend then ascend (not signed). Pass a Picnic Site and Car Park on left and in 3½ miles turn left on to the A6088. After ¾ mile descend (1 in 8) and continue to Bonchester Bridge. At the windmill turn right on to the B6357 (sp. Jedburgh). After a further 1¼ miles cross the river bridge and bear left. In 4¾ miles, at the trunk road, turn left on to the A68. After a further 1⅔ miles turn left (sp. Town Centre) to re-enter Jedburgh.

The setting sun illuminates the millpond smoothness of Kielder Water

OUTDOOR ACTIVITIES

Pennine Way

In the final stages of its journey to the Scottish border the Pennine Way passes through Bellingham before threading lonely moorlands northwards to Redesdale and the Cheviot. It can be sampled at various places - Bellingham, the B6230 crossing, and north of Byrness.

Hareshaw Linn

The Hareshaw Burn flows through a wooded valley north of Bellingham. A footpath, crossing many bridges, leads in a mile to a waterfall (linn) in a rocky amphitheatre at the head of the gorge. There are some steep sections and the track can be muddy.

Leaplish

This, on Kielder Water's southern shore, is the main activity centre catering for all major watersports. Angling facilities can be enjoyed from boat or bank at nearby Matthews Linn, as well as other beats around the shore. A forest play area has been provided for children, and there are lakeside and woodland walks together with a caravan and camp site.

BY HADRIAN'S WALL

53 miles

Rich farmlands and parks in three river valleys contrast with wild fell country of the northern Pennines. Forts, milecastles, turrets and sections of the Roman Wall,

fortified houses, castles and priories are reminders of a turbulent and sometimes peaceful past. Always, wide views lead to skylines of hills.

The priory gatehouse still stands proud at Wetheral although the priory is long gone

The Cumbria-Northumberland boundary follows the Pennine watershed for miles. Rain falling on lonely heights runs east to the South Tyne, west to the Eden or north to the Irthing which joins the Eden near Warwick Bridge. Before the Ice Age the Irthing flowed eastwards to the South Tyne, but glacial deposits closed this route, diverting its course westwards at Gilsland. Hadrian's Wall followed the uplands along the northern side of its new valley.

Villages are concentrated in the lower, fertile parts of valleys; higher landscapes show scattered farmsteads. Castles at Thirlwall and Naworth are reminders of border fighting, and even Lanercost Priory was regularly regarded either as a convenient military base or a place to be despoiled. Peaceful conditions of the 17th and 18th centuries allowed the planting of gracious parklands, the construction of better roads, and the development of the attractive market town of Brampton.

ON THE TOUR

Carlisle

See page 168.

Wetheral

Attractive houses, mainly of red sandstone or brick, many colour-washed, are grouped round a spacious triangular green, and a tall, five-arched early railway viaduct spans the river. South of the village only the 15th-century gatehouse survives from the Benedictine priory, although the adjoining farmyard may occupy the site of the former cloister.

Featherstone Castle

Beautifully situated in wooded parkland by the South Tyne, this courtyard house developed from a medieval pele tower, first in early Jacobean times, but more extensively and romantically early last century. It is worth strolling along the riverside path through the park to enjoy the best view, and to note a plaque commemorating the use of Featherstone Park as a POW camp for German officers, 1945-8, whose interpreter, Captain Sulzbach, dedicated himself to Anglo-German reconciliation.

Gilsland

Poltross Burn Milecastle, near the railway bridge in Gilsland village, is one of the best preserved on the Wall, with remains of north and south gates, walls, and two small barrack blocks. The River Irthing flows through a wooded gorge north of the village. Chalybeate and sulphurous springs were discovered nearby early in the 19th century, and a small pavilion and bath-house were built, followed by Spa Hotel (burnt down in 1859) but replaced by a much grander building, now a convalescent home. A short way up the gorge is the Popping Stone, where Sir Walter Scott proposed to Charlotte Carpenter.

Birdoswald Fort

Excavations continuing at this only visible fort on the Turf Wall section of the Roman Wall have revealed granaries and a west gate. Other good stretches of masonry walls and a gate make this one of the four best forts (out of 16) to visit. The view south from its farther end shows a landscape of green fields and trees, and the Irthing Valley with the Pennines rising beyond.

Lanercost Priory

Extensive remains of this priory of Augustinian Canons, founded in the 12th century, form a memorable group of buildings, all in local, warm red sandstone. At the dissolution the nave of the priory church was retained for use as the parish church of a scattered rural community, and contains some William Morris glass.

The chancel, transepts and crossing tower of the church still survive at an impressive height, and there are good remains of the cloister and its associated buildings, including the cellars beneath the refectory. The Prior's House was altered at the dissolution to make a dwelling house for the Dacre family who then acquired Lanercost. All the ruined parts of the priory now belong to English Heritage. Repeated sackings by the Scots between 1296 and 1346 are a distant memory.

Naworth Castle

The minor road through mature parklands at Naworth looks private, but is not. However, it gives an excellent view of Naworth Castle, which is neither a ruin nor a museum, but has been the family home of the Earls of Carlisle and their ancestors for over six centuries. Medieval corner towers were modified and added to in the 16th and early 17th centuries, and the interior shows remarkable architectural details, augmented by fine tapestries and paintings. Statuary illustrate characters from *Alice Through the Looking Glass.*

Brampton

An unusual, octagonal Moot Hall of 1817, at the centre of the Market Place, is the focal point of this extremely attractive little town. Family shops, inns and hotels exude a welcoming atmosphere, as does one of the home bakeries. Everything is on the right scale, and the main road just misses the centre. St Martin's Church is the only one built by the Victorian architect, Philip Webb, and contains some exquisite Morris glass.

Talkin Tarn is a safe place for children to master a range of watersports

ROUTE DIRECTIONS

Leave **Carlisle** (map 15NY35) from the station by following the signs Penrith, The South A6. In $3\frac{1}{3}$ miles, at the roundabout, take 2nd exit on to the B6263 (sp. Wetheral) to Cumwhinton. Continue to **Wetheral** and follow signs Brampton, then in $1\frac{1}{2}$ miles, at the trunk road, turn right on to the A69 (sp. Newcastle). Cross the river bridge and pass the road to Great Corby and Corby Castle before entering Warwick Bridge. Here, turn right, unclassified (sp. Castle Carrick) then take 1st turning left (sp. Hayton). In $2\frac{1}{2}$ miles branch left (sp. Talkin) and in a further mile keep left under the railway bridge. In $\frac{1}{2}$ mile cross the main road (B6413) and continue to Talkin. Go forward (sp. Halbankgate, Midgeholme) and in $\frac{1}{4}$ mile turn right to Halbankgate. Here, turn right on to the A689 (sp. Alston) and continue to Midgeholme and Halton Lea Gate. In a further $1\frac{1}{4}$ miles turn left, unclassified (sp. Coanwood) then in $2\frac{1}{4}$ miles, at the crossroads, turn left (sp. Haltwhistle). In $\frac{3}{4}$ mile turn left and shortly enter Featherstone Park. At the foot of a descent pass **Featherstone Castle** on the left and in a further $\frac{1}{2}$ mile, at the bridge, keep forward. After $\frac{2}{3}$ mile turn left (sp. Haltwhistle) and pass Bollister Castle on the right. Take the next left turn and, shortly, cross the river bridge then, in $\frac{1}{4}$ mile turn left on to the A69 (sp. Carlisle). In $2\frac{2}{3}$ miles turn right on to the B630 for Greenhead, then bear left on to the B6318 to **Gilsland**. Here, at the trunk road turn right (sp. Wilton) then cross the River Irthing and bear left. In $1\frac{1}{4}$ miles turn left, unclassified (sp. Brampton, Lanercost) and pass **Birdoswald Fort** on the left. Continue beside Hadrians Wall. On descending, bear left and in $1\frac{1}{4}$ miles bear left to pass **Lanercost Priory** on the left. In $\frac{1}{3}$ mile cross the river bridge then branch left and ascend through Naworth Park and pass **Naworth Castle** on the left. Bear right and in $\frac{1}{2}$ mile, at the crossroads, turn right on to the A69 (sp. Carlisle) to **Brampton**. Keep forward on to the B6264 (sp. Carlisle Airport), pass the road to Carlisle Airport on the right, and in 6 miles turn left on to the A7 to re-enter Carlisle.

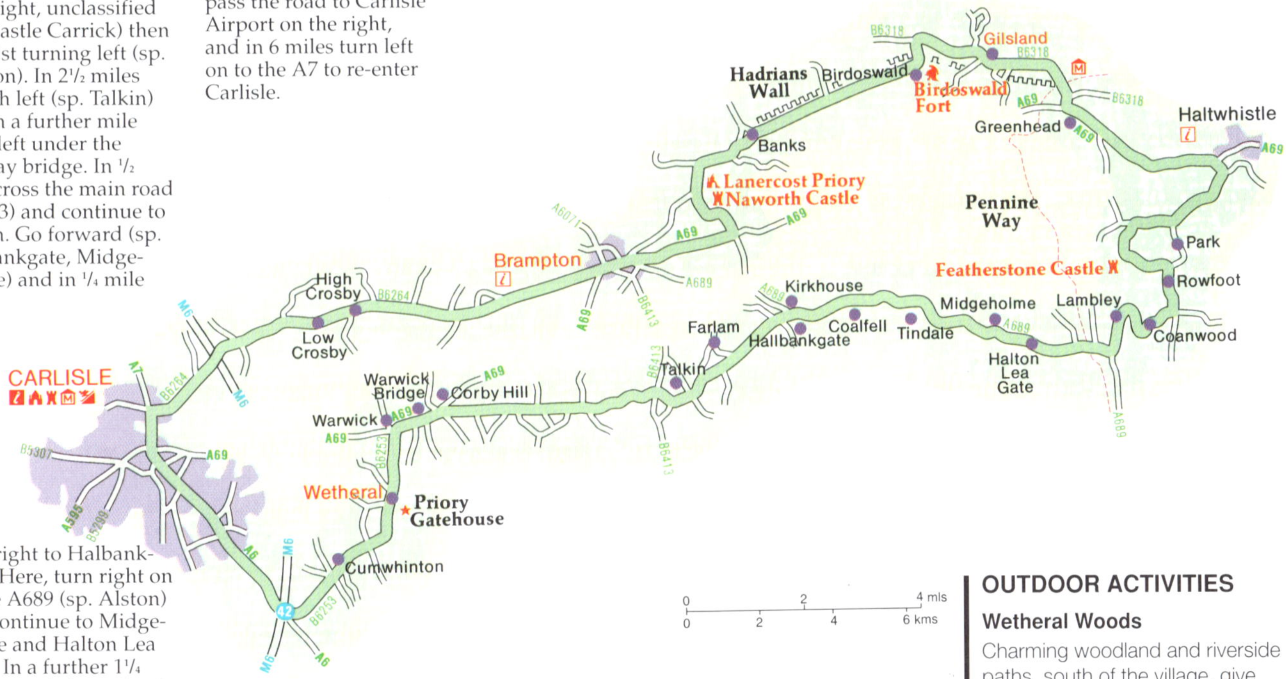

OFF THE TOUR

Corby Castle

Dramatically situated above the east bank of the Eden, and best seen from the opposite bank south of Wetheral, Corby Castle originated as a 14th-century pele tower. It came into the Howard family in the 17th century, added to it. The present stately mansion owes its elegant appearance to Henry Howard's changes early last century, although the beautiful terraced gardens which are open to the public in summer were laid out by Thomas Howard around 1740.

Cawfields

From Greenhead head eastwards on the B6318, turning left after $3\frac{1}{2}$ miles. An old quarry has been landscaped to form a car park and picnic area and information panels about the Wall. There is easy access to an impressive section of the Wall on Cawfields Crag where Milecastle 42 retains its broad foundations and shows many courses of masonry.

Carvoran Roman Army Museum

Near the unexcavated fort of Carvoran this museum and visitor centre has been designed to introduce, through models, life-size figures, exhibits and audio-visual displays, the history of the Roman Wall and the way of life of the people associated with it. Carvoran was once the home of the Wall's only garrison of archers; men from far-off Syria. School parties appreciate its comprehensive educational programme.

OUTDOOR ACTIVITIES

Wetheral Woods

Charming woodland and riverside paths, south of the village, give views of the Eden, and picturesque Corby Castle on the opposite bank (NT).

Talkin Tarn Country Park

North of Talkin off the B6413 this pleasant woodland, with a nature trail, adjoins a 65-acre lake, where fishing and boating can be enjoyed. Sandy bays will please youngsters and provide opportunities for swimming. There are fine views from a wooded hillock behind the Victorian boathouse.

Thirlwall Castle

An unclassified road off B6318, a half-mile north of Greenhead, gives closer access to Thirlwall Castle, which can also be reached by following a short stretch of the Pennine Way footpath (PW sign) from nearer Greenhead. The stark ruin above the Tipalt Burn is that of a 14th-century pele tower built of Roman masonry, which explains the absence of any Wall remains nearby.

THE CUMBERLAND PLAIN AND SOLWAY COAST

86 miles

Cumbria's plain and coast is the land beyond the mountains. Its shore faces north and west across the broad waters of the Solway Firth. Between the Eden in the north and Derwent in the south, little-known rivers - Wampool, Waver and Ellen - trace slow, meandering courses through wide pastures and farmland.

William Rufus began building Carlisle Castle in 1092, but the keep is Norman

Carlisle, at the north-eastern apex of the triangular area of the Cumberland plain, is the focal point to which all roads seem to lead. Historically, as well as in size and importance, it claims pride of place. Westwards, the Roman Wall continues to its Solway terminus, Bowness, but although its shore-hugging course can at times be recognised, masonry remains are few and far between.

Wide views and wildlife along the Solway coast make it more attractive to walkers and naturalists than to bathers, to whom muddy sands and treacherous tides are generally uninviting. For centuries there was a thriving salt trade from the coastal marshes in the north, but to the south shingle beaches and stretches of sand between Silloth and Maryport have encouraged visitors since Victorian times.

Inland there is rich farming on the coastal plain, with important local markets developing at Cockermouth and Wigton. A simple austerity characterises local buildings, although the nearness to Scotland necessitated the building of fortified church towers at Burgh-by-Sands and Newton Arlosh.

ON THE TOUR

Maryport

Founded in the middle of the 18th century by a local landowner, Humphrey Senhouse, and named after his wife Mary, the town flourished for almost 200 years on exports of coal and iron. Today, those industries have gone, but little has replaced them. An increasing number of leisure craft, for which a new marina is being developed, use the old docks.

A gridiron pattern of streets survives, and a cobbled market square suggests earlier elegance. Near the harbour a former dockside pub houses a fascinating maritime museum whose exhibits include a brass telescope from the *Cutty Sark*, as well as many reminders of Fletcher Christian, leader of the Bounty mutineers, who was born at Cockermouth in 1764.

Cockermouth

Situated on the River Cocker near its junction with the River Derwent, Cockermouth developed as a market town beneath the mainly 14th-century castle (not normally open). Two rows of trees give particular distinction to Main Street, where continuous frontages of houses, shops, inns and hotels show many original façades. Market Place is even more impressive, with handsome, three-storey buildings. An open-air market brings additional liveliness to a busy, friendly town each Monday. A maze of yards and alleyways leading off these streets reveals another aspect of Cockermouth's character, and in one of these (Bank's Court, Market Place) the Ethnic Doll and Toy and Model Museum has imaginative displays to delight children and fill adults with nostalgia. William Wordsworth was born in Cockermouth in 1770, his sister Dorothy a year later. Wordsworth House, in Main Street (NT) is open to the public.

Wigton

A small, unpretentious market town at its liveliest on Tuesdays. Modest, colour-washed houses and family shops create a homely atmosphere. Melvyn Bragg, born here in 1939, is probably Wigton's most famous son.

Carlisle

In Roman times it was Luguvalium, and Hadrian's Wall ran to its north. After the Romans' departure it reverted to Caer-luce, gradually becoming Carlisle, the only English city with a genuine British, or Celtic name. It is also the only historic town or city not mentioned in Domesday Book, for when that was written it belonged to Scotland. William Rufus reclaimed it in 1092 when the present castle and city walls were started. Edward I held parliaments in the castle, Mary, Queen of Scots lodged there, and prisoners-of-war scratched their marks on cell walls in the 14th and 15th centuries.

The city is sufficiently compact to explore on foot. The recently-pedestrianised Market Square is the central traditional meeting-place, where the beautiful 18th-century Old Town Hall is only a few yards away from The Lanes, a restored, modern shopping precinct. Specialist malls cater for most tastes. After centuries as a garrison town and the scene of many Anglo-Scottish battles, finally ending in 1745, Carlisle began to prosper as a textile town, and late 18th-century prosperity resulted in many streets of elegant Georgian and Victorian houses. The Museum and Art Gallery in the Jacobean mansion of Tullie House is the Museum of the Border and includes a fine Roman collection.

Abbey Town

The 12th-century Cistercian monastery of Holme Cultram gave its name to the village which grew around it. After the 1538 dissolution, when most of the abbey was destroyed, part of the nave of its church survived to become the parish church. With its aisles, transepts, chancel and tower it would originally have been slightly larger than Carlisle Cathedral.

Silloth

This small seaside town, which developed as a holiday resort when the railway came in 1856, retains cobbled streets and mid-Victorian buildings exuding the leisurely atmosphere of those days. A large open space, The Green, has 40 acres of lawns and flower gardens. There is a small, working harbour serving local flour mills.

ROUTE DIRECTIONS

Leave **Maryport** (map 14NY03) on the A594 Cockermouth road, passing by the edge of Dearham. In 4 miles, at the roundabout, take 2nd exit and descend to cross the River Derwent into **Cockermouth.** Here, turn left on to the B5292 and continue forward. Pass the castle then turn left (sp. Isel) and descend to follow the Derwent Valley. In 3½ miles turn left and descend beside Skiddaw Forest. Cross the river, turn left and in ¾ mile see Isel Hall House on the left and turn right (sp. Bothel). In 1¼ miles turn left and ascend, passing through Sunderland. Continue and, at the T-junction, turn left on to the A591 (sp. Bothel). At the edge of Bothel turn right on to the A595, continue through Mealsgate and in 4 miles, turn left on to the B5304 to **Wigton**. Here, turn right on to the A596 (sp. Carlisle) to Thursby then join the A595 to reach **Carlisle**. Follow the A595 Workington road, and in ½ mile, by the church, turn on to the B5307 Kirkbride road. In 1 mile further, branch right, unclassified, on to the Burgh road (sp. Kirkandrews). At Kirkandrews-upon-Eden bear left, pass through Monkhill and on to Burgh-by-Sands. Pass the road to the King Edward I Monument on the right and in a further ½ mile bear right (sp. Port Carlisle). Beyond Drumburgh follow the shore and pass through Port Carlisle to reach Bowness-on-Solway. Continue to Cardurnock and pass through Anthorn. In 2¾ miles turn right and cross the river to reach the edge of Kirkbride then turn right again on to the B5307. Continue through Newton Arlosh to **Abbey Town**. Here, at the crossroads keep forward on to the B5302. In 3½ miles turn right, unclassified (sp. Skinburness) and cross Calvo Marsh. At the Skinburness Hotel keep left and continue to **Silloth**. Here, continue on the B5300 Maryport road. Pass through Mawbray and Allonby and in 4¾ miles turn right on to the A596 for the return to Maryport.

OFF THE BEATEN TRACK

Skinburness

A large hotel dominates this tiny village, which Edward I chose as his base from which to attack the Scots. A retreating sea has now left large areas of salt-marshes to the east, and a walk along the mile-long spit of Grune Point gives marvellous views across Moricambe Bay and the many species of wading birds and wildfowl that live along its fretted shoreline and mudflats.

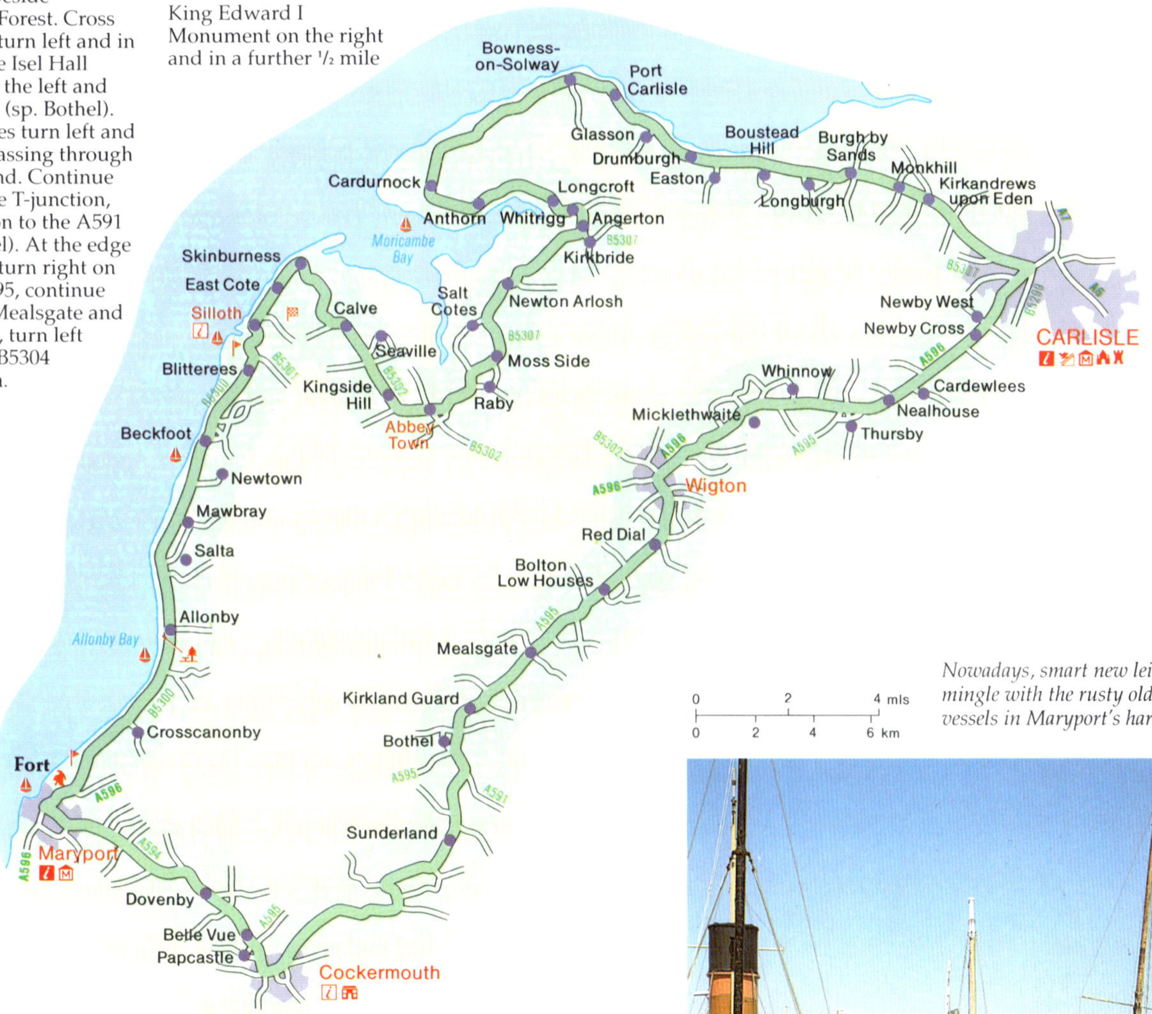

OFF THE TOUR

Edward I Monument

Signposted from Burgh by Sands along an unclassified road, from which a half-mile walk leads to a tall, isolated sandstone pillar marking the spot where Edward I - the first Prince of Wales, known as Hammer of the Scots - died in 1307, while marching northwards to fight Bruce's army. Afterwards his body lay in state in Burgh's church. The monument was erected in 1685, rebuilt in 1803 and restored in 1876.

Wythop Mill

Five miles east of Cockermouth, off the A66, colour-washed cottages of this tiny, enchanting village are grouped round a stone bridge spanning Wythop Beck. Nearby is an old mill, where visitors can see vintage water-powered woodworking machinery and a display of hand tools used by craftsmen centuries ago. Visitors can enjoy delicious home-made fare available in the coffee shop, and there are delightful walks up the wooded Wythop Valley.

Nowadays, smart new leisure craft mingle with the rusty old fishing vessels in Maryport's harbour

KESWICK, THE NORTHERN LAKES AND MOUNTAINS

59 miles

Four lovely lakes mirror majestic mountains amid the spectacular scenery of northern Lakeland. Towering crags above Honister Pass contrast with Borrowdale's sylvan charms and the gentle Vale of Lorton. Sheep graze high, lonely fells north of Skiddaw in John Peel's country of scattered farms and villages.

The old market town of Keswick is at the heart of northern Lakeland. Behind it the smooth slopes of Skiddaw rise to over 3,000ft, the site of a warning beacon at the time of the Armada, while southwards lie Derwentwater, Borrowdale's green valley and England's noblest group of mountains.

Beyond Honister's now silent slate quarries, Buttermere and Crummock Water are gracious jewels in a glaciated valley sheltered by mountain ranges on each side. Lakeside footpaths offer more intimate views, while on Whinlatter Pass the man-made landscapes of Forestry Commission plantations present a different scene.

Bassenthwaite Lake, like Derwentwater, has roads along each side, giving ever-changing views. The remote, upland country behind Skiddaw echoed to the calls of John Peel and his hounds last century. Today these hills are left to the sheep, the farmers, and those who seek their splendid solitudes.

A lovely footpath can be followed right round Buttermere, passing through pine trees and bracken

OFF THE TOUR

Lingholm Gardens

On the wooded western shore of Derwentwater, easily reached via Portinscale, the gardens of Lord Rochdale's home are probably at their best in spring and early summer, when the spectacular rhododendrons and azeleas are in bloom. Daffodils create a golden glow; many varieties of plants and trees flourish in a sheltered setting.

Watendlath

Reached by the unclassified road which also leads to Lodore Falls, Watendlath's whitewashed farms and cottages are as remote as when novelist Sir Hugh Walpole wrote about them in the early 1930s. Green hills enfold a shimmering, trout-rich tarn whose outlet beck flows beneath a neat packhorse bridge. Well signposted footpaths abound. Ashness Bridge and the 'Surprise View' in the woods above are best left to the return from Watendlath, otherwise you might not progress beyond them!

Castlerigg Stone Circle

Turn left off the A66 at Threlkeld, after the B5332, and follow the unclassified road (sp. Castlerigg Stone Circle). Thirty-eight stones survive of the 100ft diameter Bronze Age stone circle, erected about 1500BC. Situated almost with a sense of dramatic theatre, in a grassy field, with an epic panorama of mountains - Skiddaw and Saddleback to the north, the Helvellyn range to the south and the Derwentwater fells to the west - the Castlerigg circle (NT) marries prehistory with matchless natural beauty.

ON THE TOUR

Keswick

The capital of northern Lakeland, Keswick's history has deep roots, for Edward I granted a market charter over 700 years ago. After enjoying a boom for a century before the Civil War, based on mining metal ores in the nearby hills, the town declined for a century before its fortunes revived with the discovery and exploitation of graphite in Borrowdale, used for making 'lead' pencils. The Cumberland Pencil Factory now uses imported material, but its Museum portrays the industry's development.

Lakeland scenery was 'discovered' around 1770, first by Gray, followed by Hutchinson, Gilpin, West, and then the Romantic poets, Coleridge, Southey and Wordsworth. Later, Scott, Tennyson, Ruskin and R L Stevenson all stayed in the town. The Keswick Museum and Art Gallery has a rare collection of manuscripts, as well as the remarkable set of Musical Stones covering almost seven octaves of notes. Keswick is largely an early Victorian town, with most buildings of the attractive green slate-stone. The Moot Hall of 1813 dominates a lively Market Place, where good shops, inns and hotels cater for the tastes of thousands of visitors, augmented each July by Christians attending the Keswick Convention. Outside the town is the parish church of St Kentigern, named after a 6th-century saint. Nearby walks are superb, with Derwentwater featuring in most views.

Borrowdale

At Grange, once the site of a sheep farm and grain store of Cistercian monks from Furness Abbey, the clear Derwent flows beneath a twin arched bridge towards the lake. Bracken and turf cover soaring crags overlooking this charming village. Borrowdale, above, is enchanting; a symphony of silver birch and outcrops of knobbly rock, opening out southwards into a smooth-floored valley by Rosthwaite's whitewashed cottages. By Seatoller the hills close in and Honister's ruggedness lies ahead.

Whinlatter Visitor Centre

At the summit of Whinlatter Pass the Forestry Commission has established a car park, picnic site and Visitor Centre displaying and selling a range of items about forestry and wildlife. Nature trails, waymarked walks and special activities for children are available.

Caldbeck

Loosely-grouped stone cottages comprise this friendly village above Cold Beck, centred on another church dedicated to St Kentigern. A

ROUTE DIRECTIONS

Leave **Keswick** (map 12NY22) by following the signs Borrowdale B5289. Continue along **Borrowdale** to Seatoller. Ascend (1 in 4), pass Honister Pass Summit and car park, and descend (1 in 4) to Buttermere. In 4⅓ miles turn right (sp. Lorton, Cockermouth) then in 2 miles further turn right, unclassified. In ¼ mile, at the crossroads, go forward to High Lorton. At the end of the village turn right (sp. Keswick) and shortly, at the trunk road, turn right on to the B5292. Ascend and descend Whinlatter Pass, pass **Whinlatter Visitor Centre** on the left and continue the descent to Braithwaite. Here, turn left, unclassified (sp. Cockermouth A66) then in ¼ mile turn left on to the A66. After 5¼ miles turn right on to the B5291 (sp. Castle Inn), then right again. In ¾ mile further turn right across the river bridge to Castle Inn. Turn right then left over the main road, unclassified (sp. Uldale, Caldbeck) and in 2¼ miles bear right and continue to Uldale. Go over the crossroads and ascend, then in 2¼ miles join the B5299. In 1⅔ miles further bear left to **Caldbeck**, branch right, unclassified to **Hesket Newmarket**, then bear left. In ½ mile bear right (sp. Mungrisdale), pass the Horse and Farrier, and cross the river bridge then turn right to Mungrisdale. Keep forward and in 2½ miles turn right on to the A66 (sp. Keswick). In a further 6 miles branch left on to the A591 to re-enter Keswick.

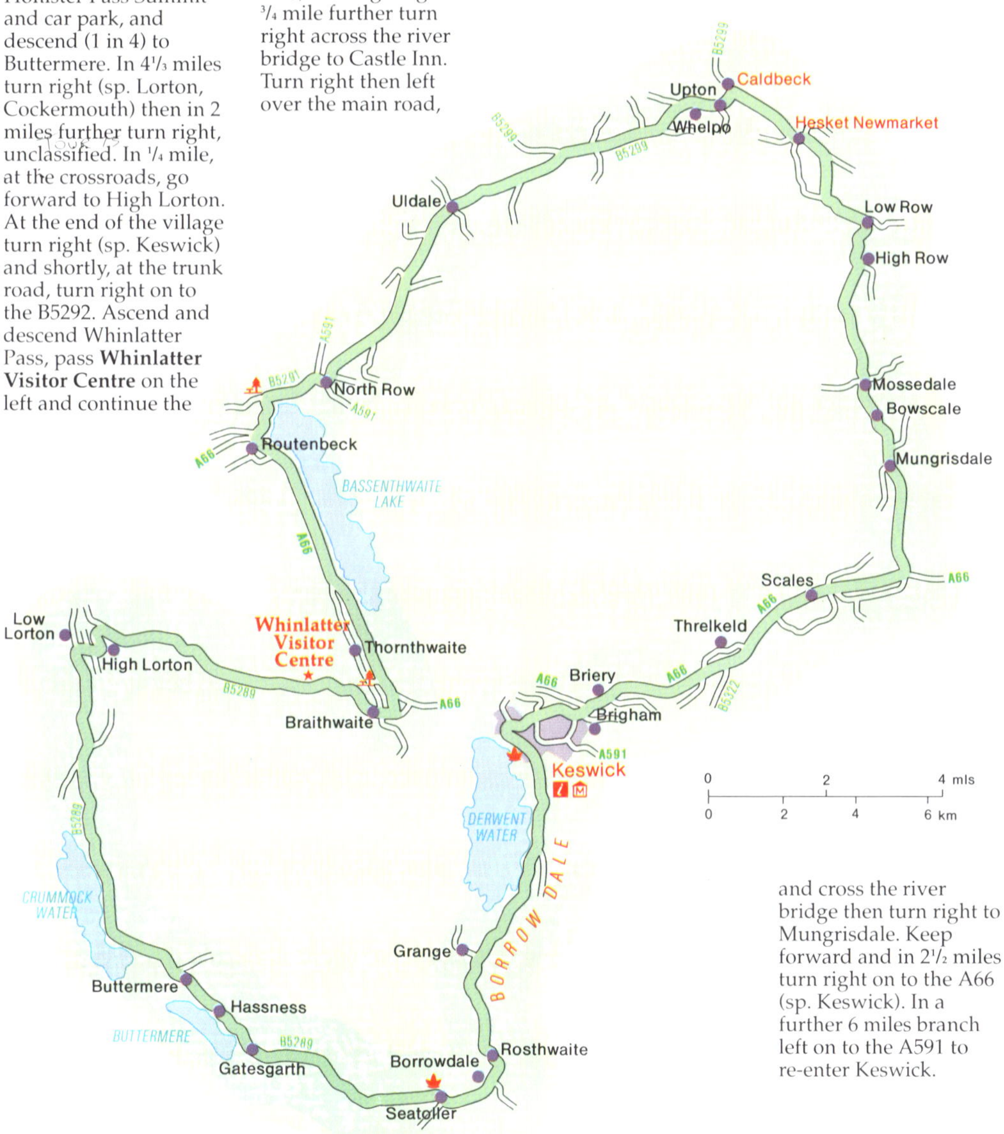

OUTDOOR ACTIVITIES

Derwentwater

In addition to a regular, round-the-lake launch service stopping at various points, boats can be hired from the Keswick landing stage, and launching facilities for visitors' boats are available here, and at Portinscale.

Friar's Crag Nature Trail

This is a short trail from one of the most famous viewpoints in the Lake District, and continues through mixed woodland along the eastern shore of Derwentwater, giving sight of many typical birds and plants of wood, shore and water habitats.

Bowder Stone

From a car park beyond Grange a short walk leads to this 2,000-ton boulder, apparently balanced on its edge. You can shake hands beneath it or, more rewardingly, climb a ladder to the top for almost a bird's-eye view of the 'Jaws of Borrowdale' to the immediate north.

Johnny Wood Nature Trail

The National Park Information Centre at Seatoller is a good starting-point for this walk through woodland and scrub to the viewpoint of High Doat. For part of the way the track winds along an old sheep trod. Johnny Wood is an old lakeland oak-forest to which other trees have been introduced.

Buttermere

Park at Buttermere village to enjoy this fairly level walk - through woods and keeping close to the shore most of the way - always with the lake's quiet charms in view, cradled by encircling hills. Nearly 4 miles.

white-painted, highly-decorated headstone in the churchyard commemorates John Peel, born locally in 1776, whose hunting exploits were immortalised in a song with words by John Graves, Peel's friend and drinking companion. Priests Mill, near the church, has working waterwheel machinery, while to the west, the Howk is a limestone gorge with waterfalls and a ruined Bobbin Mill. Other mill buildings of the 18th century have been converted to new uses.

Hesket Newmarket

A fine, wide street has many 18th-century houses fronting on to a well kept village green, with a slate-roofed, cobble-floored Market Cross as its focus. Hesket had its New Market in 1751; its trading activities, sheep and cattle fairs continued for a century before dying out, but the bear-baiting ring is still there. A surviving pub, the Old Crown Inn is a good village local hostelry complete with its own brewery.

Hesket Newmarket flourished after gaining its market charter in the 18th century

SOUTH-WESTERN LAKELAND

44 miles

Tranquil lakes, shapely hills and craggy mountains, lonely tarns, high passes and attractive valleys dotted with whitewashed farms, known and loved by Wordsworth and thousands of others since, are little-changed since the poet's time. This is the quintessence of the Lake District.

Wordsworth wrote most of his best-known poetry during his 'golden decade' at picturesque Dove Cottage

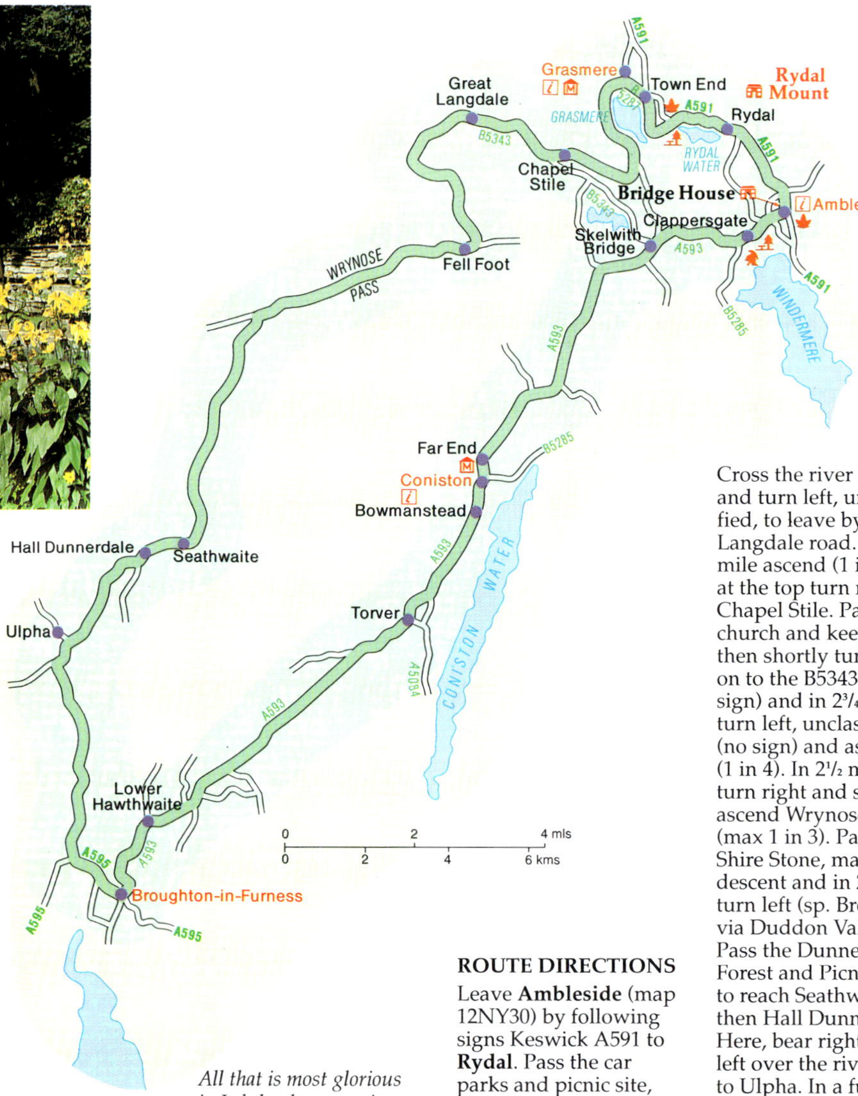

All that is most glorious in Lakeland scenery is found at spectacular Tarn Hows

The Lake District remained a virtual secret to the rest of Britain until the 18th century, but since then has increasingly become a place of pilgrimage. Prehistoric man knew it, the Romans established forts at Ambleside and Hardknott, with a road linking them. Viking settlers left a legacy of place names and language; the basis of Cumbrian dialect. They and their successors farmed what is, mainly, poor-quality land. Norman and medieval monks turned farming into an industry; wool from sheep, fishing on the lakes, and woodland management to feed the iron trade of Furness.

By the 17th and 18th centuries farmers had become more independent. Mineral ores in the fells above Coniston have long been exploited, but slate-quarrying, still flourishing in a number of places, has been the most continuous industry, although scars are few. Natural beauty overrides all, in spite of mass-tourism and the popularity of fell-walking. Ambleside, Grasmere, Langdale and Coniston are small, busy holiday centres, and boating enthusiasts will find Coniston and Windermere lakes have much to offer.

ROUTE DIRECTIONS

Leave **Ambleside** (map 12NY30) by following signs Keswick A591 to **Rydal**. Pass the car parks and picnic site, then the road to Dove Cottage on the right. Here, turn left on to the B5287 to **Grasmere**.

Cross the river bridge and turn left, unclassified, to leave by the Langdale road. In 1¹/₄ mile ascend (1 in 4) and at the top turn right to Chapel Stile. Pass the church and keep left, then shortly turn right on to the B5343 (no sign) and in 2³/₄ miles turn left, unclassified (no sign) and ascend (1 in 4). In 2¹/₂ miles, turn right and shortly ascend Wrynose Pass (max 1 in 3). Pass Three Shire Stone, make a long descent and in 2 miles turn left (sp. Broughton via Duddon Valley). Pass the Dunnerdale Forest and Picnic Area to reach Seathwaite and then Hall Dunnerdale. Here, bear right then left over the river bridge to Ulpha. In a further ¹/₄ mile bear left over the river bridge and in 2³/₄ miles descend (1 in 5). In ¹/₂ mile, at the trunk road, turn left on to the A595 (sp. Lancaster) then ¹/₂ mile further at the top of an ascent bear left to enter **Broughton-in-Furness**. From the square turn left on to the A593 (sp. Coniston) to Torver, then **Coniston**. Cross the river bridge and turn left (sp. Ambleside) then make a long descent (1 in 8) to Skelwith Bridge. Cross the bridge and bear right, then in 2 miles cross the river bridge and turn left to re-enter Ambleside.

ON THE TOUR

Ambleside

Encircled by sheltering hills on three sides, and facing southwards to the head of Windermere, Ambleside enjoys an enviable situation on the main `spinal' road through the Lake District. Granted a market charter in 1650, its markets and fairs were almost extinct two centuries ago, when the coming of the railway to Windermere boosted a developing tourist trade.

Now predominantly a small Victorian town, whose villas are small hotels and guest houses - augmented by 18th-century inns and hotels - Ambleside has a pleasant atmosphere, and among its many good shops there is an excellent bookshop for browsers, while Sheila's Country Cottage Restaurant will please gourmets.

Old Ambleside is focussed on the Market Place, and on the south bank of Stock Ghyll, whose waters powered a succession of mills. The tiny, unusual Bridge House was originally a summer house for Ambleside Hall, and down Lake Road, Hayes' Garden World is famous for its wonderful flower displays.

Rydal Mount

Wordsworth's home from 1813 until his death in 1850 is open most days, and has family portraits, personal possessions, some first editions, and four acres of gardens which he landscaped. The great and the good, writers and artists, visited Wordsworth here. Other tourists merely came in the hope of a glimpse of the poet, who had become a national figure.

Grasmere

The village of grey stone houses and its nearby little lake, set in an amphitheatre of woods and craggy hills, can still justify Wordsworth's description as 'the loveliest spot that man hath ever found'. His most creative years, 1799-1808, were spent at Dove Cottage, one of a cluster of cottages outside the village by the old road to Ambleside. Preserved as it was in his day, with furniture and relics, this is the main pilgrimage centre. A converted barn nearby contains the major manuscripts, first editions and personal possessions. In the village W Heaton Cooper's Studio has a permanent display of this modern artist's characteristic Lake District watercolours. The famous Grasmere ginger-bread is still available in a small shop by the churchyard. Grasmere church has a puzzling but lovable interior; outside, in the churchyard by his beloved Rothay, Wordsworth is buried.

Broughton-in-Furness

Centred on a cobbled Market Square with chestnut trees, a drinking-trough, stocks and an obelisk marking George III's jubilee in 1810, Broughton's ambience is of modest Georgian prosperity, perhaps slightly faded by now. Buildings are all of grey, slaty stone, some colour-washed.

Coniston

The 5½ mile-long lake and the village near its northern end are dominated by the shapely, 2,600ft mountain known as the Old Man of Coniston. Large quantities of copper ore were mined on the mountain's lower slopes, especially in the mid-19th century. Hotels and whitewashed cottages line Coniston's main street; Ruskin is buried in the churchyard and there is a Ruskin Museum in the village. Donald Campbell, whose jet-powered *Bluebird* crashed at 300mph on the lake in 1967, is commemorated by a simple plaque. In recent years the National Trust has restored steam-yacht *Gondola* to its mid-Victorian opulence; it now provides the only regular steam-powered service in the Lake District.

OFF THE BEATEN TRACK

Swinside Stone Circle

Reached by a minor road off the A595 west of Broughton, followed by a mile walk from Crag Hall, this compact circle of 55 stones dates from the Bronze Age, and is set in a lonely area of open, grassy fells.

OUTDOOR ACTIVITIES

Loughrigg Nature Trail

This nature walk of 2½ miles starts from Ambleside, taking in riverside scenery, grass meadows and arable fields, with the upland landscapes of Loughrigg Fell giving different habitats and rewarding views.

White Moss Common Nature Trail

A large car parking area by the A591 between Rydal Water and Grasmere is the starting-point for a ¾ mile nature trail which samples a range of lakeland habitats, chiefly lake shore, river and broad-leaved woodland. Bluebells in May and autumn colours in October are seasonal highlights.

Dudden Valley Picnic Site

Immortalised by Wordsworth, the Dudden Valley reveals beautiful views of riverside, woodland and mountains. The Forestry Commission car park and picnic site near Birks Bridge is the starting-point for five waymarked woodland walks. There is also good access to the fells.

OFF THE TOUR

Waterhead

Ambleside's 'port', a mile away at the head of Windermere Lake, has a regular `steamer' (diesel) boat service that operates the length of the lake. Comfortable smaller launches offer local trips; boats may be hired and there are launching facilities for private vessels.

Stagshaw Gardens

This woodland garden on the hillside above Waterhead to the south, created by the late C H D Acland, Regional Agent for the National Trust, has a fine collection of azaleas, rhododendrons and other trees and shrubs, amid thinned oak woodlands. Car parking is limited, but the gardens are not far from the large, public car park at Waterhead.

Hardknott Fort

From Cockley Beck, at the foot of Wrynose, turn right. Be prepared for very severe gradients and hairpins. The Roman fort, garrisoned by 500 troops in the 2nd century, has remains of watchtowers, a granary, a parade-ground, and breathtaking views into Eskdale.

Tarn Hows

From the B5285 (Hawkshead road) at Coniston, an unclassified road leads to Tarn Hows, which encapsulates the elements of Lakeland scenery. There are superb views across water, rock, grass, bracken and trees to northern mountains, and easy walks above and around the small lake. Tree screened car parking illustrates the National Trust's care of this lovely place.

Brantwood

Found off the B5285, down the eastern side of Coniston, this home of John Ruskin's from 1872 to 1900 is one of the finest-situated houses in the Lake District. It has displays of Ruskin drawings and watercolours, a Wainwright Exhibition and other Art Exhibitions. There are lovely woodland walks.

Ambleside's tiny Bridge House

WINDERMERE AND ULLSWATER

62 miles

High mountains look down on Ullswater's three beautiful but distinctive reaches; lesser hills, richly wooded, cradle Windermere's northern half. An exciting road over

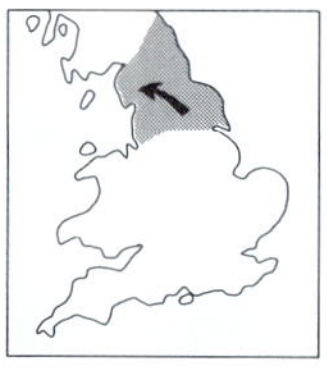

Kirkstone Pass links England's two largest lakes, and on Lakeland's eastern fringes quiet villages and farms continue pastoral farming patterns.

A boat trip aboard the steamer Lady of the Lake *is the best way to explore Ullswater, the second-largest lake in the Lake District*

ON THE TOUR

Windermere

Until early Victorian times there was a hamlet called Birthwaite in the old parish of Windermere. In April 1847 the railway from Kendal to Windermere was opened. Almost immediately the place grew up around the station and what is now the Windermere Hotel. The little town spread gradually down the hill towards the older lakeside village of Bowness, and the two places are now linked. Today they cater for the holiday trade, with many hotels, guest houses, holiday flats, and a wide range of shops. Many water-speed records have been attempted on the lake, and there are excellent facilities for boating and water sports. Orrest Head, above Windermere, gives a superb panorama of the lake. Off the A592 (Rayrigg Road) north of Bowness church, the Windermere Steamboat Museum shows, mainly under cover, Victorian and Edwardian steam launches and other craft all regularly maintained. Trips are available in the steam launch *Osprey*, and there is a museum shop.

Kendal

See page 177.

Shap Abbey

Just ½ mile off the road to Bampton is Shap Abbey, beautifully situated by the River Lowther; the 15th-century ruins of this small abbey are dominated by a graceful 16th-century tower.

Lowther Wildlife Park

140 acres of parkland provide a glorious setting for a rich variety of wild life, from wolves and wild cats to flamingoes and storks. There is sanctuary for rare British breeds of farm animals, an adventure play-ground, an assault course, and many picnic

West from Shap Fell the land rises steadily, reaching over 2,700ft on High Street - which has Britain's highest stretch of Roman road running for miles along its windy crest. North of Shap the River Lowther, turning its back on the hills, passes charming villages and splendid parklands. The ruins of Shap Abbey and, nearer Penrith, Brougham, evoke contrasting aspects of the medieval past. Kendal's roots are based on continuing successful local trades, but Windermere town is a creation of Victorian times, when the railway brought visitors in their thousands to sample Wordsworth's Lake District.

Industry has touched Ullswater and Windermere; tourism dominates today, but farming continues and sheep sound from the hillsides.

OFF THE TOUR

Wetheriggs Pottery

Three miles south-east of Eamont Bridge on a minor road off the A6, this 19th-century industrial site has a steam engine driving a potter's wheel, where traditional earthenware is made. There are weaving and leather workshops, a small museum and a children's play area.

Brougham Castle

Extensive remains of a late Norman castle, with later buildings set around a courtyard by the River Eamont, lie east of Eamont Bridge off the A66 and the B6262. Lady Anne Clifford restored the castle in the 17th century. There is a small display of Roman tombstones from the cemetery of a nearby fort.

Dalemain

Take the A592 from Penrith roundabout, and Dalemain is 2 miles along this road to Pooley Bridge. A medieval, Tudor and Georgian house, with fine furniture and portraits. Museums devoted to the countryside, agriculture and the county yeomanry cater for varied interests, and there is an adventure playground and a picnic area.

Brockhole National Park Visitor Centre

Just 2½ miles north of the A591/A592 junction at Windermere, Brockhole, a 1900 mansion, is set in 30 acres of terraced gardens and grounds stretching down to the lake. Interpretative displays and exhibitions illustrate all aspects of the Lake District. Audio-visual presentations and lectures are given regularly. There are picnic-places, shore walks and special activities for children, as well as a cafeteria, shops, and an Information Centre.

ROUTE DIRECTIONS

Leave **Windermere** (map 12SD49) by following the signs Kendal A591 to the junction for Staveley. Then, in 3½ miles, take the left-hand lane, A5284, to enter **Kendal**. Follow the signs Penrith A6 to Shap Summit and on to Shap. Here, at the end of the village, turn left, unclassified (sp. Ullswater, Brampton). Pass the road to **Shap Abbey** on the left and bear right to Brampton Grange. Here, cross the river bridge and bear right (sp. Askham). Continue to Bampton and bear right to the edge of Helton. Continue to Askham and then turn right (sp. Lowther). In a further ½ mile cross the river bridge then bear left to enter **Lowther Wildlife**

areas, plus the spectacular shell of an early 19th-century mansion, Lowther Castle.

Ullswater

This 7½-mile-long lake, with the A592 keeping close to its western shore for most of the way, divides scenically into three sections. The northern section, from Pooley Bridge, is fringed with low hills and is favoured by watersports enthusiasts. Wooded banks and higher hills give the middle section its particular charm, while the third section reaches a climax at the head of the lake - cradled beneath a grand group of mountains, dominated by the Helvellyn range to the west - reaching to over 3,000ft. A regular steamer service operates between Pooley Bridge and Glenridding, calling at Howtown.

Glenridding

A small steamboat pier, other boating facilities, good access to the lake shore, a few shops and hotels all combine to underline the popularity of Glenridding as a small holiday centre at the head of Ullswater. By Red Tarn Beck above the village are the remains of the Greenside Lead Mine, whose busiest years were from 1830 until 1870.

Kirkstone Pass

Named after a huge boulder shaped like a small church tower the Kirkstone Pass climbs to 1,489ft, with the famous Kirkstone Pass Inn at the summit dispensing good hospitality and giving extensive views, particularly back down towards Brotherswater.

Troutbeck

This mile-long village lies just off the main road and consists of a series of hamlets, clusters of farms and cottages dating from the 17th and 18th centuries, strung along a narrow road.

At its southern end Town End (NT) is the most interesting and important house in the village. Built around 1626 as a 'statesman's' farmhouse, it remained in the Browne family for over 300 years, and contains carved furniture and woodwork, much of it home-made, as well as books and papers collected by the family during that time.

Victorian pleasure craft can be seen at the Steamboat Museum at Bowness-on-Windermere

Park. In a mile, at the crossroads, turn left then in ½ mile turn left on to the A6 (sp. Penrith). Continue to Clifton and on to Eamont Bridge, then turn left on to the B5320 (sp. Ullswater). Continue through Tirril to Pooley Bridge then in ½ mile further join the A592 and continue beside **Ullswater**. Pass the car park and Aira Force on the right and continue through **Glenridding** to Patterdale. In a further 3¼ miles, make a long ascent (1 in 5) over **Kirkstone Pass** to Kirkstone Inn. Then, make a long descent (1 in 6) and in 3 miles branch right, unclassified (sp. Ambleside). Continue to **Troutbeck**, pass Town End on the right, and branch left (sp. Windermere). In 1¼ miles turn left on to the A591 and cross Troutbeck Bridge. In a further ⅔ mile, at the mini-roundabout, go forward for the return to Windermere.

OFF THE BEATEN TRACK

Keld Chapel

Turn left off the minor road after Shap to see this pre-Reformation chapel, owned by the National Trust, in a remote hamlet, still used for occasional services. A notice on the door indicates where the key is available.

Hartsop

Two miles south of Patterdale turn left off the A592 to see a little-changed farming hamlet in a secluded valley. Some of the 17th-century houses retain their old, covered spinning galleries. This is altogether a rare survival.

OUTDOOR ACTIVITIES

Aira Force

Off the A592, a car park by the A5091 is the start of a short, easy walk to the deep, wooded, rocky glen where Aira Force tumbles almost 70ft, by two stages, into a dark, shaded pool. A footbridge spans the top of the waterfall.

Howtown Walk

For one of the most rewarding walks in the Lake District take the steamer from Glenridding to Howtown, and walk the lakeside (or above lakeside) path back to Patterdale; about 6 miles, so allow 4 hours, full of superb views all the way.

KENDAL AND SOUTH EAST CUMBRIA

70 miles

Two fine rivers, the Lune and its tributary the Rawthey, have carved valleys that almost embrace the Howgill Fells between the Lake District and the northern Pennines. Grey stone market towns and villages sit comfortably in open, hilly, sheep-farming countryside.

This is upland country, largely of Norse settlement from the centuries before the Conquest. Villages are few and far between, farmsteads widely scattered. Except around Kirkby Lonsdale in the south there is little woodland or afforestation, so views are open and wide-ranging. The country between Kendal and the Lune Valley is broken and hummocky, but to the east the high fells rise above Barbon with their Pennine characteristics.

To the north, beyond Sedbergh, the Howgills reach well over 2,000ft; a compact mass of rounded, grassy hills separated by long, narrow valleys, unenclosed country above the walls and hedges of the fringing farms. Northwards again, between Kirkby Stephen and Tebay, a vast limestone plateau with many gleaming outcrops, scars and pavements, provides another landscape contrast, but still enjoys panoramic views to distant hills and mountains.

ROUTE DIRECTIONS

Leave **Kendal** (map 12SD59) by following signs Skipton, then branch left on to the B6254 (sp. Oxenholme) to Oxenholme Station. Cross the railway (sp. Kirkby Lonsdale) to Old Hutton and on through Old Town to **Kirkby Lonsdale**. Here, bear left then right and at the end of the town turn left on to the A65 (sp. Skipton). Cross the River Lune then turn left on to the A683 (sp. Sedbergh) to Casterton. In a further 1/2 mile branch right, unclassified, to Barbon. Turn right (sp. Dent) and ascend (1 in 7) then in 5 miles descend (1 in 7) to Gawthrop along **Barbondale**. Here, turn right, cross the river bridge and descend. In 1/4 mile, at the trunk road, turn right to **Dent**. Return, unclassified (sp. Sedbergh) and in 5 miles bear left over the river bridge into **Sedbergh**. Here, turn right on to the A683 (one-way) and at the end of the town go forward (sp. Brough). In 11 3/4 miles, at the trunk road, turn right on to the A685 to **Kirkby Stephen**. Here, at the end of the town, turn left, unclassified (sp. Soulby) and in 1/4 mile bear right to Soulby. At the crossroads turn left (sp. Great Asby) then in 3 miles branch right over the crossroads and in 2 miles further descend then turn left into Great Asby. Here, bear right then turn left over the river bridge and at the end of the village, go forward (sp. Orton). In 3 miles turn left on to the B6260 (no sign) to Orton. Continue forward (sp. Kendal, Tebay) to the Tebay roundabout and take 2nd exit, A685 to return to Kendal.

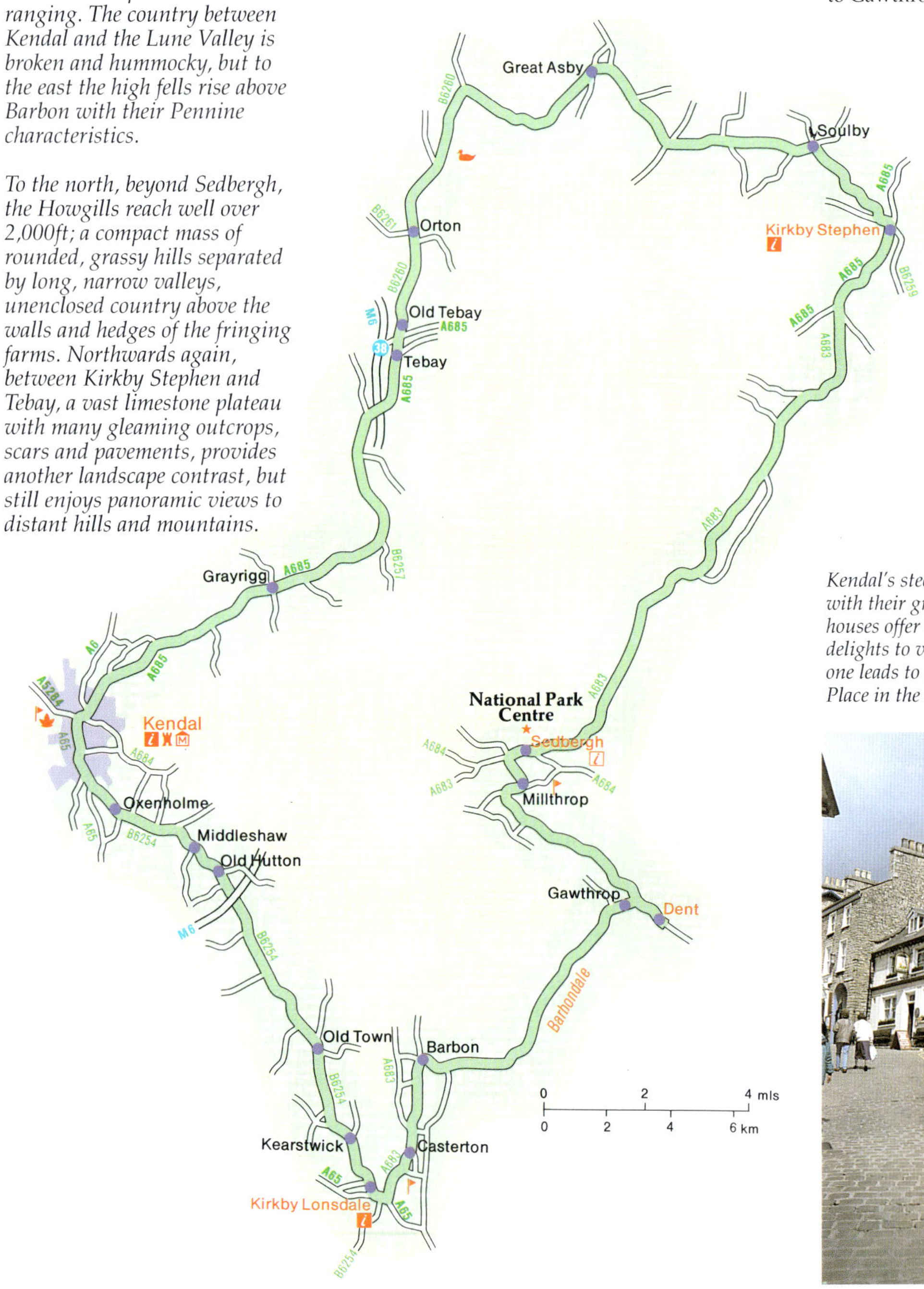

Kendal's steep streets with their grey limestone houses offer many delights to visitors. This one leads to the Market Place in the town centre

OFF THE TOUR

Sizergh Castle

Just 3½ miles south of Kendal (off the A6) the family home of the Sticklands for 700 years is a beautiful example of a 14th-century fortified tower; added to in the 15th, 16th and 18th centuries to become the gracious house it now is. Containing fine furniture, china and portraits it is noted for its superb panelling and ceilings. There are extensive wooded grounds.

Levens Hall

Five miles south of Kendal by the A6, this Elizabethan home of the Bagot family is famous for its unique late 17th-century topiary garden; superbly maintained in its original form, with colourful herbaceous borders. The house contains fine Jacobean furniture, paintings and needlework. There is a collection of working model steam engines from 1820 to 1920.

Brigflatts

A mile west of Sedbergh, off the A683, lies one of the most famous of the early Friends' Meeting Houses. Dated 1675 it is modest and homely and evokes, in its setting and simple beauty, the quiet purposefulness of Quakers in the years of their persecution. The area has many associations with George Fox, founder of the Society of Friends.

Brough Castle

Found 5 miles north of Kirkby Stephen (by the A685) this Norman royal castle was destroyed by the Scots in 1174, rebuilt and subsequently granted to the great Clifford lords. The redoubtable Lady Anne Clifford extensively restored it in the 17th century; much of her work survives together with some from the 14th century. The keep is a magnificent viewpoint.

Barbondale's landscape is divided by the drystone walls so typical of this part of Cumbria. Views from here are superb

ON THE TOUR

Kendal

Kendal takes its name from the River Kent and is rightly regarded as the southern gateway to the Lake District. In spite of modern developments Kendal has remained true to its character of a working town rather than a tourist centre. With a lively weekly market and a good range of shops, inns, restaurants and hotels - mainly late Georgian - Kendal continues to serve its own population of over 20,000. Its weaving trade developed in the 14th century and continued to bring prosperity. By the 18th century many associated trades were added, and people lived and worked in the narrow, enclosed yards behind the frontages of Highgate and Stricklandgate, many of which survive.

The Abbot Hall Gallery, housed in an elegant 18th-century mansion, displays paintings by Raeburn, Reynolds, Romney and Turner, as well as modern sculptures, while in the stables is the Museum of Lakeland Life and Industry.

Kirkby Lonsdale

This country and market town (market day Thursday) of dark grey stone houses is always enjoyable to wander through. Nothing is spectacular, all is modest and of human scale, with friendly inns and hotels, and family shops selling quality products. Two market crosses add characteristic touches and the church, full of variety and interest, contains richly-carved Norman doorways. Ruskin, a good judge of landscape, described the view of the Lune Valley from this churchyard as 'one of the loveliest scenes in England'. A different aspect is obtained at the 15th-century Devil's Bridge, south-east of the town, with its three graceful arches spanning the Lune's rocky course.

Barbondale

Once past the woodlands of Barbon Park, Barbondale becomes a lovely narrow valley between high green fells. Sheep-cropped sward makes a popular picnic place by a lively beck, with the stone cairn of Jossy's Pike a steep, challenging scramble up the opposite hillside.

Dent

A spacious car park west of the village enjoys a superb view across Dentdale's green fields to sweeping fells beyond. Narrow, winding streets are cobble-carpeted from wall to wall. Sturdy stone cottages, mainly whitewashed, have roofs of heavy stone flags. The Sun Inn looks across to St Andrew's Church which has some Jacobean box pews. Behind it is the old grammar school, attended by Adam Sedgwick at the end of the 18th century. He subsequently went to Cambridge, became a great geologist, and is commemorated near the churchyard's southern entrance by a memorial fountain in rough Shap granite. John and Eliza Forder's gallery adjoining contains superb photographs of Dentdale scenes.

Sedbergh

Although, like Dent, in Cumbria, this grey town is the western gateway to the Yorkshire Dales, and has a good range of shops, hotels, inns, guest houses, and a National Park Visitor Centre. It also has a famous school, founded as a chantry school in 1525, and made a public school in 1874. School buildings and playing fields cover most of Sedbergh's southern edge, while to the north rise the steep flanks of the Howgill Fells. Garsdale, Dentdale and the Rawthey Valley meet nearby before their waters join the Lune. Domestic knitting flourished here from the 17th to 19th centuries, with a cotton industry adding to Sedbergh's industrial history.

Kirkby Stephen

This grey stone market town of the upper Eden Valley (market day Thursday) has an impressive church whose churchyard is approached from the Market Place through a cloister-screen of Tuscan columns built in 1810. The town developed last century with the growth in demand for local limestone as a building material.

OFF THE BEATEN TRACK

Cautley Spout

From the Cross Keys Inn (NT unlicensed), by the A683 5 miles from Sedbergh, a good grassy footpath leads for a mile to Cautley Spout: a series of pencil-like cascades totalling nearly 600ft, rather obscured by rocks and trees. The frowning mass of Cautley Crags to the south is the only large, rocky outcrop in the Howgills.

Lune Gorge

At Lune's Bridge, a mile south of Tebay, the river rushes through a rocky gorge, into a series of dark pools favoured by anglers. The M6 and the main railway line add to the drama of the setting, at the western foot of the Howgills. A riverside track continues down the east bank of the Lune to Low Borrowbridge, site of a Roman fort.

OUTDOOR ACTIVITIES

Asby Scar Nature Reserve

Two miles south-west of Great Asby, where the road bends right, a track ahead over a common leads to Asby Scar. This 400-acre nature reserve comprises wide limestone pavements set in grassland, or as long, low cliffs. Deep fissures (grikes) in the pavement make tiny gardens of shade-loving plants.

YORKSHIRE DALES

57 miles

Three lovely rivers - the Swale, Ure and Wharfe - with their tributaries, flowing east from the high Pennines, create green valleys, separated by long upland ridges. Grey stone

villages, farms and barns harmonise with some of our most treasured landscapes, where pastoral farming follows the changeless pattern of the seasons.

Here, moorland ridges sweep upwards to Pennine summits reaching over 2,000ft high fells, and form some of our last wilderness areas, where fierce winds sough through grass and heather. Spongy peat and squelching moss generate lively becks which tumble down hills and over waterfalls; meeting and mingling to form beautiful rivers in serene, green valleys whose floors were smoothed by glaciers. Limestone scars etch the hillsides, often darkened with broad-leaved woodlands. Colours are muted, greys and greens, purple heather, tawny bracken, silver birch, with bright wild flower accents on limestone pastures.

Villages have remained for a thousand years, their names evoking Anglian, Danish and Norse settlers. The seemingly ageless buildings seen today are mainly the product of the past three centuries, and the stone walls were added between 1780 and 1850. Life here follows its seasonal rhythms - lambing, shearing, haymaking, winter foddering - with the annual sheep sales, weekly market and daily milking in between.

ON THE TOUR

Hawes

Most market towns in the Dales are situated towards their lower ends. Hawes is the exception, being in upper Wensleydale, about 850ft above sea level, with high fells north and south. It is a relative newcomer, with a Market Charter granted in 1700. Now, the A684, one of the few trans-Pennine main roads, passes through the town on its way from Leyburn to Sedbergh, and minor roads climb high passes to Wharfedale and Swaledale. The weekly livestock mart reaches its operational peak with the autumn lamb sales from late August. The Wensleydale Creameries, not open to the public, is the 'home' of Wensleydale cheese, stocked in local shops, while the Ropeworks, where visitors can see ropes being made, also sells many other craft products. Nearby is a National Park Information Centre, and also occupying former railway premises the Dales Countryside Museum houses a very impressive display. The Pennine Way passes through Hawes, thus adding to the popularity of the town, and its modern youth hostel.

Hubberholme

A tiny village noted for its unusual church, in a superb setting by the Wharfe. A background of fells make an ideal frame for its broad, low profile and sturdy tower. The medieval atmosphere of its rough-walled interior is enhanced by a rood-loft of 1558, painted in bright colours. Almost all other woodwork is modern, by Robert Thompson, whose 'mouse' sign on most pieces never fails to satisfy. The George Inn opposite was once the vicarage, and, each New Year's Day hosts the ancient ceremony of letting the 'Poor Pasture', when farmers bid for the tenancy of a 16-acre field.

Aysgarth

A National Park car park and Information Centre add to the honeypot of attractions here. They include glorious, wooded riverside scenery, terraced waterfalls extending half-a-mile, and the Middle and Lower Falls; reached by a pleasant walk through Freeholders' Wood, where coppicing has been re-introduced. The Yorkshire Carriage Museum now occupies the large premises of 19th-century Yore Mills.

Castle Bolton

A massive castle dominates a tiny village along a green. Dating from 1379 Wensley-dale's largest building, a huge manor-house with four corner towers, was, for six months

OFF THE TOUR

Muker

One mile down Swaledale, left off the B6270 from Thwaite, Muker is the largest of the trio of villages near the head of Swaledale. Beyond it, the Swale follows a quiet, curving valley east of Kisdon, an isolated hill. Clustered stone cottages, a popular pub, a church built during Elizabeth's reign, and a chapel and Institute dating from last century's lead-mining days, comprise Muker. Nothing is outstanding, but its setting and its groupings are memorable. All around are the finest traditional haymeadows in the Dales.

Hardrow Force

A mile north of Hawes, by the minor road along the north side of Wensleydale. Access to this waterfall is through the Green Dragon Inn (small fee). Various rock strata have eroded deeply back to allow Hardrow Beck to fall 80ft in a single leap. There is sufficient space by the worn shale base to allow adventurous visitors to walk behind the waterfall. The natural auditorium of the gorge is a setting for annual band concerts, usually in early summer.

ROUTE DIRECTIONS

Leave **Hawes** (map 12SD88) on the A684, Sedbergh road and near the end of the main street turn left, unclassified (sp. Gayle and Kettlewell). Shortly, cross the Duerley Beck and ascend through Sleddale to reach the summit. Make a long descent into the valley to Oughtershaw Beck. Continue through Oughtershaw and follow the Kettlewell road beside the river to enter Langstrothdale. At the George Inn in **Hubberholme** keep forward and continue to the village of Buckden.

The Pennine Way takes in many fine views across Swaledale

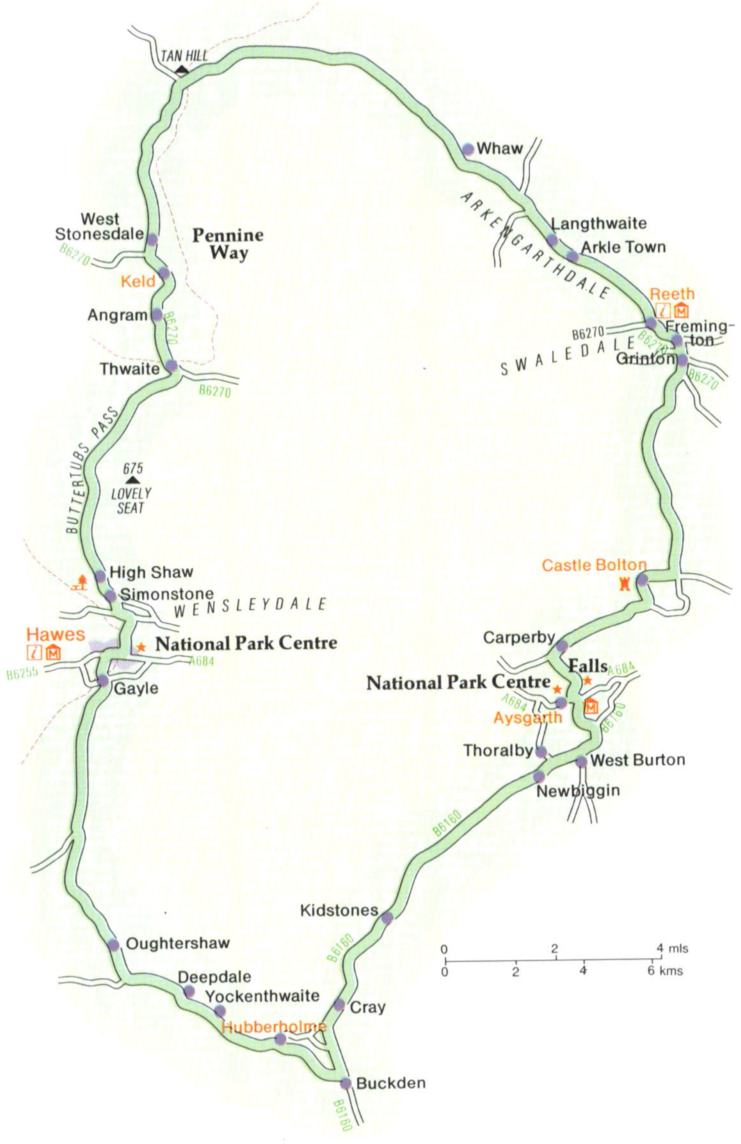

Kisdon Force, found below the village at Keld

Turn left on to the B6160 (sp. Aysgarth) and climb along Kidstones Pass. Descend to Bishopdale to reach the edge of West Burton. Here, turn left, branch left, unclassified (sp. Aysgarth) and in ¾ mile, turn left on to the A684. Pass **Aysgarth** and, in ¼ mile turn right, unclassified (sp. Aysgarth Falls). Pass the Yorkshire Museum of Carriages and Horse Drawn Vehicles, cross the River Ure and then pass the Yorkshire Dales National Park Centre on the left. Continue, unclassified, and in ¾ mile turn right (sp. Castle Bolton) and enter Carperby. In a further 2 miles, turn left for **Castle Bolton**. Follow the Reeth/Redmire road for ¾ mile then, at the crossroads, turn left (sp. Grinton and Reeth). Make a long climb, then at the foot of the hill turn left to Grinton. Here, turn left on to the B6270 and cross the River Swale for **Reeth**. At the Buck Hotel turn right, unclassified, on to the Langthwaite road. Half a mile beyond Langthwaite keep forward (sp. Tan Hill). Cross Arkengarthdale Moor for 7½ miles to reach Tan Hill Inn. Here, turn left (no sign) and follow the moorland road to enter West Stonesdale. Make a steep descent before crossing the River Swale and turning left on to the B6270 to the edge of **Keld**. Continue to Thwaite then turn right, unclassified (sp. Hawes) and ascend the Buttertubs Pass. Descend to Wensleydale and proceed through Simonstone. In ½ mile, at the T-junction, turn left then next right to return to Hawes.

in 1568, the comfortable prison of Mary, Queen of Scots. It was partially dismantled after the Civil War. Now open to the public, it houses a local history folk museum and a good restaurant.

Reeth

Reeth stands on a commanding position on the slopes of Calva, where Swaledale is joined by its feeder valley, Arkengarthdale. For two centuries after receiving its market charter in 1695 it prospered as a centre of farming and lead mining. Houses, good inns and hotels around its large green date from the 18th century, and a wide range of exhibits in the Swaledale Folk Museum, housed in a former Methodist schoolroom, illuminate various aspects of Reeth's past. All around, field and riverside paths are an invitation to walkers.

Keld

Green hills enfold this small stone village astride the 1,000ft contour at the head of Swaledale. Two chapels, the school and the youth hostel - in a former shooting-lodge - are its largest buildings, and the sound of flowing, falling or rushing water its ever-present background. Behind the village a path leads to the gorge of the Swale beneath wooded limestone cliffs, and the Pennine Way begins its long, lonely course on to the peaty fells around Tan Hill.

OFF THE BEATEN TRACK

Yockenthwaite Stone Circle

Above Yockenthwaite, in Deepdale, the Wharfe is a laughing, enchanting river; a delight for youngsters and readily accessible. On the north bank a footpath (part of the Dales Way) passes a small Bronze Age stone circle, about 25ft in diameter, consisting of rough limestone boulders placed in a circle.

OUTDOOR ACTIVITIES

Semerwater

One mile east of Hawes along the A684 take the unclassified road to Burtersett, continuing climbing eastwards then descend to Semerwater, Yorkshire's largest natural lake. The only access is at the short north shore, where the lake attracts canoers, wind-surfers, yachtsmen, fishermen, children and picnickers. Swimmers brave the cool, shallow waters in summer; wildfowl like it in winter.

Pennine Way

This long-distance footpath from Edale, Derbyshire to Kirk Yetholm, across the Scottish border, runs northwards through the Yorkshire Dales. This tour touches it at Hawes, Tan Hill, Keld and Thwaite, each useful access points for sampling some of its contrasts.

Buckden

A track climbing through Raikes Wood above the car park follows the line of a Roman road which linked a fort at Bainbridge with the camp at Ilkley. Other paths from the village lead to the surrounding hills and along riverside meadows.

MORECAMBE, LUNESDALE, INGLETON AND LANCASTER

68 miles

One of the loveliest northern rivers, the Lune carves a gracious valley in its south-westerly course from the Pennines to the sea in Morecambe Bay. Green pastures and limestone uplands contrast with the wild moors of Bowland Forest, while historic Lancaster links beautiful countryside with a holiday coast.

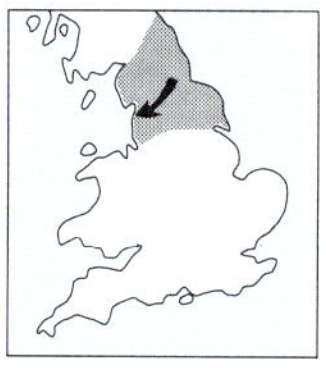

Long, white scars etch the limestone hills above Ingleton and Clapham whence the Lune's tributary, the Greta, is born. To the south, the River Wenning's gathering-grounds are largely on the fells of Bowland, also joining the Lune between Kirkby Lonsdale and Lancaster. Attractive, stone-built villages are regularly spaced out across vale landscapes; well farmed and generously wooded. Limestone scenery at a lower level gives particular charm to the pleasant, undulating countryside between Kirkby and Carnforth, to whose west are the mosses above Morecambe Bay's indented shoreline, with its vast skies and low horizons. There could scarcely be greater contrasts than those between the lonely fells, isolated farms, and quiet villages east of the M6, and the concentrated tourist pressures and popularity of Morecambe and its neighbours to the west. Nature, history and man have contributed individual themes to create an unusual and fascinating harmony.

ON THE TOUR

Morecambe

Fishing-boats still bob in the vast bay as though to remind the thousands of visitors that Morecambe developed from three fishing villages in Victorian times. Railways once brought crowds from Lancashire's mill towns. Now they come from everywhere, by road and rail, to sample the bay's natural beauty, the breezes and the boisterous fun. Four miles of promenade, ablaze with dazzling light each autumn, are supplemented by facilities and entertainment for all ages, particularly during the holiday season. Marine-land, Frontierland, Leisure Park, Superdrome, swimming pools, shows - they're all here in their colourful, frenetic, noisy, joyous, salty brashness.

Steamtown Railway Centre

Not only is there an impressive assembly of British locomotives here - large and small, main-line and industrial, but also carriages and freight wagons, an engine shed, signal box and coaling plant. Lower down the scale are a 15" gauge railway operating on a mile-long track, and a model railway layout. Three types of activity days offer a choice - static displays only, a minor operating day with the 15" gauge working, and a full operating day.

Warton Old Rectory

The ruins of this 14th-century rectory suggest it was like a small manor house, with hall, buttery and kitchen; giving a shadowy hint of medieval life in this village of stone houses and cottages below Warton Crag.

Kirkby Lonsdale

See page 177.

Clapham

Trees and grey stone houses line streets on both sides of Clapham Beck, which is crossed by four bridges. Clapham has three diverse claims to fame: James Faraday, father of electrical pioneer Michael, was village blacksmith; Reginald Farrer, of Ingleborough Hall, travelled the world seeking plants, and in 1939 the *Yorkshire Dalesman,* now *Dalesman* was founded here, where it is still published. The Farrer Nature Trail commemorates the botanist; the National Park Information Centre has excellent interpretative displays, with detailed information about the many superb walks in the woods and limestone hills.

Lancaster

Despite its Roman roots, medieval past and a modern shopping area, Lancaster is predominantly a comfortable, Georgian county town with a University added in recent years. On Castle Hill the medieval castle is part of a prison, but the 18th-century Shire Hall (Crown Court) cells and 'drop' room are open to the public. Nearby, the stately Priory Church is sole survivor of a Benedictine priory, and at the head of Church Street the Judges' Lodging houses two museums; of Gillow furniture, and the Museum of Childhood.
The Maritime Museum on St George's Quay, in the old Custom House, has displays illustrating the history of the Port of Lancaster, and at the opposite side of town the Ashton Memorial's swaggering dome commands the scene. The Old Palm House near it in Williamson Park has been transformed into a superb Butterfly House. Lancaster's intricate street network offers a rewarding exploration. Few buildings are more than three storeys, and there is a pleasant mix of large and small shops and a fascinating market.

A gleaming red engine lovingly cared for inside the engine shed at Carnforth's Steamtown Railway Centre; part of a fine collection

OFF THE TOUR

Leighton Hall

Turn left in Yealand Conyers. This castellated house, built of gleaming white limestone, has a fairy-tale quality enhanced by its glorious setting against a background of woods and the distant hills of Lakeland. It is the home of the Gillow family, famous Lancashire furniture makers, and contains examples of their early work, together with paintings, clocks and other *objets d'art*. Gardens, woodland walks and a new maze provide outside interests, while the Leighton Hall eagles, which give daily flying displays, are a particular attraction.

Heron Corn Mill

After Yealand Redmayne turn left on to A6 to Beetham. This 18th-century traditional corn mill on the banks of the River Bela was used for grinding corn until 1955. Now restored as a working, water-powered mill, producing stone-ground flour, it shows all aspects of milling operations. To coincide with the 500th anniversary of UK papermaking, a new display tracing the history of papermaking has been created.

The undulating hills of the Forest of Bowland, near Slaidburn

ROUTE DIRECTIONS

Leave **Morecambe** (map 12SD46) from the Central Pier and follow the A589 Marine Road East to Hest Bank. In 1 mile, at the traffic signals, turn left on to the A6 (sp. Kendal) to Bolton-le-Sands and Carnforth. Here, branch left, unclassified (one-way, sp. Warton, Silverdale) and in $\frac{1}{4}$ mile, at the T-junction, turn right. Pass the **Steamtown Railway Centre** on the left and continue to **Warton**. Go forward (sp. Yealand Conyers) and in $1\frac{1}{3}$ miles bear right then left into Yealand Conyers. Pass the road to Leighton Hall on the left and continue forward to Yealand Redmayne. Pass the road to Leighton Moss RSPB Reserve ahead and turn right (sp. Milnthorpe, Kendal). In $\frac{2}{3}$ mile cross the main road, then in $1\frac{1}{4}$ miles, further, at the T-junction, turn left then immediate right (sp. Hutton Roof, Kirkby Lonsdale). In $4\frac{1}{3}$ miles turn left, pass Sellet Hall Herb Garden on the right and bear left. In a further mile cross the main road and in $\frac{1}{4}$ mile further, at the T-junction, turn right then branch left (one-way). Shortly, at the foot of a descent, turn right on to the B6254 to Kirkby Lonsdale (see page 177). Go forward to the main road then turn left on to the A65 (sp. Skipton). Reach Cowan Bridge and in $4\frac{1}{4}$ miles cross the River Greta and, at the Bridge Hotel, turn left, unclassified, and continue to Ingleton. Bear right (sp. Hawes B6255) then shortly, at the T-junction, turn left on to the B6255 (sp. Hawes). Take 2nd turning on the right, unclassified, to **Clapham** and at the T-junction turn left then right into Station Road. In a further $\frac{1}{4}$ mile cross the main road (sp. Keasden) and 1 mile further bear left under the railway bridge and keep right (sp. Slaidburn). Make a long ascent, then a descent (1 in 7) and pass Gisburn Forest Car Park on the right. In 2 miles, at the crossroads, turn right on to the B6478 (sp. Slaidburn) and in $2\frac{1}{2}$ miles further descend (1 in 8) and cross the river bridge to enter Slaidburn. Here, bear left (sp. Lancaster) to Newton and go forward, unclassified, for Dunsop Bridge. Go forward to the T-junction then turn right and ascend to Trough of Bowland Summit. Make a gradual descent to Jubilee Tower and in $1\frac{1}{2}$ miles descend (1 in 6). After $1\frac{1}{4}$ miles further ascend (1 in 6) and at the top, go over the crossroads. In $1\frac{1}{2}$ miles at the T-junction turn right then pass the entrance to Ashton Memorial on the right.

In $\frac{1}{3}$ mile, at the crossroads, turn left (sp. Kendal) to **Lancaster**. Here, turn left on to the A6 (one-way) then take the right-hand lane and follow the signs A6, North. At the end of the one-way system follow the signs for Morecambe and cross the River Lune to join the A589. In 2 miles, at the roundabout, take 2nd exit B5274 (sp. Town Centre) to return to Morecambe.

OUTDOOR ACTIVITIES

Leighton Moss RSPB Nature Reserve

Beyond Yealand Redmayne (sp. Nature Reserve) this man-made fen, drained about 1920, now has open water, reed-beds, marshes, scrub and woodland, a variety of habitats with abundant bird life, as well as many mammals.

Eaves Wood Nature Trail

Near Silverdale, 2 miles beyond Leighton Moss, this limestone woodland consists of oak, ash, lime, beech and yew covering an understorey of buckthorn, spindle and privet. A 2-mile trail, with a short cut if necessary reveals a surprise view at the highest point.

Ingleton – The Falls Walk

In 1884 local residents created miles of paths, with steps and bridges, along the wooded valley of the Rivers Doe and Twiss (later amalgamating in the Greta). Waterfalls abound, and there are fine open views revealing limestone uplands.

Caves at Ingleton & Clapham

White Scar Caves by the B6255 north of Ingleton, and Ingleborough Cave, a half-mile walk from Clapham, are commercial caves, with footpaths and electric lighting, showing classical features of limestone caves - passages, rock formations, waterfalls, stalactites and stalagmites, and exposed fossils.

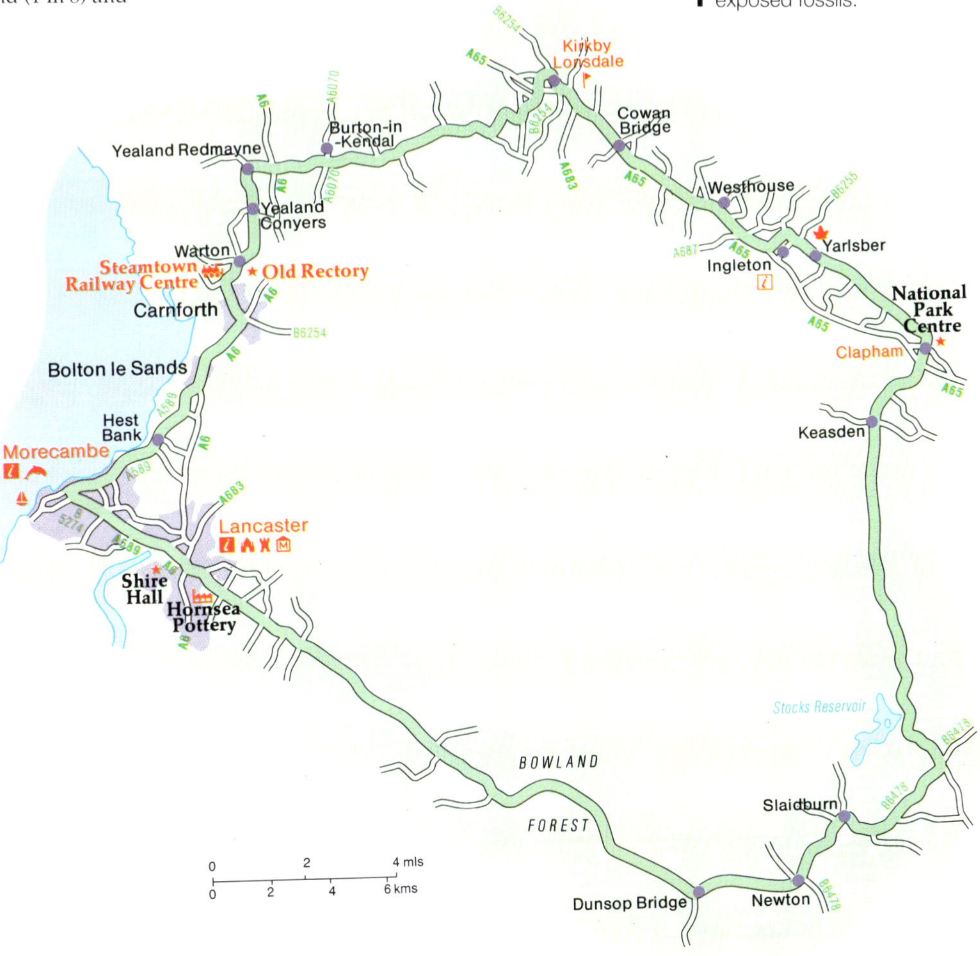

CLITHEROE TO SKIPTON

71 miles

Limestone uplands of the Yorkshire Dales nourish the rivers Aire and Ribble. The Aire flows south-east towards industrial Yorkshire, while the Ribble, taking a westerly course across Lancashire through a broad vale of stone villages and market towns, maintains a longer affinity with the hills.

Ribblesdale is predominantly farming country presenting a picturesque, pastoral landscape of fields, hedgerows and small woodlands against a background of hills rising to over 1,700ft. A network of roads links historic villages, usually of dark stone houses and cottages. The upper valley beyond Settle shares with upper Airedale, above Gargrave, the clean-limbed characteristics of the Craven Pennines, where the limestone bones of landscape are close to the surface - creating cliffs, and etching long scars. White stone walls edge green hillsides - sheep and cattle graze rich pastures, and sturdy stone barns store summer's hay for winter feed.

South of the Aire and Ribble dark moors rise to flowing skylines, limestone gives way to dour Pennine gritstone, and below the hills compact villages, towns and mill chimneys show evidence of a recent industrial past. Pendle country may still be associated with dark days of witchcraft but today's visitors are more likely to appreciate the wide views, flowing skylines, varied scenery and friendly people of Ribblesdale.

ROUTE DIRECTIONS

Leave **Clitheroe** (map 12SD74) on the B6478 (sp. Waddington) for Waddington church. Follow signs Newton, Slaidburn and ascend then descend (1 in 6) to Newton. Go forward to the T-junction turn right, staying on the B6478 to **Slaidburn**. Here, turn right (sp. Settle) and in ¼ mile cross the river bridge then ascend. In a further mile branch right, unclassified (sp. Bolton-by-Bowland) to the Copy Nook. Here turn left and in ¼ mile bear right to Bolton-by-Bowland. Turn left (sp. Hellifield) and in 6½ miles, at the T-junction, turn left on to the A682 (no sign). In 2 miles further, at the T-junction turn left on to the A65 (sp. Settle) to Long Preston. In a further 3 miles, at the roundabout, take 2nd exit on to the B6479 to **Settle**. In ½ mile turn right (sp. Horton in Ribblesdale) to Langcliffe. Turn right, unclassified (sp. Malham) and ascend (1 in 5). In 3 miles bear right then in a further mile branch right. In ½ mile, at the crossroads, turn right and then descend to **Malham**. At the Buck Inn go forward (sp. Skipton) to Kirkby Malham, and bear left to Airton. In ⅔ mile bear left then in 3 miles further bear right to Gargrave. Here, at the T-junction, turn left on to the A65 (sp. Skipton) and in 3 miles, at the roundabout, take 2nd exit, unclassified. In 1 mile further, at the T-junction, turn right, then at the next roundabout take 2nd exit A6131 (not shown) to **Skipton**. At the roundabout take 2nd exit (sp. Keighley) and in ⅓ mile turn right, unclassified (sp. Carleton, Lothersdale). In a further mile bear right then in ½ mile bear right for Carleton. Make a long ascent and descent over Elslack Moor then in 7½ miles bear left. After ⅔ mile further turn right and follow signs Colne A6068. Continue to Colne and the junction with the A56. At the traffic signals go forward and in ½ mile, at the gyratory, continue with Burnley signs. Shortly, turn right on to the B6247 (sp. Barrowford). Pass the **Pendle Heritage Centre** on the left then at the George and Dragon turn left on to the A682 to Barrowford. Here, turn right, unclassified, ascend and descend to the Bay Hourse at Roughlee. Turn left (sp. Burnley) and in ½ mile turn right (sp. Barley). In a further mile, at the end of the village, bear left (sp. Downham) and in 1½ miles further, at the crossroads, turn left and descend to Downham. Continue to Chatburn and, at the T-junction turn left (sp. Clitheroe). In 1¼ miles, go over the crossroads on to the A671 (no sign) and return to Clitheroe.

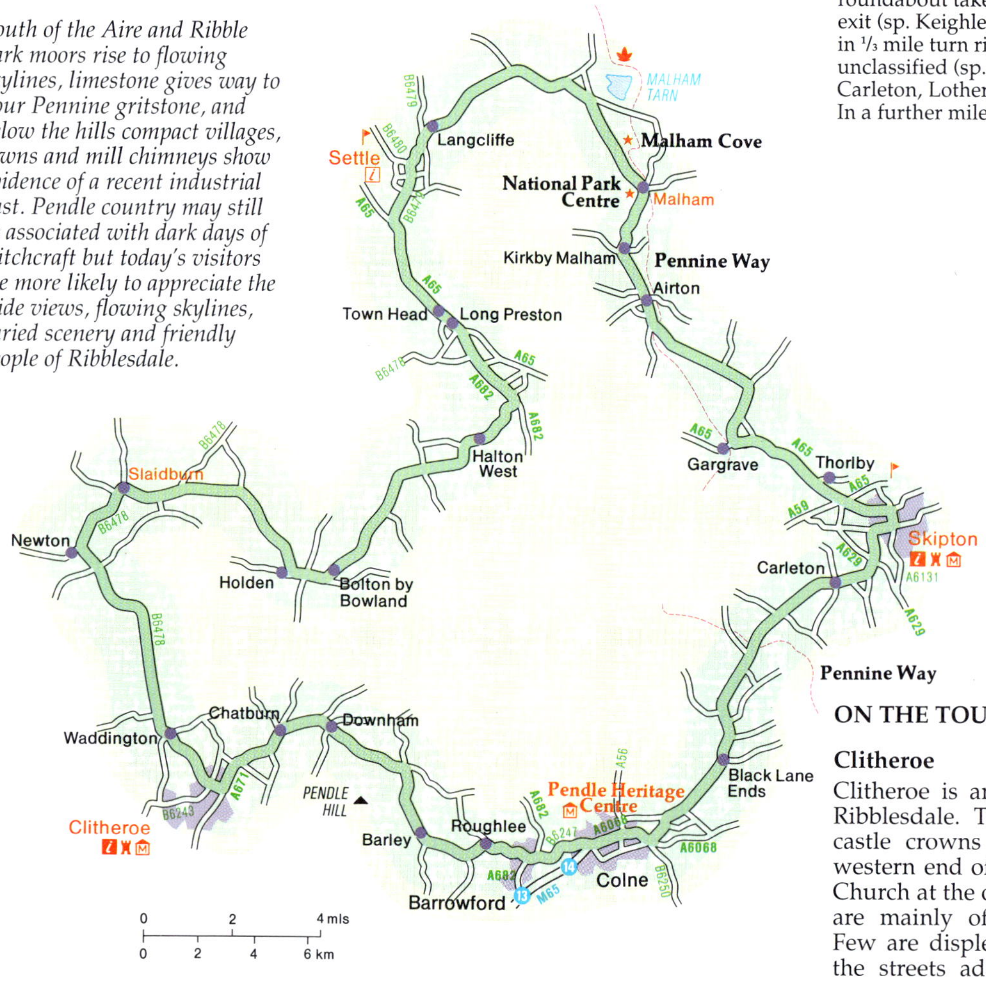

ON THE TOUR

Clitheroe

Clitheroe is an ancient town at the heart of Ribblesdale. The small keep of its Norman castle crowns an isolated rocky hill at the western end of its main street, with St Mary's Church at the other end. Buildings in the town are mainly of stone, and modest in scale. Few are displeasing, and changes in level of the streets adds to the interest. Shops and inns give friendly service; Castle House Museum contains much of interest relating to the town's long history. The market is open on Tuesdays and Saturdays, and there is an excellent Tourist Information

OFF THE TOUR

Browsholme Hall

Take the first turn left after Waddington to see this home of the Parkers, traditional bow-bearers of the Forest of Bowland, who have lived there since 1507. The house contains family portraits, fine furniture, arms and armour, textiles and stained glass. A member of the family shows you round. Opening times are limited.

Embsay Steam Railway

One mile east of Skipton, off the A59, Embsay's station of 1888 now re-lives its past and houses a railway shop and café, with a nearby picnic area. Trains, usually steam-hauled by an industrial tank engine, take passengers on a pleasant 2-mile trip to the rural Holywell Halt.

Earby Mines Museum

1¼ miles past the WT aerials on Elslack Moor, turn right, descending steeply into Earby. The voluntary-run Mines Museum in School Lane, housed in the old grammar school, shows many aspects of 19th-century lead mining: tools, old pictures, working models and a large mineral collection. It is open on Sunday afternoons and Thursday evenings.

Sawley Abbey

Turn right in Chatburn and in 1½ miles turn left off the A59. The meagre ruins of a Cistercian monastery, founded in 1147, show the outline of various buildings, including walls of an unusually small church. Although it was a poor foundation the monks owned extensive sheep farming estates in upper Ribblesdale.

Malham Cove is the focal point of Craven's limestone country; natural beauty mingles with miles of man-made limestone walls

Centre. An old limestone quarry at Salthill now offers an important geology trail, although this is increasingly overshadowed by recent industrial development.

Slaidburn

Scenically enfolded by the Bowland hills, in the upper Hodder Valley, Slaidburn is a gem. Stone cottages line its two streets, cobble-edged. St Andrew's Church has good 18th-century woodwork and the nearby Grammar School bears the date 1717. Church Street and Chapel Street meet by the famous Hark to Bounty Inn, named, apparently, after a foxhound belonging to a 19th-century squarson who often drank there. Outside stairs lead to the Court Room where the Forest of Bowland Courts meet.

Slaidburn, unspoilt at the heart of Bowland

Settle

This lively market town in upper Ribblesdale is full of fascinating corners. Dated houses, inns and shops illustrate its importance in the 17th and 18th centuries. Local crafts proliferate in stalls and family-owned shops in this small, compact, friendly town which has been faithful to its past. Modernity does not impinge, and a short stroll round Settle still reveals its old yards, squares, small workshops, and the extravaganza of its grandest house, The Folly, with the towering Castlebergh Rock (well worth a climb) above. The famous Leeds to Carlisle railway passes through the town.

Malham

Limestone scenery achieves high drama at Malham, where the Cove, reached by an easy footpath, is a huge cliff nearly 300ft high, surmounted by a superb 'pavement'. Gordale Scar, a mile east, is an impressive gorge. Field and riverside walks abound, and the National Park Information Centre, with a large car park, is well worth visiting. A chuckling beck graces the village, whose sloping green is dominated by the Lister Arms of 1723. Limestone cottages, farms and barns sustain architectural interest.

Skipton

Many trunk roads meet and cross at Skipton adding to its market importance, with four market days each week. It developed as a Norman castle-town. Lady Anne Clifford restored the castle in the 17th century and it is now one of the best-preserved medieval castles. The parish church adjoining looks down the busy High Street, where yards leading off each side had terraces along them formerly, housing workers at the 19th-century cotton-spinning mill. The Leeds to Liverpool Canal had earlier brought more industry and prosperity, but is now used as a leisure waterway. Excellent shops, inns and hotels, and its situation as the southern gateway to the Dales, add to Skipton's popularity.

Pendle Heritage Centre

Occupying the 17th-century home of the Bannister family, this emphasizes the architectural heritage and textile history of the area. Displays of all aspects of Pendle life are being amassed, including regional farming. Even the Pendle witches are not overlooked! A walled garden has been planted in 18th-century fashion, and across the road an early 19th-century tollhouse has been admirably restored. There is a shop, picnic area, guided tours, and study courses are offered.

OUTDOOR ACTIVITIES

Pennine Way

Britain's first long-distance footpath passes northwards through the Yorkshire Dales on its 250-mile journey from Derbyshire to the Scottish border. Between Gargrave and Malham - both good access points - it follows parkland and riverside paths giving very pleasant walking; far more tranquil than most of its route.

The Ribble Way

This recently-designated middle-distance footpath (70 miles) follows the valley of the Ribble from its wild source at Ribble Head to the sea at Longton, near Preston. Good access points all along its route enable it to be sampled in short sections.

Malham Tarn

Minor roads running north from Malham pass south of Malham Tarn (NT). The Pennine Way footpath runs past the eastern and northern edges of this important Nature Reserve where there is a nature trail. Malham Tarn House is used as a Field Studies Centre.

Barley Picnic Site

Adjoining the road, this is a good base from which to walk the many footpaths all around, linking Barley to neighbouring villages and hamlets. Pendle Hill offers a challenging climb; and the Information Centre at the picnic site has other suggestions for local exploration in this area of the Lancashire witches.

VALE OF YORK, HAREWOOD & FOUNTAINS ABBEY

56 miles

Three lovely rivers - the Ure, Nidd and Wharfe - reach maturity in the fertile Vale of York. Historic towns and castles, majestic monastic ruins, and great houses amid gracious parklands make their own contribution to this favoured countryside with the spa town of Harrogate at its heart.

From the Vale of York the land rises gently westwards reaching over 800ft around Brimham Rocks, where there is heather moorland. Hedged arable fields give way to stone walls, grassy pastures, and brick-built villages and farms of the Vale contrast with their stone counterparts to the west.

Successive generations have left their marks: a Saxon monastery at Ripon, and one which was to achieve greater fame (at nearby Fountains) followed in Norman days. Baronial castles in their turn gave way to stately country houses, parks and gardens, and the north's premier spa developed around mineral springs at Harrogate. Racecourses at Wetherby and Ripon are particular attractions. Throughout, a network of lanes links villages still retaining a hint of timelessness. There, and at many wayside pubs, good food and hospitality can be enjoyed; much of it with a characteristic Yorkshire flavour.

One of England's most palatial homes, Harewood House's rooms by Robert Adams are unrivalled in elegance and style

ROUTE DIRECTIONS

Leave **Harrogate** (map 12SE35) on the A61, Leeds road and after 6 miles cross the River Wharfe and ascend, passing **Harewood House** to reach Harewood. Here, turn left on to the A659 (sp. Wetherby A58) to Collingham. Here, turn left with the A58 then in 1¾ miles, at the roundabout, turn left on to the A661 to enter Wetherby. Cross the river bridge, and turn left with the A661 (sp. Harrogate). Continue to Spofforth. Here, keep forward, unclassified (sp. Follifoot) and pass **Spofforth Castle**. Continue to the village of Follifoot and turn right on to the Knaresborough road. In a further mile turn left on to the A661, turn right on to the B6163. Cross the river bridge and ascend to **Knaresborough**. At the traffic signals turn left (sp. Town Centre). At the end of the main street, at the traffic signals, turn right and leave by the A6055, Boroughbridge road. After 6 miles reach Minskip. Beyond the village cross the A1 and, at the roundabout, turn right. Then, turn left, unclassified, to enter Aldborough (see page 187). Pass the village maypole and shortly keep left. Enter Boroughbridge (see page 187) and join the B6265. Follow the signs North, through the town, and at the end of main street turn right and cross the river bridge. At the roundabout, take 1st exit (sp. Ripon). In nearly ¼ mile turn left again, unclassified (sp. Skelton). At Skelton-on-Ure turn right (sp. Ripon). Continue with the Ripon road and after 2¼ miles turn left on to the B6265. Re-cross the River Ure and then enter **Ripon**. Here, follow the signs to Pateley Bridge to leave by the B6265 and in 1½ miles turn left, unclassified (sp. Fountain's Abbey). Enter Studley Roger, and continue to the **Studley Royal Country Park and Fountain's Abbey**. Return to Studley Roger, turn left to re-join the B6265 Pateley Bridge road and in another 1½ miles turn left, unclassified (sp. Fountain's Abbey). In 1¼ miles, at the west entrance to Fountain's Abbey, turn right and cross the River Skell. Continue (sp. Harrogate) and in 2¾ miles, at the T-junction, turn left. In a further 2¾ miles turn left on to the B6165 then, at the roundabout, take 3rd exit, unclassified, to enter **Ripley**. At the end of the village turn right on to the A61 and return via Killinghall to Harrogate.

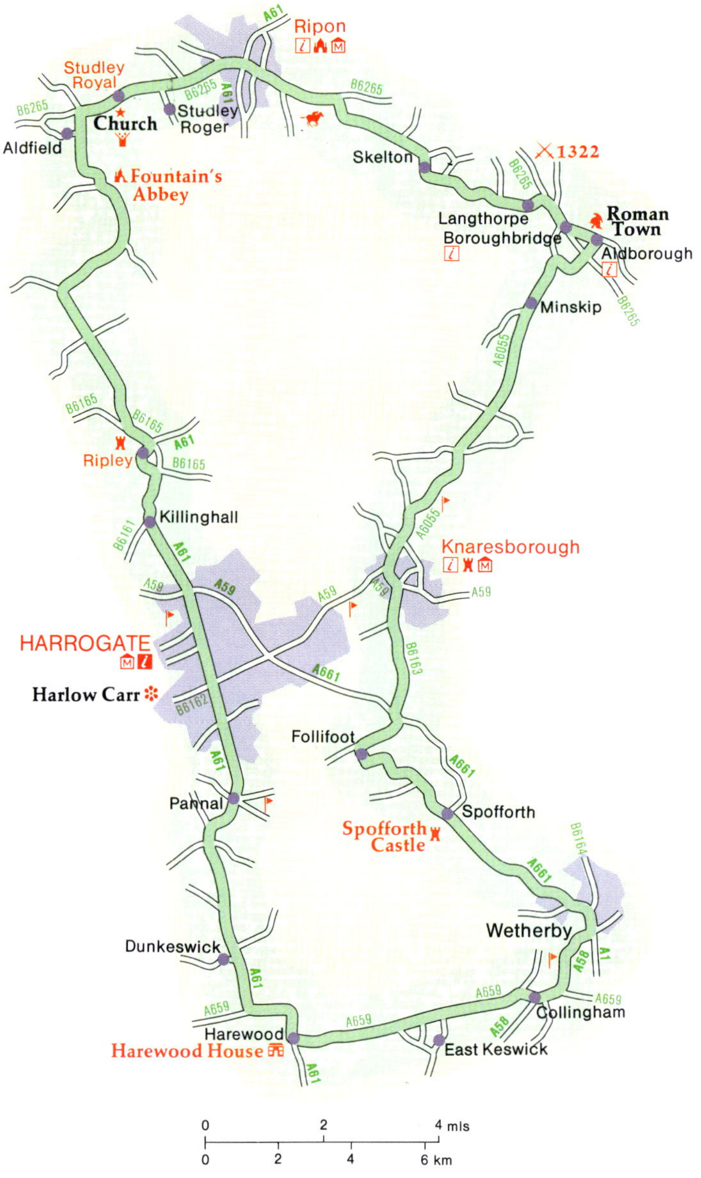

ON THE TOUR

Harrogate

About 400 years ago the medicinal properties of the waters bubbling from 88 different springs were beginning to be realised. During the 17th and 18th centuries increasing numbers of travellers came and drank or bathed in the waters, but Harrogate's growth accelerated from the middle of last century to reach a climax early this century, and it is predominantly a late Victorian and Edwardian town. Today it is many things rolled into one: a spa and health resort, a very fashionable shopping and residential town, and, with its marvellous Valley Gardens and unique Stray - 200 acres of open grassland – a floral resort. Excellent hotels and restaurants, together with large exhibition and meeting halls, contribute to its popularity as a cultural and conference centre.

Harewood House

Yorkshire's greatest architect, John Carr, designed Harewood House for Edwin Lascelles, and saw its completion in 1771. In 1843 Sir Charles Barry made additions. Robert Adam's elegant interiors contain fine ceilings, plasterwork and Chippendale furniture, English and Italian paintings and Sèvres and Chinese porcelain. Landscaped grounds include lakeside and woodland walks and the new tropical houses produce a rain-forest atmosphere and display threatened tropical birds and plants. There is also a bird garden and adventure playground. Harewood village has terraces of stately houses, in dark stone, also designed by Carr; all very formal.

Spofforth Castle

Ruins of the great hall and solar wing of the Percy's early 14th-century home suggest that it was more a fortified house than a fully defensive castle and, unusually, was shaped like a parallelogram.

Knaresborough

This ancient, historic town is an English rarity; occupying a hillside site overlooking a river. Georgian houses and pantile-roofed cottages line narrow streets, and steep steps lead down to the Nidd, dominated by a proud viaduct. The 14th-century castle ruins crown a cliff-top near the market place. This is a good 'walkabout' town with a variety of shops, inns and restaurants, a good museum, boats on the river, and the famous Dropping Well - where a curious assortment of everyday objects have been petrified by lime-rich water. The legendary Mother Shipton, a 16th-century prophetess, lived in a nearby cave. Her prophecy of the world ending in 1981 casts doubts on her reliability!

Ripon

The medieval minster became a cathedral in 1836. Beneath its central tower is the remarkable crypt of St Wildred's 7th-century cathedral, one of England's earliest Christian survivals, now housing the cathedral treasury. Narrow streets, and their names, recall the city's ancient origins. At the foot of the tall obelisk dominating a large market place the Ripon Hornblower sounds his forest horn at 9pm each evening. The Prison and Police Museum in St Marygate illustrates the twin themes of law and order.

Studley Royal & Fountains Abbey

The impressive ruins of Britain's largest Cistercian monastery, founded 1132, form a superb, dramatic climax to the great 18th-century landscape gardens of Studley Royal; with their woodlands, vistas, lakes, temples and follies, the creation of John Aislabie and his son William. To appreciate the abbey as the climax, approach from Studley Royal and walk through the gardens. From the western car park the abbey commands attention, but the great gardens are ignored. The Elizabethan mansion of Fountains Hall was built of stone from the ruins *c.*1610, and is open. Herds of deer roam the park, and St Mary's Church is a High Victorian masterpiece by William Burges.

Ripley

A vaguely continental air pervades this village of dark stone houses aligned on two streets, shaped like a T, with the market cross and stocks at their broad intersection. An early Victorian lord of the manor modelled it on the lines of a typical French village, even calling its largest building Hotel de Ville. Ingilbys still live at Ripley in the part-medieval, part-18th-century castle west of the square. Lavishly decorated rooms look out to the lakes and woods of Ripley Park.

OUTDOOR ACTIVITIES

Brimham Rocks

From Fountains Abbey return to B6265 and head west for 4 miles before turning left on a minor road. In an area of open heather moorland, with bracken and silver birches, 50 acres of fantastically-shaped rock formations form a natural adventure wonderland. Weathering has sculptured huge masses of Millstone Grit into weird shapes, many given appropriate names by Victorians who thronged here - Idol, Anvil, Dancing Bear. Children and adults enjoy the challenge of scrambling on the hard, gritty outcrops with superb views west to upper Nidderdale. There is a good Information Centre and shop.

The haunting ruins of Fountains Abbey – once an impressive edifice paid for by the monks who amassed their wealth from wool

Montpellier Parade, one of Harrogate's many pleasant shop-lined streets, still retains its smart, old-fashioned atmosphere

OFF THE TOUR

Harlow Car Garden

Lying just off the B6162 Beckwithshaw road a mile west of the centre of Harrogate, the Northern Horticultural Society's show and trial gardens at Harlow Car cover about 60 acres of formerly marginal land, 450-500ft above sea-level. This display ground for northern gardeners offers ideal opportunities for seeing ordinary plants growing in ordinary conditions. It succeeds in combining a public garden's planning and freedom with the intimacy and friendly welcome of a private garden, where every season brings its own joys.

Newby Hall

Newby Hall is a family home standing between Boroughbridge and Ripon, south of the B6265. Begun in 1705, but largely completed between 1767 and 1780 by Robert Adam, it shows some of his finest interiors. Designed to display antique sculpture these rooms also include much exquisite Chippendale furniture. There is also the unique Gobelin's Tapestry Room. The 25 acres of gardens contain many rare and beautiful plants, and, specially for children, there is a woodland discovery walk, adventure gardens, a riverside railway and a steamboat on Sundays, making something for all the family.

VALE OF YORK AND HOWARDIAN HILLS

71 miles

Taking their name from that of the landowners whose great mansion dominates one of Yorkshire's fairest countrysides, these low hills

form a gracious landscape, sloping gently south and west to the Vale of York, liberally sprinkled with neat villages, and a few market towns.

These are contrasting landscapes. Slow, winding streams drain into the broad, sluggish River Ouse, so-named only below Aldwark Toll Bridge. Fertile arable land, with shelterbelts, hedgerow trees but few woodlands, breaking a level skyline. Small, compact villages of mellow brick cottages have histories going back to centuries before the Conquest, and there are few great estates.

Yet the undulating hills, measuring little more than 15 miles from east to west, and five from north to south, formed of shelly (well-drained limestone) have something of a Cotswold character. The 17th- and 18th-century landowners favoured them; built great houses, created huge parks, and rebuilt for their tenants many 'estate' villages. Mature woodlands add sylvan maturity contrasting, towards the west, with darker plantations of the Forestry Commission.

The towers of the great Minster are visible from the southern part of the hills and from the vale, so visually, architecturally and historically, York is the dominant focus and the place from which all main roads radiate.

ON THE TOUR

York

York is simply the most historic and fascinating of English provincial cities. There are plenty of car parks outside its walls, but within them it must be explored on foot.

Since the Romans, all newcomers to York have left their mark, but the medieval character predominates; centred on the great Minster, seen in 15th-century churches, guildhalls, and streets such as Stonegate, Petergate, Goodramgate and the Shambles. York's walls are the longest in Britain, almost a 3-mile circuit above the streets and houses, with the north-eastern sector perhaps the best. Four great bars or gateways, with other openings, breach the walls.

Castle Museum, first and still the best of our folk museums, is unique. The Treasurer's House (NT) and Fairfax House, show superb 18th-century elegance, St Mary's Abbey ruins evoke a different calm. Inns, good restaurants and interesting shops abound.

Sutton Park

This early Georgian house contains fine English and French furniture, paintings and porcelain. Capability Brown designed the extensive parkland, which has an ice house, woodland walks and a nature trail.

Sheriff Hutton

Ruins of the Neville's 14th-century castle, open Monday to Friday, stand slightly aloof from the large village. A mile to the south-east Sheriff Hutton Park has surviving oak from the old forest of Galtres, with walks, picnic areas, and statuary.

Ancient half-timbered shops and inns overhang the cobblestones of The Shambles in York

Castle Howard

Vanbrugh, with help from Hawksmoor, designed this enormous Baroque mansion for the third Earl of Carlisle, 1700-1730. Breathtakingly beautiful in appearance and landscaped setting, its palatial interior has rooms filled with collections of statuary, furniture and pictures, and the Costume Galleries covering fashions from the 18th to 20th centuries have displays changed each year. Park and grounds have nature walks, temples, a mausoleum, a rose garden and a children's adventure area. The televising of *Brideshead Revisited* brought additional fame.

Hovingham

An irregular green has a short avenue of lime trees leading to the entrance to Hovingham Hall, via the Riding School. This, and the

OFF THE TOUR

Nunnington Hall

Keep straight ahead, north of Hovingham, at the sharp bend on B1257, for Nunnington. The mainly late 17th-century manor house by the River Rye has beautifully panelled rooms, with tapestries and china.

Byland Abbey

At Oswaldkirk continue along the minor road past Ampleforth to Byland Abbey. In a glorious setting, extensive ruins of this 12th-century Cistercian monastery, with the very distinctive west front, still retain sections of medieval floors, with yellow and green glazed tiles.

Beningbrough Hall

Approached through its parkland from Newton-on-Ouse, this early 18th-century house of warm red brick has a dramatic interior based on axial corridors, handsome state rooms and elaborate woodwork. A major exhibition of portraits from the National Portrait Gallery is shown in the principal rooms. The stable block, bell-tower and Victorian laundry have displays illustrating domestic life there last century.

ROUTE DIRECTIONS

Leave **York** (map 13SE65) via the Inner Ring Road on the north side of the city centre and follow signs Helmesley to leave on the B1363. Continue to Sutton-on-the-Forest and, at the trunk road, turn right and pass the entrance to **Sutton Park**. At the end of the village turn left (sp. Helmesley) and continue to Stillington. At the trunk road turn right, then near the end of the village turn right, unclassified (sp. Sheriff Hutton) to Farlington. Continue to the edge of **Sheriff Hutton** and go over the crossroads (sp. Bulmer). In 2½ miles descend, then ascend (1 in 6) to Bulmer. In 1 mile, at the crossroads, turn left (sp. Castle Howard) and, at the gateways, go forward through the grounds of **Castle Howard**. At the Obelisk go forward, passing the entrance to the house on the right, and continue to the edge of Slingsby. Here, turn left on to the B1257 (sp. Helmesley) to **Hovingham**. Continue to Stonegrave then in 2¼ miles turn left on to the B1363 (sp. York) and descend to the edge of Oswaldkirk. Keep left to **Gilling East** and in 4 miles descend (1 in 7) to Brandsby. Near the end of the village turn right, unclassified (sp. Crayke) to Crayke. Here, turn right (sp. Easingwold) and in 2 miles keep left (sp. Market Place) into Easingwold. Join the one-way traffic and, at the trunk road, turn right on to the A19 (no sign). At the end of the main street, at the crossroads, turn left, unclassified (sp. Boroughbridge) to Raskelf. Keep left to the edge of Brafferton and, at the Oak Tree, turn right (sp. Boroughbridge). In 1 mile cross the River Swale and turn left. In 2½ miles keep left then bear right and in another mile, at the trunk road, turn left. At the roundabout take 1st exit on to the B6265 and cross the river bridge into Boroughbridge. Here, turn left (sp. York) and shortly left through the Market Place. Pass **The Devil's Arrows** on the right and the road to **Aldborough** on the left and in 3 miles turn left, unclassified, for Great Ouseburn. In a further ½ mile turn left for Aldwark Toll Bridge. Cross the River Ure and shortly turn right (sp. Linton Newton-on-Ouse) for Linton-on-Ouse, then Newton-on-Ouse. Keep left (sp. Shipton, York) and in 1½ miles at the trunk road, turn right. In 2 miles further cross the railway bridge and turn right again on to the A19. At the edge of Skelton, at the roundabout, go forward to return to York.

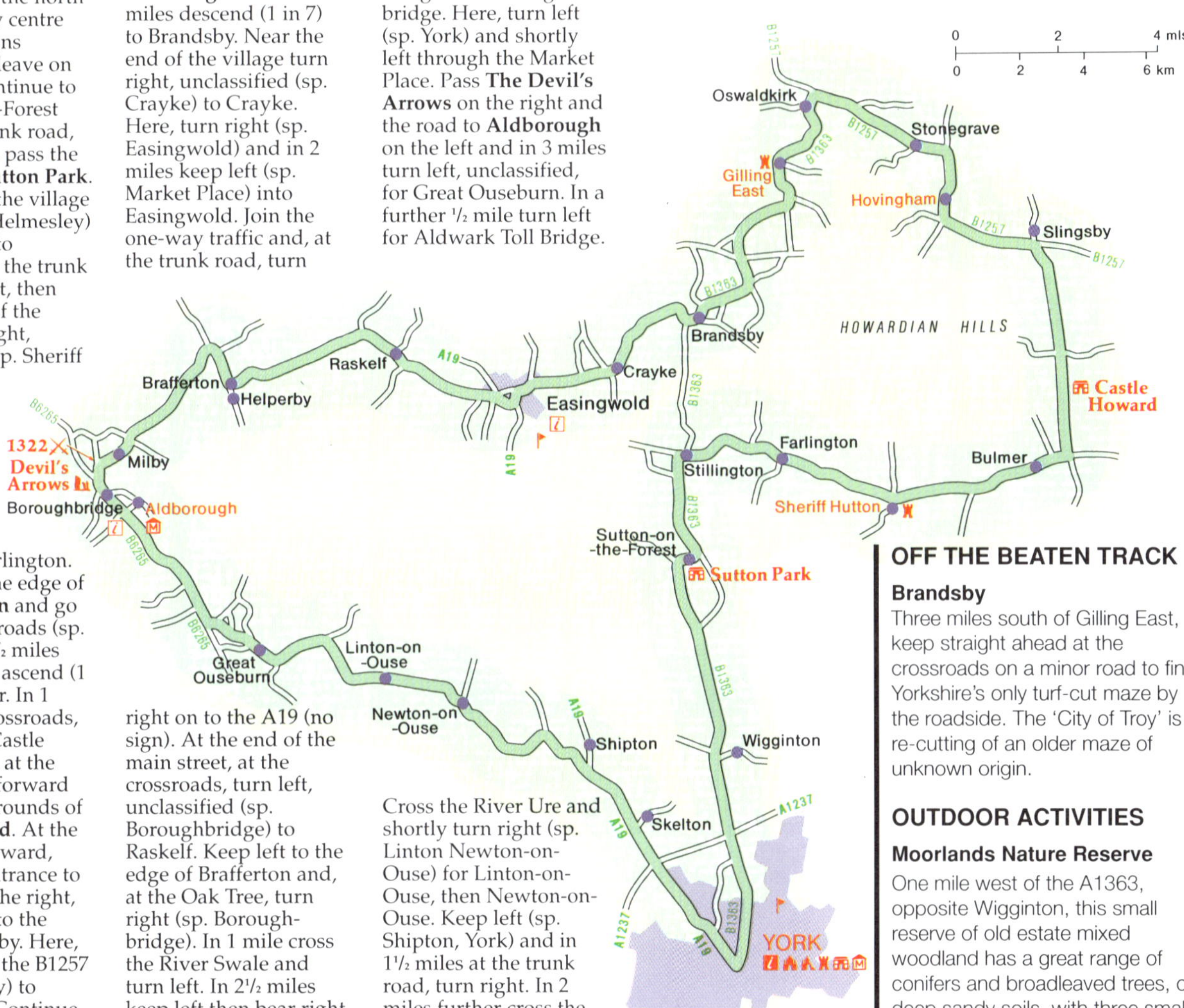

OFF THE BEATEN TRACK

Brandsby

Three miles south of Gilling East, keep straight ahead at the crossroads on a minor road to find Yorkshire's only turf-cut maze by the roadside. The 'City of Troy' is a re-cutting of an older maze of unknown origin.

OUTDOOR ACTIVITIES

Moorlands Nature Reserve

One mile west of the A1363, opposite Wigginton, this small reserve of old estate mixed woodland has a great range of conifers and broadleaved trees, on deep sandy soils, with three small pools. Daffodils, narcissi, azaleas and rhododendrons make a fine display in spring and summer.

house, are open only to booked groups. The attractive village of estate housing is largely focussed on the popular Worsley Arms. To the north, stream-side cottages make a pleasant group beyond the church.

Gilling East

Gilling Castle, west of the B1363, is used as a preparatory school for younger boys at nearby Ampleforth. Buildings round three sides of a courtyard date from the Fairfax occupancy 1492-1793. Only two rooms are open, on weekdays. The Elizabethan Great Chamber has glorious woodwork, with a menagerie of animal carvings, figures of squires and ladies, and over 370 coats of arms.

The Devil's Arrows

In an arable field west of Boroughbridge and uncomfortably close to the A1, three prehistoric monoliths stand in a straight alignment about 570ft long. Respectively 18, 20 and 22ft tall, they are of the Bronze Age.

Aldborough

The village, east of Boroughbridge, largely occupies the site of a Brigantian capital and Roman town. Parts of a Roman town wall and two mosaic pavements can be seen *in situ*, and a good museum displays major finds and features.

Castle Howard's art treasures and superb grounds are world renowned

HEARTLAND OF THE WOLDS

49 miles

Historic Beverley is the south-eastern gateway to Britain's most northerly area of chalk country, where broad, sweeping Wolds are broken only by secretive, green, dry valleys. Hedged roads and lanes link the few, scattered villages in ordered landscapes of the 18th century.

Rising gently from east to west, reaching over 600ft near Huggate and Sledmere, the Wolds were formerly one vast sheep-walk. Between about 1730 and 1810 enclosures were made, usually by hawthorn hedges, and arable crops replaced thousands of sheep-grazed acres. At the same time landowners enclosed and developed their estates, planted shelter-belts and woodlands, added hedgerow trees and rebuilt their houses. They created new landscaped parks and were instrumental in providing new roads. Many farms were rebuilt at the centre of their newly-enclosed fields, away from the villages. In the 19th century successive members of the Sykes family of Sledmere rebuilt village churches on their estates. Although Market Weighton became a locally important little town, Beverley's historic roots are deeper, so it claims pride of place, historically and architecturally. Now by-passed, it ranks as one of the most gracious of English country towns.

A solitary gatepost is a poignant reminder of once-great Londesborough

ON THE TOUR

Beverley

Only one of the town's former five gateways survives. The decorative brickwork of North Bar, built in 1409, is the most satisfying approach to this attractive, historic town - proud possessor of two of England's finest churches. Beverley Minster, at the south-eastern edge, became a parish church in Elizabeth I's reign, and has the size, dignity and splendour of a cathedral. St Mary's, another parish church just north of the town centre, though smaller, is a superb example of Gothic architecture.

Fine shops, many with Georgian fronts, grace the centre of Beverley, lining the larger of its market places, Saturday Market, which has a handsome Market Cross of 1714, with columns and a fanciful roof. Leading from the centre are medieval streets dignified by Georgian buildings, houses, inns and hotels. The small, triangular Wednesday Market is a quiet contrast to its larger counterpart, and beyond it terraces of Georgian brick houses lead to the Minster.

Good restaurants and pubs abound, and the Museum of Army Transport appeals particularly to children, with vehicles you can get in as well as admire from a distance.

Bishop Burton

Embowered in trees, graced with a large green and two ponds with well-fed ducks, stately beeches, chestnuts and sycamores, and groups of attractive brick or half-timbered cottages, Bishop Burton is a gem of a village. By the main road the famous 'Altisidora' pub is named after a local racehorse which won the St Leger in 1813. Two centuries ago John Wesley preached on the village green, and a carved wooden bust of him is in the parish church. Since 1965 an open-air service is held on the green on a Sunday in late July; music is usually provided by a splendid fairground organ.

Market Weighton

An unpretentious but typical small market town with some attractive corners, particularly north of the main road and behind the church, one of whose many monuments commemorates William Bradley who died 1820 aged 33. Measuring 7ft 9ins tall and weighing 27 stones he made a fortune in the show-business world of fairground freaks.

Londesborough

The third Earl of Burlington, a famous architect and friend of writers and artists, laid out the park in the early 18th century, but the Hall was demolished in 1819. George Hudson the 'railway king' bought the estate in 1845, but lost it four years later when his financial empire collapsed. Gone, too, is his private

station near Shiptonthorpe, but the parkland survives, and the Wolds Way footpath passes through it.

Nunburnholme

This straggling village along a chalk stream has white-painted brick cottages with pantiled roofs, a tiny church with a fine Saxon cross, and a feeling of great quiet. The Reverend Francis Morris was rector from 1854-93 and wrote his famous six-volume *History of British Birds* here.

Sledmere

The vast Sykes estates spread across the Wolds around Sledmere, where successive baronets have cared for and improved their land since the mid-18th century. The present elegant house dates largely from the late 18th and early 19th centuries. Memorials in the church and village commemorate members of the family. The 'Wagoners Memorial' on the green is beautiful and unique, while to the south a 120ft-high tower which dominates the Wolds sky-line is the tenants' memorial of 1865 to the legendary Sir Tatton Sykes, lover of racing and breeder of racehorses.

Beverley Minster, although just a parish church, has all the pomp and splendour of a major cathedral

OFF THE TOUR

Goodmanham

Goodmanham village, reached by a minor road north of Market Weighton, was an early site of Christianity in northern England. In 627 King Edwin and his pagan high priest Coifi were here converted to the Christian faith by the missionary Paulinus. The squat, Norman church, with a superb font of *c*.1533, supposedly stands on a former pagan temple site.

Burnby Hall Gardens

At Pocklington, 3 miles from Nunburnholme, these attractive gardens contain small lakes with 50 varieties of water-lilies, totalling 5,000 plants, and are richly stocked with fish.

Driffield

By staying on the A166 at Garton-on-the-Wolds, it is a short detour to Great Driffield which became an important market town because of the arrival in 1772 of the Driffield Navigation - a 5-mile link to the navigable River Hull. The waterway no longer operates; the head of the canal is a landscaped waterside open space with warehouses converted into flats.

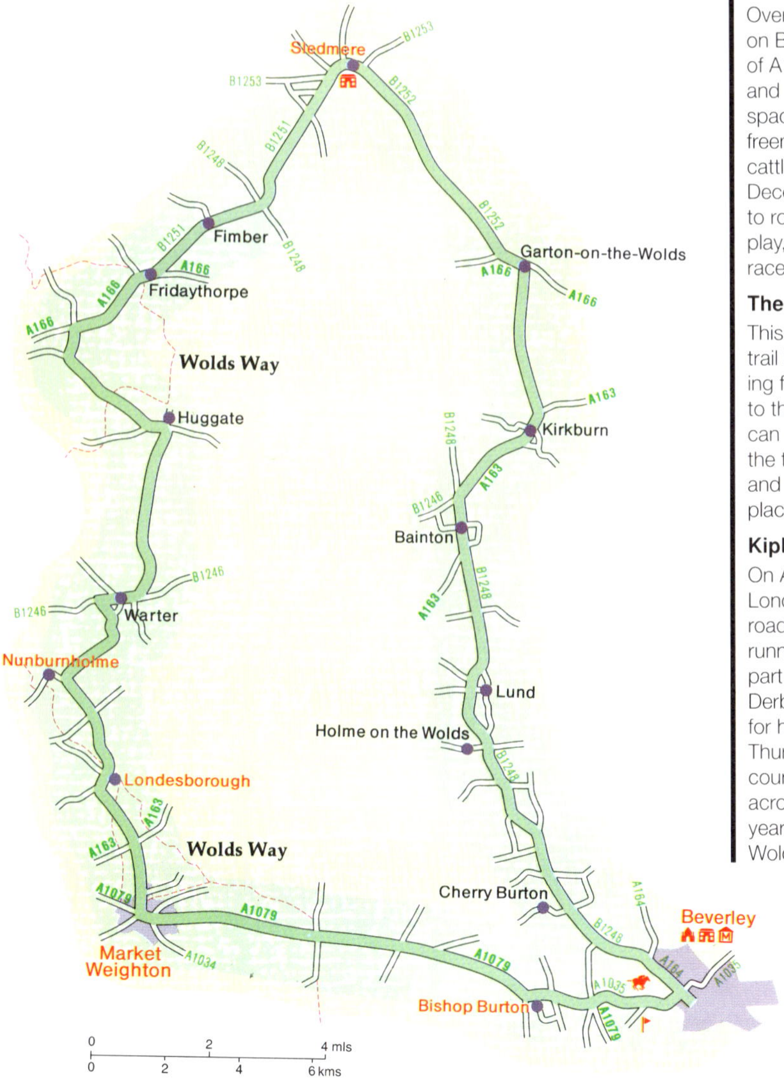

ROUTE DIRECTIONS

Leave **Beverley** (map 13TA03) by following the signs York (A1079) and in $1\frac{3}{4}$ miles, at the roundabout, take 3rd exit A1079 for **Bishop Burton**. Continue to **Market Weighton** and, at the near end of the main street, turn right unclassified (sp. Duffield) into Londesborough Road. In $1\frac{1}{4}$ miles, at the roundabout, keep forward (sp. Londesborough), then in $1\frac{1}{4}$ miles further, at the trunk road, turn right for the edge of **Londesborough**. Go over the crossroads (sp. Nunburnholme) and in $1\frac{1}{4}$ miles, at the crossroads, go forward. Descend to the outskirts of **Nunburnholme** and by the nearside of the village turn right (sp. Warter). In $1\frac{2}{3}$ miles turn right (sp. Huggate) into Warter. Here, turn right on to the B1246 (sp. Driffield) and shortly turn left, unclassified (sp. Huggate). At the edge of Huggate turn left (sp. Millington) then in $\frac{1}{3}$ mile turn right (sp. Fridaythorpe). In $1\frac{2}{3}$ miles turn right, then in $\frac{1}{2}$ mile turn right again on to the A166 (sp. Bridlington) for Fridaythorpe. At the end of the village, turn left on to the B1251 (sp. Bridlington, scenic route) to Fimber. In $\frac{3}{4}$ mile, at the roundabout, take 2nd exit to **Sledmere**. At the end of the village go forward on to the B1252 (sp. Driffield). Pass Sir Tatton Sykes Monument and in $1\frac{2}{3}$ miles turn left on to the A166 into Garton-on-the-Wolds. Here, turn right, unclassified (sp. Kirkburn) and in $2\frac{1}{2}$ miles, at the trunk road, turn right on to the A163 (sp. Market Weighton) for the edge of Kirkburn. In $1\frac{2}{3}$ miles, at the roundabout, turn left to Bainton. At the far end branch left on to the B1248 (sp. Beverley) and 9 miles further, at the roundabout, take 2nd exit A164 and return to Beverley.

OFF THE BEATEN TRACK

Wharram Percy

At the roundabout past Fimber turn left on B1248 and in 4 miles left again on a minor road for Wharram Percy Deserted Medieval Village (EH). A short walk leads to the earthworks and ruined church of the former settlement, where continued, and meticulous excavations have revealed the complex and changing history of a small village, from Saxon times until the 15th century. The church continued in use, by people of neighbouring Thixendale, until 1870.

OUTDOOR ACTIVITIES

Beverley Pastures

Over 1,000 acres of open pastures on Beverley's western edge, south of A1079, given between the 12th and 14th centuries, are an open-space asset to the town, whose freemen have grazing rights for cattle and sheep from May to December. Walkers enjoy freedom to roam, children to romp and play, and there is a golf course and racecourse.

The Wolds Way

This officially-designed national trail is a 79-mile footpath stretching from the Humber west of Hull to the North Sea coast at Filey. It can be joined at several points on the tour, Londesborough, Huggate and Fridaythorpe being good places to choose.

Kiplingcotes Racecourse

On A163 north-east of Londesborough, and opposite the road to Warter, a grassy track running south-eastwards forms part of the course of Kiplingcotes Derby; the oldest known flat-race for horses, held on the third Thursday in March, over a 4-mile course, mainly a rough track across fields. For the rest of the year the track offers pleasant Wolds walking.

NORTH YORK MOORS

54 miles

Vast areas of heather moorland extend northwards from the Vale of Pickering to the Esk Valley, broken only by steep-sided valleys.

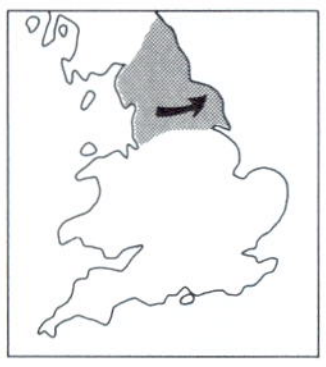

Afforestation darkens much of the southern parts, and attractive stone villages in the dales have character and special appeal.

The central moors form an upland plateau reaching 1,400 ft between Castleton, in Eskdale, and the southern-facing valleys of Rosedale and Farndale. No roads follow the east-west watershed, and, apart from A169 Pickering-Whitby, only a few minor ones cross it from north to south. Treeless moorland ridges extend to far horizons, but below them bright greens of new grass lighten the sheltered valleys, ripening to hay in summer months. Sheep voices, curlew-call and the rasp of grouse are characteristic sounds of the moors; timeless, but relieving the sense of isolation.

Prehistoric sites litter the moors. Later settlers favoured the dales, and Eskdale's string of villages are linked more conveniently by railway than by roads. Castle-towns like Pickering and Helmsley are the natural southern gateways to the 553 square miles of the North York Moors National Park, whose logo shows, appropriately, the best-known of the many stone crosses so characteristic of this beautiful area.

ON THE TOUR

Pickering

Pickering is an attractive market town whose sloping market place has a lively street market every Monday, on the site of which was the village green. The church is famous for its remarkably complete series of 15th-century wall paintings, vividly depicting biblical and historic events. Most English kings visited Pickering Castle between 100 and 1400 to hunt in the former forest nearby, and the ruins include an impressive keep, curtain walls and towers.

The Beck Isle Museum, once the home of William Marshall, agricultural pioneer, now houses a display depicting local history and folk life. Pickering is the southern terminus of the North Yorkshire Moors Railway, one of the longest private railways in the country, operating steam and diesel services throughout the season. (See Grosmont entry).

Goathland

Sheep graze the greens of this bracing moorland village, with its station on the Moors Railway. Many varied walks nearby, include a woodland one to the waterfall of Mallyan Spout, while the charming hamlet of Beckhole has two quoits pitches, and Birch Hall Inn has a sign painted by an accomplished Victorian artist, Sir Algernon Newton.

Grosmont

This former industrial Esk Valley village is the northern terminus of the North Yorkshire Moors Railway, whose locomotive sheds are reached by a short walk which passes through the short tunnel on George Stephenson's original line of 1836.

Glaisdale

Near the road and railway bridges spanning the Esk at Glaisdale, Beggar's Bridge is a narrow, graceful arch believed to date from 1619 and built by a Thomas Ferries, poor son of a sheep-farmer. He loved the daughter of a wealthy landowner, who would not allow the marriage unless Thomas became rich. He went to sea, acquired riches in the West Indies, returned to claim his bride. It is said he built the bridge as a memorial to her after her death in 1618. On earlier courting occasions presumably he used stepping stones, or swam!

The Moors Centre

Adapted from a Victorian shooting lodge, The Moors Centre at Danby is the National Park's main visitor centre and provides an ideal introduction to the area. With a picnic meadow, nature trails, activity trails, an adventure playground, various exhibitions and displays, facilities for brass-rubbing, and with miles of waymarked walks nearby, it offers something for everybody - and has a large, free car park.

Rosedale Abbey

Scarcely anything remains of the former nunnery, but there are many more survivals of the industry which turned Rosedale into an ironstone Klondyke from 1865 until 1926. A group of calcining kilns at the top of Chimney Bank stand close to one end of the mineral railway which contoured the dale, and carried the iron ore across the moors, down to Battersby and the main line.

Hutton-le-Hole

Wide greens with a stream down the middle, and stone houses with pink, pantiled roofs, make this the most attractive of the moorland villages. The Ryedale Folk Museum has spacious grounds containing reconstructed examples of various local buildings, including cottages, shops, workshops and farm buildings, as well as a collection of farm implements, tradesmen's tools and domestic articles. The World Merrills Championships (Nine Men's Morris) are held here each summer.

Hutton-le-Hole's spacious village green is divided by a moorland brook and kept in trim by the sheep which roam freely among the cottages

OFF THE TOUR

Dalby Forest Drive

Turn right at the Fox and Rabbit, 4 miles out of Pickering on A169, and in 2 miles turn left to Low Dalby. The Forestry Commission's Dalby Forest Drive (Toll) is a 9-mile scenic drive providing a through route to Hackness in the east. It has several car parking areas, picnic sites, a visitor centre, play areas and forest walks. Particular features include Staindale Lake and Crosscliffe viewpoint. The Bridestones are strangely-eroded rock pillars at the heart of a 625-acre Nature Reserve (NT), reached by an easy walk from Staindale.

Flamingo Land Zoo & Fun Park

South of Pickering, off the A160 Malton road, Flamingo Land Zoo and Fun Park near Kirby Misterton incorporates a large, privately-owned zoo with lions, tigers, elephants, polar bears, dolphins, chimps, and has countless different attractions, outdoors and under cover, with special appeal for children.

This well-preserved stretch of Roman road on the edge of Wheeldale Moor is known as Wade's Causeway. Made from large, flat stones on a bed of gravel, it runs for $1\frac{1}{4}$ miles and measures 16ft across

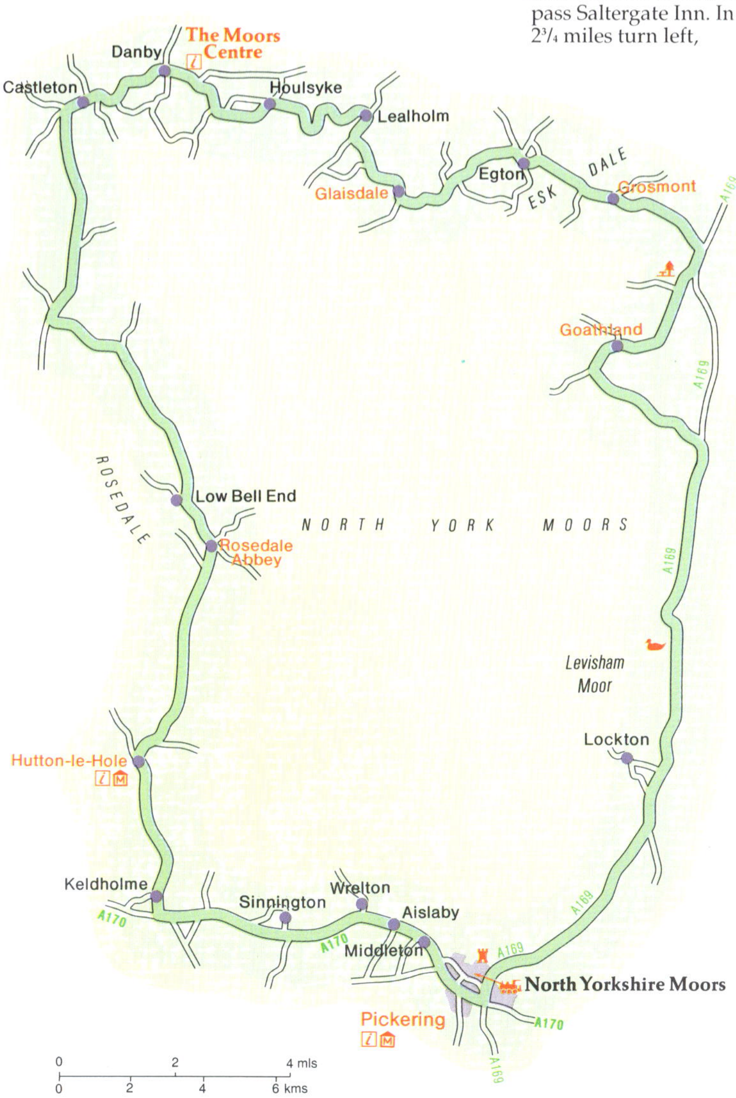

ROUTE DIRECTIONS

Leave **Pickering** (map 13SE78) by following the signs Whitby A169. Pass the Fox and Rabbit Inn on the right then, in $3\frac{1}{2}$ miles, pass the Hole of Horcum on the left and descend (1 in 8) to pass Saltergate Inn. In $2\frac{3}{4}$ miles turn left, unclassified (sp. Goathland). Pass through **Goathland**, cross the railway bridge, and ascend (1 in 4). In $1\frac{2}{3}$ miles, at the trunk road, turn left on to the A169 and take the next turn left, unclassified (sp. Grosmont). Descend (1 in 3) to **Grosmont**, go over the level crossing then in $\frac{1}{3}$ mile cross the River Esk and ascend (1 in 4) to Egton. Bear right at the Wheatsheaf Inn and turn left (sp. Glaisdale) then in $1\frac{2}{3}$ miles descend (1 in 7). Cross the river bridge and ascend through **Glaisdale**. Continue with the Castleton signs and in 1 mile bear right, then in $\frac{2}{3}$ mile, at the trunk road, turn right (sp. Lealholm) to Lealholm. Here, cross the river bridge and turn left (sp. Houlsyke, Danby) for Houlsyke. Pass the **The Moors Centre** and enter Danby. Here, go over the staggered crossroads (sp. Castleton) to Castleton. Follow the signs Rosedale and keep left on ascending. In 4 miles turn left (sp. Rosedale Abbey) and then descend to **Rosedale Abbey**. At the end turn right and ascend Rosedale Chimney Bank (1 in 3). After $3\frac{1}{4}$ miles, at the trunk road, turn right for **Hutton-le-Hole**. Here, turn left (sp. Kirkby Moorside) and in $2\frac{3}{4}$ miles turn left on to the A170 (sp. Scarborough). Continue through Wrelton and Middleton before re-entering Pickering.

OFF THE BEATEN TRACK

Wheeldale Roman Road

At the southern end of Goathland keep right at the Mallyan Spout Hotel, and shortly left to Hunt House where the road ends. From there it is a short walk to an impressive stretch of Roman road on Wheeldale Moor. The uneven appearance is misleading, for the large slabs of surface stone between ditches represent only the foundations for a final gravel layer which has long since been washed away. Some kerb-stones and culverts remain.

Botton Hall

Two miles south of Castleton on the ridge road, a minor road drops steeply left into Danby Dale, passing Botton Hall. This is a centre of a small community operated by the Camphill Village Trust to help the adult mentally handicapped. It has a coffee bar, gift and book shop, a bakery, and creamery products.

Cawthorn Roman Camps

Four miles north of Pickering, between Cropton and Newton-on-Rawcliffe, these marching or training camps, now cleared of trees, can be reached by a short, waymarked walk, and are of speciali archaeological interest.

OUTDOOR ACTIVITIES

Levisham Moor

Over 2,000 miles of Levisham Moor are a nature reserve now owned by the National Park Authority. Reached only by foot-paths from above the remarkable, basin-like Hole of Horcum by A169, or from Levisham village, the reserve has a variety of habitats including heather moor, valleys, oakwoods and streams, with a range of wildlife.

DURHAM AND THE TYNE VALLEY

66 miles

Between the maturing courses of two great northern rivers, the Tyne and the Wear, Durham's countryside shows surprising contrasts, with a mixture of agricultural and former industrial landscapes reflecting rich soils and the mineral wealth of older coal measures, all centred on the historic city at its heart.

Durham Cathedral towers above the tree-filled gorge of the River Wear, and dominates the city

ROUTE DIRECTIONS

Leave **Durham** (map 15NZ24) by following the signs Consett A691 and in $^{1}/_{4}$ mile pass under the railway bridge. In a further $^{1}/_{3}$ mile, at the roundabout, take 2nd main exit on to the B6532 (sp. Sacriston). At the next two roundabouts take 2nd exit and pass under the A167 road bridge to enter Sacriston. Continue forward (sp. Stanley) to Edmondsley and in $^{1}/_{2}$ mile turn right, unclassified (sp. Grange Villa). In a further mile turn right on to the B6313 (no sign) and in $^{1}/_{2}$ mile turn left, unclassified, to Grange Villa, and on to West Pelton. In $^{1}/_{4}$ mile further, at the trunk road, turn left on to the A693 (sp. Stanley) and in $^{1}/_{2}$ mile further turn right, unclassified (sp. Beamish Hall). Reach **Beamish Museum** and pass Eden Place Picnic Area on the left, then in $^{2}/_{3}$ mile, at the trunk road, turn right (no sign). Pass the Causeway, Mill Picnic Area and the Causeway Arch then, at the trunk road, turn right on to the A6076 to reach the edge of Sunniside then, at the trunk road, turn left on to the A692. Pass the Pack Horse then turn right on to the B6310 (sp. Gibside Chapel). In a further $^{1}/_{3}$ mile turn right on to the B6314 (sp. Rowlands Gill). Pass the road to **Gibside Chapel** on the right and cross the River Derwent to Rowlands Gill. Here, at the trunk road, turn left on to the A694 then in $^{1}/_{3}$ mile turn right on to the B6315 for High Spen. Continue to Greenside, turn left (no sign) and descend to Ryton. Here, turn left on to the A695 to Crawcrook and then Prudhoe. Turn right, unclassified (no sign) and pass **Prudhoe Castle** on the right, then in $^{1}/_{3}$ mile go over the level crossing, cross the River Tyne by a narrow bridge to Ovingham. Here, turn left (sp. Hexham) and descend (1 in 7) then, in $^{3}/_{4}$ mile, turn left (sp. Bywell). In $1^{1}/_{2}$ miles turn right to Bywell, then at the crossroads go forward, unclassified (sp. Corbridge). In 3 miles, at the trunk road, turn left on to the B6530 and continue to **Corbridge**. Turn left, follow signs Prudhoe B6321 and cross the River Tyne then, at the roundabout, take 1st exit B6529. In $^{1}/_{2}$ mile further, at the trunk road, turn left on to the A695 to Riding Mill. In $^{2}/_{3}$ mile, at the roundabout, take 3rd exit A68 (sp. Darlington) to reach Kiln Pit Hill. In $4^{3}/_{4}$ miles, cross the River Derwent to Castleside and on to Tow Law. Here, at the trunk road, turn left and in $^{1}/_{2}$ mile go forward on to the B6299 (sp. Willington). Continue to Sunniside and on to Stanley Crook then in $^{3}/_{4}$ mile further turn left, unclassified (sp. Brancepeth). In 3 miles, at the trunk road, turn left on to the A690 (sp. Durham), through **Brancepeth.** At Nevilles Cross, go forward over the crossroads, to re-enter Durham.

To the west the Pennines rise to distant skylines reaching 2,000ft, to the east the sea. County Durham, with which this tour is largely concerned, is rural; most of the older coal-mining and steel-making having either ended, or now concentrated towards the coast, leaving a landscape of pleasant, open views across woodlands and fields. Its roots lie much deeper, in Roman times, while Saxon churches and Norman castles point to the continuity of settlement.

From the Conquest until 1832 Durham was unique, a county palatinate ruled by its Prince Bishops (authorised to exercise almost kingly powers) enacting their own laws, levying their own taxes, raising their own army. Exploitation of mineral wealth, started in medieval times, peaked last century. Old villages grew, new ones arose, and a network of railways was established. Although much of the industry has gone, the Beamish Museum's working recreation of local life around 1900 ensures it is not forgotten, and a few miles away Durham city remains the proud capital of a remarkable county.

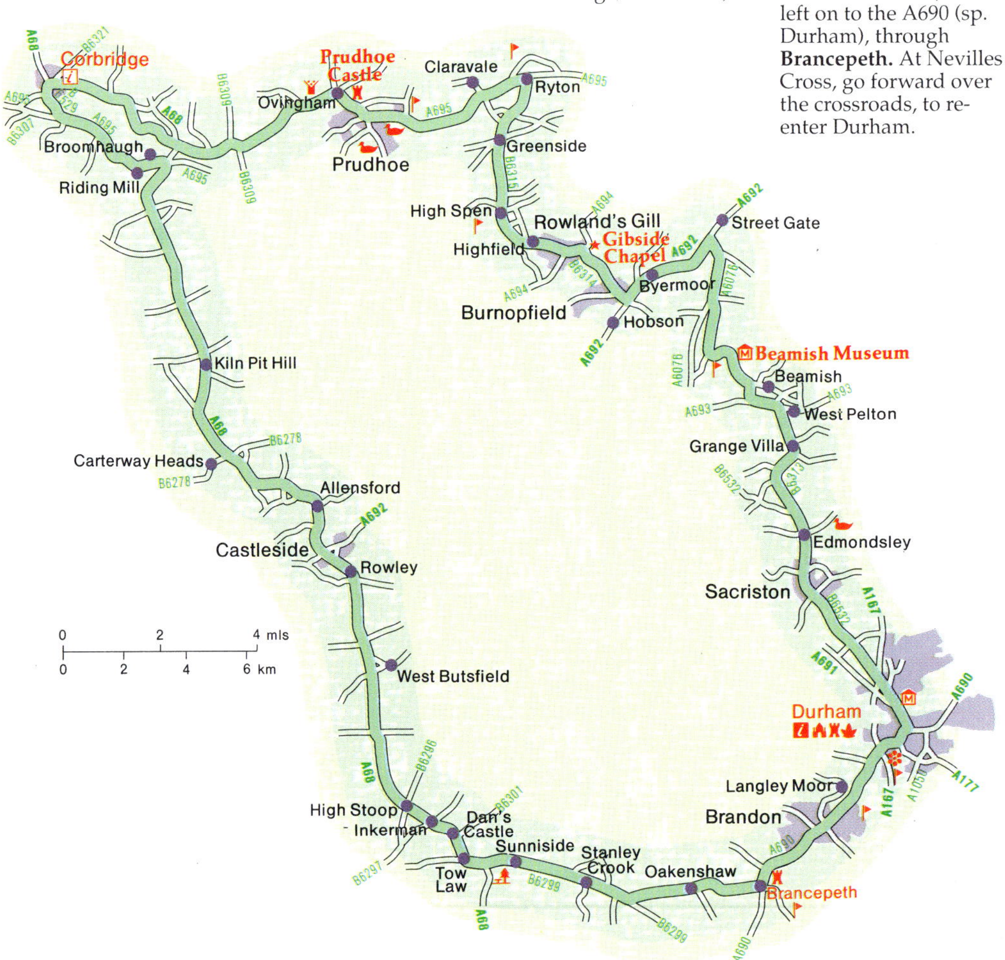

ON THE TOUR

Durham

Traffic is largely excluded from the heart of this small, compact city, occupying a high, rocky, wooded peninsula within a narrow horseshoe loop of the River Wear. The great Norman cathedral and neighbouring Norman castle are now designated a World Heritage Site. Walk the wooded banks on the west to see why. The 18th-century Prebends' Bridge gives the best, most famous, view. The approach to the cathedral via Palace Green is breathtaking. Inside, the Norman majesty is awesome, but the shrine of St Cuthbert and the tomb of Bede, at opposite ends, achieve sublime simplicity.

Most buildings around Palace Green and in North and South Bailey are now used by the University - England's oldest after Oxford and Cambridge. Durham is predominantly a Georgian and Victorian city, the capital of Northumbria and the seat of the Prince Bishops, whose throne is higher than any other in Christendom. Happily escaping the Industrial Revolution but remaining an administrative centre and an increasingly good shopping centre, Durham is also a city of today. Hotels and inns abound and there are many excellent museums. College boat crews are regularly out on the river. Lesser mortals appreciate what is available from Brown's Boathouse by Elvet Bridge. Annually, in mid July, the Miner's Gala, with its bands, banners and marching miners, are a reminder of Durham's industrial past. A market takes place on Saturdays.

Beamish Museum

Set in 300 acres of woodland and rolling countryside, based on Beamish Hall, the North of England Open Air Museum is a working example of local life early this century. Everything is authentic, the colliery village, town, railway station, home farm, the cattle, pigs, sights, sounds, smells, shops, houses, trams and trains.

Gibside Chapel

This beautiful Palladian chapel (NT) in the form of a Greek cross, built by James Paine (1760-1812) for millionaire coal-magnate Sir George Bowes, stands in wooded parkland landscaped by Capability Brown. All masonry and furnishings are superb; delicate, detailed, and restrained.

Prudhoe Castle

In wooded surroundings and protected on its north by the Tyne, the d'Umfraville barons started this castle in the 12th century, but it passed into Percy hands in the late 14th century. It has a small, free-standing keep in the inner bailey, and an unusual gatehouse protecting the outer bailey. A 13th-century window in the gatehouse chapel is probably the earliest oriel in England. Part of the inner bailey had a Gothick house built in it early last century, and this now contains an exhibition illustrating Prudhoe's history.

Corbridge

One of the Northumberland's most attractive small towns, Corbridge has deep roots, for Dere Street, the Roman road from York to Edinburgh, runs through the town. Half-a-mile to the west Corstopitum, established as fort and supply base, has ranges of ruined Roman buildings including granaries and a strong-room. St Andrew's Church, by the Market Place, was built mainly of stones taken from the Roman fort, as was the adjacent Vicar's Pele - a fortified tower of about 1300 now housing the Tourist Information Centre. A smaller pele, attached to a Jacobean house, graces the east end of Main Street. Although it no longer has a market Corbridge has two market crosses, and a number of 'pants': sources of the town's water supply last century.

Brancepeth

With its grand church, championship golf course - sham, but impressive - castle, and attractive layout, Brancepeth is worth stopping to explore on foot. The church stands in its own wooded grounds and its splendid furnishings are well documented in the leaflets inside. Although now privately owned, the castle can be visited on application.

The Open Air Museum at Beamish offers a walk, or a tram ride, down memory lane. It represents life in the early part of the century

OFF THE TOUR

Bewick Birthplace Museum

At Prudhoe, keep on the A695 to Mickley Square then turn right (sp). Thomas Bewick, artist, wood engraver and naturalist, was born at Cherryburn in 1753 and the cottage birthplace and its small farmyard buildings have been restored. The nearby larger house he later lived in has displays of his work, and most afternoons there are printing demonstrations, using wooden blocks in the traditional way.

Aydon Castle

Take the B6321 north east from Corbridge, turning left in 2 miles. Aydon Castle is a perfect example of a little-changed medieval, fortified manor house, illustrating the domestic living conditions of six centuries ago, and of its use as a farmhouse from the 17th century until 1960. Sensible information panels explain the architecture and uses of various rooms.

Derwent Reservoir

Turn right off the A68 at Carterway Heads, and right in Edmundbyers village. Pow Hill Country Park, a car park and picnic area, has fine views over the Derwent Reservoir, with walks and bird watching opportunities.

OFF THE BEATEN TRACK

Stephenson's Birthplace

Two miles north of Crawcrook, a riverside footpath leads from Wylam to George Stephenson's birthplace (NT) where the 'Father of Railways' was born in 1781. Only one room is open, on some afternoons during the season.

OUTDOOR ACTIVITIES

Waldridge Fell Country Park

Near Edmonsley nearly 300 acres of Pennine-type heathland - with characteristic vegetation enriched by bog-plants in wetter areas, and some semi-natural oak woodland - has many footpaths crossing it.

Causey Arch Picnic Site

By the A6076, this has walks leading to a wooded gorge with cliffs on each side, spanned by the world's first railway bridge, built to carry coal wagons in 1726. The walk goes across this.

Thornley Wood Country Park

Along the A694 beyond Rowlands Gill. This has good car parking, picnic areas and a playground. It is also one of many access points to the Derwent Walk which follows the track-bed of the former Derwent Valley Railway.

Collier Wood Nature Trail

By the A68, south of Tow Law, a car park has a short woodland nature trail leading from it. A notice board, plus seasonal leaflets, explains the ecology and life of this mixed woodland through the year.

SCOTLAND

From the Rhinns Peninsula in the extreme south-west to John o'Groats in the far north-east, where mainland Britain's most northerly village crouches on the cliff ramparts of Caithness, the country roads of Scotland are highways to splendours of scenery and the heritage of a romantic and violent past. Nurtured by the Gulf Stream, palm trees and tropical ferns flourish in the Rhinns gardens, while seabirds in their tumultuous thousands whirl and cry round the beetling cliffs of the Mull of Galloway.

To the east memories of saints and smugglers linger along sandy beaches and stony coves, while the rose-red ruins of Caerlaverock Castle guard the mudflats and marshes on the edge of the Solway Firth. Inland the stag and the wildcat roam the Galloway Forest Park, and further east lie the paps of the magical Eildon Hills and the bewitching Border country Sir Walter Scott loved, with its ruined abbeys and grim, grey holds.

North of the Highland Line, where the snowy Cairngorms rear up 4,000ft above royal Deeside and the valley of the Spey, mountain roads insinuate their way past glimmering, peak-reflecting lochs and climb to high passes between obdurate granite walls, remote corries and lonely lochans. In the west the glowering gates of Glen Coe open the routes to the Isles and the crossings to Skye and the sinister black spires of the Cuillins. To the north are Sutherland and Wester Ross, where the sea-lochs sparkle between cloud-capped summits in a wilderness of peat moors and swift burns on the way to far Cape Wrath.

Left: *Eilean Donan Castle, Highland – beautifully set, with Dornie, on Loch Duich*
Above: *Beinn Eighe and Liathach, Highland – two peaks in the National Nature Reserve*

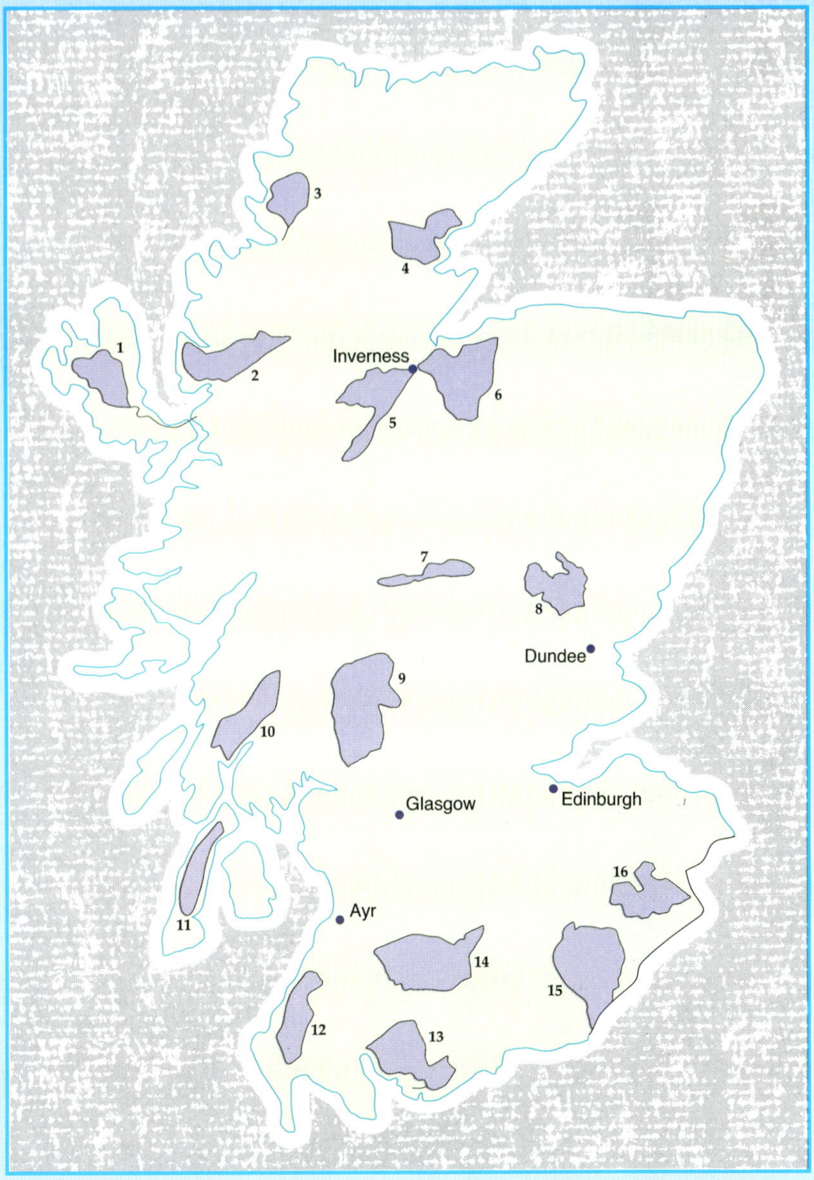

THE ISLE OF SKYE

104 miles

Skye is the Misty Isle, from its weather, or the Winged Island – Eilean a'Cheo in Gaelic – from the shape of its many long peninsulas.

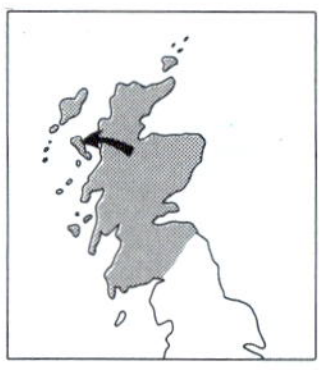

Whatever its name, this is Britain's most spectacular island, with soaring peaks and a multitude of lovely bays.

Sometime in the 1990s there will be a bridge to Skye. Until then the main access is by ferry from Kyle of Lochalsh on the mainland. Skye has an unexpectedly good main-road network, but these routes are never crowded; so there is usually an opportunity to pull in and admire the grand mountain views to the peaks of the Cuillin, or the more modest Red Hills. Skye has dozens of deeply indented sea-lochs, and its coastline is astonishingly long. After Culloden, Bonnie Prince Charlie, with a price of £30,000 on his head, evaded the Redcoats here, helped by Jacobite supporters and the splendid Flora MacDonald. Guided walks from several centres are an ideal way to learn about history and wildlife. The weather may be Atlantic and unpredictable, but Skye is a special experience – not just somewhere to visit.

ON THE TOUR

Kyle of Lochalsh

Until the Dingwall and Skye Railway arrived in 1897 this was just a bare and rocky headland. Now Kyle of Lochalsh is the main ferry port for Skye, the focus of several mainland roads and the shopping centre for a wide area of Wester Ross.

Kyleakin

The corresponding village on Skye, where the ferry lands, also has a fishing boat quay. Behind the houses and hotels which line its main street lies an unexpected inland lagoon. Kyleakin Island was once owned by Gavin Maxwell, author of the otter books such as *Ring of Bright Water.*

Broadford

This holiday resort looks north to a cluster of smaller islands and the lonely coast of Applecross. There are shore, hill and forest walks. The Isle of Skye Environmental Centre includes a museum devoted to landscape and wildlife issues, and there is a sanctuary for injured seals.

Luib

Skye folk museums illustrate life on the island in different eras. The Old Skye Crofter's House, in this hamlet above Loch Ainort, is a thatched cottage furnished in early 20th-century style.

Sconser

The Victorian sporting lodge here is now a hotel overlooking the sea. Beside it is the only public golf course on the island; a nine-hole layout sometimes drenched by rain that sweeps down from Glamaig and Marsco, two of the rugged Red Hills to the south-west.

Sligachan

The isolated hotel here, once a coaching inn, is a base for climbers and anglers. From it, footpaths approach the Cuillin range which is one of the toughest mountaineering prospects in Britain. The view south from the hotel shows the peaks soaring above foreground moorland.

Portree

The only town on Skye, this is well supplied with hotels and visitor facilities. There is a woollen mill to visit, and a variety of craft shops. Colour-washed houses overlook the harbour. It was here that Flora MacDonald bade farewell to Bonnie Prince Charlie, who had come over from the Western Isles disguised as her maid 'Betty Burke'. Meall House, the tourist office which is backed by a wooded hill threaded with footpaths, was once the town jail.

Dunvegan Castle

Home of the MacLeods for more than 750 years, this imposing castle is based on a 13th-century tower. From the sea it reveals itself as not only a stately home in gardens and woodlands, but also the clifftop fortress of the chief of a major clan. Portraits and family treasures including a spellbinding 'fairy flag' feature in the castle tour. Among the displays is a showcase about St Kilda, the remote group of islands and rock stacks evacuated of its population in 1930. Now the property of the

The Kyle of Lochalsh overlooked by the scant ruins of Castle Moil. This was once a lookout post and fortress against raiding Norsemen

OFF THE TOUR

Kylerhea Otter Haven

About 3½ miles after Kyle House, a left turn off the A850 leads to Kylerhea on the Sound of Sleat. Otters can often be seen from a Forestry Commission hide, open to visitors, on the rocky shore.

Raasay

Reached by car ferry from Sconser, Skye's largest offshore island is a glorious mixture of farm, forest and open hill land. There are exhilarating moor and forest walks, a striking ruined castle of the Macleods of Raasay, and relics of early 20th-century ironstone mining.

Stein

Before Dunvegan on the A850, the B886 turns off to this settlement built for fishermen in 1780. Stein is now a sea-angling and watersports centre. Its 350 year-old inn pre-dates the rest of the village. On the Stein road the Fairy Bridge is connected with the story concerning a certain Macleod chief who left his fairy wife here.

Talisker Distillery

At the village of Carbost; on the B8009, which turns off the A863 at the head of Loch Harport, the only malt whisky distillery on Skye was founded in 1830 and rebuilt after a damaging fire in 1960. All the processes are explained in a recently expanded visitor centre.

National Trust for Scotland, and a missile tracking station, it was once the farthest-flung outpost of MacLeod of MacLeod's domain. Boats sail from Dunvegan Castle to the brown and grey seal colonies in Loch Dunvegan.

Bracadale

Norsemen named Bracadale and its loch, which shows Skye in its non-mountain mood: all sea-bays, peninsulas and a scattering of islands.

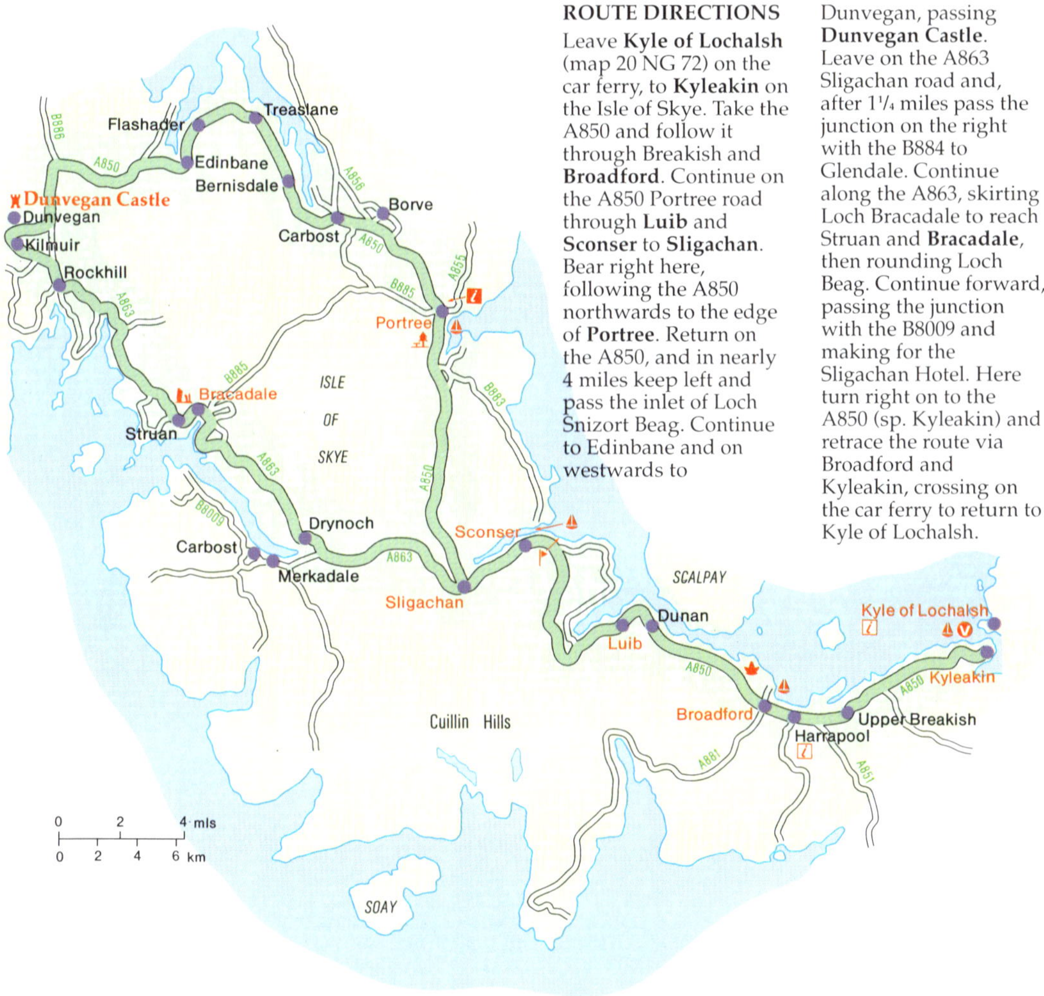

ROUTE DIRECTIONS

Leave **Kyle of Lochalsh** (map 20 NG 72) on the car ferry, to **Kyleakin** on the Isle of Skye. Take the A850 and follow it through Breakish and **Broadford**. Continue on the A850 Portree road through **Luib** and **Sconser** to **Sligachan**. Bear right here, following the A850 northwards to the edge of **Portree**. Return on the A850, and in nearly 4 miles keep left and pass the inlet of Loch Snizort Beag. Continue to Edinbane and on westwards to Dunvegan, passing **Dunvegan Castle**. Leave on the A863 Sligachan road and, after 1¼ miles pass the junction on the right with the B884 to Glendale. Continue along the A863, skirting Loch Bracadale to reach Struan and **Bracadale**, then rounding Loch Beag. Continue forward, passing the junction with the B8009 and making for the Sligachan Hotel. Here turn right on to the A850 (sp. Kyleakin) and retrace the route via Broadford and Kyleakin, crossing on the car ferry to return to Kyle of Lochalsh.

OFF THE BEATEN TRACK

After Kyleakin, the wooded grounds of Kyle House have a fine collection of flowering shrubs, grottoes and a water garden.

At the head of Loch Ainort, a bypassed stretch of old main road provides an alternative coastal route to Sconser.

A parking loop off the A863 gives a high-level view over the fiord-like Loch Harport.

OUTDOOR ACTIVITIES

At Broadford, the Isle of Skye Environment Centre may have places for day visitors on its geology and wildlife walks. Phone 047 12 487 to check.

Hebridean Venture Holidays, based near the folk museum at Luib, sometimes take day visitors on their pony-trekking, sea-angling and orienteering courses, as well as on guided hill walks. Phone 047 12 564 to check.

There are Forestry Commission walks in the Glen Varragill plantations beside the main road south of Portree.

Walks at Portree include paths along and up the steep hillsides on the north side of the bay, looking eastwards to Raasay.

Skye and the Kyle of Lochalsh, the ferry port for this, the most spectacular of Britain's islands

VIEWS OF THE INNER SOUND

91 miles

This is a journey through a landscape of superlatives. A drive over Scotland's most dramatic mountain pass road leads to one of

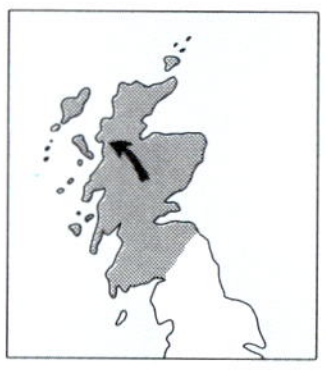

the west coast's most stunning views; to the Cuillin peaks of Skye. No mainland mountain range surpasses those of Torridon.

The Nature Conservancy, the National Trust for Scotland and other owners preserve much of the superb landscape in Wester Ross. Britain's oldest National Nature Reserve includes the multiple summits of Beinn Eighe, valuable enough to be graded as a Biosphere Reserve. Peaks, pinnacles and swooping scree-runs are all part of the vast NTS property in Torridon. Upper Loch Torridon is one of the most beautiful sea-inlets in Britain, just as Loch Maree is often considered Scotland's finest inland water.

Most of the people who once lived here, though, have left no local descendants to admire the scene. In the 19th century, thousands moved or were moved off the land to make way for more lucrative flocks of sheep which were themselves later cleared from sporting estates more concerned with raising deer.

Awesome Beinn Eighe, as seen from wild and beautiful Glen Torridon

ROUTE DIRECTIONS

Leave **Lochcarron** (map 20 NG 83) on the A896 Shieldaig road and ascend along a single-track road on to high ground, then descend to Loch Kishorn. Continue beside the Loch for 1½ miles then turn left, unclassified (sp. Applecross). Climb the Bealach na Ba, the **Pass of the Cattle**, to follow the narrow, winding lane with hairpin bends. Maximum gradient 1 in 5. Follow the descent down to the village of **Applecross**. Leave on the Shieldaig road and round Applecross Bay. After Fearnmore the tour turns south-eastwards. By-pass Kenmore and follow Loch Shieldaig to the junction with the A869. Turn left to reach the edge of **Shieldaig** and continue on the double tracked Torridon road. Pass through Annat to reach the turning for **Torridon** village on the left. Turn right here and follow a single-track road through Glen Torridon (sp. Kinlochewe). At **Kinlochewe** turn right on to the A832 (sp. Achnasheen), passing Loch a'Chroisg to reach the edge of **Achnasheen**. Turn right on to the A890 (sp. Kyle of Lochalsh) and continue forward past Lochs Gowan and Sgamhain. Proceed along Glen Carron, passing **Achnashellach Lodge** and then join the A896 for the return to Lochcarron.

OFF THE TOUR

Strome Castle

South-west from Lochcarron, this fortress of the Macdonells of Glengarry was blown up early in the 17th century and never rebuilt. Close by is the slipway for the historic Strome Ferry crossing, abandoned in 1970.

Rassal Ashwood

On a rare limestone outcrop, this reserve beside the A896 north of the Applecross turn-off is the most northerly ashwood in Britain, carpeted with wild flowers seen nowhere else in the district.

Diabaig

The minor road high above the north shore of Upper Loch Torridon plunges down one of the steepest hills on any road in Britain to reach this dramatically located village on its rocky amphitheatre by the sea.

Beinn Eighe National Nature Reserve

From a car park on the A832 north-west of Kinlochewe, the Woodland Trail explores lower pine, birch and alder woods. The much tougher Mountain Trail climbs to 1,770ft. In the territory of red and roe deer, pine marten, ptarmigan and golden eagle there are magnificent views over Loch Maree and the outstanding peak of Slioch.

ON THE TOUR

Lochcarron

Facing east to the striking hills of the Attadale deer forest, this spread-out village has a lochside frontage and several pleasant little bays. A favourite game here is shinty, the more robust, Highland form of hockey, and there is a level-ground golf course. A nature reserve occupies the ravine of the Allt nan Carnan burn flowing through the village. On the road to Strome, Lochcarron Weavers demonstrate their techniques.

Pass of the Cattle (Bealach na Ba)

The dramatic road to Applecross peaks at 2,053ft after passing the site of an incongruous construction yard built for North Sea Oil work. The narrow road rises past tremendous cliffs, then hairpins to a summit where an AA indicator describes the breathtaking view.

Applecross

This crofting village has a lovely outlook to Skye and its satellite island of Raasay. Plantations around the mansion house provide the only substantial tree cover in the whole vast Applecross peninsula. Southwards lies more natural scenery around the beautiful rocky bays beyond Camusterach. Until the 1970s the Pass of the Cattle, often closed in winter, was the only road to Applecross. Then the new coastal route was opened, partly to serve a Royal Navy torpedo range; but it allows a circular drive round North Applecross, past a number of hamlets by the sea, for some of which the new road came too late to be of use.

Shieldaig

Neat whitewashed houses here look over a sea loch to the pine-covered Shieldaig Island reserve, owned by the National Trust for Scotland since 1970. Shieldaig has a curious history. It was established in the early 19th century as part of a government policy to settle villages whose young men could be conscripted into the navy.

Torridon

More than 14,000 acres of mountains on the north side of Upper Loch Torridon are owned by the NTS: Beinn Alligin and the spectacular ridge of Liathach. This area shows natrue's sculpting of the landscape to best advantage, with some impressive sights. The rock terraces and pinnacles on Liathach reach a height of 3,457ft. A huge scree-slope teeters above the houses in the village. At the junction with the Diabaig road there is a Trust visitor centre with a deer museum closer to the lochside.

Kinlochewe

Set on a little flat valley floor among the mountains, Kinlochewe is a road-junction village with hotels, climbing routes starting nearby and places where angling permits are available for Loch Maree, as well as other lochs in lonelier locations.

Achnasheen

This smaller settlement has a station on the scenic Kyle of Lochalsh railway which opened to Achnasheen in 1870. The hotels here are also well-known to anglers.

Achnashellach Lodge

Originally a Victorian sporting lodge, this is now a hotel in splendid woodland. Day visitors stroll around the 2½ miles of paths through rhododendrons, azaleas and many other flowering shrubs. The River Lair cascades through the grounds and there is a picnic area by Loch Dughaill.

OFF THE BEATEN TRACK

A footpath up the east bank of the little River Balgy east of Shieldaig leads to some rocky falls well known to trout and salmon anglers.

On the summit level of the A896 east of Shieldaig there is one of the most glorious viewpoints in Scotland, over the bays of Upper Loch Torridon to the great massif of Beinn Alligin.

South-east of Kinlochewe, a parking area in Glen Docherty provides a chance to look back down the steep-sided valley gouged out long ago by retreating glaciers.

After Achnasheen, to the left of the road, Loch Sgamhain is the Loch of the Lungs. An old folk tale recounts how a magic 'water horse' used to drag its victims to the bed of the loch. It ate everything but their lungs, which later floated to the surface.

OUTDOOR ACTIVITIES

Lochcarron is a pleasant centre for sailing, sea angling and other watersports.

The car park in Glen Torridon is one of the access points to an exhilarating 8-mile trek on comparatively low ground, on tracks behind Liathach to the Diabaig road.

From the A896 east of Loch Clair one of the classic rights of way in Wester Ross follows the Coulin Pass to Achnashellach.

Looking over Loch Carron and Plockton to the mountains of Applecross. The sheltered village is a haven for yachtsmen

HIGHLAND PEAKS AND LOCHS

68 miles

Ullapool on Loch Broom is a trim village laid out to a regular Georgian street plan; but north of it lies the wild, outlandish landscape of two mountain districts with secret inland lochs and views to rocky islands where seals and seabirds thrive.

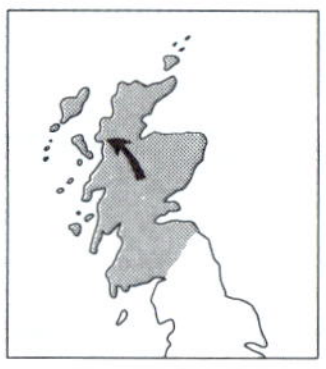

In any judgement about the mountain scenery of Scotland, remote Coigach and Assynt must rate very highly. Over moors and foothills, great sugarloaf silhouettes rear up to the skyline. Quinag, Canisp, Suilven and their neighbours may be long, substantial ridges when seen from one angle; end-on they dramatise the landscape even more. Much of the country here is safeguarded by nature reserves. Visitor trails explain both the unique geology and the wildlife. Cavers, anglers, hill-walkers, climbers and bird-watchers all find these districts special. What they lack is people. Inland valleys never recovered their old population after the 19th-century Clearances, when they were emptied to make way for sheep. In some places there may have been economic imperatives; but the silent mountains still offer their own reproach.

ON THE TOUR

Ullapool

Retaining its original 18th-century grid layout of streets with Gaelic and English names, Ullapool is a fishing port and the car ferry terminal for Stornoway on Lewis. White-washed houses, shops and hotels face Loch Broom. An old fish curing shed is now the fascinating local museum. Cruises from Ullapool visit bird-sanctuary and seal-breeding islands.

Strathkanaird

Here the River Kanaird meanders down a mountain valley; a tributary tapped for one of Scotland's smallest hydro-electric schemes. A track leaves the car park at Blughasary for the ruins of 2,000 year-old Dun Canna, a fort over-looking the beach.

Knockan Cliff Visitor Centre

The vast Inverpolly National Nature Reserve covers mountain, loch and shoreline, moors and birch-hazel woodlands in the heart of Assynt. Two trails from the centre explore the landscape that lies close at hand, one of them reaching the 1,500ft viewpoint summit of Knockan Cliff itself.

Ullapool, where factory ships buy huge quantities of mackerel for freezing and processing

Elphin

This village was laid out in 1812, to provide smallholdings for tenants cleared from the cattle-grazing areas which were given over to sheep. Attempts were made to evict the people even from here in 1851, but they resisted strongly. Now Elphin is a pony-trekking, hill-walking and angling centre, with a watercolour gallery and a farm, open to visitors, stocked with Highland livestock and rare breeds from elsewhere.

Inchnadamph

The scattered village here is set in a green oasis where Loch Assynt curves away between the mountains to the north-west. Its hotel is a popular resort for salmon and trout fishermen. Inchnadamph National Nature Reserve is a famous limestone area with caves opening off the Traligill gorge, and an abundance of wildflowers. Access may be restricted during the deer-stalking season after mid-July.

Ardvrech Castle

MacLeods of Assynt once held sway from their fortress here. In 1650 the Marquis of Montrose, most dashing commander on the royalist side in the Civil War, was held captive at Ardvrech, then sent south for his trial and execution.

Lochinver

Approached by a downhill stretch of road past waterfalls and angling pools, this village was founded in 1812 to house families evicted from their holdings inland. Lochinver, a popular base for tourists, is the main centre of population in Assynt, with hotels and craft shops, a school curiously located on a peninsula in the freshwater Loch Culag and, from the far side of Loch Inver itself, an amazing view of the great summit ridge of Suilven over foreground hills.

Inverkirkaig

Here the road south from Lochinver passes a sandy bay before snaking through the Inverpolly reserve. Achins Bookshop concentrates on Scottish, wildlife and mountain themes. From it a path leads to the tumbling Falls of Kirkaig.

Loch Lurgainn

On the southern fringe of the reserve, a chain of lochs lies in a glacial valley. Lurgainn is the largest, with a car park looking south to the mountain-shrouded loch itself, and north to the high pinnacles on the summit ridge of Stac Polly.

The ruins of Ardvreck Castle stand on the shores of Loch Assynt, with Quinag in the background

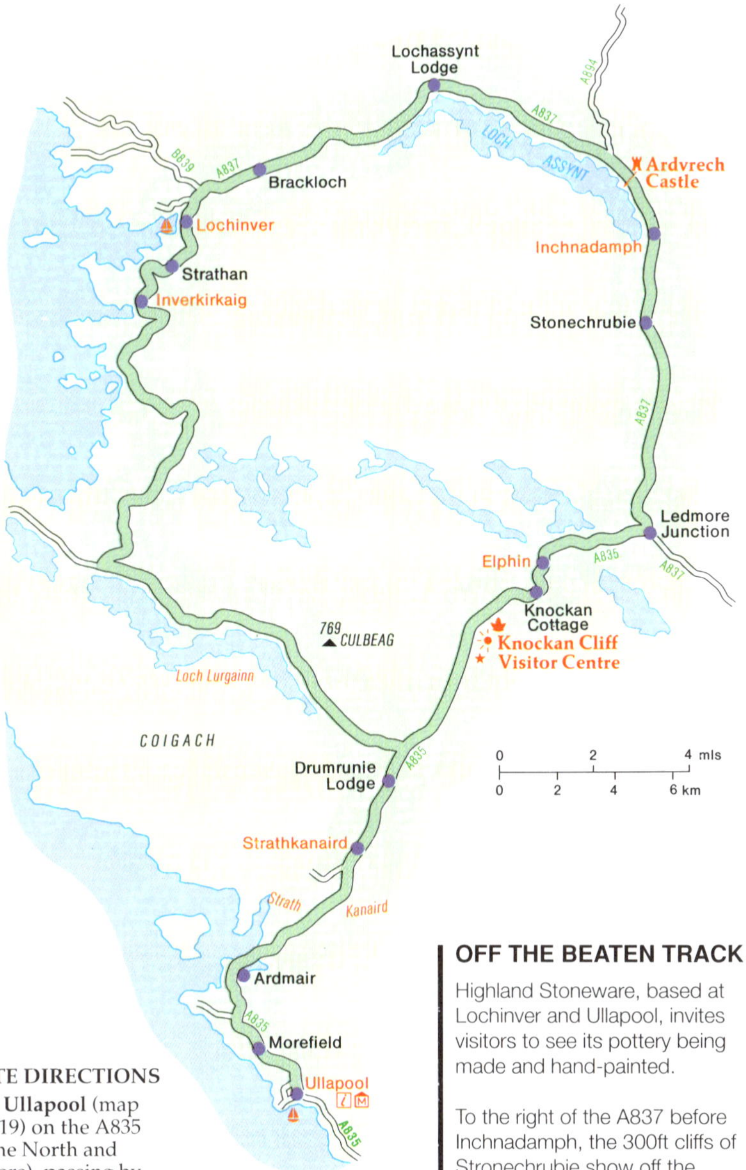

ROUTE DIRECTIONS

Leave **Ullapool** (map 20NH19) on the A835 (sp. The North and Ledmore), passing by Ardmair Bay and through **Strathkanaird**. After a further 5 miles turn right and continue up to the viewpoint and the **Knockan Cliff Visitor Centre**.

Continue forward through **Elphin** to the Ledmore Road junction and turn left on to the A837 (sp. Lochinver). Continue beyond the settlement of **Ichnadamph** and pass the ruins of **Ardvrech Castle** before reaching Skiag Bridge and the junction with the A894. Bear left to continue on the A837 to **Lochinver**. Keep forward here by the side of Loch Inver, then cross a bridge and turn left, unclassified, towards **Inverkirkaig.** Follow the winding road and, after 8 miles, at the T-junction, turn left on to the Ullapool road, unclassified, to pass beside **Loch Lurgainn**. Continue to the junction with the A835 and turn right (sp. Ullapool) and retrace the route via Strath Kanaird and Ardmair Bay for the return to Ullapool.

OFF THE TOUR

Altnaharrie

A private ferry runs from Ullapool to a hotel on the wild and otherwise uninhabited west coast of Loch Broom. There is a steep walk up an old road, now closed to traffic, to a viewpoint hill.

Kylesku

In the 1980s a sweeping modern bridge over the narrows of the loch here, with parking and picnic places nearby, replaced the last ferry on the west-coast main road network. Found north of the Skiag Bridge on the A894, Kylesku pier is still used for boat trips to the head of Loch Glencoul and the highest waterfall in Britain.

Achnahaird Bay

At the Badnagyle junction, turn right, right again and right at Brae of Achnahaird to one of the rare sandy beaches on this rocky coast.

Achiltibuie

This long, strung-out crofting village high above Badentarbat Bay is reached by turning right at Badnagyle then left at every junction until the first houses appear. At the Hydroponicum, visitors are shown how flowers, fruit and vegetables are grown in soil-free cultures. There are cruises to the Summer Isles which lie intriguingly offshore.

OFF THE BEATEN TRACK

Highland Stoneware, based at Lochinver and Ullapool, invites visitors to see its pottery being made and hand-painted.

To the right of the A837 before Inchnadamph, the 300ft cliffs of Stronechrubie show off the limestone beds typical of the area. Look for the Allt-nan-Uamh – the Burn of the Cave – appearing from a cavern below the cliffs after flowing underground.

OUTDOOR ACTIVITIES

On the pebbly spit of Ardmair Point, north of Ullapool, a boat centre provides facilities for canoeing, sailboarding, windsurfing and sea angling.

Lochinver Wildlife Cruises sail from the Culag pier to seal colonies and bird islands. There are also sea-angling trips.

Assynt Angling Club, based at Lochinver, has fishing rights on more than thirty lochs. Some are close to roads, others involve a trek into the hills.

From a car park at Loch Lurgainn, a footpath heads north to Stac Polly, one of the most spectacular of the Assynt mountains. The approach is easy, but the pinnacled ridge is for experienced hill people only.

SOUTH EAST SUTHERLAND

69 miles

Here, Sutherland is a county of contrasts. Sandy beaches separate holiday resorts on the coast. Inland there are huge areas of sheep farms and deer forests. Two vastly wealthy men – a duke and an industrialist – cast very different shadows.

Some of Scotland's finest beaches follow the coast along the Dornoch Firth and sweep away to the north. Dornoch, Golspie and Brora revel in fine sands and top-class golf links on the springy turf. However, apart from the old cathedral town of Dornoch itself, most of the coastal settlements were created for inland tenants dispossessed in the great Sutherland Clearances of the 19th century; families used to looking after cattle were forced either to emigrate or to learn an alien way of life as fishermen. Agents of the first Duke of Sutherland, the 'Leviathan of Wealth', supervised the evictions. Yet, when an even richer man, Andrew Carnegie, settled here, it was to arrange the giving away of a vast fortune in the greatest exercise in personal philanthropy that the world has ever seen.

ROUTE DIRECTIONS

Leave **Dornoch** (map 21 NH 78) on the A949 Castle Street, and at the war memorial turn right on to the B9168 (sp. Wick). After a further 2 miles turn right on to the A9. Continue forward and cross the head of Loch Fleet by a causeway, **The Mound**, still on the A9. After 2 miles pass a statue of the first Duke of Sutherland and continue into **Golspie**. Continue on the A9 past **Dunrobin Castle** and Cairn Liath and on along the coast of **Brora**. Pass the clock tower, then cross the river bridge and turn left, unclassified (no signs). Continue as the road becomes a single track. Pass through **Rogart** and, at the main road, turn right on to the A839 (sp. Lairg). In **Lairg** follow the Lochinver signs and turn right across the River Shin to leave by the A839. In 3/4 mile branch left on to the B864 (sp. Inveran) and follow a single-track road through Achany Glen and past the Falls of Shin. Continue on the B864 and, in 1 1/4 miles turn left on to the A837 (sp. Bonar Bridge) and re-cross the River Shin. After 1/2 mile join the A836 for Invershin and continue forward to **Bonar Bridge**. Here turn left on to the A9 (sp. Wick) passing by **Spinningdale** to reach Clashmore. In a further 1 1/2 miles turn right on to the A949 for the return to Dornoch.

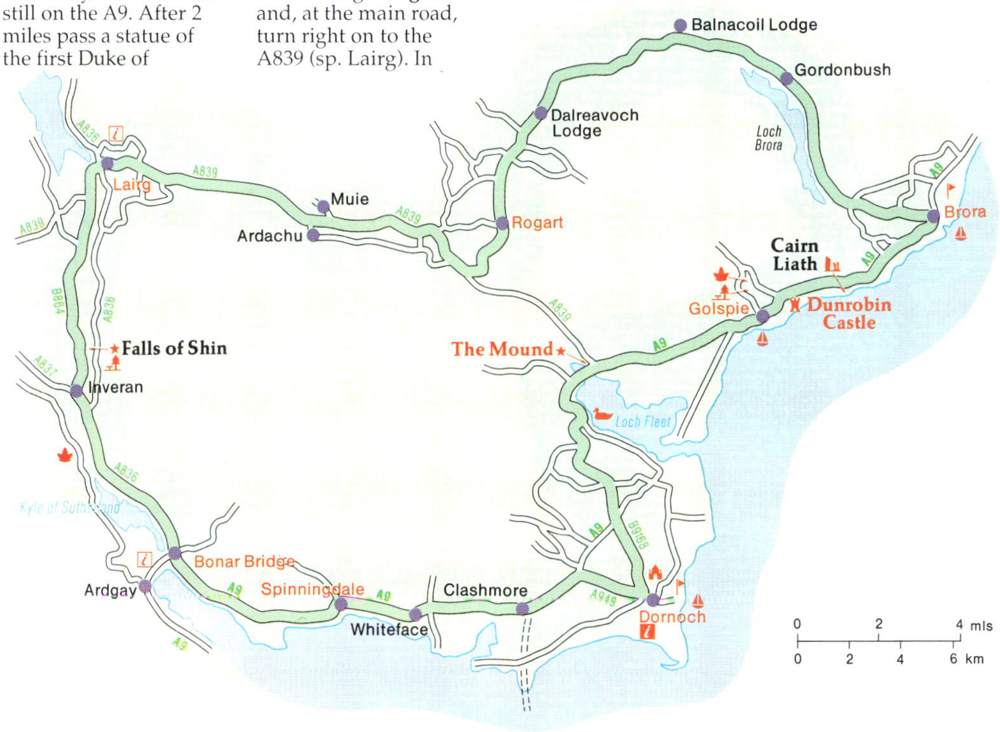

Superb Dunrobin Castle, set in lovely gardens, was originally a 13th-century keep, but was extensively rebuilt in 1856

OFF THE TOUR

Embo

Once a year during the holiday season, the little 19th-century fishing village, off to the right of the minor road north from the old station at Dornoch, celebrates the anniversary of its 16 July 1988 'declaration of independence'. Embo visas are needed by visitors to the village, which for that day issues its own banknotes, named 'cuddies' after a local fish. There is an Embo national anthem, and the whole event has royal approval.

Littleferry

The road past Golspie golf course leads to an old ferry port, past a kart racing circuit and the wildfowl haven in the tidal basin of Loch Fleet.

Raven Rock

About 5 1/2 miles south-west of its junction with the B864, a left turn off the A839 leads to a dramatic forest walk following the precipitous gorge of the Allt Mor burn through old estate woodlands.

Carbisdale Castle

At Bonar Bridge turn right on the A9, then right through Ardgay for Culrain station and the only castle built in Europe this century. A forest walk here goes through Sitka spruce, Scots and Lodgepole pine.

ON THE TOUR

Dornoch

Golfers come to Dornoch from all over the world. The Royal Dornoch course lies between a long sandy beach and colourful banks of gorse. A footpath overlooks it on the way to Embo. In the attractive square, Dornoch Cathedral was first used for worship in 1239. One group of stained glass windows commemorates Andrew Carnegie, the multi-millionaire philanthropist who retired from business in America to spend most of his time at nearby Skibo Castle. In a garden in the Littletown district, a stone marks the spot where in 1722 poor, demented Janet Horne was the last 'witch' burned in Scotland.
The craft centre in the square at Dornoch is also the entrance to the old town jail. There are displays in most of the original cells. The most unusual workshop in the industrial estate at the Dornoch station site is one which makes boomerangs.

The Mound

In 1816 Thomas Telford's causeways and bridge over the River Fleet here made the dangerous ferries on the coastal route redundant. Later, The Mound was also used by the Dornoch Light Railway which branched off the main line to the north.

Golspie

Created from a few fishing huts to house victims of the Sutherland Clearances, Golspie is now a comfortable town with a long beach and a golf course, as well as magnificent walks around the waterfalls in Dunrobin Glen. St Andrew's church dates from the 16th century and includes the 'laird's loft' of the Sutherland family.

Dunrobin Castle

In mid-Victorian times the second Duke of Sutherland commissioned Sir Charles Barry, architect of the House of Commons, to remodel the ancient family seat. It was originally a square keep, but as it now stands, Dunrobin is almost a palace in the French style, and the grandest house in the north of Scotland. It has many public rooms, a museum and smaller displays including the estate's old steam-powered fire engine. Beautiful formal gardens border the sea.

Brora

A mixture of holiday resort and industrial town, Brora has an exhilarating breezy beach, a good golf course and excellent salmon fishing, as well as a malt whisky distillery and a woollen mill to visit.

Rogart

A scattered crofting village in a maze of roads above the upper valley of the River Fleet, Rogart is a stop on the long Lairg loop of the Inverness to Thurso railway. There is a monument to Sir John Macdonald, first prime minister of Canada. His family originated in the area and were among those turned out at the time of the Clearances.

Lairg

This road-junction village and angling centre holds the biggest one-day sheep sales in Europe. There are forests, and the dammed waters of Loch Shin power a hydro-electric station. The little hill known as The Ord is a good viewpoint, and the site of many ancient habitations.

Bonar Bridge

Telford built the first bridge over the Kyle of Sutherland here, but the modern structure dates from 1973. Salmon in great numbers swim through the narrows on their way to the spawning grounds, and the Kyle is also a fine sea trout water. Fish passes here allow salmon free passage upstream; there is a famous salmon leap at the Falls of Shin.

Spinningdale

In 1792 David Dale, one of the great Lowland cotton magnates, joined forces with a local laird to build the first northern mill here. It was burned out in 1806 and now only its jagged ruins remain.

OFF THE BEATEN TRACK

Dornoch Light Railway operated from 1902 until 1960. The town station site is now an industrial estate, but the trackbed can still be seen as it wanders past long-lost stops such as Embo, Skelbo, Cambusavie Halt and The Mound.

Off the A9 north of Dornoch, Skelbo picnic place is at the start of a walk through woodlands in a little valley.

Opposite the entrance to Dunrobin Castle, a rustic railway halt which was once the private station of the second Duke of Sutherland still has occasional stopping trains.

Grandest sight on the River Shin south of Lairg are the Falls of Shin in the winding gorge that lies east of the B864.

OUTDOOR ACTIVITIES

One easy hill walk from Golspie is up an estate road to the viewpoint summit of Ben Bhraggie, loomed over by a massive statue to the first Duke of Sutherland.

Dornoch, Golspie and Brora golf courses are all highly regarded. Royal Dornoch is rated as one of the top 12 courses in the world.

The smooth, still waters of Dornoch Firth. Around the graceful little town of Dornoch are miles of safe, sandy beaches

AROUND THE SHORES OF LOCH NESS

91 miles

Two narrow valleys, Strathglass and Glen Urquhart, slice through forested and deer stalking hills to arrive at Loch Ness, a place

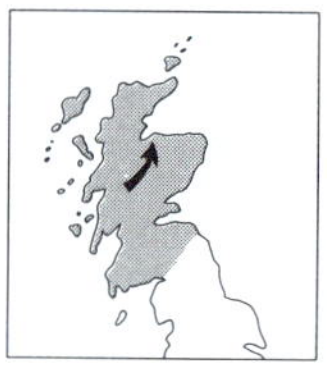

of mystery and the longest waterway in the Great Glen, the huge geological fault dividing the Highlands coast to coast.

Forests and hydro-electric schemes are impossible to avoid in this part of the Highlands, but they have left the valley of the River Beauly and its tributaries the Glass and the Farrar, ancestral land of Frasers and Chisholms, places of remarkable natural beauty. Hillsides above Loch Ness are also heavily forested, though fringed with birches, and there is hydro-electricity here too. Loch Ness is most famous, though, for the so-far unidentified creature – 'monster' is a word not much appreciated by some local people – which may inhabit its chill and phenomenally deep waters. There is, at least, something rather odd here.

Inverness, the Highland capital, is the only town in the area. Away from the bustle of its commercial and industrial districts, it is a place of fine buildings, attractive parkland, elevated views and lovely riverside strolls.

ON THE TOUR

Inverness

The most attractive parts of the Highland capital are on its south-west side, where footpaths follow both banks of the fast-flowing River Ness and link up with the wooded islands in mid-stream. Cruises on the Caledonian Canal start from the town, overlooked by the forest walk to Craig Phadrig, site of a hilltop fortress of the Pictish kings.

Whin Park at Inverness has a boating lake with bridges and islands, a play area and a miniature railway.

Cluanie Deer Farm Park

High above the River Beauly, not only red deer browse on this hillside, but also rare breeds of farm animals, llamas and angora goats. There is an indoor visitor centre in case of bad weather.

Aigas House and Field Centre

Residential courses here involve expeditions to the hills, but Aigas also has woodland walks, a fishing loch, a garden and specimen Victorian trees. Highland cattle and Jacob sheep roam the grounds.

Cannich

Near the head of Strathglass, this village is the access point for the lonely hill road up Glen Cannich to Loch Mullardoch, and the beautiful route past the wooded Dog Falls into Glen Affric.

Drumnadrochit

The Loch Ness Monster Exhibition includes an account of the expeditions – using methods from sonar to mini-submarines – which have tried to probe the mysteries of that strange stretch of water. The site also includes the International House of Heraldry. A side-road off the A82 leads to the car park for a walk to the Divach Falls.

Urquhart Castle

From its 13th-century heyday this ruined stronghold on a rise of ground above Loch Ness played its part in many historic campaigns. Several sightings of the 'monster' have been made from here.

Canal lock gates at Fort Augustus at the southern end of Loch Ness. Rising from the trees can be seen the tower and spire of St Benedict's Abbey which incorporates the Abbey School, built in 1876

Invermoriston
A 19th-century Telford bridge still crosses the Moriston upstream of the A82. Beside it, the rocky ledges by the river are a pleasant picnic place. Downstream there is a short walk to a wooded gorge.

Fort Augustus
Unfeelingly named after the Duke of Cumberland, the original fort is incorporated in the Victorian St Benedict's Abbey which includes a boys' school. Its peaceful cloisters give no clue to the abbey's martial past. Watching yachts and cruisers pass through the locks on the Caledonian Canal is a lazy occupation in mid-village.

Foyers
The twin villages of Upper and Lower Foyers were built for a pioneering aluminium works powered by a hydro-electric scheme started in the 1890s. Now much reduced in flow, the Falls of Foyers are reached by footpaths which show off their dramatic location in a precipitous wooded gorge.

Inverfarigaig
An exhibition centre in the narrow defile of the Farigaig gorge explains the workings of the local forest plantations, and there are specimen trees by the roadside. The most energetic road in Scotland reaches a glorious viewpoint over Loch Ness.

OFF THE BEATEN TRACK

In the old church at Drumchardine on the A862, Highland Aromatics shows visitors how its soaps and toiletries are made with scents such as honeysuckle, jasmine and heather.

On summer afternoons, the fish ladder at Aigas dam is open to visitors, as salmon swim to their upstream spawning grounds.

On the A831, before Cannich, St Ignatius's Well is a Victorian wayside shrine.

After Urquhart Castle, the John Cobb memorial commemorates the Land Speed Record holder killed on Loch Ness in 1952 while trying to beat the Water Speed Record in the jet-powered *Crusader.*

Suidhe Chuimein is an impressive viewpoint over hills and forests north-east of Fort Augustus on the B862.

OUTDOOR ACTIVITIES

Off the Auchterawe road at Fort Augustus the River Oich forest walks cover level ground through alder, birch, beech and rowan, as well as conifer plantations.

From the exhibition centre at Inverfarigaig, forest trails climb to marvellous viewpoints over Loch Ness and the forbidding cliff face in the River Farigaig gorge.

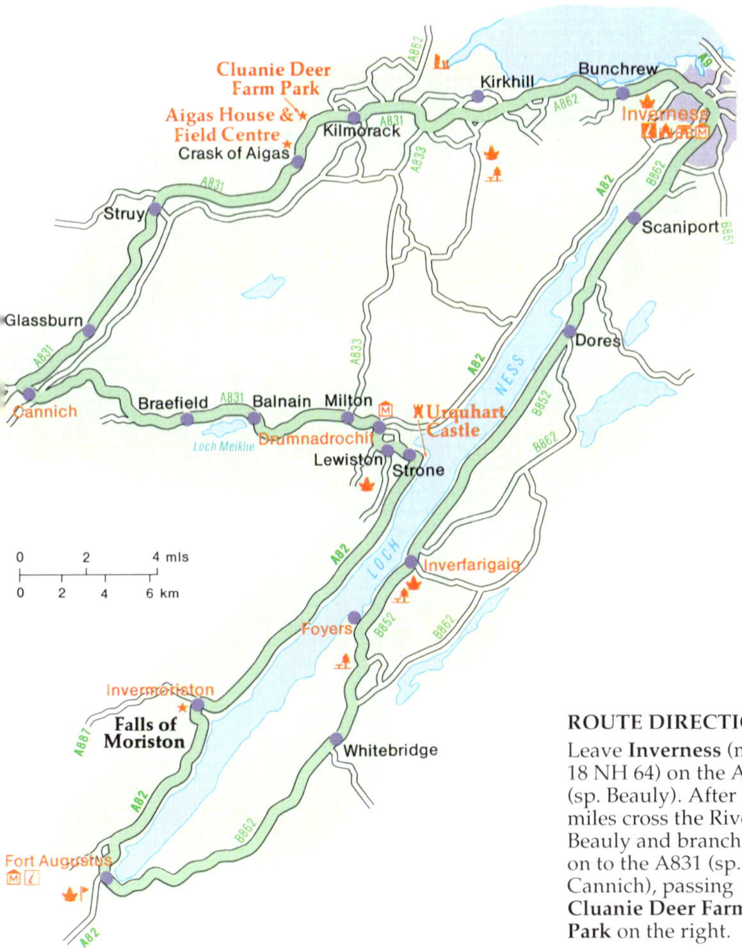

ROUTE DIRECTIONS

Leave **Inverness** (map 18 NH 64) on the A862 (sp. Beauly). After 11 miles cross the River Beauly and branch left on to the A831 (sp. Cannich), passing **Cluanie Deer Farm Park** on the right.

Continue through Kilmorack and past **Aigas House** and **Field Centre** to Struy Bridge. Cross the river and continue to **Cannich**. Leave on the Drumnadrochit road and follow the River Enrick into Glen Urquhart passing Lochs Meiklie and Milton to reach **Drumnadrochit**. Turn right on to the A82 (sp. Fort William) and after Lewiston, join the western shoreline of Loch Ness at **Urquhart Castle**. Continue to **Invermoriston** and turn left with the A82 to reach **Fort Augustus**. At the far end of the village turn left on to the B862 (sp. Whitebridge and Dores). After 3 miles the road becomes a single track. Continue forward until 1 mile beyond Whitebridge, then turn left on to the B852 (sp. Foyers). Continue beside Loch Ness, past **Foyers**, through **Inverfarigaig** and on to Dores. Here re-join the B862 and follow a two-lane road for the return to Inverness.

OFF THE TOUR

Moniack Castle Winery
About ²/₃ mile after the B9164 junction, turn left off the A862, then left at a T-junction and first right for Moniack Castle. It produces wines and liqueurs from local ingredients such as elderflower, birch and honey. There are guided tours and wine tastings.

Strathfarrar
Although the 14-mile road from Struy bridge on the A861 to the Monar dam is private, from Easter to October cars may use it, except on Sunday and Tuesday mornings. Despite its use for hydro-electricity, this remains a beautiful valley with historic stands of Caledonian pine.

Corrimony Chambered Cairn
After the A831 climbs away from Cannich, a minor road on the right leads to a fine burial cairn of the same style and era as the ones at Clava.

McBain Memorial Park
About 1¹/₂ miles after the road junction at Dores, turn right onto a minor road then right again uphill to a little garden created in 1961 by the 21st chief of Clan McBain. It provides a splendid high-level view for miles down Loch Ness.

Although now a ruin, 13th-century Urquhart Castle is still impressive. The castle was in use until 1689, when it was blown up after the Jacobite Rising

SOUTH OF THE MORAY FIRTH

89 miles

From the saddest battlefield in the Highlands, across bare and breezy upland moors, this route returns by richly wooded lower-ground estates, castles, riverside towns and a lavish playground in the pines.

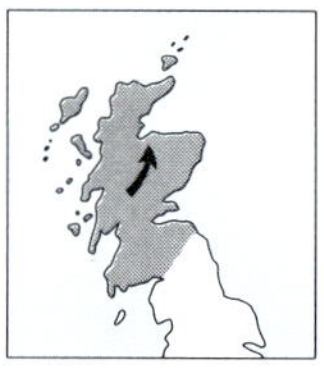

It is important to appreciate that the battle fought in 1746 on Culloden Moor, which crushed the last attempt to restore the House of Stuart to the British throne, was not Scots against English or even Highlanders against Lowlanders. It pitted the Jacobites – the supporters of the Stuarts – against the Hanoverian establishment of George II, and it destroyed a Highland way of life for ever. Away from the royal line, though, the Stuarts have flourished and there are fine houses and estates here still in their hands.

Landscapes differ greatly in this area. On lonely Dava Moor, moraines and tiny lochs were left by glaciers. The coast offers sandy beaches and the pine-woods stretch for miles. Lovely deciduous woodlands clothe the banks of the Findhorn, and rich farmlands enhance the valley of the Nairn.

The River Findhorn at Tomatin

ON THE TOUR

Culloden Battlefield

The battle here on 16 April 1746 was the last one fought on British soil. Prince Charles Edward Stuart – Bonnie Prince Charlie – was badly advised, and the battle was a rout in favour of the government troops commanded by the Duke of Cumberland. His name is still hated in the Highlands because of the atrocities his men committed in the days to follow. A visitor centre at Old Leanach Cottage describes both the battle and the history of the Jacobite risings. Most poignant memorials are the graves of the clans.

Clava Cairns

Situated on the south bank of the River Nairn, this group of Neolithic burial cairns is one of the most impressive burial sites in the Highlands; including three concentric rings of great stones.

Tomatin

Bypassed by the main road, this is a village with a whisky distillery open to visitors and one of the impressive civil engineering features of the Perth-Inverness railway – the Findhorn Viaduct.

Carrbridge

Set in pinewoods at the edge of the village, Landmark opened in 1970 as the first visitor centre in Europe. There are exhibitions on Highland life, sculptures, a Scottish Forestry Heritage Park and a woodland maze with almost a mile of confusing alleyways, and a treetop trail in the pines.

Lochindorb

In the 14th century the ruined island castle here was the lair of Alexander Stewart, the Wolf of Badenoch. Time and again he and his men swept down on unsuspecting towns, as in 1390 when they plundered Elgin and sacked its cathedral.

Forres

Moray calls itself Scotland's floral district, and here in Forres public and private gardens entrance the eye. The lawns and flower beds of Grant Park are backed by Cluny Hill, whose woodland paths climb to the viewpoint Nelson Tower; built to commemorate the victory at Trafalgar. Nearby, the 9th-century Sueno's Stone, standing 23ft high, tells in supremely detailed carvings the story of an unidentified battle, the enemy's flight and the execution of captives. Since 1990 it has been encased in a transparent canopy to fend off further weathering.

Brodie Castle

Brodies have lived in this area for around 950 years, but the earliest part of the present square-towered castle was built in 1567. It has a superb plasterwork ceiling and a fine art collection, and stands in extensive farm, forest and parkland grounds. There is also an adventure play area in the grounds.

Auldearn

Boath Doocot, or dovecote, is a viewpoint over the 1645 battlefield of Auldearn; a Royalist defeat of the Covenanters.

Nairn

From the handsome Victorian main street, a heritage trail wanders round Nairn's most prominent buildings. The old Fishertown has been largely preserved, with its own museum. The harbour, mostly given over to recreational use, has recently been revitalised. There are riverside walks and long silver sands.

Cawdor Castle

Shakespeare's Macbeth was Thane of Cawdor, but not in the present building centred on a 14th-century tower. There is a story that it was sited beside a hawthorn, and that deep in the heart of the castle a dried-out spike of tree can still be seen. This is a comfortably furnished castle with alternately grand and lived-in rooms. Home of the Earl of Cawdor, it stands in splendidly kept gardens.

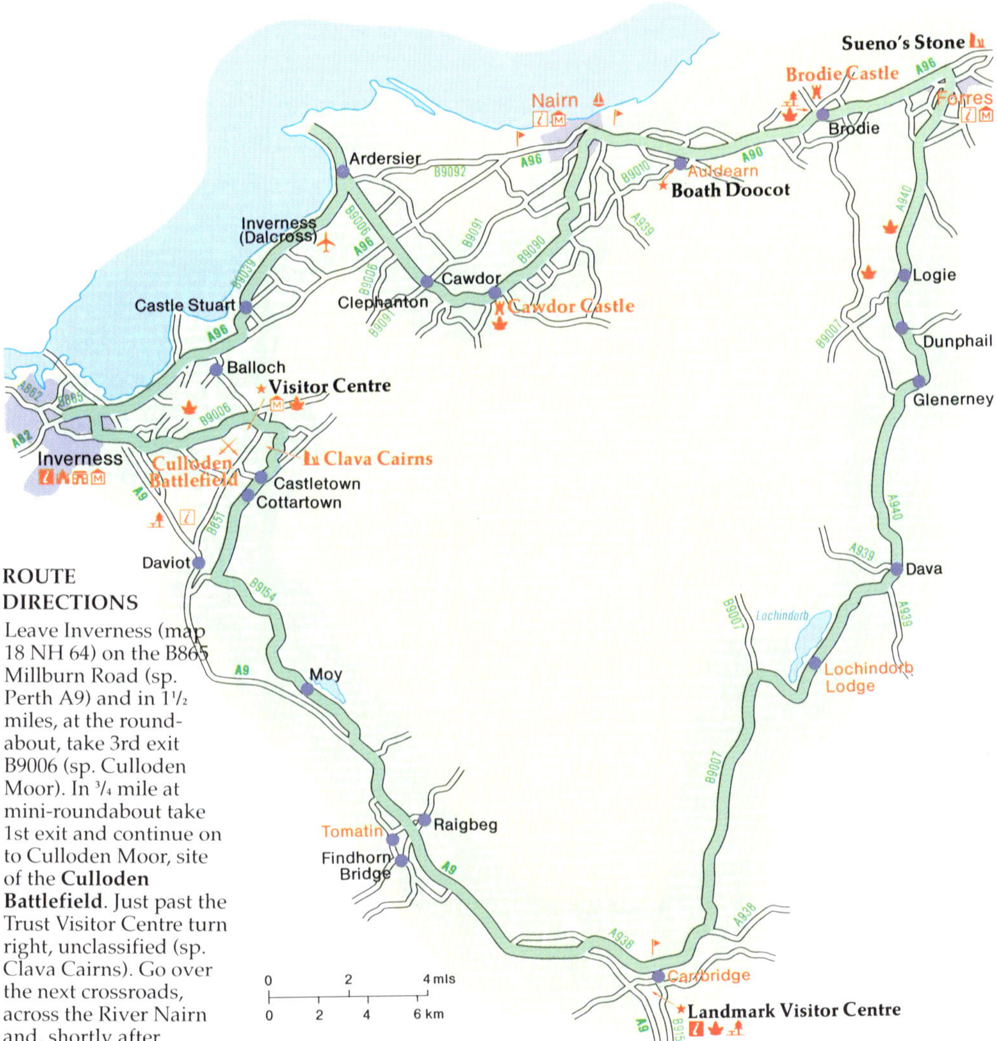

ROUTE DIRECTIONS

Leave Inverness (map 18 NH 64) on the B865 Millburn Road (sp. Perth A9) and in $1\frac{1}{2}$ miles, at the roundabout, take 3rd exit B9006 (sp. Culloden Moor). In $\frac{3}{4}$ mile at mini-roundabout take 1st exit and continue on to Culloden Moor, site of the **Culloden Battlefield**. Just past the Trust Visitor Centre turn right, unclassified (sp. Clava Cairns). Go over the next crossroads, across the River Nairn and, shortly after passing the railway viaduct on the left, turn right to pass the **Clava Cairns**. In 1 mile turn right (sp. Daviot) and after $3\frac{1}{4}$ miles turn left (no signs) on to the B9154. Continue past Loch Moy before turning left on to the A9 (sp. Perth). Cross the River Findhorn, passing the right hand turning to **Tomatin,** climb the valley to Slochd Summit, descend and, after $3\frac{3}{4}$ miles, turn left on to the A938 (sp. Carrbridge). From **Carrbridge** follow the A938 (sp. Dulnain Bridge) and after $1\frac{3}{4}$ miles turn left on to the B9007 (sp. Forres). After $6\frac{3}{4}$ miles turn right, unclassified (sp. Lochindorb). Descend to the shores of **Lochindorb** and continue across Dava Moor. At the junction with the A939 turn left (sp. Forres) then bear right on to the A940, along the Dorback Valley and on to **Forres**. Leave on the A96 Inverness road and in $1\frac{1}{2}$ miles cross the River Findhorn and continue through **Brodie** to **Auldearn**. In $2\frac{1}{4}$ miles cross the River Nairn to enter **Nairn**. Leave by the B9090 (sp. Cawdor) and in 2 miles re-cross the Nairn. After 1 mile turn right to reach Cawdor, passing **Cawdor Castle** on the left. Continue with the B9090 and, after $1\frac{1}{4}$ miles, turn right (sp. Inverness) and re-cross the Nairn. After $\frac{1}{2}$ mile, at Clephanton crossroads, keep forward on to the B9006 then cross the A96 and continue to Ardersier. From here turn left on to the B9039 (no sign) and, after $4\frac{1}{2}$ miles pass Castle Stuart. On reaching the A96 turn right (sp. Inverness). After 4 miles, take 2nd exit to re-enter Inverness.

OFF THE TOUR

Randolph's Leap

Before Forres, a left turn on to the B9007 leads to a beautiful part of the Findhorn Valley. Falls and whirlpools take the river through a wooded, rocky gorge well supplied with pathways.

Darnaway Farm Visitor Centre

On the A96 west of Forres, turn left for the farm where a major local estate explains its history, timber and dairying activities. On certain days there are visits to Darnaway Castle, home of the Earl of Moray.

Fort George

On the B9006 north of Ardersier, one of the last great military fortresses of its kind constructed in Europe which is still an army base. It retains its fine Georgian gateway and central buildings, 18th- and 19th-century barrack rooms complete with waxwork figures, the museum of the Queens Own Highlanders, and a splendid collection of weapons and equipment.

OFF THE BEATEN TRACK

Beyond Cawdor, Nairnside is the only sheep dairy farm in Scotland open to visitors. Sheep milking takes place in the afternoon, and the farm makes hard and soft cheeses, yoghurt and even ewes'-milk ice cream.

On certain days Culloden Pottery, where the B9090 meets the A96, allows visitors the opportunity to throw their own pots.

OUTDOOR ACTIVITIES

South of Forres, the Sluie Walk off the A940 crosses farm and forest land to the winding Findhorn Gorge.

Walks in Brodie Castle woodlands circle a pond with a wildlife hide.

Nairn is one of Scotland's principal golfing resorts. Gorse, pine and heather flank the seaside courses.

Cawdor Castle nature trails follow two chattering burns through extensive woods with a great variety of birdlife, roe deer and squirrels.

Ardersier Activity Centre offers sailing, canoeing, windsurfing and other outdoor sports. Phone 0667 62592 for the timetable.

Imposing Cawdor Castle, home of the Thanes of Cawdor since the 14th century, is surrounded by beautiful gardens

HEART OF THE HIGHLANDS

67 miles

The words of the popular Scottish song The Road to the Isles *say 'by Tummel and Rannoch and Lochaber I will go . . .'. No road*

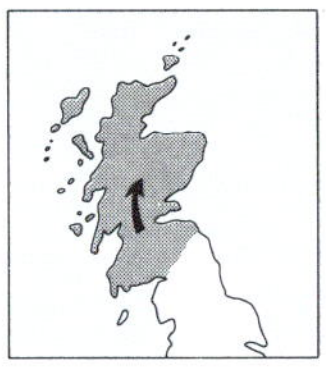

links Rannoch and Lochaber, but Tummel and Rannoch are neighbouring districts of lochs, forests and splendid mountain views.

Here is the heartland of the historic Highlands. Territory of Menzies and Robertson, Stuart and MacDonald; scene of the very first battle in the long and unavailing toil to restore to the throne of Britain the luckless Royal House of Stuart.

In modern times water-power and forestry have vastly changed the landscape, but their effects have been generally benign. Many forests in the Highlands welcome walkers and, while every river and loch on this journey supplies the vast Tummel-Garry hydro-electric scheme, the lovely and accessible Loch Faskally did not exist before 1950.

There are well-travelled holiday valleys here, as well as breezier, lonelier hills. Westward lies Rannoch, where the wilder landscape recalls the times 250 years ago when it was said to be in 'an uncivilised barbarous state, under no check, or restraint of laws'.

The Falls of Bruar at Blair Atholl rough and tumble their way down a tree-covered hillside

A red deer stag at Glengoulandie Deer Park, where Highland cattle and rare sheep can also be seen

ON THE TOUR

Pitlochry

A holiday resort since Victorian times, Pitlochry has hotels and craft shops, a fine footpath network, a good golf course, and boating and angling on the beautifully wooded reservoir of Loch Faskally. A malt whisky distillery welcomes visitors but Pitlochry, curiously enough, has only one pub – in a partly restored watermill. The design of the famous Pitlochry Festival Theatre, whose repertory offers a different play six evenings per week in summer, recalls the marquee where its first plays were produced in 1951.

Pass of Killiecrankie

Above this spectacular wooded defile, a visitor centre tells the story of the Battle of Killiecrankie in 1689. That was the first major engagement in the campaign to restore the Stuarts to the throne, which lasted until Bonnie Prince Charlie's defeat at Culloden in 1746. At Killiecrankie the Jacobite army won the day but, in a piece of typical Stuart ill-luck, its commander Viscount Dundee was killed by a wayward bullet at the very moment of triumph.

Blair Atholl

A restored 17th-century corn mill still operates here. The Atholl Collection is an exhibition on farming, domestic life, rural trades and the significance of the horse in the countryside of days gone by.

Blair Castle

The white towers of this impressive castle, home of the Duke of Atholl, stand proud of its wooded parkland. The oldest part is Cummings Tower, 1269. More than 30 public rooms display swords and muskets, portraits and furnishings, intricate plasterwork, relics of the Jacobite risings and a splendid porcelain collection. The Duke's Atholl Highlanders are the only private army in Europe; a distinction conferred by Queen Victoria.

Bruar

Clan Donnachaidh – the Robertsons, Reids and Duncans – have their clan museum here. Up the glen of the Bruar Water a magnificent walk takes in tumbling waterfalls, rock pools and footbridges on a hillside covered with larches and birch.

Kinloch Rannoch

It is a mystery why the village whose name means 'Head of Loch Rannoch' is actually at its foot. This is the shopping centre for Rannoch as well as a small resort with several hotels, one having a dry-ski slope.

Loch Rannoch

Along the north shore, the road hugs the waterline past sweeping forests with open deer-stalking country above. Near Bridge of Gaur, Rannoch Barracks was an 18th-century military outpost whose troops brought the area's notorious thieves and cattle-rustlers brusquely under control. On the south side are the Black Wood of Rannoch, which was once a den of whisky smugglers; Carie with its forest walks; and pleasant picnic sites among the lochside birches.

Queen's View

Queen Victoria admired this glorious outlook west over Loch Tummel to the towering summit of Schiehallion. Near the Forestry Commission visitor centre a 'conservation walk' explores mixed woodland by the lochside. The Allean forest walks make for higher levels and pass a long-abandoned, but now partly restored, 17th-century farming settlement.

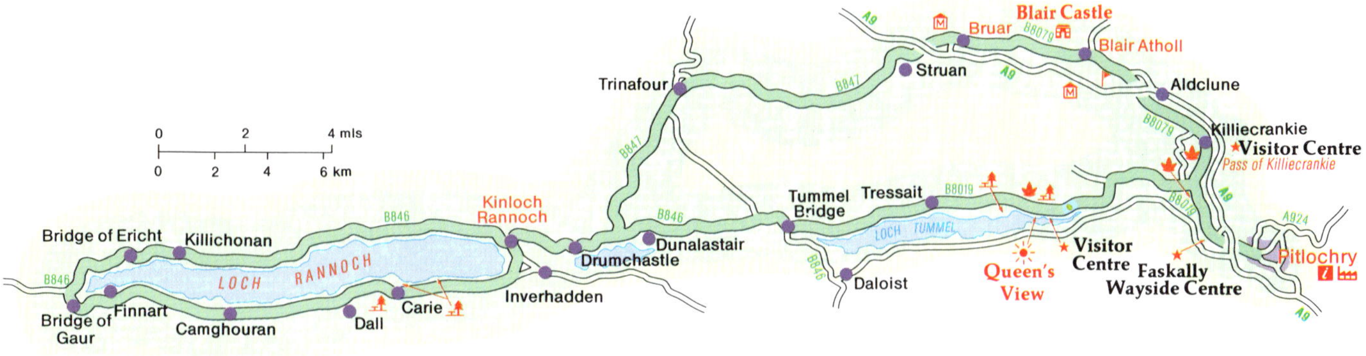

ROUTE DIRECTIONS

Leave **Pitlochry** (map 19 NN 95) on the A924 (sp. Inverness) and pass under the A9 road bridge. Keep left (sp. Killiecrankie B8019), and continue forward along the **Pass of Killiecrankie** to the B8079 to Killiecrankie. Further along Glen Garry pass under the A9 road bridge, to **Blair Atholl,** passing **Blair Castle** on the right to **Bruar**. Turn right on to the B847 (sp. Calvine), pass under the A9 road bridge and, in $1^1/_4$ miles, at Calvine, turn left (sp. Kinloch Rannoch). Follow the B847 through Glen Errochty to Trinafour. Leave the glen and descend into Tummel Valley. Turn right on to the B846 to **Kinloch Rannoch**. Keep forward on the B846 (sp. Rannoch Station) along the north shore of **Loch Rannoch**. In 9 miles pass through Bridge of Ericht. In $1^3/_4$ miles further turn left, unclassified, along the south Loch Rannoch road passing through Bridge of Gaur. After 11 miles turn left and return to Kinloch Rannoch. Turn right on to the B846, Aberfeldy/ Pitlochry road and, in $2^1/_2$ miles, keep forward (sp. Tummel Bridge). Before the bridge bear left on to the B8019, Pitlochry road, along the north side of Loch Tummel. At $1^3/_4$ miles beyond **Queen's View** bear right and, after a further $2^1/_4$ miles, cross the Bridge of Garry and turn right for the return to Pitlochry.

OFF THE TOUR

Edradour Distillery

Leave Pitlochry on the A924 through Moulin and Kinnaird, then keep right for Scotland's tiniest malt whisky distillery. Annual production at Edradour, founded in 1825, equals a single week's at one of the 'majors'.

Pitlochry Power Station

A walkway from Pitlochry across the dam leads to the power station on the far bank of the River Tummel. There are displays on the history of hydro-electricity in the Highlands, and a fascinating view into the 900ft fish ladder which gives salmon access to their spawning grounds upstream.

Glengoulandie Deer Park

On the B846 about 6 miles south of Tummel Bridge, Glengoulandie is home to Highland cattle and rare breeds of sheep, as well as its herd of red deer.

Schiehallion

On the B846 about $4^1/_2$ miles south of Tummel Bridge, a minor road on the right leads to the start of a stiff three-mile hill walk to the 3,547ft landmark summit of Schiehallion. A memorial recalls the 1777/78 visits by Dr Maskelyne, the Astronomer Royal, who lived in a turf hut on the summit ridge while making observations to calculate the weight of the Earth.

OUTDOOR ACTIVITIES

In the Pass of Killiecrankie a walk from the visitor centre shows off, at the narrowest part of the chasm of the River Garry, the fearsome rocks where, after the battle in 1689, one of the government troops managed to jump for his life across the dizzy gap called the Soldier's Leap.

West of Carie, on the south side of Loch Rannoch, the Forestry Commission arranges guided walks in the Black Wood of Rannoch, a cherished remnant of the old Caledonian pine forest.

Off the B8019 the Faskally forest walk goes through Douglas fir, oak and beech trees, sycamore, ash and lime as it circles Dunmore Hill above Loch Faskally. It also skirts the smaller Loch Dunmore, which was once an estate-owner's private fishing water.

On the south side of Loch Rannoch the Carie forest walks offer three routes through spruce plantations, birch and Scots pines on the banks of a tumbling burn. The high 5-mile walk opens up some extensive views.

From the Garry car park on the B8019 the National Trust for Scotland's Linn of Tummel nature trail follows paths in the steep deciduous woods where the rivers Garry and Tummel meet. This is a fine area for woodland birds.

White-turreted Blair Castle, seat of the Duke of Atholl, was restored by successive dukes as a splendid baronial-style mansion

STRATHMORE AND THE GLENS OF ANGUS

68 miles

The Lowlands meet the Highlands here, where the rich arable farms of Strathmore look north to the hills and forests of the Angus glens. In this land of contrasts, one of Scotland's grandest castles is near tiny hamlets which the casual tourist never sees.

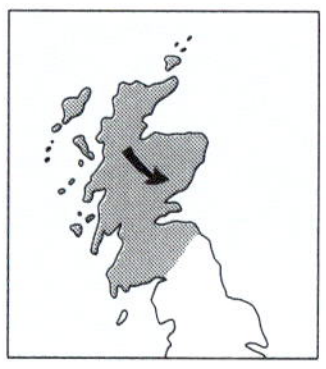

A relief map shows the two faces of landscape and land use on either side of the Highland Boundary Fault. To the south are the ploughed fields and estate woodlands of Strathmore. Rivers such as the Isla meander over a flood plain. Lines of soft fruit canes mark this as the greatest raspberry-growing district in Europe, and mysteriously carved Pictish stones show that this was a settled area – with its own sophisticated art forms – 1,500 years ago. Weaving was the staple trade of several towns and villages, in a county which was the childhood home both of the Queen Mother and of the author of Peter Pan.

To the north lie the far more sparsely populated Angus glens. Now given over mostly to sheep grazing and commercial forests, they were once the alleyways down which Highland raiders swooped to plunder the settlements of Strathmore.

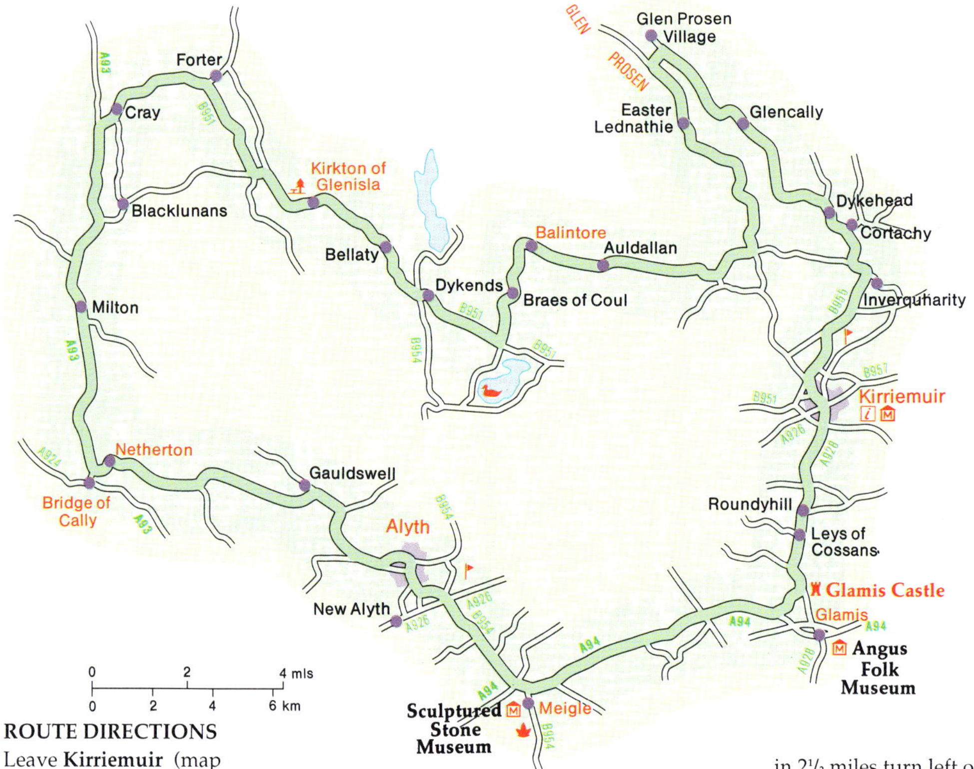

ROUTE DIRECTIONS

Leave **Kirriemuir** (map 19 NO 35) on the B955 (sp. Blairgowrie A926, Glen Cova, Glen Prosen) to reach Dykehead. At Dykehead turn left, unclassified (sp. Prosen). In 1 mile pass memorial to Scott of the Antarctic and enter **Glen Prosen**. After 4½ miles turn left (sp. Kirriemuir) and cross the river bridge, then turn left to follow the west bank of Prosen Water. In 5¼ miles, at the crossroads, turn right (sp. Glenisla), and in 1 mile turn right again. Continue through **Balintore** and, at the T-junction, turn right on to the B951 (sp. Glenisla). Pass through **Kirkton of Glenisla** and in 3¾ miles turn left (sp. Glenshee/Braemar). Ascend 1,200 feet to enter Glen Shee then, at Cray, bear right to cross Shee Water. Shortly, turn left on to the A93 Perth road, continue forward for 8 miles then turn sharp left at **Bridge of Cally**, unclassified (sp. Drimmie). Re-cross the river to pass through **Netherton**, bear right and ascend the valley. In ¾ mile turn right, then in 1¾ miles turn left (sp. Alyth). After 3 miles, at the T-junction, turn right and continue to **Alyth**. Leave Alyth on the B952 Dundee road and, at the end of the town turn left. In ½ mile, at the roundabout, take 3rd exit, B954, and in 2½ miles turn left on to the A94 into **Meigle**. Bear left on to the A94 Aberdeen road and, in 6 miles, turn left, unclassified, to reach the edge of **Glamis**. At the T-junction opposite the gates of **Glamis Castle**, turn left on to the A928 for the return to Kirriemuir.

The celebrated playwright J M Barrie was born at Kirriemuir. This is his boyhood home, now a museum

OFF THE TOUR

Reekie Linn

Turn left off the B951 along the B954 for Bridge of Craigisla and, soon after, the start of the footpath to the falls where the Isla crashes down a rocky gorge. The 'reek' is the haze caused by the spray.

Backwater Reservoir

After the village of Dykends, turn right off the B951 towards this reservoir, dammed to supply the city of Dundee. Backed by heathery slopes and larch plantations, and with parking places provided, it offers extensive south-facing views.

Drumore Loch

Before Bridge of Brewlands on the B951 divert straight on along a minor road and take the first right, across a pass loomed over by a dramatic bouldery hillside, to this artificially created little fishing loch. Lay-bys overlooking its wooded location make pleasant picnic spots.

ON THE TOUR

Kirriemuir

A textile town of warm red sandstone buildings such as the lovely St Mary's Church, Kirriemuir has a Peter Pan statue as a reminder that it was the birthplace of the celebrated playwright J M Barrie. His boyhood home is a fascinating museum. A hilltop park features one of only three camera obscuras in the whole of Scotland and offers superb panoramic views.

Glen Prosen

One of the quietest of the Angus glens, Prosen has steeply sloping fields, forests and strips of 'muirburn' where the heather grouse moors are set alight to encourage early growth. High-set Airlie Memorial Tower commemorates the 11th Earl of Airlie who was killed leading a cavalry charge in the South African War. The outward route passes a memorial to the South Polar explorers, Captain Scott and Edward Wilson, who planned their tragic final expedition here. Scott's famous last letter from the doomed camp on the icecap was written to his friend J M Barrie.

Balintore

Literally one of the high spots of the Angus foothills, 19th-century Balintore Castle stands derelict. From the roadside, motorists can share its magnificent view to Strathmore and the faraway Sidlaw Hills.

Kirkton of Glenisla

In the bright, open and most westerly of the Angus glens, this village is a centre for angling, pony-trekking and other outdoor sports. There is a riverside picnic area, and two hotels provide alfresco garden meals in suitable weather.

Bridge of Cally

Terraced above the wooded gorge of the River Ardle, this village on the Braemar road has an old coaching inn which caters for summer tourists and winter skiers.

Netherton

Down below the high sheep farms, the churchyard in this riverside hamlet overlooks rapids on the Black Water – which flows from the ski slopes of Glenshee.

Alyth

Like Kirriemuir, a one-time handloom weavers' town, Alyth lies on both sides of a burn crossed by road and footbridges, such as the preserved packhorse bridge above Market Square. Alyth Folk Museum with its local history displays is nearby.

Meigle

The glory of this village is its museum of Pictish sculptured stones. Their intricate symbols suggest that the so-called Dark Ages are a mystery not because of their unimportance, but because of our inability to read their messages.

Glamis

Off the pleasant square beside the Strathmore Arms, the Kirkwynd is well known for the Angus Folk Museum in a row of 19th-century weavers' cottages. Fine modern oakwood, carved by members of the congregation, enhances the parish church.

Glamis Castle

Seat of the Earl of Strathmore, this soaring castle, with its towers and ornamented roofline, was the childhood home of the Queen Mother. It owes its current aspect to the period 1675-87. The castle contains royal apartments as well as a richly decorated chapel, portraits, tapestries and silver. There are Dutch and Italian gardens, a woodland nature trail and a fantastically complex 17th-century sundial with 84 faces!

OFF THE BEATEN TRACK

Instead of turning left to go down the west side of Glen Prosen, go straight on into Prosen Village; an out-of-the-way place clustered on a wooded slope above the chattering Prosen Water. The little whitewashed church has some carved memorial oakwood, and a few particularly gloomy graveyard inscriptions.

From the church in Prosen Village there is a right of way footpath that starts in woodland and then, for well prepared walking parties, climbs on to open ground and heads exhilaratingly over the hills to Glen Cova.

OUTDOOR ACTIVITIES

Upstream from Alyth, the burn which shares its name runs through a deep cutting of the Old Red Sandstone from which many local houses were built. The beech, oak, hazel, ash and alder woods flanking the Den of Alyth form a public park with high- and low-level footpaths. A leaflet available on the site explains the geology and wildlife of this attractive walking area.

Ornately turreted Glamis Castle, probably the setting for Shakespeare's Macbeth, *is the Queen Mother's family home and Princess Margaret's birthplace*

THE TROSSACHS AND LOCH LOMOND

98 miles

Close to the Lowland cities, here is a stirring Highland landscape of lochs, mountains and forests in the homeland of Rob Roy MacGregor

and the characters of Sir Walter Scott, in whose footsteps the first tourists enthusiastically came.

Loch Lomond and Loch Lubnaig are two of the most beautiful inland waters in Britain. The mountain mass which surrounds them, rising spectacularly from shores and narrow passes, includes many peaks above 3,000ft.

Rob Roy MacGregor – chieftain, outlaw and cattle-raider – lived here, and this is the place to find out about him, not in the offhand criticisms of non-Scottish writers with no clear idea about his life or his historical context. Sir Walter Scott, though a Borders man, loved this area and used it as the setting for Rob Roy *and* The Lady of the Lake.

Much of this magnificent landscape is owned by the Forestry Commission, Strathclyde Regional Water Board and the National Trust for Scotland. All three organisations go out of their way to provide public access and amenities.

ROUTE DIRECTIONS

Leave **Callander** (map 18 NN 60) on the A84 (sp. Crianlarich). Continue through the Pass of Leny, through **Strathyre** and forwards. At Lochearnhead keep forward on the A85 (sp. Crianlarich) which eventually turns westwards towards **Crianlarich**. Here turn left on to the A82 (sp. Glasgow). Continue through Inverarnan to Ardlui at the head of Loch Lomond, then make a 20 mile run along its entire western side. Continue on the A82 (sp. Glasgow) through **Luss**, and 1¾ miles past Duck Bay, at the roundabout, take 1st exit on to the A811 (sp. Stirling) to reach the edge of **Balloch**. At the next two roundabouts take 2nd exits and then pass the turning for Balloch Castle Country Park. Continue on the A811 to Gartocharn, then in 3¼ miles, at the T-junction, turn left to pass **Drymen**. Four miles on bear left to join the A81 (sp. Aberfoyle). In 6¼ miles bear left on to the A821 and enter **Aberfoyle**. At the Bailie Nicol Jarvie Hotel turn right (sp. Trossachs and Callander) to take **The Duke's Road** and shortly pass the entrance to David Marshall Lodge. After another 3¾ miles turn left for Loch Katrine. Return along the same road and keep forward with the A821 (sp. Callander A84). Pass **Brig o'Turk** and then cross the River Leny and turn right on to the A84, to return to Callander.

Ben Lomond as seen from the bluebell-smothered slopes bordering Loch Lomond. The loch, praised in both song and poem, is the largest stretch of inland freshwater in Britain; it is studded with 30 islands

ON THE TOUR

Callander

A gateway to the Trossachs, with the beautiful area of mountains, lochs and forests to the west, Callander's 18th- and 19th-century main street runs parallel with the meadows by the River Teith. Victorian St Kessog's Church is now the Rob Roy and Trossachs Visitor Centre. Paths thread through the woodlands at the foot of Callander Craigs, which are themselves climbed by forest walks to an outstanding viewpoint ridge. Callander Heather Centre has a miniature railway running round the gardens.

Strathyre

Beyond the forests and towering cliffs of Loch Lubnaig, Strathyre packs hotels and restaurants along its main street. One spectacular walk from the forest centre climbs to the dominating summit of Beinn an t-Sithean, the Hill of the Fairies.

Crianlarich

A road and rail junction under the looming bulk of 3,843ft Ben More; this is where the West Highland Railway splits for Oban and Fort William. The privately-run station tea-room is popular.

Luss

In the most attractive village on Loch Lomondside, Victorian sandstone cottages line the road to the pier. St Kessog's Church was built in 1875 in memory of a Colquhoun laird drowned in the loch. Luss Highland Gathering in July is a lively social and sporting occasion.

Balloch

The River Leven here is crammed with boats and boatyards. In summer the *Countess Fiona* cruises from Balloch pier; zigzagging through the islands to Luss, Rowardennan, Tarbet and Inversnaid. Balloch Castle Country Park offers picnic lawns, woodland walks, a visitor centre and a quiet walled garden.

Drymen

Named from the *druim* – in Gaelic, the ridge – on which it stands, this is a village with a fine range of shops, hotels and inns. The Clachan Inn, facing the green, is said to be one of the oldest in Scotland.

Aberfoyle

Few places in Scotland have such a dramatic approach. Behind the village soar the rugged Menteith Hills where old woodlands and forest plantations mix with rocky crags and abandoned quarry faces. From the crossroads at the Bailie Nicol Jarvie Hotel, named after a character in Scott's *Rob Roy*, the road south makes for a group of forest walks. Doon Hill forest trail recalls a parish minister spirited away by fairies.

The Duke's Road

Originally built in 1821 by a Duke of Montrose, the A821 from Aberfoyle covers 5½ miles of the grandest Highland scenery: mountains, forests and chattering burns. There are picnic places, waymarked walks and superb long-distance views. The major stopping point is the high-set visitor centre, with its own network of walks, at the David Marshall Lodge.

Brig o'Turk

This tiny Trossachs village was a haunt of artists in Victorian times. The Byre Inn, just off the main road, was converted from farm buildings in the 19th century. Beside the post office there is a small display describing the wildlife of the area; a hint that *tuirc* is the Gaelic word for wild boar.

OFF THE BEATEN TRACK

A handloom weaver works at Inverhoulin, north of Tarbet.

Inchmurrin Hotel on Loch Lomond's largest island offers meals – and a return ferry crossing.

OUTDOOR ACTIVITIES

Forest paths in the Pass of Leny lead along an old charcoal-burners' track, to a hilltop viewpoint and to salmon-leap falls.

Lochearnhead is a major water-sports centre with tuition and hiring services for sailors, wind-surfers and water-skiers.

The Glen Ogle Trail uses riverside paths and an old military road, then returns towards Lochearnhead along a disused high-level railway.

Loch Lomond ferries, cruises and/or boat hire are available at Ardlui, Inveruglas, Tarbet, Inverbeg and Luss.

From Gartocharn it is a short walk to the glorious viewpoint summit of Duncryne.

Below: *summertime strollers in the picturesque village of Luss, Loch Lomondside*

Bottom: *parkland and lush green meadows border the River Teith in Callander*

OFF THE TOUR

Balquhidder

Due west of Kingshouse this striking valley heads for a maze of high peaks and tangled glens. Closer at hand the village churchyard holds the grave of Rob Roy MacGregor, who died in 1734 at his Balquhidder farm. Other memorials show that this is also the heartland of the MacLarens.

Balmaha

A left turn in Drymen leads to this Loch Lomondside village at the foot of Conic Hill; surface evidence of the great Highland Boundary Fault. There are walks in spruce and larch plantations, and a splendid nature trail on the high and thickly wooded offshore island of Inchcailloch. Balmaha is the starting-point for the fascinating mailboat cruises on the loch.

Achray Forest Drive

Turning right off the Duke's Road, forest roads swoop through spruce, pine, larch and birch woods to picnic sites by Loch Achray and Loch Drunkie.

Loch Katrine

A reservoir since 1859, this deep-water loch is reached by a left turn off the A821 north of the Duke's Road. In summer the elegant little 1900 steamer, *Sir Walter Scott*, cruises from rustic Trossachs Pier.

LOCH FYNE AND LOCH AWE

67 miles

These two beautiful lochs; both long, narrow and flanked by forested hills, are nevertheless quite different. Fyne is lapped by sea-tides,

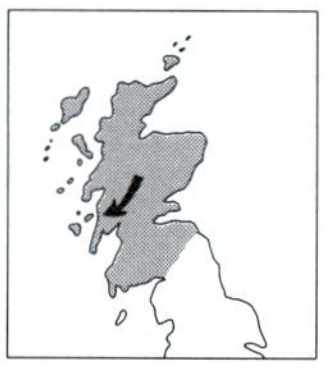

while Awe lies entirely inland. Here is Campbell country, and the lovely valley where Scotland began.

Inveraray on Loch Fyne is the home of the Duke of Argyll, chief of the great Clan Campbell, although the Campbells' first strongholds can still be seen in ruins on Loch Awe. Pre-dating even the Campbells' rise to power, the valley of Kilmartin was where the original Scots – who came from Ireland – established their 6th-century kingdom of Dalriada. Perhaps 4,000 years ago Kilmartin Valley was the site of a Neolithic culture that has left its standing stones and burial cairns to be wondered at even yet.

Loch Awe is a famous angling water sailed by a little steamboat. Crinan, at the end of a 19th-century canal, is a sailing haven with a superb island view. This part of Argyll has forest walks, gardens, a wildlife park and a folk museum where a way of farming life long-gone is lovingly preserved.

Autumn at Loch Awe. Kilchurn Castle on the shore became even more derelict in 1879 when a gale toppled one of its towers

ROUTE DIRECTIONS

Leave **Inveraray** (map 16 NN 00) on the A819 Oban road, passing **Inveraray Castle,** until it descends towards Cladich, then turn left, unclassified (sp. Cladich Ford). In $\frac{1}{4}$ mile, at the edge of Cladich, turn left again on to the B840 (sp. Portsonachan Ford). Continue through **Portsonachan**, and on to the Loch. One mile past the Loch's end, opposite the **Ford** hotel, turn left (sp. Lochgilphead). In $2\frac{3}{4}$ miles, at the A816, turn left (signposted Campbeltown). Go on past **Carnassarie Castle** on the right, to **Kilmartin**. One mile south of the village turn right on to the B8025 (sp. Crinan), and cross Moine Mhor. Cross the River Add and the Crinan Canal, then turn right on to the B841, following the canal. Keep forward for $1\frac{1}{4}$ miles, then branch left, unclassified, and after $\frac{1}{2}$ mile bear right to reach the hotel at **Crinan**. Return by the same roads, passing, after 2 miles, the junction with the B8025. Continue forward on the B841 (sp. Lochgilphead) alongside the canal. Pass two flights of locks and, at Cairnbaan, cross the canal, then turn right on to the A816. In $1\frac{3}{4}$ miles turn left for Lochgilphead. In $\frac{1}{2}$ mile bear right into **Lochgilphead**. Leave on the A83 Glasgow road and, after $7\frac{1}{2}$ miles, pass the Lochgair Hotel. Continue on the A83 through Minard, past **Crarae Glen Gardens** and Furnace, and through **Auchindrain** before re-entering Inveraray.

OFF THE TOUR

Lochawe Pier

The village of Lochawe is reached by going straight on along the A819 past Cladich and then turning left on the A85. From the pier by the lochside station, the ex-Windermere steamboat *Lady Rowena* runs summer cruises; through the lovely wooded islands below the looming mass of Ben Cruachan, and on certain days takes lunch parties to Portsonachan. A West Highland railway carriage has been converted into a restaurant.

Kilchurn Castle

This massive ruined stronghold of the Campbells of Glenorchy, built on a promontory in the loch, is best reached by ferry from Lochawe pier.

Dunadd

Once a headland lapped by the sea, this atmospheric outcrop, off the A816 south of Kilmartin, was once the rock fortress of the Dalriadan kings.

Loch Coille-Bharr

Before reaching Crinan, turn left on to the B8025 then bear left at a war memorial for two fine forest trails. The longer route goes around the loch, pronounced 'Coolivarr', which follows the north-east/south-west alignment of all the sea inlets and freshwater lochs in Knapdale.

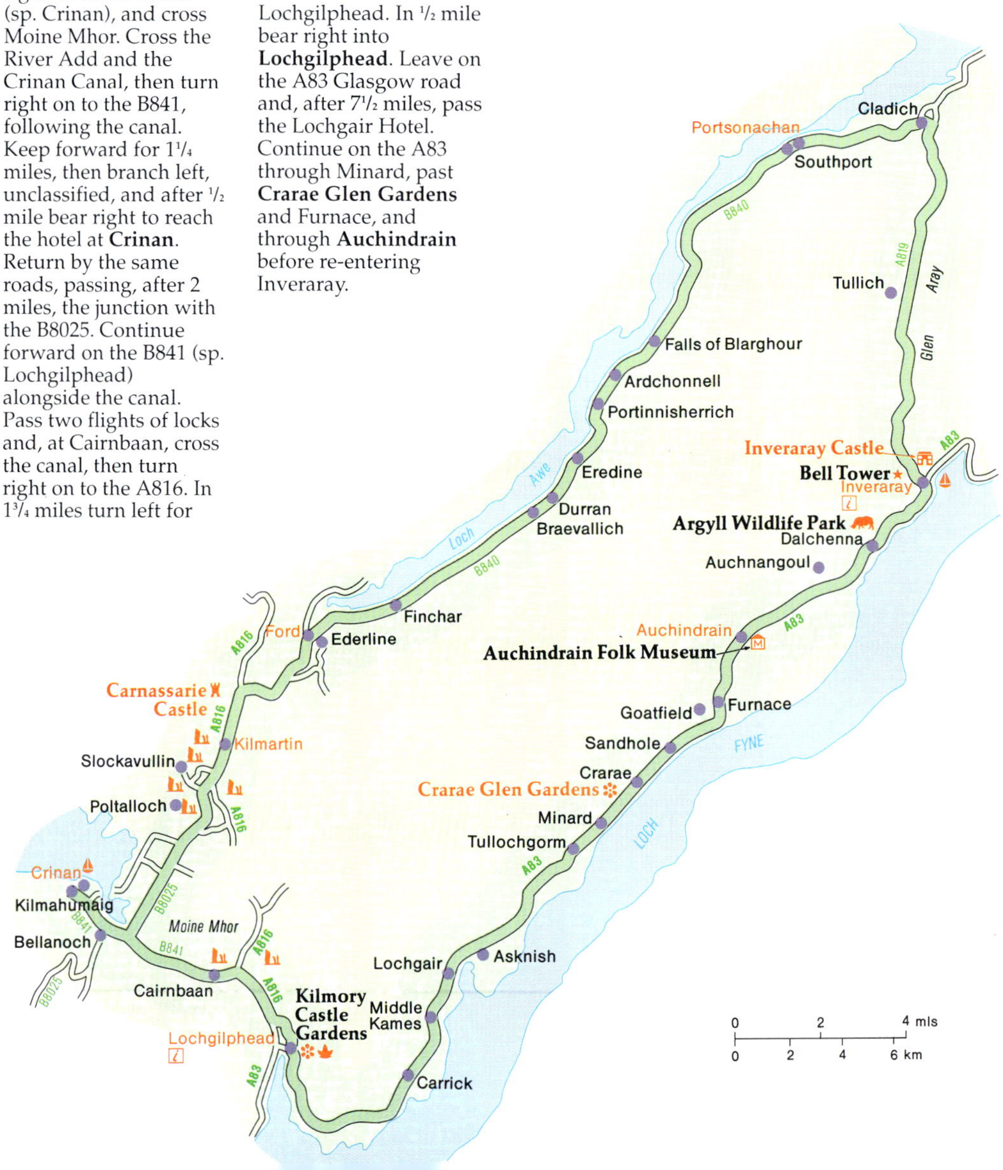

ON THE TOUR

Inveraray

Two 18th-century Dukes of Argyll created Inveraray as one of the finest Georgian towns in Scotland; with well-proportioned houses, public buildings and archways. The sandstone 1920s bell tower is the Clan Campbell war memorial. It has a notable peal of bells, and a display on bell-ringing on the ground floor. Inveraray Jail is one of the most imaginative museums in Scotland. There are displays in almost every cell, and a tape-recorded trial in the restored courtroom.

Inveraray Castle

The seat of the Duke of Argyll, stands in parkland beside the River Aray. It features an imposing armoury hall, valuable tapestries and portraits, handsome public rooms, a grand Victorian kitchen and an exhibition on the far-flung connections of Clan Campbell. In the grounds, the Combined Services Museum illustrates Inveraray's role as a training area for amphibious landings. Glenaray Fish Farm, north of Inveraray, has a children's play area and a pets corner as well as a fish hospital, feeding pools and two fishing lakes.

Portsonachan

Once the port where Highland cattle were ferried across Loch Awe on their way to Lowland markets, this is now a much less hectic village. Portsonachan Hotel, on the site of the 15th-century ferry inn, is a well-known angling centre.

Ford

In the full translation of its Gaelic name this would be Ford of the Hazelnuts. Another anglers' hotel stands near the junction where a minor road turns north for the forest walks, picnic sites and viewpoints on the west side of Loch Awe.

Carnassarie Castle

High above the main road, this 16th-century tower was where a Bishop of the Isles wrote the first Gaelic book ever printed. There is a dramatic view into the narrow glen which brings the road from Loch Awe.

Kilmartin

The church here displays impressive medieval stone carvings. Also in view are the standing stones and cairns of a much earlier era. Four burial sites in a straight line form a 'linear cemetery' near the church. Many of the antiquities can be visited.

Crinan

The village at the western basin of the Crinan Canal is much frequented by yachts and fishing boats. There is a level towpath walk looking across to the wild Poltalloch hills. Crinan harbour is a separate sheltered anchorage nearby.

Lochgilphead

This popular holiday centre is the bustling shopping and market town for a wide area of mid-Argyll. It has access to the canal towpath walk, a picnic area on a grassy sward beside Loch Gilp, a pottery to visit and – around the council offices at Kilmory Castle – rock, rose and water gardens, nature trails and masses of rhododendrons.

Crarae Glen Gardens

This woodland glen is a 'must' in any visit to Argyll. Rare trees and flowering shrubs, as well as springtime bulbs, give a variety of colour from early in the year until the final glory of autumn.

Auchindrain

The forests of mid-Argyll have not been allowed to encroach on this 19th-century farming settlement, restored as an open-air museum. Individual cottages are furnished in contemporary style, and there is a visitor centre to explain the simple farming life of generations gone by. Just south of Inveraray, Argyll Wildlife Park is home to red, roe and fallow deer, wallabies, wildfowl and an avenue of owls.

OFF THE BEATEN TRACK

North of Inveraray, a monument above the A819 commemorates author Neil Munro, creator of Para Handy and his erratic coaster the *Vital Spark*.

A massive ivied ruin, not open to visitors, on an islet south of Portsonachan, Innischonnell was the original 12th-century fortress of the Campbell chiefs.

The Crinan Canal runs between Knapdale Forest and low-lying Crinan Moss. It has 15 locks. 'Lock 16' is the seafood restaurant at Crinan Hotel.

Quarry Point is a lochside picnic area before Crarae.

OUTDOOR ACTIVITIES

Woodland walks at Inveraray Castle climb to a summit viewpoint tower overlooking castle, town and loch.

From Crinan harbour a walk on a forest road leads to a superb viewpoint over the Sound of Jura.

Left: *sheltered Crinan harbour from where a network of forest walks start, leading most notably to a superb viewpoint across the Sound to the mountainous islands of Jura and Scarba*

Right: *view from Duniquaich Hill of Inveraray Castle and town, where whitewashed houses are reflected in the waters of Loch Fyne*

AROUND THE KINTYRE PENINSULA

76 miles

Attached to the rest of Scotland only by a slim isthmus, where Tarbert's two sea-lochs almost meet, Kintyre is a long peninsula of forests,

sheep and dairy farms and tiny coastal villages once cheekily made part of the territory of the Viking kings.

By the treaty of Tarbert in 1098 the Scottish king granted the Vikings control of all the western islands they could take their ships around. Magnus Bareleg made the magnificent gesture of having his galley hauled, himself at the tiller, overland at Tarbert, thus claiming the whole of Kintyre as his domain. Even now, Kintyre place-names ending in 'dale' reveal a Viking past, just as those starting with 'Kil' were the locations of Celtic churches.

Kintyre's two coastlines are far from being mirror images. On the west, a low road below the cliffs of the old raised beaches keeps close to the shore and offers long views over well-tilled farmland to the open sea. The narrower east coast road dives and jerks its way through forests and river valleys, looking across Kilbrannan Sound to the huge bulk of Arran.

ROUTE DIRECTIONS
Leave **Tarbert** (map 16 NR 86) on the A83 Campbeltown road, passing West Tarbert and Kennacraig Ferry Terminal before moving inland past Whitehouse and Clachan. Continue on the A83 through **Killean**, past **Glenbarr** and on to **Westport**, Kilchenzie, then **Campbeltown**. Leave Campbeltown on the B842 (sp. Carradale), pass through **Peninver** and then **Saddell**. Still on the B842 continue, passing near Carradale, then follow the road inland before descending (1 in 7) to the coast at **Grogport**. In 9¼ miles, at Claonaig, where a summer car ferry sails to Arran, go forward on to the B8001 (sp. Tarbert). At the T-junction go right on to the A83 (sp. Glasgow) and, passing Kennacraig Ferry Terminal and West Tarbert, again re-enter Tarbert.

Tarbert harbour and castle on Loch Fyne. This little town was once an important herring-fishing centre, but now only echoes remain of the bustle of earlier days

ON THE TOUR

Tarbert

In Gaelic, this name indicates a narrow neck of land across which a boat can be dragged. In the 14th century, Robert the Bruce repeated Magnus Bareleg's act as he formally reclaimed Kintyre for Scotland. He also garrisoned Tarbert Castle, which stands as a viewpoint ruin, overlooking East Loch Tarbert's sheltered fishing and yachting harbour, and around which the main part of the town is clustered. About 12 miles beyond Tarbert, at Ronachan, a car park overlooks some rocks where grey seals bask.

Killean

The graveyard of the ruined parish church here displays some intricately carved medieval grave-slabs. One shows a sword and hunting scenes, another a mail-clad knight. The tradition lasted for many centuries: a gravestone carved in 1810 shows the deceased farmer ploughing with a team of horses.

Glenbarr

Glenbarr Abbey in this little village by the Barr Water is a Gothic mansion-house owned by the Clan Macalister. It is a museum with an information centre about the clan. Families connected with the Macalisters include Alexander, Allison, Lester and Saunders. Farther south, a guessing game can be held about the pronunciation of the village name Bellochantuy. Ask locally for the answer!

Westport

Beside the A83 there are many picnic and parking places, by the rocky shore where Atlantic rollers come creaming in. The one at Westport provides a striking view over the Links of Machrihanish to the great headland of the Mull of Kintyre; sometimes wreathed in low cloud.

Campbeltown

The only town in Kintyre stands at the head of its sea-loch around a fishing harbour overlooked by farmed and forested hills. Campbeltown Cross, near the pier, is a fine example of Highland stonework and the jaunty 18th-century Town House features an octagonal steeple. In the museum there are displays not only on the town itself but also about the fascinating archaeology of Kintyre. On certain days, the Creamery shows off its cheddar cheese-making with milk from the dairy farms of Kintyre and Gigha. In summer, Campbeltown hosts the Kintyre Music Festival, Highland Games, its own Festival Week and a bustling agricultural show.

Peninver

One of many pleasant little places along the east coast of Kintyre, Peninver is reached, like so many of them, by a steep descent on the B842. There is a parking area, close to a sandy beach, which looks across Kilbrannan Sound; to the hills and forests of Arran which fill the eastern horizon for many miles to come.

Saddell

A very steep, downhill hairpin bend leads into another tiny village where a river tumbles down from the forested hills above. Saddell Abbey, a ruined 12th-century Cistercian house, preserves several striking grave-slabs, again including knights in mail. This is the burial place of Somerled, Lord of the Isles and founder of the great family of Clan Donald.

Grogport

Here is another steep descent, to a burn flowing into the sea at a sand and shingle bay. A picnic site looks across the Sound to the northern peaks of Arran. Grogport was once, as its name implies, a secret haven on the whisky-smugglers' trail.

OFF THE BEATEN TRACK

The most remarkable walk in Kintyre is across the tidal bank to Island Davaar in Campbeltown Loch. There is a Crucifixion painting in one of the caves. Tide tables are available from the Campbeltown tourist office.

Traces can still be seen of the route of the Campbeltown and Machrihanish Light Railway, which ran from 1906 until 1932.

OUTDOOR ACTIVITIES

Day permits are available for trout and salmon fishing on the rivers and hill lochs of the peninsula.

From the Grianan picnic place on the B842 there is access to the Carradale forest walks.

Below: *bright white yachts and their sailors have taken the place of the old brown-sailed fishing luggers and the herring gutters in Tarbert's harbour*

Bottom: *winter reflections in Loch Fyne and the surrounding mountains from Glen Kinglas at Cairndow*

OFF THE TOUR

Gigha

A car ferry from Tayinloan sails several times every day on the 20-minute run to this fascinating island of dairy farms, quiet beaches and antiquities. The sheltered woodland gardens at Achamore House are stocked with rhododendrons, azaleas and many other flowering shrubs.

Machrihanish

On the B843 off the A83 west of Campbeltown; this is a golfing resort with a very fine course on the springy turf behind a 3½ mile beach. Inland, scheduled flights from Glasgow share an extensive RAF base.

Carradale

A right turn after Saddell leads to this fishing and holiday village which offers angling and golfing, a south-facing beach, watersports, forest and coastal trails, and informal walks in the wild garden of Carradale House.

Skipness

This village is reached by turning right on to the B8001 at Claonaig, where the Skipness River meets the sea. Its ruined 13th-century castle was a stronghold of the MacDonalds. Nearby, the roofless Kilbrannan Chapel was named for St Brendan, the 6th-century missionary explorer.

CARRICK AND THE RHINNS

70 miles

The rocky shoreline, cliffs and old raised beaches of the Carrick coast ease off to sheep-grazed hills and forests inland. In the south, quiet river valleys lead to the dairy farms of the Rhinns of Galloway and the ferry ports for Northern Ireland.

Gulls wheel raucously over the fish-landing quays at Girvan. Out in the Firth of Clyde looms the huge isolated rock of Ailsa Craig. Inland, Carrick offers many pleasant stopping places: an outstanding Pre-Raphaelite castle contrasts with a riverside village where afternoon teas are de rigueur *in summer.*

Lonely moors and forests take the route across the Wigtown border. In the 17th century this was great Covenanting country. 'Peden the Prophet' was just one parish minister forced to preach to congregations gathered doggedly in the hills. Loch Ryan, a hectic place in wartime, is the ferryway to Ireland. An exhilarating road with wide-ranging views sweeps high above the sea, then dashes down again along the Carrick shore, where travellers once went fearfully in the domain of the dreaded cannibalistic Beans.

ON THE TOUR

Girvan

A fishing and boat-building port as well as a holiday resort, Girvan has a fine exposure to the Firth of Clyde, a lively riverside harbour, a sailing club and a links golf course. Knockcushan Gardens at Girvan harbour is a sheltered park with a small aviary. Jazz and folk festivals, a major cycle race and athletics meetings are held every year.

Penkill Castle

In the 19th century, artists of the Pre-Raphaelite Brotherhood – William Morris, Burne-Jones and Holman Hunt among them – worked in this glorious house above a wooded ravine with a view of the sea. They left paintings and tapestries, decorated the house and created many garden features. Now Penkill offers guided tours, booked in advance by phoning 046 587 261.

Barr

In summer this quiet and sheltered conservation village, where cottages and an inn look down on the rocky Water of Gregg, is a favourite place with visitors for a stroll and an afternoon tea.

Barrhill

Here the route turns off on a lonely road, past some Covenanting memorials and Barrhill's remote station, to follow the railway over the moors to Galloway. In the valley, Kildonan is a former convent turned country house hotel.

New Luce

The first village in Galloway is a quiet place where the two main sources of the Water of Luce combine. A 17th-century parish minister here, Alexander Peden, was one of the many forced out of his church because of his adherence to Covenanting ways. As Peden the Prophet he became one of the finest of the hunted preachers; who held services in faraway locations with guards posted in case troops suddenly swept down.

Castle Kennedy Gardens

In the mild climate of the Rhinns, many splendid gardens have been created. Here they cover the peninsula between two inland lochs. Footpaths link banks of azaleas and rhododendrons, a monkey puzzle avenue, a waterlily pond and a sunken garden.

Cairnryan

As the alternative Irish ferry port to Stranraer, Cairnryan served in the Second World War as

In spring and early summer the Castle Kennedy gardens are ablaze with flowers

Number 2 Military Port. Loch Ryan was also a flying-boat base. Later, surplus ammunition was loaded here onto ships taken out into the Atlantic and scuttled. Ship-breaking was also a major industry.

Ballantrae

Ardstinchar Castle, a ruined stronghold of the Kennedys, dominates the approach to this pleasant, one-time smugglers' village. It stands, as its name implies, on a hill overlooking the River Stinchar; a beautiful and well-known angling water. The shingly lagoons at the mouth of the river – nestling ground for terns – are a nature reserve. The spectacular drive over Bennane Head can be enlivened by blood-curdling tales of the infamous Sawney Bean, head of a cave-dwelling family here, executed for dining off murdered passers-by.

Lendalfoot

Much of this hamlet is attractively old-fashioned: the Carleton Fishery dating from 1832, and the sturdy stone cottages. In recent years, many wooden chalets have been built, sheltering from the easterly winds below the raised-beach cliffs. On a rock-spiked shore, a little walled-in memorial commemorates a boat crew drowned in 1711.

A peaceful summer scene at Girvan's popular riverside harbour and gardens

ROUTE DIRECTIONS

Leave **Girvan** (map 14 NX 19) on the A77 (sp. Ayr). At the end of the town, at the round-about, take 2nd exit to join the B734 Barr road. On approaching Old Dailly turn right (sp. Barr), to pass **Penkill Castle**, then in ¾ mile turn left. At **Barr** turn right with the B734 (sp. Pinwherry and Barrhill) then cross the river bridge. After some 5½ miles, at the junction with the A714, turn left (sp. Newton Stewart). In Pinwherry turn right to cross the Duisk River and continue on the A714 to the outskirts of **Barrhill**. At Barrhill turn right, unclassified (sp. New Luce). After 9 miles cross the river bridge, turn left and continue. At **New Luce** turn right (sp. Stranraer) and cross the river bridge. In nearly 5 miles pass **Castle Kennedy Gardens** and then turn right on to the A75 and, after nearly 1 mile turn right on to the A751 (sp. Ayr). In 1¾ miles turn right on to the A77. Continue through **Cairnryan, Ballantrae** and **Lendalfoot**. Approaching Girvan, at the round-about, turn left to complete the tour.

OFF THE BEATEN TRACK

Ailsa Craig, 10½ miles out to sea, can be reached from Girvan. There are old quarries, a light-house and a ruined castle on a hairpinned pathway to the summit. Thousands of birds nest in one of Europe's greatest gannet colonies.

While the village of Old Dailly has all but faded from the scene, the ruined parish church retains Covenanting memorials and the grave of William Bell Scott, one of the Pre-Raphaelites of Penkill.

North of Cairnryan, Finnarts Bay picnic site offers a good view of the Irish ferries. A salmon farm welcomes visitors.

OUTDOOR ACTIVITIES

As well as the sail to Ailsa Craig, the harbour at Girvan is a starting-point for sea-angling trips.

The early part of the 212-mile Southern Upland Way includes many easy stretches in the Rhinns, on farm tracks, forest roads and even the driveway to Castle Kennedy Gardens.

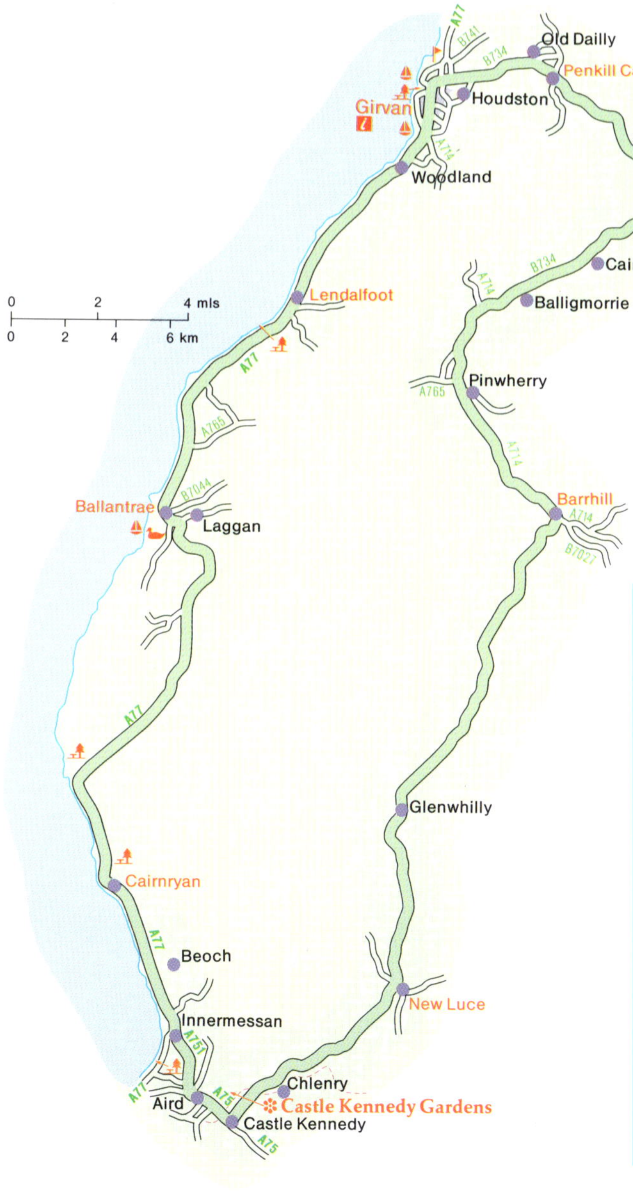

OFF THE TOUR

Turnberry

North of Girvan where the A719 leaves the A77, this is a famous golfing resort whose luxury hilltop hotel looks out towards Ailsa Craig. A walk along the beach leads to a lighthouse beside the ruins of the castle which was Robert the Bruce's boyhood home.

Bargany Gardens

About 1½ miles east of Old Dailly crossroads, these woodland gardens provide glorious colours and centre on an ornamental lake.

Glenluce Abbey

Quietly located south of New Luce, this ruined Cistercian abbey has a graceful chapter house and memorials to the families of Gordon and Hay.

Stranraer

Reached by following the A75 beyond Castle Kennedy, Stranraer is the railhead and one of the ferry ports for Larne in Northern Ireland. Its medieval town-centre castle, once the headquarters of the Covenanters' persecution and then a 19th-century courthouse and jail, is now a visitor centre with a good rooftop view. In the old town hall museum nearby, one room is dedicated to the Ross family of Polar explorers.

QUEEN'S WAY AND SMUGGLERS' COAST

90 miles

This part of Dumfries and Galloway combines the atmospheric Solway Coast, where many a boat with muffled oars landed cargoes at dead of night, with attractive towns, intriguing villages and a hinterland of lochs, rivers, hills and forests to explore.

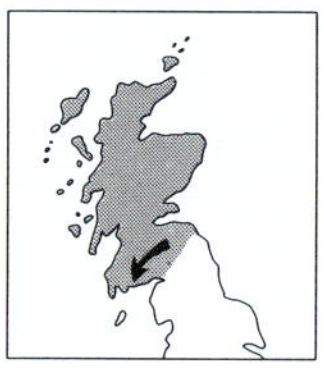

Kirkcudbright is an 18th-century architectural gem of elegance, colour and interest, where several painters and craftworkers live. Gatehouse of Fleet reveals its unexpected industrial past only to observant visitors, and Castle Douglas is the epitome of a busy market town.

Parts of the coastline are among the most beautiful in the south of Scotland, but for generations their proximity to the tax-free harbours of the Isle of Man attracted whole companies of smugglers. Secret pony-trains hustled contraband to customers who asked no questions about how the wines, silk and lace arrived in the Lowland cities.

Inland, the massive Galloway Forest Park provides walks and nature trails, picnic places, viewpoints and a chance to watch wildlife at the closest quarters.

Below: *the Galloway Window by Brian Thomas is one of many exhibits at the Deer Museum on the shore of Clatteringshaws Loch*

Below right: *the four-storeyed tower of Threave Castle, on an island in the Dee, was completed in 1690 by Archibald the Grim, Lord of Galloway*

ON THE TOUR

Kirkcudbright

This is one of the finest Georgian county towns in Scotland, thanks to its well-proportioned and often colour-washed houses. Edward Hornel, one of many artists who settled here, bequeathed Broughton House; backed by a hidden Japanese garden, as a gallery and museum. There is a riverside harbour on the Dee. Close by, MacLellan's Castle was a stately 16th-century town house, while the Stewartry Museum illustrates Kirkcudbright's social, military, sporting and mercantile past.

Gatehouse of Fleet

From the late 18th century, Gatehouse, on the River Fleet, was briefly a cotton boom town and it is intriguing to see which houses were once connected with breweries, tanneries or bobbin mills. Gatehouse has several hotels with a history. Robert Burns wrote the stirring *Scots Wha Hae* in the Murray Arms. A footpath leads to the viewpoint of Venniehill. Farther on, 15th-century **Cardoness Castle,** built by the MacCullochs, has survived the family's notoriously fiery tempers. After Gatehouse, Skyreburn Aquarium is a simple but fascinating place with fish from Galloway's lochs, rivers and coast.

Creetown

Once a great granite-producing centre, Creetown has craft shops and a leisurely walk in the woodlands of King George V Park, returning by the trout stream of the Moneypool Burn. However, its high spot is the amazing Gem Rock Museum of semi-precious stones.

Newton Stewart

This is a market town with a fine low-arched bridge over the well-fished River Cree. The museum concentrates on domestic furnishings of days gone by. In the attractive attached village of Minnigaff, a footpath leads along the narrow, wooded peninsula between the Penkiln Burn and the Cree. Just after Talnotry, at Craigdews, is a wild goat park.

Galloway Deer Museum

This stopping point on the Queen's Way, as the A712 is called where it passes through the Galloway Forest Park, has exhibits far wider-ranging than its name suggests; on all of Galloway's wildlife, its forests and hydro-electric scheme.

Castle Douglas

A substantial market centre with busy livestock auctions, Castle Douglas has coaching and market inns dating back 200 years. An extensive public park includes Carlingwark Loch with its wooded islands, boating and windsurfing.

Palnackie

Once a river port on the Urr, Palnackie specialises in the unexpected: glass-blown mushrooms, rocking camels (not horses) for Arab children, and the world flounder-tramping championship.

Dundrennan Abbey

In 1568 Mary Queen of Scots spent her last night on Scottish soil at Dundrennan; before sailing to England, exile and death. The early history of the 12th-century abbey is vague, but even in ruins the arcaded chapels and chapter house, and the soaring transepts, show a mastery of masonry and design.

ROUTE DIRECTIONS

Leave **Kirkcudbright** (map 14 NX 65) by Bridge Street, A755 (sp. Gatehouse of Fleet). Follow this road to a crossroads with the A75. Go forward on to the B727. Pass through **Gatehouse of Fleet**, and by **Cardoness Castle** ruins before turning right to re-join the A75. Pass by **Creetown** and through Palnure. Three miles on, at the round-about, take 3rd exit, A714, and enter **Newton Stewart**. In the town centre turn right on to the B7079 (sp. New Galloway A712) and cross the River Cree. One mile further on turn left on to the A712 and, passing the Craigdews Hill Wild Goat Park and the **Galloway Deer Museum**, continue to New Galloway. Leave on the A762 Kirkcudbright road and pass through Mossdale and Laurieston. At Ringford turn left on to the A75 Dumfries road. In 3½ miles cross the River Dee. Further along the A75 turn right, unclassified, towards Threave Gardens and continue to **Castle Douglas**. At the end of the Town, at the roundabout, take 2nd main exit on to the A745 (sp. Dalbeattie). After 5 miles turn right on to the A711 (sp. Auchencairn). Skirt the village of **Palnackie** and continue on through Auchencairn. After a further 3¾ miles, in Dundrennan, turn left to follow the A711 past **Dundrennan Abbey** and on into Kirkcudbright.

OFF THE BEATEN TRACK

Carsluith Castle, left of the A75 before Creetown, is a 16th-century tower whose gun ports contrast oddly with its current location beside a farm.

In summer the Forestry Commission's Raiders Road forest drive, off the Queen's Way, follows a track once used by old-time cattle thieves.

OUTDOOR ACTIVITIES

Before Gatehouse, Fleet Forest Oakwood Trail takes in one of the finest deciduous woodlands in Galloway.

To the right of the A75 at Palnure, forest trails fan out from the Kirroughtree Forest Classroom which explains the harvesting and uses of timber.

Talnotry is the start of steep forest walks to the old Edinburgh-Wigtown coaching road, a waterfall, and abandoned lead and nickel mines.

On the Threave estate just before Castle Douglas, the National Trust for Scotland's gardens are open to visitors all the year round.

OFF THE TOUR

Tongland Power Station

Tours of the spick-and-span generating centre, on the A711 north of Kirkcudbright, explain the history and workings of the Galloway hydro-electric scheme. Also, visit the 29-pool salmon ladder in a wooded glen which lets fish reach their spawning grounds above the Tongland dam.

Cairn Holy

About 4 miles after Skyreburn Aquarium, a side road right off the A75 climbs to this Neolithic burial site, at least 4,000 years old, whose upright stones mark the tombs high above Wigtown Bay.

Threave Castle

The little adventure of reaching this 15th-century stronghold of the Black Douglases involves turning left off the A75 beyond Ringford to a car park, walking along a farm track then being rowed to the castle on its island in the River Dee.

Orchardton Tower

It is a puzzle why this little 15th-century fortified house, on a minor road south from Palnackie, is the only one in Scotland built to the round Irish plan. A spiral staircase leads to a fine roof-level viewpoint.

Balcary Bay

The most desirable stretch of the Solway Coast, south-east of Auchencairn, was a favourite hideaway for contraband from the Isle of Man. The present-day hotel was built by an 18th-century smuggling company, and off-shore Hestan Island was another smugglers' den.

Part of the walk along the Solway Coast takes in beautiful Balcary Bay. The area here was popular with 18th-century smugglers as a hiding place for the booty they brought over from the Isle of Man

NITHSDALE AND THE LOWTHER HILLS

89 miles

This is typical Southern Uplands country. Arable valleys and breezy moorlands mix with places where coal, lead, gold and silver once paid the wages. The pedal cycle was invented here, and Britain's highest scheduled railway once steamed through.

If you believe one of the inscriptions in the graveyard at Leadhills, the fresh air of the Lowthers is remarkably beneficial: one local man died at the age of more than 130! At its higher levels – and the highest village in Scotland is here – this area is exhilarating hill country, as many of its walks will prove.

It is also intriguing for the industrial archaeologist. Relics of many abandoned mining enterprises wait to be explored, and the track of the old Leadhills Light Railway can still be seen. The oldest post office in Britain still functions in one of the Nithsdale towns.

Elsewhere, Drumlanrig is one of Scotland's finest castles open to visitors, while expatriate Scots all over the world know the love song about Maxwelton and the daughter of the house, bonnie Annie Laurie.

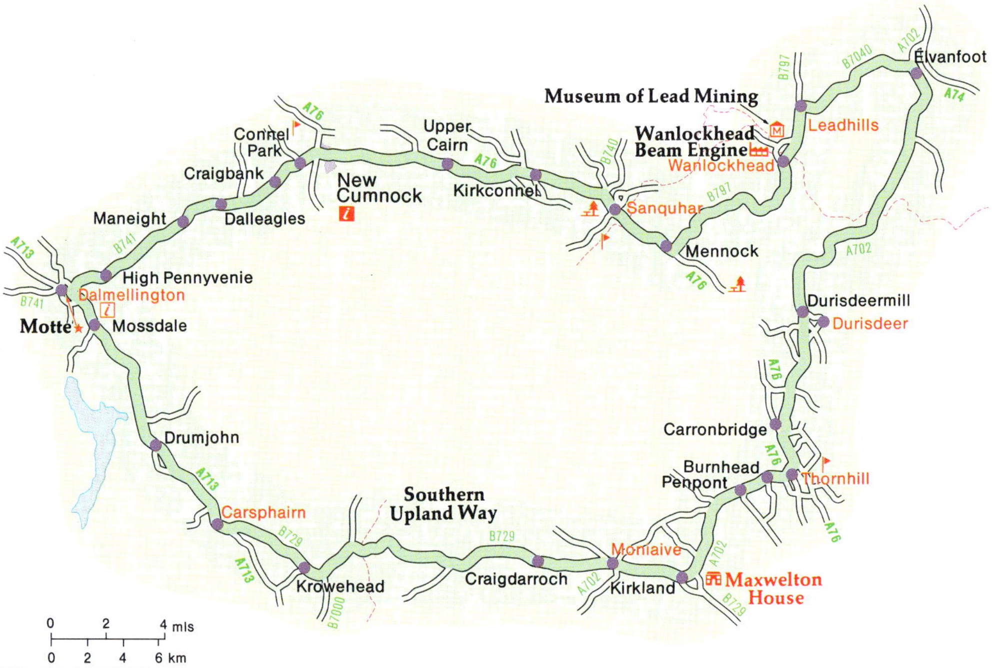

ROUTE DIRECTIONS

Leave **Thornhill** (map 14 NX 89) on the A76, Kilmarnock road. At Carronbridge turn right on to the A702 (sp. Edinburgh) and continue forward past the right turn to **Durisdeer**. Just beyond the village of Elvanfoot cross the river bridge and turn left on to the B7040 (sp. Leadhills). At **Leadhills** turn left on to the B797 (sp. Wanlockhead). Continue through **Wanlockhead** and, after 6½ miles, at the T-junction, turn right on to the A76 through **Sanquhar** and Kirkconnel. At New Cumnock turn left on to the B741 (sp. Dalmellington). In **Dalmellington**, at the roundabout, take 1st exit (sp. Dumfries), then in ½ mile turn left on to the A713 to **Carsphairn**. In ¼ mile beyond this village turn left on to the B729 (sp. Moniaive). After 3¾ miles turn left with the B729 and join a stretch of single-track road across moorland before descending to **Moniaive**. At Moniaive join the A702 (sp. Thornhill) and, passing **Maxwelton House**, near the junction with the B729 Dumfries road, continue along the A702 to Penpont. One mile beyond Penpont, at a telephone kiosk, bear right, still on the A702, to cross the River Nith and return to Thornhill.

The entrance to an old lead mine at Wanlockhead, where there is a fascinating museum of mining

ON THE TOUR

Thornhill

A Duke of Queensberry built this handsome little Nithsdale town. His emblem of a winged horse tops a column in the spacious main street. Thornhill is a good shopping centre, and in summer outdoor café tables give it a mildly Continental air.

Durisdeer

Roman legionaries and 18th-century coach travellers came through this now-bypassed village at the foot of a green Lowthers glen. Durisdeer's 17th-century church houses ornate Queensberry tombs. In the square a plaque shows where the total re-surveying of Britain's maps ended in 1982.

Leadhills

Romans took gold from the Lowthers, as did later Scottish kings. From the 17th century, lead and silver were mined. The curfew bell which tolled the hours of the changing shifts in the lead mines has been restored. An obelisk commemorates steamboat pioneer William Symington, and the claim on John Taylor's grave that he was 137 when he died in 1770 is considered only slightly optimistic. Founded in 1741 as one of the first subscription libraries in Europe, the Allan Ramsey Library preserves accounts of the lead-mining operations.

Wanlockhead

This other lead-mining village is the highest in Scotland at around 1,400ft. Its fascinating museum – in and out of doors – explores mines, smelters and the stately beam engine used to pump out flooded galleries. The walk-in Loch Nell mine shows figures of miners at work underground.

Sanquhar

A visitor centre in the tolbooth records local history and how the 17th-century Covenanters demanding freedom from government control of the church were hunted down. The coal mines are closed, but Sanquhar has an unexpected industry in firework-making. Its 1763 post office is the oldest in Britain. The Southern Upland Way climbs way up into the Lowther Hills.

Dalmellington

Weaving and coal-mining have both gone, but the Cathcartston Interpretation Centre features a handloom weaving room and also tells the story of the town. At Minnivey the Ayrshire Railway Preservation Group holds Open Days when its industrial locomotives are 'in steam'.

Carsphairn

Among green and part-forested hills, Carsphairn is a pleasant stopping-off place for a snack, meal or picnic. This was Covenanting country, and later the boyhood home of the famous road-builder John Loudon MacAdam.

Moniaive

A village of brightly painted houses and colourful gardens, Moniaive preserves its 17th-century market cross, and the Reverend James Renwick, last of the Covenanting martyrs, is commemorated. Only disused bridges, cuttings and embankments in the fields show the line of the old Cairn Valley Railway to Dumfries.

Maxwelton House

This gracious mansion was the home for many generations of the Laurie family. In the 18th century Anna, a daughter of the house, was courted by a young man her father rebuffed. They eventually married other people, but some verses her first suitor had composed were later re-written as one of scotland's most famous love songs, *Annie Laurie*. A courtyard museum displays domestic ware, kitchen, garden and dairy tools, and there is a charming Victorian chapel.

OFF THE BEATEN TRACK

The Leadhills Light Railway ran between Elvanfoot and Wanlockhead from 1902 until 1938 over the highest standard-gauge summit in Britain – 1,498ft. Part of it is being relaid as a narrow-gauge line.

A road at Minnivey leads to the sites of two remote, abandoned hill villages – Benwhat and Corbie Craigs – built in the 1850s for local ironstone miners.

While most of the gold has gone from the Lowthers, local advice should be asked about where some modest panning of the burns may be done.

OUTDOOR ACTIVITIES

The Southern Upland Way offers two walks out of Wanlockhead: along the valley of the Wanlock Water and to the aircraft radio base on the 2,378ft summit of Lowther Hill.

Carsphairn heritage trails visit several historical sites and also extend to the wild hill country of the Rhinns of Kells.

OFF THE TOUR

Drumlanrig Castle

Signposted from the A76 north of Carronbridge, the Duke of Buccleuch's Dumfries-shire home is an outstanding pink sandstone, 17th-century castle. Louis XIV furniture is matched by Rembrandt and Leonardo paintings, and a massive silver chandelier. Craftspeople have a range of workshops here. Drumlanrig Castle grounds include an adventure play area in the woodland.

Loch Doon

South of Dalmellington, a side road off the A713 leads to the reservoir where, during the First World War, there was a crazy scheme to create an aerial gunnery range. Some traces remain. In the 1930s when the water level was raised, 14th-century Loch Doon Castle was rebuilt on dry land.

Tynron

Reached by a hill road north-east from Moniaive, Tynron church has a memorial to a Covenanter shot during the religious strife of the 1680s. Tynronkirk whisky is a lost brand once stocked in House of Commons bars.

Keir Mill

At Penpont, turn right off the A702 for this village where, in 1839, blacksmith Kirkpatrick MacMillan built the first pedal cycle. He never bothered to patent his invention and lies unacclaimed in the quiet churchyard.

Sparkling Tynron water was once used in the making of unique Tynronkirk whisky

LIDDESDALE AND ESKDALE

83 miles

Divided by the watershed which separates the rivers destined for the North Sea and the Solway Firth, these rolling hills and

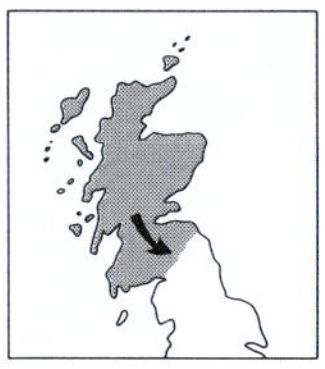

valleys feature notable textile towns, angling rivers, memories of famous men and an unexpected hint of Tibet.

The towns here are in different local authority regions, but Hawick and Langholm share interests in rugby and horse-riding, and owe their status to woollen mills powered at first by their rivers – the Teviot and the Esk. The invigorating grassy hills, which used to be the preserve of shepherds, are covered with vast areas of state and private forests. However, round much of the route, sheep and hillside sheepfolds are still often in view. Villages are few and far between, and the winding riverside roads offer many tempting picnic spots.

The people here are just as important as the places, and many have spread their fame abroad. By birth or by descent, Eskdale has produced a famous modern poet, a pioneering civil engineer and the first man on the moon.

Landscape near Newcastleton, a late 18th-century 'planned' village which is unusual in having three squares and a rectangular pattern of streets

ROUTE DIRECTIONS

Leave **Hawick** (map 15 NT 51) on the B6399 (sp. Newcastleton) and continue forward. At the turn off for **Hermitage Castle**, bear left over the river bridge. In $3\frac{3}{4}$ miles, at the river bridge, bear right across it, on the B6357 to **Newcastleton**. In 10 miles keep forward over the river bridge to **Canonbie**. At Canonbie take a sharp right and in $\frac{1}{4}$ mile, at crossroads, go right on to the A7 (sp. Galashiels). At **Langholm** turn left on to the B7068 (sp. Eskdalemuir) and go forward, past the **Scottish Explorers' Museum**, and on to the B709. Nearly 2 miles beyond **Bentpath** bear left, unclassified (sp. Lockerbie), and in $2\frac{1}{2}$ miles bear right (sp. Eskdalemuir). At **Eskdalemuir** go forward on the B709 (sp. Ettrick), continue beyond Ettrick to **Tushielaw Inn**, then turn right on to the B711 (sp. Hawick). In $3\frac{1}{2}$ miles beyond Roberton cross the river bridge, turn left on to the A7 (sp. Galashiels) and return to Hawick.

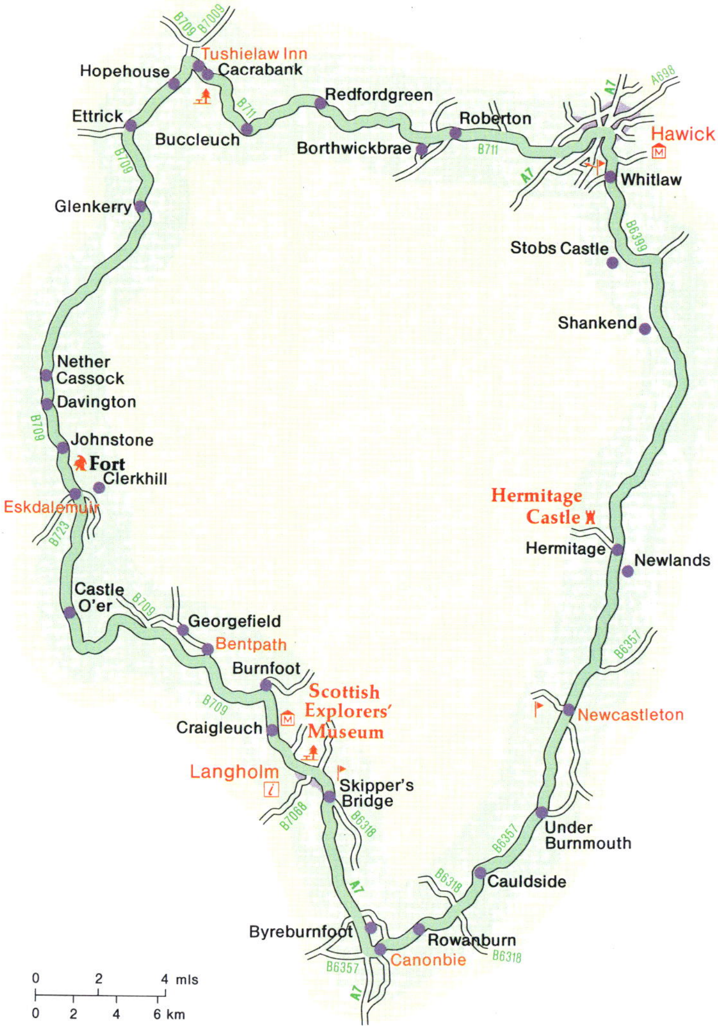

OFF THE TOUR

MacDiarmid Memorial

Hugh MacDiarmid was Scotland's most famous 20th-century poet. On the hill road to Newcastleton – off the A7 north of his home town of Langholm – stands a bronze memorial, arranged like the pages of an open book.

Meggat Water

By turning right off the B709 at Bentpath, then left after one bridge and right before another, the road leads into this narrow pastoral valley where Jamestown, at its head, was the site of an 18th-century antimony-miners' village. Thomas Telford, the great Scottish engineer, was brought up on a sheep farm here.

Wolfcleugh Waterfall Trail

On the B711 just under 10 miles after Tushielaw Inn, a right turn at a T-junction leads for $6\frac{1}{2}$ miles up the valley of the Borthwick Water to a picnic site and this Craik Forest walk.

ON THE TOUR

Hawick

Straddling the River Teviot which powered its early woollen mills, Hawick is famous for its high-quality knitwear. There is a strong sense of history here; notably at the Common Riding, whose ceremonies centre on the memorial to the Hawick men who made a successful border raid in 1514. Riverside Wilton Park includes a mansion-house museum with intriguing exhibits on the town's woollen trade, and also a memorial to the Grand Prix motor-cyclist Jimmy Guthrie. Locally-born James Paris Lee, designer of the Lee-Enfield rifle and the Remington typewriter, is commemorated in St Mary's churchyard. Rugby is the dominant modern sport. A popular outing in Hawick is to Teviotdale Leisure Centre which has swimming pools for various ages, and children's water chutes.

Hermitage Castle

This forbidding 14th-century castle was the stronghold of the Soulis, Dacre and Douglas families; about whom many grisly stories are told, including how one Lord Soulis was boiled alive in a vat of lead!

Newcastleton

After the rather wild country which precedes it, this 'planned' village of 1793, with its three squares and regular street pattern, comes as a surprise. There are hotels and restaurants, and a picnic site beside the Liddel Water. A Traditional Music Festival is celebrated here every summer.

Canonbie

Two traditional hotels here cater for trout and salmon anglers who come regularly to fish the River Esk.

Langholm

The Muckle Toon – the Big Town – produces cashmeres and the most expensive woollen twist cloth in the world. Border Fine Arts' hand-painted figurines of shepherds and their dogs, birds and animals, are not unlike the *santons* of Provence. There are walks and riverside picnic places, and the Common Riding in July features a storming gallop up Whita Hill to a memorial to a local man who became Governor of Persia. Thomas Telford, the famous civil engineer, worked as an apprentice on the bridge over the Esk. Astronaut Neil Armstrong, the first man to walk on the surface of the moon, is descended from a local family and is the only freeman of the town.

Scottish Explorers' Museum

In the mansion of Craigcleuch, this amazing collection of travellers' trove includes carvings from Sri Lanka, American Indian pipes, oriental jade and paintings, and beautiful African figurines, massed like a miniature tribal gathering.

Bentpath

This little village, with its school, church and row of cottages descending towards the Esk, displays a roadside memorial to Thomas Telford, who was born nearby in 1757.

Eskdalemuir

Sheep farming and forestry are the main activities of this scattered village, but the fluttering prayer flags announce the unexpected presence of a Tibetan Centre. The gold-roofed Buddhist temple of Samye Ling, founded by refugee monks from Tibet, is the most remarkable building in Eskdalemuir – and, indeed, the whole district. As well as being a haven of meditation and retreat, Samye Ling has its own pottery, woodwork shop and printing press. Eskdalemuir Observatory monitors seismic disturbances and gathers data on acid rain.

Tushielaw Inn

Roads converge from four directions on this hamlet, where anglers come to fish the Ettrick Water. The inn was once a well known and welcome sight to cattle drovers and coach travellers on the Selkirk Mail.

Below: *grim-looking Hermitage Castle is a 14th-century stronghold with a vivid, sometimes cruel, history. Outwardly it is almost perfect*

Bottom: *Langholm and the bridge over the Esk on which Thomas Telford worked as an apprentice*

OFF THE BEATEN TRACK

South of Hawick, after the summit of the B6399, the road is crossed by the track of the old Waverley railway line from Edinburgh to Carlisle, which closed in 1969. Lost in the forest to the left of the road is Riccarton Junction, a now-abandoned railway workers' village built with no road access.

OUTDOOR ACTIVITIES

Langholm is a fine centre for exhilarating walks. One climbs steeply from the town centre, up the grass and heather slopes of Whita Hill – territory of kestrels, skylarks, grouse and curlews – to the 1,162ft summit with its extensive views to the Border valleys, the Lake District hills and, in the very best conditions, the faraway outline of the Isle of Man.

THE BORDERS

78½ miles

Pleasant river valleys, rich farmland and green hillsides always in view make this a peaceful scene; but it was devastated by recurring Border wars. Four great abbeys were destroyed, although their stately ruins remain to be cherished and admired.

Although this area has been part of Scotland since 1018, Scots and English fought bitterly over it in the days of the later Border wars, with set-piece battles and constant minor raids. Hence the number of fortified tower houses and the ruinous state of the once powerful abbeys of Jedburgh, Dryburgh, Melrose and Kelso. Later, in more settled times, wealthy Border landowners built lavish mansions, many of which now welcome visitors.

This is Sir Walter Scott's country, and modern travellers find themselves, almost everywhere, following in the footsteps of the greatest Borderer of all.

Roman legions left traces here, and so did the settled tribes whose land they invaded. Among the well cared-for farms and woodlands are many attractive towns and villages with curious tales to tell.

ON THE TOUR

Kelso

Built around a preserved Georgian square, Kelso is well-known for its angling on the Tweed and Teviot, and for its horse races. Its livestock sales are world-renowned. The Norman abbey is a graceful ruin. Nearby, the Turret House is a local history museum with slightly gruesome illustrations of Kelso's old skinning trade.

Town Yetholm

Off the usual tourist trail, the village looks south to the Cheviot Hills, across which illicit whisky used to be pack-trained over the English border. Turn left in Town Yetholm for its twin across the Bowmont Water. Kirk Yetholm was the 'capital' of the gypsy kings, whose cottage-sized palace can still be seen. This is the northern end of the Pennine Way.

Jedburgh

This fine historic town is centred on the impressive ruins of a 12th-century abbey. The life and exciting times of Mary Queen of Scots are illustrated in Queen Mary's House. High-set Jedburgh Castle is a jail museum. Napoleonic prisoners in the town may have inspired the Jethart (or Jedburgh) snails which are actually mint-flavoured sweets.

Springtime at Dryburgh Abbey, resting place of Sir Walter Scott. Little of the church remains other than some of the 12th-century cloister buildings

Denholm

Two old coaching inns and the Text House, with its admonitory inscriptions, face Denholm's spacious green. The round-the-village walk no longer calls for the stilts once used here for wading across the Teviot.

Selkirk

Although the mills and rugby grounds which are among its preoccupations lie by the banks of the Ettrick Water, the centre of Selkirk is higher up – beside the courthouse where Sir Walter Scott once heard cases. Halliwell's Museum in a lane off the square combines a local history display with a collection of vintage ironmongery. Clapperton's Daylight Studio is a photographer's shop decorated and equipped in Victorian style.

Abbotsford

Sir Walter Scott invested most of his literary earnings in this baronial mansion by the Tweed, still owned by his family. His historical collections and extensive library are on display to the public.

Melrose

Most mellow of the Border towns, Melrose lies between the lofty Eildon Hills and the meadows by the Tweed. Beside its lovely ruined abbey, Priorwood Gardens re-create the monastic orchards. There is a motor museum here, and an exhibition on the abandoned Border railways.

Newstead

In the 12th century the stonemasons building Melrose Abbey were housed here. Long before that, Newstead was the site of the Roman camp of Trimontium; named after the three summits of the Eildons.

Dryburgh

Sir Walter Scott and First World War commander Field-Marshal Earl Haig are buried in Dryburgh Abbey, the most beautifully situated of the ruined Border abbeys on a curve of the River Tweed.

Greenknowe Tower

This sturdy 16th-century edifice was once the home of the Gordons and Setons. To this day it retains its turnpike staircase, upstairs main hall and the crowstepped-gable roof.

Floors Castle

The seat of the Duke of Roxburghe was exuberantly remodelled in Victorian times. Corbels, castellations and pepperpot towers run riot. Valuable tapestries, furniture and porcelain are on show, and Floors has an *alter ego* on film as the home of the fictional Lord Greystoke – Tarzan!

ROUTE DIRECTIONS

Leave **Kelso** (map 15 NT 73) on the A698 (sp. Hawick), passing the Abbey and crossing the river bridge. In $^1/_3$ mile keep forward on the B6352 (sp. Yetholm), then $1^1/_2$ miles further on bear right. After $5^1/_2$ miles turn right on to the B6401 (sp. Morebattle) and into **Town Yetholm**. In $3^1/_2$ miles, at the river bridge, turn right, then after $^1/_3$ mile bear left into Morebattle. In $1^3/_4$ miles turn left, unclassified (sp. Cessford), and $1^1/_2$ miles further turn left then right. In $1^3/_4$ miles go forward (sp. Jedburgh) and in another $1^3/_4$ miles, at the crossroads, go forward for another 2 miles. After a further $^1/_4$ mile bear right (sp. Jedburgh) and $1^1/_4$ miles further, at the trunk road, turn right on to the A68. In $^1/_4$ mile turn left (sp. Town Centre) and continue into **Jedburgh**. Leave by turning left on to the B6358 (sp. Hawick). In 4 miles, at the river bridge, go forward on the A698 (sp. Hawick). At **Denholm** turn right on to the B6405 (sp. Hassendean) and, at the river bridge, turn left across it. After 2 miles turn right on to the B6359 (sp. Melrose). In $1^1/_3$ miles, at the edge of Lilliesleaf, turn left on to the B6400 (sp. Selkirk). After $1^1/_4$ miles, cross river bridge and, after a further mile, turn right, unclassified (sp. Selkirk). In 2 miles, at the trunk road, turn right on to the A7. At **Selkirk** turn right (sp. Galashiels) then in $2^3/_4$ miles turn right on to the B6360 (sp. **Abbotsford**). In $^1/_3$ mile at the roundabout, take 3rd exit, A6091 (sp. Jedburgh) then after 1 mile, at a roundabout, take 2nd exit, for **Melrose**. Continue forward through Melrose, passing **Newstead** to the left (sp. Jedburgh) for $2^1/_3$ miles. At the trunk road turn right on to the A68 through Newton St. Boswells. In $1^1/_4$ miles turn left on to the B6404 (sp. St Boswells). Go into St Boswells and in $^1/_2$ mile bear left (sp. **Dryburgh Abbey**), then in $1^1/_4$ miles turn left on to the B6356 to the Abbey. In $^3/_4$ mile beyond the Abbey, turn left and ascend 1 mile further, then turn left again to ascend to Scott's View. In $^1/_2$ mile bear right (no signs), after $^1/_3$ mile, at trunk road, turn right (no signs), then left (sp. Earlston). At Earlston trunk road, turn right on to the A6105 and in $1^1/_3$ miles bear left (sp. Berwick-on-Tweed). Continue forward, passing **Greenknowe Tower** and, at Gordon turn right on to the A6089 (sp. Kelso). In 2 miles turn right, unclassified (sp. Mellerstain). In $1^1/_3$ miles turn left on to the B6397 (no signs). Turn left then right, through Smailholm. Turn left then right (sp. Kelso), past **Floors Castle**. In $^1/_3$ mile, at the trunk road, turn right on to the A6089, and, after 2 miles, at the mini-roundabout, take 3rd exit (sp. Town Centre) into Kelso.

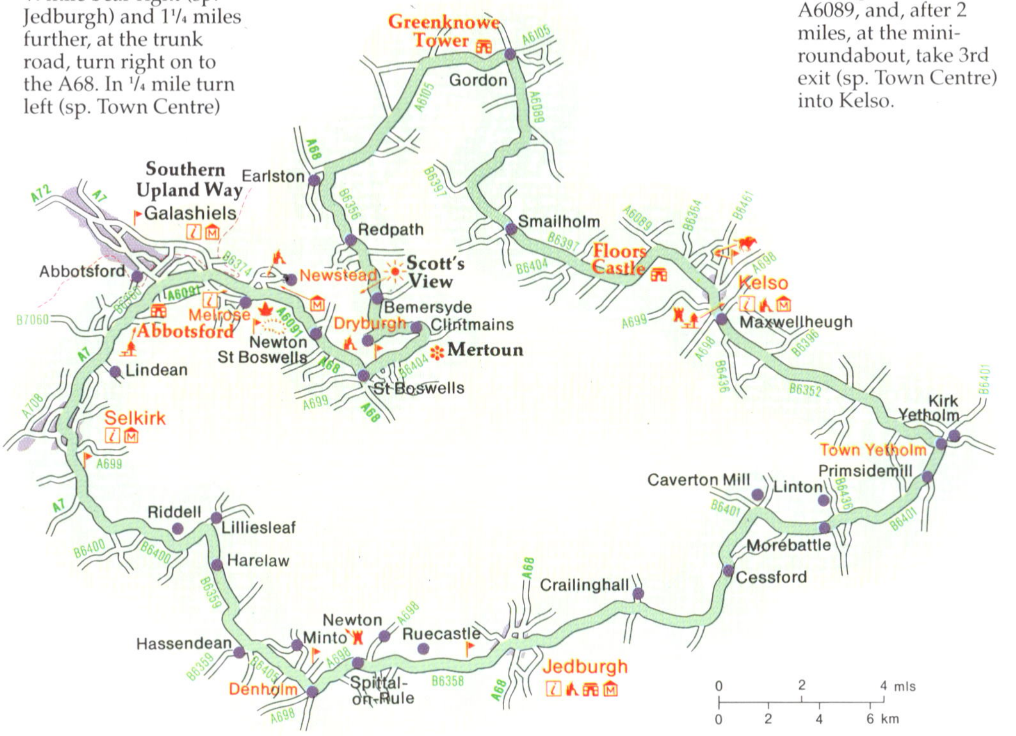

OFF THE BEATEN TRACK

East of Newstead, Leaderfoot has been a river crossing since Roman times. The modern main road bridge is alongside its graceful 1780 predecessor, and the railway viaduct of 1865 crosses the Tweed by 19 elegant arches.

High above the Kale water, Cessford Castle was left in ruins after three sieges in the 16th-century Border wars.

Just before returning to Jedburgh, the route crosses Dere Street, the Roman road from the Cheviots to Newstead. Lengths of it are signposted.

OUTDOOR ACTIVITIES

At Melrose, both banks of the River Tweed include footpaths on the long-distance Southern Upland Way. They lead to Gattonside, where the abbey monks introduced fruit farming.

One of the most exhilarating walks in the district is from Melrose to the glorious viewpoint summit of Eildon Hill North. It was a Roman signalling camp, and also, with a population of around 2,000, the hilltop capital of the Selgovae.

OFF THE TOUR

Bowhill

Follow the A708 and then the B7039 from Selkirk to the Borders home of the Duke of Buccleuch. The splendid 19th-century mansion displays paintings by Van Dyck, Gainsborough, Reynolds and Canaletto as well as valuable tapestries and Louis XV furniture. Two woodland trails wander past ornamental lochs and alongside the lovely Yarrow Water. Bowhill's grounds include an adventure playground which is a popular place for working off children's excess energy.

Mellerstain

Following the A6089 out of Gordon, after 1 mile turn right to reach this masterpiece of Georgian design. The home of the Earl of Haddington, this Adam mansion contains contemporary furniture, friezes and plasterwork. It stands in attractive terraced grounds with a rose garden and a lake.

Smailholm Tower

Turn right off the B6397 in Smailholm, following signs to the outstanding 16th-century tower house on its rocky plateau. Sir Walter Scott knew it well. Costumed figures and tapestries illustrating his works are on show.

The ancient market town of Kelso on the River Tweed, close to the Berwickshire border, is among the most beautifully situated of the Border towns. Kelso Abbey, which was once large and splendid, but is now ruined, was founded by David 1 in 1128

KEY TO ATLAS

The start towns for each tour can be located on the following map pages by using the National Grid reference given in the tour route directions.

The two letters after the map page refer to the major grid square marked by the heavier blue lines on the atlas pages. Each of these grid squares is sub-divided into 100 smaller squares marked in fainter blue and used for a more precise location. The base of the major grid square is divided into 10 sections reading west to east and the vertical into 10 sections reading south to north.

So, for example if the reference is Map 3NZ12, the town is to be found on page 3 of the atlas, in major grid square NZ 1 division along from the west side and 2 divisions up from the south.

- Motorway with number
- Motorway junction with/without number
- Motorway junction with limited access
- Motorway service area
- Motorway under construction
- Primary route single/dual carriageway
- Other A road single/dual carriageway
- B road single/dual carriageway
- Unclassfied road
- Road under construction
- Narrow primary road with passing places (Scotland)
- Narrow other A road with passing places (Scotland)
- Narrow B road with passing places (Scotland)
- Road toll
- Distance in miles between symbols
- County boundary
- National boundary
- Tidal constant (London). For more detailed and accurate information consult a Nautical Almanac
- Vehicle ferry - Great Britain
- Vehicle ferry – Continental
- Hovercraft ferry
- Heliport
- Airport

- AA Shops Mon – Fri 0900 – 1700hrs (Tues 0930 – 1700hrs) Sat 0900 – closing times vary
- AA Roadside Shop, limited services
- AA Port Shop, open as season demands
- AA and RAC – telephones
- BT telephone in isolated places
- Spot height in feet
- AA viewpoint

Atlas scale 1:633,600 — 0 10 20mls; 0 10 20 30kms — 10 miles to 1 inch

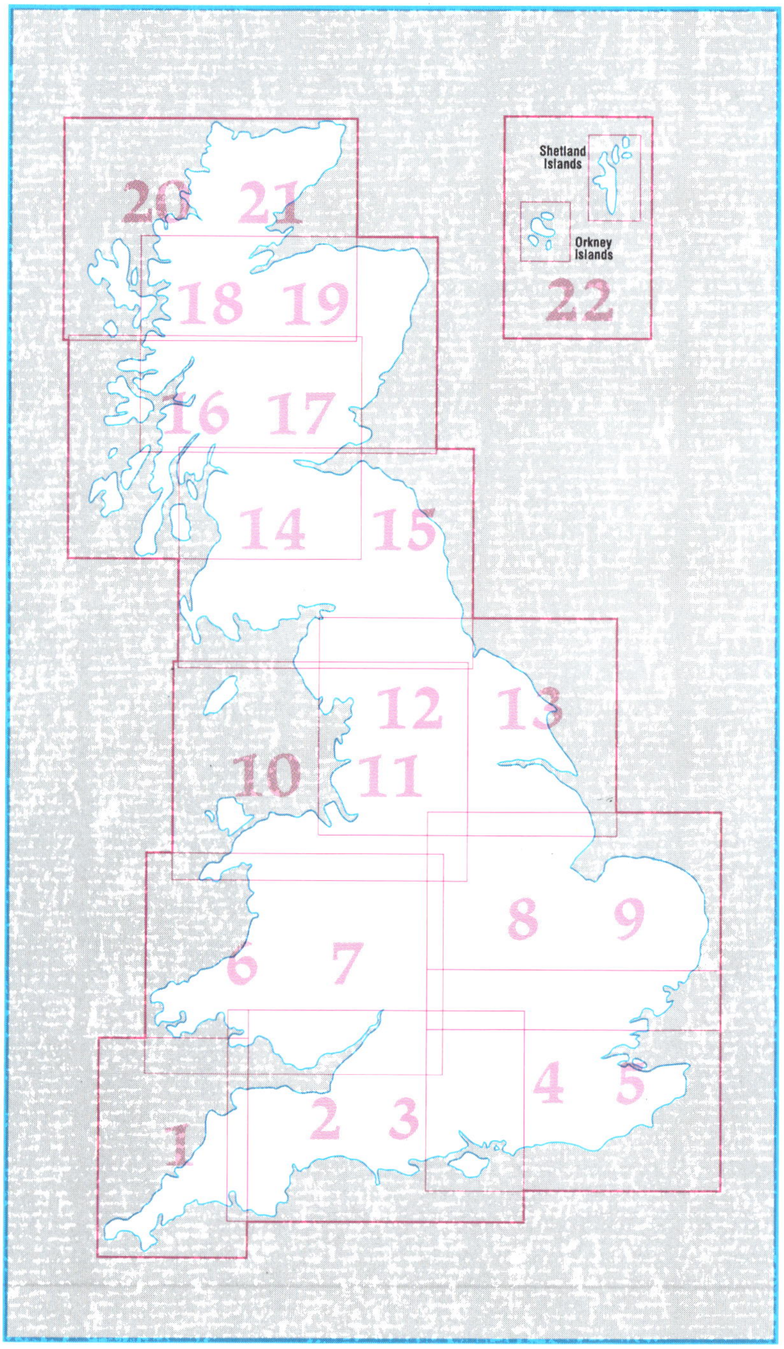

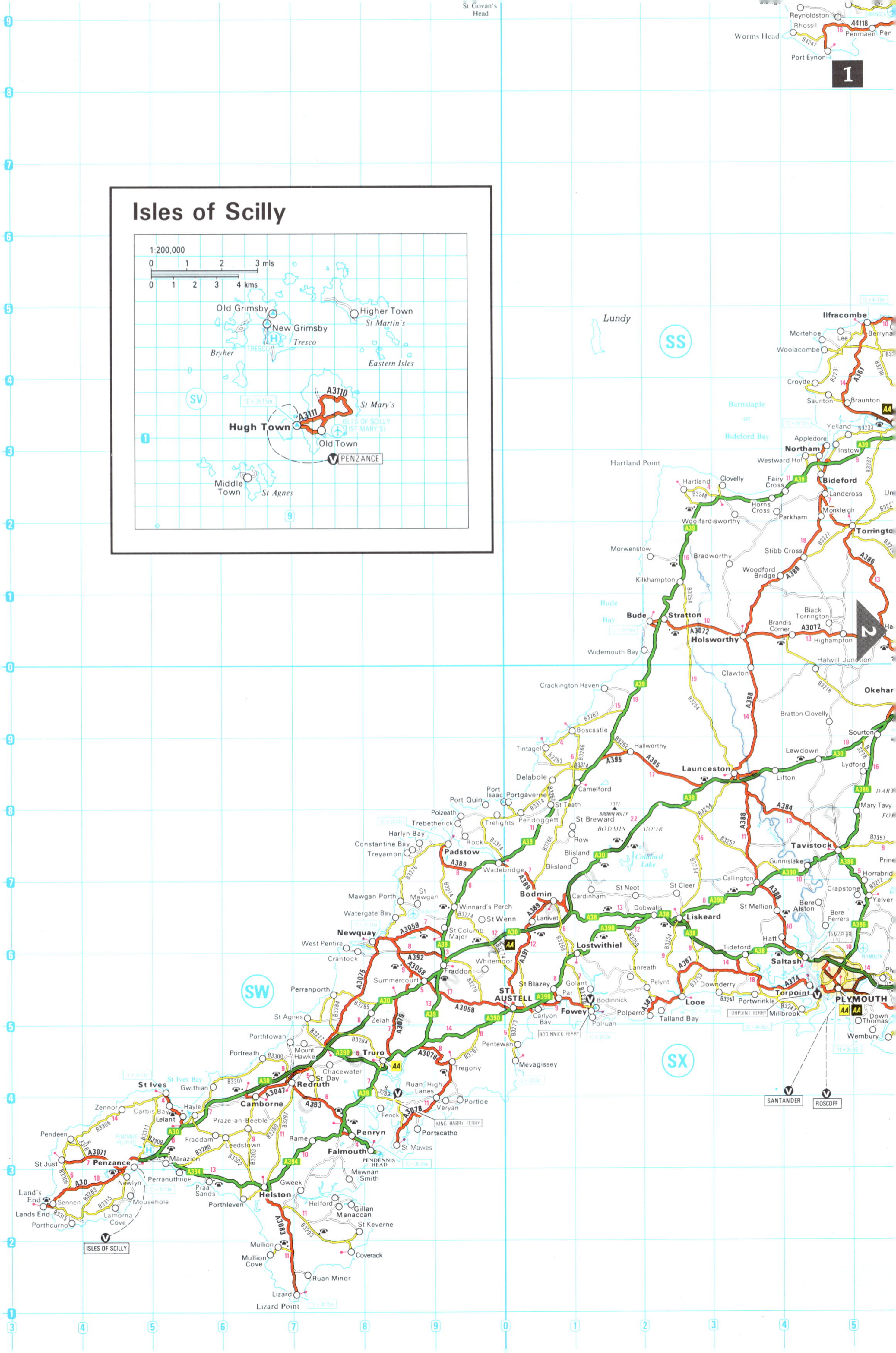

Isles of Scilly
1:200,000
0 1 2 3 mls
0 1 2 3 4 kms
Old Grimsby
New Grimsby
Higher Town
St Martin's
Tresco
Bryher
Eastern Isles
SV
A3110
St Mary's
A3111
Hugh Town
Old Town
ISLES OF SCILLY (ST MARY'S)
PENZANCE
Middle Town
St Agnes
1
St Govan's Head
Reynoldston
Rhossili
Worms Head
A4118
Penmaen
Port Eynon
B4247
Lundy
SS
Ilfracombe
Mortehoe
Lee
Berrynarbor
Woolacombe
Croyde
Saunton
Braunton
A361
B3231
Barnstaple or Bideford Bay
Yelland
Appledore
Northam
Instow
Westward Ho!
Hartland Point
Hartland
Clovelly
Fairy Cross
Bideford
Landcross
Horns Cross
Monkleigh
Parkham
Torrington
Woolfardisworthy
Morwenstow
Bradworthy
Stibb Cross
Woodford Bridge
A386
A388
Kilkhampton
Bude Bay
Bude
Stratton
A3072
Holsworthy
Black Torrington
Brandis Corner
Highampton
Widemouth Bay
Halwill Junction
Clawton
Crackington Haven
Okehampton
Bratton Clovelly
Boscastle
Sourton
Tintagel
Hallworthy
A395
Lewdown
Launceston
Lifton
Lydford
Delabole
Camelford
Port Isaac
Portgaverne
Port Quin
St Teath
Poizeath
Trebetherick
Trelights
Pendoggett
St Breward
BODMIN MOOR
Harlyn Bay
Rock
Row
Constantine Bay
Treyarnon
Padstow
Blisland
A389
Wadebridge
Colliford Lake
Mary Tavy
A384
Tavistock
Gunnislake
Callington
Horrabridge
Crapstone
Bodmin
Cardinham
St Neot
St Cleer
Mawgan Porth
St Mawgan
Watergate Bay
Winnard's Perch
St Wenn
Dobwalls
Liskeard
St Mellion
Bere Alston
Bere Ferrers
Lanivet
Newquay
A3059
St Columb Major
A39
A30
A38
A390
Lostwithiel
West Pentire
Crantock
A392
A3058
Fraddon
Whitemoor
Lanreath
Tideford
Saltash
Hatt
Summercourt
St Blazey
Golant
Pelynt
Downderry
Torpoint
PLYMOUTH
Perranporth
A3075
ST AUSTELL
Par
Fowey
Bodinnick
Polperro
Looe
Talland Bay
Portwrinkle
Millbrook
TORPOINT FERRY
Carlyon Bay
Polruan
BODINNICK FERRY
Down Thomas
Wembury
St Agnes
Zelah
A3076
Pentewan
Porthtowan
Mevagissey
SX
SW
Portreath
Mount Hawke
Truro
A3078
Tregony
Chacewater
St Day
St Ives
St Ives Bay
Gwithian
Redruth
A3047
Camborne
A393
Ruan High Lanes
Portloe
Veryan
Zennor
Carbis Bay
Hayle
Lelant
Praze-an-Beeble
Feock
KING HARRY FERRY
Penryn
Portscatho
Pendeen
Fraddam
Leedstown
Rame
Falmouth
St Mawes
PENDENNIS HEAD
St Just
A3071
Penzance
Marazion
A394
Perranuthnoe
Newlyn
Mawnan Smith
A30
Gweek
Land's End
Sennen
Mousehole
Praa Sands
Helston
Porthleven
Helford
Gillan
Manaccan
Lands End
Lamorna Cove
Porthcurno
St Keverne
ISLES OF SCILLY
A3083
Mullion
Mullion Cove
Coverack
Ruan Minor
Lizard
Lizard Point
SANTANDER
ROSCOFF
2

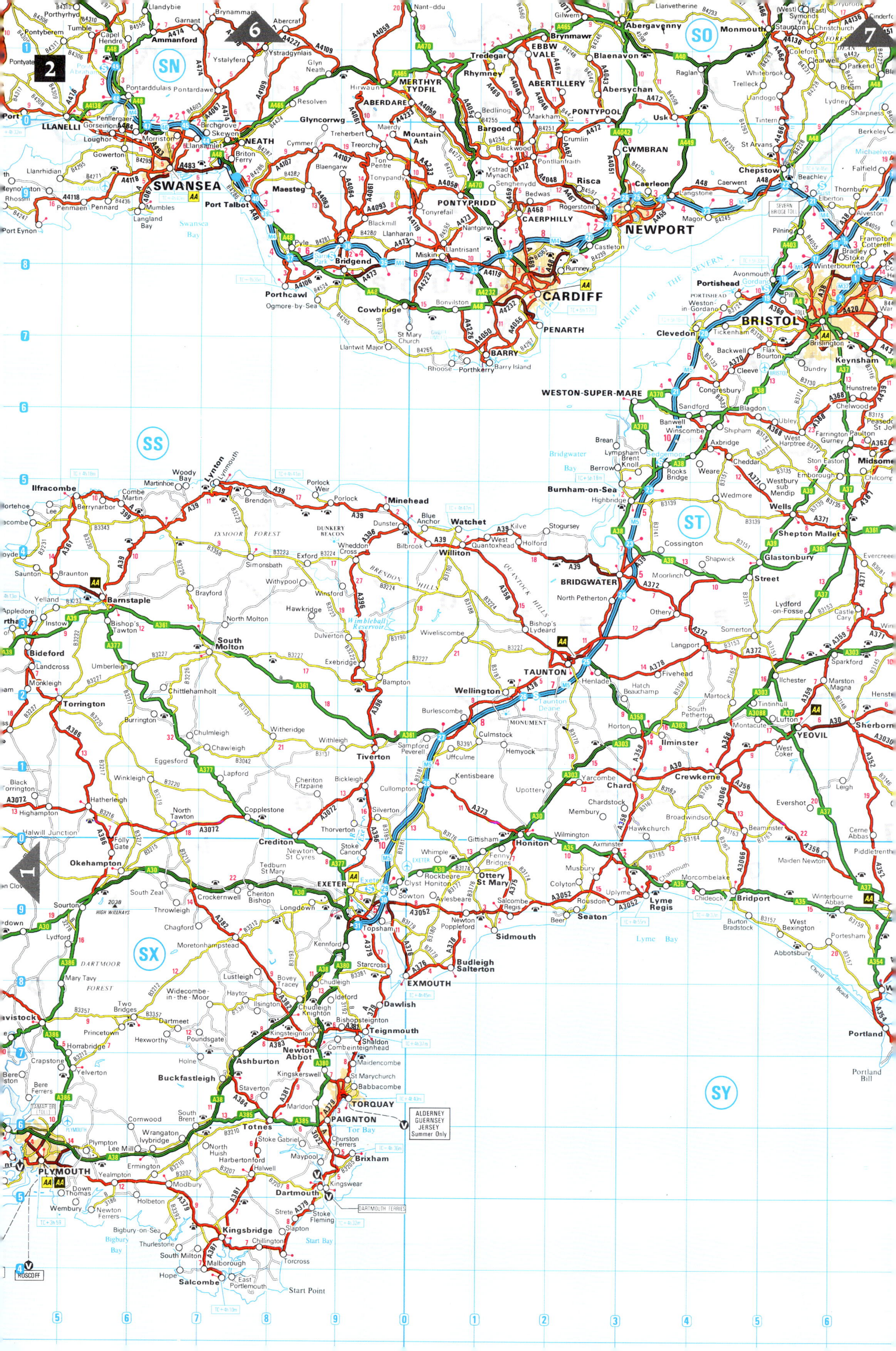

Llandybie
Brynamman
Porthyrhyd
Garnant
Abercraf
Nant-ddu
Gilwern
Llanvetherine
Abergavenny
Monmouth
Staunton
Symonds Yat
Christchurch
Pontyberem
Tumble
Capel Hendre
Ammanford
Ystalyfera
Ystradgynlais
Glyn Neath
Tredegar
Brynmawr
EBBW VALE
Blaenavon
Raglan
Coleford
Clearwell
Parkend
Bream
Whitebrook
Trelleck
Llandogo
Lydney
Tintern
Sharpness
St Arvans
Berkeley
Chepstow
Beachley
Thornbury
Falfield
Alveston
Pilning
Frampton Cotterell
Bradley Stoke
Winterbourne
Avonmouth
Portishead
Weston-in-Gordano
BRISTOL
Clevedon
Tickenham
Brislington
Keynsham
Backwell
Flax Bourton
Cleeve
Dundry
Congresbury
Hunstrete
Chelwood
Blagdon
Sandford
Banwell
Winscombe
Shipham
Ubley
Farrington Gurney
Paulton
West Harptree
Axbridge
Cheddar
Ston Easton
Midsomer
Emborough
Westbury sub Mendip
Wedmore
Wells
Shepton Mallet
Glastonbury
Street
Evercreech
Lydford -on-Fosse
Castle Cary
Somerton
Langport
Sparkford
Ilchester
Marston Magna
Tintinhull
Martock
South Petherton
Lufton
YEOVIL
Sherborne
Montacute
West Coker
Crewkerne
Evershot
Leigh
Cerne Abbas
Piddletrenthide
Maiden Newton
Beaminster
Broadwindsor
Winterbourne Abbas
Bridport
Chideock
Morcombelake
Charmouth
Lyme Regis
Burton Bradstock
West Bexington
Portesham
Abbotsbury
Chesil Beach
Portland
Portland Bill
Lyme Bay
Pontyates
Port
LLANELLI
Penllergaer
Gorseinon
Loughor
Gowerton
Pontarddulais
Pontardawe
Morriston
Llansamlet
Birchgrove
Skewen
NEATH
Briton Ferry
Resolven
Hirwaun
MERTHYR TYDFIL
ABERDARE
Rhymney
ABERTILLERY
Abersychan
PONTYPOOL
Usk
CWMBRAN
Caerleon
Langstone
Caerwent
Magor
NEWPORT
Risca
Crumlin
Pontllanfraith
Blackwood
Bargoed
Bedlinog
Markham
Glyncorrwg
Treherbert
Treorchy
Maerdy
Mountain Ash
Cymmer
Ton Pentre
Tonypandy
Blaengarw
Maesteg
Port Talbot
SWANSEA
Mumbles
Langland Bay
Swansea Bay
Llanrhidian
Reynoldston
Rhossili
Penmaen
Pennard
Port Eynon
Ystrad Mynach
Senghenydd
Bedwas
Rogerstone
PONTYPRIDD
Tonyrefail
Nantgarw
CAERPHILLY
Blackmill
Llanharan
Pyle
Bridgend
Llantrisant
Miskin
Castleton
Rumney
CARDIFF
Porthcawl
Ogmore-by-Sea
Cowbridge
Bonvilston
St Mary Church
Llantwit Major
Rhoose
Porthkerry
BARRY
Barry Island
PENARTH
WESTON-SUPER-MARE
Brean
Lympsham
Brent Knoll
Berrow
Rooks Bridge
Weare
Burnham-on-Sea
Highbridge
Cossington
Bridgwater Bay
Stogursey
Kilve
Holford
West Quantoxhead
BRIDGWATER
Moorlinch
Shapwick
North Petherton
Othery
Watchet
Williton
Blue Anchor
Minehead
Dunster
Porlock
Porlock Weir
Lynton
Lynmouth
Woody Bay
Martinhoe
Combe Martin
Ilfracombe
Berrynarbor
Lee
Brendon
EXMOOR FOREST
DUNKERY BEACON
Wheddon Cross
Exford
Simonsbath
Withypool
Winsford
BRENDON HILLS
QUANTOCK HILLS
Bishop's Lydeard
Wiveliscombe
Bilbrook
Braunton
Saunton
Barnstaple
Yelland
Instow
Appledore
Bideford
Bishop's Tawton
Landcross
Monkleigh
Torrington
Umberleigh
Brayford
North Molton
South Molton
Hawkridge
Dulverton
Wimbleball Reservoir
Exebridge
Bampton
TAUNTON
Henlade
Hatch Beauchamp
Fivehead
Wellington
Burlescombe
Taunton Deane
MONUMENT
Culmstock
Hemyock
Horton
Ilminster
Chard
Yarcombe
Chardstock
Membury
Hawkchurch
Axminster
Uplyme
Wilmington
Honiton
Upottery
Kentisbeare
Uffculme
Sampford Peverell
Tiverton
Withleigh
Witheridge
Chittlehamholt
Chulmleigh
Chawleigh
Burrington
Eggesford
Lapford
Winkleigh
Cheriton Fitzpaine
Bickleigh
Cullompton
Silverton
Thorverton
Copplestone
North Tawton
Crediton
Newton St Cyres
Tedburn St Mary
Stoke Canon
Whimple
Gittisham
Fenny Bridges
Ottery St Mary
Rockbeare
Clyst Honiton
Aylesbeare
EXETER
Sowton
Topsham
Cheriton Bishop
Crockernwell
Longdown
Kennford
Newton Poppleford
Sidmouth
Salcombe Regis
Colyton
Musbury
Rousdon
Beer
Seaton
Budleigh Salterton
EXMOUTH
Starcross
Dawlish
Ideford
Chudleigh
Chudleigh Knighton
Bishopsteignton
Teignmouth
Shaldon
Kingsteignton
Newton Abbot
Combeinteignhead
Maidencombe
St Marychurch
Babbacombe
TORQUAY
PAIGNTON
Tor Bay
Kingskerswell
Marldon
Churston Ferrers
Brixham
Kingswear
Dartmouth
DARTMOUTH FERRIES
Stoke Fleming
Strete
Slapton
Start Bay
Torcross
Start Point
Chillington
Kingsbridge
Malborough
East Portlemouth
Salcombe
Hope
South Milton
Thurlestone
Bigbury-on-Sea
Bigbury Bay
Newton Ferrers
Holbeton
Modbury
Yealmpton
Ermington
Halwell
Harbertonford
North Huish
Stoke Gabriel
Maypool
Totnes
South Brent
Staverton
Ashburton
Buckfastleigh
Holne
Bovey Tracey
Lustleigh
Haytor
Ilsington
Widecombe-in-the-Moor
Poundsgate
Dartmeet
Hexworthy
Two Bridges
Princetown
Moretonhampstead
Chagford
Throwleigh
South Zeal
HIGH WILLHAYS
DARTMOOR FOREST
Okehampton
Sourton
Lydford
Mary Tavy
Tavistock
Horrabridge
Crapstone
Yelverton
Bere Ferrers
Cornwood
Wrangaton
Ivybridge
Lee Mill
Plympton
PLYMOUTH
Down Thomas
Wembury
Halwill Junction
Folly Gate
Hatherleigh
Highampton
Black Torrington
ALDERNEY GUERNSEY JERSEY Summer Only
ROSCOFF
SEVERN BRIDGE TOLL
SN
SO
SS
ST
SX
SY
M4
M5
M32
A48
A470
A465
A4042
A449
A39
A361
A377
A30
A38
A303
A35
A37
A358
A373
A3052
A3072
A386
A380
A385
A381
A379

OXFORD
READING
SWINDON
SOUTHAMPTON
PORTSMOUTH
BOURNEMOUTH
POOLE
CHRISTCHURCH
SALISBURY
WINCHESTER
BASINGSTOKE
NEWBURY
ANDOVER
AYLESBURY
HIGH WYCOMBE
MAIDENHEAD
WINDSOR
SLOUGH
BRACKNELL
CAMBERLEY
FARNBOROUGH
ALDERSHOT
FARNHAM
WOKING
EGHAM
CHICHESTER
BOGNOR REGIS
HAVANT
FAREHAM
GOSPORT
EASTLEIGH
LYMINGTON
RYDE
Cowes
Newport
Sandown
Shanklin
Ventnor
ISLE OF WIGHT
Swanage
Wareham
Cirencester
Stroud
Malmesbury
Chippenham
Devizes
Marlborough
Trowbridge
Westbury
Warminster
Shaftesbury
Wimborne Minster
Blandford Forum
Romsey
Petersfield
Alton
Haslemere
Abingdon
Wantage
Witney
Thame
Marlow
Henley-on-Thames
Wokingham
Melksham
Calne
SP
SU
SZ
8
3
4

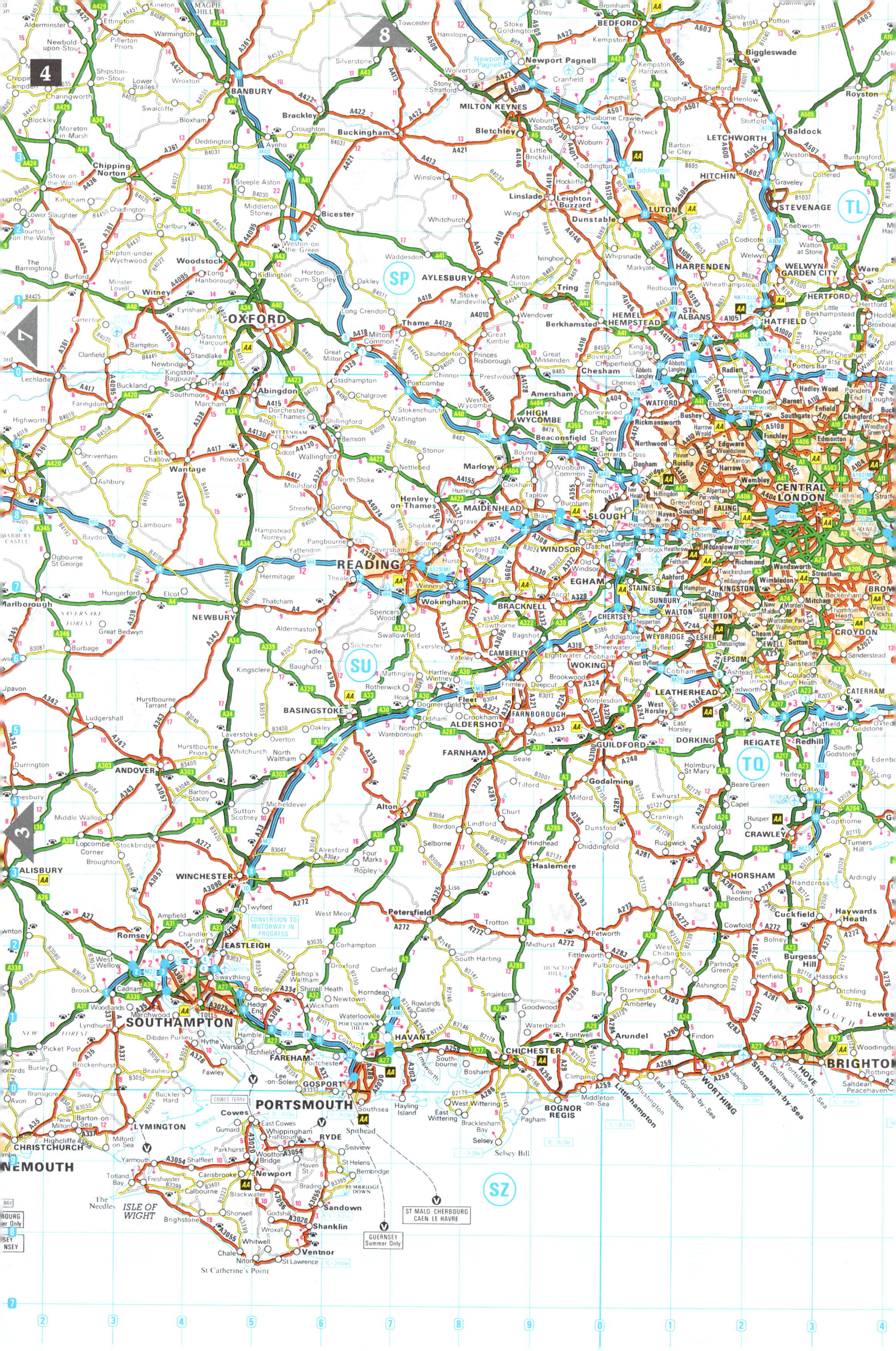

8
4
7
3
SP
SU
SZ
TL
TQ
BEDFORD
Biggleswade
Royston
Newport Pagnell
MILTON KEYNES
Bletchley
Buckingham
BANBURY
Brackley
Chipping Norton
Moreton-in-Marsh
Stow-on-the-Wold
Bicester
LETCHWORTH
HITCHIN
Baldock
STEVENAGE
LUTON
Dunstable
Leighton Buzzard
HARPENDEN
WELWYN GARDEN CITY
HERTFORD
Ware
ST. ALBANS
HATFIELD
HEMEL HEMPSTEAD
Berkhamsted
Tring
AYLESBURY
Thame
OXFORD
Woodstock
Witney
Burford
Abingdon
Didcot
Wantage
Wallingford
Henley-on-Thames
Marlow
HIGH WYCOMBE
Beaconsfield
Amersham
Chesham
WATFORD
Rickmansworth
Uxbridge
CENTRAL LONDON
Wembley
Edmonton
Enfield
Barnet
Harrow
EALING
Richmond
Wimbledon
KINGSTON
CROYDON
SLOUGH
MAIDENHEAD
WINDSOR
EGHAM
STAINES
READING
Wokingham
BRACKNELL
CAMBERLEY
WOKING
Weybridge
EPSOM
LEATHERHEAD
DORKING
REIGATE
Redhill
CATERHAM
GUILDFORD
FARNBOROUGH
ALDERSHOT
Fleet
FARNHAM
Godalming
Haslemere
Crawley
CRAWLEY
HORSHAM
Haywards Heath
Cuckfield
Burgess Hill
BRIGHTON
HOVE
Shoreham-by-Sea
WORTHING
Littlehampton
BOGNOR REGIS
Arundel
CHICHESTER
Petworth
Midhurst
Petersfield
HAVANT
PORTSMOUTH
GOSPORT
FAREHAM
SOUTHAMPTON
EASTLEIGH
Romsey
WINCHESTER
Alton
BASINGSTOKE
NEWBURY
Hungerford
Marlborough
ANDOVER
SALISBURY
LYMINGTON
CHRISTCHURCH
Cowes
Newport
RYDE
Sandown
Shanklin
Ventnor
ISLE OF WIGHT
The Needles
St Catherine's Point
Selsey Bill
Hayling Island
ST MALO CHERBOURG CAEN LE HAVRE
GUERNSEY Summer Only
CONVERSION TO MOTORWAY IN PROGRESS
SAVERNAKE FOREST
NEW FOREST

9
IPSWICH
Woodbridge
Orford
Orford Ness
Butley
Shottisham
Hadleigh
Hintlesham
Bildeston
Lavenham
Long Melford
Sudbury
Clare
Cavendish
Haverhill
Linton
Duxford
Little Abington
Great Chesterford
Saffron Walden
Steeple Bumpstead
Great Yeldham
Castle Hedingham
Radwinter
Newport
Thaxted
Finchingfield
Wethersfield
Quendon
Halstead
Bures
Nayland
Stoke by Nayland
Dedham
Manningtree
Felixstowe
Shotley
Parkeston Quay
Harwich
Dovercourt
Ramsey
Wix
KRISTIANSAND (Summer Only)
ESBJERG HAMBURG HOEK VAN HOLLAND GOTEBORG
The Naze
Walton-on-the-Naze
Frinton-on-Sea
Holland-on-Sea
CLACTON-ON-SEA
ZEEBRUGGE
TM
Ardleigh
West Bergholt
Marks Tey
COLCHESTER
Elmstead Market
Great Bentley
Thorpe-le-Soken
Brightlingsea
St Osyth
Stansted
Broxted
Great Dunmow
Braintree
Coggeshall
Kelvedon
Silver End
Tiptree
West Mersea
Tolleshunt D'Arcy
Tollesbury
Witham
BISHOP'S STORTFORD
Hatfield Heath
Leaden Roding
HARLOW
CHELMSFORD
Writtle
Boreham
Maldon
Bradwell-on-Sea
EPPING
Ongar
Ingatestone
Mundon Hill
Latchingdon
Southminster
Burnham-on-Crouch
South Woodham Ferrers
Rettendon
BILLERICAY
Wickford
Rawreth
BRENTWOOD
RAYLEIGH
Rochford
Romford
Hornchurch
East Horndon
Laindon
Pitsea
BASILDON
South Benfleet
Hadleigh
Leigh-on-Sea
SOUTHEND-ON-SEA
Great Wakering
Shoeburyness
Canvey Island
Upminster
Dagenham
Rainham
South Ockendon
Orsett
North Stifford
Bulphan
ONE TREE HILL
Coryton
Aveley
GRAYS
Erith
Purfleet
West Thurrock
Tilbury
Bexleyheath
Crayford
DARTFORD
Bexley
Northfleet
GRAVESEND
Allhallows-on-Sea
Grain
VLISSINGEN (FLUSHING)
Cliffe
Sheerness
Eastchurch
Leysdown-on-Sea
Isle of Sheppey
Queenborough
Chattenden
Hoo
Shorne
Strood
ROCHESTER
GILLINGHAM
CHATHAM
Rainham
Newington
Iwade
Sittingbourne
Faversham
WHITSTABLE
Tankerton
HERNE BAY
MARGATE
Westgate-on-Sea
Birchington
Cliftonville
Kingsgate
Broadstairs
St Nicholas at Wade
Sarre
Minster
Manston
RAMSGATE
DUNKERQUE
Swanley
Farningham
Orpington
Brands Hatch
Snodland
Aylesford
Detling
Otford
Dunton Green
Borough Green
Wrotham Heath
Larkfield
MAIDSTONE
Hollingbourne
Doddington
Boughton
Dunkirk
CANTERBURY
Fordwich
Littlebourne
Wingham
Sandwich
SEVENOAKS
Wateringbury
Hadlow
Yalding
Boughton Monchelsea
Sutton Valence
Lenham
Charing
Challock
Barham
DEAL
Walmer
Kingsdown
St Margaret's at Cliffe
Hildenborough
East Peckham
TONBRIDGE
Leigh
Penshurst
Southborough
Paddock Wood
Marden
Staplehurst
Headcorn
Hothfield
ASHFORD
Stelling Minnis
Selstead
Temple Ewell
Lyminge
Hawkinge
DOVER
TR
TUNBRIDGE WELLS
Goudhurst
Lamberhurst
Biddenden
Bethersden
High Halden
Woodchurch
Cranbrook
Tenterden
Ham Street
Hythe
FOLKESTONE
ZEEBRUGGE OOSTENDE CALAIS BOULOGNE
CALAIS BOULOGNE
BOULOGNE
Hartfield
Crowborough
Wadhurst
Flimwell
Hawkhurst
Rolvenden
Mayfield
Burwash
Hurst Green
Newenden
Northiam
Peasmarsh
Brenzett
New Romney
Dymchurch
St Mary's Bay
Littlestone-on-Sea
Greatstone-on-Sea
Lydd
Rye
Camber
Dungeness
STRAIT OF DOVER
Uckfield
Cross-in-Hand
Heathfield
Robertsbridge
Rushlake Green
Sedlescombe
Winchelsea
Battle
Halland
Boreham Street
Ninfield
HASTINGS
St Leonards-on-Sea
BEXHILL-ON-SEA
Hailsham
Stone Cross
Pevensey
Cooden Beach
Berwick
Polegate
Alfriston
Newhaven
Seaford
Eastdean
EASTBOURNE
Beachy Head
DIEPPE
TV
5
6
7
8
9
0
1
2
3
4
5
6
7

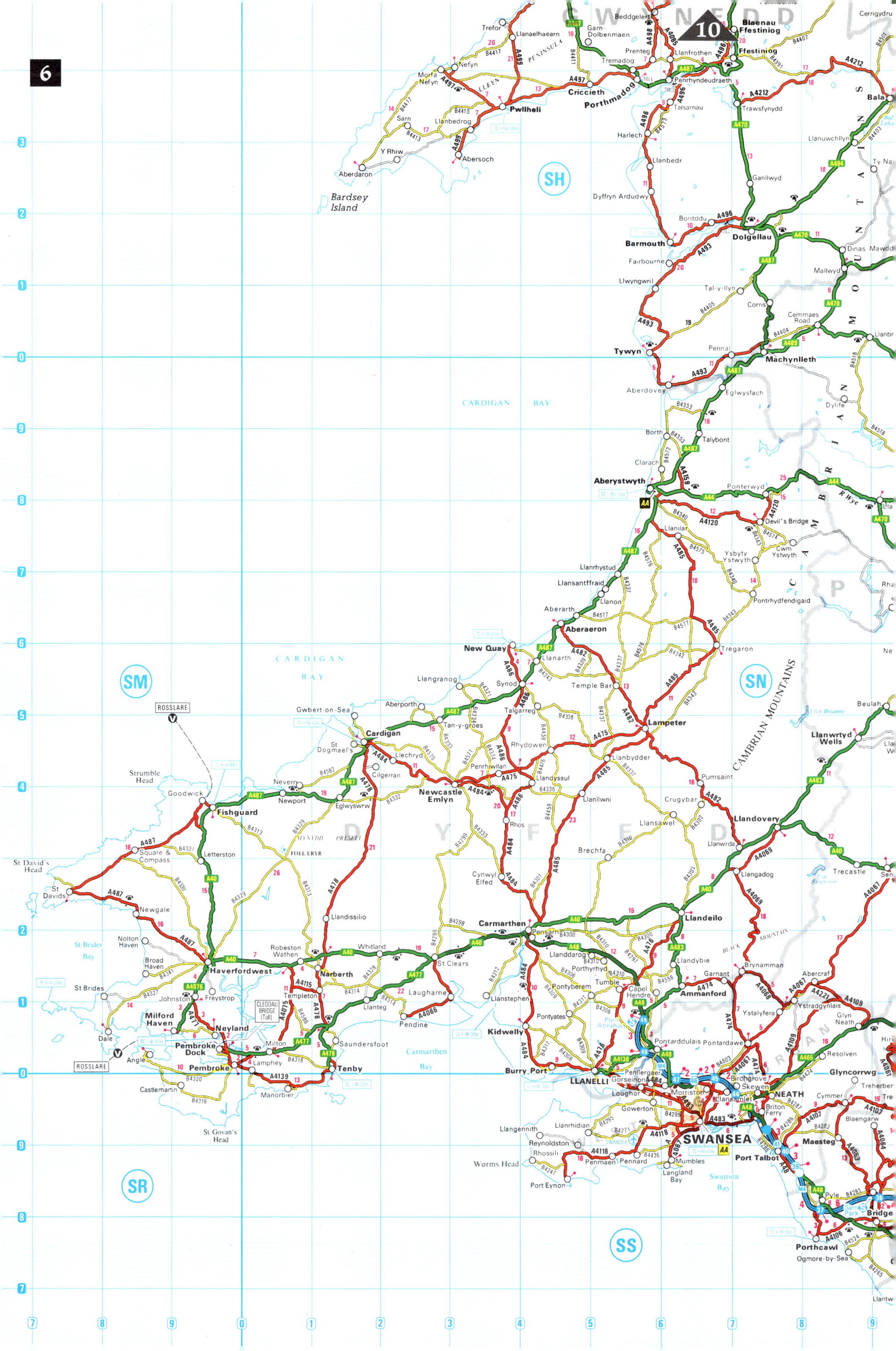
GWYNEDD
10
Blaenau Ffestiniog
Ffestiniog
Trefor
Llanaelhaearn
Garn-Dolbenmaen
Beddgelert
Prenteg
Tremadog
Llanfrothen
Nefyn
Morfa Nefyn
LLEYN PENINSULA
Criccieth
Porthmadog
Penrhyndeudraeth
Talsarnau
Pwllheli
Llanbedrog
Sarn
Y Rhiw
Abersoch
Aberdaron
Bardsey Island
Harlech
Llanbedr
Dyffryn Ardudwy
SH
Trawsfynydd
Bala
Llanuwchllyn
Ganllwyd
Bontddu
Barmouth
Dolgellau
Fairbourne
Llwyngwril
Tal-y-llyn
Corris
Dinas Mawddwy
Mallwyd
Cemmaes Road
Tywyn
Pennal
Machynlleth
Aberdovey
Eglwysfach
Dylife
CARDIGAN BAY
Borth
Talybont
Clarach
Aberystwyth
Ponterwyd
Devil's Bridge
Llanilar
Ysbyty Ystwyth
Cwm Ystwyth
Llanrhystud
Llansantffraid
Llanon
Pontrhydfendigaid
Aberarth
Aberaeron
Tregaron
New Quay
Llanarth
Synod
Temple Bar
CAMBRIAN MOUNTAINS
SN
Llangranog
Aberporth
Talgarreg
Gwbert-on-Sea
Cardigan
Tan-y-groes
Lampeter
Beulah
Llanwrtyd Wells
St Dogmael's
Llechryd
Cilgerran
Rhydowen
Penrhiwllan
Llandyssul
Llanybydder
Pumsaint
Nevern
Newport
Eglwyswrw
Newcastle Emlyn
Llanllwni
Crugybar
Llandovery
Strumble Head
Goodwick
Fishguard
ROSSLARE
SM
MYNYDD PRESELI
FOEL ERYR
Rhos
Llansawel
Llanwrda
St David's Head
Square & Compass
Letterston
Brechfa
Trecastle
St Davids
Newgale
Cynwyl Elfed
Llangadog
Llandissilio
Carmarthen
Pensarn
Llandeilo
Nolton Haven
St Brides Bay
Robeston Wathen
Whitland
St Clears
Llanddarog
Porthyrhyd
Llandybie
BLACK MOUNTAIN
Brynamman
Broad Haven
Haverfordwest
Narberth
Tumble
Garnant
Abercraf
St Brides
Johnston
Freystrop
Templeton
Llanteg
Laugharne
Llanstephan
Pontyberem
Capel Hendre
Ammanford
Ystradgynlais
Glyn Neath
Milford Haven
Neyland
CLEDDAU BRIDGE (Toll)
Pendine
Pontyates
Ystalyfera
Dale
Pembroke Dock
Milton
Saundersfoot
Carmarthen Bay
Kidwelly
Pontardulais
Pontardawe
Resolven
Angle
Pembroke
Lamphey
Tenby
Burry Port
LLANELLI
Penllergaer
Gorseinon
Birchgrove
Skewen
Glyncorrwg
Castlemartin
Manorbier
Loughor
Morriston
Llansamlet
NEATH
Treherbert
Cymmer
Gowerton
Briton Ferry
Blaengarw
St Govan's Head
Llangennith
Llanrhidian
SWANSEA
Maesteg
Reynoldston
Rhossili
Penmaen
Pennard
Mumbles
Port Talbot
Worms Head
Langland Bay
Swansea Bay
Port Eynon
Pyle
Sarn Park
Bridgend
SR
SS
Porthcawl
Ogmore-by-Sea
Llantwit

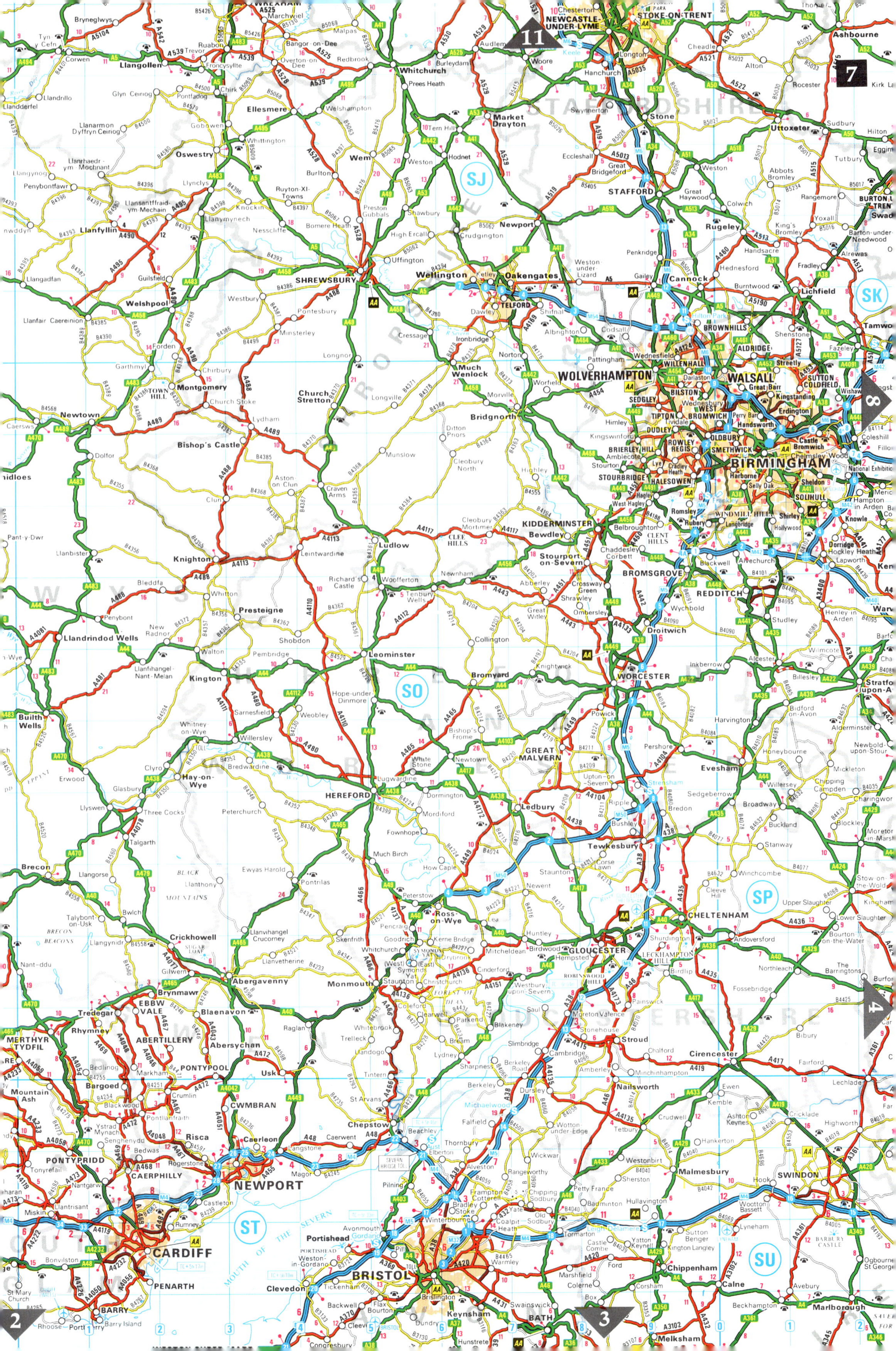

STOKE-ON-TRENT
NEWCASTLE-UNDER-LYME
11
Ashbourne
7
Wrexham
Llangollen
Whitchurch
Market Drayton
Uttoxeter
Stone
STAFFORD
Ellesmere
Oswestry
Wem
SJ
Newport
Rugeley
Lichfield
SK
Llanfyllin
SHREWSBURY
Wellington
Oakengates
TELFORD
Cannock
Welshpool
WALSALL
WOLVERHAMPTON
Much Wenlock
Montgomery
Church Stretton
Bridgnorth
SUTTON COLDFIELD
BIRMINGHAM
8
Newtown
Bishop's Castle
SOLIHULL
KIDDERMINSTER
Ludlow
Knighton
Bewdley
Stourport-on-Severn
BROMSGROVE
REDDITCH
Presteigne
Llandrindod Wells
Leominster
Droitwich
WORCESTER
Kington
Bromyard
SO
Stratford-upon-Avon
Builth Wells
Hay-on-Wye
GREAT MALVERN
Evesham
HEREFORD
Ledbury
Tewkesbury
Brecon
Ross-on-Wye
CHELTENHAM
SP
Crickhowell
Abergavenny
GLOUCESTER
Monmouth
4
MERTHYR TYDFIL
Tredegar
EBBW VALE
ABERTILLERY
Stroud
Cirencester
PONTYPOOL
CWMBRAN
Usk
Nailsworth
Chepstow
PONTYPRIDD
CAERPHILLY
Risca
NEWPORT
Malmesbury
SWINDON
ST
CARDIFF
PENARTH
BARRY
BRISTOL
Clevedon
Portishead
Chippenham
SU
Calne
Keynsham
BATH
Marlborough
Melksham
2
3

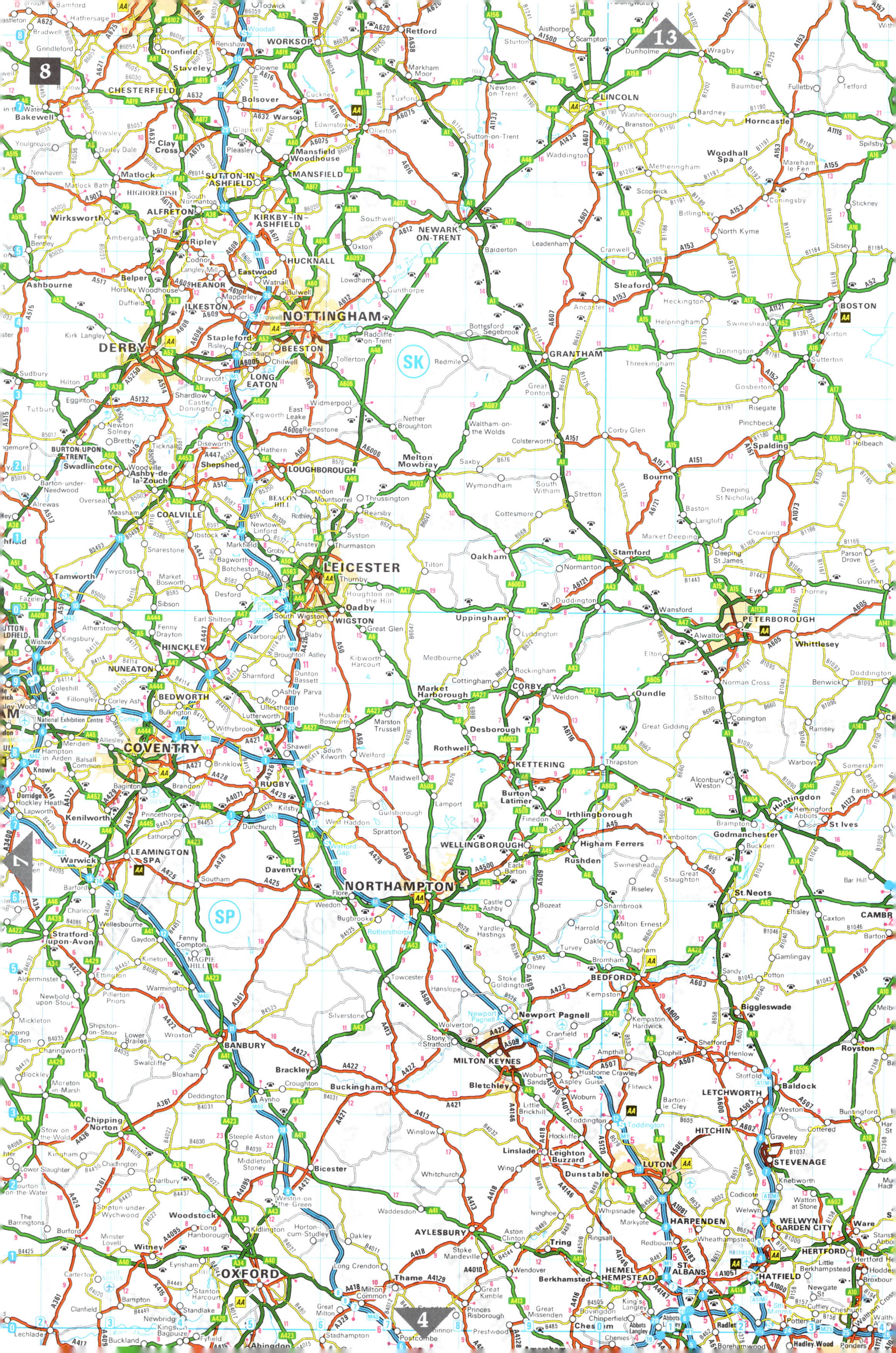
8
13
7
4
SK
SP
WORKSOP
Retford
CHESTERFIELD
Bakewell
Bolsover
LINCOLN
Horncastle
Woodhall Spa
MANSFIELD
SUTTON-IN-ASHFIELD
Matlock
ALFRETON
KIRKBY-IN-ASHFIELD
NEWARK-ON-TRENT
Wirksworth
Ripley
HUCKNALL
Sleaford
BOSTON
Ashbourne
Belper
HEANOR
ILKESTON
NOTTINGHAM
BEESTON
DERBY
GRANTHAM
LONG EATON
Melton Mowbray
Spalding
LOUGHBOROUGH
BURTON UPON TRENT
Swadlincote
Ashby-de-la-Zouch
COALVILLE
Bourne
Stamford
Oakham
LEICESTER
Tamworth
Uppingham
PETERBOROUGH
Oadby
WIGSTON
HINCKLEY
NUNEATON
BEDWORTH
Market Harborough
CORBY
Oundle
Desborough
COVENTRY
Rothwell
KETTERING
RUGBY
Kenilworth
Huntingdon
St Ives
Burton Latimer
LEAMINGTON SPA
Warwick
Daventry
WELLINGBOROUGH
Higham Ferrers
Rushden
Godmanchester
NORTHAMPTON
St Neots
Stratford-upon-Avon
BEDFORD
Biggleswade
BANBURY
Newport Pagnell
Brackley
Buckingham
MILTON KEYNES
Bletchley
Royston
Baldock
LETCHWORTH
HITCHIN
STEVENAGE
Chipping Norton
Bicester
Leighton Buzzard
Dunstable
LUTON
Woodstock
HARPENDEN
WELWYN GARDEN CITY
AYLESBURY
Tring
Witney
OXFORD
HEMEL HEMPSTEAD
ST ALBANS
HATFIELD
HERTFORD
Thame
Berkhamsted
Abingdon

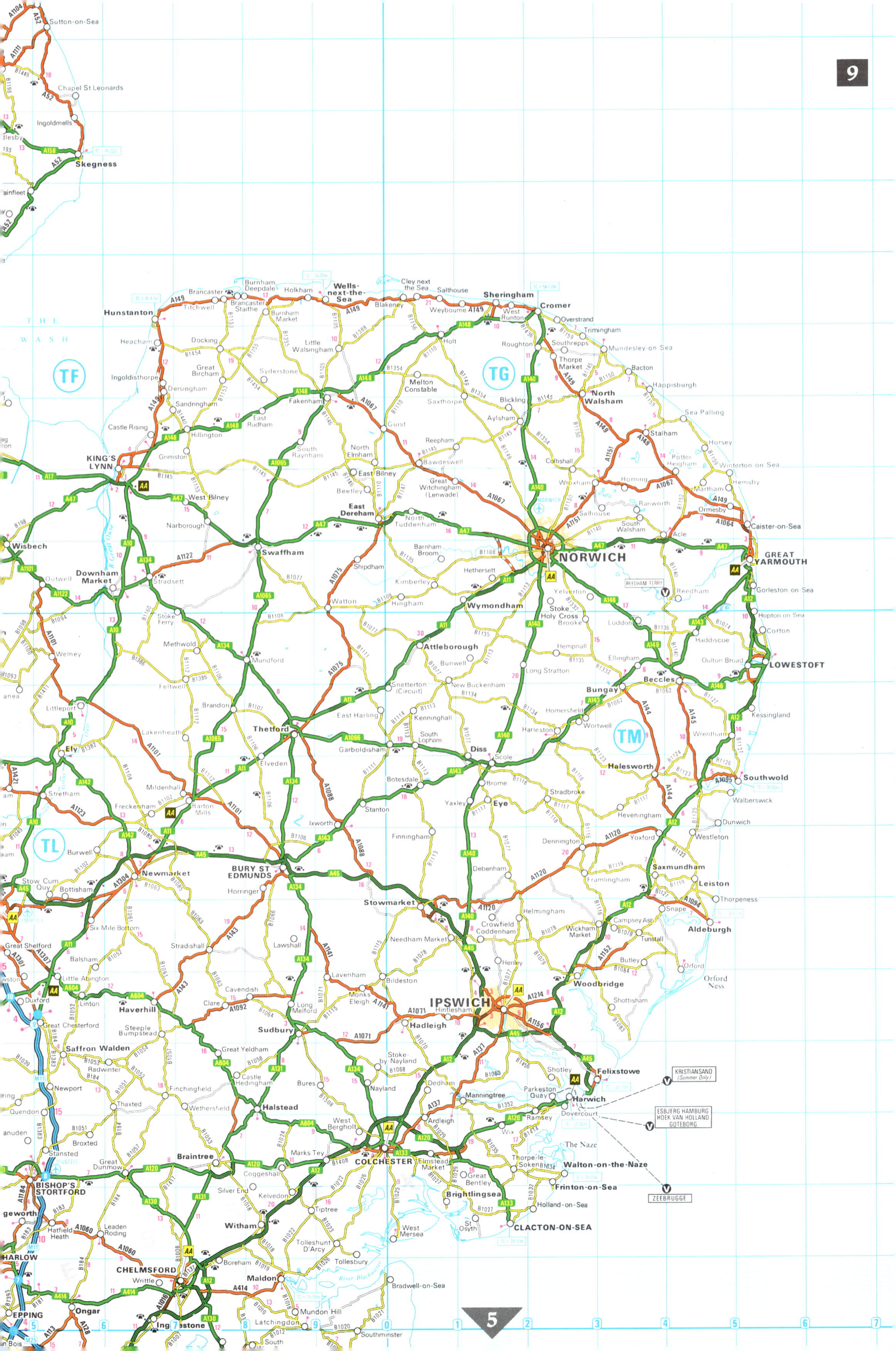
Sutton-on-Sea
Chapel St Leonards
Ingoldmells
Skegness
THE WASH
TF
TG
TM
TL
Hunstanton
Brancaster
Burnham Deepdale
Brancaster Staithe
Titchwell
Burnham Market
Holkham
Wells-next-the-Sea
Blakeney
Cley next the Sea
Salthouse
Weybourne
Sheringham
West Runton
Cromer
Overstrand
Trimingham
Roughton
Southrepps
Mundesley-on-Sea
Thorpe Market
Bacton
Happisburgh
North Walsham
Sea Palling
Stalham
Horsey
Potter Heigham
Winterton-on-Sea
Hemsby
Martham
Ormesby
Caister-on-Sea
Heacham
Docking
Little Walsingham
Holt
Great Bircham
Syderstone
Melton Constable
Ingoldisthorpe
Dersingham
Sandringham
Fakenham
Saxthorpe
Blickling
Aylsham
Castle Rising
Hillington
East Rudham
Guist
Reepham
Coltishall
Grimston
South Raynham
North Elmham
Bawdeswell
Horning
KING'S LYNN
East Bilney
Beetley
Great Witchingham (Lenwade)
Wroxham
Ranworth
West Bilney
East Dereham
Salhouse
South Walsham
Narborough
North Tuddenham
Acle
Wisbech
Swaffham
Barnham Broom
NORWICH
GREAT YARMOUTH
Downham Market
Outwell
Stradsett
Shipdham
Hethersett
REEDHAM FERRY
Reedham
Gorleston-on-Sea
Kimberley
Yelverton
Watton
Hingham
Wymondham
Stoke Holy Cross
Brooke
Hopton on Sea
Loddon
Corton
Stoke Ferry
Haddiscoe
Welney
Methwold
Attleborough
Hempnall
Oulton Broad
LOWESTOFT
Mundford
Bunwell
Ellingham
Long Stratton
Beccles
Feltwell
New Buckenham
Snetterton (Circuit)
Bungay
Brandon
Homersfield
Littleport
East Harling
Kenninghall
Wortwell
Kessingland
Lakenheath
Thetford
Harleston
Wrentham
Ely
South Lopham
Diss
Garboldisham
Elveden
Scole
Halesworth
Southwold
Mildenhall
Botesdale
Brome
Stradbroke
Walberswick
Stretham
Freckenham
Barton Mills
Yaxley
Eye
Heveningham
Stanton
Dunwich
Ixworth
Burwell
Finningham
Dennington
Yoxford
Westleton
Newmarket
BURY ST EDMUNDS
Debenham
Saxmundham
Stow Cum Quy
Bottisham
Horringer
Framlingham
Leiston
Stowmarket
Thorpeness
Six Mile Bottom
Helmingham
Snape
Crowfield
Coddenham
Campsey Ash
Aldeburgh
Great Shelford
Stradishall
Lawshall
Needham Market
Wickham Market
Tunstall
Balsham
Henley
Butley
Orford
Orford Ness
Little Abington
Lavenham
Bildeston
Woodbridge
Duxford
Linton
Cavendish
Haverhill
Clare
Long Melford
Monks Eleigh
IPSWICH
Hintlesham
Shottisham
Great Chesterford
Steeple Bumpstead
Hadleigh
Sudbury
Saffron Walden
Great Yeldham
Stoke-by-Nayland
Shotley
Felixstowe
Radwinter
Castle Hedingham
Bures
Nayland
Dedham
KRISTIANSAND (Summer Only)
Newport
Finchingfield
Parkeston Quay
Harwich
Manningtree
Thaxted
Wethersfield
Halstead
Dovercourt
Quendon
ESBJERG HAMBURG HOEK VAN HOLLAND GOTEBORG
West Bergholt
Ardleigh
Ramsey
Wix
Broxted
The Naze
Stansted
Marks Tey
Thorpe-le-Soken
Great Dunmow
Braintree
COLCHESTER
Elmstead Market
Great Bentley
Walton-on-the-Naze
BISHOP'S STORTFORD
Coggeshall
Frinton-on-Sea
ZEEBRUGGE
Silver End
Kelvedon
Brightlingsea
Holland-on-Sea
Tiptree
Hatfield Heath
Leaden Roding
Witham
West Mersea
St Osyth
CLACTON-ON-SEA
HARLOW
Tolleshunt D'Arcy
Tollesbury
Boreham
CHELMSFORD
Writtle
Maldon
River Blackwater
Bradwell-on-Sea
Ongar
Mundon Hill
EPPING
Ingatestone
Latchingdon
Southminster
South
5

14
NX
SC
SH
6
ISLE OF MAN
Point of Ayre
The Lhen
Bride
Sartfield
Andreas
Jurby West
Ramsey Bay
Sandygate
St Judes
Ballaugh
Ramsey
Sulby
Kirk Michael
Maughold
Barregarrow
SNAEFELL 2034
Knocksharry
The Bungalow
Dhoon
Peel
Laxey
Injebreck
Patrick
Baldrine
St John's
Crosby
Glenmaye
Onchan
Union Mills
DOUGLAS
St Marks
Port Soderick
Colby
Ballasalla
Port Erin
Derbyhaven
Cregneish
Port St Mary
Castletown
Calf of Man
RONALDSWAY
BELFAST
HEYSHAM
DUBLIN Summer Only
LIVERPOOL FLEETWOOD Summer Only
Head
Moor
Egremont
St Bees
Calder Bridge
Wasdale
Gosforth
Seascale
Eskdale
Holmrook
Ravenglass
Bootle
Millom
Dalton-in
Vickerst
DOUGLAS (Summer Only)
BELFAST
DOUGLAS (Summer Only)
DUBLIN DUN LAOGHAIRE
Cemaes Bay
Amlwch
Llanfaethlu
Llanerchymedd
Marianglas
SOUTH STACK
Holyhead
Llanfachraeth
Benllech Bay
Red Wharf Bay
Trearddur Bay
Valley
Llangoed
Four Mile Bridge
Llangefni
Beaumaris
Rhosneigr
ANGLESEY
Menai Bridge
Bangor
Llanfair P.G.
Aberffraw
Newborough
Port Dinorwic
Bethesda
Caernarfon
Llanrug
Cwm-y-Glo
Caeathro
Llanberis
CARNEDD LLEWELYN 3484
SNOWDON 3560
Llanwnda
Caernarfon Bay
Groeslon
Pen-y-gwryd
Rhyd-ddu
Pen-y-groes
Clynnogfawr
Beddgelert
Trefor
Llanaelhaearn
Garn-Dolbenmaen
LLEYN PENINSULA
Nefyn
Morfa Nefyn
Prenteg
Tremadog
Llanfrothen
Criccieth
Porthmadog
Penrhyndeudraeth
Pwllheli
Llanbedrog
Sarn
Talsarnau
Harlech
Y Rhiw
Abersoch
Llanbedr
GT ORMES HEAD
Llandudno
Deganwy
Rhos-on-Sea
COLWYN BAY
Mochdre
Conwy
Llandudno Junction
Penmaenmawr
Llanfairfechan
Abergele
Roewen
Tal-y-Cafn
Tal-y-Bont
Trefriw
Llanrwst
Capel Curig
Betws-y-Coed
Dolwyddelan
Penmachno
Blaenau Ffestiniog
Ffestiniog
GWYNEDD
Trawsfynydd
Prestatyn
Gronant
RHYL
Mostyn
Dyserth
Rhuddlan
St Asaph
Llanfair Talhaiarn
Llangernyw
Llansannan
Henllan
Bodfari
Denbigh
Bylchau
Llanrhaedr
Ruthin
Pentrefoelas
Cerrigydrudion
Bryneglwys
Tyn-y-Cefn
Corwen
Bala
Bala Lake
Llandderfel
Llandrillo
Llanuwchllyn
Llanarmon Dyffryn Ceiriog
Ty Nant
Llanrhaedr-ym-Mochnant
CLWYD

15
11
13
7
NY
NZ
SD
SE
SJ
SK
DISTRICT
Ambleside
Windermere
Kendal
Richmond
Northallerton
Ulverston
Carnforth
MORECAMBE
Heysham
LANCASTER
Skipton
HARROGATE
Knaresborough
Ripon
FLEETWOOD
Cleveleys
ACKPOOL
LYTHAM-ST-ANNES
PRESTON
BLACKBURN
BURNLEY
ACCRINGTON
KEIGHLEY
BRADFORD
LEEDS
HALIFAX
HUDDERSFIELD
WAKEFIELD
SOUTHPORT
CHORLEY
BOLTON
WIGAN
ROCHDALE
OLDHAM
MANCHESTER
STOCKPORT
SHEFFIELD
LIVERPOOL
BIRKENHEAD
ST HELENS
WARRINGTON
RUNCORN
WIDNES
CHESTER
WREXHAM
MACCLESFIELD
CHESTERFIELD
NEWCASTLE-UNDER-LYME
STOKE-ON-TRENT
DERBY
STAFFORDSHIRE

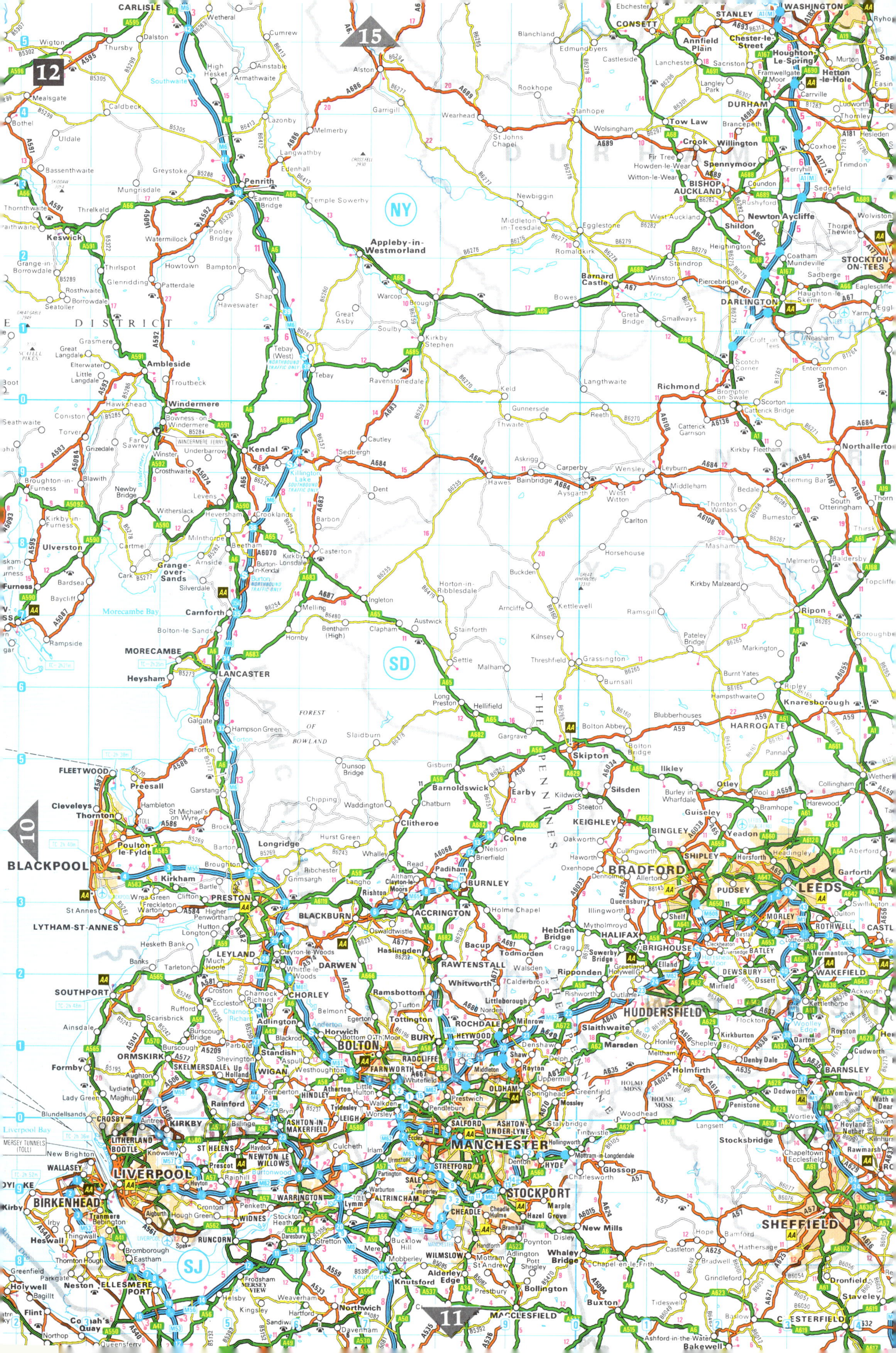

15
12
10
11
NY
SD
SJ
CARLISLE
Penrith
Keswick
Ambleside
Windermere
Kendal
LAKE DISTRICT
Appleby-in-Westmorland
Kirkby Stephen
Alston
DURHAM
WASHINGTON
STANLEY
CONSETT
BISHOP AUCKLAND
Newton Aycliffe
DARLINGTON
STOCKTON-ON-TEES
Barnard Castle
Richmond
Northallerton
Ripon
Knaresborough
HARROGATE
Skipton
Settle
Sedbergh
Hawes
Leyburn
Ulverston
Barrow-in-Furness
Morecambe Bay
MORECAMBE
Heysham
LANCASTER
Carnforth
FLEETWOOD
Cleveleys
Thornton
BLACKPOOL
LYTHAM-ST-ANNES
PRESTON
LEYLAND
SOUTHPORT
CHORLEY
BLACKBURN
ACCRINGTON
BURNLEY
Clitheroe
Colne
KEIGHLEY
BINGLEY
BRADFORD
SHIPLEY
LEEDS
PUDSEY
HALIFAX
HUDDERSFIELD
WAKEFIELD
DEWSBURY
BATLEY
BARNSLEY
ROCHDALE
OLDHAM
BURY
BOLTON
WIGAN
ORMSKIRK
ST HELENS
LIVERPOOL
BIRKENHEAD
WALLASEY
BOOTLE
MANCHESTER
SALFORD
STOCKPORT
WARRINGTON
WIDNES
RUNCORN
ELLESMERE PORT
ALTRINCHAM
CHEADLE
WILMSLOW
Knutsford
MACCLESFIELD
Buxton
SHEFFIELD
CHESTERFIELD
Bakewell
FOREST OF BOWLAND
THE PENNINES
DURHAM
NORTH YORKS

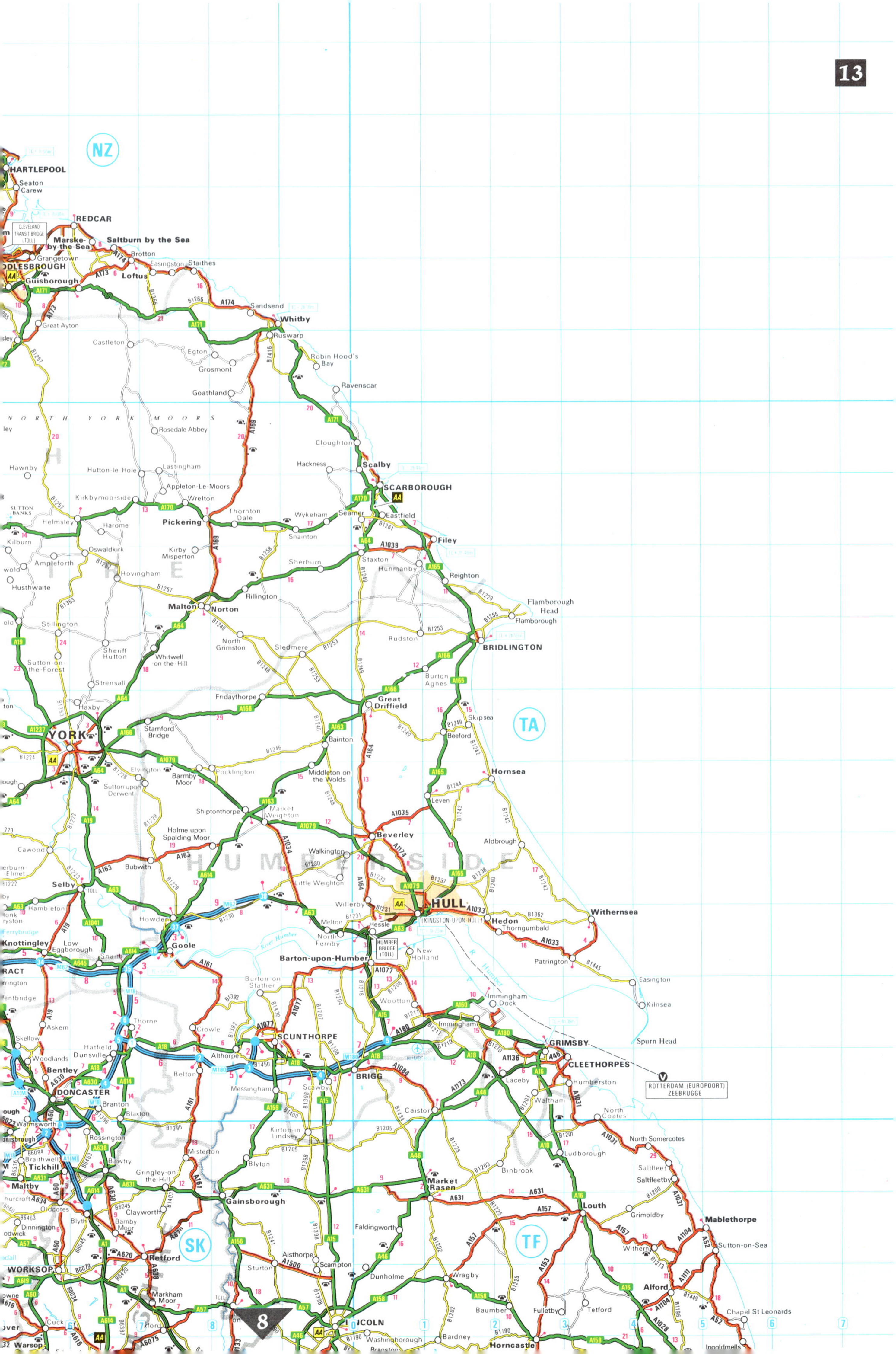
NZ
HARTLEPOOL
Seaton Carew
REDCAR
CLEVELAND TRANSIT BRIDGE (TOLL)
Marske-by-the-Sea
Saltburn by the Sea
Brotton
Grangetown
Loftus
Easington
Staithes
Guisborough
Sandsend
Whitby
Great Ayton
Ruswarp
Castleton
Egton
Grosmont
Robin Hood's Bay
Ravenscar
Goathland
NORTH YORK MOORS
Rosedale Abbey
Cloughton
Hawnby
Hutton-le-Hole
Lastingham
Hackness
Scalby
SCARBOROUGH
Appleton-Le-Moors
Kirkbymoorside
Wrelton
SUTTON BANKS
Helmsley
Harome
Pickering
Thornton Dale
Wykeham
Seamer
Eastfield
Snainton
Kilburn
Oswaldkirk
Kirby Misperton
Filey
Staxton
Sherburn
Hunmanby
Ampleforth
Hovingham
Reighton
Husthwaite
Rillington
Flamborough Head
Flamborough
Malton
Norton
Stillington
North Grimston
Rudston
BRIDLINGTON
Sheriff Hutton
Whitwell on the Hill
Sledmere
Sutton-on-the-Forest
Burton Agnes
Strensall
Fridaythorpe
Great Driffield
Haxby
Skipsea
TA
YORK
Stamford Bridge
Beeford
Bainton
Elvington
Barmby Moor
Pocklington
Middleton on the Wolds
Hornsea
Sutton upon Derwent
Shiptonthorpe
Market Weighton
Leven
Holme upon Spalding Moor
Beverley
Aldbrough
Cawood
HUMBERSIDE
Walkington
Bubwith
Selby
Little Weighton
Hambleton
Willerby
HULL
KINGSTON UPON HULL
Hedon
Withernsea
Howden
Melton
Hessle
Thorngumbald
Knottingley
North Ferriby
HUMBER BRIDGE (TOLL)
Low Eggborough
Snaith
Goole
Barton-upon-Humber
New Holland
Patrington
River Humber
Burton on Stather
Easington
Immingham Dock
Kilnsea
Wootton
Thorne
Askern
Immingham
Crowle
SCUNTHORPE
Spurn Head
GRIMSBY
Skellow
Hatfield
Dunsville
Althorpe
Woodlands
Bentley
Belton
CLEETHORPES
BRIGG
Humberston
Messingham
ROTTERDAM (EUROPOORT) ZEEBRUGGE
DONCASTER
Branton
Scawby
Laceby
Waltham
Blaxton
Caistor
Warmsworth
Kirton in Lindsey
North Coates
Rossington
Misterton
North Somercotes
Ludborough
Bawtry
Tickhill
Blyton
Braithwell
Gringley-on-the-Hill
Binbrook
Saltfleet
Saltfleetby
Maltby
Market Rasen
Gainsborough
Louth
Oldcotes
Clayworth
Grimoldby
Dinnington
Blyth
Barnby Moor
Faldingworth
Mablethorpe
SK
TF
Sutton-on-Sea
Withern
Retford
Aisthorpe
Scampton
WORKSOP
Sturton
Dunholme
Wragby
Alford
Markham Moor
Tetford
Baumber
Fulletby
Chapel St Leonards
Cuckney
LINCOLN
Washingborough
Bardney
Horncastle
Ingoldmells
Warsop
8

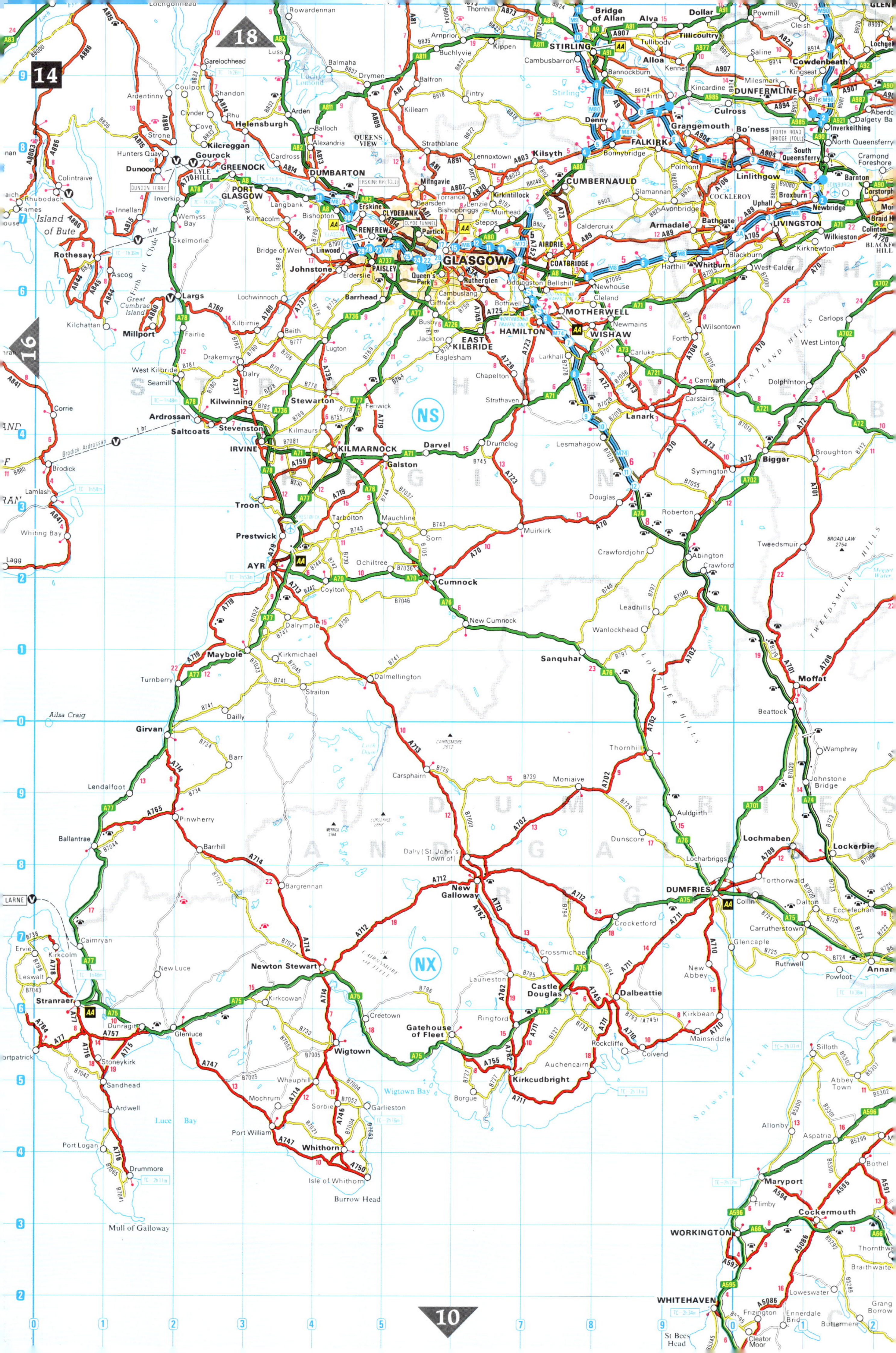
18
14
16
10
Rowardennan
Luss
Garelochhead
Ardentinny
Coulport
Shandon
Rhu
Clynder
Cove
Helensburgh
Kilcreggan
Strone
Hunters Quay
Dunoon
Gourock
Greenock
Lyle Hill
Dunoon Ferry
Port Glasgow
Colintraive
Rhubodach
Island of Bute
Rothesay
Ascog
Innellan
Inverkip
Wemyss Bay
Skelmorlie
Largs
Great Cumbrae Island
Millport
Kilchattan
Fairlie
West Kilbride
Seamill
Ardrossan
Saltcoats
Stevenston
Irvine
Kilwinning
Dalry
Kilbirnie
Beith
Lochwinnoch
Drakemyre
Balmaha
Drymen
Balfron
Killearn
Fintry
Arden
Balloch
Alexandria
Cardross
Dumbarton
Queens View
Strathblane
Lennoxtown
Kilsyth
Milngavie
Bearsden
Torrance
Lenzie
Kirkintilloch
Bishopbriggs
Muirhead
Stepps
Clydebank
Clyde Tunnel
Erskine
Erskine Bridge (Toll)
Renfrew
Bishopton
Langbank
Kilmacolm
Bridge of Weir
Linwood
Johnstone
Elderslie
Paisley
Partick
Glasgow
Queen's Park
Rutherglen
Cambuslang
Giffnock
Barrhead
Busby
Eaglesham
East Kilbride
Jackton
Uddingston
Bellshill
Bothwell
Hamilton
Motherwell
Wishaw
Newmains
Cleland
Newhouse
Coatbridge
Airdrie
Caldercruix
Cumbernauld
Slamannan
Stirling
Bridge of Allan
Alva
Dollar
Tillicoultry
Tullibody
Alloa
Kennet
Cambusbarron
Bannockburn
Airth
Denny
Falkirk
Bonnybridge
Grangemouth
Bo'ness
Polmont
Linlithgow
Avonbridge
Armadale
Bathgate
Livingston
Whitburn
Harthill
Blackburn
West Calder
Uphall
Broxburn
Newbridge
Kirkliston
Cockleroy
Kincardine
Culross
Dunfermline
Cowdenbeath
Kingseat
Saline
Cleish
Powmill
Lochgelly
Inverkeithing
North Queensferry
South Queensferry
Forth Road Bridge (Toll)
Cramond Foreshore
Dalgety Bay
Barnton
Corstorphine
Colinton
Wilkieston
Kirknewton
Thornhill
Arnprior
Buchlyvie
Kippen
Carlops
West Linton
Wilsontown
Forth
Carluke
Carnwath
Carstairs
Dolphinton
Lanark
Larkhall
Chapelton
Strathaven
Lesmahagow
Douglas
Symington
Biggar
Broughton
Roberton
Abington
Crawford
Crawfordjohn
Tweedsmuir
Pentland Hills
Lugton
Stewarton
Fenwick
Kilmaurs
Kilmarnock
Darvel
Drumclog
Galston
Troon
Prestwick
Tarbolton
Mauchline
Sorn
Muirkirk
Ayr
Ochiltree
Cumnock
Coylton
New Cumnock
Dalrymple
Maybole
Kirkmichael
Dalmellington
Straiton
Turnberry
Ailsa Craig
Daily
Girvan
Barr
Lendalfoot
Pinwherry
Ballantrae
Barrhill
Bargrennan
Leadhills
Wanlockhead
Sanquhar
Thornhill
Carsphairn
Moniaive
Dalry (St John's Town of)
New Galloway
Dunscore
Auldgirth
Locharbriggs
Dumfries
Moffat
Beattock
Wamphray
Johnstone Bridge
Lochmaben
Lockerbie
Torthorwald
Collin
Dalton
Ecclefechan
Carrutherstown
Glencaple
Ruthwell
Annan
Powfoot
New Abbey
Kirkbean
Mainsriddle
Crocketford
Dalbeattie
Castle Douglas
Crossmichael
Laurieston
Ringford
Gatehouse of Fleet
Kirkcudbright
Auchencairn
Rockcliffe
Colvend
Creetown
Newton Stewart
Kirkcowan
Glenluce
Wigtown
Wigtown Bay
Whauphill
Sorbie
Garlieston
Whithorn
Isle of Whithorn
Burrow Head
Mochrum
Port William
Luce Bay
New Luce
Cairnryan
Kirkcolm
Ervie
Leswalt
Stranraer
Portpatrick
Dunragit
Stoneykirk
Sandhead
Ardwell
Port Logan
Drummore
Mull of Galloway
Larne
Corrie
Brodick
Lamlash
Whiting Bay
Lagg
Silloth
Abbey Town
Allonby
Aspatria
Maryport
Flimby
Cockermouth
Workington
Whitehaven
Bothel
Loweswater
Braithwaite
Frizington
Ennerdale Bridge
St Bees Head
Cleator Moor
NS
NX
Solway Firth
Strathclyde Region
Dumfries and Galloway Region
Lowther Hills
Tweedsmuir Hills

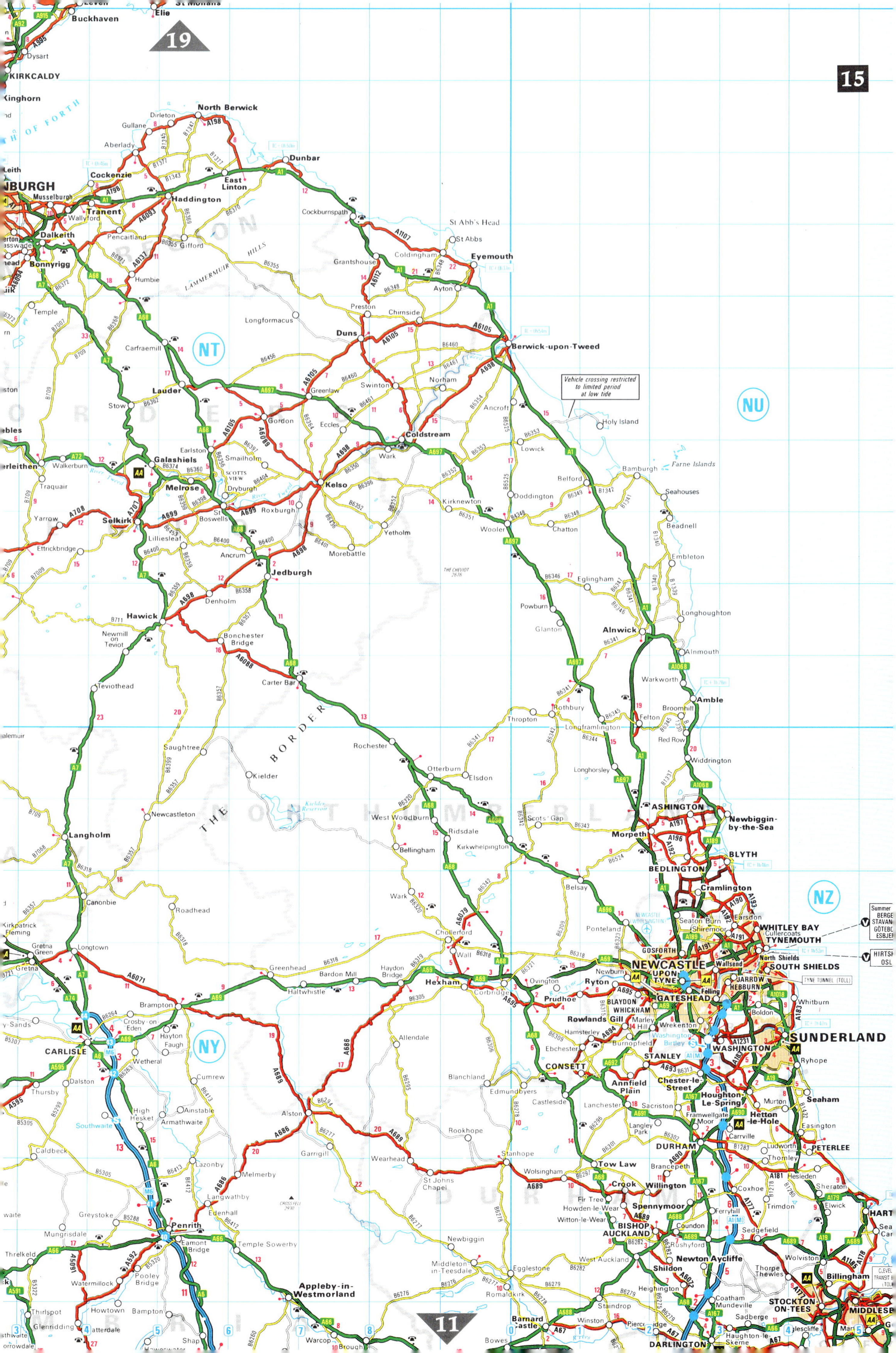

15
19
11
Buckhaven
Elie
Dysart
KIRKCALDY
Kinghorn
FIRTH OF FORTH
North Berwick
Dirleton
Gullane
Aberlady
Leith
Cockenzie
EDINBURGH
Musselburgh
Tranent
Wallyford
Haddington
East Linton
Dunbar
Dalkeith
Bonnyrigg
Pencaitland
Gifford
LAMMERMUIR HILLS
Humbie
Temple
Cockburnspath
St Abb's Head
St Abbs
Coldingham
Eyemouth
Grantshouse
Ayton
Preston
Chirnside
Longformacus
Duns
Berwick-upon-Tweed
Carfraemill
NT
Lauder
Stow
Greenlaw
Swinton
Norham
Vehicle crossing restricted to limited period at low tide
NU
Ancroft
Holy Island
Gordon
Eccles
Coldstream
Wark
Lowick
Earlston
Galashiels
Walkerburn
Innerleithen
Smailholm
SCOTTS VIEW
Melrose
Dryburgh
Kelso
Traquair
Belford
Bamburgh
Farne Islands
Seahouses
Doddington
Kirknewton
Yarrow
Selkirk
St Boswells
Roxburgh
Wooler
Chatton
Beadnell
Lilliesleaf
Yetholm
Ettrickbridge
Ancrum
Morebattle
Jedburgh
THE CHEVIOT 2676
Embleton
Eglingham
Denholm
Powburn
Hawick
Longhoughton
Newmill on Teviot
Bonchester Bridge
Glanton
Alnwick
Alnmouth
Carter Bar
Warkworth
Teviothead
Amble
Rothbury
Broomhill
Thropton
Felton
Longframlington
Red Row
Saughtree
Rochester
THE BORDER
Widdrington
Otterburn
Elsdon
Kielder
Longhorsley
Kielder Reservoir
Newcastleton
West Woodburn
Ridsdale
Scots' Gap
ASHINGTON
Newbiggin-by-the-Sea
NORTHUMBERLAND
Langholm
Bellingham
Kirkwhelpington
Morpeth
BLYTH
BEDLINGTON
Belsay
Cramlington
Canonbie
Roadhead
Wark
NZ
Seaton Burn
Earsdon
WHITLEY BAY
Cullercoats
Shiremoor
TYNEMOUTH
Kirkpatrick Fleming
Ponteland
Chollerford
Gretna Green
Gretna
Longtown
Wall
GOSFORTH
NEWCASTLE UPON TYNE
Wallsend
North Shields
SOUTH SHIELDS
TYNE TUNNEL (TOLL)
Greenhead
Bardon Mill
Haydon Bridge
Haltwhistle
Hexham
Corbridge
Ovington
Newburn
Ryton
JARROW
HEBBURN
Felling
GATESHEAD
Prudhoe
BLAYDON
WHICKHAM
Brampton
Whitburn
Boldon
Rowlands Gill
Marley Hill
Wrekenton
Crosby-on-Eden
Hayton
Fauch
Allendale
Hamsterley
Washington
Birtley
SUNDERLAND
CARLISLE
Wetheral
NY
Burnopfield
Ebchester
STANLEY
WASHINGTON
CONSETT
Ryhope
Dalston
Cumrew
Blanchland
Edmundbyers
Annfield Plain
Chester-le-Street
Thursby
High Hesket
Castleside
Lanchester
Sacriston
Houghton-le-Spring
Murton
Seaham
Southwaite
Armathwaite
Ainstable
Alston
Framwellgate Moor
Hetton-le-Hole
Rookhope
Langley Park
Carrville
Easington
Caldbeck
Garrigill
DURHAM
Ludworth
PETERLEE
Thornley
Lazonby
Stanhope
Melmerby
Wearhead
St Johns Chapel
Wolsingham
Tow Law
Brancepeth
Hesleden
Sheraton
Langwathby
CROSS FELL 2930
Crook
Willington
Coxhoe
Elwick
HARTLEPOOL
Greystoke
Edenhall
Fir Tree
Howden-le-Wear
Witton-le-Wear
Spennymoor
Ferryhill
Trimdon
Mungrisdale
Penrith
Eamont Bridge
Temple Sowerby
Newbiggin
BISHOP AUCKLAND
Coundon
Sedgefield
Rushyford
Threlkeld
West Auckland
Newton Aycliffe
Wolviston
Pooley Bridge
Middleton-in-Teesdale
Eggleston
Shildon
Thorpe Thewles
Billingham
Watermillock
Appleby-in-Westmorland
Romaldkirk
Heighington
Coatham Mundeville
STOCKTON-ON-TEES
MIDDLESBROUGH
Howtown
Bampton
Staindrop
Thirlspot
Glenridding
Patterdale
Shap
Warcop
Brough
Barnard Castle
Winston
Piercebridge
Sadberge
Bowes
Haughton-le-Skerne
Egglescliffe
Marton
DARLINGTON
Summer
BERGEN
STAVANGER
GÖTEBORG
ESBJERG
HIRTSHALS
OSLO

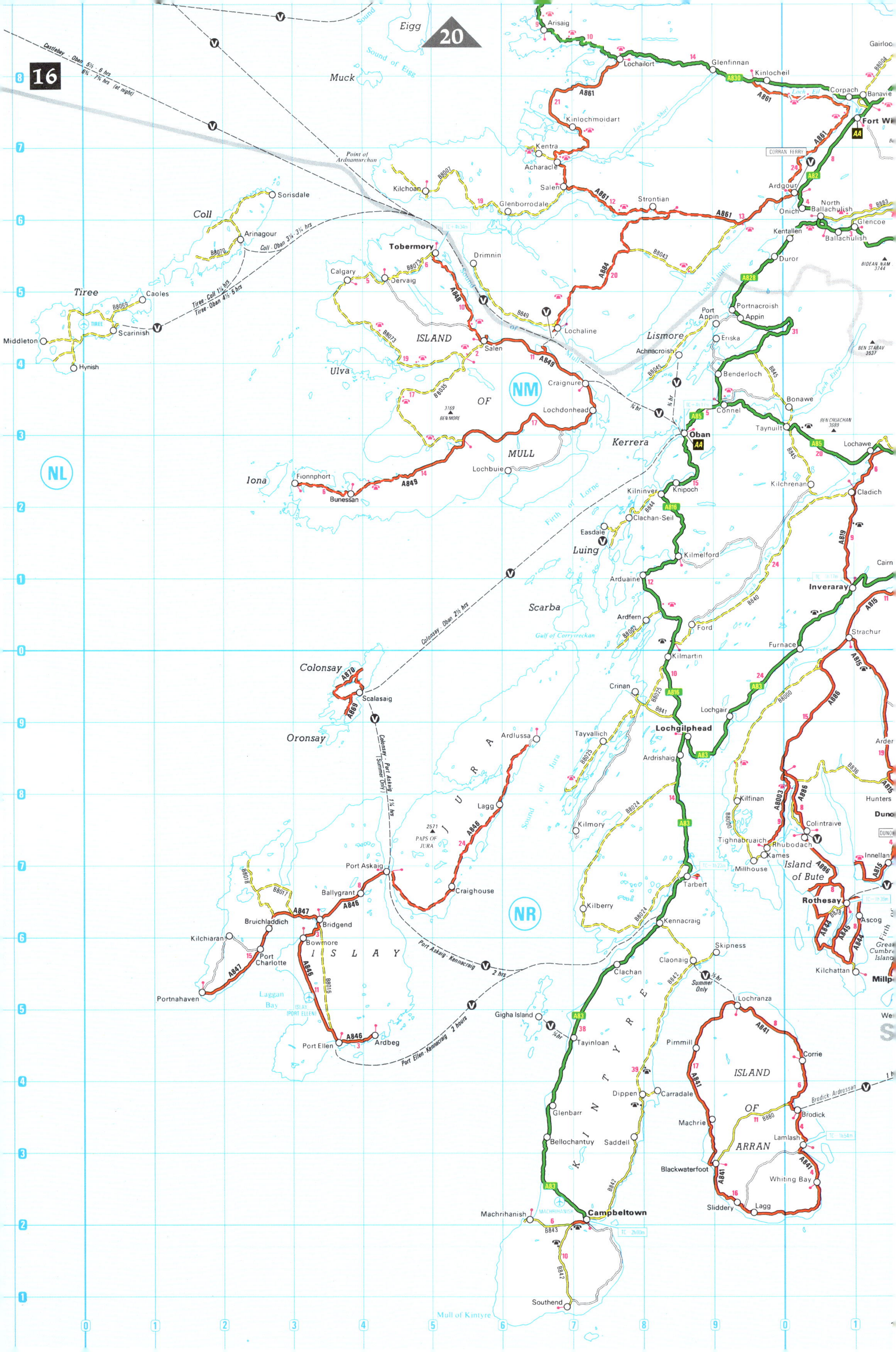
16
20
Eigg
Muck
Sound of Eigg
Castlebay - Oban 5½ - 6 hrs
6¾ - 7½ hrs (at night)
Point of Ardnamurchan
Arisaig
Lochailort
Glenfinnan
Kinlocheil
Corpach
Banavie
Fort William
Gairloch
Loch Eil
Loch Shiel
Kinlochmoidart
Kentra
Acharacle
Salen
Strontian
Corran Ferry
Ardgour
Onich
North Ballachulish
Ballachulish
Glencoe
Kentallen
Duror
Bidean Nam 3744
Kilchoan
Glenborrodale
Sorisdale
Coll
Arinagour
Coll - Oban 3¼ - 3¾ hrs
Tiree - Coll 1¼ hrs
Tiree - Oban 4½ - 5 hrs
Tiree
Caoles
Scarinish
Middleton
Hynish
Tobermory
Drimnin
Calgary
Dervaig
Sound of Mull
Lochaline
ISLAND OF MULL
Salen
Ulva
Craignure
Lochdonhead
3169 Ben More
Fionnphort
Bunessan
Iona
Lochbuie
Kerrera
Lismore
Achnacroish
Port Appin
Appin
Portnacroish
Eriska
Loch Linnhe
Benderloch
Bonawe
Connel
Taynuilt
Oban
Ben Cruachan 3689
Ben Starav 3537
Lochawe
Kilchrenan
Cladich
Kilninver
Knipoch
Clachan-Seil
Easdale
Luing
Kilmelford
Firth of Lorne
Arduaine
Scarba
Gulf of Corryvreckan
Ardfern
Ford
Inveraray
Cairn
Furnace
Strachur
Kilmartin
Crinan
Colonsay
Scalasaig
Oronsay
Colonsay - Oban 2½ hrs
Colonsay - Port Askaig (Summer Only) 1¼ hrs
Lochgair
Lochgilphead
Ardrishaig
Tayvallich
Ardlussa
JURA
Sound of Jura
Lagg
2571 Paps of Jura
Craighouse
Kilmory
Kilfinan
Tighnabruaich
Kames
Millhouse
Rhubodach
Colintraive
Island of Bute
Rothesay
Ascog
Kilchattan
Port Askaig
Ballygrant
Bruichladdich
Bridgend
Kilchiaran
Bowmore
Port Charlotte
ISLAY
Portnahaven
Laggan Bay
Port Ellen
Ardbeg
Port Askaig - Kennacraig 2 hrs
Port Ellen - Kennacraig 2 hours
Tarbert
Kilberry
Kennacraig
Skipness
Claonaig
Clachan
Summer Only
Lochranza
Gigha Island
Tayinloan
Pirnmill
Corrie
KINTYRE
ISLAND OF ARRAN
Brodick
Brodick - Ardrossan
Carradale
Dippen
Machrie
Lamlash
Glenbarr
Bellochantuy
Saddell
Blackwaterfoot
Whiting Bay
Campbeltown
Machrihanish
Sliddery
Lagg
Southend
Mull of Kintyre
Great Cumbrae Island
Innellan
Hunters
Arden
NM
NR
NL
A830
A861
A82
A828
A849
A848
A884
A85
A816
A819
A815
A83
A886
A8003
A844
A845
A847
A846
A870
A869
A841
B8007
B8070
B8069
B8073
B8035
B8043
B849
B8045
B845
B8044
B840
B8002
B8025
B841
B8000
B836
B8024
B8018
B8017
B8016
B842
B880
B843

21
17
19
15
14
GRAMPIAN MOUNTAINS
TAYSIDE REGION
CENTRAL REGION
LOTHIAN
STRATHCLYDE REGION
BORDERS REGION
SIDLAW HILLS
PENTLAND HILLS
TWEEDSMUIR HILLS
FIRTH OF FORTH
NN
NO
NS
NT
Spean Bridge
Roy Bridge
Dalwhinnie
Inverey
LOCHNAGAR 3786
GLAS MAOL 3504
Tarfs
Clova
Glenshee (Spittal of)
Calvine
Blair Atholl
Killiecrankie
Pitlochry
Kirkmichael
Kinloch Rannoch
Strathtummel
Tummel Br
QUEENS VIEW
Rannoch Station
Loch Rannoch
SCHIEHALLION 3547
Ballinluig
Ballintuim
Bridge of Cally
Kirriemuir
Forfar
Tannad
Grandtully
Coshieville
Fortingall
Aberfeldy
Bridge of Balgie
Fearnan
Kenmore
Alyth
Blairgowrie
Rattray
Meigle
Glamis
Newtyle
Coupar Angus
Auchterhouse
Dunkeld
Caputh
Kinclaven
Burrelton
Muirhead
DUNDEE
BEN LAWERS 3984
Lawers
Ardtalnaig
Ardeonaig
Amulree
Bankfoot
Stanley
Bridge of Orchy
BEN DORAIN 3523
Killin
Tyndrum
Crianlarich
BEN LUI 3708
BEN MORE 3843
Balbeggie
Scone(New)
Methven
PERTH
Glencarse
Newport-on-Tay
Wormit
Lochearnhead
St Fillans
Loch Earn
Gilmerton
Comrie
Crieff
Balquhidder
Strathyre
BEN VORLICH 3224
Muthill
Forteviot
Bridge of Earn
Dunning
Newburgh
Abernethy
Cupar
Letham
Auchtermuchty
Ardlui
Auchterarder
Gleneagles Hotel
Blackford
Braco
Glenfarg
Strathmiglo
Ladybank
Craigrothie
Stronachlachar
Inversnaid
Callander
Greenloaning
Falkland
Freuchie
Arrochar
Tarbet
DAVID MARSHALL LODGE
Kinlochard
Port of Menteith
Aberfoyle
BEN LOMOND 3192
Kinbuck
Doune
Deanston
Dunblane
Milnathort
Kinnesswood
Kinross
Lundin Links
Upper Largo
Markinch
Leslie
Leven
Buckhaven
Yetts o'Muckhart
Rowardennan
Thornhill
Bridge of Allan
Alva
Dollar
Powmill
GLENROTHES
Cleish
Luss
Arnprior
Kippen
Buchlyvie
STIRLING
Tillicoultry
Tullibody
Alloa
Kennet
Auchterderran
Lochgelly
Dysart
KIRKCALDY
Garelochhead
Balmaha
Drymen
Cambusbarron
Bannockburn
Saline
Cowdenbeath
Kingseat
Shandon
Balfron
Fintry
Airth
Kincardine
DUNFERMLINE
Culross
Kinghorn
Burntisland
Aberdour
Dalgety Bay
Inverkeithing
North Queensferry
FORTH ROAD BRIDGE (TOLL)
Killearn
Rhu
Arden
Helensburgh
Balloch
Alexandria
QUEENS VIEW
Denny
FALKIRK
Grangemouth
Bo'ness
South Queensferry
Cove
Kilcreggan
Gourock
Strathblane
Lennoxtown
Kilsyth
Bonnybridge
Polmont
Cramond
Foreshore
Leith
EDINBURGH
Cockenzie
Aberlady
Gullane
GREENOCK
Cardross
DUMBARTON
ERSKINE BRIDGE (TOLL)
Milngavie
CUMBERNAULD
Linlithgow
Barnton
Corstorphine
Musselburgh
Tranent
PORT GLASGOW
Langbank
Erskine
CLYDEBANK
Bearsden
Torrance
Lenzie
Kirkintilloch
Bishopbriggs
Slamannan
Broxburn
Uphall
Newbridge
Morningside
Braid Hills
Wallyford
Kilmacolm
Bishopton
CLYDE TUNNEL
RENFREW
Partick
Stepps
Muirhead
Caldercruix
Avonbridge
Armadale
Bathgate
LIVINGSTON
Wilkieston
Colinton
BLACKFORD HILL
Gilmerton
Lasswade
Dalkeith
Pencaitland
Bridge of Weir
Linwood
GLASGOW
AIRDRIE
COATBRIDGE
Harthill
Whitburn
Blackburn
Kirknewton
Loanhead
Bonnyrigg
Johnstone
Elderslie
PAISLEY
Queen's Park
Rutherglen
Uddingston
Bellshill
Newhouse
West Calder
Penicuik
Largs
Lochwinnoch
Barrhead
Cambuslang
Giffnock
Bothwell
Cleland
MOTHERWELL
Newmains
WISHAW
HAMILTON
EAST KILBRIDE
Busby
Jackton
Eaglesham
Larkhall
Carluke
Forth
Wilsontown
Carlops
Leadburn
Temple
Kilbirnie
Beith
Lugton
Fairlie
Drakemyre
Dalry
Kilwinning
Stewarton
Fenwick
Chapelton
Strathaven
Carnwath
Carstairs
Lanark
West Linton
Dolphinton
Eddleston
Stevenston
Saltcoats
Kilmaurs
IRVINE
KILMARNOCK
Darvel
Galston
Drumclog
Lesmahagow
Biggar
Broughton
Peebles
Innerleithen
Walkerburn
Traquair
Troon
Tarbolton
Mauchline
Sorn
Douglas
Symington
Roberton
Prestwick
Muirkirk
Tweedsmuir
BROAD LAW 2754
Yarrow
Selkirk
Ettrickbridge
AYR
Ochiltree
Cumnock
Crawfordjohn
Abington
Crawford
Coylton
St. Mary's Loch
Megget Water
Leadhills
Wanlockhead
Dalrymple
New Cumnock
Maybole
Kirkmichael
Sanquhar
Moffat
Straiton
Newmill on Teviot
Teviothead
Hawick
A9
A86
A82
A85
A84
A93
A924
A923
A926
A94
A929
A928
A827
A822
A826
A984
A90
A91
A92
A913
A914
A912
A983
A916
A915
A911
A977
A907
A873
A811
A81
A821
A809
A80
A803
A891
A814
A813
A8
A761
A737
A736
A760
A71
A73
A70
A72
A74
A76
A77
A78
A79
A719
A713
A759
A726
A723
A749
A725
A721
A706
A705
A704
A89
A904
A905
A908
A985
A994
A823
A977
A720
A702
A701
A703
A68
A7
A708
A6091
A199
A198
A1
M8
M9
M73
M74
M80
M90
M876

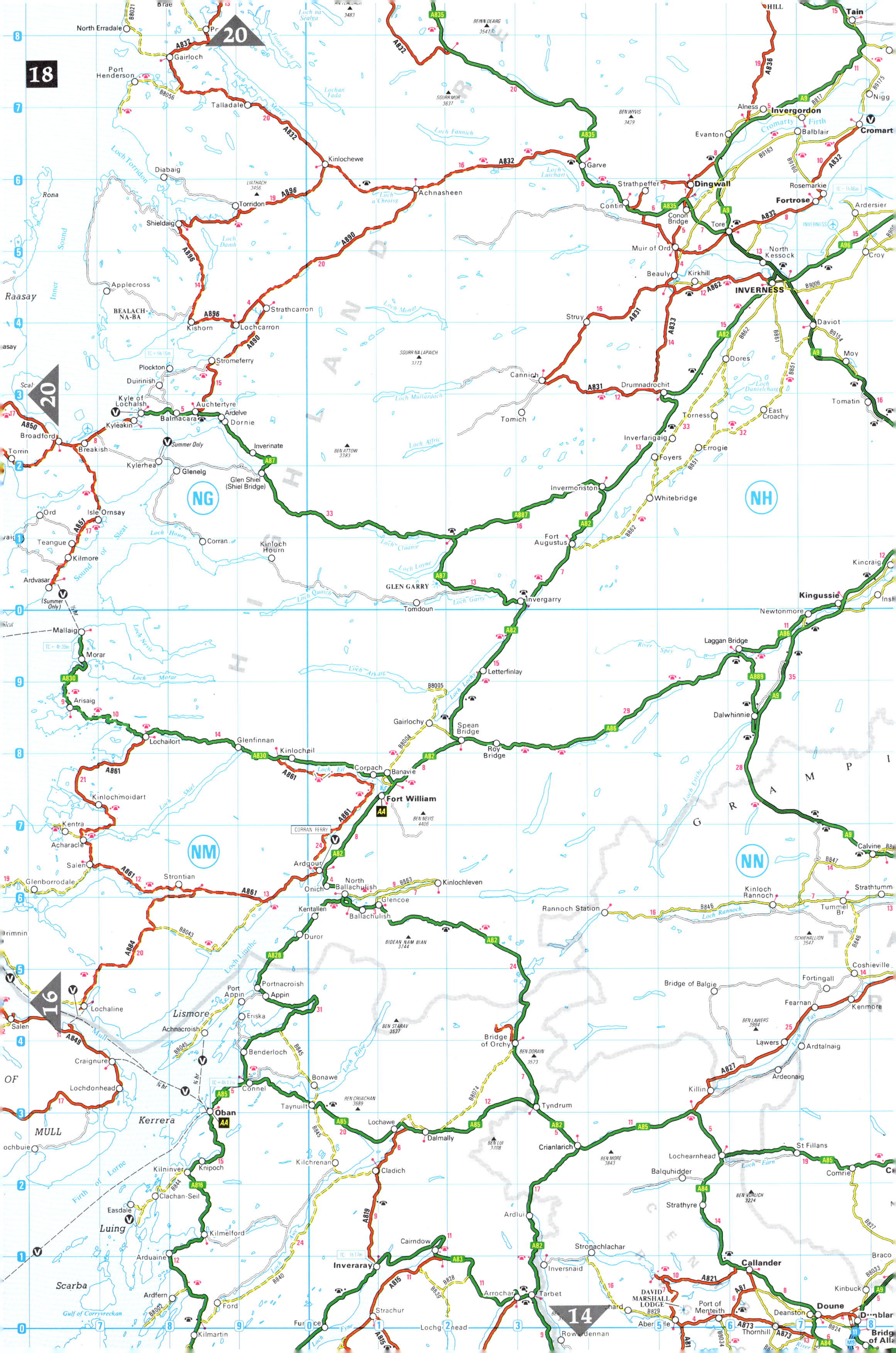
North Erradale
Gairloch
Port Henderson
Talladale
Loch Maree
Kinlochewe
Diabaig
Loch Torridon
Torridon
LIATHACH 3456
Shieldaig
Loch Damh
Rona
Raasay
Inner Sound
Applecross
BEALACH-NA-BA
Kishorn
Lochcarron
Strathcarron
Stromeferry
Plockton
Duirinish
Kyle of Lochalsh
Kyleakin
Balmacara
Auchtertyre
Ardelve
Dornie
Broadford
Breakish
Torrin
Kylerhea
Summer Only
Glenelg
Invernate
Glen Shiel (Shiel Bridge)
Ord
Isle Ornsay
Teangue
Kilmore
Ardvasar
Sound of Sleat
Corran
Kinloch Hourn
Loch Hourn
Loch Quoich
Tomdoun
GLEN GARRY
Loch Garry
Invergarry
Loch Cluanie
Loch Loyne
Mallaig
Morar
Loch Morar
Loch Nevis
Arisaig
Lochailort
Glenfinnan
Kinlocheil
Loch Eil
Corpach
Banavie
Fort William
BEN NEVIS 4406
Loch Arkaig
Gairlochy
Spean Bridge
Roy Bridge
Letterfinlay
Loch Lochy
Kinlochmoidart
Kentra
Acharacle
Salen
Glenborrodale
Strontian
Loch Shiel
CORRAN FERRY
Ardgour
Onich
North Ballachulish
Ballachulish
Glencoe
Kinlochleven
Kentallen
Duror
BIDEAN NAM BIAN 3744
Loch Linnhe
Portnacroish
Appin
Port Appin
Lismore
Eriska
Achnacroish
Lochaline
Salen
Sound of Mull
Craignure
Lochdonhead
Benderloch
Connel
Oban
Kerrera
MULL
Bonawe
Taynuilt
Loch Etive
BEN STARAV 3537
BEN CRUACHAN 3689
Lochawe
Dalmally
Kilchrenan
Cladich
Kilninver
Knipoch
Clachan-Seil
Easdale
Luing
Firth of Lorne
Kilmelford
Arduaine
Scarba
Gulf of Corryvreckan
Ardfern
Ford
Kilmartin
Loch Awe
Inveraray
Cairndow
Strachur
Loch Fyne
Lochgoilhead
Arrochar
Tarbet
Ardlui
Stronachlachar
Inversnaid
Rowardennan
Crianlarich
BEN MORE 3843
Tyndrum
Bridge of Orchy
BEN DORAIN 3523
BEN LUI 3708
Lochearnhead
Balquhidder
Strathyre
BEN VORLICH 3224
Callander
St Fillans
Loch Earn
Comrie
DAVID MARSHALL LODGE
Port of Menteith
Thornhill
Deanston
Doune
Braco
Kinbuck
Killin
Ardeonaig
Lawers
Ardtalnaig
BEN LAWERS 3984
Loch Tay
Kenmore
Fearnan
Fortingall
Bridge of Balgie
Coshieville
SCHIEHALLION 3547
Tummel Br
Kinloch Rannoch
Loch Rannoch
Rannoch Station
Strathtummel
Calvine
Dalwhinnie
Loch Ericht
Laggan Bridge
River Spey
Newtonmore
Kingussie
Kincraig
GRAMPIAN
Invermoriston
Fort Augustus
Whitebridge
Foyers
Errogie
Inverfarigaig
Torness
East Croachy
Dores
Loch Duntelchaig
Drumnadrochit
Tomich
Cannich
Loch Mullardoch
Loch Affric
BEN ATTOW 3383
SGURR NA LAPAICH 3173
Loch Monar
Struy
Beauly
Kirkhill
Muir of Ord
Inverness
North Kessock
Daviot
Moy
Tomatin
Croy
Ardersier
Fortrose
Rosemarkie
Tore
Conon Bridge
Contin
Strathpeffer
Dingwall
Evanton
Alness
Invergordon
Cromarty Firth
Balblair
Cromart
Nigg
Tain
Garve
Loch Luichart
Achnasheen
Loch a' Chroisg
Loch Fannich
SGURR MOR 3637
BEN WYVIS 3429
BEINN DEARG 3547
Loch Fada
Loch na Sealga
HIGHLAND
NG
NH
NM
NN
A832
A835
A896
A890
A87
A887
A82
A830
A861
A884
A828
A85
A816
A819
A815
A83
A86
A9
A889
A827
A84
A821
A81
A873
A831
A833
A862
A96
A836
A850
A851
A849
20
16
14

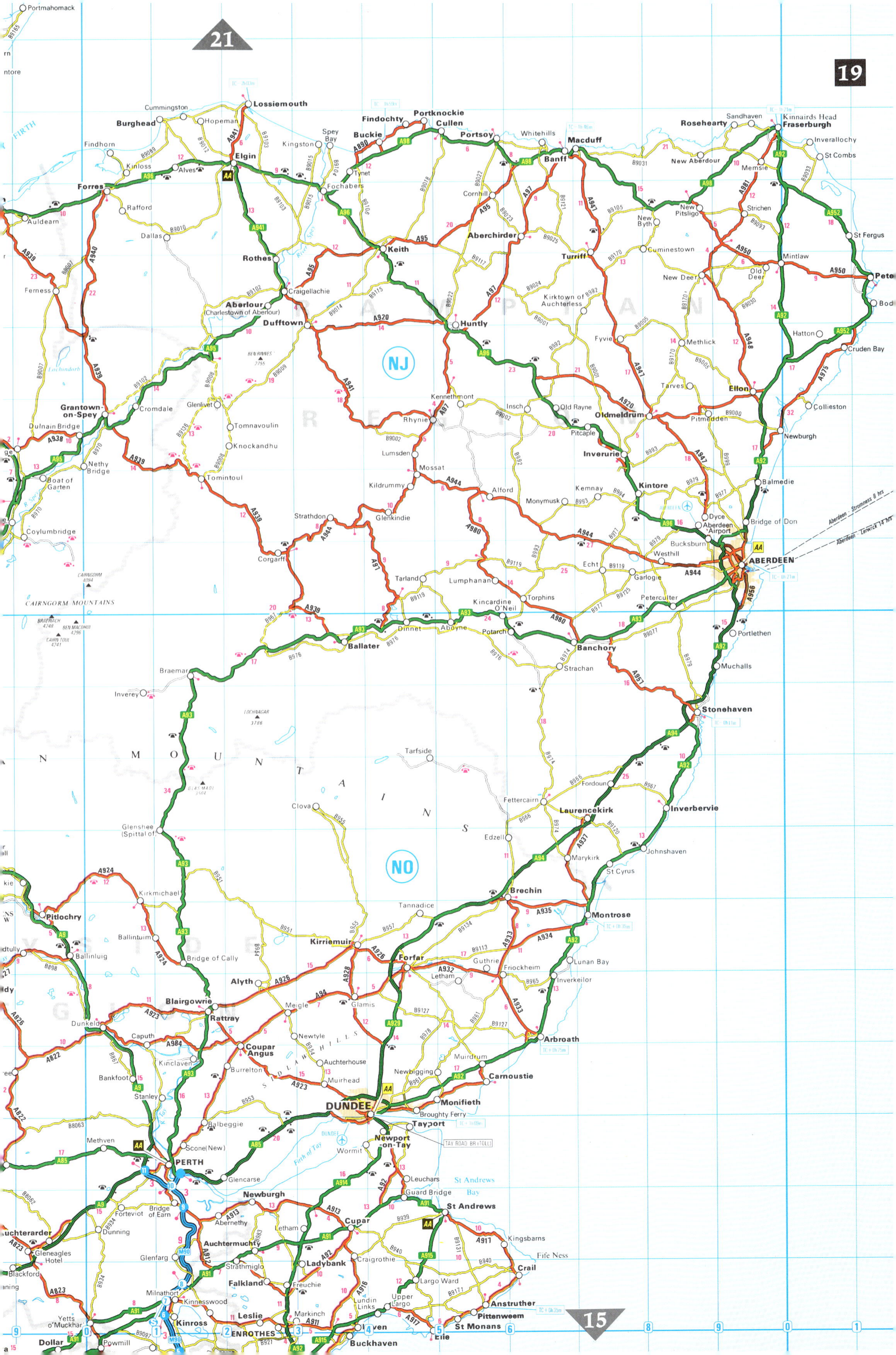
21
15
Portmahomack
Lossiemouth
Cummingston
Burghead
Hopeman
Findhorn
Kinloss
Alves
Elgin
Forres
Rafford
Auldearn
Dallas
Rothes
Findochty
Portknockie
Cullen
Buckie
Spey Bay
Kingston
Tynet
Fochabers
Portsoy
Whitehills
Macduff
Banff
Cornhill
Keith
Aberchirder
Turriff
Craigellachie
Aberlour
(Charlestown of Aberlour)
Dufftown
Huntly
Ferness
Grantown-on-Spey
Cromdale
Glenlivet
Tomnavoulin
Knockandhu
Tomintoul
Dulnain Bridge
Nethy Bridge
Boat of Garten
Coylumbridge
CAIRNGORM MOUNTAINS
Corgarff
Strathdon
Glenkindie
Kildrummy
Lumsden
Rhynie
Kennethmont
Mossat
Alford
Insch
Old Rayne
Oldmeldrum
Pitcaple
Inverurie
Kintore
Kemnay
Monymusk
Rosehearty
Sandhaven
Kinnairds Head
Fraserburgh
Inverallochy
St Combs
New Aberdour
Memsie
New Pitsligo
Strichen
New Byth
Cuminestown
New Deer
Mintlaw
Old Deer
St Fergus
Peterhead
Boddam
Hatton
Cruden Bay
Kirktown of Auchterless
Fyvie
Methlick
Tarves
Ellon
Collieston
Pitmedden
Newburgh
Balmedie
Dyce
Aberdeen Airport
Bridge of Don
Bucksburn
Westhill
ABERDEEN
Echt
Garlogie
Peterculter
Tarland
Lumphanan
Torphins
Kincardine O'Neil
Potarch
Banchory
Strachan
Aboyne
Dinnet
Ballater
Braemar
Inverey
Portlethen
Muchalls
Stonehaven
Tarfside
Clova
Fettercairn
Fordoun
Laurencekirk
Inverbervie
Edzell
Johnshaven
Marykirk
St Cyrus
Brechin
Montrose
Glenshee (Spittal of)
Kirkmichael
Pitlochry
Ballintuim
Ballinluig
Bridge of Cally
Tannadice
Kirriemuir
Forfar
Guthrie
Friockheim
Letham
Lunan Bay
Inverkeilor
Alyth
Blairgowrie
Rattray
Meigle
Glamis
Arbroath
Dunkeld
Caputh
Kinclaven
Coupar Angus
Newtyle
Auchterhouse
Burrelton
Muirhead
Bankfoot
Stanley
Newbigging
Muirdrum
Carnoustie
Monifieth
DUNDEE
Broughty Ferry
Tayport
Newport-on-Tay
Wormit
Balbeggie
Scone (New)
Methven
PERTH
Glencarse
Leuchars
Guard Bridge
St Andrews
Newburgh
Abernethy
Bridge of Earn
Forteviot
Dunning
Auchterarder
Gleneagles Hotel
Blackford
Auchtermuchty
Letham
Cupar
Ladybank
Craigrothie
Kingsbarns
Fife Ness
Crail
Glenfarg
Strathmiglo
Falkland
Freuchie
Largo Ward
Lundin Links
Upper Largo
Anstruther
Pittenweem
St Monans
Elie
Milnathort
Kinnesswood
Yetts o'Muckhart
Kinross
Leslie
Markinch
GLENROTHES
Leven
Buckhaven
Dollar
Powmill
NJ
NO
GRAMPIAN REGION
GRAMPIAN MOUNTAINS
SIDLAW HILLS
BEN RINNES 2755
CAIRNGORM 4084
BRAERIACH 4248
BEN MACDHUI 4296
CAIRN TOUL 4241
LOCHNAGAR 3786
GLAS MAOL 3504
Firth of Tay
St Andrews Bay
TAY ROAD BR (TOLL)
Aberdeen - Stromness 8 hrs
Aberdeen - Lerwick 14 hrs

Outer Hebrides

16

Cape Wrath
Durness
Strathy Point
Scrabster
Thurso
Dunnet
John o'Groats
Castletown
Freswick
21
Keiss
Strathy
Melvich
Reay
Bettyhill
Tongue
Eriboll
Rhiconich
Laxford Bridge
Halkirk
Mybster
Watten
Westerdale
Wick
Thrumster
Syre
Forsinard
BEN HOPE 3040
Loch Loyal
Loch Naver
Loch Shin
Kylestrome
Kylesku
Unapool
Altnaharra
NC
ND
Kinbrace
Latheron
Lybster
Dunbeath
Borgue
Berriedale
Inchnadamph
BEN MORE ASSYNT 3273
Helmsdale
Ledmore Junction
KNOCKAN CLIFF
Lairg
Rogart
Brora
Rosehall
Golspie
Invershin
Embo
Bonar Bridge
Dornoch
Dornoch Firth
Edderton
STRUIE HILL
Tain
Portmahomack
BEINN DEARG 3547
Hill of Fearn
Balintore
Nigg
SGURR MOR 3637
BEN WYVIS 3429
Alness
Invergordon
Cromarty Firth
Cromarty
Evanton
Balblair
NH
Lossiemouth
Cummingston
Burghead
Hopeman
Findochty
Buckie
Spey Bay
Kingston
Findhorn
Kinloss
Alves
Elgin
Garve
Strathpeffer
Dingwall
Rosemarkie
Fortrose
Nairn
Forres
Rafford
Fochabers
Tynet
Contin
Conon Bridge
Ardersier
Auldearn
Dallas
Tore
Muir of Ord
North Kessock
Croy
Cawdor
Rothes
Keith
Beauly
Kirkhill
INVERNESS
Ferness
Craigellachie
NJ
Aberlour (Charlestown of Aberlour)
Dufftown
Struy
Daviot
Dores
Moy
BEN RINNES 2755
Cannich
Drumnadrochit
Tomich
Tomatin
Grantown-on-Spey
Cromdale
Glenlivet
19
Torness
East Croachy
Dulnain Bridge
Tomnavoulin
Inverfarigaig
Carrbridge
Knockandhu
Foyers
Errogie
Nethy Bridge
Boat of Garten
Tomintoul
Kildrummy
Invermoriston
Whitebridge
Strathdon
Glenkindie
Aviemore
Coylumbridge
Fort Augustus
Corgarff
CAIRNGORM 4084
Kincraig
CAIRNGORM MOUNTAINS
Invergarry
Kingussie
Insh
BRAERIACH 4248
BEN MACDHUI 4296
CAIRN TOUL 4241
Newtonmore
Ballater
Laggan Bridge
Braemar
Letterfinlay
17
MORAY FIRTH
A836
A838
A897
A882
A9
A895
A839
A837
A894
A835
A832
A862
A831
A833
A82
A887
A86
A889
A96
A941
A940
A939
A938
A95
A920
A944
A97
A93
B874
B876
B870
B871
B873
B801
B869
B864
B9175
B9165
B817
B9163
B9160
B9006
B862
B851
B861
B9154
B9091
B9090
B9007
B9010
B9089
B9012
B9103
B9015
B9104
B9102
B9008
B9009
B9136
B970
B9152
B9002
1 2 3 4 5 6 7 8 9 0 1 2 3 4

KEY TO SCOTTISH ISLANDS

Shetland Islands

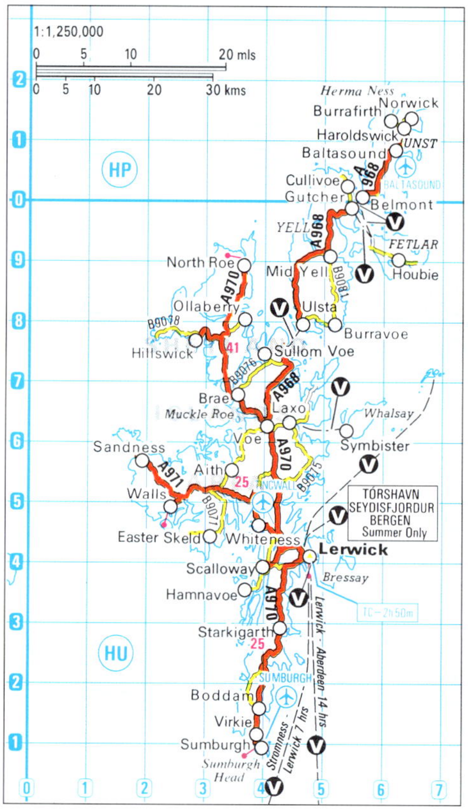

Orkney Islands

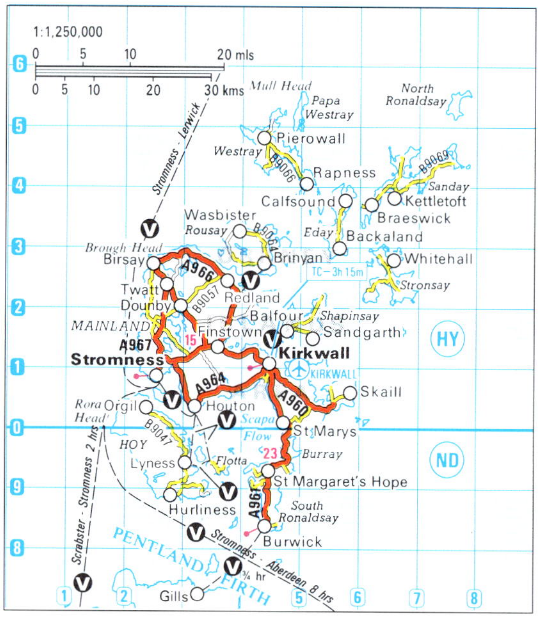

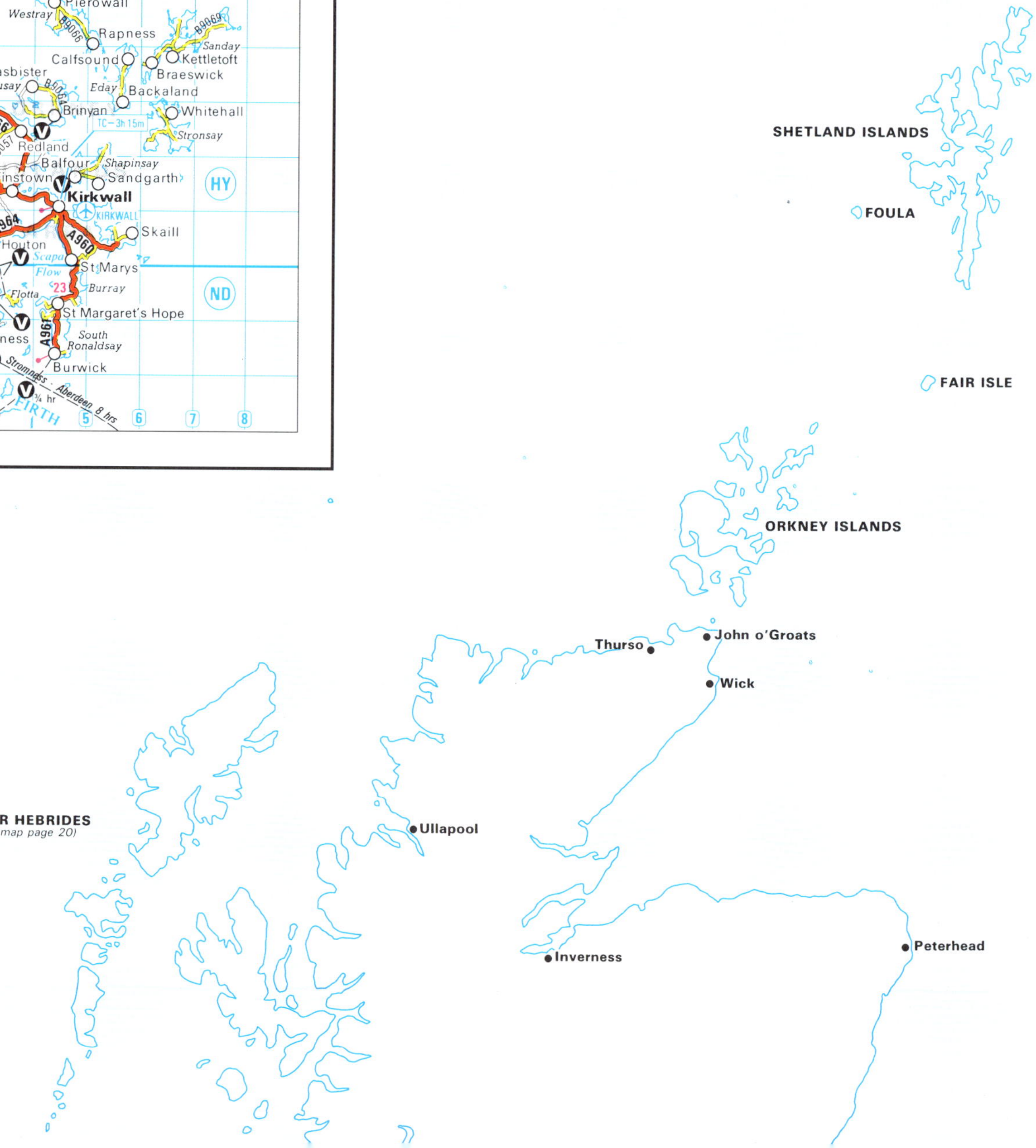

INDEX

A

B

C

D

E

F

G

N

O

P

Q

R

S

T

U

V

W

Y

Z

The Automobile Association would like to thank the following photographers and libraries for their assistance in the preparation of this book:

E BOWNESS
168 Carlisle Castle, 169 Maryport Harbour

D HARDLEY
212 L. Lomond, 213 Luss, Callander, 216 Tarbert Harbour, 217 Glen Kinglas, 219 Girvan Harbour

MARY EVANS PICTURE LIBRARY
8 Roman Road, Wansdyke, 9 Bradford on Avon, 10 Stagecoach, 11 Mailcoach, 12 George Hotel Huntingdon, 13 Highwayman, 14 Travelling Circus, 15 Gypsies, 16 Tollgate at Stanmore, 17 Margate, 19 Shillibeer's Omnibus, 22 Stagecoach

SPECTRUM COLOUR LIBRARY
14 Sir Robert Fossett Circus, 21 Glamis Castle

R WEIR
196 Castle Moil, 197 Isle of Skye, 199 L. Carron, 201 Ardvreck, 203 Dornoch Firth, 206 R. Findhorn at Tomatin, 217 Tarbert, 218 Castle Kennedy, 220 Threave Castle, 226 Dryburgh Abbey

WELSH TOURIST BOARD
130 Blaenau Ffestiniog, 132 Maes Artro & Crafts Centre, 133 Harlech Castle, 135 Llywernog Silver-Lead Mines, 136 Devil's Bridge, 141 Drefach Felindre, 142 Fishguard, 143 Cilgerran Castle, 144 Picton Castle, 146 Cefn Coed Coal & Steam Centre

The remaining pictures are held in the AA Photo Library, with contributions from:

M Adleman, M Allwood-Coppin, D Austin, A W Besley, J Beazley, M Birkitt, E Bowness, R Czaja, P Davies, R Eames, P Enticknap, R Fletcher, D Forss, S Gibson Photography, D Hardley, R Hayman S King, A Lawson, S & O Mathews, E Meacher, C & A Molyneux, R Newton, R Surman, M Trelawny, W Voysey, R Weir, H Williams, T Woodcock, J Wyand